Cult Movies

The Classics, the Sleepers
the Weird, and the Wonderful

Danny Peary

A DELTA BOOK

A DELTA BOOK

Published by
Dell Publishing Co., Inc.
1 Dag Hammarskjold Plaza
New York, New York 10017

Stills from the motion picture TRASH, courtesy of
Cinema 5 Ltd.

Excerpts from the screenplay of TWO FOR THE
ROAD by Frederic Raphael (Volatic Limited, proprietor). Every effort has been made to locate the proprietor
of this material. If the proprietor will contact the publisher, formal arrangements will be made.

Delta (R) TM 755118, Dell Publishing Co., Inc.
Printed in the United States of America

First printing—November 1981

A hardcover edition of this work
is available from Delacorte Press,
1 Dag Hammarskjold Plaza,
New York, New York 10017.

Designed by Bob Fitzpatrick
Research assistant, Henry Blinder

Library of Congress Cataloging in Publication Data

Peary, Danny, 1949–
    Cult movies.

    "A Delta book."
    Includes index.
    1. Moving pictures—Plots, themes, etc.   I. Title.
PN1997.8.P37   791.43'75   81-9785
ISBN 0-440-51647-1   AACR2

To Suzanne and Zoé
and
Laura, Joe, and Bea

Acknowledgments

If I had tried to do this book alone, it still would be in the planning stages. Therefore, I greatly appreciate the help I received from friends and strangers alike: Henry Blinder, my researcher and lone guest contributor; Bob Fitzpatrick, who I hope will design all my books; John Robert Christopher, Doug Marshall, Bob Nowacki, and Gerald Peary, who tracked down elusive photographs; my wife, Suzanne Rafer, who supported me in every way possible during the writing of this book despite her thinking my criticism of *The Red Shoes* unfair; my daughter, Zoé, who learned to sleep to the sound of a typewriter; and my agent Chris Tomasino, who had faith in this project and said, "I'm surprised no one thought of it before." Other individuals I must thank include Monty Arnold, John Bean, Eddy Brandt, Michael Carr, Carlos Clarens, Mary Corliss, Jane Covner, Robert C. Cumbow, Crittendon Davis, Jonathan Demme, Maxine Fleckner, Karyn Kay, Paula Klaw, Ira Kramer, Joseph H. Lewis, Wendall Mahler, Rita Mandelman, Rand Marlis, Mark Ricci, Ruth Robbins, Reid Rosefelt, Dana Schreiber, Kathy Stevens, Rhea Tabakin, and Bruce Trinz.

Photo credits go to the following: New Yorker Films, 20th Century-Fox, New World Pictures, Warner Bros., Cinerama Releasing, Allied Artists, Universal, Cinema 5, Columbia, Mitchell Brothers Film Group, Walt Disney Productions, PRC, ABKCO, Libra Films, Corinth, New Line Cinema, American International Pictures, Embassy Pictures, United Artists, Janus Films, Brandon Films, RKO Radio Pictures, Paramount, Metro-Goldwyn-Mayer, Sigma III, Compass International, Jack H. Harris Enterprises, the Walter Reade Organization, Republic Pictures, Bryanston Pictures, DCA, Ralph Mack Advertising, Movie Star News, Eddy Brandt's Saturday Matinee, the Memory Shop, the Museum of Modern Art Film Archive, and the Wisconsin Center for Film and Theater Research.

Finally, I would like to express my gratitude to the nice people at Dell Publishing, especially Chris Kuppig, Linda Jordan, Jack Ennis, Sandy Choron, Ann Spinelli, Johanna Tani, MaryJane DiMassi, Frances Dominguez, Michael Carney, Peter Weissman, and Allan Gale. Most of all, I would like to thank Cynthia Vartan, the rare editor who can convince you to change things for the better without damaging your ego.

Contents

Foreword

Of the tens of thousands of movies that have been made, only an extremely small number have elicited a fiery passion in moviegoers that exists long after their initial releases. *Cult Movies* contains one hundred special films which for one reason or another have been taken to heart by segments of the movie audience, cherished, protected, and, most of all, enthusiastically championed. Cultists don't merely enjoy their favorite films; they worship them, seek them out wherever they are playing, catch them in theaters even when they have just played on television, see them repeatedly, and are intent on persuading anyone who will listen that they should be appreciated regardless of what the newspaper or television reviewers thought. Strike up a conversation about movies anywhere in the country and the titles found in this book soon will be flying back and forth in frenetic debate. And as likely as not you'll end up forcing someone to watch *The Late Late Show* to see a special favorite of yours or find yourself being dragged to some repertory theater to see a picture your well-meaning abductor has viewed ten, twenty, or a hundred times.

When you speak of cult movies, you speak in extremes. Hard-core cultists, ranging from polite to lunatic, insist that their favorite films are the most intriguing, unusual, outrageous, mysterious, absurd, daring, entertaining, erotic, exotic, and/or best films of all time. Also they point out that cult films differ radically from standard Hollywood films in that they characteristically feature atypical heroes and heroines; offbeat dialogue; surprising plot resolutions; highly original story lines; brave themes, often of a sexual or political nature; "definitive" performances by stars who have cult status; the novel handling of popular but stale genres. Outstanding special effects, spectacular camerawork, and a willingness by the filmmakers to experiment distinguish many cult films, but adoration for some, like *Plan 9 from Outer Space*, has absolutely nothing to do with admiration for the filmmakers' skills—it's often to the contrary.

The typical Hollywood product has little potential for becoming a cult favorite because it is perceived by *everyone* in basically the same way. Almost everyone agrees on the quality of these films, on what the directors are trying to say, and on the correct way to interpret the films' messages. On the other hand, cult films are born in controversy, in arguments over quality, themes, talent, and other matters. Cultists believe they are among the blessed few who have discovered something in particular films that the average moviegoer and critic have missed—the something that makes the pictures extraordinary. They grasp the elusive points of their favorite films, the filmmakers' most personal visions, the cult stars' real selves coming through; and they find glory that they are among the few on the same wavelength as the people involved in making these films. While word of mouth certainly plays a large part in the growth of cults for individual films, what is fascinating is that *in the beginning* pockets of people will embrace a film they have heard nothing about while clear across the country others independently will react identically to the same picture. There is nothing more exciting than discovering you are not the only person obsessed with a picture critics hate, the public stays away from en masse, and film texts ignore.

I have included prime examples of various types of cult films. You will find pictures that daily newspaper reviewers attacked and, almost as a reflex action, film enthusiasts rallied around; pictures hated by the average moviegoer as much as by the daily press that have been saved from oblivion by a cult of out-of-the-mainstream critics and film scholars; pictures underrated or neglected by everyone at the time of their releases that recently have been rediscovered and reevaluated; pictures that have gained popularity because they star performers who have become cult stars or were made by filmmakers who likewise have become cult figures; pictures for which we have nostalgic feelings because they had great impact on us when we were kids; pictures that are so out of the ordinary that attending them has become a communal event—as it is with Midnight Movies, a godsend for financially troubled theater owners.

To hold myself to one hundred films, I was forced to limit the number of titles which feature a cult star such as Bruce Lee, Humphrey Bogart, Marilyn Monroe, James Dean, Louise Brooks, and Judy Garland or which were made by cult producers and directors such as Stanley Kubrick, Robert Altman, Nicolas Roeg, Val Lewton, Brian De Palma, Anthony Mann, Budd Boetticher, and Sam Fuller. Also, since I am aware that almost every science fiction and horror film has at least a minor cult, I have painstakingly kept the number of such films in check. I have included films that were financially successful upon their initial releases only in cases where I believe the reasons for a film's current cult are divorced from the reasons the film was once a box office hit. Although *Gone With the Wind* and *Star Wars* have fanatical followings, I have not included them because they are still distributed (by MGM and Twentieth Century-Fox, respectively) with the intention of attracting the masses rather than devotees on the fringe of the mass audience; the word *cult* implies a minority, and the studios are well aware that *Gone With the Wind* and *Star Wars* still attract the *majority* of the movie audience. Once these two pictures join such films as *All About Eve, Singin' in the Rain, Casablanca,* and *The Wizard of Oz*—all popular with the mass audience but today theatrically distributed primarily for their hard-core fans—on repertory theater schedules and on the Midnight Movie circuit, they, too, will be classified as legitimate cult movies.

Aguirre, the Wrath of God

1972 Germany Distributed in the U.S. in 1977 by New Yorker Films
Director: Werner Herzog
Producer: Werner Herzog

Screenplay: Werner Herzog
Cinematography: Thomas Mauch
Music: Popol Vuh
Editor: Beate Mainka-Jellinghaus
Running Time: 90 minutes

Cast: Klaus Kinski (Don Lope de Aguirre), Ruy Guerra (Don Pedro de Ursúa). Del Negro (Brother Gaspar de Carvajal), Helena Rojo (Iñez), Cecilia Rivera (Flores), Peter Berling (Don Fernando de Guzman), Danny Ades (Perucho)

Synopsis: In 1560, a large party of Spanish conquistadores under the command of Gonzalez Pizarro, their lavishly dressed ladies, and Indian bearers march from Quito across the Andes in Search of El Dorado, the legendary city of gold. It is a frightful journey. Men in full armor must drag cannons on narrow mountain paths and through scorching jungles. Pizarro decides it best to send an expeditionary force ahead to see if there are hostile Indians lurking about and if El Dorado is in the direction they are going. Meanwhile, the rest of the party will make camp and await its return.

Pizarro appoints nobleman Pedro de Ursúa to lead the expedition, with soldier Lope de Aguirre as his second in command. Ursúa is to be accompanied by his beautiful, brave wife Iñez, and Aguirre by his fifteen-year-old daughter Flores. Also going will be Brother Gaspar de Carvajal, who wants to spread Christianity in this new world, fat warrior Don Fernando de Guzman, and about forty soldiers, servants, and Indian bearers.

The journey down river on the rafts is perilous. One raft gets caught in a whirlpool and will not move forward or backward. Ursúa sends some men to the far side of the river to throw the stranded men ropes. But when they get there the next morning, they find that all the men on the raft have been killed by poison darts. Ursúa orders the dead men be given a proper Christian burial. Aguirre, realizing that they will have to stay in this dangerous area to perform the ceremonial burial, tells one of his cohorts to "accidentally" set off the cannon while it is aimed at the raft. The corpses are blown to bits and there can be no burial. Iñez tells Ursúa that Aguirre is responsible for what has happened to the raft.

The expedition continues. The men are terrified of Indians. The water rises, and most of the provisions are damaged. Ursúa decides they ought to give up the exploration and march back to Pizarro. Aguirre says they should continue down river to glory. Ursúa orders Aguirre put in chains. Aguirre and his followers rebel. Ursúa is badly injured by a bullet. Aguirre takes over the command and everyone is too scared to protest. Iñez asks Brother Gaspar to help Ursúa rally the men, but Gaspar thinks it wiser to side with Aguirre. Aguirre arranges for Guzman to be elected leader and the "Emperor of El Dorado" with himself second in command but controlling Guzman. El Dorado is declared free of Spanish rule.

Ursúa is put on trial. Although he is condemned to hanging, Guzman—much to Aguirre's chagrin—grants Ursúa clemency. Travel down river resumes. Many men are picked off by poison darts and arrows aimed by unseen Indians on shore. Food runs out and no one wants to risk landing to look for more. Only Guzman, the emperor, eats well. Then he is killed by an arrow. Aguirre, now in command, orders Ursúa hanged. This is carried out.

The men come ashore and walk through a deserted village. Many are killed by spears thrown by unseen Indians and Iñez walks into the jungle, never to be seen again.

The journey continues. Almost everyone is either dead or dying. Gaspar is shot by an arrow but thinks it an illusion. Flores is killed. Aguirre decides he will conquer Mexico, marry Flores, and found a pure dynasty. His only live companions, now, are the monkeys which overrun the spinning raft.

One of the most exciting cultural developments of the seventies was the spectacular renaissance of the once proud German cinema that had been decimated by the rise and fall of Hitler. Joining veteran filmmakers Volker Schlöndorff and Alexander Kluge in the vanguard of the resurgence were three brilliant young West German screenwriter-directors: Rainer Werner Fassbinder, an incredibly prolific filmmaker whose films were the first to make inroads in North America; Wim Wenders, whose Western influences range from American movie director Sam Fuller to the Kinks, the long-active English rock music group; and Werner Herzog, the most idiosyncratic and eclectic of the three. In time, the films of these directors may be accepted by the general public as enthusiastically as the once-considered-esoteric works of Bergman, Fellini, and Truffaut, but today (1981) in most parts of the world, including America, their appeal is limited to cult adulation.

Herzog hoped that *Nosferatu* (1979), riding the crest of the vampire-films wave, would at last lift him from obscurity and give him the satisfaction of having his films sought out by larger audiences, but for a vampire film it was simply too sublime, too sedate, and too nonviolent for general tastes, and it fizzled at the box office. *Heart of Glass* (1976), a film for which Herzog hypnotized all his actors before turning on the camera, and *Woyzeck* (1979), which like *Nosferatu* stars Klaus Kinski, were released in America at about the

Aguirre and his precious daughter Flores, with whom he wishes to mate and begin a new, "pure" race.

Symbolic of a journey to nowhere: a raft gets caught in a whirlpool allowing neither advancement nor retreat.

same time but didn't fare any better. One of his earlier films, *Aguirre, the Wrath of God*, appears to be his lone film with a decent chance of catching on with the average moviegoer. It is an enormous cult favorite in such places as Mexico, Venezuela, Algiers, Paris, and America, where its distributor, New Yorker Films, reports that it is the one picture in its catalog that is never out of circulation.

To see *Aguirre* for the first time is to discover a genuine masterpiece. It is overwhelming, spellbinding; at first dreamlike, and then hallucinatory. It is among the few nondocumentaries and non-Hollywood multi-million-dollar extravaganzas in cinema history—*Children of Paradise* (1945) and *The Battle of Algiers* (1966) are others which immediately come to mind—whose very production seems too remarkable to comprehend.

Aguirre was filmed in unexplored regions of South America, in jungles, on mountains, and on an Amazon tributary. There were enormous production difficulties shooting in this isolated, inhospitable region. Tempers flared, and at one point either Kinski or Herzog drew a gun on the other. It was filmmaking under the most trying circumstances, but the results are priceless; Thomas Mauch's camera has gone back in time to a lost world that is at once both beautiful and terrifying.

The picture opens with an incredible image. Far below the camera, scurrying like ants around narrow mountain paths, are conquistadores in full armor, pulling cannons, and their ladies being carried in sedans by Indian bearers. Suddenly, several of the caravan pass within feet of the camera that is stationed above the clouds and we realize that there must be more than a thousand people Herzog has somehow coaxed into walking this dangerous footing. Further shots establish that this stumbling caravan does indeed stretch unbroken from where the camera is to as far as the camera can see. The movie closes with an equally stunning sight: the camera, aboard a motor boat, speeds around the raft where Aguirre stands among his dead party, his craft overrun by wild monkeys—an ironic comment on the "success" of evolution. Critic David Ansen has called this "the grandest, most chilling image of raging solipsism ever filmed."

The journey down river is full of haunting images: ghostly figures moving in the brush; abandoned cannibal villages; the small raft trapped in a whirlpool, the stranded soldiers' voices drowned out by the roaring water; nature itself—the swirling, murky water, the birds, the eerie jungle so calm but full of death for intruders. This is not the Disneyland jungle cruise found in *Apocalypse Now* (1979), where we round each bend wondering what the special effects department has dreamed up, but a scary realistic trip into the unknown, the effect being that both the conquistadores and the film crew have somehow gone through a time warp and neither have any idea what lies ahead. The most mesmerizing shot in the film comes when the raft moves down river, leaving behind a hooded black horse that has jumped off and now stands motionless at the water's edge, surrounded by the prehistoric jungle— looking as out of place in this landscape as Godzilla in Tokyo.

Herzog adapted *Aguirre* from the diary of Brother Gaspar de Carvajal, who accompanied the real-life Aguirre and the expeditionary force on their ill-fated

The gloomy demeanor of the disposed leader Ursúa and his loyal wife Iñez is typical of all characters in Herzog's film.

search for El Dorado.* Whether Herzog stuck to the "factual" account or made the alterations he did, the plot seems ideal for what could be a colorful epic full of action and adventure—entertainment for the whole family. But Herzog was creating "art," not entertainment. As usual, he filmed with great reserve, even detachment, concentrating on character and setting and deemphasizing the exploitable death scenes. The journey down river becomes not so much an adventure as a somber funeral procession— complete with Popol Vuh's haunting choral music—in which the unhappy participants are floating toward their own deaths. In Herzog's first film, *Signs of Life* (1968), three German soldiers are garrisoned in a Greek Island fortress, slowly going mad while waiting for battle; in *Fata Morgana* (1971), the Sahara Desert wears down the characters that pass through. Again, in *Aguirre*, Herzog reveals his fascination for placing characters in hostile environments where, having nothing tangible to fight, they are unable to cope with their inevitable deaths. Neither their draconian training nor religion has prepared them for this trip down river, surrounded by unseen Indians who fling spears, blow poison darts, and shoot arrows from the jungle. They have no choice but to stay on the raft,

---

*Exactly what happened remains unclear, but it is believed that Aguirre murdered Pedro de Ursúa, whom Gonzalez Pizarro (the half-brother of the dead Francisco) had placed in charge of the expedition, and then declared the party independent of Spain and crowned his puppet Don Fernando de Guzman "Emperor of El Dorado." Later Aguirre killed Guzman and assumed command, but then he was murdered by his men, who eventually made their way to the northeast coast of South America. This all sounds very similar to Magellan's trip around the world: his men came back but he didn't. In Herzog's film there are some changes: Guzman is killed by an Indian arrow; Aguirre kills Ursúa *after* the death of Guzman, who had granted Ursúa clemency; Aguirre is the sole survivor as the film fades out, although his doom, too, is sealed.

where they will slowly die of starvation or fever if the Indians don't get them. The farther they go down river, the more their minds become mush. They see a great ship stuck high in a jungle tree—are they imagining it? They are shot by arrows and believe that they are illusions. Aguirre speaks of conquering Mexico although he should know he will never leave this river, and of marrying his daughter Flores. The movie becomes increasingly delirious. The characters barely communicate with one another. It's as if they have sunstroke or have been shot up with morphine. They endure their great suffering and deaths in silence, not even wincing when arrows penetrate their flesh. Their constant horror, depression, and fear of death have reached such abominable proportions that these feelings have become numbingly tedious—even to themselves.

As always, Herzog allows his viewers to supply the thoughts and emotions that his (subtly expressive) characters conceal beneath their impassive visages. Aguirre has little dialogue, and that is delivered mostly in a dry-throated monotone, but seconds after the camera first studies Klaus Kinski—sneering and snarling, gnarled like Richard III, standing at an angle as if to signify he is at odds with the world, twisting his head before moving his body—one immediately understands him to be contemptuous of the world and the men around him, and tortured by inner demons.

Since Herzog is a German filmmaker, it is not surprising that many critics have surmised that he has tried to make an analogy between Aguirre and Hitler, two megalomaniacs who convinced their followers to share their delusions of personal greatness. As it would be with Hitler in Depression Germany, Aguirre rises out of destruction and despair and convinces his men to move forward to fulfill their glorious destiny; having nothing to lose, they follow. As it would be with Hitler,

Aguirre treats Iñez with contempt but she refuses to be intimidated. Behind them on the raft is the horse that will be left behind in the forest.

Aguirre dreams of a "pure dynasty" and of amassing land and fame through conquest. Hitler's downfall began with his unsuccessful Russian campaign, where his troops were defeated by guerilla ambushers and a hostile environment; Aguirre's men suffer the same fate. Hitler ended up awaiting death in an underground bunker, his country crumbled around him, his dreams wrecked. Aguirre ends up on a raft, his dead men scattered around him, his dreams wrecked.

The analogy with Hitler holds up, but it also applies to other figures who sought out the greatness they were not capable of attaining. General George Armstrong Custer, like Aguirre, was a longhair who ventured amongst Indians, intent on exterminating an entire race of people in hopes of catapulting himself into power —in his case, the presidency. He, too, went into hostile territory and was ambushed. As legend has it, by the time he met his death at the Little Bighorn, his entire command, like Aguirre's, lay dead around him. Custer, Hitler, Aguirre: all mad visionaries who led loyal followers down an insane path to destruction. . . . Oddly, Aguirre's poor leadership reminds me of a scene in Buster Keaton's classic Civil War comedy, *The General* (1927): a foolish Union officer on horseback orders a train to cross a burning bridge, insisting that the bridge will be able to hold the great weight. His orders are followed, the bridge gives way, and the train crashes. Keaton quickly cuts back to the officer, whose expression changes ever so slightly but enough for us to know that he is feeling the complete horse's ass in front of his regiment. Aguirre's subtle facial grimaces each time disaster occurs because of a poor decision he has made remind me of that officer with egg on his face.

The allusion to Keaton is not off the wall. I believe that *Aguirre* is to a great extent a comedy. Herzog takes delight in presenting a film to document one of the most embarrassingly unsuccessful expeditions in history— carried out, not by heroic figures, but by nefarious Spanish imperialists who wiped out entire Indian nations while in search of wealth and glory. He mocks their silly proclamations so ceremoniously delivered; the monk who tries to spread Christianity in a land into which God knows better than to travel; the nobleman Guzman, who spends his time eating, drinking river water from gold containers, and going to the raft's outhouse; Aguirre's inability to give an intelligent order; the great Spanish invaders who are so dumb that they travel through a tropical environment in full armor, and pull cumbersome cannons through the mud. And is there a more mocking scene than that skinny musician standing by Aguirre, playing one note repeatedly on a reed instrument which has as much musical tone as a bunch of straws strung together? If this film had a second raft full of movie good guys, one could see the comedy more easily—and laugh as these bad guys are killed off so ridiculously and as Aguirre, a great comic villain, becomes increasingly frustrated. Herzog believes these men deserve their doom. And he thinks it fitting that a scoundrel who saw himself becoming another Cortez or Francisco Pizarro ends up a mere historical footnote, known insultingly as "Aguirre, the Madman."

All About Eve

1950 20th Century-Fox
Director: Joseph L. Mankiewicz
Producer: Darryl F. Zanuck
Screenplay: Joseph L. Mankiewicz
Based on a story and radio play, "The Wisdom of Eve," by Mary Orr
Cinematography: Milton Krasner
Music: Alfred Newman
Editor: Barbara McLean
Running Time: 138 minutes

Cast: Bette Davis (Margo Channing), Anne Baxter (Eve Harrington), George Sanders (Addison De Witt), Celeste Holm (Karen Richards), Gary Merrill (Bill Sampson), Hugh Marlowe (Lloyd Richards), Thelma Ritter (Birdie), Marilyn Monroe (Miss Caswell), Gregory Ratoff (Max Fabian), Barbara Bates (Phoebe), Walter Hampden (aged actor), Randy Stuart (girl), Eddie Fisher (stage manager)

Synopsis: As Eve Harrington receives the Sarah Siddons Award for the year's best performance by a theatrical actress, Karen Richards, the wife of playwright Lloyd Richards, thinks back to the previous October, to the night she first met Eve. That meeting took place outside the theater where Karen's best friend, Margo Channing, Broadway's greatest actress, was appearing in *Aged in Wood*, a play written by Lloyd and directed by Bill Sampson, Margo's boyfriend. Eve told Karen that she had been to every performance over the past six months so she could watch her idol, Margo. Charmed by the young girl's lack of pretense, Karen decided to introduce Eve to Margo. Displaying a great deal of charm, Eve told Margo, Karen, Lloyd, and Birdie (Margo's aide and live-in companion) her sad life story, which Birdie said had "everything but bloodhounds snappin' at her rear end." All four of them, and Bill, who entered after the story was finished, were very taken with the girl. Even the very hostile Margo developed a "protective feeling" for her young admirer, and decided to take her under her wing, and into her home. Eve began doing Margo's chores, and, although she was always helpful and kind, Birdie warned Margo that Eve seemed to be studying her. The forty-year-old Margo, who was very sensitive to her age in regard to her Broadway stardom and to keeping the love of the thirty-two-year-old Bill, began to think that Eve was trying to steal Bill away from her, and that Bill was becoming interested in Eve as well. Margo and Bill fought repeatedly, with Margo always refusing to believe Bill's commitment to their relationship—especially if her career ended. With Karen's unwitting help, Eve first became Margo's understudy and then replaced her when Margo couldn't make it to the theater one night. After her tremendous performance, Eve tried to seduce Bill. When he rejected her, while swearing his love for Margo, Eve gave herself to the vile critic Addison De Witt, who set about promoting her career. In his newspaper column he lashed out at Margo for selfishly wanting to star in Lloyd's next play when Eve was more proper to play the young lead.

Although he had broken up with Margo during an argument, Bill returned to console her after reading De Witt's harsh words about her. Margo and Bill announced their marriage plans, and Margo told Lloyd that he should give his new lead to Eve.

During rehearsals Eve won Lloyd's heart and convinced him to break up with Karen after opening night. However, when Addison learned that Eve was going to leave him for Lloyd, he told Eve that he would reveal her shady past and ruin her career if she went through with her plan. So Eve told Lloyd to go back to his wife. The play, which Bill directed, was a great success, and Eve receives the Sarah Siddons Award. Neither Margo nor Karen applauds her victory. Instead of going to the party after the ceremony, Eve returns to her hotel. In her room she discovers Phoebe, an aspiring actress who idolizes her. Phoebe starts to do things for Eve—just as Eve once did things for Margo.

Publicity shot of standout cast:
(L-R) Bette Davis and then-husband Gary Merrill, George Sanders, Anne Baxter, Hugh Marlowe, Celeste Holm.

Where there is a repertory movie theater, you can bet even money that Joseph L. Mankiewicz's *All About Eve* is somewhere on its schedule. It is one of the most enduring of all American films, that rare "instant classic" and Best Picture Oscar winner that has maintained its popularity through the years—earning a reputation, along the way, as a "cult film" before that term was fashionable. Its enormous appeal for today's moviegoers is quite obvious: for the curious, there's Bette Davis and Gary Merrill, in love on screen, falling in love off-camera—anticipating the celebrated Elizabeth Taylor–Richard Burton hijinks during the making of Mankiewicz's *Cleopatra* (1963); for movie buffs, there's Davis and Marilyn Monroe, one former and one future box office queen, in their only film together; for Davis cultists, there's the great resurrected actress breathing fire into what is, arguably, her greatest role; for Monroe cultists, there's a glowing young contract player more than holding her own among an intimidating veteran cast; for connoisseurs, there are delectable supporting performances by George Sanders and Thelma Ritter, whose sharp, witty deliveries—his full of venom, hers full of warmth— are finally used to full advantage; for the discriminating, highbrow viewers, there's a clever, highly intelligent script (its merits can, at the very least, be debated), remarkably performed by an outstanding ensemble. Moreover, most film fans, having by nature an antitheater bias, can delight in having their worst suspicions confirmed about theater people; as Mankie-

wicz takes us behind the Helen Hayes–Mary Martin–Rosalind Russell shroud (or curtain) of graciousness and into the pompous, snobbish, claws-bared world of the Bankheads and the Chattertons, where jealousy, insecurity, and in-fighting over parts and partners reign supreme, and where women aren't necessarily ladies because that's what they play on the stage.

While each succeeding generation of moviegoers since 1950 has received *All About Eve* with unbridled enthusiasm, post-fifties critics in general have been less magnanimous. While very few of them actually dislike the film in its entirety, they do have strong gripes.

Critics blame Anne Baxter's lack of depth as an actress for making Eve Harrington come across as an essentially shallow character, too weak a personality to compete with the gloriously sophisticated Margo Channing. But it is more likely that Eve is shallow by design—not because of Baxter's acting deficiencies. For Eve's villainy to come through as it should, the audience must be one step ahead of the other characters in recognizing that underneath Eve's gentle, ingratiating veneer is a ruthless, manipulative, self-perpetuating woman—and, literally, nothing more. As it happens to Peter Sellers's simple gardener in *Being There* (1979), other characters keep reading grand qualities into Baxter's Eve which we know don't exist. Eve is nothing more than the other side of Miss Caswell, trying like her to make it or, better, fake it to the top, despite a lack of personal substance; while Caswell is resigned to "playing the game" by allowing herself to be used by produc-

Eve, Karen, and Lloyd look on while Margo and Bill put on one of their frequent real-life performances.

ers and the like, Eve *uses* everyone, especially those who are good to her, as stepping-stones on her road to stardom. In truth, Eve is no more a threat to Margo than is Miss Caswell. Margo may be deceived, at first, by Eve's confident, laid-back, wait-until-Margo-sticks-her-foot-in-her-own-mouth-again attitude into thinking that Eve has gained the upper hand on her, particularly with Bill, but ultimately she sees what we all do: that Eve can't lay down a victorious trump card because she has none; that Eve is limited by her own superficiality and can only hope for victory (conquest) by bluffing Margo—a woman of no limitations—into defaulting.

Writing in *New York* magazine (October 16, 1972) Mankiewicz explained Eve's constant need to go after whatever belongs to others as her way of "servicing a bottomless pit . . . [an] inner emptiness [she] can never fill—but must continue to feed merely to exist."* It is only to such an artificial, amoral creature that a Mephistopheles character like Addison De Witt could be attracted. If Eve were the strong character some critics wanted Anne Baxter to play her as, she could never have wound up as the kept woman of a man who only selects from the bottom of the barrel. Baxter is by no means a

great actress, but her Eve is perfect: externally cool, calculating, and controlled, yet empty at the core.

Mankiewicz has often chastised movie fans for having lost their ability to *listen*. This has been his way of saying flashy camera technique is no replacement for good dialogue. In 1973, in *Variety*, Lee Beaupre rebutted Mankiewicz: "That the film has aged less well than the script can be attributed to Mankiewicz's visual lapses—an inability to place characters in a meaningful spatial relationship to each other, not a failure to use 'arty' camera trickery (his frequent, nearsighted reply to critical charges that he is only a dialogue director)." Beaupre may be correct that Mankiewicz's weaknesses as a director are related to where he places his characters within his frame and how he moves them about in relation to one another. But it is hardly likely that the majority of critics who have objected to Mankiewicz's directorial style have made a picture-by-picture study of his handling of these spatial relationships. No, Mankiewicz is correct in assuming that many movie critics resent him primarily because he uses his frame as if it were a stage and because, in most cases, he will use dialogue rather than the camera to make a point.

All About Eve is not particularly inventive in its use of space or in how the camera is used, but since the acting is so marvelous and the quotable dialogue so

---

*For another portrayal of a manipulative social climber, see the gifted Joan Fontaine in *Born to Be Bad*, also released in 1950.

much fun to *listen* to, it hardly makes a difference. But to be fair, there are a few times when Mankiewicz proves that he is a proficient *film*maker, capable of cinematic touches: when Eve tells her fabricated life story in Margo's dressing room, everyone moves to one side of the room to face her—as if they are an audience and Eve is an actress giving a performance (which is exactly what she is doing); when Margo is about to kiss Bill good-bye at the airport, the camera pans to find the sneaky Eve standing just inches from them, intentionally jarring them out of their intimacy; when Margo confronts Bill at her party, she suavely puts an olive into her mouth to punctuate her verbal attack—and is so surprised by Eve's sudden appearance that she freezes with the olive halfway in her mouth and a silly look on her face, appearing the fool in front of the man she loves.

The genesis for *All About Eve*'s script was a story actress Elisabeth Bergner and her husband, producer-director Paul Czinner, told actress-writer Mary Orr about an experience they "had had with an unscrupulous young actress they had befriended." Mary Orr's resulting short story, "The Wisdom of Eve," appeared in *Cosmopolitan* in May 1946. In 1949, Orr's radio play, "The Wisdom of Eve," was performed on NBC's *Radio Guild Playhouse*. Mankiewicz's loose adaptation of the Orr short story and radio play was written in ten days. It was quickly hailed as one of the best scripts in cinema history, and the following spring won Mankiewicz an Oscar to go along with his Best Director award. In addition, in 1951, it became the first movie script to be published (by Random House) as a hardcover book. It is a script that is too often clever just for the sake of being clever; but except for an ending which wrongly has Eve rather than Margo as the focal character, it is always fascinating, particularly in its portrayal of women.

Unlike *A Double Life* (1947) and *The Saxon Charm* (1948), two of its antecedents, *All About Eve* is about the women of the theater. The men—the writer, the director, the producer—are all in stable situations throughout the film, having reached the peak of their professions and knowing that they will stay there. (It was very intentional that there is no major character who is an *actor*.) It is different with the women—the star who is growing too old for certain parts, the unknown actresses trying to get a break by hook or crook, an ex-vaudevillian who has no place on stage in modern theater, the playwright's wife who must be prepared to be set adrift if some ambitious young actress sets her

As usual, Bill tries to console the angry Margo and assure her that he loves only her.

While Margo threw the party, predictably she was the first to leave. But she's still the topic of conversation when Max (standing), Eve, Bill, Karen, De Witt, and Miss Caswell (played by a young Marilyn Monroe) gather in this famous scene.

sights on her husband. These women are all in transitional periods of their lives, and neither we nor they know how they will end up.

All About Eve is mostly about Margo Channing, perhaps the most dynamic woman ever to appear on the screen. Margo is intelligent, opinionated, high-strung, temperamental, and the only lead female character in the movies other than Hildy Johnson in *His Girl Friday* (1940) adept at unleashing funny one-liners. As all multidimensional characters should be, Margo is quite contradictory: she is vain, but self-effacing; strong enough to hold her own during the course of an argument ("Fasten your seat belts. It's going to be a bumpy night"), but vulnerable to its aftereffects; self-reliant one minute and dependent the next, wanting to be stroked like an alley cat that finds it too difficult to fend for itself all the time. Addison De Witt, Mankiewicz's mouthpiece, who seems to have the right words for describing everyone in the film, tells her: "You're maudlin and full of self-pity. You're magnificent."

Since almost every one of these traits mentioned above immediately makes one think of the image projected by Bette Davis, screen personality, it is hard to believe that Claudette Colbert—not one to play bitchy parts—was the first choice to play Margo. Davis was a last-minute replacement when Colbert hurt her back and was forced to withdraw. Of course, what particularly makes *All About Eve* such a treat is that in 1950, Davis, like Margo, was at a crossroads of her career and romantically involved with a younger man. (Merrill is six years younger than Davis, Bill eight years younger than Margo.)

After a string of tepid soapers, Davis was having a hard time convincing producers that at age forty-two she could still play leading ladies. Margo, forty, feels that she is being eased out of leading parts to make room for rising stars like Eve Harrington; and she worries that if she is stripped of her stardom Bill will find her lacking as a woman. Like Davis, Margo must do some soul-searching as she looks toward the future. At the film's end, Margo realizes that even if she retires, she is still, as the supportive Bill insists, "a beautiful and intelligent" woman; now that she acknowledges her value for the first time in her life, she can forget about Eve—importantly, their competition stops when Margo agrees to marry Sampson—and concentrate on her marriage *and* on keeping her career going. As for Davis, she reestablished her rightful claim to be Hollywood's queen with her sterling performance as Margo. In doing so, she proved to producers, long before Fonda, Wood, MacGraw, Jackson, and Audrey Hepburn, that actresses over forty can play romantic leads in commercially successful films.

What is interesting about the final section of the picture—after Margo and Bill announce their engagement—is that Bill and Lloyd, with Margo's blessing, work with Eve in a new play. (By this time everyone realizes what a despicable character Eve is.) Mankiewicz's point: in the theater, talented people are accepted, regardless of character. As Margo has learned, there is room at the top.

Andy Warhol's Bad

1971 A New World Pictures release of a Factory (Andy Warhol) Film
Director: Jed Johnson
Executive Producer: Andy Warhol
Producer: Jeff Tornberg
Screenplay: Pat Hackett and George Abagnalo
Cinematography: Allan Metzger
Music: Mike Bloomfield
Editors: Franca Silvi and David McKenna
Running time: 100 minutes

Cast: Carroll Baker (Mrs. Aiken), Perry King (L. T.), Susan Tyrrell (Mary Aiken), Stefania Cassini (P. G.), Cyrinda Foxe (R. C.), Mary Boylan (grandmother), Charles McGregor (detective), Tere Tereba (Ingrid Joyner), Brigid Polk (Estelle), Susan Blond (young mother)

Synopsis: Mrs. Aiken is a middle-aged Queens housewife who shares her home with a useless husband, a mother who has lung cancer but still smokes, and Mary, a dumpy daughter-in-law and her messy, always crying baby. To make money she runs a facial-hair removal business in her kitchen and an out-call murder-for-hire organization that specializes in doing away with kids and animals. While she performs the electrolysis herself, she has four young female employees who carry out the assassinations (or other acts of mayhem): the blond R. C., the Spanish P. G., and Glenda and Marsha, a sister act. Mrs. Aiken is always on the phone making appointments for murder or hair removal.

L. T. comes into town, and although Mrs. Aiken usually doesn't take men into her employ or into her house as boarders, she allows him to rent a room from her while he waits for a call from Mrs. Joyner to give him the go-ahead to kill her autistic child. Mrs. Joyner hopes that with the problem child dead, her husband will stop drinking. L. T. is physically attracted to the much older Mrs. Aiken, but she is not happy to have him around, watching television, eating, staring at her. When she discovers that he has slept with P. G., and that he has drugs and girlie magazines in his suitcase, she raises his rent to a hundred dollars a day—twenty-five more than the American Plan charges.

During L. T.'s stay at Mrs. Aiken's house, Mrs. Aiken removes hair from a lot of women's faces and sends her female assassins on various assignments. Mrs. Aiken becomes irritable during this time because the overly emotional Mary and her crying baby sit around the house all day and annoy her, her hit squad arrives too late to kill a baby that its impatient mother had already done away with, client Sarah's nose hairs are growing back, and a crooked black cop is pressuring her to let him arrest one of her employees, perhaps L. T., who she insists is her nephew. At last, L. T. receives his call. While the Joyners pretend to sleep, he goes into the room of their autistic son. Since L. T. was unloved as a child, he relates to this neglected boy and is unable to bring himself to murder him. Nevertheless, he takes the money and goes back to Mrs. Aiken's, telling her that all he was given for committing the murder was an IOU. Because she wants her share of the money, Mrs. Aiken calls the Joyners to demand payment—only to find out that the boy is still alive.

L. T. leaves Mrs. Aiken's house. The angry woman walks into the kitchen and discovers the black cop rummaging through her drawers. When she calls him a "stupid nigger," he drowns her in the kitchen sink.

Too impatient to wait for assassins Glenda and Marsha, a young mother disposes of the intended victim by tossing him out a window.

In the surprisingly funny *Andy Warhol's Bad*, poor Mary's rare outing to a picture show proves disastrous when the film turns out to be in Spanish, and her two irritated female companions, Glenda and Marsha (both members of Mrs. Aiken's assassination-for-hire squad) burn down the theater and drive off in a stolen car—leaving the befuddled Mary miles from home in the middle of the night. When Mary finally makes it home to Mrs. Aiken's house, crying and totally bedraggled, L. T. notices her sorry condition and asks, quite seriously, "Bad movie?" The point director Jed Johnson and screenwriters Pat Hackett and George Abagnalo could be making is that L. T.'s question is not so foolish in a world where there exist Andy Warhol films—like *Andy Warhol's Bad*—which indeed have had a disturbing effect on many unprepared viewers.

In fact, it has always been the intention of Warhol and his directors to "disturb" the American audience's movie-watching sensibilities as conditioned over the years by the dominant Hollywood product. Warhol forces us to accept *his* redefinition of cinema. In *Andy Warhol's Bad*, for instance, we are treated to doses of graphic violence (always with comic overtones) and to the typical Warhol images and language that many viewers have always found repulsive, and we must either adjust to his taste (or lack of it) or flee the theater— perhaps looking as disturbed as Mary does to L. T.

Warhol's wish is not to do away with the Hollywood-type film that he and his talented directors—especially film buff Paul Morrissey (an Anna Magnani fan), his most frequent director—obviously have knowledge of and appreciation for, but to *expand* the American cinema so it will include films not limited in terms of theme, subject, and method by Hollywood standards.

Beginning with *Heat* (1973), Paul Morrissey's superdecadent homage to the already-decadent *Sunset Boulevard* (1950), and followed by Morrissey's *Andy Warhol's Frankenstein* (1974) in 3-D, and *Andy Warhol's Dracula* (1974), Warhol has more and more acknowledged his debt to Hollywood films and revealed his interest in creating not so much parodies as "parallel" films that use familiar story lines yet are made in the singular Warholian manner (which explains his name in the title, a la Fellini). Made for $1.5 million (more than three times the budget of his most expensive prior film), starring name performers Carroll Baker, Susan Tyrrell, and Perry King, and using a union crew, *Bad* is the closest Warhol has ever come to making a film that at least *looks* like a "legitimate" Hollywood film. If some enterprising European distributor dubbed the film with serious dialogue it could pass (almost) as a tough Hollywood melodrama—much in the way Woody Allen turned that Japanese film he bought into a comedy by dubbing it with silly dialogue for *What's Up, Tiger Lily?*

P.G. gets her kicks by covering the excitable Mary with aerosol spray.

(1966). That's how low-keyed the performers play their absurd parts in *Bad*, and how serious they look as they recite preposterous lines like "I want you to kill a dog, and I want you to kill it viciously." *Bad* may very well be the most ridiculous film ever distributed by a Hollywood company (Roger Corman's New World Pictures), but it is amazingly consistent in its ridiculousness, with characters, as weird as they are, acting within strict guidelines. First-time director Jed Johnson, just twenty-six, always keeps things under control, resisting

Mrs. Aiken has been responsible for countless murders; now she is about to meet her own end.

the temptation to let his characters run wild (and improvise); as a result this one-gimmick (the absolutely absurd being played absolutely straight) black comedy beats the odds and works beautifully. It is Corman's *The Little Shop of Horrors* (1960) with all the humor but without all the mugging.

"Like all Warhol movies, especially *Trash* [1970] and *The Chelsea Girls* [1966]," writes *New York Times* critic Vincent Canby, "*Bad* means to bewilder the audience by presenting, without moral comment and with a certain amount of glee, a picture of an absolutely rotten society." The characters in *Bad*, whether motivated to perform evil by a desire for money or a need to fulfill a natural yearning to do wrong, are so nasty that they'd give that Richard Widmark villain of *Kiss of Death* (1947), who kicks an old lady in a wheelchair down a flight of stairs, a good run for his money. Working on a contract for Mrs. Aiken, P. G. lowers a car on a garage mechanic's legs; too impatient to wait for the hired assassins, Sarah tosses her crying baby out the window herself; Glenda and Marsha even go so far as to stab a dog with a sharp knife. But these are the only major crimes.

Bad is full of incidents where characters are mean to one another or pull cruel jokes merely to *irritate* those people they don't like. The film opens with the beautiful R. C. intentionally clogging a drugstore's toilet to make it overflow. When L. T. comes to the drugstore, he steals candy. Why? Because it's there. P. G. cuts off the mechanic's thumb for no reason and stuffs it in Mrs.

Aiken's ketchup bottle, then laughingly attacks Mary with a can of aerosol spray. Fat Estelle physically attacks a dog's owner because he wears the same blue pants every day and still has the nerve to comment that she looks ugly in shorts.

The meanest character is Mrs. Aiken, equally obsessed with her hair removal business and the murder-for-hire racket she runs on the side. She flicks lit cigarettes at her ineffectual husband, places broken glass on the floor where she knows her unwanted boarder L. T. will stand, and tells him when the damage has been done to "milk the wound." (At this point, P. G. tells her "You're so cruel.") She constantly reminds Mary, who is married to her prisoner son, that he will never return to her and her ugly baby; chastises Sarah, who calls her to arrange a contract, for allowing hair to grow back on her nose; and, of course, arranges the murders of kids and animals. She is the breadwinner in the family and like most American housewives devotes her life to making ends meet. She holds down two jobs, rents rooms to her assassin employees, takes Mary's welfare check for allowing her to live in a room in the basement, puts a lock on her phone so no one will make toll calls without her permission, and tells a blind newsdealer that she handed him a five-dollar bill when she actually gave him a one.

The Mrs. Aiken role is probably the only part turned down by Shelley Winters in the last twenty-five years. Carroll Baker is an inspired second choice, playing the dowdy character in a beautician's robe and pin curlers, emoting all the compassion of a prison warden. She is terrific—much better than Winters could have been—in what is her best role since *Baby Doll* (1956), her debut film. Baker came back to America from Europe after a ten-year self-imposed exile to work for

Warhol and proved that her real calling wasn't as a sex symbol but as a comedienne.

The part of L. T. was originally intended for drag queen Jackie Curtis. Perry King plays it soberly and somberly, like one of those many insane boarders found in movies since Hitchcock's *The Lodger* (1925). Wearing a leather jacket and carrying a switchblade, L. T. reminds one of the title character King played in *The Possession of Joel Delaney* (1972), only this time instead of carving up bodies he uses his knife to core an apple, whittle away at Mrs. Aiken's chair, and slice a doughnut. The L. T. sequence is the most peculiar in the film, because it has serious undercurrents. He is hired by Mrs. Joyner to assassinate her autistic son so her unhappy husband will stop drinking. But when L. T. enters the boy's room he is unable to commit the crime. (He tosses the kid around the room but produces no emotional response.) Having had a bad childhood himself, neglected by his mother and kept alone in a room, L. T. relates to the plight of this unloved child. He carries the boy into the parents' room where they pretend to sleep while the murder takes place. He throws the boy on the floor and yells at the Joyners to kill the child themselves—knowing that they don't have the courage. This scene is quite poignant, even sentimental, and what is truly remarkable about it is that in a film that is otherwise a complete comedy it is not disruptive; what this sequence does is show us that in scenes that count—the ones that are realistic—Warhol and Johnson do not treat sensitive subjects irresponsibly.

Andy Warhol's Bad is not for everyone. It is made to be a cult film, and I predict that in the next few years, if it receives the exposure it deserves, its cult will grow to enormous proportions.

The film's one serious scene: L. T. feels compassion for an autistic boy.

Badlands

1974 Warner Bros. release of
Jill Jakes production
Director: Terrence Malick
Executive Producer: Edward
Pressman
Producer: Terrence Malick
Screenplay: Terrence Malick

Cinematography: Bryan Probyn
and Steve Larner
Music: Carl Orff, Erik Satie,
and George Tipton
Editor: Robert Estrin
Running Time: 95 minutes

Cast: Martin Sheen (Kit), Sissy Spacek (Holly), Warren Oates (Holly's father), Ramon Bieri (Cato), Alan Vint (deputy), Gary Littlejohn (sheriff), John Carter (rich man)

Synopsis: In Fort Dupre, South Dakota, in the late fifties, Kit Carruthers, a twenty-five-year-old garbageman, starts courting fifteen-year-old Holly Sargis. Holly, who reads pop music and movie magazines, is infatuated with Kit. She thinks he looks like actor James Dean. But her widower father, a sign painter, shoots her dog when he finds out she's been seeing Kit, and forbids him to come near her. While Holly watches with mixed emotions, Kit kills her father with a pistol. They burn down her house and run off.

For several weeks they live in a treehouse they build in a grove of cottonwoods. When several deputies come after the two fugitives, Kit ambushes them and kills them all. Kit and Holly go to the house where Cato, Kit's former work partner, is living. When Cato acts suspiciously and runs toward his truck, Kit shoots him. A young man and a woman drive up to the house. Kit forces them into an underground shelter and fires at them, not knowing if he kills them.

An alert is out for Kit and Holly throughout the Midwest, and they head for Montana. They go to a rich man's home for supplies. They lock him in a closet but do him no harm. They even give him a list of all the things they are borrowing from him, including his Cadillac.

By the time they reach the badlands of Montana, Holly has tired of Kit and no longer pays attention to him, preferring to spend her time, she says, "spelling out entire sentences on the roof of my mouth." They drive on toward Canada, where Kit wants to get a job with the Mounties.

When they stop for gas at an oil rig, a police helicopter swoops toward them from above. Kit kills a policeman in the helicopter and rides off in the Cadillac. Holly, who refuses to go with him, turns herself in. A sheriff and his deputy chase Kit at high speeds across dusty roads. Kit gets away. He then stops his car, makes a stone monument to himself, and on that spot allows himself to be captured. "He's no bigger than I am," says the deputy of his legendary prisoner.

At a military base, where Kit is regarded as a celebrity by soldiers and police, Kit is reunited with Holly. Like him, she is handcuffed. He tells her, "It's too bad about your dad. We're going to have to sit down and talk about that sometime."

Kit and Holly fly off to prison and to stand trial. She will marry the son of the lawyer who defends her. Kit will be executed.

In 1958, Charles Starkweather, nineteen, and his girlfriend, Caril Fugate, just thirteen, made national headlines as they sped through Wyoming and Nebraska and apparently without motivation—not for money or thrills—gunned down ten innocent people. Neither showed remorse when apprehended or when sentenced for their crimes, he to be electrocuted in 1959, and she, who killed no one herself, to serve a long prison term. Director-screenwriter Terrence Malick's independently made first feature, *Badlands,* based on the Starkweather-Fugate murder spree, is a grim study of two similar human by-products of an American society that during the apathetic, lethargic Eisenhower era is so emotionally, morally, and culturally bankrupt that it not only spawns and nurtures heartless killers but makes them folk heroes as well. (Charles Starkweather fan clubs actually sprang into existence, just as years later there would be a run on "Son of Sam" T-shirts.) The murders committed in *Badlands* by Kit and Holly, the screen counterparts of Starkweather and Fugate, are shown by Malick to be a function of their yearning to escape the vacuum that is the American Midwest of 1958.

Like other girls of fifteen in Fort Dupre, South Dakota, the motherless Holly is a virgin, has a pet dog and a fish, twirls a baton, takes music lessons, and studies Spanish (which probably no adult in town speaks other than her teacher). To relieve the boredom of her banal existence, Holly reads about the lives of the stars in her movie magazines. The flowery words and images make a great impression on the lonely girl—her cliché-ridden narration of *Badlands* sounds as if she were trying to compose a story that could be submitted to one of these magazines. Her attraction to Kit (Martin Sheen) is predictable: he looks like movie actor James Dean reincarnated—he even dangles a cigarette from his lips and wears an open jacket over a white T-shirt, the way Dean does in *Rebel Without a Cause* (1955), a title that aptly describes Kit.

Holly doesn't run off with Kit simply because she loves him—she continues to wonder about the type of man she will actually marry—but because by doing so she believes she will become a star in an adventure story. She only *plays* at being Kit's girl, necking with him in

One of Malick's many stunning shots of the landscape with the aimless Holly and Kit starting to drift apart.

Kit and Holly leave a rich man's home with many of his possessions.

the back seat of a car (people neck in fifties movies) but probably not making love to him after the first time (people don't have sex in fifties movies); setting up house (a play house) with him in the wilderness; and learning to load and fire a gun "if I have to carry on without him." Nothing that happens on the journey is real to her—not even the killings; it is all a "movie," and the people killed along the way are seen only as characters in her story "the adventures of Kit and Holly" (or of James and Priscilla, the aliases they take on but never use). At times she admits that living with Kit is as exciting as sitting in a bathtub with the water draining out, but most of the time her narration reveals that she is mentally turning the most mundane events (the movie's visuals) into episodes full of drama, adventure, and meaning. She even makes their ride across South Dakota and Montana, which realistically couldn't take more than a couple of days, sound like a trek of epic proportions. Holly is a fantasizer of the first order, and her greatest wish is that she "be taken off to some magical land." Ironically, at the film's end, when she is being transported to jail, her plane flies among the clouds, and at this moment she must believe that her dream is coming true.

Like ghetto teenagers who decorate their paths with graffiti just to show the world they exist, Kit is obsessed with leaving behind a record of his life, not only to prove he was here but also to show he was *special* in an era that bred conformists. For posterity he buries a bucket full of mementos, sends off other mementos in a balloon, makes a record for the police to find in which he confesses he killed Holly's father, tape-records his personal philosophy (which is surprisingly conservative) on a number of issues, gives a rich man a list of what he is taking from him (including a trophy), tells Holly that

he wants a girl to shout his name when he dies, builds a rockpile at the site where he is taken prisoner, and donates his body to science. Kit believes that by becoming a "celebrity" he can give significance and immortality to a life that otherwise is doomed to be unnoted in the history of the world. Sadly, only by becoming a murderer can Kit achieve his goal.

The beginning of *Badlands* is very similar to Noel Black's *Pretty Poison* (1968), another film in which a director intends his characters to embody a sociological "sickness" that is spreading through America's heartland. The first time we see Holly, she is twirling a baton; the first time we see Sue Ann (Tuesday Weld) in *Pretty Poison,* she is carrying a flag and marching with her high school band. Holly is attracted to Kit, an older stranger who reminds her of a movie star; Sue Ann is attracted (or so we are led to believe) to Dennis (Anthony Perkins), an older stranger who professes to be a secret agent, an equally glamorous occupation. Both girls lose their virginity to their new boyfriends (although it's likely that Sue Ann only pretends she is a virgin) in an outdoor setting, and both find the experience unexciting. Both girls have strict single parents who order these male suitors to stay away from their daughters or face harsh consequences. The murder sequences of Holly's father and Sue Ann's mother (Beverly Garland) begin much the same way: the respective daughters pack their clothes in their upstairs' bedrooms; a parent comes home, goes upstairs and finds the boyfriend there, and is confronted with a gun and killed. The twist in *Pretty Poison* is that Dennis is unable to shoot Sue Ann's mother, and Sue Ann gleefully does it herself. In *Badlands,* Kit kills Holly's father while Holly stands by, mildly upset. But the real difference between the films comes next. Kit tells Holly she can call the police and

Holly's father looks at Kit for the first time and doesn't like what he sees.

turn him in for the murder—which is exactly what Sue Ann does to the innocent Dennis—but Holly chooses not to, deciding instead to run off with her boyfriend—something Sue Ann promised Dennis she would do, but had no intention of carrying out.

Pretty Poison ends a little while later, but *Badlands* has a long way to go. Unfortunately, Kit and Holly have already been totally defined, and for the remainder of the film they will not waver in the least from what we already know about them and expect of them. They lack the unpredictability, the intelligence, the spark, and the emotion that make Dennis and Sue Ann so interesting to watch. When they finally split up at the oil rig, Kit and Holly express disappointment in each other, having discovered what we learned even before they fled Fort Dupre: that they are both dull, empty people.

Malick intentionally made Kit and Holly artificial catatonic characters, of course, to make the point that criminals of their ilk are not worthy of the adulation Americans traditionally bestow upon them. Likewise, their murders are deglamorized, trivialized, and made antiheroic, filmed with the same detachment with which the couple carries them out; Kit and Holly get no sexual charge or power sensation from causing death. (Some critics hailed Malick's dispassionate approach to the killings; others condemned it for being too cold and manipulative.) Malick's intent may be valid, but it seems to me that he has forgotten what is told to all first-year writing students: a story about dull, emotionless people and unexciting events need not be dull, emotionless, and unexciting.

Badlands was the surprise hit of the New York Film Festival in 1973, when response was so enthusiastic that Warners bought world distribution rights—only to see its film make almost every critic's Top Ten list the following year and still flop at the box office. It has never caught on with the public despite a cult of critics who have praised this film like few others of the seventies. In fact the critics who select films for the New York Film Festival even brought it back in 1979 in hopes of giving it the exposure it still hadn't received.

There is much in *Badlands* that impresses me greatly. Sissy Spacek, as always, is splendid—though I believe that her haunting evocation of Holly has the effect of promising us more from the character than the script is able to deliver. As in *Days of Heaven* (1978), Malick pays wonderful attention not only to the plants and trees of the landscape but to nature's sounds, like the swirling breezes and even the chirping crickets (he is the only director besides Nicolas Roeg who understands that insects are a dominant force in most environments). The visuals are extraordinary: the enormous sky and the large full moon and red clouds that fill it; indoor settings lit by the sun filtering through the windows; great gobs of dust sweeping across the barren land at twilight. Malick even gives the desolate badlands a beautiful, ethereal quality that is something to behold.

But I have strong reservations about *Badlands*. I find it a self-consciously artistic film that panders to an intellectual art-house audience. My major complaint is the same one I have with Michael Cimino's *The Deer Hunter* (1978): the director treats his characters with condescension, indicating a belief that their "inferior" cultural and intellectual backgrounds prevent them from comprehending the sociological and political implications of what is happening in *their* lives as thoroughly as a sophisticated movie audience can. Films about a particular cultural type shouldn't be purposely over the head of that type.

Their murderous odyssey over, Kit and Holly show no remorse but a lot of pride as they are escorted by policemen and soldiers.

Beauty and the Beast

(La Belle et la Bête)

1946 France Released in the U.S. by Lopert Films
Director: Jean Cocteau
Producer: Andre Paulve
Screenplay: Jean Cocteau
From a fairy tale by Mme. Leprince de Beaumont
Cinematography: Henri Alékan
Music: Georges Auric
Editor: Claude Ibéria
Running Time: 90 minutes

Cast: Jean Marais (Avenant/The Beast/The Prince), Josette Day (Beauty), Marcel André (The Merchant), Mila Parely (Adelaide), Nane Germon (Félice), Michel Auclair (Ludovic)

Synopsis: Beauty lives in a big country house with her merchant father, her rotter brother Ludovic, and her two wicked, socially conscious sisters Adelaide and Félice. Because her sisters refuse to do any work, she takes it all upon herself and never complains. She loves her brother's reckless, handsome friend Avenant but won't marry him because she believes her father needs her too much.

The Merchant goes to the city on business and discovers that he is bankrupt. He travels home at night in a harried state and gets lost in the forest. He takes refuge in a decaying castle which appears to him when the thick shrubbery suddenly opens up. In the morning he picks a rose in the garden to take home to Beauty. A hideous Beast wearing nobleman's clothes steps out. It is his castle and his garden, and he tells the Merchant that he must die for stealing a rose, his most prized possession. The terrified Merchant gets the Beast to allow him to return home to say good-bye to his children. The Beast tells him that he can send one of his daughters to be killed in his place.

At home, the Merchant tells his horrible story. Beauty volunteers to take her father's place and returns to the castle. The first time she sees the Beast, she screams and faints. When the Beast sees Beauty, he falls in love and gives up all thoughts of killing her.

As time goes on, Beauty begins to enjoy the Beast's company. But every night when he proposes, she turns him down, as she loves Avenant.

The Beast gives Beauty permission to return home to visit her sickly father. He tells her that if she doesn't return when she promises, he will die of grief. To show her that he trusts her, he gives her the key to Diana's Pavilion, where he keeps all his earthly treasures.

Beauty returns home. When she cries while speaking kindly about the Beast, her tears become diamonds. Excited by the possibility of acquiring great wealth, Beauty's sisters steal her key. They give it to Avenant and Ludovic, who ride to the Beast's castle.

Because she cannot find the key, Beauty returns to the castle after the time she had promised the Beast she'd return. She has discovered she loves him, but when she comes upon him he is dying of grief. At the same time, Avenant climbs into Diana's Pavilion. Diana's statue comes to life and shoots him with an arrow. As he dies, Avenant takes on the appearance of the Beast. The Beast dies in Beauty's arms and suddenly comes to life as a Prince who looks much like Avenant. The Beast is no longer cursed, because Beauty has agreed to marry him—he has become the handsome Prince he was meant to be. Beauty and the Prince ascend magically to a heavenly home where they will be joined by the Merchant and Beauty's sisters, who will be her servants for a change.

One of the screen's great couples:
Beauty and the equally beautiful Beast.

The movie screen is the true mirror
reflecting the flesh and blood of my dreams.
—Jean Cocteau

Jean Cocteau considered himself a poet who made films, painted, and wrote plays, novels, scenarios, and essays as the means through which to express his poetic vision. He directed only a few films during his long, illustrious artistic career— the experimental short *Blood of a Poet* (1930), *Beauty and the Beast* (1946), *L'Aigle à Deux Têtes* (The Storm Within) (1948), *Les Parents Terribles* (1948), *Orpheus* (1950), and *The Testament of Orpheus* (1959), all of which he wrote—but his small body of work encompassed several traditions (the avant-garde, surrealism, naturalism, classical drama) and had the impact, as Sheldon Renan points out in *An Introduction to the Underground Film* (Dutton, 1967), of "introducing film as a medium that [can] transform reality into living, subjective poetry." His films are totally unique to the cinema, "personal past all practicality," writes Renan, "and poetic with a vitality that surpasses preciousness"— all wonderfully exciting alternatives to the factory-line commercial Hollywood product.

Beauty and the Beast, Cocteau's first feature, is the cinema's most "poetic" work, a beautiful, dreamlike

(T) The overworked Beauty loves the handsome Avenant but refuses to leave her father so she can marry him. She is happy when the Beast becomes a Prince (R) who looks much like the dead Avenant, but this Jean Marais incarnation looks like a clown compared to the majestic Beast.

telling of the classic French fairy tale. Long held dear by critics and film historians, it has turned up with increasing regularity over the last few years in repertory theaters, as well as being featured on the Public Broadcasting Service's *Film Classics* series, the result being that nowadays it seems to be the *new* "all time favorite film" of about every other person you meet. Its popularity is not too hard to explain. First-time viewers are invariably impressed and surprised that such an unusual film exists; that Cocteau dared make a fairy tale without drastically changing the content of the original story; that he dared make a film with "art" and not box office success as the ultimate goal; and that he dared approach his film as a poet rather than as a typical movie director.

That Cocteau intentionally and somewhat defiantly went against the cinema grain is documented in the journal he kept during production, most recently published as *Beauty and the Beast: Diary of a Film* (Dover, 1972). In regard to the film's glorious music, he wrote:

> At my request, Georges Auric has not kept [the score] to the rhythm of the film but cut across it so that when film and music come together it seems as though by the grace of God.

About the photography:

> Alékan tells me that all the material I think is admirable is considered by some people at the studio as hopeless, badly lit, white cheese. Doesn't he know yet what I have been used to for years?—every time anybody tries anything out of the ordinary, people go blind and can see only what looks like things they've already seen. People have decided once and for all that fuzziness is poetic. No, since in my eyes

poetry is precision, numbers, I'm pushing Alékan in precisely the opposite direction from what fools think is poetic.

And about the lighting:

> Nothing seems so dreary to me as the photographic uniformity of a film which the know-alls call style. A film must distract the eye with its contrasts, with effects which attempt, not to copy those of nature, but to find the truth which Goethe contrasts with reality. Sometimes I light one face more than another, light a room more or less strongly than it would be naturally, or give a candle the power of a lamp. In the Beast's park I use sort of a twilight which doesn't correspond to the time of day when Beauty goes out. If it suits my purpose, I will link up twilight with moonlight. And it's not just because I'm dealing with a fairy story that I treat realism in such a high-handed way. A film is a piece of writing in pictures, and I try to give it an atmosphere which will bring out the feeling in the film rather than correspond to the facts.

Cocteau was excited by film because it gave him the chance to "explore," as he put it, "the reality of the unreal." An example of this is when Beauty's wicked sister looks in the Beast's magic mirror and a monkey is reflected back at her; while the monkey image is "unreal" (impossible) it reveals the *truth* (the "reality") about her. Cocteau felt that only by filling his films with surreal imagery—human beings who have been turned into Beasts; statues that have life; mirrors (Cocteau's most frequently used symbol) that are doorways between life and death or between the earth and the netherworld; death as a physical presence; the dead walking the earth and the living visiting the dead; characters who move at strange speeds—could he convey the precise emotions, feelings, and atmosphere that he believed represented an absolute truth. He was anxious that viewers would find madness in this method and felt compelled to explain what he was trying to accomplish with his surreal imagery. In *Orpheus*, for instance, the dead Heurtebise, who has come back to life, may well be speaking to the audience when he tells the confused Eurydice: "It's not necessary to understand, it's necessary to believe." *Beauty and the Beast* begins with a note from Cocteau asking his audience to revert to their childhood so they will be able to accept the fantastic elements of his story. He needn't have worried; no one in the film thinks it odd that such a Beast exists, and neither do we.

Much of the charm of *Beauty and the Beast* is that it is presented so simply, without self-indulgence or pretense. Film scholars can read the picture as a Freudian tale: Beauty has too strong an attachment to her father; the Beast and Avenant (who does not exist in Leprince de Beaumont's story) represent the split parts of *one* personality, that of the Prince. But it is such a magical, pleasing work that I prefer to take it at face value as being a totally innocent, literal adaptation of a children's story.

The picture's major strengths are its visuals. Christian Bérard's atmospheric castle sets, fanciful costumes, and magnificent mask and wardrobe for the Beast (who looks like an elegant werewolf) make the fairy tale come to life. Alékan's photography is deliberately supersharp so that if the picture were in color it might look like a filmed comic book. His camera rarely moves, yet within his fixed frame comes a mesmerizing panorama of movements (most haunting are the billowing curtains in the castle's hallway), shadows, darkness, the clear white sky, and characters who, set against that sky, are filmed as if they were moving statues. There are countless striking visual passages; among the particularly memorable are the Merchant's terrifying visit to the Beast's dark, forbidding castle, in which statues move and unattached arms extend from the walls and hold candelabra; Beauty's arrival at the castle, in which she floats / walks trancelike through the various rooms and hallways; Beauty pacing impatiently while awaiting the Beast's nightly visit, as a statue behind her moves its head back and forth to follow her strides; Beauty taking the sad Beast's hand from his face and holding it high as she respectfully walks him down the park steps, the camera pulling back at full speed; Beauty looking into the magic mirror, seeing her calm face replaced by that of grieving beast, and then seeing her own image again, which is now sad. There are two scenes in which magnificent visuals are complemented by strong dialogue: when the smoking, bloody Beast orders Beauty back to her room so she won't see him in such an inhuman state; when the Beast is told by Beauty that she loves Avenant and upon hearing his name reacts as if he had been pierced in the heart.

Josette Day is perfectly cast as one of literature's great heroines: innocent, strong of character, honest,

The Beast carries Beauty through Cocteau's surrealistic castle set.

loyal, exquisite, and so virtuous that even while she is wearing pearls and a lavish gown she volunteers to do the family laundry. I am less taken with Jean Marais, Cocteau's protegé and housemate, who went on to become one of France's top romantic idols because of this film. He plays three parts (which in itself is enough to convince many of a brilliant performance), but I don't think he distinguishes himself in any of them. (I particularly dislike his rasping voice as the Beast.) Perhaps the problem lies in the characters: the obnoxious, foolish rapscallion Avenant, the wimpish, self-pitying Beast, and, worst of all, the Prince, an effeminate, conceited fellow who looks like he plays the harp, stuffs snuff in his nostrils, and spends much time at the hairdresser's. I find the Beast insufferable groveling at Beauty's feet and always apologizing for his ugliness,* and I can't understand why she falls in love with him; but at least the Beast is physically imposing and, in his own way, handsome. He is certainly more interesting than Avenant. So when the Beast becomes a human being who looks like Avenant with a permanent, our immediate reaction is anger. We understand why Beauty says that she is a bit disappointed in the resemblance and that there is no more Beast—we assume that she misses the Beast's face, which she finally realizes was beautiful. But then, in this terrible, unnerving finale, Beauty suddenly becomes flirtatious, as if all along she had only pretended to be an innocent, and concedes that she is pleased with the physical change in her fiancé. We aren't pleased by any means. This transformation, the worst scene in the picture, almost ruins what went before it: a true king has been demoted to a prissy prince.

---

*Life does imitate art. While making *Beauty and the Beast*, Cocteau suffered from numerous ailments, including impetigo, a terrible skin infection, which ravaged his face and put him in the hospital for a time. These words in his diary could have been written by the Beast: "I look at myself in the mirror. It's awful. . . . It would be criminal to make a film suffer from my suffering and ugliness." And: "The pain is now torture, a torture so horrible that I am ashamed of ever showing myself."

Bedtime for Bonzo

Publicity shot for this surprisingly amiable comedy shows stars Diana Lynn, Bonzo, and Ronald Reagan.

1951   Universal
Director: Frederick de Cordova
Producer: Michel Kraike
Screenplay: Val Burton and Lou Breslow
From a story by Raphael David Blau and Ted Berkman
Cinematography: Carl Guthrie
Music: Frank Skinner
Editor: Ted J. Kent
Running Time: 83 minutes

Cast: Ronald Reagan (Professor Peter Boyd), Diana Lynn (Jane), Walter Slezak (Professor Hans Neumann), Lucille Barkley (Valerie Tillinghast), Jesse White (Babcock), Herbert Heyes (Dean Tillinghast), Herbert Vigran (Lt. Daggett), Brad Johnson (student), Ann Tyrrell (operator)

Synopsis: Professor Peter Boyd teaches psychology at Sheridan College. He is engaged to Valerie Tillinghast, the dean's daughter. But the dean has reservations about Peter when he learns Peter's father was a habitual criminal. The dean is a former genetics teacher and believes Peter may have acquired some of his father's "criminal" genes. Peter thinks the dean's theory is way off base. He believes that environment and not heredity is the major influence on a human being. When the dean breaks off his engagement to Valerie, Peter realizes that he had better prove his theory.

Without the dean's knowledge, Peter borrows the university-owned Bonzo, an unhappy baby chimpanzee, from friendly professor Hans Neumann. He takes Bonzo home with him, planning to raise him as if he were a human child. To make the home setting even more conducive for rearing a "child," Peter hires a nanny named Jane to act as surrogate mother. But since Jane is young and pretty, Peter keeps Valerie away from the house. Jane and Peter clothe Bonzo, let him sleep in a crib, and feed him at the kitchen table. By bringing up Bonzo in an atmosphere of love and kindness, Peter hopes to teach him morality, the difference between right and wrong. Jane falls in love with Peter. She is upset that he considers the happy life the three of them lead together as papa, mama, and child an experiment and that he plans to give Bonzo back to the university once he has proved his point—and that he plans to marry Valerie.

Valerie walks out on Peter once she discovers Jane is living with him. Jane walks out on Peter once she realizes he can never feel the way she does about their "family." Bonzo becomes upset that his peaceful house is falling apart. In his distressed state, he breaks into a jewelry store and steals a valuable necklace. Peter tries to return the necklace but is caught with it in his pocket. The police will not believe that Bonzo is capable of such a crime.

Jane returns when she finds out what has happened to Peter. The college has made a deal to sell Bonzo to Yale for research, but Jane and Hans refuse to let the chimp be sold. Hans, knowing he will lose his job, says he will buy the champanzee for the same high fee Yale was offering.

Jane brings the chimp to the police station. She tells Bonzo to return the necklace. While the stunned police watch, Bonzo climbs into the jewelry store and returns the necklace to its proper place. Peter is cleared. Bonzo has learned the difference between right and wrong. Peter and Bonzo are heroes around the college. (And Hans is not fired). Peter and Jane drive off on their honeymoon. Bonzo plays in the back seat.

The day after Ronald Reagan was elected president, there was an item on the all-news television network that caught my suspicious eye. A chimpanzee named Dena, wearing boots, jeans, and a plaid shirt, was shown walking into a Dallas bank and depositing a large sum of money. There was no mention of how Dena came by this money; nor was there a discussion of political payoffs—in fact, the reporters who covered the Dallas event didn't even hint that there was a connection between the Reagan victory and the chimp making a bank deposit. Apparently, they weren't familiar with *Bedtime for Bonzo* and how much Reagan's simian costar in that picture contributed to his election. Not that Dena is Bonzo using an alias to avoid autograph hounds—the original Bonzo (worth $50,000) and his four stand-ins died in a trailer fire in the early fifties on the day he was supposed to help present the first Patsy Awards. But Dena might very well be one of Bonzo's descendants to whom Reagan feels obligated.[*] After all, their famous ancestor—talented, extremely likable Bonzo—has been a help to Reagan throughout his political career.

In 1966, Reagan ran for governor of California against Edward "Pat" Brown, the incumbent. Brown came up with the not-so-bright idea of using part of his advertising money to sponsor late-night television showings of *Bedtime for Bonzo*.[†] He probably figured that those people who couldn't stay up to see the picture would at the very least see it listed in the paper and think that the man who wanted to be their governor once played a character named Bonzo—possibly a close

---

[*]After Reagan's victory, Bonzo creators Raphael David Blau and Ted Berkman presented Bonzo II, a chimp that looks remarkably like the original. They also announced that "Bonzo" merchandise was selling like crazy.

[†]In 1980, all Reagan movies were kept off television because of the equal-time rule that was not in effect in 1966.

cousin of Bozo the Clown. If people did tune in the film, Brown expected them to laugh at an actor so lightly regarded in the industry that he was reduced to playing papa to a chimp, and to start comparing his acting talents unfavorably to those of the scene-stealing Bonzo. Either way, confident Brown believed that the picture would reduce Reagan's credibility as a serious governor, actor, and human being. In 1980, some Democrats across the country came up with a plan similar to Brown's and booked *Bedtime* for Democratic fundraisers. Universal 16, the current distributor of the picture, announced that all prints of the film were booked solid for all of 1980. (Admittedly, some groups—the smart ones—that booked *Bedtime* were pro-Reagan). Of course, as history records, Reagan soundly defeated Brown in the California gubernatorial election of 1966 and won the big one, by a really big margin, in November of 1980. In both election campaigns, the attempt by Democratic politicians and anti-Reagan film exhibitors to demean Reagan by screening his pictures, especially *Bedtime for Bonzo*, completely backfired.

Many voters who saw Reagan's films conceded he was a thespian of limited range but that fact, they argued, proved he hadn't the skills to "act" honest and therefore must really *be* honest. Others who watched the actor they had heard such terrible things about were surprised that, with the exception of his work in a few awful films, he wasn't that bad. Reagan was certainly one of the dreariest romantic leads in cinema history—as a heartthrob he fell somewhere between Hugh Marlowe and Richard Carlson—but undeniably he had an amiable, appealing screen personality. Mitch Tuchman accurately wrote in *Film Comment* (July-August 1980):

> . . . Within a particular range of characters he was quite a creditable performer with a pleasing personality—a normal, healthy boy, more playboy than lover, incapable of malice. His was the enormous appeal of the "natural," free of fussy artifice, highfalutin airs, or pansy make-believe.
>
> He wasn't bad; he was chicken-hearted. He lacked daring. He never played a lumbering hunchback or devious Nazi spy. He had no talent for

Peter saves the depressed Bonzo from a suicide attempt and returns him to Professor Neumann.

dialects and never wore a putty nose. He sprang from no theatrical tradition. . . . If he resumbled anyone at all, it was Glenn Ford or James Garner, sympathetic, unremarkable, and complacent; brave, clean, and reverent; wholesome, handsome, and dull, but occasionally good enough to suggest he had been underestimated.

Reagan's major importance to the movie industry was not as an actor but as two-time president of the Screen Actors Guild. (He brought about better wages for actors but helped break a major craft union strike by having Guild members cross picket lines and testified before HUAC that he was trying to eliminate Communist content in scripts.) Nevertheless, he did turn in several fine performances in his long career: as the ill-fated Notre Dame football star George "Win One for the Gipper" Gipp in *Knute Rockne—All American* (1940); as George Armstrong Custer in *Sante Fe Trail* (1940), supporting Errol Flynn; as a double amputee ("Where's the rest of me?") in *King's Row* (1941), his most famous role; as a disgruntled farm laborer in *Juke Girl* (1942); as a liberal southern prosecutor taking on the Ku Klux Klan in the much underrated *Storm Warning* (1950); as baseball great Grover Cleveland Alexander in *The Winning Team* (1952); as an undercover government agent in *Cattle Queen of Montana* (1954); as a cowpoke in *Tennessee's Partner* (1955); in his only outright villain role in Don Siegel's *The Killers* (1964), his last film; and—unfortunately for Reagan's political enemies—as a psychology professor trying to raise a chimpanzee as if it were a human child in *Bedtime for Bonzo*. One critic went so far as to say that Reagan, as well as Diana Lynn, proved to be "an excellent farceur" in *Bedtime* and was very instrumental in helping the picture do well at the box office.

Bedtime for Bonzo has a silly title, but it is certainly not as ridiculous as *Bonzo Goes to College* (1952), the sequel Reagan refused to appear in, and a picture that might well have harmed his future in politics. *Bedtime* is much better than its sequel. For one thing it deals with a legitimate, interesting premise based on actual scientific experiments. The effects of heredity and environment on human beings are analyzed by rearing chimps from birth as if they were human beings. (Interestingly, the script by Val Burton and Lou Breslow requires Reagan

to play a character who believes environment is the key to a person's personality. While Peter insists that his father would have been a good man if he hadn't come from the slums, he doesn't discuss "environment" in Marxian terms and speak of social-political-educational-economic factors on individuals from the day they are born; he thinks of "environment" only in terms of the amount of attention, love, and kindness a child receives at home. While Peter is no socialist, this script —ironically—probably contributed to Val Burton's subsequent blacklisting in the industry as a suspected communist.) *Bedtime* asks the question: *Can a monkey be taught morality through an upbringing based on love and kindness?* The picture doesn't really answer this question, but at least it provides more food for thought than the sequel's *Can Bonzo lead his college football team to victory?* (If Francis the Talking Mule can do it, then surely Bonzo will have no trouble.)

Except for moviegoers who don't like animal films, most viewers will find *Bedtime for Bonzo* quite enjoyable, as its good reviews attest. Bonzo is fun to watch whether he is riding his tricycle in his cowboy garb, doing flips in his crib, making cooing noises while Reagan hums to him, sloppily eating his morning mush, wearing glasses, or running away from an out-of-control vacuum cleaner. He is truly a cute, sweet chimp, and very affectionate—one of the better screen animals. It is, of course, inadvisable to compete with an animal for audience attention because the actor will lose— doubtlessly, that is why in Tarzan films Johnny Weissmuller rarely allowed himself to be in the same frame with Cheetah when the chimp did his amazing tricks. But Reagan proves to be an adequate screen partner for Bonzo, only rarely being his foil, and never being the fool anti-Reaganites expected to find when they rented the picture sight unseen. As usual, Reagan is reliable, friendly, earnest, and an all-around good sport—all admirable qualities. If Bonzo has an advantage over Reagan as a screen performer it is that Bonzo has the comedic range to surprise us every now and then. After Reagan's first moment on the screen, he is *predictable*. Perhaps this is what viewers (voters), who often confuse the character on the screen with the actor who plays him, find so comforting about Ronald Reagan's screen image.

Behind the Green Door

1972 Mitchell Brothers Film Group
Directors: Jim and Art Mitchell
Producers: Jim and Art Mitchell
Screenplay: Jim Mitchell and Ed Karsh
Cinematography: Jon Fontana
Music: Not original
Editor: Jon Fontana
Running Time: 72 minutes

Cast: Marilyn Chambers (Gloria),
George S. McDonald (Barry),
Johnny Keyes (stud), Ben Davidson
(doorman), Jim and Art Mitchell
(kidnappers)

Synopsis: Two truckdrivers tell a
diner counterman a strange
experience they had. While sitting
on the terrace of a resort hotel,
they watched helplessly as two men kidnaped a pretty young blond
woman. That night they went to a secret night club and took their
seats facing the stage. They were surprised to see the blond, Gloria,
being led onto the stage through a green door by six young women
dressed in nuns' habits. There was an announcement that Gloria
would be forced to participate in various sexual acts and, as a result,
would achieve great pleasure and forget her fears and anger.

The six women undressed Gloria and themselves. They kissed
her all over and performed cunnilingus on her in preparation for what
was to follow. In spite of her fears, she became sexually aroused.

To an African beat, a black man appeared wearing a leotard from
which his long penis stuck out. He made love to the confused Gloria,
slowly at first, but then much faster. Her passion built, and finally
she had a tremendous, satisfying orgasm.

Meanwhile, everyone in the audience became excited and partici-
pated in an orgy.

Gloria was led to three men who sat on trapezes, their penises
jutting out of holes in their leotards. Completely taken over by her
sexual impulses, Gloria became a participant in the sexual activities.
She willingly gave hand jobs to the men on her right and left and
performed fellatio on the man who sat in front of her. He had an
orgasm, shooting his sperm into her mouth.

*To take advantage of Marilyn Chambers's fame following the
successful releases of* Behind the Green Door *and* The Resurrection of
Eve, *the Mitchell Brothers put together the documentary* Inside
Marilyn Chambers, *which features sizzling footage from those two
films plus interviews. This is a handbill passed out in Los Angeles.*

In the late sixties, when I lived in Madison, Wisconsin, there was a theater (the Majestic) in the center of
town, near the capitol, that usually showed foreign
films. Most often it showed a Bergman or a Truffaut, but on occasion it played an X-rated sex film of
foreign or domestic origin that had no artistic pretensions. Trash: Isabel Sarli movies, Kim Pope in *The Love
Object* (1969), etc. Soft-core skin flicks that had much
heavy breathing, some nudity, a little pubic hair. Everyone familiar with the theater was aware that for some
reason *bright* lights would go on the *exact second* the
picture ended. Consequently, about a half minute be-

The fantasy begins: women dressed as nuns lick Gloria's body.

fore the conclusion of the sex films, almost all the men in the theater would jump up and make a mad dash down the dark aisle toward the exits so no one would be able to identify them. I still remember one well-dressed businessman or legislator frantically beating his fists against a door that wouldn't open.

All across the country at this time, raincoated men were sneaking in and out of theaters showing skin flicks—particularly those tawdry grind houses in San Francisco and New York featuring 8-mm and 16-mm hard-core shorts (stag films and "beaver" loops).* But this would change in a hurry due to public acceptance of a number of soft-core sex films as "legitimate" mainstream motion pictures. *Russ Meyer's Vixen* (1968), Radley Metzger's *Therese and Isabelle* (1968) and his subsequent *Camille 2000* (1969) and *The Lickerish Quartet* (1970), the earlier Swedish-made, Metzger-imported *I, a Woman* (1966), and the inept but money-making 3-D film *The Stewardesses* (1970) were major breakthrough films. These made filmmakers aware that for a sex film to be commercially successful it must attract women as well as men, and that the best way to arouse female interest was to make films about *women* striving for sexual fulfillment.

The commercial success in America of the Swedish *I Am Curious (Yellow)* (released in the United States in 1969), a political film that contains a couple of moments of explicit sex, proved that women would come to hard-core sex films provided they played in first-run theaters. The first hard-core films to get bookings in suburban and neighborhood theaters were quasi-documentaries and "educational" marriage-manual films. The release of Bill Osco's *Mona* (1970), about a girl who

---

*According to *Sinema* (Praeger, 1974), by Kenneth Turan and Stephen F. Zito, in 1969 there were approximately twenty-five theaters in the United States playing hard-core films.

can't get enough of fellatio, marked the first time a 16-mm hard-core narrative feature played in theaters. A precursor to *Deep Throat* in terms of subject matter, *Mona* and Paul Gerber's *School Girl* (1970), a fairly good sex comedy about a girl who enters the sexual underground so she can gather information for a college term paper, both made inroads into attracting a mixed audience. But of course it was Gerard Damiano's *Deep Throat* (1972) that finally managed to make hard-core porno fashionable. Major critics reviewed it. A few even liked it. Everyone saw it. Children discussed it. Star Linda Lovelace became a household name, and instead of being treated as a leper, as performers in stag films of the past had been, she became an instant celebrity. She even was a popular, much-in-demand guest on the talk show circuit. As *Deep Throat* moved up *Variety*'s top-grossing films list, it was not uncommon for there to be long lines in front of (showcase) theaters where it played, and the men and women in those lines came from every socioeconomic group.

Deep Throat made it acceptable for middle-class men and women and their college-age children to attend porno films that played in legitimate theaters. But there would only be a few other hard-core films that would attract mixed audiences before *attending* porno was no longer chic. (Porno films, however, would be the best sellers, come the advent of the cassette industry.) Without question, the three most important hard-core films of the period were *Deep Throat*, Damiano's *The Devil in Miss Jones* (1973), and Jim and Art Mitchell's *Behind the Green Door*, considered the *classiest* porno film ever made. All three are better made than the run-of-the-mill porno flick; each contains a variety of sexual acts that are illegal in many states; each features a woman in the lead part; each is about a woman who becomes sexually liberated. *The Devil in Miss Jones* is the only one of the three I liked when it came out, and I think that was because actress Georgina Spelvin was the only one of the three lead actresses who looked as if she'd enjoy the sex even if the camera were turned off. The other two films, especially *Deep Throat*, seem lazy and lacking in imagination.

To me, *Behind the Green Door* is just an elaborate stag film, and more boring than many of that dreary lot. But it does have special appeal to many people, including those women who prefer sex films to be *erotic* rather than raunchy like Damiano's. I don't find *Green Door* erotic, but at least that is what the Mitchell brothers strived for. Damiano, on the other hand, worked for impact. He hoped that his strong images would elevate his films to the top of the porno list and force critics to consider them legitimate *independent* productions— thus making them commercially more viable in terms of distribution. At least the Mitchell brothers, while entrepreneurs, seemed as concerned with artistry as with making money. I don't think them as talented as Damiano, but I like them better. One reason: Linda Lovelace (who today contends that she was forced to make porno films) received a straight salary for her work in *Deep Throat*, a picture that has made countless millions of dollars; Marilyn Chambers was given a salary plus residuals for participating in *Green Door;* when the picture took off at the box office she justifiably made a great deal of money.

The story for *Green Door* was taken from a male-written pamphlet that circulated around army barracks during World War II, but it was filmed in a hypnotic, dreamlike fashion in hopes that women seeing the film might recognize their own sexual fantasy. I believe that if *Green Door* continues to be popular among women —who were a major part of the film audience in 1972 and today buy *Green Door* video cassettes—it could be that they can identify with the character of Gloria. Screenwriter Ed Karsh spoke about this when interviewed by *Adam Film World* (Vol. 4, No. 7, 1973):

> Here is a woman who is kidnaped, is brought through that barrier and goes through the process whereby she is not only a participant, but a *willing* and active participant. She abandons the fear that brought her into the circumstances, and that is an exhilarating kind of thing, and transforms all that energy into a tremendous sexual response to the circumstances. It builds from the beginning to the end. A woman has got to empathize with the woman on the screen. Obviously that is a male chauvinist point of view; I can't speak to the issue of what women feel, so this is my assumption, based on the women I have spoken to.

If women do indeed identify with Gloria, it could be because they see themselves as star Marilyn Chambers, who is pretty enough to be a regular motion picture heroine. (Not until her *Green Door* follow-up, *The Resurrection of Eve* [1973], did Chambers talk; then it was discovered by all that she can't act.) Chambers, who did a famous nude dive into a pool in the film *Together* (1971), doesn't look anything like the ugly, hunchbacked, pimply-faced women who populated stag films. She is good-looking, blond, shapely, and healthy. She is a middle-class WASP who has adorned boxes of Ivory Snow with a baby on her knee. How All American can you get? It is no secret that much of the initial success of *Behind the Green Door* was the result of people wanting to see the 99⁴⁴/₁₀₀% pure "Ivory Snow Girl," a minor celebrity whose face they knew well, participate in sex acts. As it was with Lovelace and Georgina Spelvin, women were curious about Chambers, but once they saw her I believe she was the only one whose sexual activities many could relate to. Chambers's trapeze act (she performs fellatio on one man and simultaneously gives two others hand jobs) may be difficult, but, in comparison, Damiano's women have *amazing* sexual talents.

I suppose the trapeze scene is the most erotic sequence in the film, although some viewers undoubtedly consider the scene in which Gloria is seduced by several women (dressed as nuns) more stimulating. I find the sex scene between Gloria and the black stud (played by ex-boxer Johnny Keyes) too self-conscious. The orgy among the spectators is more realistic than the ritualistic sex on stage, but there's a really fat guy in there who spoils the whole effect. The climax of the film is a literal sexual climax, taking ten minutes of screen time; it is described in *Sinema* this way: "The image of one of the men ejaculating into the heroine's mouth is shot in extreme slow motion, and it is repeated and reworked by means of dissolves, overprinting, and reverse printing. The color solarizes and the image becomes brilliant, abstract, changeable." This sequence is fascinating for those interested in special effects, but considering what is happening in the shot, I found it erotic, then embarrassing (because of its extreme length), and finally boring. And because of the abstract way it is filmed, you're not even sure if Marilyn Chambers is the female in the frame.

Now that Linda Lovelace has disavowed her association with porno films, Georgina Spelvin has aged into her forties and is no longer given leads, and Desiree Cousteau threatens to retire from sex films, Marilyn Chambers is the undisputed queen of pornography, the industry's fantasy girl. She has long been a regular contributor to a popular adult magazine, and in 1980 made a comeback picture, *Insatiable,* that did good business due to her extensive promotion campaign (she did several radio talk shows in the buff). But it is *Behind the Green Door,* now one of the top-selling video cassettes, that continues to be her entry into middle-class homes when those doors—sometimes green—have been closed to other top porno stars.

The fantasy ends: Gloria services several men in the notorious trapeze sequence.

Beyond the Valley of the Dolls

1970 20th Century-Fox
Director: Russ Meyer
Producer: Russ Meyer
Screenplay: Roger Ebert
From an original story by Roger
Ebert and Russ Meyer
Cinematography: Fred J.
Koenekamp

Music: Stu Phillips
Songs: Bob Stone and Stu
Phillips, Lynn Carey and Stu
Phillips, and Paul Marshall
Editors: Dann Cahn and Dick
Wormel
Running Time: 109 minutes

Cast: Dolly Read (Kelly MacNamara), Cynthia Myers (Casey Anderson), Marcia McBroom (Pertonella Danforth), John LaZar (Ronnie "Z-Man" Barzell), Michael Blodgett (Lance Rocke), David Gurian (Harris Allsworth), Edy Williams (Ashley St. Ives), Erica Gavin (Roxanne), Phyllis Davis (Susan Lake), Harrison Page (Emerson Thorne), Duncan McLeod (Porter Hall), Jim Iglehart (Randy Black), Charles Napier (Baxter Wolfe), Henry Rowland (Otto), Haji (Cat Woman), the Strawberry Alarm Clock

Synopsis: Kelly, Casey, and Pet (Pertonella) are an aspiring all-woman rock group. Harris, their manager and Kelly's boyfriend, convinces them to go to Los Angeles to see if they can make it big. Once there, Kelly looks up her generous aunt Susan, who offers her part of a family inheritance despite the objections of her conservative lawyer, Porter Hall. They all go to a party given by rock producer Ronnie "Z-Man" Barzell, who takes a liking to Kelly. Harris gets jealous. With Ronnie's help the band, now called The Carrie Nations, becomes bigger and better. Kelly has less and less time for Harris. When Kelly starts to date gigolo Lance Rocke, Harris is miserable and starts an affair with porno star Ashley St. Ives, who likes to make love anywhere but in bed.

Casey, confused about why she is unattracted to men, becomes friends with Roxanne, a lesbian fashion designer. Pet, although in love with Emerson, a young law student, has an affair with heavyweight boxing champion Randy. Randy beats Emerson up twice and Pet kicks him out of her life and asks Emerson to forgive her. He does. Z-Man holds many parties. At one, Baxter Wolfe, an old love of Susan's, comes back into her life and she agrees to marry him. She fires Porter when she discovers he has slept with Kelly in order to get her to waive her share of the inheritance.

Ashley breaks up with Harris and calls him gay, which hurts him terribly. Drunk and on drugs, he goes into Z-Man's house and fights with Lance. When Lance beats him up, Kelly tells Lance she is through with him. The depressed Harris goes to Casey's apartment. She, too, has been taking pills. Harris makes love to her while she sleeps. She wakes up angry, and pregnant. Roxanne arranges for Casey to have an abortion and the two women become lovers.

The Carrie Nations perform on television. Harris attempts suicide by diving from the rafters onto the stage. He suffers traumatic paralysis and is confined to a wheelchair. Kelly realizes she loves him. She becomes loyal to Harris and plays chess with him.

Z-Man invites Roxanne, Casey, and Lance to his house for a party. They get high on drugs. Roxanne and Casey go into a bedroom and make love. Z-Man ties Lance up and then reveals his female breasts—Z-Man is truly a woman. Although tied up, Lance mocks Superwoman, who takes a sword and cuts off Lance's head. Totally berserk, Superwoman kills his Nazi butler Otto. He then puts a gun in sleeping Roxanne's mouth. She wakes up, and Superwoman blows her brains out. Superwoman chases Casey through the house and shoots her in the head. Too late to rescue Casey, Kelly, Pet, and Emerson charge into the house, and in the ensuing struggle Superwoman shoots herself. Harris discovers that he has feeling in his toes. Kelly and the recovering Harris, Susan and Baxter, and Pet and Emerson have a triple wedding.

From 1959 to 1963, Russ Meyer was known as King of the Nudies. During this period he made a fortune as the independent producer-director-cameraman-editor-writer-distributor of such cheapie harbingers of the Naked Cinema as the ground-breaking *The Immoral Mr. Tees* (1959), *Naked Gals of the Golden West* (1962), and *Europe in the Raw* (1963). Some were fiction and others were stylized documentaries. Infinitely more ambitious were several tongue-in-cheek potboilers he turned out later in the decade that served as the basis for the pre-*Beyond the Valley of the Dolls* Meyer cult: *Lorna* (1964), *Mud Honey* (1965), *Motor Psycho* (1965), *Faster Pussycat, Kill Kill* (1966), *Russ Meyer's Vixen* (1968), and my favorite, *Cherry, Harry, and Raquel* (1969). Set in rugged terrains (swamps, back country, timberlands, deserts) that are inhabited by sexually driven buxom beauties (Meyer's trademark), strong-jawed, no-nonsense heroes, and an assortment of religious zealots, rapists, and sweaty lowlifes, these films from Meyer's second cinematic phase are essentially fake morality plays, in which the numerous sinners either repent or are punished severely. Full of nudity, infidelity, and scenes of extreme violence, they might well have been made by some shrewd, larcenous country preacher to use as object lessons in sermons for which he charged admission.

As skin flicks, Meyer's 1964–1969 films were far superior to those of his competitors. They are extremely well photographed: the first four are in black and white; the final two are in bright color and the characters look as if they are garbed in Disney-cartoon clothes. They contain some truly erotic fantasy-fulfilling soft-core sex scenes (especially those with Lorna Maitland in *Lorna* and the aggressive Erica Gavin in *Vixen*) and fine, sharply edited action sequences (particularly in *Cherry, Harry, and Raquel*) that recall the raw power of the early Don Siegel. But what really gives these pictures their uniqueness—and what impressed early Meyer cultists—is Meyer's willingness to inject his "sex" films with wild, absurd visual humor, dialogue that makes no sense (i.e., *Vixen's* final tirade), and ridiculous plot situations—while his actors play their parts straight. It is as if Meyer is winking at us and saying "Let the voyeurs enjoy the exploitation elements of my films. Both you and I know that I'm too talented to be making skin flicks, but as long as the motion picture establishment ignores me, I might as well have fun by making my films even sillier than the sex film genre dictates." He is like Denholm Elliott in *The Apprenticeship of Duddy Krav-*

The red-hot Carrie Nations, who sing and sleep their way to stardom. Kelly (L) sings lead; Casey (R) backs her up; Pet plays the drums.

itz (1974)—a frustrated filmmaker who, resigned to earning a living making short documentaries of bar mitzvahs, fills them with symbolism in an attempt to turn "home movies" into art films.

Following the tremendous financial success of *Vixen*, Meyer's first film to play in first-run theaters as well as drive-ins and attract females as well as males, Meyer signed a three-picture deal with Twentieth Century-Fox. His first project was to be *Beyond the Valley of the Dolls*, a major, multi-million-dollar production. Initially, *BVD* (as it was called in the industry) was intended to be a sequel to the horrible, money-making Fox film based on Jacqueline Susann's trashy best seller; but soon it was decided that *BVD* would have nothing to do with the original.* Given almost free reign by Fox

*Having received filthy letters from people who believed she had written the script for the X-rated *BVD*, Susann later sued Fox for using the title of her book in the movie's title. Posthumously, she won a $2 million settlement.

to film whatever story he came up with, at last Meyer had the opportunity to showcase the talent and ideas that had supposedly been untapped during his sex film years. Like many of his fans, I believed that *BVD* would rescue Meyer from a lifetime career turning out trivial "sex" films.

To many moviegoers who hadn't seen a Russ Meyer film, *BVD* was a revelation—a film that they (mostly college students) considered to be on their own "far-out" wave length, evidence that there was a genius in their midst whose earlier works deserved investigation. (Thus began the numerous Meyer retrospectives and tributes at colleges and festivals.) But many of us who had been Meyer admirers prior to the release of *BVD* concluded that we'd overestimated his talents. *BVD* may take place in a big city and deal with "sophisticated" characters instead of hicks, but it is certainly no improvement on Meyer's earlier works. Instead of making a cliché-filled parody of skin flicks, Meyer now

COPYRIGHT © 1970 TWENTIETH CENTURY-FOX FILM CORP. ALL RIGHTS RESERVED.

Everyone has several sexual partners in BVD. Among the most relevant couplings are: Kelly and Harris (TL); Kelly and Lance (TR); Pet and Emerson when she professes she loves him and is through with Randy (BL); and Roxanne (L) and Casey, moments before their deaths (BR).

made a cliché-filled parody of overblown Hollywood soap operas like *Valley of the Dolls* (1967). In addition, as screenwriter Roger Ebert has pointed out in *Film Comment* (July-August 1980), Meyer wanted the movie to "simultaneously be a satire, a serious melodrama, a rock musical, a comedy, a violent exploitation picture, a skin flick, and a moralistic exposé of what the opening drawl called 'the oft-times nightmarish world of Show Business.'" I had thought Meyer inventive; he turned out to be conservative and lazy. There's nothing worse than a multi-million-dollar spoof of movies that are already self-parodies.

Meyer is known for his outrageousness, but his timidity is what I see in *BVD*—a fear that if he tests himself his limited talents will be revealed. Instead of aiming high in *BVD* he returned to his skin flick womb and relied on tricks that had succeeded in the past, counting on them to win over a new audience, making no attempt to turn out original, solid work. Once again he avoids using real characters and populates his picture with caricatures. And as if he were embarrassed to be making exploitation films, he tempers scenes of sex and violence with absurd humor so no one will take them seriously enough to judge his writing and directing talent. For instance, if an intimate scene between Pat and Emerson plays badly, he just puts on soap opera music in the background and has them do a few bits that are obviously silly; when Lance is decapitated, Fox logo music can be heard; when it is announced that Casey is dead, crippled Harris immediately announces that he can wiggle his toes and Casey is forgotten. Meyer will just never play a scene straight because he wants to leave himself an out if it doesn't work. Consequently, one scene after another is full of intentionally exaggerated dialogue, clichés, non sequiturs, unresolved and unmotivated plot twists. Then, when the film makes no sense, Meyer laughs that it was intended that way. In fact, it was at the last moment that Meyer and Ebert decided to have BVD end in confusion and to turn Z-Man into a transvestite. At the climax, they have him running around his house executing people (a la the Tate-LaBianca murders) but they did not bother to alter earlier scenes in order to make the switch from Z-Man to Superwoman seem logical. This is no artist at work. In an interview I did with Erica Gavin, the star of Vixen and a costar in BVD, she commented:

> Russ Meyer's not a director, he's a cameraman. He's great at shooting that slick look, having colors very good, the light very bright, with no muted tones and everything looking sharp. As a director, I don't think he really knows what he's doing when he does it. He doesn't really set out to make campy films. To him they're all serious, but they come out that way. The reviews come out saying "It's great, beautiful camp," and he goes along with them: "Yes, it's all camp. It's all a big joke." That's bullshit. His thinking is just so back in the sixties that his work seems to be camp.

I agree, only I believe that from BVD on, Meyer has been content to have his pictures regarded as nothing more than camp. That is an attitude that is hard to respect.

BVD is really a terrible film, energetically but poorly acted by ex-Playboy bunnies Dolly Reed and Cynthia Myers, model Marcia McBroom, and under-emoting or overemoting stars. (I do have a special fondness, however, for Charles Napier, Erica Gavin, and Michael Blodgett.) Roger Ebert is a fine critic with the Chicago Sun-Times and cohost of the TV series Sneak Previews, but his script is crude, stupid, and boring. As a critic he attacks films which show scantily clad women being terrorized by maniacs; so how does he justify the offensive scene in which Z-Man puts a gun into the mouth of sleeping nude Roxanne, who fellates it a few seconds without waking, and then has her head blown apart (shown graphically)? Or when Z-Man chases Casey with a gun while she wears a see-through nightgown? BVD is a smug film full of lines that are meant to show off Meyer's and Ebert's clever grasp of screen clichés: "Don't bogart that joint"; "Hang cool, teddy bear"; "Why don't you lose your laundry, Peter?" Even new lines are meant to sound like clichés; when Harris tells Ashley that he wants a woman who will lick him between the toes (he's joking, of course), she suddenly becomes Confucius: "Boys who wear sandals probably don't get many offers."

Cryptic jargon and Meyer's rapid-fire editing techniques are meant to camouflage the picture's emptiness. But the holes in the script come through. The biggest problem is that the final murder sequence has the effect of overwhelming what up to that point had been the thrust of the film: the problems that Harris and Kelly have been having with their deteriorating relationship. Also, what is all the fuss about Kelly's share of the inheritance? Once she's a big rock star, as the lead singer of a group that sounds like the Partridge Family, she certainly doesn't need the money.

There is little in BVD to recommend. The only thing I enjoy is counting the numerous combinations of people that get into bed together. BVD is a flashy, artificial snow job. Most disturbing is that Meyer's "put-on" morality of his sixties films has been carried over to his biggest production. Those people killed in the film are those that Meyer considers deviates; so not only do a Nazi and a murderous transvestite die, but also a bisexual and two lesbians who haven't really harmed anyone. Those characters who have repented for their misdeeds and amoral behavior are the ones who survive. The world has been cleansed. Is Meyer parodying "movie morality" or does he really believe this?

BVD signaled the demise of Meyer as a talent critics had to take seriously. It proved that what we had seen in his early films was everything Meyer had to offer. He made one more big studio film after BVD, the extremely dull The Seven Minutes (1972), purporting to be a protest against censorship. The picture flopped. Then by choice (!), Meyer returned to making independent sex films—in the Vixen mold but not as good. This unfortunately is the milieu to which he is best suited.

Russ Meyer explains how he wants "Z-Man"/"Superwoman" to kill Lance.

1971 Warner Bros. release of a
National Student Film Corp. production
Director: T. C. Frank
Producer: Mary Rose Solti
Screenplay: Frank and Teresa Christina
Cinematography: Fred Koenekamp and John Stephens
Music: Mundell Lowe
"One Tin Soldier" written by Dennis
Lambert and B. Potter; sung by Coven
Editors: Larry Heath and Marion Rothman
Running Time: 112 minutes

Cast: Tom Laughlin (Billy Jack), Delores Taylor (Jean Roberts), Clark Howat (Sheriff Cole), Bert Freed (Posner), Julie Webb (Barbara), Kenneth Tobey (Deputy), Victor Izay (Doctor), Debbie Schock (Kit), Stan Rice (Martin), Teresa Kelly (Carol), David Roya (Bernard), Katy Moffatt (Maria), Susan Foster (Cindy), Paul Bruce (councilman), Lynn Baker (Sarah), Susan Sosa (Sunshine), Gwen Smith (Angela), John McClure (Dinosaur), Cissie Colpitts (Miss Eyelashes), Howard Hesseman and members of the Committee

Synopsis: An ex-Green Beret in Vietnam and a hero in a war he didn't like, Billy Jack, a half-breed, has returned to the Arizona reservation near Wallich. He has turned his back on an unjust, racist society and lives in some ancient ruins with an old holy man who prepares him for a sacred initiation ceremony. A hapkido expert, he protects the Indians, wild horses which town boss Posner tries to round up illegally and sell for meat, and Jean Roberts's Freedom School. The Freedom School is under constant criticism from the conservative Wallich townspeople and Posner because it takes in any kid with a problem, whether the kid is black, white, Indian, or Chicano. Jean is grateful that Billy Jack watches over the kids who love him, but, being a pacifist, she worries that Billy's violent nature will serve as a bad example. It is because of his enormous fondness and respect for Jean that Billy tries to control his temper.

Mike, Sheriff Cole's deputy, who like most people in town (but not Cole) is controlled by Posner, beats up his teenage daughter Barbara when she tells him she became pregnant while a runaway in San Francisco. She runs away again, and Billy, Cole, and her doctor arrange for Barbara to live and study at the Freedom School without Mike's knowledge. She is an unhappy girl who has never liked anyone—but soon she mellows from being around Jean and the kids.

In town, several kids from the school are denied service in an ice cream parlor because some of them are Indians. Bernard, Posner's son, who is always trying to do one thing his father will be proud of, pours flour on the children and beats Martin, an Indian who is a pacifist. Billy Jack arrives, beats up Bernard, and in turn is attacked by Posner and several men. Billy is overcome but not until he has kicked Posner in the face and delivered karate blows to several others. Cole breaks up the fight before Billy gets too badly hurt.

Posner supports an ordinance to restrict the hours during which kids from the school will be allowed in town. Most council members support Posner as the school has a bad image. When two members visit the school, however, they are impressed and invite several people from the school to perform street theater in the town. As a result, animosity between the townspeople and the long-haired schoolkids lessens. Jean is raped by Bernard, but she won't tell Billy because she knows that he would kill the boy and be arrested and the school would be closed down.

Barbara falls off a horse and loses her baby, which the doctor says would have been white. The baby is cremated. Bernard convinces Mike that Martin was the father, and the prejudiced man becomes furious. He kidnaps Martin and beats him. Barbara, who loves Martin, agrees to go back home if Martin is freed; but before this takes place, Martin escapes. Bernard gives chase and kills him.

Billy, who has figured out that Bernard has raped Jean in addition to killing Martin, goes after the boy despite Jean's protests. Bernard shoots him, but Billy kills the boy with a karate blow. Mike tries to ambush the wounded Billy, but Billy kills him. Now wanted by the police for two killings, Billy holes up in a church surrounded by police and reporters. Jean visits him and they express their love for one another. She convinces him to stand trial. He agrees to this if Barbara is put in Jean's custody and the Freedom School is funded for ten years. Kids salute him as he is driven to jail.

Billy Jack

I remember first seeing Tom Laughlin in William Wellman's 1958 film *Lafayette Escadrille*. There is a comical baseball game among the flyers that ends when a short, wise-guy pitcher conks a tall skinny batter on the head and is chased by him off the field. Years later, when I again saw the picture, I learned that the tall skinny unknown was Clint Eastwood and the short unknown was Tom Laughlin. Around this time Laughlin appeared in several other films without making a name for himself, including *Tea and Sympathy* (1956), *South Pacific* (1958), *Gidget* (1959), and *Tall Story* (1960). He also wrote and directed *The Proper Time* (1960), a film about college and premarital sex that probably hasn't been shown anywhere in twenty years. The first real inroads Laughlin made into the film industry came in 1967 with the release of American International's *Born Losers*, considered by many to be the best "biker" film ever made. Laughlin (under his T. C. Frank pseudonym) directed this antiviolence picture (which has a lot of gratuitious violence) and appeared in it as Billy Jack for the first time.

The financial success of *Born Losers* convinced Laughlin and his wife Delores Taylor to make another film using the Billy Jack character, but this time, instead of aiming for the drive-in audience they would go after

A hero who believes that violence is the only way to bring about peace.

Jean with the teen-age girls who admire her. Unlike Billy Jack, she believes in passive resistance.

the enormous alienated-youth audience. Because they would be dealing with such personally felt subjects as Indian mysticism (they were both students of Indian culture) and alternative education (they had founded a Montessori school in California), the Laughlins (again under various pseudonyms) directed, produced, edited, and wrote Billy Jack, as well as playing the two leads. And it was their insistence on having absolute control over all phases of production that resulted in what they have termed "one of the weirdest success stories in modern cinema history."

Billy Jack began filming under the auspices of AIP, but when the studio ignored the contracts and started interfering with what the Laughlins were trying to do, Laughlin and Taylor chose to shut down production. Eventually they worked out an amicable agreement with AIP whereby they could take the property to another company. Joseph E. Levine of Avco Embassy agreed to finance the picture after AIP's withdrawal, but on the day contracts were to be signed—six weeks after a verbal agreement had been made—Avco changed its mind without explanation and refused to sign. Next Twentieth Century-Fox gave financial backing to the Laughlins to complete filming. Laughlin got Richard Zanuck, studio chieftain at the time, to agree that Twentieth was not to edit the film in any way until Laughlin had turned in his completed version of the film; but Laughlin found

out that Zanuck had taken the print of the film from the studio vault before Laughlin was finished editing it and was planning to cut it on his own. So Laughlin sneaked the soundtrack out of the lab and left Zanuck with an expensive film that had no sound. When Laughlin threatened to erase a reel a week off the soundtrack, Zanuck gave in and agreed to sell Laughlin his picture.

Finally, the Laughlins took their $650,000 completed film to Warners, which bought it for $1.8 million, and the picture was released in 1971, almost three years after production began. It quickly became known as the sleeper of the year, with people (mostly juveniles and college students) going back to see it four and five times. While it did badly in major markets, it hit it so big in places like Dayton, Duluth, St. Louis, Kansas City, Minneapolis, and Omaha that it earned a phenomonal $30 million; and a year after its release there were still three thousand prints in exhibition.

But the Laughlins were not satisfied, and filed a $51 million breach-of-promise (and antitrust) suit against Warners for improperly publicizing the film. Laughlin greatly embarrassed the studio by taking his "cause" to the people. Just as he promoted Billy Jack as the messiah of the counterculture, he portrayed himself as the "Billy Jack" of the industry—a rebel who was trying against great forces to get his film shown to the public. At first glance, it seemed that Laughlin was trying to achieve

Billy Jack holds his own against racist Wallich townspeople who are angry at him for sticking up for Indians.

justice for all filmmakers, but many of us became suspicious that there was primarily a profit motive behind his actions when we noticed that among Laughlin's chief complaints was that Warners had improperly merchandized "Billy Jack for President" buttons, and Billy Jack magazines, posters, records, and pamphlets.

Warners and the Laughlins settled out of court, the end result being that Wearners agreed to re-release the picture in 1973, and this time give it a massive publicity campaign. In an unprecedented move, Laughlin and Warners rented sixty-five theaters from exhibitors in Los Angeles (designated the advertising campaign's test city) into which they placed *Billy Jack*. (This *rental* procedure is called four-walling, and the distributor takes in all the proceeds.) In the month-long Southern California trial run *Billy Jack* grossed an amazing $2.9 million, which Warners and the Laughlins split fifty-fifty. Knowing their advertising methods paid great dividends, Warners and Laughlin then rented 389 theaters in August-September 1973 in New York, Philadelphia, Chicago, and Detroit at a cost of $1.1 million a week; they spent another $750,000 a week on ads. Within two weeks, *Billy Jack* had made $6 million in these four cities alone. From there, *Billy Jack* went on to rake in another fortune during its full release throughout the country. The industry shook its collective head in disbelief.

In their introduction to the *Billy Jack* screenplay, the Laughlins, with vanity that their respective characters in the picture do not possess, wrote: "Billy Jack did indeed become a most influential and successful picture with the young people of America, making it the greatest youth culture picture of our times." Its popularity with the youth of America cannot be disputed, but I wonder if it wasn't less the result of the young being on the same wavelength as the Laughlins than it was because the Laughlins had calculatingly catered to the "politics" of this socially conscious younger generation. I always felt there was a trace, or more, of dishonesty connected with the Warners-Laughlin promotion (in their publicity releases) of the honesty and sincerity that is, according to them, present in every frame of the film; I can't help believing that (whatever the Laughlins' politics) this picture was specifically designed to financially exploit the youth market. *That* is why it gives them everything it wants. There is a "do-your-own-thing" mentality that dominates the film, as well as continuous praise for youthful idealism and independence. The picture, like its audience, is for justice and equality, yoga, the creative arts, meditation, role-playing therapy, wild horses, gun control. It is against bigotry, bullies, child-beaters, formal education. Nothing controversial. (One thing it does do that other films have shied away from is aim criticism at specific targets *by name*: the Nixon cabinet, the Bureau of Indian Affairs.) It preaches pacifism, but what really excites audiences is the violence generated by Billy Jack.

The half-breed Billy Jack serves as the link between the white world and that of the Indian; the theme of the picture is that the disenchanted youth of America have an ally in the Indian: "The whole spiritual wisdom of the great holy men, the Indian tradition is now what the young people of the world are looking for." Becoming an Indian is not impossible. Billy tells us it is not even a matter of blood. But he doesn't really tells us what "being an Indian" means. (Stripping oneself of an ego? Being bitten repeatedly by rattlers?) Most Indians are kept in the film's background—except for the nebbish Martin, who carries around a saying by St. Francis of Assisi, and allows the girl he loves to learn to ride a horse while she's pregnant. The only Indian audiences want to be like after seeing this film is Billy Jack, and that's only because he goes around beating up and shooting their enemies. At the beginning of the film the kids from the school put on a skit in which the new Christ is born (and is black) and the kids give him a "Power" salute. At the end of this film Billy Jack is taken from the church and off to prison (Calvary), and all along the road kids give *him* the same "Power" salute. It is eerie that these pacifist-taught (by Jean) children regard the violent Billy Jack as *their* savior. And it is especially disturbing because the picture and its ad campaign were designed to make Billy Jack and Tom Laughlin be one and the same in the public eye. Such narcissism would not appear again until Sylvester Stallone and *Rocky* (1976).

The film itself isn't so badly made. It's an entertaining action movie—like a fair low-budget western or, like *Born Losers*, a motorcycle film. If it is pretentious at times, it is also energetic at others. And it has several pretty good sequences: I particularly like the very realistic city council meeting scene during which both the kids and adults show their worst qualities; and all those scenes in which Jean and Billy discuss pacifism and violent retaliation (the Laughlins definitely have a chemistry that is appealing).

The plot has flaws. For instance, Billy's demands to the governor would never be met. The one flaw that I find unforgivable is having the city council members and then the townsfolk become impressed with the work being done at the school solely because they are amused by the improvisational skits (which I'd seen elsewhere before they were supposedly "improvised" for this film) done by school members whom we recognize as being the famous improvisational group, The Committee. These people should become impressed with the school because of the *children* who are living, learning, and creating there—not on account of these overaged "Ringers" (who are like pros playing in a college sports contest). My only other objection is that Bernard is killed. For much of the film, we are made to feel sorry for him because of the harsh treatment he is given by his father. We sense that he will end up becoming friends with kids at the school who were also *victims* of poor unbringings. But Laughlin turns him into an outright villain, having him kill Martin and rape Jean; and he

Billy Jack takes part in a sacred Indian ceremony.

thus becomes deserving in Billy's eyes of being killed.

Laughlin is a good, charismatic action hero—his hapkido is spectacular—and he is believable, except when he does a bad Brando imitation (as in the ice cream sequence). Taylor is fine, too, although her face and voice are always *too* full of emotion. As Joan Mellen wrote in *Cinéaste*, "Only Jean, whose rough-hewn features bespeak the pioneer woman rather than the ingenue, escapes the Hollywood mold." Pauline Kael, whose positive reaction to the film was based mostly on the performance of Taylor and the Jean Roberts character, was especially taken with the manner in which Jean discussed being raped. In *The New Yorker* (November 27, 1971) she wrote:

> I can't remember another movie in which the rape victim explained what the invasion of her body meant to her or how profound the insult and humiliation were. This woman isn't young . . . and it's never suggested that she's a virgin, and she hasn't been beaten or injured. This kind of rape might be treated jeeringly, as of no consequence. Yet the film pauses for these emotions, which were perhaps improvised by Delores Taylor.

In a 1975 interview in *Cinéaste* (Vol. VI, no. 4), Jane Fonda called *Billy Jack* an "extremely *progressive* film." She explained: "Billy Jack takes the American superman as its main image, and that has to be improved on, but here you have a Vietnam veteran who comes to the aid of a minority people and you have a real debate about pacifism versus armed resistance. Why think what it means that people in [ultraconservative] Orange County [California] are lined up to see it. That's fine."

In the same interview, Fonda spoke of how the sequel, *The Trail of Billy Jack* (1974), goes even further in dealing with concrete politicial issues. But after a tremendous test run in California, due mostly to another heavily financed ad campaign, the picture died at the box office. *Billy Jack Goes to Washington* (1977) was not even released. America's love affair with Billy Jack—or is it Tom Laughlin?—had apparently ended.

At the end, Sheriff Cole leads martyr Billy Jack to prison, where he must await trial for murder.

Black Sunday

Also known as *La Maschera del Demonio (The Mask of the Demon)*

1960 Italy A Galatea-S.P.A. production released in the U. S. in 1961 by American International Pictures
Director: Mario Bava
Producer: Massimo de Rita
Screenplay: Ennio De Concini and Mario Bava
From the story *The Vij* by Nikolai Gogol
Cinematography: Ubaldo Terzano
Music: Roberto Nicolosi (Italian version); Les Baxter (English version)
Editor: Mario Serandrei
Running Time: 83 minutes (but it may vary according to print)

Cast: Barbara Steele (Asa and Katia), John Richardson (Dr. Andre Gorobec), Ivo Garrani (Prince Vaida), Andrea Checchi (Dr. Choma), Arturo Dominici (Javuto*), Enrico Olivieri (Constantin), Antonio Pierfederici (the Pope), Clara Bindi (the innkeeper)

Synopsis: In Moldavia in 1630, the beautiful witch princess Asa and her lover Javuto are put to death by Asa's brother. Asa, who is a vampire, puts a curse on her brother's descendants and vows to get her revenge. A spiked demon's mask is hammered into her face.

In 1830, Dr. Choma and his young assistant, Dr. Andre Gorobec, travel through Moldavia. As they are traveling by coach through the frightful woods, a coach wheel breaks. The two doctors continue on foot in the direction of a howling noise. They enter a crypt on the Vaida estate and discover the tomb of Asa. Her mask breaks and a decomposed head can be seen. When a bat attacks Choma, he cuts his hand. His blood drips onto Asa's face.

Leaving the crypt, the doctors meet Katia, who looks exactly like Asa. She tells them that she, her father (Prince Vaida), and her brother (Constantin) live a sad life on land the people of Moldavia think is haunted. The two men drive on to an inn.

Asa is revived by Choma's blood. She calls for Javuto to rise from his grave, and he does so by turning his grave site upside down. He goes to the castle and enters the Prince's room. The Prince drives him away by holding up his crucifix but is so terrified by the ordeal that he becomes deathly ill. Katia and Constantin send their servant Boris to bring back the doctors. But Boris doesn't arrive at the inn. It is Javuto who brings Choma to the castle. He takes Choma through a secret passage in the fireplace to the crypt. Asa sucks blood from his neck. Choma goes to the Prince and kills him. Asa tells Javuto that she wants the blood of Katia—only that can make her immortal.

Andre arrives at the castle. He is suspicious of Choma, who acts very mysteriously. He comforts Katia. They fall in love.

Boris is discovered along the road, drained of his blood. A little girl tells Andre that she saw a man with a mustache pick up Choma at the inn. She points to a picture on the castle wall. A priest recognizes Javuto's painting. He and Andre go to Javuto's grave. They find Choma inside. Realizing Choma is a vampire, the priest drives a stake through his eye.

Katia searches the castle for Andre and Constantin. She sits by her father's body. Her father sits up and tells her he is a vampire and wants to drink her blood. Javuto intervenes and destroys the Prince by throwing him into the fireplace. He takes Katia to Asa. Just as he is about to bite into Katia's neck, he hears Andre in the castle. He goes to fight him. Asa grabs Katia, but when she goes to drink the blood from Katia's neck, she finds a crucifix there.

After a brutal fight, Andre tosses Javuto down into a pit where Constantin is. Constantin crawls out. Before he dies, he urges Andre to save Katia.

Andre enters the crypt. Asa pretends to be Katia and tells him to drive a stake through the real Katia who is lying on a rock slab unconscious. He is about to do so when he notices that Katia is wearing a crucifix. He opens the robe that Asa wears and sees only bones. The priest arrives with the townspeople. They burn the screaming Asa at the stake. Andre and the priest pray for Katia to return to life. Their prayers are answered.

*Listed in some sources as Javutich

In 1630, witch Asa is about to be executed; already her lover Javuto (on the other stake) has been killed by a spike-studded mask that was driven into his face.

The prints I have seen of Mario Bava's Italian horror classic begin with a producer's warning that "the picture will shock you like no picture ever has," that it may be "harmful to the young and impressionable," and that it shouldn't be viewed by anyone younger than fourteen. Twenty years after its release, *Black Sunday* is far more interesting for its stunning evocation of a malefic environment than for its shock content—scores of excessively violent horror films, some even directed by Bava, have understandably lessened its impact. Yet I recall seeing it as late as 1969 and finding the imagery so strong that I could see why England would ban it for eight years. The spiked demon's mask being driven into Asa's face, the maggots crawling around the eye sockets of Asa's skeleton, the older doctor being drawn toward the reborn Asa's face, which is covered by holes from the spikes, Andre pulling back Asa's robe and discovering her body is all bones—if there were even more gruesome images like these, then perhaps it would still be banned in England.

(But other than these shocks, there is little in *Black Sunday* that couldn't be found in Universal horror movies of the thirties.)

Black Sunday was the first film directed by Bava, considered before his death Italy's greatest fantasy filmmaker. Previously he had been cameraman on Ricardo Freda's *I Vampiri* (1957), the first picture of Italy's vampire cycle, and Freda's *Caltiki, the Immortal Monster* (1960), one of my favorite schlock horror films. *Black Sunday* is as impressive as it is because it reveals Bava's background—almost everything is conveyed visually. Bava's world consists of dark mountains set against a gray sky; mist-shrouded forests where limbs from trees seem to reach out to grab those who dare pass through; two-hundred-year-old graveyards where the soil is too cursed for anything to grow; ancient crypts where bats fly about in the darkness, spiders spin their webs, and decaying walls crumble; and shadowy, ice-cold castles full of secret passageways and enormous hidden chambers. It is a world where light (i.e., the fires

In 1830, Andre and Dr. Choma stand near Asa's crypt. This is one of several glorious sets in Bava's film that represents a decaying universe.

used to burn witches) fights a losing battle against oppressive darkness, and even the pure (priests, virgins) wear black. It is with his camera that Bava, working closely with his gifted art director Giorgio Giovannini, creates an atmosphere where the living and dead coexist (but not harmoniously). In *The Vampire Film* (Barnes, 1975), Alain Silver and James Ursini write:

> The world which Bava conveys . . . is a mutable one, composed of shifting contrasts and colors, of complements and atonalities, a world which moves like Spenser's "ever-whirling wheel" from real to unreal and back again, from life to death and death to life in an unstable landscape of phantasmagorical sights and sounds.
>
> Bava's characters are often thrust into the mutable middle ground between these two existential extremities, where figures glide through misty, opulently decorated yet insubstantial and illusionary settings, a universe of semidarkness where shadows and hallucinations are as graphically actualized as the personages, a special passageway linking the natural and supernatural.

Black Sunday was shot in black and white, and this helps considerably in establishing the haunting mood of the film, as well as working allegorically in a tale about good versus evil. Probably even more effective is Bava's use of a mobile camera to explore his nightmarish world. The film's most interesting moments all contain camera movement. The two doctors enter Asa's crypt, and the camera turns 360 degrees around the spooky, crumbling, cobweb-covered chamber. The doctors ride off in their coach, but the camera returns to the crypt, where after a long tracking shot it settles on Asa's face. Maggots crawl in her eye sockets; her mouth is slightly open and she calls to Javuto to rise—lightning flashes outside, a tomb breaks open, dust flies, and rocks crumble as Javuto returns from his grave. Soon the mobile camera follows the path taken by the now invisible Javuto through the castle toward the Prince's chamber; as it moves along we see things topple over as if a gust of wind was blowing through the castle. Dr. Choma rides in the carriage driven by Javuto. The journey is in slow motion, but paradoxically the coach looks as if it was going as fast as the wind, as the foreground and background seem to whiz by the panning camera. (Where other horror scenes are accompanied by sounds—suspenseful music, bells, wind howling through a broken organ's pipes—this carriage ride takes place in absolute silence and captures the exactness of a nightmare like no other sequence in the picture.) Once in the castle, the doctor follows Javuto, and Bava's camera follows the doctor. Doors automatically close. It is dark. Javuto disappears, but his lantern hangs by itself in the air. A door creaks open, then slams shut. From out of the dark passageway, Choma has entered the crypt. The top of Asa's tomb quivers and bursts off, revealing Asa on her back, panting. It's a great sequence, and, like the other fine moments in the film, it has no dialogue. (In a *dubbed* film, which *Black Sunday* is, moments *without* dialogue can be appreciated.)

Black Sunday convinced many of us that Mario Bava would be a force to be reckoned with in the horror field for many years to come. Unfortunately, he never made another picture half as good. *Planet of the Vampires* (1965), though silly, and *Blood and Black Lace* (1965), though replete with gratuitous violence, can be recommended with some hesitation, but most of his films, like the terrible *Baron Blood* (1972), make me wonder if there were really two Mario Bavas. It may be, as some critics contend, that Bava's mistake was to switch from black and white to color; after *Black Sunday* he preferred showing blood (in bright red) to creating an atmosphere for terror—his forte.

Black Sunday is blessed with the presence of Barbara Steele, the most fascinating actress ever to appear in horror films with regularity. This was the English actress's first starring role—she was under contract to AIP in America but was loaned to Bava—and she proved to be the ideal choice to play the dual role of Asa and Katia. Her beauty is mysterious and unique: her large eyes, high cheekbones, jet-black hair, thick bottom lip, and somewhat knobby chin don't seem syn-

Javuto tries to strangle Andre. It is Asa or Katia who lies by them?

chronized, and as a result her face can be looked on as being either evil (Asa) or sweet (Katia), depending on the beholder. Steele played heroines and villainesses with equal believability in numerous horror films after *Black Sunday* all over Europe, and earned the distinction of being the unofficial queen of the genre. One critic called her "the only girl in films whose eyebrows can snarl"; *Variety* said that she resembled Jackie Kennedy; Eugene Archer of the *New York Times* described her as "a blank-eyed manikin with an earthbound figure, and a voice from outer space." Critics weren't the only ones to take note. Fellini used her in *8½* (1963); her one-time husband, screenwriter James Poe, wrote a part for her in his script of *They Shoot Horses, Don't They?* (1969) which went to Susannah York once the property was taken out of Poe's hands; Jonathan Demme wrote a part for her which she did play in *Caged Heat* (1974). Like a few other actresses who aren't box office sensations—Caroline Munro, Linda Hayden, Beverly Garland, Jenny Agutter, Erica Gavin, Stella Stevens, Angie Dickinson, Glynnis O'Conner, Tuesday Weld, Blythe Danner, Diana Rigg, Barbara Hershey—Steele has a strong cult following. Her fans revere her for her talent, her wit, her emotional range, her intelligence, and her mysterious quality as much as for her beauty, and wish she wouldn't keep accepting minor roles in minor films when she should be doing significant work. After twenty years, her star has not faded, and it is because of Steele, probably even more than Bava, that *Black Sunday,* in which her screen persona was established, remains a cult favorite.

Javuto emerges from his grave.

The Brood

1979 New World
Director: David Cronenberg
Producer: Claude Heroux
Screenplay: David Cronenberg
Cinematography: Mark Irwin
Music: Howard Shore
Editor: Alan Collins
Running Time: 91 minutes

Cast: Oliver Reed (Dr. Hal Raglan), Samantha Eggar (Nola Carveth), Art Hindle (Frank Carveth), Cindy Hinds (Candice Carveth), Nuala Fitzgerald (Julianna), Henry Beckerman (Barton Kelly), Susan Hogan (Ruth), Michael McGhee (Inspector Mrazek), Gary McKeehan (Mike Trellan), Bob Silverman (Jan Hartog), Nicholas Campbell (Chris)

Synopsis: Dr. Hal Raglan's Somafree Institute of Psychoplasmics is a controversial retreat outside of Toronto where patients are taught to physically manifest their inner hostilities toward various individuals (whose parts Raglan plays in psychodramas) as welts and sores on their skins. Raglan loves one of his patients, Nola Carveth, a very insane woman who was beaten as a child by her mother Julianna. He keeps Nola in strict isolation, not permitting her husband Frank to see her, but he insists that she be granted weekend visits from her five-year-old daughter Candy. Frank is very upset that after one of her weekend visits Candy has bumps and bruises on her back—just like Nola did as a child. He decides that the only way the law will grant him the right to keep Candy away from the institute—and her mother—is by finding evidence to discredit Raglan. He visits a former patient of Raglan's, Jan Hartog, who tells him that many former patients are suffering physical deformities.

Nola has a session with Raglan during which she recalls her harsh treatment from her mother when a child. Julianna investigates loud noises and is brutally attacked and killed by a dwarf-sized figure in a red coat. Candy sees who killed her grandmother but is too upset and terrified to talk about it, even to her father, whom she loves dearly. Nola has a session with Raglan during which she complains that her father, Barton Kelly, never protested when her mother beat her. Barton arrives in Toronto to attend the funeral of his ex-wife Julianna. He stays in Julianna's house. The dwarflike creature emerges from under a bed and brutally kills Barton. Frank finds Barton's body and is almost killed by the creature. It jumps on Frank's back but suddenly falls to the ground and dies. The doctor at the autopsy says that the malformed creature died because it simply "ran out of gas." He points out that since the creature has no naval it couldn't have been born like human beings are born.

Meanwhile Ruth, Candy's teacher, babysits for Candy. She gets a rude telephone call from Nola, who is jealous that she is in Frank's house and assumes that they are having an affair. The next morning, two dwarflike creatures come into Candy's classroom. They brutally kill Ruth and take Candy away with them. Nola tells Raglan that she no longer has any hostility toward Ruth and she doesn't know why. From Michael, a tormented former patient at the institute, Frank learns that Raglan has sent all the patients home except for Nola. Michael tells him that she takes care of a large group of children at the institute. That night Frank arrives at the institute. Raglan, who carries a gun, stops him and tells him that it would be safer if he went upstairs to the children's ward to get Candy. He tells Frank that the strange creatures are Nola's children and that they will attack anyone if she is angry. For his safety and Candy's, he tells Frank to lie to her to keep her calm so the Brood, the children of Nola's rage, will be neutralized.

While Raglan goes into the Brood's sleeping quarters to try to rescue Candy, Frank tells his wife how much he still loves her and how he wants them to get back together. She is happy to see him at first, but then decides she hates him and is lying to her. She becomes angry.

The Brood attacks Raglan and kills him. Nola reveals that she has an umbilical cord and an amniotic sac that grows outside her body. She gives birth to a new creature. Frank is disgusted. She tells him that she would rather see Candy dead than go away with him. Upstairs the Brood goes after Candy. Frank strangles Nola. The Brood dies. Frank takes the crying Candy to his car. He doesn't see the welts that grow on her arm—signs of her inner rage.

In one of the more interesting scenes in *The Brood*, Frank Carveth visits Jan Hartog, a former patient at Dr. Raglan's Psychoplasmics Institute, where he was taught to manifest his mental disorders *physically* as welts on the skin. Revealing a hideous lymphosarcoma that dangles from his neck and resembles a cancerous growth on a horny toad, the deathly ill Hartog angrily contends that Raglan's treatment has "encouraged my body to revolt against me." This is a key phrase, because all of Cronenberg's Canadian-made horror films—*They Came From Within* (1975), *Rabid* (1977), *Scanners* (1981), and *The Brood*—are about our bodies in revolt; our bodies becoming our enemies by creating and, sometimes, transmitting "monsters" that literally destroy our flesh and our sanity. It is probably a morbid fascination for disease, as well as an awareness that nothing scares us more than sudden changes in our physical composition, that makes Cronenberg fill his pictures with so many unpleasant images of bodies in open rebellion: open sores, lesions, bumps and bruises, malformations, abnormal growths, and quickly spreading infections that are embodied by living parasites working their way into our systems and moving about under the skin. This suspicion seems confirmed by the fact that Cronenberg sets his pictures in hospitals, private clinics, and other sterile, orderly environments such as the self-sufficient apartment complex in *They Came From Within*. (All houses, schools, apartments, and even outdoor locales in his films are hospital clean.) For what makes less sense and is at the same time more realistic than to have your body or mind suddenly run amuck in places geared to promote health, where people—scientists, doctors, and psychiatrists—are supposed employed to do everything in their power to see to your physical and mental well-being? The unfortunate characters in Cronenberg's work remind me of (and usually are) the victims of not only the wrong operations (or therapy) but botched operations as well.

While I like *The Brood* and am intrigued by the premises of all Cronenberg's films, I question his judgments and directorial maturity—I get the feeling that what he considers to be his films' high spots are those elements I find the least admirable. I think Cronenberg is at his best when building suspense and creating a malevolent atmosphere, and wish that he didn't get so much juvenile pleasure from trying to jolt viewers by repelling them with blatant, often ridiculous, images. For instance, in *The Brood*, he not only has Nola reveal her physical abnormality but has her give birth on the spot just so that when Frank strangles Nola a moment later it will be all the more gruesome because a monster baby gets crushed between them. That's overdoing it. Often Cronenberg is offensive—too often he is downright vulgar; he seems to be getting kicks trying to disgust us. (He's like a kid who puts a green pea in his nose at dinner.) Furthermore it is objectionable that he repeatedly shows that sexual contact leads to "monsters" and infectious diseases. In *They Came From Within*, the violence-inducing parasite enters Barbara Steele's vagina while she bathes; later she passes it to her lesbian lover via an open-mouthed kiss (we see a swelling move from

Nola's children: Candy (L) and the deadly Brood.

her throat to her lover's). In *Rabid*, quasi-vampire Marilyn Chambers, who has a bloodsucking needlelike spine in her armpit, gives a virulent strain of rabies to whomever she kisses. And in *The Brood*, the sexual union of the sadistic Julianna and the weak Barton resulted in producing Nola, who because of her parents' upbringing became progressively insane, and the "symbolic" sexual union of Nola and Raglan has produced the malformed, murderous Brood.

They Came From Within is the picture that gave birth to the David Cronenberg cult. (The cult includes director John Carpenter, who considers Cronenberg the best director of horror films working today.) I think this film has a great setting (an enormous, isolated apartment complex), an interesting premise (a parasite that turns people into raving maniacs moves from tenant to tenant), but is an absolutely terrible picture, one of the worst. It begins promisingly enough with humor and slowly building suspense, but Cronenberg suddenly seems to say "to hell with subtlety" and lets everything get out of hand. About halfway through the picture, the "story" ends—also gone are the rules by which we can judge what is logical in Cronenberg's world—and the remainder of the picture is devoted to one repetitive scene after another in which bands of crazy tenants tear through the building and brutally kill those unaffected by the parasite. *Rabid* is a very similar picture.

The Brood is Cronenberg's best film, his *one* good film. He still tries to shock us with grotesque imagery

(included are several close-ups of bloody, crushed heads), and makes up rules as he goes along so viewers can never get their bearings, but there is much in the picture that is noteworthy. For one thing, we care about the characters. We root for Frank as he tries to save his child; we feel sorry for Nola because of her terrible upbringing and because her incurable insanity prevents

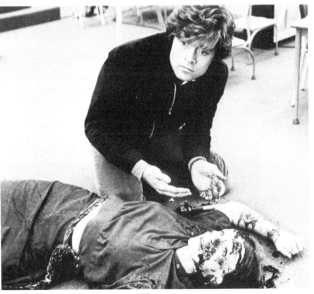

Frank discovers that the Brood has killed Ruth and kidnapped Candy.

To keep Nola's horrible secret until the end, Cronenberg films her throughout from the shoulders up.

her because all through the film he has Frank hugging her, kissing her, comforting her, talking to her in a gentle voice, offering to tell her bedtime stories, tucking her in, leaving the hall light on so she won't be scared, zipping up her coat, taking her to and from school, trying to protect her. And it's incredibly poignant when she hugs him and says in her sweet soft voice "Oh, Daddy, Daddy," or expresses how relieved she is when he tells her that the creature who killed Julianna is dead and won't bother her again. She's such a delicate, vulnerable child, it makes me angry that Cronenberg ends the film by showing welts on her arm (signifying that her rage is building up as it did in her insane mother when she was a child)—why can't contemporary film-makers *ever* let us leave the theater thinking it's all over and all is well?

There are several terrifying sequences in *The Brood*, particularly the murders of Julianna and Barton. When Julianna enters her mysteriously ramshackle kitchen, looks up toward the ceiling, and spots a little crouched figure in red atop the cupboards about to leap on her, or when Candy sees the hooded figure (who may remind you of the dwarf assassin in *Don't Look Now*, 1973) hiding on the stairwell, you are likely to jump. Many of the other scenes with members of the Brood will also give you the creeps. The most chilling of these scenes are when two of them brazenly enter Candy's classroom pretending to be her classmates; and when they walk with Candy hand in hand along the highway in the snow.

her from being the wife and mother she would like to be; we even feel sympathy for the pathetic Julianna and Barton, who try to drink away their guilt. And we love Candy, a sweet, gentle, adorable little girl who is being pulled in too many directions; she is scared and is suffering. It is obvious that Cronenberg also cares for

Frank tells Dr. Raglan that he doesn't like Candy being forced to spend time with her insane mother at the institute.

The Brood turns on Candy.

Perhaps what is most remarkable about *The Brood* is the sinister quality that Cronenberg establishes. He does this by staging intense psychodramas between Raglan and Nola; by creating a restrictive atmosphere around the Psychoplasmics Institute; by making his characters humorless and setting the picture in cold, snowy weather (where everyone wears coats and scarves, and walks under gray skies) to suit their icy dispositions and give us chills*; by giving Hartog a progressively worsening cancer; by giving the autocratic Raglan a henchman; by making us aware of the history of child abuse in Nola's life; and by giving his characters unusual otherworldly surnames—looking in the large Manhattan directory, I was unable to find most character names from the film: Carveth, Raglan, Mrazek, Trellan, Desborough, or Birkin.

I have no real complaint about *The Brood* until the final sequence. I think that the "revelation" that Nola gives actual birth to the Brood is a bit anticlimactic. We know that she created the Brood children and that they are murderers—it makes no difference to us whether they were produced typically, parthenogenetically, or by her willing them into existence. But what I would like to know is, to what extent does Nola control the Brood's actions? If, as Raglan tells Frank, she doesn't realize that the Brood brought Candy back to live in their "dormitory" at the institute, then that means they acted on their own in kidnaping the girl. But if the Brood can act on its own, then why does it take Nola's rage to initiate its actions against Raglan? Then again, if it does take Nola's rage to instigate the Brood's violent actions, as Raglan says, why doesn't Raglan allow Frank to go secretly into the dormitory? Since Nola doesn't feel threatened, there is no reason for her to have an attack of rage at this time. It is in fact Frank's appearance that sets her off; now feeling persecuted, paranoid, and guilty (like most characters in the picture), she shouts at her husband, "You hate me!" and the Brood swings into action, killing Raglan and attacking Candy. This sequence makes no sense to me, but at least it is spooky, lively, and comes after about an hour and a half of absorbing, solid cinema.

---

*The only other recent horror film to exploit the horror elements of a cold environment is Bob Clark's *Black Christmas* (1975), also made in Canada.

Burn!

Also known as *Queimada*

1970   Italy-France   United Artists release of a Produzioni Europee Associates–Les Productions Artistes Associés film
Director: Gillo Pontecorvo
Producer: Alberto Grimaldi
Screenplay: Franco Solinas and Giorgio Arlorio
From an original story by Gillo Pontecorvo, Franco Solinas, and Giorgio Arlorio
Cinematography: Marcello Gatti
Music: Ennio Morricone
Editor: Mario Morra
Running Time: 112 minutes (North American version); 132 minutes (elsewhere)

Cast: Marlon Brando (Sir William Walker), Evaristo Marquez (José Dolores), Renato Salvatori (Teddy Sanchez), Norman Hill (Shelton), Tom Lyons (General Prada), Wanani (Guarina)

Synopsis: In 1845, Great Britain sends secret agent Sir William Walker to the Portuguese-controlled island of Queimada. Great Britain wants to take control of the island because of its sugar crop, but doesn't want to risk a war with Portugal. Three centuries before, the Portuguese had wiped out the native Indians during a rebellion by burning the entire island. Then they had brought blacks from Africa to work on the sugar plantations. The intellectual, foppish Walker convinces the owners of the plantations that they could make greater profits if the Portuguese were kicked off the island. He also befriends a defiant black dock porter named José Dolores and preaches to him about freedom for the black population. He persuades José to rob a bank of a large quantity of gold. The naive José doesn't equate this action with politics, but Walker does. Walker informs the Portuguese government that José is responsible for the robbery so they will track him into the hills. While awaiting the arrival of troops in a small village, Walker teaches the black men of the village how to use firearms. The men wipe out the Portuguese soldiers. Now believing that they can have a successful revolution, Dolores and his men form an army. More and more people join and Dolores becomes a hero. During an annual festival, Walker and Teddy Sanchez, a mulatto with political ambitions, sneak into the governor's mansion. As Walker holds his shaky arm, Sanchez kills the Portuguese governor. Portugal withdraws from Queimada and the island is open to world trade. José expects to be declared leader but Walker points out that he is not equipped to do so. He gets José to disband his army. Sanchez becomes president. He will give preferential treatment to Great Britain in return for keeping him in office. José says good-bye to Walker on the docks. They are still friends.

Ten years pass. Walker has dropped out of society. He is a drunkard and a brawler who haunts the shadiest parts of London. He is hired by the British to return to Queimada. They want him to quell a rebellion being led by José Dolores. Walker employs the methods used by the Portuguese in the sixteenth century. He burns most of the island and shoots rebels as they run from the flames. When Sanchez objects to the British using him and the island for their own interests, Walker has him arrested as a traitor and shot. He adds Sanchez's army to his British forces. The burning and killing continues. There is no food left on the island for the rebels and no villages left in which to hide. At last all the rebels are tracked down and killed in the mountains. Walker captures José. He is surprised that José won't talk to him. This galls him. He likes José and offers him a chance to save his neck. He must renounce his politics, Walker says, and he can go free. Walker is stunned when José says he'd rather be a martyr because he believes that is what revolutions need. Sad that his friend will die, Walker walks across the dock to board a ship back to England. Someone calls him. He smiles because he knows it to be José and this will rid him of his tremendous guilt. But it is not José. A dock worker stabs Walker with a knife. Walker falls to the ground, dead. The revolution will continue.

If a man gives you freedom, it is not freedom.
Freedom is something you take for yourself.
—José Dolores in Burn!

In America, where commerciality determines a film's distribution and "political" films are regarded as box office poison, most moviegoers regard any film that has any antiestablishment sentiments as being political and controversial. But when American filmmakers make so-called political films which criticize once-sacred cows—the President, people in government, the FBI, the CIA, the police, the military, the courts—they typically wait until such criticism becomes fashionable, as in the post-Watergate era when the press attacked these very targets. Their films aren't really controversial but reflect the popular sentiments of the time. More significantly, American filmmakers emphasize that their villains are *individuals* whose actions in the name of America go against everything the American system stands for: they are rotten apples in an otherwise perfect barrel. We are told that if these men who have overstepped the bounds of power entrusted to them are removed from their powerful positions—and we are shown to have a system which can remove such men—and are replaced by decent men, then the system will work again. Though antiestablishment on the surface, these pictures reenforce our faith in the American way of life, in the American political process. They suggest that it is *not* a sociopolitical system rooted in corrupt, antihumanistic activities that is the real villain, but the opportunistic, fascistic men who take advantage of such a system.

These American-made films are not *truly* political because the stories they tell are to be taken as isolated incidents peculiar to one place and time and are not meant to be seen in the light of history or as explanations of the political processes and forces that have determined the course of human events. Therefore, whatever one's politics, it is instructive for American moviegoers to see alternative pictures which attempt to give us a

The Portuguese overthrown, Walker makes sure the new leader will be a pawn of the British; thus he makes sure revolutionary José (R) turns over the island's rule to the weak Teddy Sanchez.

A political irony: Former slaves now employed in Sanchez's army gun down their brothers of the revolution that brought Sanchez to power.

better understanding of history (which does indeed repeat itself and which has indeed shaped the present), where the stories told reveal important political truths about countless occurrences in the past all over the globe, and where such terms as imperialism, colonialism, racist policies, counterrevolution, systematic oppression, systematic torture, nationalism, liberation movements, political conciousness-raising, popular uprisings, terrorism, guerilla warfare, and revolution are defined and placed in historical context. Such pictures, I believe, *are* political. Since so few of this kind of film are made in America and receive adequate distribution, it is fortunate that on occasion political films are imported.

One of the most important radical filmmakers is Gillo Pontecorvo, the brilliant Italian director whose *The Battle of Algiers* (1967) and *Burn!* have both been distributed in the United States.

Many consider *The Battle of Algiers* the best political film of all time. This remarkable work is about the nationalist struggle to oust the French army from Algeria between 1954 and 1962, the year Algeria achieved independence. While *Battle* deals specifically with what transpired in the capital city of Algiers, it is not a film about events but is instead about *tactics* employed by both the oppressors (counterrevolutionaries) and the oppressed (revolutionaries) in cities around the world

where revolutionary struggle takes place. It is a picture that has meaning for people outside of Algeria—that is why it is such an important film. In fact, the American Black Panther Party used *Battle* to teach its trainees urban guerilla warfare. Counterrevolutionaries around the world might also use the film to learn how to combat anticolonialists, but the message of *Battle* is clear: people who want freedom for themselves and their country will eventually secure what they desire no matter what the cost.

As great as *The Battle of Algiers* certainly is, *Burn!* is, I believe, its equal. A painful yet fascinating look at colonialism in both theory and practice, *Burn!* should be regarded as a classic, but because most American critics compared it unfavorably to *Battle* and its distributor, United Artists, released the picture without publicity, relatively few people have seen it and it has been relegated to cult status. In fact, I wouldn't be surprised if more people are familiar with the story of the film's production than with the film itself.

Because of the commercial success and notoriety achieved by *The Battle of Algiers*, United Artists agreed to finance *Burn!*, Pontecorvo's next project. *Battle* was filmed in black and white on grainy film stock and cast entirely with nonactors; its crowd scenes, street battles, and bombings look so authentic that viewers are con-

Walker teaches the Queimada villagers how to fight the Portuguese.

vinced they are watching documentary footage. Budgeted at $3 million, *Burn!* was to be made in glorious color (and the color is indeed glorious), have Marlon Brando in the lead role, have a *great* rousing musical score by Ennio Morricone; it was to be a combination of the romantic type of adventure film that Errol Flynn used to make at Warners—swashbucklers with revolutionary spirit—with a "film of ideas."

Like *Battle*, *Quemada* (the Spanish word for "burnt")—as *Burn!* was known during production—was inspired by historical events. In 1520, imperialist Spain set fire to a Caribbean island in order to quell a native uprising and thus exterminated the entire population. Black slaves were then brought from Africa to replace the Indians who had worked the Spanish sugar plantations. For three centuries, until its global power had waned to a point where it could no longer protect its possessions from internal revolt, Spain exploited the displaced Africans and profited greatly from the island's resources.

Quemada was filmed in Colombia, South America. Production was long and tedious, partly because Pontecorvo cast an illiterate Colombian cane-cutter in the large part of José Dolores. Not only had Evaristo Marquez never acted in a film before—he had never even *seen* a film! Reports came back that Brando was very patient and went along with Pontecorvo's tactic of kicking Marquez lightly below frame level every time he was supposed to move while the camera was running. But after nine months in out-of-the-way locations, Brando packed up and came back to America. There were conflicting reports: he had become sick; he had become bored. Brando agreed to finish the picture but wouldn't return to Colombia, so the film was completed in such locales as the Virgin Islands, France, Rome, and Morocco. Meanwhile Spain began to put pressure on United Artists to alter *Quemada* so that Spain wouldn't be portrayed as a villainous country. Afraid of a Spanish boycott like the one against *Behold a Pale Horse* (1964),

which cost Columbia Pictures several million dollars, United Artists made Pontecorvo change his story. It was then that the Portuguese were brought in and the Spanish disappeared from the movie. The title was changed to *Queimada* (the Portuguese word for "burnt"), and one unscrupulous country was let off the hook and another, whose unscrupulous imperialistic activities were far less widespread, was put on the hook in its place. Deciding that *Queimada* wasn't a title that could assure it of high grosses, United Artists changed it to *Burn!* for American distribution. They also cut twenty minutes out of the American print (which explains why there is some awkward jump-cutting). After all that, they dumped the picture, despite the fact that it seemed the ideal film for the politically conscious movie audience of 1970.

Perhaps they dumped it because it was too political. No doubt they realized that the switch from Spain to Portugal was irrelevant and that the picture still implicated the United States (though not by name) in gross misconduct in the past and in the present. Brando most definitely was attracted to the project because it did make statements that were applicable in regard to American imperialism, colonialism, and racism—and not because it was taking a swipe at the Spain or Great Britain of the nineteenth century. The parallels that can be drawn are clear. We are reminded of the systematic removal (through genocide and exile to reservations) of the American Indians; of the black Africans who were brought to America to be a slave work-force; and of black Americans who continue to seek their civil rights and their freedom more than one hundred years after the Emancipation Proclamation—we recall José Dolores's words, used as an epigraph to this article. In terms of 1970, *Burn!* makes us think of CIA involvement in overthrowing governments hostile to America. The placement of mulatto Teddy Sanchez as England's puppet ruler who represents foreign interests more than his own people obviously reminds us of America's support of an unpopular puppet regime in Vietnam. The burning of land and peasant villages conducted by Walker, of course, is similar to the war strategy of America in Vietnam. But *Burn!* doesn't only apply to American history.

Burn! is also, and maybe most significantly, the story of revolt against colonialism in Third World countries. Interestingly, Pontecorvo, a white man, makes no attempt to get into the psychology of the black. He believes that the black is beyond his or any white person's comprehension—which is why William Walker is so unnerved when José—whom he thought he understood—won't shake his hand or talk to him after he has been captured. (On the other hand, Walker, professional that he is, thinks he has won a gentleman's game from José.) Nor does Walker understand why José won't save his own life by denouncing his revolutionary activities, preferring instead to die a martyr. Walker is distressed because his self-confidence is shattered: he has failed to understand the singular nature of the black and the willingness of black people to fight into eternity for freedom. José comes across with great dignity as played by neophyte Marquez—like Paul Robeson in his better roles. He wants to be a martyr of the people—he is already a symbol of the continuing revolution. As Pontecorvo points out in *Battle*, even the leaders of revolution can be replaced; unfortunately for Walker, José's replacement can be found on the island's docks with a knife in his pocket. Pauline Kael writes:

> *Burn!* is perhaps the least condescending film that has ever dealt with slavery. No doubt the dignity of the slave victims is ideological, but clearly Pontecorvo is not distorting his vision to fit his ideology; when he endows them with nobility, it rings aesthetically true.

Marlon Brando returned home after filming *Burn!* swearing he would kill Pontecorvo if he ever saw him again. Nonetheless his E. Howard Hunt ancestor William Walker is perhaps his most interesting screen character. For the first half of the picture, he is our hero. Pragmatic, intellectual, witty. He seems to genuinely like José and to be concerned about the plight of the blacks on Queimada. Without the superior attitude he assumes when he is around white people on the island —soldiers and foreign businessmen—he teaches the blacks how to begin a "spontaneous" revolution and then how to pull it off. When Walker tells José that the freed island's presidency will go to Sanchez, José is angry but he still meets Walker on the docks and says good-bye to him. Friends.

Ten years later Walker returns to the island. We expect him to eventually join his old friend against the British troops. So why does he burn the island once more, wipe out all Dolores's men, and arrest Dolores? It may have something to do with his professionalism and his practicality. Or his amorality and cynicism. (Pontecorvo and Brando intentionally portrayed Walker as another victim of colonialism/imperialism/racism.) History is full of brilliant political men, military strategists, and philosophers like Walker who, for reasons of their own, fought on the wrong side. We see that Walker really does like José and wants him to live. He also wants José to live to exonerate himself from the guilt he feels and to prove to José and himself that his theories on these black slaves are correct. He cannot accept that in this godforsaken world people with virtues (people like José) exist—if he had known, he might have remained virtuous too. Our hero of the first half of the film has become thoroughly despicable—so despicable, in fact, he thinks José should still call him friend. He deserves being stabbed to death.

And it's good too that he sees his murderer and realizes that even when colonialists wipe out *all* the rebels—as happens in *Battle*—*new* rebels emerge. This ending in *Burn!* is just as wonderful as when the masses appear out of nowhere at the end of *Battle* and march down the steps of Algiers, living proof that revolutions against colonialists go on and on and on, until there is total success.

Walker doesn't understand why the captured José will not talk to him. All around them is the burned landscape—the result of Walker tracking down José.

Caged Heat

1974 New World
Director: Jonathan Demme
Producer: Evelyn Purcell
Screenplay: Jonathan Demme
Cinematography: Tak Fujimoto
Music: John Cale
Editors: Johanna Demetrakis and Carolyn Hicks
Running Time: 83 minutes

Cast: Juanita Brown (Maggie), Erica Gavin (Jackie Wilson), Roberta Collins (Belle), Barbara Steele (McQueen), Ella Reid (Pandora), Rainbeaux Smith (Lavelle), Warren Miller (Randolph), Lynda Gold (Crazy), Mickey Fox, Desiree Cousteau, Joe Viola, George Armitage

Synopsis: After attempting to flee the police, Jackie Wilson is arrested and charged with drug possession and accessory to attempted murder of an officer during the foiled escape. She is taken to Connersville, a tough California women's work prison.

Behind bars, Jackie becomes like the other women who are deprived of male companionship, and has wild sexual fantasies. Even McQueen, the crippled female warden, has unusual dreams with overt sexual overtones. But to those around her McQueen is prudish; in keeping with this image, when she finds a nude photo of Pandora, one of the prisoners in Jackie's cell block, she angrily puts her into isolation. Belle, Pandora's best friend, sneaks through hidden passages to bring Pandora food she has stolen from the prison's kitchen. Jackie becomes friends with Belle and Pandora, but has no such luck with Maggie, a hardened prisoner who is only out for herself. They even have a scuffle in the shower, and McQueen warns the two women not to cause any more trouble or face the consequences. While Jackie and Maggie are working in the kitchen, a female guard intentionally ruins the prisoners' food. Maggie knocks her out, and she and a fellow prisoner attempt an escape. The other escapee is killed, and Maggie is caught. Jackie is also thought to have taken part in the escape, and she and Maggie are both taken to the prison's male doctor to receive agonizing shock treatments meant to tone down their hostility.

While Belle is stealing food for Pandora, another prisoner happens along and Belle accidentally kills her while trying to quiet her down. She is discovered by the guards and is taken to the doctor for shock therapy. While working in the fields, Jackie and Maggie elude the guards, steal a car, and drive off the prison grounds. Shy prisoner Lavelle is caught, however, and is thrown into isolation. Then McQueen assigns her to work as an attendant in the doctor's office. There she sees that the doctor is insane; he fondles, kisses, and has intercourse with Belle, whom he has drugged so she can't resist his advances. He also takes pictures of Belle after he has removed her clothes and gets her to sign a form that will allow him to perform a lobotomy on her and turn her into a vegetable. Lavelle tells Pandora. Jackie convinces Maggie and her friend Crazy, whom they meet at the Society for Sexual Satisfaction, that they should return to the prison and rescue Belle from the doctor. Maggie says she'll go back if Jackie will pay her and if she doesn't have to put herself in real danger. They rob a bank to get money and then confiscate a prison van, which Jackie and Crazy drive through the prison gates.

Just as the doctor is about to operate on Belle, Pandora, holding a long knife, orders him to stop. McQueen enters with an armed guard at her side and orders Pandora to drop the knife. Jackie and Crazy charge in with rifles, Belle is freed, and the doctor and McQueen are taken hostage. McQueen's female assistant orders the prison guards to shoot at the van as it passes through the prison gates. The doctor and McQueen, who are inside the van, are shot. When Maggie sees that the van is in danger, she forgets her self-interest and drives the getaway car into the firing zone. Jackie, Belle, Lavelle, and Crazy jump in, and with bullets still flying, the five women drive off to freedom.

Caged Heat came out toward the end of the low-budget, R-rated women-in-prison cycle that was launched in 1971 with New World's *The Big Doll House*. It failed to make the huge profits of its numerous predecessors, but it is the only one of the lot that since has escaped the drive-ins and triple features to be shown in repertory theaters and such prestigious film programs as those conducted by New York's Collective for the Living Cinema and The Museum of Modern Art. *Caged Heat* is the best sexploitation film of the era, the only picture other than Stephanie Rothman's *Terminal Island* (1973) to almost completely overcome the stringent dictates of the inherently misogynist women-in-prison genre and deserve recognition on its own terms. It accomplishes this by deliberately reversing the formula which has sex and nudity being supplemented by action, and by for the most part refusing to equate violence toward women (or the threat of violence) with *sex* or use such female-in-peril/agony scenes to titillate male viewers.

Prior to *Caged Heat*, newspaper critics either ignored or attacked the women-in-prison films made by New World and other companies specializing in low-budget sex and violence (of the R variety) flicks, but I confess to having had an ongoing curiosity and fondness for the genre. For one thing, it provided first-time directors an opportunity to make films when major studios wouldn't give them the chance, and it was exciting to "discover" talented new filmmakers like *Caged Heat*'s Jonathan Demme before their careers took off.* Equally significant is that this genre featured women as the stars of *action* films—a major breakthrough. Women in bikini outfits or minidresses may look a little strange when in the climactic rebellion scenes they pick up machine guns or rifles—but at least, at last, these are *women* who have seized what, in films, have traditionally been male possessions. It seems disconcerting to see these women with guns pointed at the men who had held them captive, but this is not a surprising reaction, for in a sense what we are witnessing is the symbolic castration of men who had earlier sexually violated and abused these women. Now that the rebellious women have taken their guns away, the men have lost their ability to dominate them physically, and are metaphorically impotent; moreover, now that the women have the guns—used here as male substitutes—they no longer consider asking men to help them with their escape. As most of the women were tossed into prison because of some "crime" against a man and most have suffered male abuse in prison, they gladly accept responsibility for their own destinies and conclude that they must rely on each other and not men to attain their freedom.

The first half of most of these films is about female bondage (which is what the exploitative poster ads for the films stress), with scantily clad women at the mercy of sexually perverse, sadistic (male and female) prison guards, doctors, and wardens; but I see these films not

---

*Demme has since directed a number of critically acclaimed pictures including *Handle with Care* (1978) and *Melvin and Howard* (1980).

so much as bondage films as films in which women ultimately *break the bonds* of oppression and confinement. As John Dorr wrote of *Caged Heat* in *The Hollywood Reporter:* "Prison is a ready metaphor for the repression of modern life, and the women who break their way out . . . suggest a positive, even militant, reaction to sexist victimization."

Similar sentiments were expressed in an unexpected (semi)endorsement for *The Big Doll House* and *Women in Cages* (1972), the two formula-setting films of the genre, in the feminist magazine *Women & Film* (No. 2, 1972). In the article "Bondage Series," the writer Donnie condemned the genre for "the excessive amounts and varieties of tortures as well as the prurient, repetitious exposure of female breasts—a seeming fetishistic convention of these male-directed female films"; but she seemed surprised that in such an exploitative genre there are films which give the audience an accurate view of the "squalor and vileness of prison life and its desperate need for radical change," and also contradict the "traditional image of the helpless, passive female."

Caged Heat, though released after Donnie's article was written, contains everything she found praiseworthy in the earlier women-in-prison films—strong, intelligent, clever women involved in a *group* action; women as lead characters; a not unflattering glimpse at lesbianism and transvestism; prisons shown as cruel, dehumanizing, and terrifying as they really are—minus much that she found objectionable—emphasis on female breasts; the disproportionate use of white and black characters which typically has only one black actress in a lead role.

There is a great deal in *Caged Heat* that distinguishes it from the rest of the genre. For one thing, director-screenwriter Jonathan Demme set the picture in the United States (filming took place in California's Lincoln Heights Jail), significantly making it clear that his attack on inhumane prison conditions is specifically directed against *America*'s prison system rather than at some fictional Latin American country's, as has been the

A tantalizing publicity still from the best of the women-in-prison pictures: (Top, L-R): Rainbeaux Smith, extra, Juanita Brown, Ella Reid, extra; (Bottom, L-R): Roberta Collins, Erica Gavin, extra.

case in the other pictures. Rather than striving for sheer entertainment, Demme dealt with some real issues facing the American prisoner: that they lack privacy, so that even their toilets are in the open, and their persons are subject to embarrassing searches conducted by members of the opposite sex; that some prisoners who are considered hostile are given shock treatments or lobotomies; that drugged prisoners, like indigent hospital patients, are tricked into signing forms that allow doctors to perform hideous, permanently debilitating, operations on them. The ending of the film, during which prison guards fire on the escaping prisoners and inadvertently kill the prisoners' hostages, McQueen and the prison doctor, also has its basis in fact. Demme tells me that his inspiration for this scene was the escape by prisoners on trial from a California courthouse several years back, during which the police accidentally killed the prisoners' hostages and tried to charge the escapees with their murders.

While most films of the genre seem to have been created in a cinematic vacuum by directors who had never seen a movie in their lives, *Caged Heat* makes Demme's cinematic roots quite evident. Several prison sequences remind one of Raoul Walsh's *White Heat* (1949). Demme's use of John Cale's fine blues score (with harmonica whining during outdoor sequences) is similar to Arthur Penn's playing of Flatt and Scruggs's "Foggy Mountain Breakdown" during the speeding-car sequences in *Bonnie and Clyde* (1967). When Jackie, Maggie, and Crazy go to rob a bank and find another group of bankrobbers already there, we might easily flash back to the bungled bank robbery in Woody Allen's *Take the Money and Run* (1969), when two gangs simultaneously pull out their guns. When we are presented with a close shot of a wall in the prison mess hall which has on it the writing "Don't Throw Food"

Cult figure Barbara Steele in one of her oddest roles: Prison Warden McQueen, a cripple who has wild sexual fantasies such as the one seen here in which she dances in the bathroom with top hat and cane.

The thrilling getaway. While Crazy covers her, Pandora jumps out of a prison truck.

and the wall is immediately struck by flying food, I recall the opening of Mark Robson's *Youth Runs Wild* (1944) with its street sign reading "Drive Slowly—We Love Our Children" immediately knocked over by a carelessly driven truck. When the camera pans around McQueen's room and we discover a revealing photo from her pre-wheelchair days when she had a happy family, we may recall the finale of Roman Polanski's *Repulsion* (1965), in which the camera similarly finds a family photo that gives insight into Deneuve's present mental state.

But I don't want to give the impression that the style and content of *Caged Heart* is not singular to Demme; overall, *Caged Heat* is like few other films. The last time I saw it, I was impressed by the film's rare ability to work extremely well as visceral entertainment —the poor soundtrack on the 16-mm print made it difficult to hear the dialogue, but it didn't seem to matter because there is so much movement, and so much action. Most spectacular is the razzle-dazzle escape sequence, in which Jackie, Pandora, Crazy, and Lavelle leap from the prison truck, firing guns at the guards and dodging the storm of bullets heading their way. As each woman lands on the ground, Demme changes momentarily to stop-action, single-frame photography, dramatically heightening the tension and catching the individual characters at their most defiant moments in the film. Here they are the most exciting action heroines since Emma Peel of *The Avengers*. Then these four women race to Maggie's getaway car, still dodging bullets, and climb inside. Demme freezes the frame before all the car doors are closed, before we know if the women will escape—and we hold our breath and hope the film hasn't ended. It hasn't—Demme unfreezes the picture, and though the Hollywood code of years past would have insisted that these lawbreakers *pay* for their crimes, we see all five women drive off to freedom (hooray!). Demme told me: "I insisted [to New World] that all the women be allowed to escape." It is a truly rewarding conclusion.

The sex and nudity in *Caged Heat* are handled well by Demme, who takes measures not to debase his female characters. It is likely that Demme was influenced in this regard by producer Evelyn Purcell, editors Johanna

Demetrakis and Carolyn Hicks (would-be sex scenes at times seem to come to an abrupt halt), and the predominantly female cast. What sex and nudity there is appears to be there only as a means of compromise between Demme and New World, which specializes in distributing R-rated films. The nudity is casual and often takes place while Demme directs our attention elsewhere in the frame. As if to counterbalance his forced use of nudity, Demme intentionally deglamorizes the women on several occasions, showing them on the toilet and looking ill, or with food in their mouths, or even dressed up like baggy-pants male comics, mustaches and all. The only unfortunate bit is when the doctor takes photos of the drugged Belle, kisses her, and rapes her, while slowly stripping off her clothes.

For once in the women-in-prison genre, the director allows his actresses freedom to *act;* and *Caged Heat* turns out to have a truly talented cast, headed by Barbara Steele, the classy cult favorite as a result of her roles in a series of European horror films. Demme wrote the part of McQueen with Steele in mind, and then convinced her to do it. Steele is fine in what may be the strangest role of her strange career, but the other, less experienced actresses do not pale in comparison. Demme gives all his characters, including McQueen, a sense of humor, and they all prove adept at comedy, especially Roberta Collins, a sexploitation film veteran who I hope someday will be cast in an A picture: she's talented and beautiful and deserves such an opportunity. Blaxploitation film star Juanita Brown and part-time acress Ella Reid also come off well; both exude a great deal of command and confidence. Most impressive are Rainbeaux Smith and Erica Gavin, whose eyes grow tougher as the film progresses—both actresses are particularly fine when they must perform without dialogue.

In 1977, I interviewed Erica Gavin for *The Velvet Light Trap* (No. 16, "From *Vixen* to Vindication"). The former star of *Russ Meyer's Vixen* (1969) and Meyer's *Beyond the Valley of the Dolls* (1970), and a cult figure as a result of these two pictures, gave her reasons as to why *Caged Heat* turned out to be such a crowd (and critics) pleaser:

> If Russ Meyer would have directed *Caged Heat*, he would have exploited the sex and violence to the nth degree, catering to males' weird fantasies. He never would have filmed it as sensitively or realistically as Jonathan. For one thing, Russ would have had the girls making it with each other in their cells— Jonathan only hinted at lesbian sex by having the girls holding hands. And Meyer's film would have been gorier. I can't knock anything Jonathan did, considering he had to use the Roger Corman formula. But I didn't even mind doing nudity because I knew Jonathan would handle it tastefully. . . . Everybody got along with each other, and even with so many actresses there was no competition among us. Evelyn did a fabulous job as producer dealing with a predominantly male crew and we all wanted to make it work for her and for Jonathan, and the money was secondary. It was so much fun to make and that feeling seemed to come across to audiences, who like us didn't want it to end.

Casablanca

1942 Warner Bros.
Director: Michael Curtiz
Producer: Hal B. Wallis
Screenwriters: Julius J. Epstein, Philip G.
Epstein, and Howard Koch
From the play *Everybody Goes to Rick's* by
Murray Burnett and Joan Alison
Cinematography: Arthur Edeson
Music: Max Steiner
Songs: M. K. Jerome and Jack Scholl
Editor: Owen Marks
Running Time: 102 minutes

Cast: Humphrey Bogart (Rick Blaine), Ingrid Bergman (Ilsa Lund), Paul Henreid (Victor Laszlo), Claude Rains (Captain Louis Renault), Conrad Veidt (Major Strasser), Sydney Greenstreet (Señor Ferrari), Peter Lorre (Ugarte), S. Z. Sakall (Carl), Madeleine LeBeau (Yvonne), Dooley Wilson (Sam), Joy Page (Annina Brandel), John Qualin (Berger), Leonid Kinskey (Sascha), Helmut Dantine (Jan), Marcel Dalio (Emil), Ludwig Stossel (Leuchtag)

Synopsis: Having been jilted without explanation by Ilsa Lund in Paris on the eve of the German occupation, Rick Blaine is disillusioned with life. He and his piano player Sam have come to Vichy-controlled Casablanca, Morocco. He runs the Café Américain nightclub and claims to be neutral in regard to the escalating war. His only friends are his employees and Captain Renault, the clever, corrupt, charming head of the Vichy police.

Casablanca is one of the few places from which European expatriates can escape the Nazis. If they have visas to Lisbon, they can go from there to America. Renault sells visas for sexual favors; Ferrari, a black marketeer, sells them for exorbitant sums. Ugarte kills two German couriers and steals two letters of transit signed by De Gaulle that he hopes to sell for much money. Rick agrees to hide the two visas for him, but doesn't protect him from arrest by Renault, who impresses the newly arrived German officer Major Strasser by apprehending the killer of the couriers. Strasser and Renault tell Rick that Victor Laszlo, a famous freedom fighter, has come to Casablanca with his wife, and they don't want him to escape the city. They imply that if Rick has the visas he shouldn't sell them to Laszlo as Ugarte intended. When Laszlo and his wife enter the club, Rick is stunned to see that she is Ilsa. That night, when they are alone, Ilsa tries to explain to Rick why she left him in Paris, but he won't listen to her. Ferrari tells Laszlo that Rick probably has Ugarte's visas. When Laszlo tries to buy them from Rick, he refuses to sell them. When asked why, Rick replies, "Ask your wife."

Strasser orders Rick's club closed down. That night Ilsa goes to Rick's room and threatens him with a gun so he'll give her the visas. But she can't shoot because she still loves him. She tells Rick that when they were in Paris she had thought Laszlo dead, only to hear on the day of the occupation that he had escaped a concentration camp. She knew that Laszlo needed her so she returned to him. She says that she will stay with Rick now if he helps Laszlo escape Casablanca so he can carry on his important political work. In private, Laszlo tells Rick to use the two visas to take Ilsa away to safety while he stays behind.

Rick, Ilsa, Laszlo, and Renault (on whom Rick has a gun) go to the airport. Much to everyone's surprise, Rick tells Ilsa to go with Laszlo so she can help him in his work. He assures Laszlo that Ilsa is a faithful, loving wife. They get in the plane. Having been warned by Renault, Strasser arrives at the airport and tries to stop the plane from taking off. Rick is forced to kill him. Renault is the only witness, but, impressed and inspired by his friend's willingness to sacrifice the woman he loves for the cause, he doesn't turn Rick in. Instead he and Rick go off together to join the Allies in the fight against Hitler.

T he *Casablanca*–Humphrey Bogart cult really took root in the early sixties in Cambridge, Massachusetts, when the Brattle Theatre started running the picture three weeks a year, year after year. It was there, long before the audience-participation phenomenon surrounding *The Rocky Horror Picture Show* (1977), that Bogart addicts came back repeatedly and joined their idol as he spoke such classic lines as "I stick my neck out for no one"; "Sam, I thought I told you never to play ... ."; "You played it for her, you can play it for me"; "Here's looking at you, kid"; "Go ahead and shoot, you'll be doing me a favor"; "But we'll always have Paris"; " . . . that the problems of three little people don't amount to a hill of beans on this crazy little planet"; and "Louis, I think this is the start of a beautiful friendship." Afterward many viewers gathered in The Casablanca, the bar located below the theater, where perhaps they would "Bogart" cigarettes and commiserate over their brews about how "pictures aren't made like that anymore."

In truth and contrary to popular impression, *Casablanca* isn't representative of what pictures were like "back then" but is maybe the *only* picture which succeeded in meeting those old-time studio heads' requirements for what all "entertainment" movies were *supposed* to be like. It contains almost every element that would appear on an audience checklist: action, adventure, bravery, danger, espionage, exotic locale, friendship, gunplay, humor, intrigue, a love triangle, a masculine hero, a mysterious heroine, patriotism, politics (without being *too* political), romance, sentimentality, a theme song, a time factor, a venomous villain, and war. With these ideal plot ingredients, plus a splendid

An intimate moment is interrupted by the first sounds of the German occupation of Paris. Amidst the Warners' stock company, Ingrid Bergman's foreignness is emphasized, and in our eyes Ilsa becomes a symbol of a beleaguered Europe.

cast—Ingrid Bergman and well-known Warner Bros. players Humphrey Bogart, Paul Henreid, Claude Rains, Peter Lorre, and Sydney Greenstreet—and Michael Curtiz, the studio's finest contract director, at the helm, making a somewhat overloaded, confusing story move along at a brisk clip, *Casablanca* is that rare *lucky* film where everything came together, clicked, and there was perfection.

The word *luck* does come into play when considering the success of *Casablanca.* For instance, it is lucky that the picture wasn't cast as first intended with Ronald Reagan as Rick, Dennis Morgan as Laszlo, and Ann Sheridan (once plans to use Hedy Lamarr fell through) as Ilsa. And it is also lucky that screenwriter Howard Koch was able to hurriedly write the script (once Julius and Philip Epstein abandoned the project) while production was underway. Part of the film's mystique is that the actors didn't know how the story would turn out until they were almost ready to shoot the final scenes. (Most pleasantly surprised was Claude Rains, who saw his character switch from villain and traitor to hero and patriot.) But the luckiest break of all is that this picture, which was shelved by Warners after a brief run late in 1942, was rereleased in 1943 for no reason other than to capitalize on the headline-making Roosevelt-Churchill summit in, of all places, Casablanca, which Eisenhower's troops had secured for the Allies during his North African campaign. Given a second chance, the picture went on to become a box office sensation, win several Academy Awards, including Best Picture, Best Director, and Best Screenplay, and take its place as an American "classic."

Of course, during production, there was no way of knowing that Americans would become familiar with a city in Morocco. It was a truly inspired choice of locale.

By setting the picture in a city where people from all over the world—Americans, Czechs, Bulgarians, Russians, French, Germans, and others, as well as the native Muslims—are crowded together, there is a great feeling of tension from the outset. Moreover, because the arrival of Major Strasser implies that a complete German takeover of Morocco is imminent, the movie takes on an exciting sense of urgency. Many people stuck in the city must get out quickly and their only hope is to attain a much-in-demand visa to Lisbon, where they can then book passage to America.

The locale automatically makes the characters more interesting. For one thing, it gives them "a past," a prerequisite for interesting, well-rounded movie characters. Everyone in Casablanca is, in one way or another, in a state of transition, between what they were before Nazi imperialism and what they will become as the war spreads throughout the world. This applies equally to those who are just passing through, as are Laszlo, Ilsa, and the numerous other European expatriates waiting for visas, and to those who live in Casablanca permanently and who have set up new enterprises either to "accommodate" the transient population, as has Rick with his Café Américain, or to take advantage of their desperate situations, as have black marketeers Ugarte and Ferrari. What is extraordinary about Casablanca in particular is that because it is still classified as "free territory" (despite increasing German dominance), it is a rare place where individuals can choose their own destinies, i.e., their own sides during the war. That the characters work themselves out of a limbo stage (symbolized by Casablanca itself) through their own hard decisions (based on philosophical idealism) and actions (taking a stand/making a choice between a life under the Nazi regime and going elsewhere to join the Allies in combatting the Nazis) is why *Casablanca* has such emotional impact on viewers; and why Rick, who in *his* limbo stage refuses to think about a few hours in the future but ultimately *chooses* to sacrifice what is most dear to him (Ilsa) for the sake of a better future for mankind (his commitment), has come to be regarded as one of the cinema's great existential heroes.

When we are introduced to Rick he is playing chess. This epitomizes Rick's laid-back attitude in the face of spreading Nazi aggression. Like all Hollywood studios, Warner Bros. made films that wholeheartedly supported Roosevelt's war effort, and its stance was that the realities of war precluded Rick or anyone else from hiding behind a cloak of neutrality. A hero who refuses to choose sides in the conflict and plans to sit out the war is totally unacceptable, so the natural course of the film was to have Rick change from someone uninterested and uninvolved in world events to being an active participant in the fight against Hitler.

First, the film establishes that Rick is worthy of our attention: he ran guns to Ethiopians in their fight against Mussolini; he fought with the Republicans against Franco in Spain; he fled France on the eve of the occupation because his reputation would have put him in grave danger with the Nazis. A man with such courage and experience fighting Nazis certainly would be of great value to our side. But Rick claims that he is no longer a political idealist willing to put himself on the line for any cause (left-wing or partisan) that battles fascism. He is cynical, callous, and embittered, relating to the world in terms of his own shattered ego. On the day Ilsa left him in Paris (and, of course, a Paris romance is far stronger than others), he withdrew into a shell, not caring what happened to him or the world—for a world without love does not matter to him.

Although Rick puts up a cold, uncaring front, we feel that there is hope Rick will rejoin "the fight" because we see glimpses into the man who Renault senses is a "sentimentalist at heart." While Rick professes little concern for Laszlo's plight, he bets Renault that Laszlo will escape from Casablanca; while he professes to be unpatriotic to the "Free World," when Laszlo tells Rick's orchestra to play "La Marseillaise" to

Renault's men capture Ugarte, who vents his fury at Rick for not helping him escape.

Ilsa tries to explain her disappearance from France, but Rick would rather wallow in self-pity than listen.

drown out the German soldiers' rendition of "Die Wacht am Rheim," a quick cut of Curtiz's camera reveals that it is Rick who nods his permission to the musicians for the French anthem to be played; while he professes not to care about the personal problems of the transients, rather than allow Annina to sleep with Renault to get visas for husband Jan (primarily) and herself, Rick rigs his roulette wheel so Jan can win enough money to buy visas.

And his reemerging sentimentalism is what makes him ask Sam to play "As Time Goes By" (a song he associates with Ilsa and Paris) repeatedly. At first we are upset that Rick doesn't protect Ugarte from Renault's police; but if Ugarte had killed the two German couriers because of political beliefs, rather than to steal the valuable letters of transit to sell, then it is likely Rick would have protected him.

All that keeps Rick from freeing his impulse to do the right thing and take his place in the Cause is self-pity and martyrdom, the results of his still feeling deserted by Ilsa in Paris. His attitude begins to improve when he comes to understand that Ilsa was not disloyal to him in Paris; she was not *his* to begin with, but Laszlo's—and (properly) she was loyal to Laszlo, her husband, once she discovered that he was still alive. Like Annina, who was willing to give up her self-respect to help Jan get out of Casablanca, Ilsa left Rick because of things more important than herself. Now in Casablanca Ilsa is willing to stay behind with Rick if he can arrange Laszlo's escape. And Laszlo (whom Rick has learned to respect) is willing to let Ilsa fly away with Rick if that means her life will be saved. Having discovered at last that war requires all people to make great personal sacrifices, Rick, not to be outdone by Ilsa or Laszlo, nobly stays behind while they fly away to safety. He knows that it is best for the Cause that Ilsa be with Laszlo to support him in his work (Ilsa had been correct in her Paris decision) and that he (Rick) be able to concentrate on fighting without having Ilsa sap his energies in what would definitely be a most consuming love affair.

What a couple Bogart and Bergman are (in their only film together)! His face is hard, dark, stubbly even after a shave, ugly; hers is soft, glowing, warm, beautiful. His eyes are cold, suspicious, narrow, introspective; her eyes sparkle, are trusting, generous, caring. He is demanding, critical, secretive; she is comforting, loving, open-armed. Rick and Ilsa are a couple who are not meant to be despite the great love they have for one another. But it is wonderful to see them have a second romantic fling in Casablanca, no matter how brief. And Curtiz pays them tribute when, after a one-shot of Rick watching Ilsa and Laszlo approach the plane door, he isolates his camera on Ilsa—keeping Laszlo out of the frame—as she looks back at Rick so that the two of them can share one last romantic moment.

If Rick can't have Ilsa, at least he gets Renault. Howard Koch wrote, "The ambiguous, cat-and-mouse relationship of the two men, each with a wary respect for the other . . . became the thread which wound its way through the story and held it together." Through most of the film Renault justifies his own corruption by using Rick as his model: if Rick with his glorious past refuses to stand up to the Germans, then why should he,

admittedly a lesser man? But Renault has a guilty streak, and truly would like his model to change so he can change himself. He repeatedly tries to coax and nudge Rick into returning to politics. Oh, he doesn't do it in an obvious way, but cleverly and subtly: by teasing Rick about how low he has fallen ("You're the only one with less scruples than me"), and constantly reminding him of his past exploits against fascism (speaking in a mocking tone lest Rick become suspicious of his intentions). Renault greatly admires Rick's hidden side, the sentimentalist ("If I were a woman . . . I'd love Rick"), and desperately wants Rick to acknowledge its existence. When Renault sees Rick put himself on the line by helping Laszlo and Ilsa (whom he knows Rick loves) escape, his suspicions about Rick are confirmed. When Rick shoots Strasser, who took Americans so lightly that he ignored Rick's gun and tried to draw his own, rather than tell his men who committed the murder, Renault says those immortal words: "Round up the usual suspects." Then Renault tosses a bottle of Vichy wine into the garbage and goes off to fight Nazis with Rick, the man who has restored his faith in humanity. Never has there been a more romantic ending.

The classic airport sequence: Rick, Laszlo, and Ilsa wait anxiously while Renault gives one of his men instructions.

1941   RKO Radio
Director: Orson Welles
Producer: Orson Welles
Screenplay: Herman J. Mankiewicz
and Orson Welles
Cinematography: Gregg Toland
Music: Bernard Herrmann
Editor: Robert Wise
Running time: 119 minutes

Cast: Orson Welles (Charles Foster Kane), Joseph Cotten (Jedediah Leland), Everett Sloane (Bernstein), Dorothy Comingore (Susan Alexander Kane), Ray Collins (James W. Gettys), William Alland (Jerry Thompson/newsreel narrator), Agnes Moorehead (Mary Kane), Ruth Warrick (Emily Norton Kane), George Coulouris (Walter Parks Thatcher), Erskine Sanford (Herbert Carter), Harry Shannon (Jim Kane), Philip Van Zandt (Rawlston), Paul Stewart (Raymond), Fortunio Bonanova (Matisti), Alan Ladd (reporter), Arthur O'Connell (reporter)

Synopsis: In 1940 Charles Foster Kane, publisher of the New York *Inquirer* and numerous other papers, and one of the richest men in the world, dies at age seventy while living in near seclusion at Xanadu, his palatial estate in Florida. He had brought about America's participation in the Spanish-American War, known politicians from Teddy Roosevelt to Adolf Hitler, run (unsuccessfully) for governor of New York, influenced America's thinking for half a century, and had made numerous enemies. Some thought him a fascist and others a communist. His own definition of himself was, "I am, have been, and always will be one thing—an American."

Magazine editor Rawlston wants to find out the real story of Kane. He tells Thompson, a reporter, to find out what Kane meant when he said "Rosebud" just before he died. He thinks it might be the key to Kane's life. Thompson reads the diary of Walter Parks Thatcher, now dead, Kane's guardian. He interviews Susan Alexander, Kane's second wife. He talks to Bernstein, chairman of the board of the *Inquirer,* and Kane's manager since the 1890s. He talks to Jed Leland, former drama critic on the *Inquirer,* Kane's college chum and best friend. And he talks to Raymond, Kane's butler for the past eleven years. He puts together the following story.

Charles Kane was born in the mid-1860s in New Salem, Colorado. He loved his mother Mary dearly, but his father, Charles Senior, used to thrash him. His parents ran a boarding house that didn't take in much money, but a boarder left Mary a deed to a "worthless" mine that proved to be a bonanza. The Kanes became fabulously wealthy and Mary arranged for bank executor Thatcher to make Charles his ward and bring him up properly. Charles didn't want to go and knocked Thatcher down with his sled.

Thatcher and Kane never got along. Kane was thrown out of many colleges. When Kane turned twenty-five, he claimed his fortune and took over the New York *Inquirer.* The first edition carried Kane's Declaration of Principles, stating he would be champion of the working man. Leland was impressed and wanted to keep the original copy of the Principles. Circulation went up sharply over the next few years as the paper published exposés. In 1900 Kane married Emily Norton, the President's niece. They had a son, Charles Junior. Kane had an affair with a nice, would-be (but untalented) singer, Susan Alexander. When it looked like Kane would be elected governor of New York, his rival exposed the affair. Kane lost the election. Emily divorced him. In 1918 Emily and Junior were killed in a car crash. He married Susan, and built an opera house for her in Chicago. She made her debut and was terrible. Leland was too drunk to finish the bad review he was writing about her. Kane finished it for him, then fired Leland. Kane made Susan continue singing, but when she attempted suicide, he agreed to let her quit. In 1929 the first Kane newspaper closed. Kane and Susan moved to Xanadu, a combination castle and museum. In 1932 she left him. He went berserk and wrecked her room. The Kane empire collapsed. No one paid attention to his word anymore. He died alone, holding a glass ball with a snow scene inside. He uttered "Rosebud," and the ball crashed to the floor and broke.

Thompson can't figure out what "Rosebud" means. But he doubts if the word would prove significant in analyzing the life of a man he now feels only sorrow for.

Useless Kane possessions are tossed in a fire. One is the sled from Kane's childhood. On it is the word *Rosebud.*

Citizen Kane

Some contemporary critics choose *The Magnificent Ambersons* (1942) above *Citizen Kane* as Orson Welles's masterpiece. Moreover, *Ambersons, The Lady from Shanghai* (1948), *Touch of Evil* (1958), and *Chimes at Midnight* (1967)— my favorite Welles film—have each been championed by Welles admirers, critics included, to a point where *Kane*'s position as *the* top Welles cult film is in jeopardy. But no one will dispute that *Kane* is still regarded as Welles's most important film. In technical virtuosity and dramatic structure it is the most influential work of the sound era, the picture to which not only Welles films but all films must, inevitably, be compared. *Kane* is a cinematic reference point which should be seen over and over again to learn the language of film, to learn its potential as a storytelling medium and as an outlet for personal and artistic expression.

In the early seventies new interest in *Kane* was sparked by Pauline Kael's long essay in *The New Yorker* titled "Raising Kane," which subsequently served as an introduction to the film's shooting script in the best seller *The Citizen Kane Book* (Little, Brown, 1971). It was Kael's thesis that Herman J. Mankiewicz deserved almost all credit for the *Kane* screenplay and that Welles's work on the script didn't warrant his being listed in the credits as coauthor, even if his name is listed second and is in smaller letters than Mankiewicz's. Since she believed that the true greatness of *Kane* lies in the script, it was her contention that Mankiewicz, not Welles, should be the person heralded for the masterwork. This claim was vehemently disputed by countless critics, most from the *auteur* school of criticism.

I agree that the *Kane* script is terrific, not *shallow* as many critics contend; if it doesn't *read* well it is because

For the fall to be great, so must be the climb. At the peak of his power and prestige Kane appears to be a sure victor in the election for governor—he will lose.

Mary Kane tells her eight-year-old son that he will be going away with Thatcher (L). Charles Sr. (back) has nothing to say in the matter, but young Charles will turn and with his sled "Rosebud" push Thatcher into the snow.

few *great* scripts read well—they *transpose* well to the screen. And considering that Welles was the lone screenwriter on *Mr. Arkadin* (1955), a Welles-directed variation on *Kane* that falls apart because of script (as well as budget-related) lapses, I am willing to concede that Mankiewicz is at the very least responsible for the *consistent* quality of the *Kane* script. In interviews with Peter Bogdanovich and others, Welles himself has said Mankiewicz's contributions to the script were invaluable (of course, he says his own were the same). He has stated that the "Rosebud"-as-sled idea was Mankiewicz's, and that Mankiewicz wrote Welles's favorite scene: when the aged Bernstein tells Thompson of a young woman in a white parasol he saw for one second more than forty years before whom he still thinks about daily. This is a wonderful, quiet passage in an otherwise boisterous film; I'm sure Mankiewicz was equally responsible for other standout moments. However, I believe the greatness of *Citizen Kane* lies not in the script but in the flamboyant, audacious (i.e., freeze-frames, deep focus, long takes, strange angles and lighting), exhibitionist, often theatrical impositions made on the story by director Welles. For the many who believe Charles Foster Kane is based more on Orson Welles than William Randolph Hearst, twenty-five-year-old Kane's words "I think it would be fun to run a newspaper" is how they think twenty-five-year-old Welles felt as a first-time movie director on *Kane*, given carte blanche by RKO to transform a jaded art form into something wild and experimental. Similarly, Kane's signing his name to the Declaration of Principles that is published on page one of his first edition of the *Inquirer* in order to let everyone "know who's responsible" probably indicates how Welles felt when he took almost all credit and responsibility for *Kane* and, without malice, shoved Mankiewicz into the background.

What might have been a simple narrative is made complex (and interesting) by having Kane's story told through a series of flashbacks representing six points of view: the documentarians' (who made the *March of Time* newsreel), Thatcher's, Bernstein's, Leland's, Susan's, and Raymond's. Because we still are missing pieces in the Kane jigsaw puzzle despite all the recollections, Welles forces us to gather information in unorthodox ways from which we will make our deductions. He proves that filmmakers can tell stories not only through dialogue and action but through the creative use of props, screen space, music, editing, lighting, sets, sound, costumes and makeup, and—as the best directors of the sound era had already discovered—camera lenses, placement, movement, and angles.

Sets are particularly important in *Kane* as storytelling devices. Welles uses very few close-ups, preferring to show his characters in medium or long shots so we can study them within the milieu they inhabit (e.g., the physical world Kane builds for himself). When characters are in the foreground or across the room, cameraman Gregg Toland uses deep-focus photography to keep us aware of the entire setting. Each set reflects the characters that dwell in it: the spare, functionally furnished Colorado home that reveals the practicality of Mary Kane; the warm, comfortable room innocent Susan rents when Kane meets her; the cluttered offices of the busy *Inquirer* staff; Xanadu's expansive, empty living room chamber where idle people lead vacuous lives. As time progresses, each set loses its human touch. They become forbidding, despairing gothic chambers, reflecting the mind of the brooding Kane or the people dominated by his will.

Toland's work is outstanding. His camera was stopped down, and a variety of wide-angle lenses were employed to create the deep-focus effect. He used excessive light in most of the expressionistic sequences. Often he had light coming from a single source to heighten the dramatic import, as when Thompson visits

Bernstein and Leland talk about Kane's statues—the first of the many possessions Kane will acquire over the years. Welles brought Everett Sloane and Joseph Cotten to Hollywood from New York, where they had been part of his Mercury Radio Theatre.

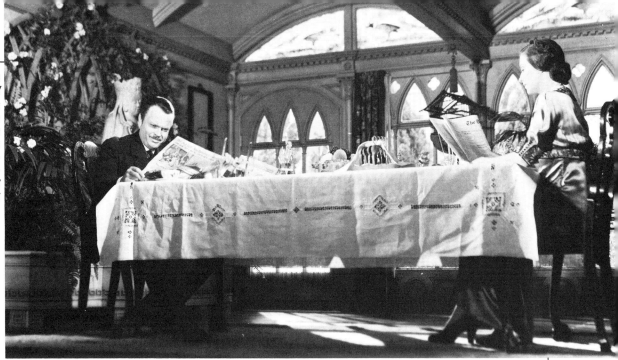

As Kane and Emily grow further and further apart, Welles shows it visually. The renowned breakfast montage ends up with the unhappy couple sitting at opposite ends of a long table and reading rival newspapers.

Thatcher's library or when Kane and Susan are in the gigantic Xanadu living room that is lit by an enormous fireplace. And how well Welles and Toland used the frame: dark areas call attention to areas in light—but after awhile, especially during long takes, we start to explore the darkness.

Similarly, when sound (e.g., the sound of voices) gets our attention in one area of the picture, other sounds (or visuals) will demand our attention elsewhere. *Kane* was a breakthrough in sound experimentation, particularly at RKO. Ex-radio director/actor Welles pays much attention to voices, which range from quietly passionate to jittery (Kane shyly telling the *Inquirer*'s society editor that he wants to announce his engagement) to hysterical. *Kane* could be one of Welles's *Mercury Radio Theater* plays, as so much about the characters is revealed through speech patterns: the nuances, the inflections, the rhythm, the balance, the texture. Notice how the voices sharpen, harden, become more defensive in the famous breakfast montage where lovebirds Kane and Emily end up sitting at opposite ends of a long table, he reading the *Inquirer*, she the *Chronicle*, neither conversing. (Here the rhythm of the *editing* is also used by Welles to summarize their deteriorating marriage with facility and economy.) Another dominant storytelling device on the soundtrack is Bernard Herrmann's versatile score, soaring in Kane's triumphs, wobbly and ominous during Kane's downfall.

Citizen Kane is about a search for the last part ("Rosebud") of a document on a man's life, a search for *subjective* truth. Welles creates "realism" (the "true" picture of Kane) through illusion and expressionism, and *Kane* thus becomes his tribute to the camera. The visuals show past events not as the storytellers remember them but as the filmmaker interprets the storytellers' words. There are contradictions between how we see Kane and how he is remembered verbally, as well as between how we conceive the personalities of various characters in the flashbacks and how they come across when interviewed by Thompson. The film is journalistic in nature: it makes *us*, even more than Thompson, investigative reporters. He can't properly sum up the testimony, but we can because we have seen the revealing visuals as well as sitting in on Thompson's interviews. (The flashback camera doesn't lie, but we must be careful because of its ability to manipulate.) Likewise, the disclosure of the "clue" to the real Kane—"Rosebud" is the name on the sled he owned as a child—is not granted Thompson, but it is a visual present to viewers from the filmmaker through his camera.

Citizen Kane was almost shelved or destroyed when associates of William Randolph Hearst put enormous pressure on RKO not to release what they thought was an unflattering portrait of Hearst. Not that *Kane* is meant to depict accurately only Hearst, the controversial yellow journalist, unsuccessful politician, empire builder. As mentioned, Kane seems based to a degree on Welles himself—a child prodigy, he was orphaned at thirteen and placed in the care of a man named Bernstein (the basis for the film's Bernstein character). Welles told Peter Bogdanovich: "Kane was better than Hearst, and [actress] Marion [Davies] was much better than Susan —whom people wrongly equate with her." As years pass, it becomes less important whom Kane is based on. What remains interesting is the picture's story: a man chases the American Dream and somewhere, somehow, his life *irrevocably*—the word Kane can't pronounce— goes wrong. The money young Kane's mother got from the silver mine dictated the course of his life. He had to leave home, get an education, and then attempt to achieve power and position in addition to his wealth. But the message is simple: success, power, riches cannot replace love and tranquility. *Kane* is a classic tragedy of a mammoth figure destroyed by a lust for power, by too much ambition; but because of Welles's nonlinear, non-Aristotelian structure, which allows us to know Kane is dead at the outset and to look backward, it becomes an American tragedy: a classic figure gains our sympathy as he is reduced to common-man terms (the poor guy misses his sled!).

Susan eavesdrops while Gettys and Emily tell Kane that he must either give up his mistress or his marriage and political ambitions.

The film's title indicates our protagonist's contradictory nature. The "Citizen" is heroic, a champion of the unprivileged class's legal and human rights, an idealist, a visionary. But the "Kane" is flawed, a self-serving, destructive opportunist, a classic tragic figure doomed to fall. He is at one time or another a patriot, a democrat, a pacifist, a warmonger, an idealist, a fascist, a communist; he is always, he stresses, "an American." He is a man of principles but is willing to forget what is right for the pleasure of swaying public opinion back and forth. (His obsession with influencing others' decisions is why his not being able to influence the major events in his personal life drives him crazy.) He is a crusader for social reform but is also a "muckraker" in the most exploitative sense of the word. He "has a generous mind," as both Leland and Susan, who hate each other but share opinions, attest, but "he never gave people what they wanted." Despite what Leland thinks, he *is* capable of love—he has love and loyalty for his mother, Susan, Leland, Bernstein, and, for a time, Emily—he is just too clumsy to express it. That he finds it more important that people love him is understandable considering how often he is rejected. Leland thinks Kane a quitter ("He never finished anything but my notice") who sold out his principles, but I see Kane's life as characterized by his having to fight battles alone after being deserted by those close to him. When he was a boy, his mother sent him away (although they had great love for each other). When Harvard expels Kane, Thatcher doesn't support him. Emily sides with her uncle (the President), the *Chronicle*, and the unscrupulous Gettys rather than her husband. She divorces him, takes away his son, and they completely "abandon" him when they are killed in a car crash. Best friend Leland blames Kane for losing the gubernatorial election and setting reform back in the process when he should have stood by Kane for admirably not allowing Gettys to force him out of the race with political blackmail. Leland also lets Kane know he prefers Emily to Susan

once she becomes his woman. Susan's voice is so unbearably shrill after she reads Leland's review of her concert debut that we barely listen to her words to Kane, who still calls Leland his friend; yet her words are *true*: "A friend wouldn't write an article like that!" Leland is a terrible, self-righteous friend who won't even write the depressed reclusive Kane when he contacts him years later. Susan is the last of the many people who walk out on Kane—not counting the American public, which turns its back on him in the thirties.

Kane had wit, charm, and good intentions, but money gave him power and power gave him a false sense of omnipotence. "Everything was his idea," Susan tells Thompson, "except my leaving him." The same words could be spoken by all the others who walked out on Kane. In his interview with Bogdanovich, Welles described Kane: "All he *had* was charm—besides the money. He was one of those amiable, rather likable monsters who was able to command people's allegiance for a time without giving much in return." Sadly, while Kane pulled people into his life and overwhelmed them, not one person was allowed close enough to know what "Rosebud" meant.

A theme of *Kane* is a variation of Kane's "If the headline is big enough, it makes the story big enough": the real stories aren't headline worthy. For example: "Rosebud." Kane's reflecting back on "Rosebud" has in part to do with his "searching for his [lost] youth"—the reason he gives Susan for claiming his family's old possessions, including the sled and glass ball containing a snow scene. But he doesn't want to go back to an "edenic" existence as many viewers assume: his father beat him, his only companion was a snowman he built. What the sled is to the dying Kane was the one *possession* he treasured *before* he got money and was able to buy everything he wanted (and simultaneously ruin his life): the *Inquirer*, the *Chronicle*'s staff, statues, and zoo animals (which unlike people couldn't run away from him), Xanadu, public opinion, "friendship," and "love." As part-idealist, part-visionary, part-pragmatist, part-cynic Kane told Thatcher years before money led to his downfall: "If I hadn't been really rich, I might have been a really great man."

The dreadful opera in which Susan (in the blond wig) makes a fool of herself.

The Conqueror Worm

One of many shocking images in Reeves's film: Suspected witches including John Lowes (R) are hanged while their condemner Matthew Hopkins looks on from his steed.

Also known as *The Witchfinder General*

1968   Great Britain   American International release of a Tigon British Film
Director: Michael Reeves
Producer: Louis M. Heyward
Screenplay: Michael Reeves and Tom Baker
Based on a novel by Ronald Bassett
Cinematography: Johnny Coquillon
Music: Paul Ferris
Editor: Howard Lanning
Running Time: 88 minutes (the British version is without prologue and epilogue narrations but this has no effect on screen time)

Cast: Vincent Price (Matthew Hopkins), Ian Ogilvy (Richard Marshall), Hilary Dwyer (Sara), Robert Russell (John Stearne), Rupert Davies (John Lowes), Patrick Wymark (Oliver Cromwell), Wilfred Brambell (horse dealer), Nicky Henson (Trooper Swallow)

Synopsis: It is 1645, and England is torn by war between the Royalists and Oliver Cromwell's Roundheads. While the country is in a state of confusion, professional witch-hunter Matthew Hopkins and his brutal assistant John Stearne ride from town to town, torturing confessions out of suspected witches and collecting money from local magistrates for every "witch" they execute.

They arrive in Brandiston, where aged clergyman John Lowes had been called a witch by some villagers. They torture him by sticking needles into his back (searching for the devil's mark) and hitting him, stopping only when Lowes's beautiful niece, Sara, whose fiancé, Richard Marshall, is off fighting with Cromwell, offers herself to Hopkins. With Lowes in prison, Hopkins visits Sara for sexual favors every night. But while he is away, Stearne rapes Sara; when Hopkins finds out, he wants nothing more to do with her and orders Stearne to continue his torture of Lowes. Before leaving the village, Hopkins and Stearne execute Lowes and two others. Marshall returns to Brandiston and realizes that he hasn't kept his oath to Sara to let "no one harm you." He vows to kill Hopkins and Stearne. After marrying Sara—at least in his eyes (no one performs the ceremony)—he sets off across the English countryside, telling Sara to go to Lavenham. Marshall eventually catches up with Stearne, but after a brutal fight he escapes. Now both Hopkins and Stearne know that Marshall is on their trail.

Marshall finds out that Hopkins and Stearne are in the town where Sara has fled. With a few of his soldier friends he gallops there. However, Hopkins, having found out that Sara is in the town, has set a trap for him: soon both Marshall and Sara are taken off to a dungeon.

While Sara is pricked with long needles, Hopkins tries to get Marshall to confess that he is a witch so he can be publicly executed. But all Marshall says is that he will kill Hopkins, so the torture continues. Hopkins orders Stearne to bring Marshall closer while he brands Sara. At this moment, Marshall kicks his boot heel into Stearne's eye, blinding him. He then grabs an ax and strikes Hopkins with it innumerable times. Arriving at the scene, one of Marshall's friends mercifully shoots Hopkins, killing him. "You've taken him from me!" yells the outraged Marshall. Sara screams uncontrollably.

During the summer of 1968, exciting reports began to filter out of Europe (beginning with West Germany) about a British "horror" film called *The Witchfinder General,* directed by the relatively unknown Michael Reeves. Oddly, the picture had played in America that spring under the title *The Conqueror Worm* and had gone virtually unnoticed. The few snoozing trade paper reviewers who saw it had treated it as just another entry in AIP's Edgar Allan Poe series starring Vincent Price, and gave it such dismal notices that future bookings were scarce. By the time anyone was alerted that *The Conqueror Worm* was not adapted from the unadaptable Poe poem, that AIP had not made the film but was only distributing it, and that it deserved our unqualified attention, it was long gone from the circuit. By the time most American critics were able to track down a print, Michael Reeves was dead.

On February 11, 1969, England's most promising director, and already its most fascinating from both a visual and thematic standpoint, committed suicide—his death being attributed to an overdose of sleeping pills.* Michael Reeves was twenty-five. While one can't necessarily understand what makes a director tick or how he perceives the world around him by studying his films, when one looks at Reeves's small oeuvre—*The Castle of the Living Dead* (1964), on which he began as the assistant director but took over in midproduction, *The She-Beast* (1965), and especially *The Sorcerers* (1967),

*Depending on the source, Reeves's death was either suicidal or accidental. His manner of death has also been debated; various reports had Reeves dying from a pill overdose, a car accident, and a fall from a high window.

One of the film's erotic images: Marshall and Sara get reacquainted when he returns from the front.

and *The Conqueror Worm*—his manner of death doesn't seem all that surprising.

It is safe to say that no director in cinema history exhibited such a consistently depressing and angry view of the world and humanity as Reeves. For that reason, politically "progressive" film critics have had difficulty dealing with his works—particularly *The Conqueror Worm*, which Reeves cultists correctly regard as his best, most ambitious film. While Reeves's talent is indisputable and his repeated condemnation of those who abuse power admirable, it is hard to fully endorse him because his attitude, as reflected in his joyless endings, was so negative, even defeatist; his heroes and heroines, who start out as likable people, full of love and tenderness, ultimately surrender to the evil Reeves felt to be the dominant part of every person's nature. Film purists may protest AIP's addition of the prologue and epilogue narration for the American print of the film, but the words of Poe that conclude this version aptly sum up Reeves's gloomy philosophy as set forth in his art: "That the play is the tragedy 'Man.' And its hero the Conqueror Worm."

All those enjoyable Poe films starring Vincent Price, like *The House of Usher* (1960), *The Pit and the Pendulum* (1961), and *The Masque of the Red Death* (1965), deal in some way or another with evil. Directed by Roger Corman, those films were intentionally claustrophobic, with almost everything taking place within secluded castles. The evil that exists, personified by the mad, hermitlike Vincent Price characters, is confined to the castles themselves, so that if the castles are destroyed the evil within their walls will be destroyed as well. These pictures end optimistically, quite the opposite of what happens in the Reeves films.

In *The Conqueror Worm* we are presented with an evil that is overwhelming, invulnerable, and that will emerge victorious. This evil is not confined to a single castle but runs rampant across all of England, contaminating the people, wiping out whatever goodness exists and replacing it with a contagious sickness characterized by each "victim's" desperate need to be cruel to his fellow human beings. Throughout the England of 1645 (and the film accurately depicts how it really was in that time) the devil's work is being done: in the countryside, Cromwell's Holy War leaves scores of bodies unburied in the forests and high grass; in the towns, Matthew Hopkins and John Stearne carry on their reign of torture and murder, also in the name of religion and with the townspeople's compliance. But it doesn't stop there. The evil is all-encompassing, as is evident when Hopkins kills suspected heretics by/in *fire*, by/in *water* (drowning), and in the *air* (hangings); and is himself brutally killed deep within the *earth*.

The real-life Matthew Hopkins was the son of a Puritan minister, a lawyer by trade. In 1645 and 1646 he and his partner John Stearne executed two hundred so-called witches. (Among his victims was John Lewis, whom the film's John Lowes is based on, and Elisabeth Clarke, actually Hopkin's first victim, though in the movie one of his last.) But in 1646 Hopkins fell into disfavor with powerful religious and political figures, and when magistrates outlawed the methods he used to get confessions of witchcraft, he retired. He wrote a defense of his two-year career called *The Discovery of Witchcraft*, completing it just before his death the next year.[*] I believe *The Conqueror Worm* is an exercise in revenge: Michael Reeves in the person of Trooper Richard Marshall (played by Reeves's friend Ian Ogilvy) achieved revenge on a historical perpetrator of evil, whom Reeves doubtlessly thought died too easily. Instead of allowing Hopkins the peaceful death he enjoyed in real life, Reeves has Marshall do him in, Lizzie Borden style.

As Matthew Hopkins, Vincent Price has never been better. Critic Robin Wood, who wrote a long, excellent tribute to Reeves for *Movie* (circa 1969) thought Price miscast, but I think it is quite the contrary. Even physically, Price is perfect: we see an intelligent face covered by a scruffy beard—symbolic of Hopkins's contempt for a world gone to the uncivilized; we are unsettled when this aging, flabby man matter-of-factly orders young women to be sent to him for sexual favors; we see him in his Puritan garb perched on his black horse and we recognize the angel of death. Hopkins comes across as a menacing figure, shrewd, arrogant, brutal, and Price properly plays him with a great deal of restraint. Reeves, who previously directed excellent performances by horror movie icons Christopher Lee,

[*]John Stearne retired in 1648. He then wrote *A Confirmation and Discovery of Witchcraft*.

Barbara Steele, and Boris Karloff, managed to keep Price from going into the ham actor routine that mars many of his performances—that in itself is an achievement. Importantly, Price conveys the scorn that someone of Hopkins's breeding and intelligence would have for a world which allows him—and even financially enables him—to commit what he knows to be monstrous, sadistic acts. Hopkins is god in an England full of greedy, hypocritical, superstitious people who he feels are inferior to him. He spits on them and debases them by raping their women, taking their money, and executing the few among them brave enough to protest the diabolical acts taking place in their country.

Over the years there have been numerous films which have dealt with a man or woman seeking revenge on those who have harmed his or her loved ones. *Death Wish* (1974), *The Bride Wore Black* (1968), *Rancho Notorious* (1952), *Nevada Smith* (1966), a few dozen mad scientist movies. The list is endless. Yet, as *Village Voice* critic William Paul perceived in 1970, "[I]f anywhere, [*The Conqueror Worm*'s] antecedents lie [not in film but in] the Elizabethan [and Jacobean] revenge play, sharing both the revenge motif and large quantities of blood spilled." In fact, one may think of *Hamlet* while watching Richard Marshall risk court-martial, the loss of his mind, and perhaps Sara's love as well in his relentless pursuit of Hopkins and Stearne. What is quite evident is that Marshall quickly forgets the reasons he is seeking revenge. While it starts as an act of "justified" vengeance on the men who killed John Lowes and raped

Sara, it soon becomes clear that his hatred for the men is less because of these crimes than because they have caused him to *break his honorable promise* to Sara that he would allow no harm to come to her. And what eventually motivates Marshall, onward and onward, is solely his second *vow* that he will kill Hopkins. It is not unexpected that in the horrifying dungeon sequence Marshall refuses to utter the confession that will halt Sara's torture taking place in front of him, choosing instead to reaffirm his vow to kill Hopkins. When Marshall's soldier friend kills Hopkins before the berserk Marshall can strike him with an ax for the umpteenth time, Marshall predictably explodes, shouting "You've taken him from me!" Now even Marshall's second oath has been broken. This is too much for him to cope with and his look of madness is genuine.

Audiences usually cheer at the end of revenge films when the villain gets his just desserts. But they inevitably groan when they see the helpless Hopkins lying on the ground, all bloody and senseless, waiting for another blow to fall. They are relieved when the soldier's gunshot prevents Marshall from continuing his sadistic revenge. They sense, as Sara does when she screams and screams, that Marshall is performing an act that would have made Hopkins proud. It is appropriate that this corruption of Marshall's soul takes place in the bowels of the earth, in Satan's playground.

Reeves's *The Sorcerers* is about a kindly elderly couple (Boris Karloff and Catherine Lacey) who, by using a mind control machine, force a depressed young man (Ian Ogilvy as Michael Roscoe) to perform crimes to which they can vicariously thrill without risking arrest. The crimes they have him commit *increase* in degree, from petty theft to brutal murder, just as the scientist's once-sweet wife's love of power and violence *increases*. For that film to work, and it does, everything depends on the tension level gradually *building* toward the fiery (everyone-is-killed) conclusion. *The Conqueror Worm* presents a challenge to a director in that it begins with a pre-credits sequence so powerful—a screaming woman being led to a scaffold where she is hanged—that the film must be kept at a high level of intensity in order to avoid a dramatic letdown. *The Conqueror Worm* is a stunning film in many ways, but

probably Reeves's greatest achievement is that he was able to maintain an extraordinary momentum throughout, until the film ends as it began with a woman (Sara this time) screaming.

Along the way there is much violence—executions, tortures, a nerve-wracking soldier-ambush sequence— and even some erotic lovemaking between Sara and Marshall. And whenever there is a chance that the hectic pace might be slowing a bit, Reeves automatically has Marshall jump on his mighty steed and race it across the countryside (an effective visual device), the sweeping music driving him on. The audience never gets a chance to relax. By the end of the film it is as if you have just run the gauntlet.

The horrifying finale begins with Stearne joyfully inserting needles into Sara's back while the chained Marshall can do nothing to stop his wife's torture except confess that he is a witch, which he will not do no matter how much she suffers.

Dance, Girl, Dance

1940   RKO Radio
Director: Dorothy Arzner
Producer: Erich Pommer
Screenplay: Tess Slesinger and
Frank Davis
From a story by Vicki Baum

Cinematography: Russell Metty
Music: Edward Ward, Chester
Forrest, and Robert Wright
Dances staged by Ernst Matray
Editor: Robert Wise
Running Time: 88 minutes

Cast: Maureen O'Hara (Judy O'Brien), Louis Hayward (Jimmy Harris), Lucille Ball (Bubbles/Tiger Lily White), Virginia Field (Elinor Harris), Ralph Bellamy (Steve Adams), Maria Ouspenskaya (Madame Basilova), Mary Carlisle (Sally), Katherine Alexander (Miss Olmstead), Edward Brophy (Dwarfie), Walter Abel (judge), Harold Huber (Hoboken gent), Ernest Truex (Bailey number 1), Chester Klute (Bailey number 2), Sidney Blackmer (Puss in Boots), Vivian Fay (lead ballerina), Erno Verebes (Fitch)

Synopsis: Judy O'Brien wants to be a ballet dancer, but she makes a living as a chorus girl in a troupe run by the kindly Madame Basilova, once a great Russian ballet instructor. One night in Akron, Judy meets and falls in love with Jimmy Harris, a rich, idle young man who drinks and broods because he and Elinor, whom he still loves, have gotten a divorce. But shy Judy watches her man-chasing friend Bubbles steal Jimmy away for the night.

The chorus girls return to New York, but only Bubbles is able to find a job, which she wins by doing a dance with a lot of oomph, and assuring the Hoboken nightspot owner: "Don't worry, I don't have an ounce of class." Judy does have class, and Basilova tries to help her realize her dream of becoming a ballet dancer by arranging for her to audition for Steve Adams, the director of the American Ballet Company. But on the day of the audition Basilova is struck by a car and killed, so it isn't until a week later that Judy goes alone, and unexpected, to the audition.

Olmie, Steve's kind, reliable secretary, tells Judy that she will convince Steve to see her, but while Olmie talks to him, Judy runs out—after having watched the American Ballet rehearse and becoming convinced that she is not good enough to audition for such a company. Steve runs into Judy in the elevator and in the street, but they do not know each other's identities. When she mistakes his kindness for freshness, she runs off.

Bubbles—now calling herself Tiger Lily White—becomes a headliner at a burlesque theater, and Judy is hired to be her preliminary act. Before Bubbles's raunchy song and striptease, Judy dances ballet and is subjected to the jeers of the male audience, becoming, in effect, Bubbles's "stooge." Judy even gets a reputation as a comic dancer, and when Steve sees her picture, he goes to the theater to see the girl he met on the street. He is impressed by her dancing. Not knowing who he is, Judy avoids him. Jimmy comes to the theater, and he and Judy have a wonderful date. However, the next night he shows his love for Elinor when he jealously punches her new husband, Puss in Boots. Jimmy gets drunk the next day, and Bubbles, discovering he is rich, takes advantage of his confused state to marry him. Judy becomes so upset when she finds out what Bubbles has done, she can't concentrate on dancing. When she is booed for her sorry effort, she tells off the audience, saying they are the ones making fools of themselves just by being there. When the audience joins Olmie and Steve in applauding Judy, Bubbles becomes jealous and comes on the stage—only to be booed. Judy wrestles her to the ground and they fight furiously. They are arrested for making a disturbance.

In court, Judy and Bubbles end their ongoing squabble. At Judy's recommendation, Jimmy and Elinor (whose marriage to Puss in Boots has been annulled) reunite—after Bubbles agrees to free Jimmy from their marriage for fifty thousand dollars. When Judy tells the judge that dance means everything to her, Steve and Olmie, who are sitting in court, realize they have found a future dancer.

At the American Ballet, Judy discovers that Steve Adams and the man she has been avoiding are the same person. He tells her that his choreographer will teach her dancing technique to assure her success. She both laughs and cries, realizing that achieving her dream of becoming a ballet dancer "could have been so easy."

One of the most significant, beneficial results of feminist inquiry into films by and about women has been the rediscovery and subsequent availability of the works of Dorothy Arzner, Hollywood's lone female director (with the exception of Wanda Tuchock, who codirected one film) during the thirties and early forties. Among the twenty films Arzner directed were such major pictures as *Fashions for Women* (1927), with Esther Ralston; *The Wild Party* (1929), one of her three films with Clara Bow; *Sarah and Son* (1930), one of her three films with Ruth Chatterton; *Merrily We Go to Hell* (1932), with Sylvia Sidney; *Christopher Strong* (1933), with Katharine Hepburn; *Nana* (1934), with Anna Sten, "Goldwyn's Garbo"; *Craig's Wife* (1936), with Rosalind Russell; *The Last of Mrs. Cheney* (1937) and *The Bride Wore Red* (1937), both with Joan Crawford; *Dance, Girl, Dance* (1940), with Maureen O'Hara and Lucille Ball; and *First Comes Courage* (1943), Arzner's last film, with Merle Oberon. What is important about these films is not so much that they star such notable actresses as that they are about *women* radically different from those found in other directors' films of the period. Although about half of Arzner's films were scripted by men, if anything her women are invariably more intelligent, witty, courageous, resilient, self-motivated, self-reliant, honorable, and ambitious than their male counterparts; moreover, these films don't deal only with how a woman relates to men, but also explore how she sees herself in relation to other women, her career, and/or what she believes to be her "mission" in life or her life's potential. As Molly Haskell wrote in *The Village Voice*, "There are other Hollywood films about women, about camaraderie among women, about career women, many of them more stylistically distinguished than Arzner's films, but she is the only director who consistently scrutinizes women who have priorities other than marriage and the family and destinies that take precedence over love." There may not be a true masterpiece in the Arzner collection, but as Haskell suggests, her thematically daring films "surpass anything that has been done since, by men or women, in picturing (within the conventions of a Hollywood film!) woman's difficult and heroic struggle to wrest her soul from the claims attached to her from the time she was born."

Dance, Girl, Dance is Arzner's cult film, the most enthusiastically received and widely written-about of her pictures. On the surface it is but another in the long line of backstage musicals in which an unknown entertainer *makes good,* but on closer examination it is revealed to be a remarkably complex film (as unpredictable as any Hollywood film) in terms of how the women—and the men—are treated.

"Making good" for Judy O'Brien does not mean

Judy is taken with Jimmy when he offers to take a collection for the women dancers who have lost their jobs during a raid. Sally looks on, sensing Judy's infatuation.

that she becomes a star, as it does with other lead characters in the backstage genre. If Judy were Vicky Page (Moira Shearer) in *The Red Shoes* (1948), a high-class backstager, that picture would end before it really begins, at the moment the girl is accepted into the ballet company—long before she achieves success and fame as the lead dancer in "The Ballet of the Red Shoes." Stardom will undoubtedly come to Judy once she gets professional training from Steve, but her moment of triumph doesn't have to be delayed until then. Her personal victory—over uncertainty, unnecessary distractions (a romantic fling), and self-doubt—comes when she understands that nothing matters more to her than dance; and that she is willing to adhere to the dying Basilova's prudent counsel and to "make the last sacrifice for art," something Vicky Page is unable to do.

At the beginning of the film, Judy knows that she wants to dance, but doesn't realize how much. When Bubbles walks off with Jimmy, on whom Judy has a crush, sad-eyed, stiff-upper-lipped Judy tells her friend Sally, "I only care about dancing." Neither Sally nor the viewer believes her. The *key*, pivotal scene comes in the middle of the film, when Judy returns from an all-night,

though innocent, date with Jimmy, who has come back into her life. They have had a wonderful, dream-come-true time together, and it appears that Jimmy is falling for her. Judy rushes upstairs to her room and looks out her window at the morning star (which is also a nickname Jimmy gave her, and the name of the ballet she has choreographed for herself). She makes a wish, and we are positive she is going to ask the morning star to make Jimmy love her as she loves him. But her wish is "Please make me a dancer." At this point, we realize, although Judy doesn't know it yet, that dancing is truly more important to her than anything—including winning the man she loves. Judy will still pursue Jimmy, and be upset when Bubbles marries him while he is drunk; but Judy comes to understand the situation as we do, and in the courtroom scene voluntarily relinquishes all claims to Jimmy, returning him to his ex-wife, whom he still loves, and telling the judge: "Dancing means everything to me." It is these words of commitment to an art that cause Steve and Olmie to look at each other happily. Steve wants to find dancers, not stars, and is aware from Judy's statement that, regardless of her inchoate talent, she was "born with more than other dancers."

The skyscraper which houses the American Ballet Company is a metaphor for Judy's success, much as the sky is a metaphor for aviator Cynthia Darrington's independence in Arzner's *Christopher Strong*. In each instance, as the women go higher, the atmosphere becomes more hostile, oxygen seems scarcer, and their heads start to spin. Judy begins the film working in a club in which you have to go *down* a few stairs to enter. Dancing in a burlesque theater later places Judy as out of her element as Cynthia is when in a gown and mixing in high society, but it is a literal step *upward* for her: at least she is up on a stage, making decent money, and dancing ballet. On her first trip *up* inside the skyscraper, she becomes frightened and rushes back *down* before she auditions. But she will try again. Just as Cynthia breaks the altitude record and simultaneously commits a "noble" suicide at the end of *Christopher Strong*, Judy makes it to the top of the skyscraper, and finds that her stomach isn't turning, her knees aren't buckling, and her talented feet are sturdy on the ground.

For some reason, critics have described Judy as being extremely passive, probably because it makes her an ideal character to contrast with man-chasing, man-catching, man-using Bubbles, just as the demure, angelic Maureen O'Hara seems the opposite of wise-cracking, hip-swinging Lucille Ball (in her finest screen role). Bubbles may spend her time figuring out how to get rich and get ahead, but when she sees Judy doing her dance exercises *she* is impressed by *Judy's* ambitious nature—which Judy doesn't deny having. And Judy proves over and over again to be tougher than Bubbles, for she never takes the easy path by using her feminine wiles to get what she wants—she just plods along. Don't let her fairy-tale-princess beauty (in the opening scene, she has sparkling eyes and a sparkling dress, and the background decor sparkles behind her) fool you, or her kind, gentle nature, tears, or devotion to a high art make you think she is soft. Throughout the film she is *aggressive* and outspoken, taking more than her share of hard knocks on her climb up that skyscraper. She works in a dive so low that *she* asks a decent *male* customer (Jimmy), "What are you doing in a place like this?"; when the cops close down the club, she's the one chorine who protests (while Bubbles keeps silent) "We're working girls who want to get paid!"; while Bubbles takes a ride with a sugar daddy, Judy thumbs from Akron to New York; trying to get her troupe work, she does a humiliating hula dance for a glaring Hoboken club owner; nightly, she is laughed at unmercifully by hecklers in the burlesque house while being

The female camaraderie that is prevalent in most Dorothy Arzner films. Roommates Sally and Judy are visited by other members of Basilova's company. On the mantelpiece is Fernando, the toy bull Judy keeps to remind her of Jimmy.

Bubbles's stooge, but refuses to quit; she finally tells off the hecklers; she slaps and wrestles with Bubbles on the stage, and admits later that she tried to kill her; and she stands up to a stern judge, although it means spending time in jail. Maybe some of her strength (and temper) can be attributed to her being Irish, but most of it comes from being a woman trying to make a living during the Depression and refusing to give up no matter what. Judy only once shows weakness—when she chickens out of the audition. But considering what she's been going through, she's certainly entitled. Since Arzner,

herself, doubted the overall quality of the movies she made, probably she thought it natural that Judy would at first doubt that she had the talent to dance with such an intimidating company as the (fabricated) American Ballet.

Of course, the greatest example of Judy's willingness to fight back and to stand up for her rights and integrity comes when, with legs spread and arms crossed, she tells off her hecklers in the burlesque house. She concludes her condemnation of *them* by saying "We'd laugh too, only we're paid to let you sit there and

The rivalry between Tiger Lily and her ''stooge'' intensifies.

roll your eyes and make your screamingly clever remarks. What's it all for? So you can go home and strut before your wife and sweethearts . . . play at being the stronger sex for a minute? I'm sure they see through you like we do!" As Karyn Kay and Gerald Peary in *Women and the Cinema* (Dutton, 1977) contend, "This utterly remarkable . . . speech is without parallel in the whole history of the cinema." It is no wonder that Olmie, the one woman in the audience, the first to comprehend the broader antisexist implications of this speech, jumps to her feet to applaud Judy's words.

When Olmie applauds Judy, this is only one of many incidents where women show their support for one another. Earlier Olmie had used her influence with Steve to get him to give Judy an audition; when he becomes annoyed that Judy is wasting her ballet talent working in burlesque, Olmie again jumps to Judy's side, chiding him, "That's right, condemn a girl 'cause she has to make her own living." Although at odds with one another, Judy and Bubbles both try to get their troupe work; and Bubbles, who secretly pays Judy's and Sally's rent, gets Judy a job with the burlesque, insisting she get a good wage. At the film's end, Judy defends Bubbles to the judge, and the look of respect between the two women indicates that their feud (like a sibling rivalry) is over. Arzner likes all her women, even Bubbles. She may be difficult but is no villain.

Likewise, Arzner's men are not villains. Jimmy is misguided, spoiled, and irresponsible, but he isn't unlikable. He takes a collection for the chorines at the closed Akron nightclub, and later yells at the burlesque customers who make fun of Judy's dancing. He leads Judy on—but he doesn't realize he is doing so and that he still wants his wife back. And as it turns out, he hasn't done anyone any harm.

Steve is a welcome change from brash, fresh Errol Flynn and Fred Astaire types in how he relates to Judy. It is never clear if he actually is pursuing a romantic involvement with her; what is clear is that he is truly a nice guy. When he first talks to Judy it is only because she is crying. When he tries to protect her with his umbrella during a rainstorm, he is doing a good deed, not coming on to her. When she runs away from him, he doesn't gaze at her full body from the rear, as most lascivious male characters would (upon a male director's instructions), but at her nimble feet "dancing" through the puddles. (Likewise, when he and Fitch watch Judy dance at the burlesque house, they don't discuss her body as most men in that audience are likely doing, but speak of her in terms of her eyes and footwork.) Even when he hugs Judy at the film's end, comforting the half-laughing, half-weeping young woman, saying "Go ahead and laugh, Judy O'Brien," we still do not know if he wants the two of them to begin a romance. It doesn't really matter, but if it happens, it will be fine with us, because we realize that Steve's main concern, like Judy's, has always been that she be given a chance to dance. This scene is reminiscent of the finale in George Stevens's much-neglected *Vigil in the Night* (1940), when dedicated nurse Carole Lombard and doctor Brian Aherne embrace and then, realizing that their great love still ranks second in importance to their work, untangle themselves and walk down the hospital corridor together to do their duty. If Steve takes Judy to the justice of the peace once the film is over, it will be on the rare day when no dance rehearsal is scheduled.

1971 Paramount release of a Maran Film and Kettledrum Productions coproduction*
Director: Jerzy Skolimowski
Producer: Helmut Jedele
Screenplay: Jerzy Skolimowski, J. Gruza, and B. Sulik
Cinematography: Charly Steinberger
Music: Cat Stevens and the Can
Editor: Barrie Vince
Running Time: 87 minutes

Cast: Jane Asher (Susan), John Moulder-Brown (Mike), Diana Dors (lady client), Karl Michael Vogler (gym teacher), Christopher Sandford (the fiancé), Louise Martini (prostitute), Erica Beer (baths cashier), Anita Lochner (Kathy), Anne-Marie Kuster (nightclub receptionist), Karl Ludwig Lindt (baths manager), Erika Wackernager (Mike's mother), Peter Martin Urtel (Mike's father)

Synopsis: Mike, a fifteen-year-old London boy, takes his first job as an attendant at the seedy Newford public baths, in the men's division. He is taught the ropes by his coworker Susan, a very pretty twenty-three-year-old redhead who gets him to agree to send male clients to her in exchange for her female clients so they can both get bigger tips. Mike doesn't provide the women Susan sends him with any sexual favors, but since he is handsome and looks older than he is, they find him suitable to just stand near them while they have sexual fantasies. He doesn't know it, but while he is taking care of Susan's clients, she is having an affair with the baths' swim instructor, his gym teacher from school.

Mike develops an enormous crush on Susan. When two teenagers at the swimming pool imply that she sleeps around, Mike fights them. While underwater, he fantasizes seeing her nude.

Susan regards Mike with friendly contempt, but when she sees him without clothes, she finds him attractive—despite his age. Although she would never consider becoming romantically involved with him, when he tells her that he is a virgin she begins to flirt with his affections and encourage his sexual interest in her.

When Susan and her fiancé go to a sex movie, Mike follows them and sits directly behind her. Susan allows Mike to caress her breast but then slaps him and sends her fiancé to get the manager. While he is gone, Susan kisses Mike on the lips.

Mike finds out that Susan has been having an affair with his gym teacher, becomes very upset, and tells Susan that he will no longer switch clients with her. He tries to sabotage a date they are having by riding his bike in front of the gym teacher's car. Susan ends up riding over Mike's bike and crushing it.

Mike steals a poster from in front of a strip joint because the bare-breasted woman on it resembles Susan. He angrily confronts Susan with the poster. She denies that it is she on the poster, but is not adamant enough about that fact to convince Mike she is telling the truth. He is very disappointed in her. However, that night he throws the poster into the swimming pool, then jumps on it, holding it in his arms, pretending it is Susan.

After a track event, Susan discovers that Mike has punctured the tires to the gym instructor's car. She scuffles with Mike, and the jewel from her engagement ring falls off into the snow. She panics, but Mike helps her carry bags of snow into the empty swimming pool, where they can strain the snow and look for the jewel. When the gym instructor appears and yells at Susan for the damage done to his car, she tells him to go away and breaks off their relationship. When she returns from calling her fiancé, she finds Mike lying naked on the pool bottom, with the jewel he has found in his mouth. Afraid that he will swallow the ring, she strips off her clothing to reward him. He gives her the jewel, and looks sad. She starts to leave, but stops and grants Mike a chance to make love to her. Meanwhile, a baths attendant who doesn't know Mike and Susan are there opens a valve that lets the water rush into the pool. Mike becomes very upset when his attempt at lovemaking fails. Susan gets up to answer the ringing phone—and to escape the rising water—but Mike won't let her leave before they have talked about what has just happened. She starts to climb out of the pool but Mike swings an overhanging lamp at her and it strikes her head. Dying, she falls into the water. Mike caresses her as he did the poster, as the water mixes with the red paint of an overturned paint can.

---

*_Deep End_ is an English-language film made by a Polish director in England and Germany. It was financed primarily by West German and U.S. money.

Deep End

Polish-born Jerzy Skolimowsky coscripted Andrzej Wajda's _Innocent Sorcerers_ (1960) when he was twenty-two, and Roman Polanski's debut film _Knife in the Water_ (1963) before he began directing his own screenplays. _Rysopis_ (1964), _Walkover_ (1965), _Barrier_ (1966), and especially _Le Départ_ (1967), his most popular film, were well received in Europe and were shown at several international festivals; but it was _Deep End,_ his second English-language film and his first released, that was expected to be Skolimowski's breakthrough film in America, not only on the art film circuit but in commercial theaters as well. Unfortunately, Paramount, which bought the distribution rights, had no idea how to market a strange little picture that critic David Thomson correctly describes as "funny, touching, sexy, surreal, and tragic—all at the same time." When _Deep End_ didn't immediately catch on, Paramount pulled it as a single attraction and booked it as a cofeature—I discovered it in an empty out-of-the way theater on the lower half of the twin bill with Lewis Gilbert's even more obscure _Friends_ (1971), starring those two box office magnets Sean Bury and Anicee Alvina. As Mitchell S. Cohen lamented in his article "_Deep End:_ Passion in a Public Bath" (_The Velvet Light Trap,_ Winter 1975), Paramount was so quick to abandon the film that "_Deep End_ never found its audience, and an unusual, complex motion picture deserving of support and detailed critical attention has for the most part gone unrecognized."

There is much to admire in _Deep End:_ the fine ensemble acting by an English and German cast; the improvisational feel to the scenes between the awkward

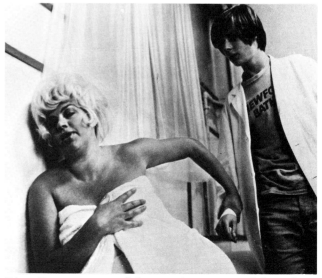

Diana Dors, once one of the screen's top sex symbols, makes a memorable appearance as a plump middle-aged client who brings herself to orgasm while keeping confused Mike by her side.

Susan and her lover watch his female students splash about in the baths' pool.

Mike and the self-possessed Susan; the sexual intensity that pervades whenever the two of them are together; wonderfully funny moments like when Mike must keep a buxom middle-aged client (fifties sex symbol Diana Dors) company while she brings herself to an orgasm by ranting and raving about soccer superstar George Best scoring a goal; and a remarkably effective use of color to heighten dramatic tension—for instance, at various times Skolimowski uses the color red to signify sex/sin (Susan's red hair falls over her virginal white coat); anger (a vertical red stripe is painted on a wall between the baths' overweight cashier and the slender Susan, who is making her jealous by deliberately eating an ice cream soda in front of her); danger (a pre-title drop of blood fills the screen); and death (red paint topples into the swimming pool where the fatally injured Susan floats, and turns the water blood red).

Skolimowski's London is striking in that it is not the *swinging* town of many English films of the period, but is instead a city whose glorious days have long passed. Porno theaters, strip joints, and seedy public baths are the order of the day. Sexual temptation is everywhere, and everyone is motivated primarily by sexual fantasies and drive. To the Polish Skolimowski, no one bothers to be faithful in such a decadent environment, or has any scruples about with whom they sleep: Susan has a fiancé her own age, but has an affair with the older, married gym instructor and at the same time

considers fifteen-year-old Mike a potential sexual conquest; likewise, the gym instructor, besides having an affair with Susan, plays sexual games (which one suspects aren't as innocent as he pretends) with his teenage female swim students. Things can no longer be taken at face value: porno movies go under the guise of being sex education films; public baths are not where people go to wash up anymore but are where they go to get hot and bothered (and live out their sexual fantasies with Susan and Mike). Sexually experienced women, like Susan, dress in white. Young boys, like Mike, live in the bodies of men.

Much in *Deep End* reminds me of the work of Skolimowski's former collaborator Roman Polanski: the absurdist humor, the overt sexual imagery and symbolism, the use of color to create mood. Yet while I like most of what Skolimowski has done with this film, I can't help thinking that Polanski would have been the ideal director for it. What Polanski does better than anyone else is make you laugh, or giggle nervously, while simultaneously preparing you for a brutally unhappy ending. Polanski's climaxes can depress you, but at least you feel as if you have been forewarned. In *Deep End*, Skolimowski makes us laugh (and giggle nervously) but neglects to give us enough ominous signs that the film—which continues to roll along whimsically—will in fact end on a tragic note. If anything, we expect an amusing finale where perhaps Mike coaxes

To Mike water is a purifying agent, but it also has sexual connotations for him and is a catalyst for his sexual fantasies. While underwater, he caresses the poster of a girl he thinks might be Susan. At the end, he will caress the dead Susan in this pool.

Susan into his bed, becomes a "man," winks at the camera, rejects Susan for being such a sexual tease, returns to his former girl friend Kathy, and lives happily ever after. But this is by no means the direction in which Skolimowski wants to take us. Unfortunately, his shift from comedy to tragedy is swift when it should be gradual, and so subtly done that until the end we simply believe that the film's humor has temporarily gone flat rather than having been virtually eliminated by design. So when Mike kills Susan we are totally shocked, even numbed by the horror of it—and we feel that we have been misled all along by the film's comedy and optimistic nature. The climactic death scene, which many critics have called overly melodramatic, is without doubt the major reason audiences didn't respond positively toward the film. But this ending is only problematic because we are not ready for it. On the plus side, it is an ending that makes us reexamine what has gone on earlier with a different perspective; because of this we discover that what could have been just another amusing film is something much more: a most interesting character study.

Mike is one in a line of autobiographical male protagonists in Skolimowski's work. But he is not as much related to the characters Skolimowski himself played in three of his films as he is to nineteen-year-old Marc (Jean-Pierre Léaud) in *Le Départ*. Both characters are outsiders/loners who are overly sensitive and easily hurt; compulsive, impulsive, and often irrational, and as a consequence sometimes end up being complete fools; rebellious and foolishly daring, but certainly not *heroic* in the movie sense of the word; sexually inhibited and frustrated, but on the prowl and not to be deterred. The significant difference between the two is that Marc's quirkiness is endearing while Mike's becomes increasingly repulsive as he gets closer to going off the metaphoric deep end—which finally happens when he kills Susan in the deep end of the baths' swimming pool.

For the first part of the film every male viewer who as a young boy had a crush on an older female student-teacher, baby-sitter, camp counselor, or best friend's sister can readily identify with Mike. At fifteen, an age when young boys are sexually curious and confused, innocent Mike works with Susan, a young woman (played splendidly by Jane Asher, best known as a former girl friend of Beatle Paul McCartney) who is so sexy and pretty that it would seem impossible for such an impressionable lad *not* to become enamored of her. We nostalgically laugh at Mike's clumsiness around Susan; at how he becomes tongue-tied when she teases him; at how he fantasizes seeing her nude; at how he follows her around and spies on her; and at how he finally manages to muster up enough nerve to ask her out—only to have her tell him that she has a fiancé. This is all familiar, amusingly painful territory. But we must applaud Mike's nerve when he touches Susan's breast in the movie theater while her fiancé sits nearby, for none among us had such derring-do. And we feel admiration and a touch of jealousy toward Mike when Susan turns and kisses him on the lips—a just reward for taking such a chance.

But from the time he discovers Susan's affair with his gym teacher, Mike's infatuation toward her becomes an embarrassing obsession with which we no longer wish to identify. As, by leaps and bounds, Mike becomes more compulsive, more possessive toward Susan, and more pathetic in how he deals with the situation, he becomes as difficult to watch as James Stewart in *Vertigo* (1958). A male acting foolish because of a woman we can smile at, but it makes us squirm to see him become as weak as jelly, and completely out of control of his actions and ability to reason, as he edges toward that deep end.

In Krishna Shah's *The Rivals* (1972), another film that ends with an unpopular death of someone who doesn't deserve killing, the point is made that a young boy who is *intellectually* the equal of an adult is not necessarily able to handle the emotional effects of sexual initiation as maturely as an adult would. In *Deep End,* it is a boy who is *physically* equal to an adult who cannot cope with failure during his first attempt at sexual intercourse. This is the darker side of *Summer of '42* (1971), also a film in which a boy fantasizes losing his virginity to a woman in her twenties and has the opportunity to fulfill that fantasy; here, Mike doesn't succeed in "coming of age," and as a result of his failure (impotency), he actually regresses in years and acts like a small child.

From the beginning, Mike's attitude toward sex is decidedly immature. He obviously associates sex with something dirty: the first thing he does when he enters the prostitute's room is wash his hands; and he spends much time scrubbing the floors and walls of the public baths, a haven for sexual activity and fantasy fulfillment. Mike is puritanical when he chides Susan for two-timing her fiancé, but he wants to make love to her himself. He is unhappy that she resembles the bare-breasted poster girl, but it excites him that she may actually be that girl. When two teenage boys tell him of Susan's well-known promiscuity, he fights them in the pool, but at the same time their words have stimulated his first sexual fantasy of her. Mike thinks Susan naughty and is disillusioned that she doesn't live up to his angelic image of her—but he cannot help that his libido is aroused by the thought that she might be a loose woman.

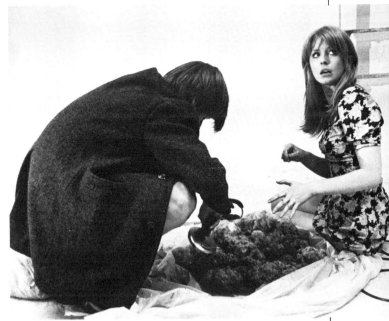

Mike and Susan search for the missing jewel in snow they brought to the empty pool.

Throughout the film, Skolimowski shows us other signs that the mature-looking Mike is still very much a child. When he catches Susan making love to his gym teacher, he becomes like a jealous child whose mother has punished him without reason, and smashes the glass of the baths' fire alarm, cutting his hand; he then goes into his room and weeps, putting his thumb in his mouth. With the planning aptitude of a two-year-old, he can think of no cleverer way to stop the date between Susan and the gym teacher than by riding his bike in front of their car. After his failure at lovemaking, his childish impulses completely take over: he cries, calls for his mother, refuses to give Susan her purse, and finally, like a destructive child who desperately wants attention, swings the overhanging lamp at Susan and kills her.

Susan is a complete tease, not only on a sexual level with her fiancé, her lover, and Mike, but in other ways as well. That is her nature. She tempts the baths cashier with that ice cream soda; she even calls a dog to her, and when it arrives zonks it with a snowball. But Susan is not a bad person, and not to be hated. If Skolimowski himself hated Susan, he would have had her make love to Mike for the express purpose of getting him to give her jewel back, and not after she has already secured it; as it is in the picture, she allows Mike to make love to her as a *kind* gesture to him. Susan's big mistake is in not paying attention to the fact that Mike is immature and must be treated with kid gloves. When he proves impotent, which is likely to happen considering the circumstances, she doesn't assume the responsibility for soothing the feelings of the boy whose affections she had no business toying with. Susan is an irresponsible person who, unfortunately for her, is irresponsible to the wrong person. That Susan is killed and that Mike, who loves her madly, is the one who kills her is a double tragedy.

Detour

Trapped in a hotel room with the despicable Vera, Roberts begins to lose his patience. She couldn't care less.

1946 PRC (Producers Releasing Corporation)
Director: Edgar G. Ulmer
Producer: Leon Fromkess
Screenplay: Martin Goldsmith
From a novel by Martin Goldsmith
Cinematography: Benjamin H. Kline
Music: Ordody
Editor: George McGuire
Running Time: 67 minutes

Cast: Tom Neal (Roberts), Ann Savage (Vera), Claudia Drake (Sue Harvey), Edmund MacDonald (Charles Haskell, Jr.), Tim Ryan (Gus), Esther Howard (Hedy), Roger Clark (Dillon)

Synopsis: In a Reno diner along the highway, depressed and ill-tempered Al Roberts thinks back on recent events. He wanted to be a classical pianist, but he eked out a living playing at a half-empty New York night spot called the Break of Dawn Club. What made it tolerable was that he loved Sue Harvey, the club's singer. She decided to put off their wedding until they had both realized their professional ambitions, and went out to Hollywood to become a star. When Roberts next spoke to her by phone, she was slinging hash in Los Angeles. They decided that waiting for success was now secondary to their being together, and agreed to marry as soon as Roberts hitched out to the Coast.

It wasn't easy for Roberts to get rides, and he ran out of money. In Arizona he was given a lift by Charles Haskell, Jr., a tough-talking man who said he would drive Roberts all the way to L.A. Haskell even bought him a meal. As they drove along, Haskell told him that the scratches on his hand were from a female hitchhiker he had tossed out of his car. During a storm, Roberts drove the car while Haskell slept. When Roberts felt himself dozing, he tried to awaken Haskell only to discover that he was dead, possibly from taking too many pills while driving. Afraid that he would be arrested for murder, Roberts dumped Haskell along the side of the road and took his wallet, clothes, and car.

Across the California state line, Roberts offered a ride to a female hitcher. Vera turned out to be a terribly cruel woman, the one Haskell tossed out of his car. When Roberts tried to explain to her how he came to be in possession of Haskell's car, Vera refused to believe him. She told him that he was under her power now, and that she would squeal to the police if he didn't sell the car in L.A. so she could get the money.

They arrived in L.A., then drove to San Bernardino, where they checked into a hotel as husband and wife. She didn't let him out of sight, which was doubly bad for him because she was awful company. She drank and traded insults with him.

Vera changed her mind about selling the car when she read in the paper that Charles Haskell, Sr., was dying. Knowing that Haskell Senior hadn't seen his son in many years, she told Roberts that he must pretend to be his son so they could collect on his inheritance.

That night Roberts and Vera argued viciously. She got drunk and kept threatening to call the police. When he saw she was serious about doing it, Roberts knocked her down. Vera took the phone into the bedroom and locked the door. In the living room Roberts tried to rip the cord apart. The wire had gotten tangled around Vera's neck and as he pulled on the wire, she was strangled to death. When he saw what had happened, he knew he'd be arrested.

Roberts walks out of the diner. Vera's body has been discovered. He wonders what life would have been like if Haskell had just passed him by. A patrol car picks him up. Roberts knows that fate has played a cruel trick on him.

In their excellent anthology on low-budget films, *Kings of the Bs* (Dutton, 1975), editors Charles Flynn and Todd McCarthy cite Edgar G. Ulmer's *Detour* as "probably the greatest 'B' film ever made." In *Dames* (Praeger, 1969), British film historians Ian and Elisabeth Cameron call *Detour* "a work well in the running to be the cheapest really good film to come out of Hollywood." Many more critics have voiced similar sentiments about the quality of this film, which has reached near-legendary status despite infrequent screenings in theaters or on television. *Detour* is truly an unusual film, far more intense and stylish than the run-of-the mill low-budget film, and featuring the oddest, most repellent symbiotic (leechlike) relationship in cinema history. This, plus the fact that it was made by Ulmer—regarded as the "master" of the B-film—in just six days, using only four characters of any signifiance (Roberts, Ann, Sue, and Haskell), and only six minimally furnished indoor sets (the Reno diner, the Break of Dawn Club, the Arizona diner, the motel room across the California state line, the San Bernardino hotel rooms, and the car dealer's office),* makes it a natural for critics impressed by quality in spite of low budgets. But my guess is that the typical moviegoer will find *Detour* disappointing, even ludicrous at times, as every line seems out of Bartlett's; and those familiar with Ulmer's films might think it much less enjoyable or consistent than *The Black Cat* (1934), *Bluebeard* (1943), which I think is his best film, *Ruthless* (1948), and *The Naked Dawn* (1955).

Beautifully filmed and ornately designed, the majority of Ulmer's films deal with a flawed male protago-

---

*I make a point of listing the major characters and the indoor sets because I have read in several places that the film has only two characters (Roberts and Vera) and one indoor set (the hotel rooms). I have also read that the picture was made in four days, although Ulmer claimed it was six days.

nist who, driven by uncontrollable passions/ambitions, ultimately meets a sad end (usually death). Typically, Ulmer films from *Ruthless* to *The Amazing Transparent Man* (1960) are about the long rises and swift falls of these characters. But in *Detour* we are presented with a character who starts out at rock bottom—he has a lousy, unrewarding job and no prospects, little money, and his fiancé Sue decides to move three thousand miles away —and falls even farther. The picture might have begun on an optimistic note if the first scene were the one in the Break of Dawn with Roberts playing the piano and Sue singing a love song meant for him, "I Can't Believe That You're in Love with Me." This scene does come first chronologically. But Ulmer and screenwriter Martin Goldsmith (and uncredited rewrite man Martin Mooney) chose to open the film at the end, with Roberts in a Reno diner thinking back over the set of circumstances that have ruined his life. So when we flashback to the Break of Dawn scene (the second scene in the film), we know that despite Roberts's happy demeanor ("I was a pretty lucky guy") he has nothing to look forward to. No wonder Andrew Sarris calls *Detour* "the most despairing" of all B-pictures. In *King of the Bs*, critic Myron Meisel writes about the fatalistic nature of the film:

> Its inevitability reminds one of [Ulmer's mentor in Germany] F. W. Murnau's *Tabu* (1931): the lighting and the camera serve as instruments of the inexorable progression to disaster, tracking shots that signal the subtle images that exist so strongly on the screen that each subsequent shot literally forces the previous one from its place on the screen. . . . *Detour* mercifully

lasts little more than an hour, during which it compulsively grasps at the intolerable, only to find it readily within its reach.

Vera may believe in the inevitability of her own death ("If I'm hanged all they'll be doing is rushing it"), but Roberts believes in the inevitability of everything. And his outlook is always bleak. When Sue tells him she's going to Hollywood to try to make it big, instead of encouraging her he says, "People go out there and start polishing cuspidors." Then he kisses her and walks into the fog, the ultimate fate symbol (along with trains and roads). After disposing of Haskell's body, he checks into a motel to sleep; he takes time to put on Haskell's pajamas and they are *striped*, which makes us believe pessimistic Roberts already sees himself in prison garb. When he picks up Vera and discovers who she is, he narrates, "No matter what you do, no matter where you turn, fate sticks out its foot to trip you." When he is picked up by police at the film's end, he narrates similar words: "Fate or some mysterious force can put a finger on you or me for no good reason at all." The truth is that while fate is most definitely at work, Roberts does nothing to ward it off. Instead he uses fate as the explanation/alibi for his downfall when his own foolishness is the *major* contributing factor. It is Roberts's foolish decision to dump Haskell; to steal his wallet, clothes, and car; to pick up hitchhiker Vera although he should be trying to keep a low profile, especially since he is riding in a stolen car and Haskell told him of a female hitchhiker *he* picked up earlier; to go along with Vera's schemes; and to not call Sue when he reaches L.A. Roberts is one of the screen's all-time great losers.

A happy Roberts plays the piano while his fiancée Sue belts out a song.

A lurid poster for Detour, *which has nothing to do with the film. The shots of Vera's murder are indeed from the film but the other pictures aren't. For instance, in* Detour *Roberts and Sue converse under a lamppost, but here we find Roberts with Vera, who is saying things that make her sound desirable, which she definitely is not in the film.*

doing her bidding, keeping him in sight at all times, and even ordering him to close the hotel window. After watching Roberts being pushed around by Vera, one can only conclude that, fate or not, he gets just what he deserves. Ironically, actor Tom Neal proved to be a loser exactly like Roberts: he killed his wife and was sent to prison.

Like Tom Neal, Ann Savage had a lackluster Hollywood career, appearing in such marvelously titled non-classics as *Two Señoritas From Chicago* (1943) and *Pygmy Island* (1950). But as Vera she was able to play the character who is quite possibly the most despicable female in movie history—even she admits she was born in a gutter. *A truly memorable character.* The nicest compliment Roberts can give her is "She had a homely beauty." The truest thing he can say is "Vera was just as rotten in the morning." When she coughs and says, "It's nothing," he remarks hopefully, "That's what Camille said." Her looks remind me of a vulture—not because she's ugly but because she appears to be thinking she'd like to rip you apart with her teeth and devour you piece by piece. Ian and Elisabeth Cameron correctly describe her: "Miss Savage looks in profile quite ordinary, though not particularly pretty—like a younger Judith Anderson—but when she turns and looks at the camera, she has eyes so terrifying that one wonders how those who beheld her in the flesh managed to avoid getting turned to stone." Even more terrifying than her face, in my opinion, is her voice. Rarely does she simply deliver a line; instead, she screams. She is loud, scratchy, vulgar, intolerable. All the time. And worse when drunk. The only screen characters whose voices are similar are the insane wife in John Waters's *Desperate Living* (1977) and Susan (Dorothy Comingore) in *Citizen Kane* (1941) when she gets bad notices for her opera debut and screams at Kane until you want to put your fingers in your ears. It is fitting that Vera dies with a telephone wire around her neck, unable to finish her final sentence.

The scene in which Vera is killed is doubtlessly the highlight of the film. Not only because it shuts Vera up once and for all, but because it exhibits Ulmer's most audacious use of the camera in the entire film. When Roberts finds Vera's dead body, the camera moves around the room, fading in and fading out (like someone between life and death) as it settles on various objects; the most dynamic shot is that of a mirror which reflects Roberts and the strangled Vera lying on the bed. What I find particularly intriguing about this death scene is that it occurs when it does. We expect Roberts and Vera to pull off the hoax on Haskell Senior whereby Roberts would pose as Haskell Junior so they could get some big money; but suddenly Vera gets mad at Roberts and picks up the phone, and he ends up killing her. I wonder: if Ulmer had more money than allotted by PRC, a true Poverty Row studio, would Vera and Roberts have had their final battle a half hour later— after they had visited Haskell Senior? More than one low-budget film had to toss out major parts of the script because of budget problems, and this might have been the case with *Detour*.

At the beginning he is a sourpuss; about money he says, "It's a piece of paper crawling with germs," "It couldn't buy what I wanted," and "Money causes problems in the world simply because there's too little of it." Of hitchhiking, he grumbles, "Emily Post should write a book for those thumb-riding." Of Murphy beds, he sneers, "I invented them." From the start we are aware that Roberts feels sorry for himself and believes that the whole world is against him; so by the time Vera tells him, "I don't like your attitude, Roberts—all you do is bellyache," we are almost on *her* side. It is when Roberts meets Vera that we come to realize that Roberts is also a weakling. Just because he believes man has no free will is not a good reason for him to let Vera make him her virtual slave ("My favorite sport is being kept prisoner," he says sarcastically), blackmailing him into

Duck Soup

1933 Paramount
Director: Leo McCarey
Producer: Herman J. Mankiewicz
Screenplay: Bert Kalmar and Harry Ruby
Additional Dialogue: Arthur Sheekman and Nat Perrin
Cinematography: Henry Sharpe
Music and Lyrics: Bert Kalmar and Harry Ruby
Editor: LeRoy Stone
Running Time: 70 minutes

Cast: Groucho Marx (Rufus T. Firefly), Harpo Marx (Pinkie), Chico Marx (Chicolini), Zeppo Marx (Bob Rolland), Margaret Dumont (Mrs. Teasdale), Louis Calhern (Ambassador Trentino), Raquel Torres (Vera Marcal), Edgar Kennedy (lemonade seller), Edmund Breese (Zander), Leonid Kinskey (agitator), Verna Hillie (Trentino's secretary)

Synopsis; Mrs. Teasdale agrees to give the small country of Freedonia twenty million dollars to save it from bankruptcy provided that Rufus T. Firefly is appointed the country's new leader. During his inaugural ceremony, Firefly courts the widowed Mrs. Teasdale, and insults her friend Trentino, the scoundrelly ambassador of neighboring Sylvania. He also sings that if Freedonians think their country is bad off now, "Just wait 'til I get through with it." Trentino schemes with the seductive singer Vera Marcal, telling her to keep Firefly out of the way while he tries to win Mrs. Teasdale's hand in marriage, thereby gaining control of Freedonia. Trentino hires hot dog and peanut vendor Chicolini and Firefly's chauffeur, Pinkie, to spy on Firefly.

Firefly presides over his cabinet. He refuses to discuss taxes or anything else that has to do with government. He reduces workers' hours by shortening their lunch break. He hires Chicolini to be his secretary of war, believing he will annoy the rest of the cabinet. Firefly and Bob Rolland, his secretary, decide that they want to start a war with Sylvania by causing a personal feud with Trentino.

Firefly interrupts Trentino's attempt to propose to Mrs. Teasdale. When Trentino calls him an upstart, Firefly slaps him with a glove and declares war between Freedonia and Sylvania. Mrs. Teasdale arranges for the two men to make peace that night. Firefly jokingly asks Trentino what he called him earlier. When he answers "upstart," Firefly slaps him again, and once more declares war.

Vera is a guest in Mrs. Teasdale's house. She talks to Trentino by phone. Trentino sends Chicolini and Pinkie to the house to steal Firefly's war plans. They both dress up as Firefly to fool Mrs. Teasdale into turning over the papers, but Firefly himself, who is fooled for a time into thinking his look-alikes are his reflections, captures Chicolini.

Chicolini goes on trial, but the chaotic proceedings come to a halt when Mrs. Teasdale tells Firefly that Trentino is on the way to the courthouse to make one final effort to avoid a war. Firefly agrees to apologize to Trentino, but has second thoughts when he considers that Trentino may refuse to shake his hand of friendship. When Trentino enters, Firefly immediately slaps him instead of suffering a possible rejection and being insulted. Trentino storms out, declaring war. There is a great war between Freedonia and Sylvania. Freedonia suffers many casualties when Firefly mistakenly shoots his own men. To get new recruits Pinkie roams the countryside with the placard "Join the Army and See the Navy." Chicolini deserts Trentino and joins Freedonia because it serves better food. Mrs. Teasdale calls Firefly and says her house is under attack. Firefly, Chicolini, Pinkie, and Bob rush to her aid. Just when it looks as if they have been defeated, they capture Trentino when he tries to break into the house. Freedonia has won the war! The four men pellet Trentino with oranges. When the happy Mrs. Teasdale sings the Freedonia national anthem, they pelt her instead.

Appreciation for the Marx Brothers has increased dramatically since the sixties, when their films were rediscovered on America's college campuses. Outrageous behavior bordering on lunacy and flagrant contempt for authority and conventions—*if* intellectually conceived—were revered at the time (and have been ever since), and no one ever embodied these characteristics more than the stoop-walking cigar smoker with the burnt-cork moustache, the happy-go-lucky phony Italian, and the diabolical, demented mute in the curly blond wig. The one surprise is that the most popular Marx Brothers film for the subsequent generations of Marx devotees is not *A Night at the Opera* (1935), a certified comedy masterpiece, but *Duck Soup*, the team's lone critical and financial flop during their peak years.

In his biography *Groucho, Harpo, Chico, and Sometimes Zeppo* (Simon and Schuster, 1973), Joe Adamson writes: "*Duck Soup* juggles logic and defies gravity, it is outrageous, it is ridiculous, it is funny, it is savage, it is silly. It is a symphony in gagtime, composed by an army and orchestrated by one man." That one man was Leo McCarey, who had already worked with such fine comics as Laurel and Hardy (whom he brought together as a team), Charlie Chase, and the much underrated Eddie Cantor, and who later would direct many gems, including *The Awful Truth* (1937), the best of the Cary Grant–Irene Dunne films, and the Oscar-winning *Going My Way* (1944). McCarey was the best director with whom the Marx Brothers were ever associated, the only one wise enough to balance the trademarked Marxian word games with visual humor—even letting Groucho and Chico enter the world of pantomime that had been Harpo's private domain—and improvisational material with what had to be done

Zeppo, Chico, Groucho, and Harpo make as formidable a fighting force as there has ever been in pictures.

according to the script. It was McCarey who gave the film its title and brought in the two *great* visual scenes: the Laurel and Hardy routine during which Chicolini and Pinkie keep aggravating Edgar Kennedy (a Hal Roach comedian) by knocking his hat from his head and hands, and finally burning it; and the much-copied Schwartz Brothers mirror routine (never done better than in *Duck Soup*) during which Firefly thinks Pinkie, who has dressed like him, is his reflection.

McCarey presents the Marx Brothers at their best, at their "purest"—at their most consistently rude and irreverent, delivering a nonstop series of gags over the film's breakneck-paced seventy minutes. The Marx Brothers' humor is derived to a great extent from the cumulative effects that their unremitting insults (Groucho), puns (Groucho and Chico), invasions of privacy, destruction of property (Harpo), and general annoyances (Groucho, Chico, and Harpo) have on the pompous boors and wealthy hypocrites who populate their world. McCarey realized it was imperative to allow this aggravation of the Marx Brothers' victims to build without the usual disruptive inclusion of an incidental love affair (the script had Zeppo's dullard romancing Vera, but McCarey didn't bother to shoot such scenes), or Chico's piano and Harpo's (tedious) harp solos. In other Marx films the musical interludes tell viewers that there is a civilizing, cultural influence on Chico and Harpo that keeps them from being totally alien. While there is a grand piano in Mrs. Teasdales's house in *Duck Soup*, Chicolini never plays it; when it seems that Pinkie is about to play the "harplike" part of the grand—as

Harpo often does in films—the piano top falls down on his fingers. McCarey knew that the Marx Brothers are funniest when they are without any redeeming or endearing traits.

Most significant, for the only time in film, the Marx Brothers, whose comedy has often been defined by their anarchist tendencies when they are involved with any institution, are appropriately allowed to run amuck in a political setting. In *We're in the Money* (New York University Press, 1971), a book about the Depression and its films, Andrew Bergman attributed *Duck Soup*'s failure to find an audience in 1933 to a belief that, a year into the New Deal, Americans, because of understandable psychological needs, wouldn't allow themselves to think of the government they were counting on to save them from financial ruin or worse as absurd. But when *Duck Soup* caught on in the sixties with people in despair over the state of America and the direction it was heading, it made perfect sense that a picture would portray war in terms of absolute madness and treat politics with complete disdain.

Duck Soup is neither pointed enough in its criticism nor didactic or moralistic enough to be termed a political satire—more likely it is a parody of the many mythical kingdom films of the era, like *Million Dollar Legs* (1932), in which W. C. Fields plays the dictator of Klopstokia. It does, however, make valid thought-provoking *points* about politics and human nature in general: leaders of nations are not chosen necessarily because they have the qualifications to "lead" a country; countries which pride themselves on the liberties al-

Firefly ruins Mrs. Teasdale's lawn party when he repeatedly insults Trentino.

Firefly has second thoughts about hiring Pinkie and Chicolini to help him run Freedonia.

lowed their people (e.g., *Free*donia, or America, the land of the free) can become authoritarian overnight if a leader with dictatorial tendencies takes office; citizens of the world must trust their welfare to self-serving, egotistical diplomats who are so sensitive that they might declare war if they suffer a personal affront; the continuation of a war may not have as much to do with principles as with economic considerations ("It's too late [to stop the war]," declares Firefly. "I've already paid a month's rent on the battlefield!").

Groucho's Rufus T. Firefly is pure dictator (even his humorous nature can't cover this up), not because he will profit by being so but because he simply believes that any country so irresponsible as to appoint him its leader deserves the worst ruler possible. As always, Groucho plays his part with an air of cynicism—as if he were trapped by the world, the Depression, and the movie itself. Since only the world as a whole upsets him, he takes nothing less than the world as a whole seriously; therefore, nothing, not the day-to-day catastrophes or even dealing with loonies like Chicolini and Pinkie, fazes him. Like Chico and Harpo, Groucho is a winner simply because he won't acknowledge any defeat he sustains. Groucho's major source of pleasure is unnerving those bores who do take things seriously and are afraid of losing their power of dignity. Nothing delights him more than making someone an unwilling participant in his comedic dialogues. It is not that the jokes he tells are funny, or the puns; what is funny is that he insists on letting fly with lowbrow humor in austere settings (his inaugural ball, cabinet meetings, Mrs. Teasdale's party for the upper classes, the Royal courtroom) among genteel company. He loves being rude in public, and one of his playful diversions is to ruin polite conversation by pretending to take offense at something innocent said to him (he twists words

around) and quickly insulting the person who said it. If an occasion demands propriety, he is at his most hostile. At Mrs. Teasdale's lawn party, for instance, Firefly marches in uninvited, past one stuffy guest, from whom he grabs a doughnut, and, still walking, past another guest, into whose tea he dunks the doughnut. When Firefly finds his romantic rival Trentino down on his knees proposing to Mrs. Teasdale, he snaps, "When you're through with her feet, you can start on mine," and then turns to us with a prideful aside, "If that isn't an insult, I don't know what is." At the inauguration, to which Firefly arrives late and enters by sliding down a pole, he sings a ridiculous ditty about how he'll ruin the country, does an embarrassing dance, makes lewd advances to pretty women, dictates a note to his dentist, rolls his pants above his knees, asks Mrs. Teasdale to "pick a card" ("Keep it. I still have fifty-one left"), and, naturally, insults Trentino.

While W. C. Fields wins the hearts of rich dowagers through lying flattery, Groucho/Firefly somehow wins Margaret Dumont/Mrs. Teasdale although he insults her repeatedly. When Mrs. Teasdale catches on to Firefly, he quickly retreats from using her as a sounding board for the insults he's been waiting to try out on somebody, and covers up, "What I'm trying to tell you is that I love you." And with these words, he wipes out her short memory of the preceding insults.

It is only because Dumont (a great straightwoman in seven Marx Brothers films) loves Groucho that this two-bit social climber can enter the upper echelons of society in film after film, and in *Duck Soup* become the leader of a country. And it is only through Groucho that such lowlifes as Chico and Harpo can gain access to important places and leave them in shambles. Firefly looks out a window, spots peanut vendor Chicolini and immediately asks him if he wants a "soft government

job." When Chicolini impresses him with his riddles, Firefly makes him secretary of war. Later, Firefly knows that Chicolini is a spy for Sylvania but he holds no grudges and continues to keep him on as his secretary of war. Firefly feels a kinship to Chicolini that he does not have with anyone else in Freedonia. Both men are hustlers and money-grabbers, tell the truth (especially if it means they'll be insulting someone), detest snobbery (and exhibit a reverse snobbery of their own against snobs), and love driving people, including each other, to distraction with intricate, often nonsensical word play. (Groucho's attitude to Chico has always been, "I probably shouldn't ask this, but here goes . . .") Firefly and Chicolini understand each other—if not the exact meaning of their pun-filled sentences, then the reasons the other is talking so funny: they both play games (Firefly plays jacks at his cabinet meeting) to amuse themselves in stodgy old Freedonia.

Firefly only tolerates Pinkie so he can have Chicolini's company. (He knows that wherever Chicolini goes, Pinkie goes too.) Chances are that if Firefly had anything of value to lose he'd worry about having Pinkie around. As it is, the fellow amazes him. In *Close-Ups* Irving Brecher, author of two of the Marx Brothers' later films, wrote: "Chico's role was always to protect and big-brother the elfin, deliciously manic mute Harpo. And he, grateful for Chico's devotion, did something no other character did—he actually believed Chico was a real Italian."

Harpo may be the team's link to silent comedy, but his character is also the missing link in man's evolution, an unsuccessful stage in man's development. He is part man, part beast, a creature whose sole concerns are eating, grabbing blondes, and destroying everything in his path. He sleeps with animals (Pinkie beds down with his horse in one bed while a woman sleeps alone in a second bed in the corner of the room), and eats everything (EVERYTHING) including cigars, telephones, and shoelaces. He is a wild man—violence personified: he cuts everything in sight with his scissors—even cutting out Kennedy's pocket and making it into a peanut bag—burns Kennedy's hats, carries a gun and a blowtorch in his remarkably well-supplied coat. When Chico and Harpo are together, it reminds you of the guy who walks his unleashed dog down the street, and cares not a hoot that it is biting people. No doubt about it: Harpo should be on a leash.

As for Zeppo, he doesn't fit in, although the *Duck Soup* press release stated: "Zeppo, despite his straight character, is a most important part of the team. He's an expert gagman and is so splendid at imitating any one of the brothers that should illness stop one from making an appearance, Zeppo can immediately take his place." Well, he never did. After *Duck Soup*, he retired from the team. But his one consolation through the years must have been that he had been part of the Marx Brothers' best film, and hadn't ruined it. (And, you know, he's even kind of funny in this film. Let's give him his due.)

El Topo

(The Mole)

1971 Mexico ABKCO release of a Producciones Panicas film
Director: Alexandro Jodorowsky
Producer: Roberto Viskin
Screenplay: Alexandro Jodorowsky
Cinematography: Raphael Corkidi
Music: Alexandro Jodorowsky
Editor: Frederico Landeros
Running Time: 123 minutes

Cast: Alexandro Jodorowsky (El Topo), Brontis Jodorowsky (Brontis as a child), Mara Lorenzio (Mara), David Silva (the Colonel), Paula Romo (the Woman in Black), Jacqueline Luis (the Small Woman), Robert John (Brontis as a man)

Synopsis: El Topo rides through the desert with his seven-year-old son Brontis. He tells Brontis to bury his first toy and his picture of his mother in the sand because he is now a man. They ride into a town where there has been a dreadful massacre. El Topo guns down several of the men responsible and castrates the leader of the bandits, the Colonel, who then commits suicide.

Mara, the Colonel's woman, pushes Brontis aside so she can ride away with El Topo. Brontis is left behind with the town's monks, never to forget his father's rejection.

El Topo and Mara make love in the desert sands. She tells him that he should prove himself "the best" by killing the Four Sharpshooter Masters who live in the desert. They go in search of these Masters. A Woman in Black who is physically attracted to Mara follows them. The First Master is a quicker draw than El Topo but El Topo tricks him and shoots him. Mara kills The Double Man—two men, one without arms, on the bottom, and the other, without legs, strapped on top—who was the Master's servant.

Mara sees her reflection in a pool and falls in love with herself. While she makes love to El Topo she looks at herself in a mirror. El Topo shoots the mirror and puts the broken glass in his pocket.

The Second Master is totally preoccupied with his mother, with whom he lives. Before the two men draw, El Topo places glass beneath the mother's foot. When she cries out from pain, the Second Master is distracted. El Topo kills him. He takes a copper ashtray the Master made and puts it under his shirt.

The Third Master shoots El Topo in the heart, but his bullet hits the copper ashtray. El Topo kills him.

The Fourth Master catches El Topo's bullets with a butterfly net and flings them back at him. To show El Topo how unimportant death is, he takes El Topo's knife and stabs himself. El Topo, feeling guilty because of the tricks he played on the other Masters, goes crazy. He retraces his journey, at last breaking through the walls of the First Master's octagon home, and frees some doves. While he stands on a bridge, the Woman in Black shoots him in his hands and feet as if he were being crucified. Then she shoots him in the side. He falls, thinking he will die. The Woman in Black and Mara go off together.

El Topo wakes up more than twenty years later. He no longer considers himself a god. He is now a humble man doing penance for his sins. He has been cared for by a Small Woman who loves him. They have been living in a closed-up cave with other retarded, deformed dwarfs who have been banned by those in the town. El Topo, with a shaved head and dressed as a monk, and the Small Woman go to the sinful town, where slaves are killed for sport. They perform mime routines and use the money they earn to help them dig a tunnel that will free the dwarfs. They are forced to make love in public. The Small Woman becomes pregnant. El Topo asks her to marry him, but when they arrive at the church they find a grown-up Brontis instead of the priest. Brontis swears to kill his father but agrees to wait until the tunnel is finished. After nine months the tunnel is completed and the dwarfs rush into town. They are massacred by the townspeople. El Topo is also shot but refuses to feel the pain. He kills everyone in town. Then he performs self-immolation. The Small Woman gives birth. She, the baby, and Brontis ride off into the desert.

The movie begins with El Topo riding through the desert with his son Brontis.

If you're great, El Topo *is a great picture; if you're limited,* El Topo *is limited.*
—Alexandro Jodorowsky

Significantly, *El Topo* became the first major Midnight Movie when it played on Friday and Saturday nights at the old Elgin Theater in New York, beginning in January 1971. There was little publicity connected with the screenings, but *El Topo* thrived because of word-of-mouth and ended up staying at the Elgin for about a year. The film was initially handled by Douglas Films, a local concern, but Beatles manager Allen Klein—at John Lennon's instigation—purchased distribution rights for his ABKCO Films and booked it for successful midnight engagements throughout America. For college students, acid freaks, and movie enthusiasts into head pictures (films that are confusing but mentally stimulating), the controversial *El Topo* became the event picture of the year. But while it attracted a great number of repeat viewers who thought it a masterpiece and its Chilean-born director-writer-star Alexandro Jodorowsky an absolute genius, more people left the theater irritated by the picture's ambiguity, numbed by the great amounts of graphic violence (including the killing of animals), and/or complaining that they had just sat through "a goddamn Jesus film."

El Topo is the kind of picture from which a narcissistic director-writer-star like Tom Laughlin might have gotten his inspiration. It is about an egotistical man ("I am God") who ends up completely humbled ("I am not a god. I am a man"), but is itself among the most self-indulgent, narcissistic films ever made. This is a shame, because its self-congratulatory, pretentious nature makes one overlook its few moments of cinematic brilliance. To give an example of Jodorowsky's lack of humility, for the scene in which Mara hugs a rock and is squirted by a stream of miracle water/urine/semen that bursts forth, Jodorowsky writes* in the script: "The

---

*All Jodorowsky quotes in this article are from his book *"El Topo": a Book of the Film* (Douglas/Links 1971). The books contains an annotated script and a long Jodorowsky interview.

Mara is seduced by the Woman in Black (here, obviously, wearing nothing) and gives up El Topo for her new lover.

stone is an exact replica of my own phallus: thick, not very long, but with a voluminous head. That's how I am. That's how the rock is. That's El Topo's sex." (That's Jodorowsky's ego.) Dennis Hopper was a big fan of *El Topo.* I suppose Jodorowsky's use of abstract images had something to do with it. And Sam Fuller wrote he liked it because of the amazing diversity of material from which Jodorowky drew. Jodorowsky stated that *"El Topo* is a library . . . of all the books I love." He also admitted the influence of *films* made by such figures as Jean-Luc Godard, Luis Buñuel, Sergio Leone, Erich von Stroheim, and Buster Keaton (whose action often takes place in front of a stationary camera). Because of the film's peculiar content, I imagine other fans of *El Topo* would have included young Jung scholars, members of Jesus cults (do they go to movies?), perhaps Jews for Jesus, students of Zen, and

the creators of David Carradine's silly old one-aphorism-per-minute TV series *Kung Fu.*[*]

It is an impossible picture to categorize, but if pressed I'd group *El Topo* with such better, more coherent films as Luis Buñuel's *Simon of the Desert* (1965), George Stevens's telling of Jesus's life, *The Greatest Story Ever Told* (1965), Sergio Leone's *A Fistful of Dollars* (1967), Sam Peckinpah's *The Wild Bunch* (1968), *Fellini Satyricon* (1969), and Gilbert Rocha's *Antonio Das Mortas* (1969), which has a bounty hunter who is heavier than, but resembles, El Topo. Each of these films contains some of the plot and visual elements found in *El Topo:* a quest/mission, spectacle,

---

[*]*El Topo* cultists became enamored with the picture in the early seventies. The cult has not grown because since then the film has been nearly impossible to see.

ritualistic violence, a desolate landscape, and allusions to history, myth, religion, and culture. *El Topo* borrows from these films, but it is one of a kind. For one thing, Jodorowsky, who is a prolific stage director, is greatly indebted to theater for the style and content of the picture. He borrows freely from passion plays, miracle plays—what begins as a quest for enlightenment and moral and physical perfection ends up with El Topo achieving spiritual salvation and sainthood—the Theater of Cruelty, the Theatre of the Absurd (particularly Becket), surrealism (a la Cocteau, in both theater and film), mime (Jodorowsky studied with Marcel Marceau), and even magic acts. Likewise, Jodorowsky takes from artists and poets. Moreover, *El Topo* is part Sartre, Jung, Reich, Neitzsche, and Lao-tsu (the Chinese philosopher who usually is credited with founding Taoism about six hundred years before Christ). It uses the Old Testament, the New Testament. It is about Moses, about Christ, about a Zen disciple, and, to make it really confusing, about Jodorowsky. There are, in fact, far too many references, Jungian and religious symbols/artifacts, parables, geometric configurations, epigrams, in-jokes, and too much obscure imagery for anyone but

Jodorowsky to know what is going on. It's as if prior to writing and making his film Jodorowsky made a long list of items he wanted to allude to: films, books, poems, symbols, etc. But rather than cut his list, he was determined to use everything and began inserting his visual references to varied sources whether they worked in the film's context or not. Nor did it matter to him if viewers would know what he intended. For instance, when Mara and El Topo wash in a pool, are we expected to agree with Jodorowsky that "Mara and El Topo are like two gigantic hands entering a wash basin" and that "perhaps they are the two hands of Pontius Pilate"? And how are we supposed to look at a Master and realize he "contemplates the spiritual center of his body"?

The film is most interesting at the beginning, when avenging angel El Topo rides into the town where hundreds of people have been massacred and kills off the scoundrels responsible. We at least understand what is going on. Ditto when El Topo rejects his son and rides off with Mara (Eve?). But the picture goes in the wrong direction when El Topo enters the desert and takes on the Four Masters. This quest to "be the best" by killing the Masters was not El Topo's idea to begin with but

El Topo shoots the First Master as he falls into a hole El Topo dug during the night.

Now bald, the humble El Topo and the Small Woman perform mime for the townspeople.

Mara's; so I am confused by his motives for pursuing a goal which, as far as we know, has never been important to him. (Mara assumes the role of the traditional hen-pecking woman who forces her man to be more ambitious than he is—and causes his breakdown.) These four meetings—talks and gunfights—seem to go on forever, and while the dialogues between the Masters and El Topo are meant to be wise and mystical, they come across as empty and simplistic. I can hear such trite lines being said to and by David Carradine's priest on kiddie show *Kung Fu*: "I don't try to win but to gain perfect control"; "The deeper you fall, the higher you get"; "Perfection is losing yourself"; "And to lose you must love"; "You don't fear death anymore. That's why you're a dangerous enemy"; and "Too much perfection is a mistake."

Some of the action sequences are exciting. Too often they are gratuitous. The same can be said for the "sex" scenes. Much of the camerawork is excellent and eerily conveys the mystical, holy world Jodorowsky wanted to attain; but too many of the visuals and camera setups call attention to themselves. At least amidst all the carnage and religious fervor, there are a few bits of funny absurd comedy—when one of the Colonel's men washes his face with his glasses on, or when it turns out the fourth Master has a pole for a house. (However, I am not sure Jodorowsky meant this pole to be taken as humorous.) There are good things in *El Topo*—it is obviously made by an intelligent man who is a talented filmmaker from a visual standpoint. But it is just too unwieldly. It reminds me of college days when you didn't have enough time to do projects for every course so handed in the same one to several classes. *El Topo* makes you wonder if Jodorowsky didn't take a number of unrelated subjects one semester and then out of desperation make the *one* film which could be handed in to any of his professors (Masters). That may explain why it is overloaded with the sum total of Jodorowsky's knowledge/learning. It should be an impressive film, but it falls flat because it lacks clarity. As Pauline Kael stated, that this film has impact doesn't make it art. My aphorism: that this film is beyond our comprehension doesn't make it profound.

Emmanuelle

1974   France   Columbia Pictures release of a coproduction of Trinacra Films and Orphee Productions
Director: Just Jaeckin
Producer: Yves Rousset Rouard
Screenplay: Jean-Louis Richard
Based on the novel by Emmanuelle Arsan
Cinematography: Richard Suzuki
Editor: Claudine Bouchet
Music: Not original
Running Time: 92 minutes

Cast: Sylvia Kristel (Emmanuelle), Alain Cuny (Mario), Marika Green (Bee), Daniel Sarky (Jean), Jeanne Colletin (Ariane), Christine Boisson (Marie-Ange)

Synopsis: Nineteen-year-old model Emmanuelle joins her new husband Jean in Thailand, where he is a member of the French embassy. Although she now lives in a beautiful estate full of servants, she is unhappy because she is bored with the people she meets, especially the unproductive women she joins for nude sunbathing. They tease her because she has never had an affair—although Jean has suggested that she do so. She wishes she could be like the teenage Marie-Ange and have sex without having guilt. That is her goal.

Although Ariane, her squash partner, constantly tries to seduce her, Emmanuelle is more attracted to Bee, an archaeologist whom the other women shun for being different and for ignoring them. Emmanuelle pursues Bee, and eventually they make love. Emmanuelle is very content in this relationship until Bee tells her that she doesn't love her, and the affair comes to an end.

Jean, who was very jealous while his wife was with Bee, is very happy to have her return to him. While he continues to have affairs with Marie-Ange and Ariane—who also has managed to successfully seduce Emmanuelle at last—he sends Emmanuelle to receive sexual instruction from the elderly Mario, who many of the women say is the best lover they know.

Upset by her experience with Bee, Emmanuelle is completely open to Mario's sexual philosophy. "Destroy all values, conformity, and morals," he tells her. "Throw away the pleasure of love, and realize the dream of eroticism." During the night, he tells a drunk stranger to remove her panties, escorts her to an opium den where she is raped, offers her as the prize in a prizefight, and proves to her that sex is best with a third person involved. He never actually makes love to her, saying "True love is erection, not orgasm." Feeling as if Mario had freed her from prison, she physically makes herself up into a sexual animal, realizing that is what she wants to be now.

Emmanuelle (R) is happiest when she is with Bee, but Bee will reject her.

Sylvia Kristel is surprisingly good in a bad film; her lack of inhibitions, particularly in the way she dresses, has an undeniably erotic effect. Kristel is one of the few actresses who has been able to make the jump from sex films to R- and PG-rated films.

Emmanuelle reminds me of those tedious "adult" films that they run on pay TV in some large hotels. You know, the type that has a beautiful, "free-spirited" young woman who seeks her identity through sexual encounters with everyone else in the cast; lots of stripping and nude sunbathing; close-ups of women in the throes of sexual ecstasy, with heavy breathing on the soundtrack—but no actual hard-core sex; lush music and plush sets. True, unlike these other foreign films, *Emmanuelle* isn't dubbed, but it took more than an hour for that fact to register with me. Putting subtitles on this film seems about as incongruous (as well as pretentious) as if I. Honda subtitled all his Japanese monster movies.* *Emmanuelle* is certainly among the best soft-core sex films ever made, but since we are now speaking of the worst genre in existence, this is not necessarily a statement of praise. That *Emmanuelle* has continued to draw

well long after its release, despite bad reviews and equally bad word of mouth, is one of the true mysteries of the cinema.

Who are the moviegoers who have made *Emmanuelle* a surefire moneymaker at America's revival houses? My theory is that its cult is made up of people who use *The Sensuous Woman* as a reference book. Not the female readers, mind you, but the men. Exhibitors consider *Emmanuelle* popular with couples, but it is likely that only men see it more than once, returning each time with new dates who they hope will follow Emmanuelle's lead and, by choice, become sexual pawns for the rest of the evening.* Fat chance. Women probably have a hard time taking this film seriously, for it is nothing other than the visualization of male fantasies: that a beautiful woman (Emmanuelle) will try to please a man (her husband Jean) who tells her to be free, yet insists on having ultimate power over her; that, in

---

*When Radley Metzger distributed the English-language version of Mac Aglberg's *I, a Woman* in 1966, he used subtitles so that it would appear to be an art film. It proved to be a very successful decision. Oddly, few distributors copied Metzger's tactic prior to the release of *Emmanuelle*.

---

*While Emmanuelle chooses to be a sexual *pawn*, the title character of director Just Jaeckin's subsequent *The Story of O* (1975) willingly becomes a sexual *slave*. Does Jaeckin hope that women in the audience will "take the hint" and figure out what the men who brought them to see his pictures desire of them in their own relationships?

"X was never like this!" was Columbia's slogan for Emmanuelle. *Here Ariane finally manages to seduce the young heroine.*

seeking sexual fulfillment, she trustingly will turn herself over to a man (Mario) to be her educator. It isn't surprising that female laughter accompanies screenings of this film.

Rarely has a foreign film been so eagerly anticipated in America as was *Emmanuelle* in 1974. Advance publicity had done the trick. We were reminded that the picture was based on a scandalous 1957 novel by the pseudonymous Emmanuelle Arsan that had been banned by De Gaulle, and that Pompidou had tried to ban the film, only to see it become France's all-time box office champ. Columbia Pictures—still smarting from its G-rated musical disaster *Lost Horizon* (1973)—had thought enough of *Emmanuelle* to make it the first X-rated film it had ever distributed, assuring viewers that they were importing, as some French critics proclaimed, "a masterpiece of eroticism." Since it was coming from the country that had given us Bardot and all her imitators, it is conceivable that some Americans were waiting on the docks for *Emmanuelle*'s arrival in the States. Licking their lips, no doubt.

Realizing that there was a major audience who

wanted to sample a sex film, preferably of the tamer soft-core simulated-sex variety, but who didn't want to go into a sleazy porno house, Columbia wisely booked *Emmanuelle* into first-run theaters, predominantly those usually reserved for prestigious foreign "art" films. It hyped the film as being *classy* porn (which probably means that there's slick photography and stars without acne), giving it a huge mass media campaign, capped by full-page ads which asked the pertinent/impertinent question "What is the most sensual part of your body?" And consequently, *Emmanuelle* became a big winner for Columbia. Fortunate, since no one particularly liked it, or recommended it. As for its being erotic, *Time*'s Jay Cocks summed up the feelings of most American critics:

> *Emmanuelle* could not cause a tingle in the Achilles tendon of a celibate scoutmaster. Why it is turning on the French . . . is a matter for the most melancholy sociological conjecture.

It should be kept in mind, of course, that the well-lathered extremes of American porn are banned in France. Without knowledge of *Deep Throat*

[1972], *Emmanuelle* might seem like pretty hot stuff. This gives the film rather much credit, however. *Emmanuelle* would have to go up against something like *The Greatest Story Ever Told* [1965] before it could be called titillating.

Emmanuelle is by no means as stimulating as Radley Metzger's best soft-core opuses like *Camille 2000* (1969) and *Therese and Isabelle* (1968), where the director's fertile imagination almost makes one forget that the sex is simulated. But I believe it does have some genuine erotic appeal—at least on a voyeuristic level. It's as if you were in the presence of a beautiful woman who presumably doesn't realize that she forgot to button her blouse, or who hasn't checked her shades before undressing. Sweet-looking Dutch actress Sylvia Kristel, as the half-innocent, half-sex-crazed Emmanuelle, is a turn-on just moving across the screen, seemingly oblivious to the fact that her casual display of her body is arousing to anyone on the screen or off. Kristel has a wonderful abandon in the way she lifts a leg and allows her robe to open fully; or leans forward and causes her blouse to shift so that a breast is in view for a second or two. Scantily clad as she always is, she keeps our eyes alert. And it is little wonder that Ariane, aware of a most revealing dress Emmanuelle wears at a party, feels compelled to put her hand over Emmanuelle's breast despite the fact that they are surrounded by other guests.

In fact, much of Emmanuelle's allure is that she isn't shy about her body, or even afraid to engage in sexual activity in semipublic places: she allows Ariane to seduce her in a locker room; jointly masturbates with Marie-Ange on her porch while her servants mill about; and makes love with Bee in sight of a bridge where people walk. These scenes may indeed make your brow sweat. However, when Mario thrusts Emmanuelle in front of an audience and turns her into an exhibitionist who is aware that her body is on display, Emmanuelle is debased in our eyes and loses the appeal which went hand in hand with her naturalness and freedom.

Undeniably, Emmanuelle's relationships with men are dull—the Mario sequence is, in addition, as anti-erotic as anything in Pasolini's *Salo* (1977), Russ Meyer's *Blacksnake* (1973), which features a whip-wielding bitch/heroine, or Jaeckin's *The Story of O* (1975), which this sequence foreshadows. Yet there is a sensual intimacy between Emmanuelle and the other women that is rare in the cinema. My favorite moment is when lollipop-sucking teen-ager Marie-Ange comes upon the nude Emmanuelle asleep. Without embarrassment, she leans forward and curiously, without thoughts of seduction, circles Emmanuelle's nipple with her finger. When Emmanuelle awakens, nothing more develops—it was just a nice, *innocent* moment. A few minutes later, they will sit in chairs facing each other and masturbate—but they don't think of one another while doing so: Emmanuelle fantasizes (or did it really happen?) about being seduced by two strangers (men) on a plane, and Marie-Ange thinks about Paul Newman! The interlude between Emmanuelle and Bee is on a more mature level, and is noteworthy because it is of a

Mario gives Emmanuelle lessons in hedonism.

more *romantic* nature than one would expect in a "sex" film. After spending quality (as opposed to quantity) time together, Bee informs Emmanuelle that she cannot return her love, and that their affair must come to an end. This seems unfair, the work of a writer out to appease the male viewers/readers who feel threatened by Bee's good influence on Emmanuelle, and prefer to see the young girl back under her unworthy husband's control and Mario's tutelage. Bee is the one special person Emmanuelle comes across in the entire film; it makes sense that the other characters don't like her: she is the smartest character, as well as being the most responsible, the most productive, the most socially conscious, and the least hypocritical. We see that she can carry on her work as an archaeologist with Emmanuelle at her side, and be happy doing so; as Emmanuelle doesn't interfere with her life negatively, it is hard to believe that Bee—if the *writer* didn't demand it—would throw her confused young lover back to the wolves.

And it is equally hard to believe that Emmanuelle would turn to Mario as soon as Bee rejects her. Mario is certainly not the logical alternative to Bee. We are aware of Mario's "quality" the first time we lay eyes on him at the party, when a woman he's propositioning says "You disgust me," and walks away. It is upsetting to see Emmanuelle putting on makeup in the extreme at the end of the film, and looking like a sexual freak when we remember how pretty and happy she was during her affair with Bee. Blame the male filmmakers for her sorry state.

Mention should be made of the interesting, beautifully shot scenes of Bangkok—wasted in such a film. Former fashion photographer Jaeckin could obviously turn out fine travelogues—and let's hope that's the type of films he will end up making.

Enter the Dragon

1973 Warner Bros. release of a Warner Bros.–Concord
Productions coproduction
Director: Robert Clouse
Producers: Fred Weintraub and Paul Heller, in association
with Raymond Chow
Screenplay: Michael Allin
Cinematography: Gilbert Hubbs
Music: Lalo Schifrin
Editors: Kurt Hirshler and
George Watters
Running Time: 98 minutes

Cast: Bruce Lee (Lee), John Saxon (Roper), Jim Kelly (Williams),
Shih Kien (Han), Bob Wall (Oharra), Ahna Capri (Tania), Angela
Mao Ying (Su-Lin), Betty Chung (Mei Ling), Geoffrey Weeks
(Braithwaite), Yang Sze (Bolo), Peter Archer (Parsons)

Synopsis: Lee, a martial arts expert from Hong Kong, is hired by an
Englishman named Braithwaite, who is connected with the government, to collect evidence that will prove master criminal Han guilty
of illegal drug trade and turning kidnaped women into prostitutes.
Lee is to infiltrate Han's island fortress as a contestant in a great
semiannual martial arts tournament. He is aware that Oharra, Han's
righthand man, had attacked his sister Su-Lin, and though she had
put up a great fight against many of his men, she committed suicide
when it was apparent he was going to rape her.

Among the other men who come to Han's island are Americans
Roper and Williams, one white, the other black, one wanted by the
mob back home and the other by the police. Ex-war buddies, they
resume their friendship, and Roper also becomes friends with Lee.

After being greeted by the evil Han at a banquet, all the men are
offered women for the night. While Roper is in bed with Tania, Han's
hostess, and Williams enjoys the company of four women, Lee talks
to Mai Ling, his contact on the island, who is pretending to be one of
Han's private female guards. She tells him that women keep
disappearing and that she doesn't have much time left. Lee sneaks
through the palace and beats up several guards while trying
unsuccessfully to find a way into Han's underground chamber.

The next day an angry Han orders the guards who let the
unknown prowler escape to prove themselves worthy of his employ
by fighting the muscular Bolo. Bolo kills all of them. Lee next fights
Oharra as part of the day's activities. Remembering what Oharra did
to his sister, Lee beats him badly. Totally flustered, Oharra resorts to
fighting with broken bottles—which even Han disapproves of—but
Lee kills him by smashing Oharra's neck with his feet. In private,
Han orders Williams to tell him who the prowler was he saw the
night before. When Williams refuses to talk, Han engages him in
combat and kills him with an attached iron hand. Han gives Roper a
tour of his underground chamber, allowing him to see the drug
manufacturing that is taking place, the prisoners he keeps for
scientific testing, and the women he is turning into prostitutes. He
tries to recruit Roper to work for him, but when Roper sees that Han
has murdered Williams he is aghast and turns him down.

Again Lee tries to sneak into the dungeon, and this time he
succeeds. With the evidence now to have Han arrested, he radios
Braithwaite to send reenforcements. But before he can get out of the
dungeon he is forced to fight with hundreds of Han's men. He
defeats them all, but Han traps him between locked doors.

Han orders Roper to fight Lee to the death. When Roper refuses,
Han orders him to fight Bolo instead. Meanwhile Mai Ling secretly
frees all of Han's prisoners. They charge into the courtyard and do
battle with all of Han's soldiers. While they win their fight, Roper
kills Bolo in a brutal contest.

Lee chases Han into a room full of mirrors in Han's private
museum. Han puts on a metal hand which has knife blades instead
of fingers. He cuts Lee badly several times, but Lee emerges
victorious, with Han impaled on a spear. Outside, Lee finds the
rebellion over. Many are dead, including Tania. He gives a "thumbs
up" sign to Roper. Now, too late to do any good, Braithwaite's men
arrive.

Between 1972 and 1975, the talk of the film
industry (in addition to porno films) was the
martial arts movies—"chop sockies," as the
genre was dubbed—that were being churned
out in Hong Kong, mostly by the Shaw
Brothers, and were inundating international markets
and raking in astronomical profits. They were influenced by ritualistic life-and-death combat found in such
diverse forms as ancient Chinese drama, opera, folklore,
and fairy tales, Jacobean revenge plays, American pulp
fiction and superhero comics, Japanese samurai pictures, Italian muscleman epics, European-made westerns, and Hollywood fantasy films. These blood-soaked
spectacles—in which every character is proficient in
kung fu and it is not uncommon for even the most
run-of-the-mill fights to include castrations, behead-
ings, disembowelments, eyes gouged out, throats slit
open, and backs and necks broken—provided thrilling
visceral escapism for ghetto kids, the unemployed, and
working-class audiences world-wide by "adding," according to Verina Glaessner, author of *King Fu: Cinema
of Vengeance* (Bounty, 1974), "a new dimension to the
iconography of violence." While the great majority of
these kung fu films are assembly line jobs, a few of the
better ones have style: the one-armed swordsman series;
those movies starring the beautiful hapkido expert Angela Mao Ying; *Five Fingers of Death* (1972), the first
kung fu film imported to America, and the one that has
the worst hero but the best villains in the genre. Without
question it was the Bruce Lee films—*Fists of Fury*
(1972), *The Chinese Connection* (1972), *Enter the
Dragon*, and *Return of the Dragon* (1973)—which highlight action and martial arts *technique* as much as
violence, that gave the entire genre a touch of respectability. (It just so happened that the most charismatic,
sexual film personality of the period was working in the
kung fu genre.)

Filmmakers in Communist China rejected traditional western cultural influences and, until a sudden
production curtailment in 1974, made political films,
often based on historical events, that take place in the
countryside and glorify a group/class (the Red Army/
the peasantry) action against, typically, Japanese invaders or bourgeois landlords of pre-Revolution China.
Directors in Hong Kong made films set in the city
(though characters may come from the country); usually
with Chinese of the same social standing—but of different martial arts schools—fighting one another; with
heroes working individually to defeat a villain who does
not represent an oppressive government as, say, the
landlord does in Shanghai-produced films, but is a
gangster, a racketeer, and a murderer, whom the government and police have no like for either.

Writing in 1974 in *Sight and Sound*, Tony Ryans
defined the kung fu hero as having gone through a long

(L-R) Jim Kelly, John Saxon, and the incomparable Bruce Lee headed the all-star cast for America's first venture into martial arts movie making. Here Williams, Roper, and Lee arrive at Han's island.

process involving meditation, breathing control, and sustained discipline; being virtuous, diligent, perceptive, patient, and stoical in misfortune; having loyalty to family, a martial arts school and its instructor, and country (on occasion the Japanese are villains here, too); and being capable of acquiring heightened powers at the moment of greatest trial, like God-given strengths. Bruce Lee, the most spectacular of the kung fu heroes, has all the attributes listed by Ryans, but he differs from the other heroes of the genre in several respects.

Lee called his unique, self-created "street-fighting" style *jeet kune do*, "the fist-intercepting way," a system whereby, through a mastery of biomechanics and reliance on speed, one strives to upset an opponent's gravity. For other heroes, influenced by Taoism and Buddhism, the martial arts are a practical application of those philosophies. Lee, however, who was often criticized because his fighting methods lacked philosophical base, said, "By martial art, I mean an unrestricted athletic expression of an individual soul. It is to be practiced [not as part of a religious-philosophical discipline] for health promotion, cultivation of mind, and self-protection. . . . It is being wholly and quietly alive, aware, and alert, ready for whatever may come."

While other heroes won their fights with the help of special-effects men, Lee refused to use gadgetry such as pulleys, trampolines, and fake props, bragging that he was the only fight choreographer who showed only what was real or at least possible. Unlike his rivals, Lee, the actor, exploits his sexuality (something only the female stars of kung fu films did with regularity), stripping off his shirt to reveal his rippling muscles, posing for battle with legs spread, knees slightly bent, his hands on his thighs—somehow looking relaxed and tense at the same time. Suddenly his hand thrusts forward and his fingers penetrate an opponent's flesh, his feet shoot upward, and he emits his *kiai* (fighting yell), which in conjunction with his acrobatic body movements reminds one of a wild animal in heat.

"Watching Bruce Lee on screen is the sheerest joy," writes Kenneth Turan in *Close-Ups* (Workman, 1978). "His physical movements—the flying kicks, the leaps, the quicker-than-the-eye hands [the cameraman on *Enter the Dragon* was unable to capture Lee's fastest movements at regular film speed] manage to be death-dealing while they remain appealing, graceful, almost balletic. . . . In presence and charisma, Bruce Lee was as good as they come. He is refreshing, youthful, invigorating, with an ingratiating grin, and a totally unexpected, totally winning personality. It is this pixie quality, coupled with his mind-boggling, deadly physical abilities, that makes him, despite the amiable dross of low-grade exploitation films, irresistible. He is bad, but not evil, a killing machine with a heart of purest gold."

Bruce Lee in action: (Above) Lee fights the blade-fingered Han to the death—Han's death. (L-R) Muscles rippling, Lee gets ready to fling one of Han's henchmen; Lee give Oharra an unfriendly kick on the jaw; again displaying his acrobatic talents in this publicity shot, Lee flies at Yang Sze, who plays Bolo in the film.

Everything in which Bruce Lee appeared during his brief life (he died mysteriously and suddenly at the age of thirty-two, possibly from an edema, or swelling, of the brain) is the object of enormous cult devotion: from the films he made as a youth when he got the nickname "little dragon"; to television shows *The Green Hornet*, in which he played Kato, and *Longstreet*, in which he was a martial arts instructor in several episodes; to a villainous scene-stealing bit part in *Marlowe* (1969), kicking apart James Garner's office and later missing a dropkick to Garner's face and flying off a high balcony to his death; to his kung fu films which made him the world's most popular star. But it is *Enter the Dragon* for which Bruce Lee will best be remembered: it is his most widely seen film—having grossed in the United States alone more than twenty times its cost—and the last film he completed before his death. (While the Lee-directed *The Return of the Dragon* was released in America after *Enter the Dragon* it was made earlier, under the title of *The Way of the Dragon*. Prior to his death, Lee filmed about ten minutes of fight sequences for *Game of Death*, which was finally released in 1979, with Robert Clouse as director and another actor in a beard and a mask playing Lee in all the other sequences. Not surprisingly, the film is a terrible mishmash, but what is disappointing is that even the fight sequences with the real Lee aren't very good, as his famous *kiai* tends to get on one's nerves after a while.)

The first American–Hong Kong coproduction, *Enter the Dragon*, directed, written, and filmed by Americans, is arguably the best, most colorful kung fu film ever made. The production values are high, the action nonstop and consistently exciting, the sets lavish, and the atmosphere rich. Particularly memorable is a brilliant evocation of crowded Hong Kong. And there is even an all-star cast of sorts, with American imports

John Saxon, Jim Kelly, who is the film's lone black, and Bob Wall joining an international ensemble which includes such Chinese kung fu stars as "The Chinese Hercules" Yang Sze; "Lady Kung Fu" Angela Mao Ying, who is exciting and deadly in a thrilling flashback sequence; and, of course, the incomparable Bruce Lee.

Lee's physical capabilities seem impossible. His fight with Oharra is particularly stunning. He does flip kicks and several of his infamous lightning one-inch paralyzing punches while his opponent looks nailed to the ground. The end of Oharra mercifully takes place below the screen where Lee's lethal feet destroy Oharra's windpipe, while an incredible close-up in slow motion of Lee's face allows us to see his face muscles quivering like waves in the ocean: he is killing the man who caused his sister's suicide, and rarely has such pure emotion—"emotion, not anger," Lee tells his pupil—been captured on a screen character's face.

The dungeon sequence where Lee takes on scores of Han's men with a *non chaku* (a two-sectional staff) and then his hands is equally spectacular. Cleverly directed by Lee, there is one terrific moment when the camera is placed tight on Lee's body, and we can only see glimpses of Lee's foes from behind as they charge him two at a time and are knocked out of the way as if they were a never-ending stream of tennis balls. Perhaps the most impressive image of Lee, however, takes place during the climactic fight in the courtyard, when Lee stands perfectly still as he eyes Han, his body tense, while hundreds of others do hectic battle behind him.

According to Linda Lee's biography of her husband, *Bruce Lee: The Man Only I Knew* (Warner, 1975), Bruce Lee considered *Enter the Dragon* a mistake in his career: "He knew his impact always lay in the fact that he was on the side of the little man; in that film he was simply an authority figure." Lee had a point, for

there is a definite problem with his character. If there is anyone in the film who relates to the oppressed of the world it is Williams, a black who fights racist cops in a flashback set in America, and who waves to poor Chinese kids in the Hong Kong harbor, lamenting "Ghettos are alike all over—they stink." It is odd that Lee and Williams are never really seen together or talk to each other—could it be that director Clouse recognized that they represented two entirely different worlds? As American screenwriter Michael Allin intended, Lee is not just a man who escaped the Chinese ghetto but a James Bond figure, just as the iron-handed Han is a Doctor No rip-off. Lee has come to Han's island *primarily* to do secret-agent work, and not, as is always part of the kung fu film formula, to avenge his sister and temple, which doesn't get dishonored in the first place.

Lee's wrongly motivated character is only one of the film's flaws. After being seemingly invincible in several fights, Oharra and Bolo prove to be disappointingly inadequate opponents for Lee and Roper. Han introduces his sexy daughters to Roper, telling him what trustworthy guards they are, but we never get to see them in action. In the Red Chinese film *Five Horses of Lang Yo Mountain*, five men jump off a cliff rather than surrender to the thousands of enemies they kept at bay while their main force withdrew. But it is completely against the formula for Hong Kong-made kung fu films to have Su-Lin commit suicide so she won't surrender to Oharra's sexual advances—everyone knows that if this film weren't written by an American she would fight to the death.

But the worst mistake is that there is an absence of a time element in the script. There is no bomb about to explode and no intended victim of Han about to be tortured—consequently, there is little of the suspense or sense of urgency so necessary to adventure films. The final rebellion on the island comes unexpectedly, without any buildup whatsoever, too quickly for what had been a well-paced film, and, unforgivably, before Han attempts anything dastardly.

While the flaws are abundant, they are trivialized by the spectacular kung fu sequences that take place every few minutes. *Enter the Dragon* is on a comic-book level for sure, but great entertainment nevertheless. And most significantly it stars the finest action hero in cinema history in one of his few roles: the one and only Bruce Lee, at his remarkable best.

Lee searches for Han in a climactic mirror sequence straight out of Orson Welles's 1948 film The Lady from Shanghai.

Eraserhead

1978 Libra Films release
Director: David Lynch
Producer: David Lynch with the cooperation of the American Film Institute Center for Advanced Film Studies
Screenplay: David Lynch
Cinematography: Frederick Elmes and Herbert Cardwell
Production Design and Special Effects: David Lynch
Special Effects Photography: Frederick Elmes
Location Sound and Re-recording: Alan R. Splet
"Lady in the Radiator" composed and sung by Peter Ivers
Editor: David Lynch
Running Time: 90 minutes

Cast: John Nance (Henry Spencer), Charlotte Stewart (Mary X), Allen Joseph (Mr. X), Jeanne Bates (Mrs. X), Judith Anna Roberts (the beautiful girl across the hall), Laurel Near (The Lady in the Radiator), V. Phipps-Wilson (landlady)

Synopsis: *A Dream of dark and troubling things.*—David K. Lynch

Ever have a dream while sleeping face down, with your mouth and nose buried in your pillow? In your discomfort you might have conjured up something that approximates *Eraserhead;* but it seems to me that the only way you can expect to duplicate this nightmare is by somehow entering the dark, uneasy dream/subconscious world of the most paranoid, depressed individual in the universe on the day he or she will either commit suicide or roam the streets wearing a doomsday placard.

This is one strange movie. "A true rarity," wrote David Bartholomew in *Cinefantastique,* "an original work that seemingly has no antecedent in the [horror] genre. It is not abstract, but it defies a coherent plot description, in fact, it defies description of any kind." It is the wedding of abstract art, surrealist painting, and minimalist cinema—a sophisticated approach to the primitive. It is the ultimate student film (financed in part by AFI and Sissy Spacek) and the ultimate experimental

The image of Henry Spencer that now adorns T-shirts.

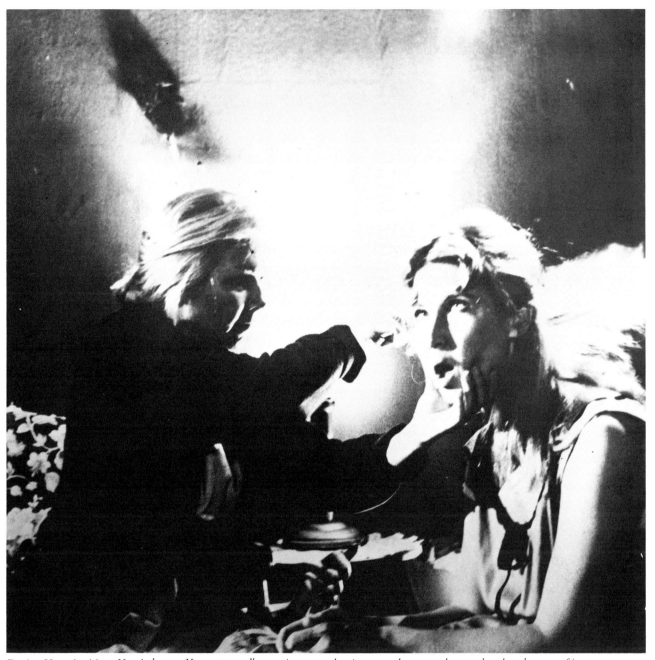

During Henry's visit to Mary's house, Mary repeatedly goes into a cataleptic state, whereupon her mother slaps her out of it.

film, dimly lit but bright with ideas and ambitiously incorporating such diverse material as spectacular frame-by-frame animation and a constant barrage of sound effects—noises that anyone who has ever tried to listen to a ball game on a radio station located two thousand miles away will immediately recognize.* And it is the final word in personal filmmaking. Former art student and animator David Lynch, in a feature debut that took a year to shoot (in an attic) and another year to edit, produced what has to be the most precisely made and deliberately paced film directed by anyone other than France's introspective Robert Bresson.

*The Academy Award–winning Alan R. Splet also did the sound effects for Lynch's *The Elephant Man* (1980).

Eraserhead is unpleasant and often repellent, but all the while it is riveting and fascinating, not unlike sideshow acts at the carnival. It is cruel and sadistic, but has moments of compassion and humor; is about all things alien, but about things that ring a responsive chord; is full of images that are in themselves ugly or bland, yet (because of some magnificent black-and-white photography) everything is touched with beauty. This is not a true narrative, but an intense mood piece. Steam blows across the frame. Smoke, too. Lights flash. And now everything is in shadows. Brooding shades of gloom. Even gray on gray—reminiscent of the unshaven Nixon in a gray suit blending into a gray background in his first televised debate with Kennedy, only more

artistic. And always noise: piercing, deliberately annoying, somehow creating an atmosphere in a vacuum.

Eraserhead presumably takes place in a post-apocalyptic age—*Newsweek*'s Jack Kroll suggested that the film deals with an "internal" apocalypse, "the ultimate corruption of matter itself throughout the universe"; when it is no longer possible to distinguish between spirit and matter, illusion and reality, the normal and the abnormal. The spooky locale is an industrial town that might be in Pennsylvania but could just as easily be in Poland. It is so dark and deserted that it is probable that those few people we see are the only ones who live here, and that the factories which constantly blow off steam are self-run, with their workers long dead, like those mammoth Krell furnace chambers in *Forbidden Planet* (1956).

Our hero is Henry Spencer, who looks like a reject from those frat house rejects huddled into a corner during fraternity rush in *National Lampoon's Animal House* (1977). The worst blind date imaginable. He dresses like a creep, but his most unendearing quality is his hair, which stands straight up as if he had just stepped out of an electric chair. Henry lives in the type of building one fears ending up in when stranded in a strange town after all the decent hotels have closed down. There is no doorman (it's a miracle there's a door); the elevator barely works and its light goes on and off; the halls are narrow, dark, and deserted; and a prostitute lives across the hall and isn't particular about whom she brings to her room. Henry's room is worse than depressing. Seaweed covers his bureau, there are containers of water in his drawers. (Sexual imagery abounds.) He puts a scratchy record on his old turntable and it skips like mad. His one window faces a brick wall. People get beat up down below. And there's noise, always noise. For escape, the (seemingly) depressed young man sits on his squeaky bed (which has ripped covers) and stares behind the radiator. There a putty-faced woman stands on a stage and sings that Henry can find happiness in heaven.

Henry visits his plain-looking, shabbily dressed girlfriend, Mary X, in a scene that outdoes every awful boyfriend-meets-girlfriend's family sequence you've seen (or experienced). It is a painful excursion into black comedy, wherein Henry must answer many embarrassing questions about himself—some twice because one entire conversation is repeated verbatim—including whether he has been having sex with Mary. Mary has several fits and is slapped out of them by her mother. Mary's catatonic grandmother sits in the kitchen with a lit cigarette dangling from her mouth (she may be dead). Mary's father slams his arm with his fist and reveals he has no feeling in it. Mary's overly passionate mother licks Henry's face and has to be pulled off him. For dinner they have man-made chicken which spurts awful slime and moves by itself. Puppies lie on the floor nursing. Lights short-circuit and flick on and off. And we learn several things: Henry is on vacation from his job as a printer in a label factory, Mary has given birth to Henry's "baby," a mutant, and Mary's parents insist that the couple marry.

Mary moves into Henry's room, as does the "baby," which a *Village Voice* critic rightly described as "a mewling, eye-rolling first cousin to the skinned rabbit from *Repulsion* (1965)." Lynch refuses to say how this being was created or how it moves; for distribution he protected his "mystery" child by not having pictures of it included in publicity stills. It must suffice to say that it is hideous—especially when it gets a rash—and it is remarkable.

The baby cries a lot; in fact, it cries all the time, turning what was never a domestic paradise into eternal hell for both parents. Finally Mary can no longer stand the baby or Henry (in the most upsetting moment of the picture she refuses to let the father of their abnormal child touch her), and she moves out. Henry is left to care for the infant, and for a while he is a surprisingly good, prideful father, even nursing the baby back to health when it is very ill. What I find interesting is that the baby never does anything bad in the picture and is actually quite loving to Henry; nevertheless we are scared of it lying in the shadows on the dresser facing a wall because of the way it looks, and the film's *horror* comes from this—our fear of what this baby will end up doing to Henry. After all, we recall the mutant baby in Larry Cohen's *It's Alive* (1974) whose hobby is genocide. But when Henry, whose "style" is cramped by the presence of a child who needs constant attention, becomes the one to cause harm and attacks the baby, we are shocked, wishing we could protect the unfortunate, harmless creature from his cruel father. Is Lynch speaking out against parents in *our* society who covet the deaths of their abnormal babies (and often bring about these deaths by legal means)? Or is he speaking up for abortions to prevent child abuse from parents who are unqualified to have children, much less abnormal children? In any case, Lynch is on the side of the child, and by the end of the film, so are we.

Before we reach the end, however, we have several visits with the Lady in the Radiator. At times we see her stepping on snakelike creatures which likely are related to sperm. Liquid spurts from each crushed creature (the abortion angle again?). The prostitute spends one night with Henry and they sink into what is literally a sexual pool in the middle of his bed. Henry has a dream in which he appears to be pulling snakes (the sperm that created the baby?) from out of Mary, and he hurls them against the wall, where they splatter. Finally there is the return of a horribly burned man (who looks like he has suffered the effects of nuclear fallout) who sits by a window, as he did at the film's very beginning when it is likely that the baby was conceived, and yanks cranks of some sort that are embedded in his floor. Is he God? Or is he the discharger of mutant-life-creating sperm in this new world?

What you will discover when talking to people who have seen *Eraserhead* is a reluctance on their part to either answer questions about the film, or attempt to explain it (though some may mumble a few words about "the astral plane" or something to that effect). Few will fully endorse the film or say flat out that you shouldn't see it; what they all seem to say is "You had better not be squeamish if you choose to see it. Remember that eye that gets slit wide open in *Un Chien Andalou* [1928]?" In fact, part of the mystique of *Eraserhead* is that it is a

In the darkness that permeates the film, a man with burned skin sits by a window and pulls on a mysterious crank lodged in the floor.

film that repulses many viewers. So I admit I had a bit of apprehension when I saw it during one of its midnight screenings in New York. (It has also played the midnight circuit in cities such as Los Angeles, San Francisco, St. Louis, and Minneapolis.) Afterwards, there was booing and clapping; one man hissed, another shouted that he had seen a masterpiece. Opinion was divided down the middle—just as it has been with critics. As for me, I had a favorable response, thankful perhaps that I didn't find anything in the film particularly nauseating (although what Henry does to his baby is as enjoyable to watch as real-life open-heart surgery). And I was not even disappointed because I had joined the swelling ranks of those who can't fully understand what was on the screen. It is apparent that while Lynch maintains a *logic* throughout his film, he does not intend for all his images to fit exactly, logically, into a giant puzzle. Intentionally, Lynch has given us too many puzzle pieces (or is it too few?) so that we are never (mentally) finished "working out" his film, never through thinking about it.

Yes, the word "Eraserhead" is explained in the film and it turns out to be a joke, overly obvious and having nothing really to do with the "story" as far as I can tell. I am reminded of a shaggy-dog story. I won't reveal the meaning of "Eraserhead" here or anything more of the plot. The less you know about *this* film before you see it, the better chance you will have to enjoy it, or at least maintain an interest in it. You may not like it, but I recommend it to you just the same . . . unless, maybe you . . .

Fantasia

1940 RKO release of a Walt Disney Productions film. (Today this film is released by Buena Vista.)
Animation Directors: Samuel Armstrong, James Algar, Bill Roberts, Paul Satterfield, Hamilton Luske, Jim Handley, Ford Beebe, T. Hee, Norm Ferguson, and Wilfred Jackson
Production Supervisor: Ben Sharpsteen
Producer: Walt Disney
Story Directors: Joe Grant and Dick Huemer
Music: Johann Sebastian Bach, Peter Ilich Tchaikovsky, Paul Dukas, Igor Stravinsky, Ludwig van Beethoven, Amilcare Ponchielli, Modest Moussorgsky, and Franz Schubert
Musical Director: Edward H. Plumb
Music performed by the Philadelphia Orchestra, Leopold Stokowski, conductor
Musical Film Editor: Stephen Csillag
Running Time: 116 minutes

Cast: Deems Taylor (himself), Leopold Stokowski and the Philadelphia Orchestra (themselves), Mickey Mouse (sorcerer's apprentice)

Synopsis: Musicologist Deems Taylor introduces *Fantasia*, explaining that it will visually interpret music that tells a story, music that paints a picture, and absolute music, or music for music's sake.

Bach's *Toccata and Fugue in D Minor*. Leopold Stokowski conducts the Philadelphia Orchestra. The superimposed images of musicians in silhouette fade into an abstract sea of colors dotted with gemlike sparkles. As the music builds, swirling circles of vaporous clouds rise into pillars in a screen full of light patterns and abstract figures.

Tchaikovsky's *The Nutcracker Suite*. Dawn breaks over a meadow. During the "Dance of the Sugar Plum Fairies," tiny fairies sprinkle drops of dew on every flower and stem. A cluster of mushrooms, dressed in long robes and coolie hats, perform the "Chinese Dance." Multicolored blossoms shaped like ballerinas perform the "Dance of the Flutes." Goldfish perform a graceful "Arab Dance." High-kicking thistles, dressed like Cossacks, and orchids, dressed like lovely peasant girls, join together for a wild "Russian Dance." In the "Waltz of the Flowers," autumn fairies color everything they touch brown and gold with their wands; then the frost fairies arrive and everything becomes part of an icy, jewellike pattern.

Paul Dukas's *The Sorcerer's Apprentice*. When the Sorcerer goes to sleep, his lazy apprentice puts on his wizard's hat and magically brings his broom to life to carry his water buckets for him. Things get out of hand and the apprentice accidentally creates an army of bucket-carrying brooms which flood the castle. The Sorcerer returns and with a wave of his hand brings the brooms under control and ends the flood. He chastises his embarrassed apprentice.

Stravinsky's *Rite of Spring*. White-hot gasses emitted from the sun drift through space and solidify into a ball of fire. As earth forms, there are boiling seas, volcanoes that spout lava, scalding fogs, smoking mud flats. Primitive life comes into being in the sea and then on land. The dinosaurs become earth's dominant species and then are made extinct during a great drought. There is an eclipse, then an earthquake, which causes mountains to thrust upward and oceans to cover the land. Everything is still.

Beethoven's *The Pastoral Symphony*. On the slopes of Mount Olympus, mischievous fauns, baby unicorns, and winged horses live in harmony. Cupids turn the thoughts of male and female centaurs to love and romance. Bacchus and his donkey arrive and there is song and revelry. After a great storm, during which Zeus hurls lightning bolts, tranquility returns.

Ponchielli's *Dance of the Hours*. In a great hall, ostriches, elephants, hippos, and alligators dance together in a slam-bang fashion, causing the castle's iron doors to crumble.

Moussorgsky's *Night on Bald Mountain* and (a choral rendering of) Schubert's *Ave Maria*. During the night of the Witches' Sabbath, Chernabog, lord of evil and death, holds court over evil spirits, witches, vampires, and skeletons on Bald Mountain, condemning them all to a fiery pit. Morning comes and the mist around the mountain fades away. As church bells ring, a procession of faithful worshipers of God moves across a meadow into a vast forest. There is a blaze of light. The powers of life and hope have triumphed over the hosts of death and despair.

The most ambitious of the Disney features and the studio's most daring project from a conceptual standpoint, *Fantasia* was made for around $3 million when the studio had only about $2 million in the bank because of investments in other projects and the construction of a new studio in Burbank. More than a thousand people were employed during the two years of production, including eleven animation directors, sixty animators, and thirty background painters. Astonishingly, more than one million separate drawings were done—meaning that there was approximately a 4½-to-1 ratio between what was drawn and what was actually used—an extremely high ratio for animation (Warners usually used everything that was drawn) and quite expensive. The elaborate "Fantasound" sound system alone cost $40,000 to install in each of the twelve showcase theaters where the movie premiered. What is ironic is that such an enormous, costly undertaking began as a simple attempt by Disney to upgrade his "Silly Symphonies," the successful series of short cartoons based on music that he had begun in the late twenties.

Most of the "Silly Symphonies" had employed original music written by the Disney Studio's resident composers Frank Churchill and Leigh Harline; but for this new short, Disney wanted to select a piece of music that already had a story that went along with it. He chose French composer Paul Dukas's *The Sorcerer's Apprentice*, which debuted in concert in 1897, having been inspired by Goethe's poem *The Apprentice of Magic*—which itself had been based on a legend by the Roman poet Lucan (39–65 A.D.). To add prestige to the proceedings, Disney invited Leopold Stokowski to come to California to conduct the music. (Thus *The Sorcerer's Apprentice* was the only segment in the feature for which Stokowski's Philadelphia Orchestra did not record the music—as Stokowski worked with Disney's own musicians.)

While there was some thought given to casting Dopey of the Seven Dwarfs as the apprentice, Disney insisted that Mickey Mouse be used. He hoped that the short would result in an upswing to Mickey's declining popularity. The new Mickey would have a bit more dignity than before and would be a little more subdued and less pleasure-bent; and, for the first time, his eyes would be given pupils.

Disney was satisfied with the completed *The Sorcerer's Apprentice*, but since it cost $125,000—three or four times the budget of a typical Mickey Mouse short—he realized that there was no way to make back his money . . . *unless* it became part of a feature cartoon. It was at this point that Disney, with Stokowski's encouragement and willingness to participate, decided to finance several more costly shorts that similarly would be designed to illustrate the partnership of fine

The sorcerer's apprentice is about to get a whack on the rear for having caused so much mischief. This segment of Fantasia *was the first completed—in fact, it was meant to be a short.*

music and the animated cartoon, and to put them all together in "A Concert Feature" (the picture's working title).

Fantasia (titled after the sound system) was to be Disney's attempt to win over the highbrow audience to (his) animation. But since Disney realized that the real money was in Middle America, he took great pains not to lose his loyal lowbrow audience in the process. Thus the hiring of popular, unintimidating musicologist Deems Taylor to act as a "folksy" emcee.

Walt Disney built his film around the notion that *music* elicits different images and emotions from different people; he was counting on viewers to be generous by understanding that what they were seeing were only personal interpretations of great music. So he must have been shocked when he was viciously attacked in print for the first time in his career for taking too much leeway with the music and for being so pretentious as to try to teach others about classical music when he himself was completely ignorant of the art. Those of us who object to the misrepresentation of country music in *Nashville* (1975); to the use of bluegrass music, created in the late thirties, as background music for *Bonnie and Clyde* (1967), set in the early thirties; to the playing of rock songs in *American Graffiti* (1973) that were not popular when the film takes place, can understand why

music experts were so touchy about Disney's sometimes careless musical interpretations (or "bastardizations," as some critics of the time wrote).

Bach's *Toccata and Fugue in D Minor*, the opening segment, was spared the harsh criticism reserved for other sequences. One reason for this is that there is no objectionable accompanying *story* to go along with the familiar music—the *Toccata* has visuals of the orchestra and during the *Fugue* the screen is filled with abstract designs and light patterns (which is why it was so popular with the psychedelic generation of the sixties). More important than the absence of a story, Leopold Stokowski, who orchestrated these pieces, was generally recognized as one of America's major interpreters of Bach. (In fact, he had conducted an orchestra which played three short Bach pieces in the movie *The Great Broadcast of 1937*.)

It is hard to criticize the music of this first sequence, but I find the visuals of the orchestra during the *Toccata* quite chilling. It's as if Leni Riefenstahl, Hitler's major filmmaker, were shooting the athletes for *The Olympiad* (1938), as the orchestra members are filmed from below, in silhouette or in glorious light, with electric-charged music jumping from their magical instruments. These musicians are heroic, as Spartan-like as Riefenstahl's athletic figures. And there's even a cloud formation

Fantasia shines during those few moments when there is superb character animation. Among the characters that are fluidly animated are (T) Bacchus and his donkey in "The Pastoral Symphony"; and the hippo and the alligator in "The Dance of the Hours."

being displaced by Stokowski: similar to Hitler emerging from the clouds at the beginning of Riefenstahl's *Triumph of the Will* (1934). These are strange images to emanate from a Hollywood studio.

The visuals from *The Nutcracker Suite*, the second segment, are charming, particularly "The Mushroom Dance," which was animated by the great Art Babbitt, and "The Waltz of the Flowers." While the animation for *The Nutcracker* has been praised by almost everyone, there has been criticism regarding the music. Purists can not tolerate that the first two movements have been omitted and that the original order of the other movements has been altered.

The Sorcerer's Apprentice is the film's most universally liked sequence. That is because, as mentioned, there already was a story that went along with the music. The animation for this sequence is wonderful. The wizard's magic, the apprentice's magic, the cosmic activity in the sky, the march of the brooms with their shadows marching behind them on the wall, and the flood lend themselves to fluid, full animation. It's an exciting sequence, and such character animation experts as Preston Blair, Les Clark, Freddie Moore, and Vlad Tytla combined to make this the equal of *The Band Concert* (1935) as the best Mickey Mouse cartoon ever made.

Walt Disney claimed that Igor Stravinsky was impressed by the segment of *Fantasia* which utilizes his

Rite of Spring, but Stravinsky, the only composer still alive from whose works Disney borrowed, hinted otherwise. His once-controversial work was written to depict life, including dances and religious rites, among a wild, almost stone-aged people in primitive Siberia. Disney's sequence is about nothing less than the creation of the world. The visuals are outstanding; the cataclysmic volcanos, lava flows, earthquakes, and floods result in a nonstop series of powerful images. The otherworldly shots of the newly formed landscape likely were an influence on Stanley Kubrick's star-gate sequence in *2001: A Space Odyssey* (1968)—a film that may also have been influenced by *Fantasia* in its use of classical music.

The most objectionable sequence is undoubtedly *The Pastoral Symphony*. Beethoven had a specific image in mind when he composed this masterwork. He wanted to express the feelings a person has when taking a trip to the country. It has to do with *human* emotions and has no place in a syrupy story about mythological creatures who live a sickeningly harmonious existence on Mount Olympus. (While some of the animation is excellent, with the exception of Bacchus and his donkey, the

The modern, surrealistic poster from the sixties meant to attract members of the drug culture. The psychedelic images are obvious: The flying horses, the dancing mushrooms, the fairies, the clouds, and the lord of evil from "The Night on Bald Mountain"—all in a rainbow of colors.

Collage of images from The Rite of Spring *wherein Disney went against science texts and attributed the demise of the dinosaurs to a lack of water rather than an Ice Age.*

characters—the cupids and the centaurs—are terribly drawn and repulsive.)

Dance of the Hours works much better. Here Disney parodies ballet by having oddly shaped animals partaking in a knockabout comic dance; he is back on familiar Disney turf, catering to the lowbrow audience that by now might be tired of the reverential treatment accorded the other musical pieces in the film. This sequence is great fun, as the acrobatic ostriches, elephants (in tutus), hippos, and alligators are all very enjoyable, likable characters. In a film which, due to the dictatorial structure of the music, too often has scenes that begin in peace, have upheaval in the middle, and end with a return to tranquility (characters are always going to sleep), it is a nice change of pace to have a sequence end with a bang, namely the crumbling of the Great Hall's iron gates as a result of the vigorous dance.

I find the *Night on Bald Mountain* sequence quite impressive, although it too has received harsh criticism. As in most good animation, there is continuous movement, and this works well in exposing the restless nature of the cursed souls that occupy the multilayered mountain—a brilliant evocation of Dante's Inferno. Vlad Tytla's Demon is magnificent, worthy of the late great artist who is known as the Michelangelo of animators. In *Cinefantastique*, John Canemaker quotes Tytla: "For the devil on Bald Mountain in *Fantasia* I did some reading about Moussorgsky. Now I'm Ukrainian and Moussorgsky used terms I understood. He talked about 'Chorni-bok'—the Black Art. Ukranian folklore is based on 'Chorni-bok'—I related to this and studied up."

The *Bald Mountain* sequence segues into the anticlimactic *Ave Maria* sequence, which is probably the worst bit in the film. As Richard Schickel writes: "As the climax of the film it seems insincere—a conventionalized invocation of religiosity, an arbitrary resort to a surefire sentiment."

Fantasia was not a success when first released. Part of its financial difficulties can be attributed to the cutback Disney suffered in regard to profitable foreign markets during World War II. Also, the distribution was poorly handled by RKO, which would also turn *Citizen Kane* (1941) into a failure the following year. (Some prints of *Fantasia* had thirty minutes cut out.) However, *Fantasia* has become an enormous hit in re-release, particularly in the sixties with the pot-smoking, acid-dropping Woodstock generation, which caused great embarrassment to the straitlaced Disney organization. "Disney was giving us a sensory experience, America's first acid happening," wrote William Zinsser in *Life* in 1970. In that same year, National General Theaters sent out a weird memo to theater owners, containing these words:

> Don't get uptight about the potential audience. These are nice, unwashed potsmoking citizens . . . the freak-out crowd. They're here for a trip. They'll head for first row seats, sit in the aisles, in the pit, and on top of each other, but down front. They'll smoke pot and offer advice to Mickey Mouse.

Seeing *Fantasia* today, one will probably be less upset by the handling of the music than by the repetition of images (e.g., characters napping, reflections in water); the lack of good personality animation (a Disney hallmark) as characters of the same type tend to act identically; and the predictable way that nature goes haywire in almost every sequence (the struggle between the profane and the sacred) and the way scenes end as they begin, in tranquility.

It is impossible not to be impressed if you see *Fantasia* on a large screen in a theater where there is a topnotch sound system. *That* is the way to view the film, and the only true way to judge it. As Philip French wrote in *The London Observer:* "What chiefly comes through today is the sheer prodigal inventiveness, high spirits, wit, and fluidity of the graphic work."

Forbidden Planet

1956 MGM

Director: Fred McLeod Wilcox
Producer: Nicholas Nayfack
Screenplay: Cyril Hume
Based on a story by Irving
Block and Allen Adler
Cinematography: George Folsey
Special Effects: A. Arnold
Gillespie, Warren Newcombe,
Irving G. Reis, and
Joshua Meador
Art Decoration: Cedric Gibbons
and Arthur Lonergan
Electronic Tonalities: Louis and
Bebe Barron
Editor: Ferris Webster
Running Time: 98 minutes

Cast: Walter Pidgeon (Dr. Morbius), Anne Francis (Alta Morbius), Leslie Nielsen (Commander Adams), Warren Stevens (Lieutenant "Doc" Ostrow), Jack Kelly (Lieutenant Farman), Richard Anderson (Chief Quinn), Earl Holliman (cook), George Wallace (Bosun), Bob Dix (Grey), Jimmy Thompson (Youngerford), James Drury (Strong), Harry Harvey, Jr., Roger McGee, Peter Miller, Morgan Jones, Richard Grant, Robby the Robot

Synopsis: In 2200 A.D., United Planets Cruiser *C-57D*, under Commander Adams, approaches Altair-4, a planet with pink sand, a green sky, and two moons. The mission of the fourteen-man crew is to find out what became of the earth colony that came there twenty years before. Before landing, the ship receives a radio message from Dr. Morbius, a member of that party. He warns the crew that he can't be responsible for their welfare if they land.

Once the men get out of their spaceship they are greeted by Robby, an amazing robot who knows one hundred and eighty-eight languages and can—among innumerable things—cook, sew, arrange flowers, drive a jeep, and make bourbon. The only thing that the enormous robot cannot do is harm human beings, as his creator Dr. Morbius has provided him with a built-in safety factor. Robby drives Adams, "Doc" and Lieutenant Farman to Morbius's house.

Morbius tells Adams and the others that he and his eighteen-year-old daughter Alta are the only human beings left on the planet. The others from the expedition, including his wife, had died years ago, one at a time, mysteriously and brutally, at the hands of some invisible force which hasn't been around since. He and his daughter have lived alone ever since with Robby and some wild earth animals that Alta treats as pets. Alta has never seen a man other than her father and becomes very curious about them. Farman teaches her how to kiss, but she is not stimulated by the experience. However, when she coaxes Adams into kissing her, she and he have a strong mutual attraction.

At night, something damages the ship's equipment, preventing the ship from taking off until repairs are made. Morbius tells Adams and Doc that the planet was once inhabited by the Krell, a great two-thousand-year-old civilization that inexplicably disappeared in one night. He tells them that he has long been experimenting in an old Krell laboratory with a brain-booster machine they left behind and that it has increased his IQ to super genius level.

At night, the invisible being kills Chief Quinn. Morbius tells Alta: "It's happening again!" The next night the creature returns to the ship site. The crew is prepared and traps it in a force field. In the laser beams they are able to make out an enormous monster. They stop it but are unable to kill it, and it lashes out at several men, dealing a death blow to Farman. It disappears. Doc puts on the Krell brain-booster machine in hopes of getting the knowledge to understand the invisible being. The strength of the machine kills him, but before he dies he tells Adams that the Krell were destroyed by monsters of the Id which they created in their search for ultimate knowledge. Morbius now understands that the monster that killed the members of the colony long ago and has killed Adams's men comes from his own subconscious. He has willed it into being.

The Id monster comes toward Morbius's house. "That thing out there. It's you!" Adams tells Morbius. The Id monster enters the lab where the three scared people have holed up. Morbius yells, "I deny you! I give you up!" The monster destroys Morbius and in doing so ceases to exist. Adams pulls a lever in the lab that starts a chain reaction of Krell furnaces. Alta, Adams, and Robby rush to the spaceship as it flees the exploding planet.

I have long been baffled as to why there is such a strong, loyal cult following for *Forbidden Planet*, just as I have been unable to figure out why film historians and critics almost uniformly regard it as being not only the best of the many science fiction interstellar films of the fifties but also one of the few "great" films the SF genre has ever produced. While there are marvelous things in *Forbidden Planet*—the electronic music, special effects (including the Id monster and Robby the Robot), and scenic design—they are all of a cosmetic nature, when what the picture needs is a total overhaul.

In my opinion there are numerous science fiction films that are more intelligent, clever, suspenseful, economical, original, witty . . . you name it. But while I consider *Forbidden Planet* grossly overrated, I do not underestimate the film's importance to its genre. A seminal work, the only SF movie of the fifties to succeed in giving the SF genre a long-denied tag of respectability within the industry, it represents several firsts: the first time a major studio (MGM) released an SF film that was meant to be a top-line production; the first time a large budget (over $1 million) was invested on an *original* SF story that had been conceived expressly as a film project; and the first SF film to be made in both glorious color *and* CinemaScope—which I guess had as much to do as the special effects and bizarre music with permanently awing the film's cultists when they were impressionable kids in 1956.

As chronicled in the monumental *"Forbidden Planet"* issue of *Cinefantastique* (Spring 1979), *Forbidden Planet* was first concocted in 1954 by Irving Block, who had helped create special effects for a number of science fiction films, including the very fine *Rocket Ship X-M* (1950), and his partner, writer Allen Adler. Together they set out to devise an SF film more sophisticated than other examples of the genre. On a surface level they realized their ambition simply by basing the film on Shakespeare's *The Tempest*, Block's favorite play, which gave it instant "class." Dr. Morbius is the counterpart of *The Tempest*'s magician, Prospero; Morbius's daughter Alta of Prospero's daughter Miranda; the officers of the *C-57D*, the first men Alta lays eyes on, of the visiting Italian noblemen, who are the first men seen by Miranda; Robby the Robot of the Spirit Ariel; and the Id monster, whose actions are orchestrated by Morbius's subconscious, of the witch-child Caliban, a virtual slave to Prospero's will. (Altair-4, of course, is the counterpart of Prospero's enchanted island.) Frederick S. Clarke and Steve Rubin write in *Cinefantastique:*

> For the Id monster, Block also dipped into Freudian psychology, then in vogue with the general public. "The idea of a bug-eyed monster is a pretty childish illusion," says Block, explaining the choice. "But

Cheers from the audience usually accompany this shot of a miniature of United Plants Cruiser C-57D landing on Altair-4.

there are real monsters and demons that exist within us that we know nothing about. We're capable of doing the most horrendous things and we're often shocked at the truism."

Rather than bring their project—then titled *Fatal Planet*—to Allied Artists, which was churning out low-budget SF films, Block and Adler took it to MGM. It so happened that studio chief Dore Schary was searching for the right property to turn into MGM's first SF venture; as he told *Cinefantastique* in 1979, he "liked the idea of the Id force and its effects on Morbius. It was an imaginative concept and I felt it could transcend the average space adventure story—the type of picture that was then being produced by everyone else." So *Forbidden Planet,* as the film was retitled, was added to MGM's production schedule.

Because MGM would later publicize *Forbidden Planet*'s million-plus budget, it is often overlooked that originally MGM planned to spend only around $500,000 on the project. While Schary intended *Forbidden Planet* to be a cut above the average SF film, he didn't have enough faith in it to give it great financing. This is very significant, because when Schary eventually became excited about the project and substantially increased its budget, he granted extra money only to the special-effects unit and scenic and art departments while all the other facets of production remained geared for the making of a relatively cheap film. Schary would have done the picture more justice if he had spread the money out a bit.

To keep finances down, MGM hired a cast that, with the exception of the worn-out, long-winded Walter Pidgeon, consisted of stiff-backed, frozen-faced nonstars—newcomer Anne Francis is fine even if her part isn't, but Leslie Nielsen as the romantic lead?—and a director, Fred McLeod Wilcox, who (and I'm not being facetious) was more capable of directing animals, as he had done in several fairly good "Lassie" movies, than human beings (especially unskilled actors). Workmanlike veteran Cyril Hume was hired to write the script. He was told by producer Nicholas Nyack to follow Block and Adler's story outline; and not to insert expensive visuals, but to add dialogue, flesh out the characters, and punch it with humor—and we must question if he did anything but add dialogue, ad nauseam. It is a very juvenile, trite script. The combined efforts of the cast, director, and writer may be adequate for a low-budget science fiction thriller (which indeed is what they were hired to be part of), but in this million-dollar production their work is overwhelmed by the special visual elements provided by the better-financed MGM units. The only bargain Schary managed was spending just $25,000 for a 25-minute score composed in New York by experimentalists Louis and Bebe Barron, which Schary decided to use throughout the film. According to Frederick S. Clarke and Steve Rubin,

The score for *Forbidden Planet* represents a great many circuits designed by the Barrons. These interesting compositions ranged from the hesitating "beta beat" of the Id monster, to the bubbly sounds

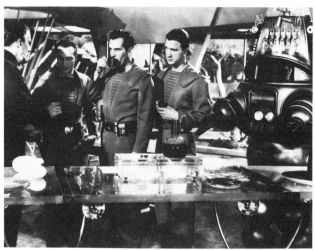

The emphasis is on (L-R) Morbius chatting with "Doc," Farman, and Adams, but all eyes are on the film's most interesting character, Robby the Robot.

design the picture the way it should be done regardless of the damn budget." Gillespie added, "This gave us a chance to create a new world outside our own solar system. Nobody could prove us wrong. We could do almost anything."

The work Lonergan and Gillespie did on *Forbidden Planet* is very impressive, to say the least. Among their units' greatest achievements, working together or independently, are the construction of six-foot-eleven, walking-talking-driving-cooking Robby the Robot; several large sets, including the interiors of the Krell laboratory and the spaceship; several precise miniatures of the spacecraft; and an astounding, beautifully painted 10,000-square-foot cyclorama, similar to the *perspective* backdrops in MGM's *The Wizard of Oz* (1939)—more than anything, this cyclorama gives *Forbidden Planet* its fairy tale look. The most stunning set is the Krell ventilation shaft, across which Morbius leads Adams, Doc, and Farman on their tour.

Dore Schary hired the Disney Studio's special-effects animation department, headed by Joshua Meador, to work on what turned out to be the most spectacular sequence in the picture. This is the night attack of the Id monster on the spaceship, during which it is caught in a force field and becomes visible for the only time in the film. (The Id monster turns out to look like a cross between the MGM lion and the Tazmanian Devil, Warners' cartoon character.)

While Schary was willing to more than double the projected budget during the course of production to finance the efforts of Lonergan and Gillespie, funds to the two men were not unlimited. Too bad. If still more money could have been spent on additional visual elements, serious, damaging voids in the film could have been filled. Lonergan's sets may be wonderful, but he only had the go-ahead to build a few. Consequently, the

associated wtih Robby the Robot. . . .Some of these themes involved as many as seven different component sounds, each representing a separate circuit. "From the beginning, we discovered that people compared them with the sounds they heard in their dreams," says Louis Barron. "When our circuits reached the end of their existence (an overload point), they would climax in an orgasm of power and die."

For the film's eventual upgrading, credit MGM's independent-minded art director Arthur Lonergan, and the studio's special-effects supervisor A. Arnold "Buddy" Gillespie. Lonergan recalled (in *Cinemafantastique*), "MGM wanted to make a cheap film. . . . Buddy and I got together, and . . . we decided we'd . . .

While Adams and Alta stand by helplessly, Morbius confronts his Id monster, which has broken into his lab.

only exteriors of Altair-4 are set around the spacecraft and Morbius's house. It would be wonderful to explore this planet. I am reminded of *Shalako* (1969), a western that takes place in the great outdoors but is composed almost entirely of close-ups of the actors. Because we see so little of Altair-4 there is no real reason the film takes place on this far-away planet—even considering the existence of the Krell centuries before, the picture could just as easily be set in a secluded area on earth (even in the present). Even the animals on Altair-4 are transplanted earth creatures.

The film's climax also suffers because of budgetary limitations. The whole sequence builds to where Morbius confronts his Id monster. Where the script notes that the Id monster should be *visible* in this sequence, which might not make total sense but is essential for audience excitement, we don't get the chance to see that it's visible—which would have required costly special effects—because while Morbius and the Id monster are on one side of the laboratory, the camera is on Alta and Adams, on the other side of the room! I would be satisfied if we could see the shadows of Morbius and the Id on some wall, but showing us nothing, though it saved money, is a copout, and totally unfair. Also it is confusing: Why is Morbius unmarked after the Id has disappeared, and why isn't he dead yet, but only dying? What happened?

Other than the lack of exterior sets and a visible monster in the climactic sequence, the most serious

In a shot not in the finished picture, Morbius and Alta hold each other closely, giving insight into the not-so-innocent feelings Morbius has for his daughter.

omission is one that was not the result of monetary limitations. Filming was done on a scene in which Alta tells Adams that she loves him, and Morbius gives her an ultimatum to choose between him and Adams. Unfortunately, editor Ferris Webster decided to cut out the scene to help speed up the picture. This scene is essential, for it is the only one in which the emotionless Morbius hints at the extent of his love for his daughter and, more important, his need to possess her. Alta was something more than just a daughter to Morbius, and it is not just fatherly concern but downright jealousy and a need to punish an "unfaithful" woman which triggers the return of his Id monster after a twenty-year hiatus. Without this deleted scene, none of Block's Freudian concepts are clear; also, the film is minus the sense of *conflict* that it so desperately needs. (This conflict would be represented by the struggle between Adams and Morbius for Alta; as well as the struggle in Alta's mind over the painful decision she must make.)

There are other problems. It seems a shame to set the film in the twenty-third century, and have the men of the *C-57D* be the norm for the Eisenhower era—white, WASPish, and, even after a year in space, even-tempered, unquestionably loyal and obedient to their captain. Their humor is all feeble, and none of these men can actually laugh—I have never heard so much snickering in one film. Why do all the men have the same haircuts? And why does everyone in the film wear dull costumes?

How can Adams be considered a near-genius and not know what the world *id* means? Doesn't he ever play Scrabble? How can Morbius be so scholarly, and

Adams watches Farman teach Alta how to kiss. Interestingly, screenwriter Cyril Hume had Dorothy Lamour receive kissing instructions from Ray Milland in 1936's The Jungle Princess, *and Debra Paget got the same from Robert Wagner in his script for the 1955 western* White Feather.

Artist's rendering of Adams and his men fighting the Id monster at the only time it becomes visible.

have a daughter who is so ignorant (and lazy to boot)? Why do the mature officers of the *C-57D* become dumb clucks as soon as they meet Alta? Why doesn't Morbius punch out Doc for his supposedly flattering remarks about his daughter? Why is there a long scene where we are led to believe that Alta is swimming nude, only to have us disappointed by a one-second insert of her climbing out of the water wearing a garment?

Why does the Id monster sabotage the *C-57D* when what Morbius wants most is for the ship and its crew to leave Altair-4? Why does the Id monster unselectively kill one person at a time instead of wiping out everyone in one night? Does the Id monster come to Morbius's house to kill Morbius, Adams, or Alta, or all three?

And then there is the problem with Robby. Because Adams is so businesslike and Morbius so cold, without even a demonic glimmer in his eye, and whose sole emotional outlet is the Id monster, Robby emerges as the most likable, "alive" character in the film. Robby *is* the star of *Forbidden Planet*, "symbolizing," as Clarke and Rubin write, "the harmonious synthesis of scientific advance and social good as at last the powerful tool which man is unable to turn upon himself." Robby illustrates Asimov's Robotic Laws, which essentially state that a robot can't cause harm to living organisms. Because Robby is denied this dramatic element the filmmakers don't know what to do with him—so they make him into the picture's major comic character (especially in his scenes with the ship's cook). This is a mistake, because when the film becomes serious toward the end with the escalating activities of the Id monster, humorous Robby is moved into the background. The Robotic Laws may preclude him from destroying the Id monster when it comes into Morbius's lab, but it would be truly fascinating to see Robby impede the Id's progress through a series of defensive measures I'm sure only he is capable of. As it is, Robby joins Adams and Alta as *observers* when they should all be at the center of the action.

Forbidden Planet was not a financial success in 1956. This was unfortunate because it would take another twenty-one years, until *Star Wars*, before it became common for SF films to be produced on a high budget. Nevertheless, today when SF films are made by the score, if you strike up a conversation about the genre, chances are someone will mention their favorite SF film and it won't be one made recently but *Forbidden Planet*.

Force of Evil

1948 MGM release of an Enterprise Productions film
Director: Abraham Polonsky
Producer: Bob Roberts
Screenplay: Abraham Polonsky and Ira Wolfert
From the novel *Tucker's People,* by Ira Wolfert
Cinematography: George Barnes
Music: David Raksin
Editor: Art Seid
Running Time: 78 minutes

Cast: John Garfield (Joe Morse), Beatrice Pearson (Doris Lowry), Thomas Gomez (Leo Morse), Roy Roberts (Ben Tucker), Marie Windsor (Edna Tucker), Howland Chamberlin (Fred Bauer), Paul McVey (Hobe Wheelock), Jack Overman (Juice), Sheldon Leonard (Ficco)

Synopsis: Joe Morse is a smart young Wall Street lawyer whose ambition in life is to make millions. He takes part in a get-rich-quick scheme with his client Ben Tucker, a numbers racket kingpin. Only he and Tucker know that on July 4, when numerous people annually bet on the number combination 776, Tucker's men have arranged for that number to come out: this will force the small, independent numbers banks to go deeply in debt because of all the winners and Tucker will be able to absorb them into his big-time operation which he would then turn into a profitable, legitimate business.

Tucker tells Joe not to inform Leo, Joe's older brother, that the small policy bank he runs will go bankrupt when the 776 combination comes up. Because Joe feels indebted to Leo, who helped him get out of the ghetto by putting him through law school, he tries to convince Leo to close his bank on the Fourth so he won't lose money. But Leo refuses, explaining that his regular customers are expecting him to stay open so they can make bets.

Joe arranges for the police to bust Leo and his staff—including Doris (who had just quit working for Leo but hadn't left the bank in time), a young woman whom Joe is attracted to—and to toss them in jail for the night, hoping this will frighten Leo into closing down his operation. Indeed, when Leo is freed, he insists that he will retire—but only after July 4.

On July 4 the combination 776 turns up and there is a run on the policy banks. Leo goes bankrupt. Joe convinces him to let Tucker take over his business; Leo will still be in charge, and for once Leo will make a lot of money because he will be involved in a bigger league operation. Bauer, Leo's accountant, becomes scared of Tucker's gangsters, who now work in the bank and who refuse to let him quit under the threat of death. Hoping to close the bank down completely so he can get out, Bauer becomes an informer for city hall, telling them when the bank is in operation so it can be raided. Meanwhile Bauer is approached by Ficco, Tucker's opposition, who wants to move in on the numbers racket, and is told to set up Leo for a hit.

After Leo is busted for a second time, Joe wants to get him out of the dangerous business. He decides to buy Leo out and become Tucker's partner by running the bank himself; for the first time he will be directly breaking the law. His romance with Doris continues, and she tries to persuade him to get out of the corrupt life he leads.

Bauer sets up Leo for Ficco in a restaurant. Leo dies of a heart attack and Ficco's men kill Bauer. When Joe finds out about his brother's death, he angrily goes to Tucker's house. He finds Tucker, who doesn't know Leo is dead, and Ficco making a deal for Ficco to be the muscleman in Tucker's numbers business. Joe and Ficco fight. Then Joe secretly takes the hook off Turner's phone, which he knows to be bugged, and coaxes Ficco into confessing to Leo's murder. Before Ficco can shoot him, Joe knocks out the lights. In the darkness, a gun battle between the three men takes place, with Ficco killing Tucker, whom he mistakes for Joe, and Joe killing Ficco.

Joe decides to help expose the numbers racket.

When Doris sees Joe for the first time, he is typically arguing with his brother Leo, her boss.

Force of Evil was the only film directed by Marxist screenwriter-director Abraham Polonsky prior to his blacklisting in Hollywood for being an "uncooperative" witness in front of HUAC in 1951. (He would not direct another film for twenty-one years.) As such it was long a curio among film historians and an underground classic. Its reputation as one of Hollywood's most realistic urban melodramas was buoyed as much by those who had only read about the picture as those who had come across a rare print.

Polonsky's film is the darkest, seediest, most claustrophobic entry to *film noir*. It is moodily scored by David Raksin and strikingly photographed so that characters seem physically dominated by their surroundings. It also has a great performance by John Garfield— whom Polonsky has called "the darling of Romantic rebels"—in the one film in which he plays an educated character; and the most rhythmic, believable "city-street" dialogue to be found in any Hollywood film. Polonsky presents us with an ugly, cynical view ("I was born dead," says Joe) of our capitalistic, money-and-power-oriented society, where even "decent" people are so trapped and poisoned by the system that they resign themselves to making a living in crime; where there is little, if any, distinction between crime and business ("I'm a businessman," protests Ficco's thug, who wants to set Leo up for a hit), law enforcers and gangsters, or what is legal and what is not (Joe and Tucker want to gain a monopoly on the numbers racket so they can "legitimize" it and make a fortune—just as in 1979 the city of New York made plans to legalize the numbers game to give itself additional revenue). *Force of Evil* "turns clichés upside down," writes Howard Gelman in *The Films of John Garfield,* "for here the ghetto achiever [Joe Morse, who has become a lawyer] uses socially acceptable values to distort and corrupt himself and those around him; and seemingly innocent people doing honest work [or, like Leo, doing work they have

A scene reminiscent of the gathering of cigar-smoking bureaucrats in Sergei Eisenstein's 1925 Russian film Strike. *Joe meets with Tucker (L) and his corrupt associates.*

deceived themselves into thinking honest] are seen as manipulated by corrupt forces in their environment."

Yet Polonsky's "autopsy on capitalism" (as he called *Tucker's People,* the book from which it is based) is, surprisingly, not all that *political.* Polonsky merely touches on some basic Marxist thought: characters are products of their environment; conflict results from the interaction of different classes (which are determined by financial-social standing); capitalism breeds decadence (courthouses are filthy, great amounts of money are passed back and forth within the slums without those who live there getting their share). While this film makes one aware of the economic shame of the cities—where the rich get richer by exploiting the poor; where the only jobs that can be found by the poor are in crime and involve further exploitation of members of their class—Polonsky shies away from making a real plea for social change or suggesting how such change could take place through *group* (class) action bent on dismantling the capitalistic power structure. Polonsky would want the poor to toss the robber barons out of their community and to stop participating in their own exploitation—so why doesn't he try to get this point across in his film? Instead Polonsky concentrates, conventionally, on *individuals;* his theme being that one can only protect his/her integrity and morality by refusing to adhere to the corruptive success-at-all-costs mentality prevalent in

a capitalistic society. Simply put, his theme is "don't sell out."

Where Polonsky himself sells out, or, as he says, compromises his convictions, is at the end. It makes perfect sense for Joe to go to Tucker's house hellbent on revenge after the murder of his brother Leo; but that he should decide to help the law clamp down on the numbers game after the deaths of Tucker and Ficco seems a bit illogical. (His rationale, I suppose, is that he must purge himself of the guilt he feels because of Leo's death.)

The scene in which Joe tells us (through his narration) that he will help the police is shot as if Joe were walking down a long flight of stairs into hell. But it is filmed with an optimistic slant; it is the only scene that takes place in *bright* sunlight—the dark cloud of moral decay no longer hovers over Joe—and there is exhilarating music on the soundtrack. Polonsky doesn't end the film with Joe down by the river's edge where his brother lies dead—that is too downbeat; he ends the film only after Joe has walked back up the stairs from this purgatory to join Doris, and has been regenerated. By all this, Polonsky tells us that Joe has learned the difference between right and wrong—just as Garfield's boxer did at the end of the Polonsky-scripted *Body and Soul* (1947) when he refused to throw his fight despite what the mob might do to him. He wants us to believe

Bauer sets Leo up for a hit by Ficco's men.

that Joe is taking a (progressive) step forward. Hog-wash! When Joe gives his allegiance to the law, which, granted, in the great majority of Hollywood films seems to be the proper thing to do, he is only moving from one evil force to another. Throughout the film Polonsky has shown us a law that is unfeeling, a pawn of the rackets (whenever a lawbreaker wants another lawbreaker thrown in jail he simply calls the cops) and oppressive: the rackets investigation is run by a man we never see (Big Brother?) called Hall (as in City Hall), who bugs phones, raids policy banks, and throws anyone on the premises in jail whether they work there or not, and makes arrests and convictions by using a network of informers and creating an atmosphere of paranoia. Why does Polonsky disregard all this in his climax? From what has transpired earlier in the film, Joe's *right* course of action is to fight corruption wherever it exists—in the rackets, in the police, etc.—just as Glenn Ford does in Fritz Lang's *The Big Heat* (1954). Better Joe go on the lam, or even join a commune, then agree to work with this police force. Neither Polonsky nor John Garfield would name names in front of HUAC, so how could they allow their hero to turn informer (assuming that is what the word "help" means)?

The ending of *Force of Evil* is not horrible, but it is disappointing in that it is so pat by Hollywood stan-dards. It is likely that Polonsky was reminded continu-ally that he was after all making a film to be distributed by a Hollywood studio (cheerful MGM). How else does one account for the typical Hollywood "meet cute" bit between Joe and Doris? It provides a needed touch of levity (Doris ends up sitting on a mantel in a lobby from which it is too high for her to climb down); but it is unfortunately out of place in such a gritty film. But to Polonsky's credit, Doris proves to be anything but an ineffectual heroine. Doris grew up in a ghetto also and the more you see her with Joe (trading brash lines with him in the intense classic one-shot taxicab sequence, swapping passionate kisses with him in his apartment) the more one gets the impression that she's been around as much as he has. She may look demure and call her mother (each time she's thrown in jail), but she has the strength to quit working in Leo's numbers bank al-though it might cause her financial hardship and allow Leo to lay a guilt trip on her (which he does), to walk out on Joe when she believes he will never come clean ("I don't want to die of loving you," she tells him), and to stay by Joe when he has shown that he wants to change for the better even after he has hit rock bottom. Just as Garfield's mother (Anne Revere) in *Body and Soul* tells her son to fight for something more worth-while than a boxing title he will have to step on a lot of people to attain, Doris advises Joe to fight his way out of the corruption that has engulfed him. And as she is someone he has learned to respect as well as love, he listens to her.

While the relationship between Joe and Doris succeeds because they are able to communicate with one another, that between Joe and Leo (wonderfully played by Thomas Gomez) is characterized by their inability to express the love and loyalty they have for each other. Leo always refuses Joe's gestures of friendship and fibs that his own kind overtures to Joe are based on duty and self-sacrifice, not love. They squabble over dinner as if Joe were the son and Leo his stereotypical ethnic mother (hard as nails), with Leo constantly reminding Joe of his many sacrifices to pay for Joe's education and of his bad heart, which he tells Joe not to aggravate. And Leo gets what he wants; he makes Joe feel guilty ("Blame me," Joe tells Doris, "everybody does."). When Leo is killed, Joe naturally feels responsible (in this case he is probably right).

But to Polonsky, Leo is the one who should feel the most guilt. He stubbornly holds on to his belief that his numbers bank is a small, benevolent business that harms no one. He pretends it is a legitimate business by keeping regular hours and a protective, familial arm over his long-time staff, and by pridefully contending that he is providing a service for his regular customers—ghetto dwellers who in reality are losing what little money they have betting on numbers in his bank at no-way-to-win odds. When his bank goes bankrupt, Leo characteristically makes Joe force him into accepting Tucker's money and a part in Tucker's lucrative operation—just so he can keep a morally superior facade and transfer all the guilt he should be feeling for accepting the money onto his brother for suggesting the deal in the first place.

But Joe and Leo are equally part of the pervading corruption; and the longer they stay in, constantly moving up the wobbly ladder of "success," the closer they come to self-destruction. At the end only Joe gets off the ladder before it is too late. But he has lost his brother. Polonsky shows us that if you take part in the game of capitalism you must expect to pay a heavy toll.

Joe and Doris look below where Leo's body lies. With her support, Joe will help expose the workings of the racketeers.

42nd Street

1933 Warner Bros.
Director: Lloyd Bacon
Producer: Darryl F. Zanuck
Screenplay: Rian James and James Seymour
From a novel by Bradford Ropes
Cinematography: Sol Polito
Music: Al Dubin and Harry Warren
Choreography: Busby Berkeley
Editor: Thomas Pratt
Running Time: 98 minutes

Cast: Warner Baxter (Julian Marsh), Bebe Daniels (Dorothy Brock), George Brent (Pat Denning), Una Merkel (Lorraine Fleming), Ruby Keeler (Peggy Sawyer), Guy Kibbee (Abner Dillon), Ned Sparks (Barry), Dick Powell (Billy Lawler), Ginger Rogers (Ann), Allen Jenkins (MacElroy), Henry B. Walthall (the actor), Edward J. Nugent (Terry), Harry Akst (Jerry), Clarence Norstrom (leading man), Robert McWade (Jones), George E. Stone (Andy Lee), Al Dubin and Harry Warren (songwriters)

Synopsis: During the Depression stage director Julian Marsh has gone broke. He jumps at the opportunity to direct the musical comedy *Pretty Lady* by Jones and Barry. Since Julian is very sick, he counts on the success of the show to take care of him for the rest of his life. Tryouts take place. Two who win lead roles are Dorothy Brock, the personal choice of Abner Dillon, the show's producer, to star in the play, and Billy Lawler, a well-known juvenile lead. Billy takes a fancy to young Peggy Sawyer, who has never been in a Broadway production before. He helps her relax during chorus tryouts when most of the other chorines are being unfriendly to her. Two chorines are friendly: "Anytime" Annie and Lorraine, the girlfriend of Andy Lee, the choreographer. All three win parts in the chorus.

When director Marsh finds out that Dorothy has been two-timing Abner and is still sweet on her boyfriend and former partner Pat Denning, he sends men to strong-arm Pat lest Abner find out and withdraw backing for the show. But Pat and Dorothy have decided to split up anyway. Pat wants to make his own success and goes to Philadelphia to work in a stock company. They hope to get back together someday. Five weeks of rehearsals speed by. The company goes to Philadelphia, where the play will open. Dorothy sees Pat with Peggy, and though they are just friends, she becomes jealous. At a party held the night before the opening, Dorothy gets drunk. She kicks Abner out of her hotel room. Abner is offended and tells Marsh that he wants to withdraw his backing. Marsh convinces him to remain with the show if Dorothy will apologize to him.

Dorothy calls Pat and tells him to come over. He arrives at her room and tries to console the drunk woman. Outside the door, Peggy overhears the writers tell each other that Marsh will once again try to get Pat out of the way. Peggy goes to Dorothy's room to tell Pat what she heard. Dorothy gets jealous and loses control of herself. She turns her ankle. Marsh arrives to find out that he has lost his leading lady the night before the play.

The next day, Abner announces that he has a new leading lady: "Anytime" Annie. Marsh is willing to use her, but Annie tells him that there is only one girl who can carry the show: Peggy. Marsh had never noticed Peggy before, but he agrees to use her. For the next five hours he works with the girl on her acting, singing, and dancing. She improves steadily.

Before Peggy makes her debut she gets encouragement from Billy, Dorothy, who says she will marry Pat, and Marsh, who tells her: "Sawyer, you're going out a youngster, but you've got to come back a star!"

The elaborate play with several large production numbers is a great success, and Peggy is a big hit. After the play, the exhausted Marsh sits on the steps in the alley. He overhears patrons saying, "Marsh will probably say he discovered her. Some guys get all the breaks."

By 1930, the musical film which had dominated the cinema since the advent of sound in 1927 was considered passé. But in 1933, the genre was revitalized in grand style from two fronts: RKO teamed Fred Astaire and Ginger Rogers for the first time in *Flying Down to Rio,* and Warner Bros. released three big musicals: *42nd Street, Gold Diggers of 1933* (both with Ginger Rogers in a supporting role), and *Footlight Parade,* all featuring extravagant production numbers choreographed by the outrageous Busby Berkeley, a putting-on-a-show plot in the *Broadway Melody* (1929) tradition, and singer Dick Powell and dancer Ruby Keeler as young lovers. The tremendous impact made by all of these films convinced their respective studios to continue making Astaire-Rogers and Busby Berkeley films for the rest of the decade; and though they were completely different conceptually, the two series would enjoy simultaneous popularity.

The best Astaire-Rogers films take place in a cheery, problemless world where gentlemen have valets and dress in top hats and tails and ladies have maids and dress in evening gowns. Their lives are spent in enormous ballrooms, expensive dinner clubs, and luxury hotels. Since no one has to worry about making money, theirs is a happy life of leisure where time is spent learning sophisticated dances (which are being done in other parts of the world), singing, and in amorous pursuit (with Astaire always chasing Rogers until she gives in). I love the Astaire-Rogers films, but as Allan Scott, who scripted six of the ten films, says, "They were modern fairy tales, far from the reality of the Great Depression."

Warner Bros. was the one studio in the thirties that tried to inject its pictures with social significance. Its best films of the era—including *42nd Street* and *Footlight Parade*—are not only set in the Depression, they are about the Depression.

As were the lumpen proletariat to whom the Warners musicals spoke, the characters in these films start out unemployed, hungry, desperate, and disillusioned. *Gold Diggers of 1933* begins with chorus girls happily chirping "We're in the Money" only to have their rehearsal end with the news that the backing for their show has been withdrawn and that they are out on the street once again. In the Depression, even when these women find work they know it might be temporary; since survival is what comes first, they often search out a rich benefactor (as does Dorothy Brock in *42nd Street*) or a rich husband (as do the Gold Diggers). Theirs is a gritty, sweaty world full of men with ulcers and women who'd stab their sisters in the backs for the right roles or men. Here life is spent in dusty old theaters, high-kicking on stages, catnapping in dressing rooms, smoking in alleys, or sharing cramped hotel rooms. Few of

"Anytime" Annie, Peggy, Lorraine, and the other chorus girls put in hours of rehearsal.

these people are formally educated, but they are all street-wise, as their snappy, slang-filled lingo attests. In this world, a leg's a gam, a dancer's a hoofer (Peggy tells Billy in *42nd Street* that to dance all you have to do is "pick 'em up and lay 'em down"), and a woman's a dame. And these dames know there's no such thing as a gent; in *42nd Street*, Lorraine snaps at her dance partner, "You've got the busiest hands," and she is only one of many dames in these films aware that in the theater world, where men control employment, women are in a position of compromise and men always try to take advantage. These are women who believe they will do anything to get a job and do more than that to achieve permanent success—but there inevitably comes a time when they refuse to be used any longer. For instance, Dorothy Brock, in *42nd Street*, becomes Abner's mistress to win the lead in *Pretty Lady*, but she kicks him out of her life the day before the play is to open, despite the consequences. And even Ginger Rogers's "Anytime" Annie, of whom it is said, "She only said no once and then she didn't hear the question," says no to the lead role and offers it to Peggy although she knows it means she will be missing out on a chance for stardom *and* also might lose the affections of rich Abner, whom she had sweet-talked into giving her the lead in the first place.

It is not a totally bleak world that these musicals portray. Despite their predicaments and fears the gum-chewing chorines maintain their self-respect and sense of humor ("It must have been tough on your mother not having any children," Annie tells a backstage rival). When the films stories are gloomy, as in the Lloyd Bacon-directed *42nd Street* and *Footlight Parade*,

the production numbers have light themes, such as "I'm Young and Healthy" and "Pettin' in the Park"; when there is a particularly depressing number, such as the remarkable "Remember My Forgotten Man" in Mervyn LeRoy's *Gold Diggers of 1933*, the story itself is lively and frivolous. The three Warner brothers were great admirers of Franklin Roosevelt, whose face actually fills the screen at the end of the patriotic finale in *Footlight Parade*, and their musicals reflected the optimism of Roosevelt's New Deal, complete with pep talks delivered by directors to their companies which were as gung-ho and reassuring as the new President's speeches. Whereas the Astaire-Rogers films are fairy tales about love, courtship, and marriage in a world where no one worries about finances and securing employment, the Warner musicals are in a sense Horatio Alger tales which assert that hard work, diligence, and a little luck will lead to success in business.

The Berkeley–Gold Diggers series deteriorated after 1933 into fluffy, innocuous musicals that only serve as excuses for the inclusion of Berkeley's spectacular production numbers, which somehow got better and more complicated with each picture. But the three films made in 1933 hold up surprisingly well. I think *Gold Diggers*

*Dick Powell and Ruby Keeler,
both with rosy cheeks
and red lips, were partnered
regularly in Busby Berkeley musicals.*

(Above) Berkeley's chorus girls model one of their revealing costumes. (Below) The climactic "42nd Street" number begins.

of 1933 is the least impressive of the three, as it lacks a strong lead character like Warner Baxter of *42nd Street* and James Cagney of *Footlight Parade;* and its silly plot doesn't seem overly concerned with whether its women characters, who unlike the men have no money, survive the Depression: it is a foregone conclusion that these women will end up with rich men and that the play (shuffled to the background) will go on.

Footlight Parade has better production numbers than *42nd Street* and it has the dynamic James Cagney, but I prefer the earlier film, as do most fans of the Berkeley series. The way *Footlight Parade* is set up, we hope Cagney's "Preludes" (live stage production numbers meant to precede movies) are successful so that Cagney will get back on his feet during the Depression. But we don't care about the cast—they are his pawns. It is the individual we root for. But in *42nd Street,* rather than rooting for Julian Marsh, whom we don't particularly like (especially when he orders Pat to be strongarmed) and who will retire after this play, we cheer the lead singers and dancers, the crew, and particularly the chorines, whom we have seen in numerous montages working endlessly, desperately driving themselves past tears and exhaustion, their faces revealing that the play's success means their survival.

The recent Broadway success of the David Merrick–Gower Champion *42nd Street* has perhaps erased the "camp" connotation given the film from which it was adapted. The picture is just too good, too skillfully made, to be regarded as camp. Sure, it has a formula *Grand Hotel* (1932) plot. Sure it contains *the* great theater cliché—an unknown goes on stage a "youngster" and comes back a star. Sure, it stars a cherubic Dick Powell, whose cheeks are rosier than Santa Claus's, and Ruby Keeler, who taps like an elephant (I was surprised that the one constant in the rave reviews the film received in 1933 was that Ruby Keeler does such a terrific job dancing). And sure, it has a final production number that like most Berkeley pieces is too elaborate ever to be performed on a real stage, with sections filmed from above, women used as props to form geometric patterns, close-ups, dollies, and pans, and an ending in which Berkeley thrusts his camera forward between the spread legs of numerous chorines who stand on a revolving stage. (Astaire seduces Rogers with his dancing; Berkeley's less subtle camera seems to perform the sexual act.) It has elements of camp, but it has unmatched vitality, a strong sense of unity among its characters, and—most important because of the period in which it was made—a great deal of honesty.

Julian Marsh points an accusatory finger at Pat, blaming him for the injury that has forced Dorothy to withdraw from the show. For Peggy destiny beckons.

Freaks

1932 MGM
Director: Tod Browning
Producer: Tod Browning
Screenplay: Willis Goldbeck and Leon Gordon
Based on the short story "Spurs," by Tod Robbins
Dialogue: Edgar Allan Woolf and Al Boasberg
Cinematography: Merrit B. Gerstad
Music: No credit
Editor: Basil Wrangell
Running Time: 64 minutes

Cast: Wallace Ford (Phroso), Leila Hyams (Venus), Olga Baclanova (Cleopatra), Rosco Ates (Roscoe), Henry Victor (Hercules), Harry Earles (Hans), Daisy Earles (Frieda), Rose Dione (Madame Tetrallini), Edward Brophy and Matt McHugh (Rollo Brothers), Louise Beavers (maid); As themselves: Daisy and Violet Hilton, the Siamese Twins; Olga Roderick, the bearded lady; Johnny Eck, the boy with half a torso; Randian, the Hindu living torso; Schlitzie, Elvira, and Jennie Lee Snow, the White Pin Heads; Pete Robinson, the Living Skeleton; Josephine-Joseph, the Half-Woman Half-Man; Martha Morris, the Armless Wonder; Frances O'Connor, the Turtle Girl; Angela Rossito, a midget; Zip and Pip; Elizabeth Green.

Synopsis: A carnival barker takes customers to look at a sideshow freak called the Feathered Hen. A woman screams. He tells the story of the freak. Cleopatra was a beautiful trapeze artist with the carnival. She knew that Hans, a midget, had a mad crush on her, and flirted with him so he'd give her money. Frieda, Hans's fiancée—also a midget—warned Hans that Cleopatra was just taking advantage of him, but he would not listen. He believed that the normal Cleopatra loved him despite his small size and often visited her in her trailer.

Venus, the carnival's pretty seal trainer, moved out of strong-man Hercules's trailer when she realized he was no good. She and Phroso, the clown, became intimate friends, but they still cared about what was going on with their friends, the carnival freaks. Among the happier events: the human skeleton and the bearded lady had a child—a hairy baby girl; Violet Hilton agreed to get married just like her Siamese twin sister Daisy; Schlitzie, one of the pinheads, got a new dress.

Hercules and Cleopatra had an affair. They laughed at Hans behind his back for thinking she was really interested in him. But when Frieda let it slip out that Hans was heir to a great deal of money, Cleopatra realized she and Hercules could become rich if she married Hans.

After the wedding there is a celebration. Cleopatra and Hercules were extremely drunk and openly cozy with each other. Frieda became very upset and walked away. Hans felt humiliated. When all the freaks started chanting to Cleopatra that they accepted her as one of them, she became hysterical at what she regarded as an insult and mocked them. Her true feelings about freaks were revealed.

After Hans's inheritance, Cleopatra began giving him poison, which she told him was medicine. But Hans was aware of her evil plot and spit out the poison when she wasn't looking. Meanwhile the other freaks spied on Cleopatra and Hercules.

One stormy night, as the circus caravan moved slowly toward the next town, Hercules tried to break into Venus's wagon to rape her, but Phroso interfered. During their fight, the wagon overturned, throwing them out. Just before Hercules got the upper hand, he was struck by a knife. Pinheads, Johnny Eck (the boy with half a torso), Randian (the Hindu Living Torso), and other freaks chased him through the forest. For Hercules, there was no escape.

Meanwhile, other freaks confronted Cleopatra with the fact that she'd been poisoning Hans. They pulled out knives and guns. She ran through the forest, but they were close behind . . .

Cleopatra is the Feathered Hen. She is so mutilated that she is more chicken than woman. She squawks.

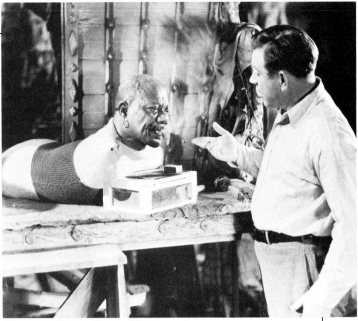

Phroso carries on a "normal" conversation with Randian, the Hindu Living Torso.

When a boy in the late 1800s, Tod Browning did what millions of lads just dream about: he quit school and ran off to join the circus. He befriended the sideshow freaks and witnessed firsthand the public's simultaneous feelings of morbid fascination, fear, and pity toward them. It was these feelings that Browning drew out of audiences when he directed a series of silent horror classics in which Lon Chaney played characters with physical abnormalities. (Sometimes Chaney would have no arms; sometimes he would have no legs; always his body was twisted and ugly.) But while these films dealt with physical grotesqueries, they were not about freaks per se; it was only when, at the suggestion of midget actor Harry Earles, he made *Freaks*, starring actual freaks, that Browning was able to adequately express his own feelings toward the strange folk he had worked and lived with as a child. Viewers of this picture will feel not only fear, curiosity, and pity toward the freaks but also warmth, respect, and amazement. "*Freaks* is moving, harsh, poetic, and genuinely tender," writes critic Penelope Gilliatt. "To enable people to look at grossly deformed human beings without ever feeling sickened or even intrigued is the sort of thing that can be done by art." Despite what Gilliatt writes, we *are* jolted and a bit sickened by our first sight of the freaks in the picture, when the twisted, deformed creatures are playing in the farmer's field. But they are presented to us so matter-of-factly (without dramatic music or close-ups) that within minutes we are, as Gilliatt contends, perfectly comfortable in their presence. In fact, we can't help but admire how well they function despite their handicaps and that they carry on pridefully, their physical aberrations notwithstanding. Freaks without hands eat with their feet; those without legs walk on their hands; and even Randian, who was born without arms or legs, gets along—he can even light his own cigar. Browning's point is that people needn't pay to see them just because of their "differentness"—with the exception of the pinheads, these freaks are *talented* show people. For one thing, they can "act" in front of a camera. Some of them even display a quirky sense of humor (especially the Hilton Siamese twins).

The first time we see the freaks they are frolicking in the woods like five-year-olds at play. When the owner of the property comes upon them, he lets them stay on his land because Madame Tetrallini, their supervisor, assures him that they are as harmless as children. But we soon learn that they are much more complex than children and that they only revert to their childlike side as a ploy to get outsiders to leave them alone. The same freaks who clutch Madame Tetrallini for protection in this early sequence will later crawl through the rain-soaked forest with guns in their pockets and long knives in their teeth to castrate Hercules (this castration is implied although the actual scene depicting this was deleted from all prints) and mutilate Cleopatra. Children? It is Cleopatra's treatment of Hans as if he were a child that makes her so insidious. "To me—you're a man," says Frieda to Hans. And he is a man, but Hans mistakenly believes that being a man means being "big"; in order for him to be convinced that he is normal/man he must meet the approval of a normal woman. The opening shot of Cleopatra shows her high on the trapeze looking down on Hans admiring her from below. She will later refer to Hans as "my little green-eyed monster," and as a "dirty, slimy freak," but we can tell immediately from this visual metaphor how "small" she thinks him to be. Her downfall, of course, is a result of her also mistaking size for a sign of manhood. When she is playing around with Hans, she isn't dealing with a child.

Browning's picture pits beautiful physical specimens against freaks of nature. But it is the freaks who become our heroes and Cleopatra and Hercules who come across as repugnant monsters. Cleopatra and Hercules are typical normal people: they are in love with physical beauty (she has a picture of a muscleman on her wall) including their own; and seek wealth and sexual gratification no matter whom it hurts. They are unfaithful every chance they get, disloyal even to each other. On the other hand, the strength of the freaks lies in their solidarity. They accept that they are not normal—this is their common bond—and have learned that there is no shame in looking like they do. (Hans *temporarily* forgets this.) It is only when someone tries to harm them or damage their self-respect that they find it necessary to defend themselves. Theirs is a community of capable individuals who watch over one another. When one is hurt, they all feel the pain and come out in force, with

Venus, played with pizzazz by beautiful Leila Hyams, gives Frieda advice on how she should treat her man Hans.

Told by the freaks that they accept her as one of them, Cleopatra is revolted. Hans (at the head of the table with his back turned) feels shame that his wife has acted so insultingly toward his friends. Only Hercules is amused by the situation.

one objective, as one—and not like little children. Their code of honor calls for retribution; it does not call for leniency.

Freaks doesn't become a horror movie until the wedding banquet. The freaks sit around the table and walk on it, dance and drink, and do tricks. The fire-eater and the sword-swallower do their routines. It is like something out of Buñuel. Cleopatra is enjoying herself smooching with Hercules and insulting Hans when the freaks begin to chant deliriously, "We accept you, one of us. (Gooble, gobble*)" and offer her a toast. She "freaks out" and chases them away for insulting her by suggesting that she could be one of them. They leave the banquet, but they don't go away. Browning places them under trailers, under trailer steps, at trailer windows—always staring at Hercules and Cleopatra, giving them the willies. Once insulted, they are all business as Cleopatra learns when they enter her trailer looking like Al Capone's hit men, pulling guns and knives from their coat pockets. The night scene when the freaks crawl under the trailers through the mud puddles and slither and hop through the woods to get to Cleopatra and Hercules is much creepier than anything in Browning's

Dracula (1931), as horrifying as anything he ever did. It has often been criticized for exploiting the physical abnormalities of the freaks to create its terror. Of course, this is true. But the freaks must be portrayed as they are in this scene: to emphasize the fact that both Cleopatra and Hercules, seeing them approach, think of them as monsters; and to remind us that freaks won't allow the world to trample on them, that they are a formidable force when united, and that despite being "exhibits" in the carnival, they are not passive beings, but capable of aggression.

It is because of the freaks that the picture has had so much trouble with censorship over the years. (It was banned in England for thirty years.) But I can think of no film from the period that is filled with more *sexual* innuendo. The relationship between the very sexy Venus and Phroso is most peculiar. "You're a pretty good kid," she tells him. "You're darn right I am," he replies, adding this unexplained line: "And you should have caught me before my operation." There is one long scene in which you believe Venus is talking to Phroso while watching him take a bath. Finally, we see that he is wearing pants and the tub we thought he was sitting in (he is standing through the tub) is just a prop for a clown routine. We don't know what went on when Venus

---

**It sounds like "gooble, gobble" to me.*

shared a trailer with Hercules, but we know what's about to happen when he visits Cleopatra. She asks how many eggs he wants her to make for him. "Not many," he says. "Six." She opens up her robe to reveal her black slip. "How do you like *them*?" she asks. He looks at her breasts and says, "Not bad." Even the Siamese twins, the Hilton sisters, take part in the suggestive humor. They each have a man (a husband and a fiancé), and we wonder what the sleeping arrangements are. An amusing moment occurs when one of the sisters is kissed on the lips and we see that the other sister is enjoying the sensation. Oddly, Browning didn't fully exploit the sexual possibilities of Josephine-Joseph the half-woman half-man. But just her presence in the sleazy sideshow atmosphere will start you thinking.

Interestingly, there seem to be at least three versions of *Freaks* in circulation. The one I always saw until a couple of years ago ends with a shot of Cleopatra turned into a chicken (just like Browning turned Chaney into a chicken for a twenties' publicity pose), squawking like Emil Jannings in *The Blue Angel* (1930). But I have seen two other versions with a tagged-on scene. In the first, Phroso and Venus, both smartly dressed, leave an office (possibly in a court house) and smile at the hugging Hans and Frieda, who smile back. In the second, a depressed Hans looks as if he is about to cry. Perhaps it's because he thought he had the beautiful Cleopatra, but now Browning has him being married off to Frieda, a character played by Daisy Earles, *his real-life sister*.

The classic shot of Cleopatra after the vengeful freaks have had their way with her.

The Girl Can't Help It

1956 20th Century-Fox
Director: Frank Tashlin
Producer: Frank Tashlin
Screenplay: Frank Tashlin and Herbert Baker
Cinematography: Leon Shamroy
Music: Lionel Newman
Songs: "The Girl Can't Help It" and "Rock Around the
Rock Pile" by Bobby Troup
Editor: James B. Clark
Running Time: 99 minutes

Cast: Tom Ewell (Tom Miller), Jayne Mansfield (Jerri Jordan),
Edmond O'Brien (Murdock), Henry Jones (Mousie), Julie
London (herself), John Emery (Wheeler), Juanita Moore (Hilda),
Barry Gordon (Barry), Ray Anthony, Little Richard, Fats Domino,
Gene Vincent and His Blue Caps, The Platters, The Treniers,
Eddie Fontaine, Abbey Lincoln, The Chuckles, Johnny Olenn,
Nino Tempo, Eddie Cochran

Synopsis: Former top agent Tom Miller drinks to forget Julie
London, whom he made into a star and still loves. Miller has not
discovered a new talent in some time when ex-slot machine king Fats
Murdock hires him to make a star out of his girlfriend Jerri Jordan. "I
can't marry a nobody," Murdock explains. Murdock turns her over
to Miller but reminds him, "Hands off."

Jerri Jordan is a sweet, statuesque blonde who goes along with
Murdock's plans because she is grateful to him for helping her father
when they were prisonmates. But she confides to Miller that all she
wants out of life is to be a wife and mother. Taking full advantage of
Jerri's stunning figure, Miller devises a plan by which every
nightclub owner in town notices her—and wants to book her without
even knowing if she has any talent.

Miller soon discovers that Jerri has no talent; her singing is
especially bad, as her off-key voice can make glass shatter. Murdock
refuses to be swayed, however, as he realizes that most singing
stars of the day don't have trained voices. He arranges for Jerri to
record a song he wrote while in prison called "Rock Around the Rock
Pile." While Ray Anthony and his band provide the vocals and
instrumentals, all Jerri must contribute is a scream that sounds like
a police siren.

Jerri and Miller, who has forgotten Julie London, fall in love, but
decide not to tell Murdock, to whom they both feel indebted. Miller
continues trying to make her into a star. He tries to get Wheeler, the
jukebox king, to sign Jerri to a contract. But Wheeler remembers his
long-time rivalry with Murdock and promises to keep Jerri's record
from being played. Murdock, with his accomplice Mousie, pressures
jukebox owners to replace Wheeler's jukeboxes with his own.
Consequently, "Rock Around the Rock Pile" becomes a big hit, and
Jerri becomes a star.

At a rock 'n' roll concert, Jerri sings Miller a love song, and it
turns out she can sing after all—she had only been pretending that
she couldn't sing so she wouldn't have to pursue a show business
career. After her song, Wheeler chases Murdock onto the stage,
vowing revenge for having all his jukeboxes broken. Murdock ends
up singing "Rock Around the Rock Pile," and the audience loves him
so much Wheeler decides to sign him to a record contract instead of
murdering him.

Murdock realizes that Jerri and Miller have fallen in love. Instead
of being angry, he asks to be Miller's best man. So Jerri becomes
Miller's wife and has several kids: and Murdock becomes a rock 'n'
roll star.

Like Jerry Lewis, whom he directed several
times, Frank Tashlin's reputation has always
been greater in France than in America. Jean-
Luc Godard was the late director's most distinguished champion, exalting him in the pages of
Cahiers du Cinema when he was a critic there, then
imitating him when he became a director. Godard's
disparaging references to Ford cars and Coca-Cola in his
own films have their roots in Tashlin's lampooning of
other "symbols" of American civilization: television,
padded bras, rock 'n' roll, superhero comic books,
Madison Avenue, and even movies; and his identifying
alienation technique, where his actors speak directly to
the audience, was influenced as much by Tashlin as by
Brecht. Truffaut and other emerging French directors of
the late fifties and early sixties were also indebted to
Tashlin, not so much for his humor itself as for his
willingness to intrude upon his linear, perfectly logical
story lines with bits of funny business that have neither
rhyme nor reason. It may be, as critic Stuart Byron
suggested, that "the [French/European] New Wave . . .
would have been impossible without Tashlin." Of
course, Tashlin had his own influences, and he borrowed heavily from Mack Sennett, the Marx Brothers,
Jack Benny, Red Skelton, Jerry Lewis, Hal Roach, and
especially Tex Avery, Friz Freleng, and Chuck Jones,
his fellow directors in Warners' cartoon unit.

Considering that Tashlin was a militant union man
at the Disney Studio in the early forties, and spent much
time picketing and organizing, it is disappointing that
his films are so apolitical. Rather than attacking the
capitalistic establishment for corrupting the values of the
American populace and alienating its workers—a course
of action Godard would have applauded—Tashlin was
more comfortable simply taking a friendly slap at individuals who get caught up in the American Dream and
whose inspiration is Horatio Alger. As his titles *Hollywood or Bust* (1956) and *Will Success Spoil Rock Hunter?*
(1957) imply, Tashlin's thematic concern was that
Americans were setting themselves up for misery and
frustration by striving for what they had misdefined as
success. He saw his countrymen joining the rat race
because they assumed that was what they were supposed
to do, and getting ulcers but little real satisfaction—all
because they had equated "success" with reaching the
top of their profession rather than leading a personally
meaningful life.

Tashlin's heroes, in both the scripts he wrote for
himself and for other directors, hold jobs that place
them far from the top of the employment spectrum. His
titles often reveal their work status: *The Fuller Brush
Man* (1948), *Kill the Umpire* (1950), *The Good Humor
Man* (1950), *The Disorderly Orderly* (1965); and his
women work: *Variety Girl* (1947), *The Fuller Brush Girl*
(1950), *Artists and Models* (1955), *The Lieutenant Wore
Skirts* (1956). His aim was to show that there is dignity
in work itself, and that fame, salary, and social position
are irrelevant. To Tashlin, it is just as valid for someone
to raise chickens or grow flowers, as do Tony Randall
and John Williams, respectively, in *Will Success Spoil
Rock Hunter?*, as it is to be president of a large ad

The famous showstopper when Jayne Mansfield holds two milk bottles in front of her chest.

Jerri asks Tom if he thinks she's equipped to be a mother. He looks into her face although his eyes are drawn elsewhere.

agency, and to quit as they both did; and perfectly acceptable to abandon a show business career in order to *work* at being a wife and mother, as does Jayne Mansfield in *The Girl Can't Help It*. Tashlin was clearly on the side of America's common working people who resist the temptation to "sell out" their ideals for material gains, and thus refuse (usually in the last scene) to become part of the "system." All his films end happily—what other director of the sound era could make such a claim?—with all his heroes and heroines maintaining their integrity.

Tashlin never made a masterpiece, but *The Girl Can't Help It* rates a near-miss. It's a highly inventive film, briskly paced and extremely colorful: one-liners are bandied back and forth, actors are in constant motion, music blares, and there's even a screen which, upon Ewell's command, switches from black and white to color and expands to CinemaScope. The off-color jokes, double entendres, and sexual innuendoes—all staples of Tashlin humor—will make you either smile or walk up the aisle cursing about adolescent humor. I bet you'll stay seated. It is a fifties comedy that seems to improve with time, and today looks much better than most highbrow comedies of the period. If it doesn't reach the peaks of *Born Yesterday* (1950), from which its plot obviously is taken, it certainly isn't embarrassed in comparison. Edmond O'Brien, in what I believe is his only comedy, proves a splendid comic actor, at least on a par with Broderick Crawford in the tough-guy role. Tom Ewell, as the fellow who helps the "dumb blonde" reach her potential, may not have William Holden's charisma or dramatic acting ability, but he is funnier; and often when Ewell's back is to the camera and he speaks lines seemingly written for Holden, it appears that Holden is playing the part. If anything, the conclusion of *The Girl Can't Help It* is the more satisfying of the two pictures because Murdock, as we were led to believe, turns out to be a nice, softhearted soul; when Crawford turns out to be a cad, we feel deceived—we only let his character make us laugh earlier in the film because we wrongly believed he'd prove to be sweet below his gruff exterior. Tashlin must have remembered how Preston Sturges wisely allowed The Boss (Akim Tamiroff) in *The Great McGinty* (1940) to return to our good graces at the end of that film after having made him an all-out villain for a few shaky minutes.

As a rock 'n' roll movie, *The Girl Can't Help It* is far and away the best of the many made during the rockin' fifties—the one film of the genre not geared exclusively for teens and the drive-in crowd. Tashlin probably thought little of rock 'n' roll. Bobby Troup's two (great) songs for the film are meant to parody the music and in his *Rock Hunter?* Henry Jones says his daughter had a nervous breakdown listening to rock 'n' roll. But Tashlin conceded that it was the dominant music of the day, and presented us with a fine sampling. Into *The Girl Can't Help It* Tashlin blended seventeen numbers without missing a beat. He even used the lyrics of certain background songs to comment on what is going on in the foreground; for instance, when Jerri, in a tight dress, slithers across a nightclub floor, Eddie Fontaine sings "She's Got It," containing the memorable words "I love your eyes, I love your lips; you taste better than potato chips."

The acts—particularly Little Richard at his peak, the Platters, Fats Domino, Gene Vincent, Abbey Lincoln, and Eddie Cochran, who like Mansfield died in a car crash—were, with the possible exception of those in *Go, Johnny, Go* (1959), the best assembled for a fifties rock 'n' roll film. It is, in fact, their presence that originally made *The Girl Can't Help It* a cult item, and convinced Twentieth Century-Fox to reissue the film in the mid-seventies at the height of the nostalgia boom. Today the film's cult has grown, partly because of the standout music, and partly because of renewed interest in Jayne Mansfield.

Murdock is upset to find Tom in Jerri's bed. Mousie stands back, knowing better than to interfere in one of Murdock and Jerri's arguments.

Tom introduces Murdock to the concert audience and, while Ray Anthony's band plays, Murdock wins the crowd over by singing his hit composition "Rock Around the Rock Pile."

MILLER *to* MURDOCK: Rome wasn't built in a day.
MURDOCK *to* MILLER: What we're talking about
is already built.

The Girl Can't Help It was the first film Jayne Mansfield made for Twentieth, which had signed her to a seven-year contract as insurance while it feuded with Marilyn Monroe. Twentieth hoped that Mansfield could be a bargain-basement Monroe, but she wisely sidestepped a losing battle and copied Mae West—both in life (she designed her home and bedroom with West in mind) and on film. Unfortunately, Mansfield never understood that West's appeal had not so much to do with her body as with her bawdy, unembarrassed attitude toward sex in general. (Bette Midler, on the other hand, understands Mae West perfectly.) West's character was confident, and always in control; and when she joked about her figure and sexual prowess she was actually praising herself and teasing the men in the audience. West kept herself on a pedestal. Mansfield was the one actress whose vulnerability worked to her disadvantage, as it weakened a character that depended on strength; she played women who were sexually innocent in the sense that they had never found the men who could satisfy them (while West had found scores of good lovers)—and thus came off as being less intimidating to men than West; when Mansfield joked about her figure, she was joining the men in the audience in teasing *her* for having an "abnormal" body rather than boasting about having "the best body around" as West surely would have done.

Because Mansfield was willing to mock herself, she was always considered a "good sport" by viewers, but since she didn't seem concerned about establishing herself as an *actress*, no one really took her more seriously than she herself did on screen. She had talent, as present-day viewings of *The Girl Can't Help It* and *The Wayward Bus* (1957) attest, but she never had a chance to challenge herself. After the first few pictures she was relegated to self-parody and never got to play anything

other than "Jayne Mansfield" as the public thought of her. Critic David Thomson commented: "Because Jayne Mansfield was widely laughed at, it is now assumed that she was happy to deride her own absurd glory. There is no evidence for or against that wishful thinking, but some to suggest that there was an actress trying to escape."

BARRY *to* MILLER: If she's a girl, I don't know
what my sister is.

Jayne Mansfield's measurements were 40-18½-36, and it is not surprising that Tashlin—whose Russ Meyer-like attitude, as expressed to Peter Bogdanovich, was "There's nothin' in the world more hysterical to me than big-breasted women"—would use her body as the basis for more than half of the film's humor. While serving Miller breakfast, Jerri leans forward, her half-exposed breasts close to his bulging eyes, and says straight-faced: "People don't think I'm 'equipped' to be a mother." The earlier, famous "mother's milk" scene has her clutching two milk bottles to her chest, one over each breast. Guess where your eyes are drawn? In a revealing red dress, she wiggles past stunned nightclub owners, who, like us, have never seen her like before. With Little Richard wailing the title tune on the soundtrack, Jerri strolls nonchalantly down the street, causing the cap of a milk bottle a man is holding to pop off and the milk to spew forth as if he were having an orgasm (how did the censors miss this?); and another man's eyeglasses to shatter. (This last sequence is reminiscent of cartoons in which male characters' eyes literally pop out of their sockets when sexy females walk by.)

Like it or not, when Mansfield is on the screen, one's eyes gravitate toward her bosom. ("The girl can't help it—she was born to please.") But Tashlin makes it easier for us: he puts her in tight outfits and shoots her from the side; he sometimes frames his picture so that she is only visible from the neck down. In tight sweaters and tight skirts, barely able to walk, she looks more like a caricature of the "fantasy blond bosom-beauty of the fifties," than a real woman. She isn't exactly sexy; in fact, she often reminds me of Bugs Bunny (whose cartoons Tashlin made) those times he's in drag, and overdoes it.

And Mansfield, the "good sport," took it all in stride, more than willing to endure sexual objectification in order to make an impression (and further her career). She is spirited, lively, and undeniably funny, even silly when the scene calls for it; and she emerges triumphant and virtually unscathed. In this *one* Mansfield film—maybe because it's the first to really exploit her physical attributes—we don't feel embarrassed for her, but rather admire her for the way she adapted to what was demanded of her. Since the sexist humor is harmless—she blunted it—we don't feel guilt when we laugh. And we do laugh many times. However, when Tashlin gave Mansfield the identical treatment in *Rock Hunter?*, their follow-up collaboration, further trapping her with an unflattering image and forever typecasting her, it stops being funny, and especially today with hindsight becomes painful to watch.

Greetings

1968 Sigma III release of a West End Film
Director: Brian De Palma
Producer: Charles Hirsch
Screenplay: Charles Hirsch and Brian De Palma
Cinematography: Robert Fiore
Music: The Children of Paradise
Editor: Brian De Palma
Running Time: 88 minutes

Cast: Jonathan Warden (Paul Shaw), Robert De Niro (Jon Rubin), Gerrit Graham (Lloyd Clay), Richard Hamilton (pop artist), Megan McCormick (Marina), Bettina Kugel (Tina), Jack Cowley (photographer), Jane Lee Salmons (model), Ashley Oliver (Bronx secretary), Allen Garfield (smut peddler), Roz Kelly (photographer)

Synopsis: Lyndon Johnson is President. The war in Vietnam is broadcast daily on the six o'clock news. Society makes little sense to friends Paul Shaw, Lloyd Clay, and Jon Rubin, three young New Yorkers. It becomes more confusing when Paul receives his draft notice. Jon and Lloyd advise him how to flunk the preinduction physical. He must purport to be either a right-wing militant or a homosexual.

While Paul waits to be drafted he tries to overcome his broken-off affair by going on a series of computer dates. The sex-crazed lad goes out with a Bronx secretary, a gay divorcée, and a mystic.

Jon is a confirmed voyeur who takes films of unsuspecting women for his Peeping Tom collection. He goes around telling strange women that he is doing a series of voyeuristic studies for the Whitney Museum and persuading them to disrobe in front of his camera. He manages to get a shoplifter to strip for him. While he explains the fantasy he wants enacted he can't see that another woman is doing exactly what he wants the woman he's with to do.

Lloyd is convinced that the Warren Commission report on the Kennedy assassination has come to the wrong conclusion. He is sure that more than one gunman killed Kennedy and spends all his time trying to prove his theory. He studies pictures, blows them up, even traces bullet trajectories on the nude body of his girlfriend.

Paul gets out of the draft. He ends up an actor in porno movies, the ideal outlet for someone with his craving for sex.

Lloyd is assassinated on the way to the Statue of Liberty. It appears to be the work of a lone, crazed maniac. But was it? Was there a conspiracy to stop Lloyd's investigations?

Jon is sent to Vietnam. He is interviewed in a rice paddy by a TV crew covering the war. He cuts off the interview to try to persuade a Viet Cong female he spots to remove her clothes and act out his fantasies.

Back home in the United States, Johnson comes on television. He announces, "We've never had it so good."

Greetings, made in two weeks by twenty-eight-year-old Brian De Palma, was one of the most popular "antiestablishment" pictures of the late sixties and early seventies. A particular favorite among college students—protesters against the Vietnam War and social injustice and/or young filmmakers—this $43,000 independent production took in a most respectable million dollars plus. Its success did not cause major studios to drop multi-million-dollar blockbusters from their production schedules to finance several low-budget youth films as would the following year's box-office smash *Easy Rider* (1969), but it is a better, more ambitious, certainly more humorous picture than *Rider*. In addition, it is a more accurate portrait of a disenfranchised, disillusioned generation trying to cope with American society, and braver in the sense that it attacks specific political targets: Lyndon Johnson (looking foolish in cartoons and televised speeches), the Vietnam War, the Warren Commission report, and the draft. Following the commercial failure of *Hi, Mom!* (1970)—a sequel in which Jon returns to New York from Vietnam and becomes radicalized—De Palma permanently withdrew from the political filmmaking arena. But it is commendable that he made these two films before *Easy Rider* made so-called "protest films" fashionable.

Greetings is about obsession (the title of De Palma's 1976 film). Paul is obsessed with sex and pursues sexual adventures through computer dating. Lloyd is obsessed with the Warren report and pursues evidence that will prove Kennedy was shot by more than one assassin. Jon is obsessed with voyeurism and pursues women to pose for Peeping Tom films he pretends he is making for the Whitney Museum. But the most obsessed person of all is De Palma, who reveals in this film that he is obsessed with and is exploring the very nature of film. (His later films suggest that his exploration continues.) Where our three heroes use "cinematic" tools—motion picture cameras, television monitors, photographic equipment—in their *pursuits*, there is a dramatic reversal and they wind up being the passive test subjects/prey in other people's "cinematic" experiments. Paul ends up as an actor in a porno movie *The Errand Boy and the Bored Housewife*—a film within De Palma's film; Jon, not Paul, is sent to Vietnam, where he tries to get Viet Cong women to pose for his films and ends up being

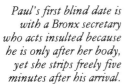

Paul's first blind date is with a Bronx secretary who acts insulted because he is only after her body, yet she strips freely five minutes after his arrival.

As Lloyd and Jon (L-R, facing the other direction) look on approvingly, Paul rehearses the Nazi act he'll try out on the Draft Board.

filmed himself by a television crew on the scene; Lloyd ends up being assassinated by a lone gunman (or was it a conspiracy to stop him from continuing his investigations?)—the maniac's gun is a camera in a metaphoric sense because it must be aimed and a trigger must be clicked/pulled. De Palma realizes the aggressive nature of film.

De Palma's studio-backed pictures of the seventies and eighties invariably call attention to Alfred Hitchcock, the filmmaker De Palma credits with teaching him the language, the grammar of film. *Greetings*, in which a copy of the Hitchcock/Truffaut book is fondled, shows that when De Palma started out there were other filmmakers who had a profound influence on him. The

cinéma-vérité look to some of the scenes and the use of news footage, and segments of Lyndon Johnson speeches ("We've never had it so good") to counterpoint the disturbing images of "reality" we see, suggest the influence of such diverse documentarians of the period as D. A. Pennebacker and Emile D'Antonio. As Lloyd starts examining photos of the Kennedy assassination and considers enlarging some to see if he can discover another gunman in Dallas's infamous grassy knoll, he becomes increasingly like the David Hemmings character in Michelangelo Antonioni's *Blow-Up* (1966) (referred to by name by Lloyd and Tina). Just like Hemmings, Lloyd concludes that blurry images in the photos are people with weapons. De Palma uses this concept several times, directing our attention to foreground action when the important image on the screen (e. g., Paul's girlfriend packing; a woman duplicating the fantasy Jon is telling another woman in the foreground) is in the background in soft focus. De Palma also borrows from Antonioni when he flirts with the notion that once a camera is introduced, reality becomes illusion.

The other filmmaker to whom *Greetings* is indebted is Jean-Luc Godard, the most influential political filmmaker of our times. The young characters who inhabit De Palma's world could very well be acquaintances of Jean-Pierre Léaud and his compadres in Godard's *Masculine Feminine* (1966) and *La Chinoise* (1967), children of Marxism and Coca-Cola. The film abounds with Godardian/Brechtian "alienation" devices, reminding us we are watching a film: Lloyd speaks directly toward the camera whether expressing his political philosophy or revealing how two women seduced him; there is no linear story and no consistent structure within individual sequences; there is jerky, New Wave-like editing (no doubt brought about by the paltry budget as much as De Palma's natural style) where one scene doesn't necessarily flow into the next; characters make asides or react toward the camera instead of toward the other characters; De Palma inserts title cards to set the action. What makes *Greetings* so special is that it is the rare film which is made for filmmakers and film students as much as it is for the young, alienated, angry generation.

Greetings is most interesting today as a testament of its times. Not only does it reflect the political unrest and malaise of 1968 America—and the despair in Vietnam—but it is also a splendid model of the type of independent films that were made back then. It has a left-wing, anti-government/society/authority/status quo bias. It is concerned with disillusioned young males who look for a direction in and meaning to life (another side to the previous year's *The Graduate*). There is some female nudity in this (then) X-rated picture, and women, all in subordinate roles, are defined by their sexuality. There are technical lapses and sloppy editing and photography throughout—but there are also moments of cinematic brilliance. The picture is often vulgar in a self-conscious sort of way. The wild, slapdash humor is at times original and hilarious and other times smug and self-congratulatory. One moment in the film is clever, the next is pretentious. Often it is breezy, but too often it becomes sluggish. Most impressive: *Greetings* is an independent picture that got made and got distributed!

Brian De Palma has become one of the industry's top directors since he left behind his *Greetings–Hi, Mom!* days and has concentrated on turning out a decidedly Hollywood product. His later pictures—the uneven comedy *Get to Know Your Rabbit* (1972); a spooky horror thriller, *Sisters* (1973); my favorite De Palma film, *Phantom of the Paradise* (1974), a rock-music update of the horror classic; *Obsession*, a variation on Hitchcock's *Vertigo* (1958); his commerical break-

A smut peddler gets Jon to buy a porno film. This hilarious scene is repeated with slight variations in De Palma's sequel, Hi, Mom!, *with Allen Garfield (Goorwitz) stealing that film as a porno filmmaker who gives Jon a job.*

through film, *Carrie* (1976), a bloody black comedy about a girl with telekinetic powers; the despicable, offensively violent and misogynist horror film *The Fury* (1978); the inept, sluggish *Home Movies* (1980), De Palma's tribute to independent productions that he put together with the help of his film class at Sarah Lawrence; and the tricky transvestite murder tale *Dressed to Kill* (1980). Oddly, the same faults turn up in De Palma's recent films that are found in *Greetings*. He is still a sexist filmmaker who includes much gratuitous female nudity (and gratuitous violence). And he is still so sloppy that when it appears that *two* "blondes" are trailing Nancy Allen through New York in *Dressed to Kill*, we automatically believe that because of De Palma's jumbled editing *one* blonde (the killer) is at two locations at the same time—but, apologies to De Palma, it turns out that there are *two* "blondes" (the killer and a female cop). Interestingly, the cult that admires De Palma's commercial films is almost entirely divorced from the cult that admires De Palma's underground classics. Only the absurd humor connects the films from the two De Palma phases.

It is of special interest that Robert De Niro makes an early screen appearance in *Greetings* a possible surprise to those who thought he debuted with Scorsese years later in *Mean Streets* (1973). Joining the flamboyant De Palma-regular Gerrit Graham and the more reserved Jonathan Warden, genial, jittery De Niro lends much humor and believability to the film through his natural improvisational manner. That films like *Greetings* get little real consideration from the mainstream newspaper press is quite clear when one reads a comment made at the time by Howard Thompson of the *New York Times*: "Of . . . Robert De Niro and Jonathan Warden, the latter gives at least some evidence of talent." Very perceptive, Howard.

Lloyd and Tina look at a blowup of Dallas's infamous grassy knoll near where Kennedy was shot.

Gun Crazy

Also known as *Deadly Is the Female*

1949 United Artists
Director: Joseph H. Lewis
Producers: Frank and Maurice King
Screenplay: MacKinlay Kantor and Millard Kaufman

From a story by MacKinlay Kantor
Cinematography: Russell Harlan
Music: Victor Young
Editor: Harry Gerstad
Running Time: 87 minutes

Cast: Peggy Cummins (Annie Laurie Starr), John Dall (Bart Tare), Barry Kroeger (Packett), Annabel Shaw (Ruby Tare), Harry Lewis (Clyde Boston), Morris Carnovsky (Judge Willoughby), Stanley Praeger (Bluey-Bluey), Nedrick Young (Dave Allister), Mickey Little (Bart Tare, age seven), Russ Tamblyn (Bart Tare, age fourteen), Don Beddoe (Cadillac driver)

Synopsis: As a young boy, Bart Tare develops a fascination for guns. He is a crack shot, but when he kills a chicken with a B. B. gun he cries; and he cannot bring himself to shot a mountain lion. He is arrested for stealing a pistol from a store window. Although his older sister Ruby, with whom he has lived since his parents' deaths, and his friends Clyde and Dave tell the judge that his love for guns is harmless, Bart is sent off to reform school.

Years later, Bart returns home to Ruby, who has married and has children. He has just gotten out of the army, and he tells Clyde, now the town sheriff, and Dave, a newspaperman, that he will take a job with a pistol company, as his love of guns has not diminished. The three friends go to a carnival. Bart is immediately attracted to a beautiful but obviously dangerous trick-shot artist named Annie Laurie Starr. He beats her in a shooting contest, but his attraction to her is so great that he joins her act and becomes part of the traveling carnival. Fired from the carnival after a run-in with the owner, Packett, who was making advances to Laurie, both Bart and Laurie hit the road. He proposes to her. She accepts, telling him that she will try to be better than she has been in the past.

Their money soon runs out, and the newlyweds become desperate. Bart wants to take a job with Remington, the pistol company, but Laurie tells him that she will leave him unless he pulls off a few robberies so they can make some real money. Rather than lose her, he acquiesces. They commit a series of armed robberies. Bart is upset by their life of crime, but is comforted by her words of love for him. Chased by police after a bank robbery, Bart fires at the police car, puncturing a tire. He tells Laurie that he killed the driver, because he knows that is what she wanted him to do.

They decide to give up their crime spree, but Laurie insists they do one more big job and then split up for several months so they can better elude the police dragnet that has spread throughout the country. They rob a Montana meat-packing plant, and during the getaway Laurie intentionally kills two people but tells Bart that she harmed no one. They find their bonds are too strong to separate and they drive off together.

They arrive in California. Bart makes arrangements for them to cross into Mexico, where they can buy a ranch and settle down. He is upset to learn that Laurie committed the two murders back in Montana. She also admits to having once killed a man in St. Louis. She tells Bart that she is no good and offers to leave. He won't hear of it. While they are out dancing, they discover that police have traced them through the money they have been spending. They flee, without being able to return to their motel room to get their money.

They travel by rail to Bart's hometown and stay at Ruby's. Dave and Clyde become suspicious that something odd is going on there, and pay a visit. When they find Bart and Laurie, they ask them to give themselves up. They refuse.

Bart and Laurie drive into the mountains, the police hot on their trail. Their car breaks down, so they race through the woods on foot. They express their love for one another and sleep huddled together. In the morning they hear footsteps, and Dave and Clyde call to them. Laurie loses her quick temper and yells back that she will kill them. She gets her gun ready. Bart shoots her. Then he is cut down in a barrage of gunfire, as the police think he has fired upon them.

As the sexual tension mounts during their first meeting, Bart gives Laurie back the ring he won from her in a shooting contest.

Forgotten for many years by all but true film connoisseurs, *Gun Crazy* has been the object of cult adulation and a regular entry at film festivals since it was "rediscovered" in 1967. That was the release year of Arthur Penn's *Bonnie and Clyde*, which its many admirers soon learned bears a remarkable resemblance to the Joseph H. Lewis picture made eighteen years earlier. There have been many fine movies about young couples driving cross country with the police on their trail, including *Bonnie and Clyde* and dating back to Fritz Lang's *You Only Live Once* (1937), but none is more fascinating or exciting than *Gun Crazy*, a low-budgeter that is supercharged with energy,

non-stop action, violence, passion, and sex. While set against a backdrop of a poor, insensitive small-town America of the forties, and reflecting a postwar malaise ("Everything in these forty-eight states *hurts* me!" sneers Laurie), *Gun Crazy* remains remarkably contemporary, especially in its portrayal of a country turned on by speed, violence, and crime.

Gun Crazy began as a story in *The Saturday Evening Post* written by MacKinlay Kantor. Kantor's 320-page script (which translates into about five hours of screen time) was pared down by Lewis and screenwriter Millard Kaufman by about 200 pages. "It was a good story," Lewis told me during one of several

Their dreams have gone astray and they are on the road to nowhere. (L) The counter man at a roadside diner feels sorry for the penniless Bart and Laurie, dressed in a style Faye Dunaway would copy in 1967's Bonnie and Clyde. *(R) The one process shot in the film: Bart is dressed in a military uniform; Laurie can't hide her despair.*

conversations we have had about *Gun Crazy,* "with the characters well laid out. And it served as the basis for the film. But we had to cut it down, and I used a director's prerogative to embellish it a bit. I can honestly say that I made the film twice as good as the Kantor script. But he never spoke to me again."

Not only did Lewis alter Kantor's story, but also he made several last-minute changes in the shooting script he had worked on with Kaufman; in each instance the new scenes noticeably improved on the originals. In the Kaufman script we are supposed to *see* the police, the dogs, and the police cars that surround Bart and Laurie on their final morning; in the picture, the camera stays tight on the frightened couple while our only knowledge of the law's presence comes by way of the voices and footsteps that emanate out of the fog. The tension is far greater because we relate to Bart and Laurie's fear of an "unseen enemy." Equally important, by showing only Laurie and Bart, Lewis allows his characters a final moment of screen intimacy.

In the Kaufman script Laurie and Bart were supposed to separate after the meat-packing plant robbery and to meet again later in the film. But at the last moment Lewis decided to have them simultaneously change their minds and in broad daylight, with the police nearby, run to each other, hug and kiss, and drive off together, leaving one of their getaway cars in the middle of the road. This scene has tremendous impact and is pivotal in that it not only confirms the characters' interdependence but also marks the point when Laurie realizes she truly loves Bart as much as he loves her.

Probably the most famous scene in the film is the one-camera-shot bank holdup. During this sequence, Laurie and Bart, in cowboy garb, drive around the block in a small western town. She is at the wheel and he is next to her giving directions, with the camera set up in the back seat and running the whole time. Laurie pulls over to the curb. Bart gets out and goes into a bank about twenty yards away. A policeman walks toward the car and Laurie gets out and keeps him occupied. A

shot comes from the bank, and when Bart runs out carrying the loot, Laurie knocks out the cop. With the bank alarm ringing, Bart and Laurie jump back into the car and speed away. All this action was done in one take with one continuously rolling camera. Lewis told me:

> Five days had been scheduled for shooting this sequence in the routine manner with several shots and numerous camera setups. I wanted to do it with one shot because I knew it would be more exciting and seem more authentic that way. I convinced my producers, Frank and Maurice King, who were wonderful, to let me do it by telling them that it would take less than one day to film. That made them happy because it meant they would save a lot of money. But I had to prove to them I could pull it off. So I did a test run using extras and filming them myself with my 16 mm camera. They did all the things Peggy and John would do, but it was all silent. And it worked. So we stripped out the back of the Cadillac Peggy would be driving—incidentally Peggy and John did all their own driving and we only used one process shot in the entire film—and we laid down some boards and a jockey's saddle for the cameraman. And four of us crowded into the back. We did the bank robbery scene without "blocking off" the street or informing pedestrians what we were up to. So when you hear someone yell that the bank has been robbed, that was not rehearsed. We drove around the block, with the camera rolling, not even knowing if there'd be a place to park. If there wasn't we were going to just go around the block again.

Lewis's achievements in *Gun Crazy* are great, ranging from maintaining a remarkable pace throughout to attaining a distinct sense of time and place. But undoubtedly his most inspired contribution to the project was casting the relatively unknown John Dall and Peggy Cummins in the leads. They both prove to be highly skilled actors who lend an intelligence to the proceedings and express such a complex array of emotions so honestly that it is truly hard to believe that they are not playing themselves. They are simply terrific.

Cummins was a British actress whom Twentieth Century-Fox was grooming to be one of its top stars in the late forties, but when she was given bad notices for her performance as the social climber in Gregory Ratoff's period film *Moss Rose* (1947), Twentieth tried to dump her. Lewis recalls: "I asked Twentieth's cutter to let me see dailies of *Moss Rose* before the film was released. I thought she was devastatingly beautiful and talented and that the fault for the picture's failure belonged to the director and producer, who just wanted to make Peggy their scapegoat. So Peggy and I had lunch together for five days straight and we just talked—not only about *Gun Crazy* but about other things as well. And I became absolutely convinced that she could play Laurie. She was a terrific actress who did everything I asked of her."

The casting of an actress as beautiful as Peggy Cummins makes perfect sense in the world of movies, and it is likely that United Artists wouldn't have been unhappy with her even if it turned out she couldn't act. What really reflects the casting artistry of Lewis is his choice of John Dall to play Bart. Tall, lanky, and a bit too introspective for leads, Dall was never before nor since given such a choice part. "A director thinks in many ways," Lewis told me. "For the character of Bart I wanted an actor who by osmosis or scent or whatever projected an inner weakness. I decided to cast a gay in the part. I didn't have to tell John Dall how to play Bart or that I wanted him to express Bart's weakness. I knew he'd betray *himself*. Subtly and gently."

When Lewis speaks of Bart's inner weakness, he is not implying that Bart is gay. Neither does he believe that Dall's *gayness* is his weakness. What I believe Lewis finds in common between any gay (in 1949) and Bart is an implied ongoing internal struggle in regard to self-identity and self-definition. To Laurie guns equal sex, money, and excitement, and to Laurie and Bart *as a couple* the firing of guns while committing crimes is how they fuel their sexual flame (evidence is Laurie's ecstatic face just after the bank holdup), just as it is with Bonnie and Clyde; but to Bart, *the individual*, guns mean something else: not a penis substitute or a sign of manliness as it is for the impotent Clyde Barrow, but a means of identity for a man who as a kid had no parents and, possibly as a result, no self-worth. His reliance on a gun as a means of elevating his status in his own eyes is clear in young Bart's words to the judge: "I've just got to have a gun. [It makes me] feel good inside, like I'm somebody."

Lewis continuously films Laurie and Bart in two-shots (as opposed to cutting back and forth between the two), sitting in their car—an image that projects both character intimacy and a feeling of movement—or standing very close together. They are constantly grabbing each other, snuggling up, kissing. Never has a relationship seemed so intense. There is a physical attraction between Bart and Laurie at *first sight*: Romeo and Juliet, both from the wrong side of the tracks. For Bart this attraction is based on love as much as sex; for Laurie it is all sex ("What do you do besides shoot?" she asks him). Lewis recalls:

In every other scene, I let the audience supply the sex, but in the carnival sequence I admit that I didn't try to hide my meaning. It's all quite in the open. I told John, "Your cock's never been so hard," and I told Peggy, "You're a female dog in heat, and you want him. But don't let him have it in a hurry. Keep him waiting." That's exactly how I talked to them and I turned them loose. I didn't have to give them more direction.

One thing Lewis and I disagree about regarding *Gun Crazy* is in our interpretations of Laurie. Lewis sees her as a totally evil character, "a beautiful demon who no man can resist or help forgiving when she does wrong; a woman who can be soft and cuddly but is really playing you for a sucker." I find Laurie to be the victim of a world that doesn't forgive past sins. She was born with three strikes against her and never recovered. (Even her honeymoon is ruined by trips to the pawn shop.) It is true that she plays men for suckers and leads the bad life, but I think she is sincere when she apologizes to Bart for being unable to control her mean temper and when she says on their wedding night "I have a funny feeling I want to be good. I'll try hard." She does try every once in a while (when she is able to compose herself), but every time she and Bart are about to retire from a life of crime she says, "Just one more job." She is like a fiend who needs a fix or an alcoholic unable to control the urge to drink. Her wickedness is an illness which she fights, with Bart's help, to overcome. It is that Bart loves her despite *her* weakness—her (gun) craziness—that ultimately attracts her to him. Both Bart and Laurie try to cover up what they believe to be their weakness in exactly the same manner. After fleeing from police, Bart tries to please Laurie by lying that he killed one of their pursuers. After fleeing from the packing plant, Laurie tries to please Bart by lying that she did *not* kill anyone during their getaway.

Lewis and I also differ in that he doesn't think Laurie ever really loves Bart. He argues: "She marries him on the spur of the moment—not for love. And her

As always, Laurie is the more aggressive when she and Bart rob a meat-packing plant.

Laurie and Bart wait for the police to surround them. They are content to die together.

opinion of him never really changes. She is too concerned with survival to think of him. He is just her means to make money."

I don't believe Laurie loves Bart when they get married. Her attraction to him is purely sexual at that time, and she fully expects (if not intends) to play him for a sucker and leave him when he starts to bore her. It is Laurie who suggests the temporary separation after the packing-plant robbery. It seems quite obvious that she intends this separation to be permanent, as Bart has decided to commit no more crimes. But it is the very scene which Lewis inserted in which Laurie finds that she doesn't want to leave Bart after all that, as I mentioned earlier, confirms her love for him. From this scene on, Laurie may waver in her decision to lead a crimeless, nonviolent life, but her love for Bart is never in question.

Gun Crazy is not only about *two* people who are deeply in love but is one of the most romantic films ever made. Has there ever been a more romantic movie sequence than the finale? Just before Bart and Laurie meet their deaths, they flee police in a speeding car which travels up a treacherous mountain road. The car breaks down, and though they realize there is no real chance of escape, they jump out and run through the woods on foot. It is rough terrain, and soon they are wet (from walking through a stream, as Bonnie and Clyde would do years later in Penn's film), bruised, exhausted, dirty, and in panic because they hear hounds on their trail. Their faces reflect the horrible strain and they can barely talk. Yet Bart still calls Laurie "honey," and as they stumble along they still take a moment here and there to hug and kiss. In the morning they wake up and realize they are surrounded and there is absolutely no way out. "We're in real trouble this time," Laurie says apologetically, believing that it was her propensity for violence which put the gentle Bart on the point of death. But Bart's response is soothing, and honest:"Laurie, I wouldn't have it any other way." They kiss passionately and hold each other one last time. A few seconds later they lie side by side, dead, like Romeo and Juliet. Heavenly music indicates their love will continue in a more hospitable environment. A true love story has come to a fitting end.

Halloween

1978 Compass International Pictures release of a Falcon International production
Director: John Carpenter
Producer: Debra Hill
Screenplay: John Carpenter and Debra Hill
Cinematography: Dean Cundey
Music: John Carpenter
Editors: Tommy Wallace and Charles Bornstein
Running time: 93 minutes

Cast: Donald Pleasance (Loomis), Jamie Lee Curtis (Laurie), Nancy Loomis (Annie), P. J. Soles (Lynda), Charles Cypers (Brackett), Kyle Richards (Lindsey), Brian Andrews (Tommy), John Michael Graham (Bob), Nancy Stephens (Marion), Tony Moran (Michael, age 21)

Synopsis: In Haddonfield, Illinois, on Halloween night in 1963, while his teenage sister Judith made love to her boyfriend upstairs, six-year-old Michael Meyers took a long knife from the kitchen drawer. After Judith's boyfriend had left, Michael went upstairs, put on a Halloween mask, and stabbed Judith to death. During the next fifteen years he was kept in isolation at a mental hospital in Smith's Grove, Illinois, under the supervision of Dr. Loomis. He never spoke a word in all that time, he just stared at the wall . . . waiting. On October 30, 1978, Michael steals a state car and escapes. Loomis, horrified because he thinks Michael the personification of evil, capable of terrible crimes, drives toward Haddonfield, believing that Michael will head there. He is correct: Michael has killed a trucker and stolen his clothes and has come back to his old house, vacant since the night of the murder. On Halloween morning he looks out his front door and sees Laurie on her way to the high school. Later Laurie, from her classroom window, sees Michael standing across the street behind a state car. He wears a mask.

When Laurie and her more outgoing friends Lynda and Annie, Sheriff Brackett's daughter, walk home from school, Laurie notices the state car drive past. It comes to a sudden halt a few yards ahead but then moves along.

Loomis arrives in Haddonfield. He goes to the graveyard, where he discovers that Judith Meyers's tombstone is missing. Loomis talks to Sheriff Brackett, who is investigating the theft of a mask, a rope, and some knives from a hardware store. Together they go to the Meyers house and wait for Michael to return. On Halloween night, Laurie baby-sits for Tommy while Annie is across the street baby-sitting for Shelley Wallace. As the girls talk on the phone, Tommy keeps interrupting the conversation to tell Laurie that he sees the boogeyman outside the Wallace house. Each time Laurie looks, he is gone.

Before Annie goes to pick up her boyfriend, she drops Shelley off with Laurie and Tommy. When Annie climbs into her car, Michael is in the back seat and slits her throat. Lynda and her boyfriend Bob arrive at the Wallace house and, finding no one there, go upstairs and make love. When Bob goes to the kitchen alone, he opens a closet and Michael jumps out and impales him with his knife high on a wall. Michael then goes upstairs and strangles Lynda.

Not understanding why Annie hasn't returned, Laurie goes to the Wallace house. She finds Annie, Lynda, and Bob all dead, with Annie's body lying ceremoniously under Judith Meyers's tombstone. Michael comes at her with a knife from out of the darkness, but misses. Laurie escapes and goes back to the house across the street. Michael follows her. Laurie thinks she kills him: first with a long knitting needle and then by stabbing him with his knife. But he keeps getting back up. Loomis, canvassing the neighborhood, sees Tommy and Shelley running from the house and goes inside. Just as Michael is about to kill Laurie, Loomis shoots him numerous times and Michael falls out the window to the ground below. Loomis tells Laurie that Michael is truly the boogeyman. He looks outside and sees that Michael has gone.

Having already earned more than $50 million on a meager $320,000 investment, John Carpenter's *Halloween* ranks as the most profitable independently made feature of all time. I am not as sold on the picture as are many critics and the picture's enormous cult following, but I don't dispute the claim that it is not only the scariest horror film since *Psycho* (1960) but also the most imaginatively directed. There have been far too many recent films about unknown assailants with knives or axes (or spears, hatchets, chain saws, etc.) who do away with teen-agers / college students in gruesome fashion. *Halloween* inspired many of them, but Carpenter's film is so much better than the others that it almost defies comparison. *Halloween* isn't merely an excuse to show people killed off but is foremost a fascinating exercise in style. Carpenter truly understands how to make a good horror film according to the rules of the genre, blending together the dark, spooky atmosphere essential to Val Lewton; the humor and suspense that go hand in hand in Hitchcock; the cheap—but fun—tricks and shocks found in William Castle (particularly in his "haunted" house films); and the graphic violence that is a staple of the post-*Night of the Living Dead* (1968) American horror film.

The most noticeable characteristic of Carpenter's technique is that his camera (in this case, the very mobile Panaglide) is constantly on the move, following young Michael from outside his house, through the kitchen and dining room, up the stairs, and into his sister's bedroom, where he stabs her to death (this is all done in one take); craning back outside the Meyers's house to reveal that Michael is just a small boy. In the present, it sweeps across a Haddonfield street, moving from a long shot to a close-up of Laurie, Annie, and Lynda walking home from school; or simply (yet cleverly) panning to follow imperiled characters as they walk past. The constant movement of the camera combined with Carpenter's quick editing gives one a sense of dislocation; because we don't have time to adjust to a particular setting we never feel secure no matter where we are. This certainly

The three teen-age girls terrorized by psychotic Michael: (L-R) the wisecracking Annie, the upbeat Lynda, and the worried Laurie.

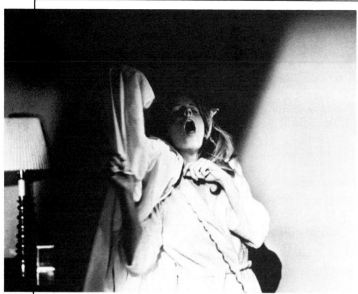

Before she can complete her conversation with Laurie, Lynda is strangled by Michael, who has fooled her into thinking it is her boyfriend under the sheet.

adds to our nervousness, though I doubt that Carpenter moves his camera so often to give us this sense of insecurity. More likely, he does it to keep the film's pace from lagging. But I do believe it is to make us feel insecure that Carpenter switches back and forth (even within the same sequence) between using the camera objectively, to make us identify with the killer or the characters in danger, and subjectively to have us be observers of events transpiring on the screen. Sometimes this effect works well, as in the opening sequence, in which the camera looks through Michael's mask's peep holes; but too often it becomes confusing, as when we think we are seeing a P.O.V. (point of view) of the killer's only to discover a few seconds later that he is somewhere else entirely. Such a use of the camera, particularly when it is placed near a potential victim's back to make it appear that someone is about to reach out and grab him/her from behind, definitely builds tension and adds to the paranoia that is desired by the filmmaker, but it is also unfairly manipulative and misleading.

Carpenter builds a sense of paranoia more legitimately through the creative use of light and shadow. With the exception of Val Lewton's films, I can think of no horror film that has fewer brightly lit shots. It is very rare in *Halloween* when some part of the frame isn't either in shadows or totally dark. This is by design and works wonderfully. I particularly like the shadowy effect caused by the trees Laurie, Annie, and Lynda walk under, which prevents them from enjoying the safety one usually feels outdoors in broad daylight. Also impressive is how Carpenter uses the color *white* in his night scenes. In fact, this color picture works so well because it is for the most part in black and white—the respective colors for evil (Michael) and good (everybody else). The Wallace house is white, and so are most of the interiors of both houses. This allows the moon to reflect

light off the woodwork and keeps the sets from being totally dark, giving the characters an excuse not to turn on a light to see. Wisely, Carpenter also has Michael wear a white mask so at times the screen is totally dark but for his mask, which is reflecting moonlight—this is creepy. It is also extremely powerful when Laurie runs out into the hall after discovering the bodies of her friends and stands crying in the doorway of a totally dark room, and suddenly the white mask materializes in that darkness. Michael's appearance at this moment is like a vision and recalls the early scene outside the mental hospital when the inmates walk around the grounds at night, their white robes in the darkness making them look like apparitions.

Carpenter's imaginative use of the wide frame (the picture was filmed in Panavision) contributes to both building paranoia and building suspense. Time and again, when we search the screen we discover more than what is taking place at the point of action. If a character is in the foreground facing the camera, Carpenter will typically have the masked Michael move into the background within striking distance only to disappear when the character looks around. One of the most frightening visuals in the film is when Annie is in the foreground looking out the stuck laundry room door and, in the background (unknown to her), Michael appears outside the window. If a character in the background is looking away from the camera, as is Laurie when she puts the key under the door of the supposedly empty Meyers house, or is preoccupied, as are make-out artists Lynda and Bob in the Wallace living room, Carpenter will place Michael directly in front of the camera—but only with his back and shoulder in frame so we can see both him and his intended prey. In most cases Carpenter will jolt us by having Michael step into the frame, but in the scene in which Lynda and Bob neck on the Wallace couch he pulls his camera back to reveal Michael in the archway staring at them.

Laurie discovers the body of Annie, her throat slit, lying on a bed in front of the tombstone of Michael's dead sister.

Wearing a mask, Michael tries to kill Laurie, the last of the girls.

In most instances Michael's appearances are accompanied by bursts of loud "shock" music, usually a note or two but sometimes driving, scary, piercing music that helps build the suspense. It has a rhythm like a timepiece or a heartbeat and by its very nature adds a *time element* to the picture that is otherwise missing. The best use of music, I think, is in the opening sequence; as soon as the upstairs light goes out, signifying that Judith and her boyfriend are having sex, a penetrating note jumps on the soundtrack. It fades slightly as the camera (Michael's P.O.V.) enters the house, but as it does it seems to vibrate; then a spooky melodic line is played on top of this vibrating note as Michael goes upstairs to perform his evil chore. My major complaint with the music is that it is played far too often, at expected moments, and with little variation. (When Michael's shadow appears on the wall behind Lynda and Bob making love in the Wallace bed, it would have been much stronger if there were no music.) John Carpenter composed the musical score and he did a fine job, but it becomes repetitive and the ringing is tiresome.

Unlike most women-in-peril pictures, *Halloween* has an interesting assortment of characters. Donald Pleasance is entertaining as Loomis, a quirky, perversely amusing doctor whose every word spreads terror about the events that might transpire now that "the evil is gone" from the asylum. He seems a bit batty after spending fifteen years with Michael, but we realize that it probably takes an insane type to want to track down the indestructible Michael. So we're glad he's on our side. Pleasance gets top billing, but the film belongs to three young female leads. Jamie Lee Curtis (the daughter of *Psycho*'s Janet Leigh and now a cult favorite of horror fans) as Laurie, Nancy Loomis as Annie, and, to a lesser degree, P. J. Soles as Lynda are first-rate, playing the most believable teenagers seen in the movies in some time. The horror aside, it's a real treat watching these three Middle America teenagers jabber away about boys, school, dates, sex, etc. They are witty (Annie: "I hate a guy with a car and no sense of humor"), smart (which is why Laurie has a hard time attracting boys), and odd in a conventional sort of way (Lynda uses the word "totally" in every sentence). Compare the teenage girls in Brian De Palma's *Carrie* (1976) with those in *Halloween*, and you'll discover that De Palma still bears hostility toward teen-age girls from his adolescence while Carpenter likes them despite their idiosyncracies.

I think Michael is an incredibly interesting character, not the typical vengeful movie psycho. Carpenter defines him as Evil itself (the real boogeyman), but I don't believe that he goes around killing people because he is evil. Insane, yes; evil, no. There is still a little boy inside the man's body, and everything he does is part of a game. In fact, his activities are less suited for Halloween than "Mischief Night" (the night after Halloween "celebrated" in many American towns when kids play dirty tricks on their neighbors). He has fun scaring characters before he kills them, or teasing them by making noises, or jumping out of closets. The scariest moment is when Michael drives past Laurie, Annie, and Lynda and stops for a moment. He could kill any of these people any time he wants to, but he prefers to hide behind bushes and in closets, peer into windows, or, as in the case with Annie, play tricks with her car door. Before he kills Lynda, he stands in the bedroom doorway with a sheet over his body and glasses on his face, to scare her before strangling her. In his never-ending struggle with Laurie, he even pretends to be dead: repeatedly he crumbles to the ground and lies lifeless only to get up like the Greek Antaeus, stronger each time he is knocked to the ground. That it is all "play" to Michael is confirmed when he stops strangling Laurie in order to put his mask back on (like an unmasked dirty wrestler). Interestingly, Michael never attacks a child (his peers). A boy even runs into him at the elementary school, and Michael lets him go immediately. That Michael is only a threat to adults is odd since by definition a boogeyman is "a hobgoblin who carries off naughty children."

I don't mind that Michael terrorizes Laurie and Annie without true motivation. Carpenter's excellent TV thriller *Someone Is Watching Me!* (1978) benefits from the fact that Lauren Hutton doesn't know the man who is spying on her. I also find it somewhat refreshing that in *Halloween* we are rooting for the female victims and would-be victims rather than siding with the killer —as is truly the phenomenon in many of these films— by wanting to see scantily clad females get their comeuppance. On the other hand, I find it a bit annoying that the preludes to Annie and Lynda's deaths are dragged on for such a long time that we *almost* hope they are killed just to get it over with; and regrettable that even this film thrives upon the deaths of pretty, half-dressed women.

In fact, *Halloween* has been criticized for its puritanical "morality," which calls for Michael to kill the sexually promiscuous Judith, Annie, and Lynda, and for Laurie, the only virgin of the group, to be the only one who survives. In *Film Comment* (March-April 1980), critic Todd McCarthy confronted Carpenter (who also wrote the script) on this point. Carpenter's defense:

> [The critics] completely missed the boat there, I think. . . . [T]he one girl who is the most sexually uptight just keeps stabbing this guy with a long knife. She's the most sexually frustrated. She's the one that's killed him. Not because she's a virgin, but because all that repressed sexual energy starts coming out. She uses all those phallic symbols on the guy. . . .
> [The other girls are so] interested in their boyfriends [that] they're ignoring the signs. She's aware of [them] because she's more like the killer, she has problems. She's uptight, a little bit rigid. She and the killer have a certain link: sexual repression. She's lonely, she doesn't have a boyfriend, so she's looking around. And she finds someone—him.

If this is truly the rationale that helped Carpenter decide what takes place in the film and why, then we can conclude that the sexually frustrated Laurie subconsciously wished Michael back to Haddonfield and into her life. When she keeps dropping the knife (a phallic symbol) by his body on the floor (while viewers scream their disbelief that she is doing something so stupid), she is actually urging on his continued "sexual" advances. Moreover, this sexual affinity between Laurie and Michael explains why Carpenter has Laurie singing "Just the Two of Us" as she walks down the street and moves Michael into the frame with her. But I don't believe any of this. Intentional or not, Carpenter made a film in which girls are killed directly after or just before engaging in sexual activity. His defense, made up after the fact, is nonsense.

Loomis finally catches up with Michael at the moment he tries to strangle Laurie.

A Hard Day's Night

Expressing a freedom desired by the youth of the world, (L-R) Paul, George, Ringo, and John were a breath of fresh air when they entered the tired movie world in 1964.

1964 Great Britain United Artists
Director: Richard Lester
Producer: Walter Shenson
Screenplay: Alun Owen
Cinematography: Gilbert Taylor
Musical Director: George Martin
Songs: John Lennon and Paul McCartney
Editor: John Jympson
Running Time: 85 minutes

Cast: The Beatles: George Harrison, John Lennon, Paul McCartney, Ringo Starr (themselves), Wilfrid Brambell (Paul's grandfather), Norman Rossington (Norm), John Junkin (Shake), Victor Spinetti (television director), Anna Quayle (Millie)

Synopsis: In beards and other disguises, the four Beatles elude their legion of wild, screaming fans and board a train to travel to their next musical engagement. As always, they are accompanied by Norm, their short, bossy road manager, whose orders the Beatles pay little attention to, and Shake, Norm's simpleton assistant, who is constantly criticized by Norm for being tall. On this trip, Paul has brought along his grandfather, who is nursing a broken heart. Everyone looks at the well-dressed, short-haired, spectacled man and comments, "He's very clean." But as they soon learn, "He's just a dirty old man from Liverpool." In a brief time, he convinces some schoolgirls that the Beatles are prisoners, plays on Ringo's inferiority complex by telling him how short he is, heightens the antagonism between Norm and Shake, and, after disappearing for a few minutes, turns up engaged to a woman on the train. For the remainder of the trip, the Beatles lock him in the luggage compartment.

That night, the Beatles, always searching for privacy, sneak out of their hotel room and go to a rock music night spot for some dancing and relaxation. Paul's grandfather sneaks off to a casino. Norm and Shake track them all down and bring them back to the hotel. Norm is becoming more and more rattled trying to keep the Beatles in line. John is the most openly hostile (in a gentle way) toward him. "It's a battle of nerves between John and me," says the upset Norm. "John doesn't have nerves," laments Shake. Before the Beatles' television concert the next day, which they will give in front of a live studio audience, Paul's grandfather speaks to Ringo. Having already reminded him that he snores, is short, and has a big nose he now tells the unhappy drummer that the other Beatles don't appreciate him and that he should run off. Ringo takes his advice. While George, Paul, and John try to find Ringo in time for the concert, Ringo walks around town, followed by a policeman who writes down all his misdeeds.

Paul's grandfather is arrested for causing a disturbance while trying to sell autographed Beatles photos outside the theater. He discovers that Ringo has also been taken to the police station. He escapes and tells the Beatles where Ringo is, and promises not to cause them any more trouble. The three Beatles help Ringo escape, and they all make it to their concert just as it is about to begin—much to the relief of the nervous stage manager. After a successful concert, the Beatles, Paul's grandfather, Norm, and Shake climb into a helicopter and fly toward their next engagement.

Considering how little film exists of the Beatles —three full-length, live-action films and a few shorts—*A Hard Day's Night* is a real treasure. It is an impressionistic cinematic chronicle of a "typical" twenty-four hours in their hectic lives, a wonderful comedic-musical showcase for the talented foursome at their peak—before they soured on each other and went their separate ways, and long before John Lennon's tragic death saddened the world. When it was released in 1964, theaters across the country were filled with contented, smiling, singing Beatles devotees, magically unified by the Beatles and their cheery music. Today, more than fifteen years later, thirty- and forty-year-old veterans of those crowds insist that their kids accompany them to see *A Hard Day's Night* in revival houses so they can nostalgically discuss the significance of the Beatles and this picture in their lives.

A Hard Day's Night was one of the truly pleasant surprises of the sixties: a breezy, captivating, joyous film made during a particularly dreary movie period; a guaranteed box office hit that turned out to be an artistic success as well. The splendid reviews that the picture received and the unexpected praise heaped upon the Beatles for their performances made the nation's young people collectively burst with pride. To have *their* Beatles, their idols who were more than symbolically central to their lives, given "legitimacy" by establishment critics, whom their elders/parents read and respected, was much more than gratifying—it was liberating. I am serious when I say it is the only time in memory when young people could point to "proof" in writing (reviews) and tell their condescending elders: "See! I am right about something, and you are wrong!"

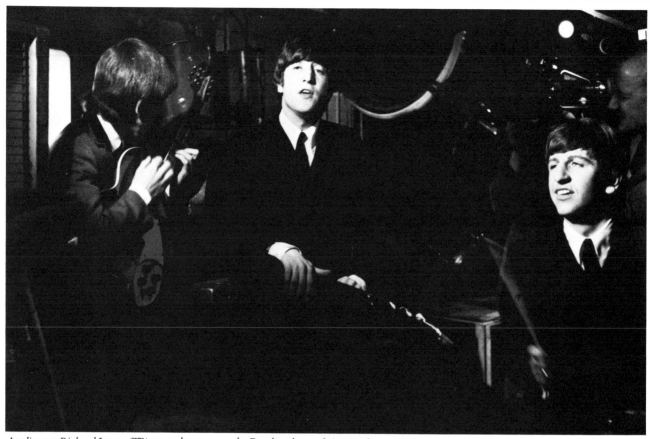

As director Richard Lester (TR) runs the camera, the Beatles play and sing in the train's baggage compartment.

What an earlier generation of Elvis admirers would have given for such testimonials. *A Hard Day's Night* gave America's youth a "moment of triumph" which they, as adults years later—balding and graying perhaps—still cherish.

Richard Lester was relatively unknown outside of England when he was approached to direct the first Beatles movie. He had made two feature films, *It's Trad, Dad!* (1962) and *Mouse on the Moon* (1963), both quite funny despite short shooting schedules, but he was more identified as a fifties television director and the maker of a series of prize-winning commercials in the early sixties. His major cinematic venture had been a hilarious short called *The Running, Jumping, and Standing Still Film* (1959), starring Peter Sellers and Spike Milligan, which won awards at several film festivals and was nominated for an Oscar. In England, at least, Lester had a reputation as being a hip, inventive, economical director, capable of turning out flashy solid work in a brief time, on a meager budget; he seemed to be an ideal choice to direct *A Hard Day's Night*, a black-and-white picture which had to be made in only seven weeks for just $580,000. And it is because of Lester that *A Hard Day's Night* bears no resemblance to the cheap exploitation picture United Artists expected to distribute.*

---

*Many other English music groups made films in the sixties but, other than the Beatles, only The Dave Clark Five was lucky enough to work with a top notch director, John Boorman. Consequently their debut film *Catch Us If You Can* (1965) was also praised by critics.

Because United Artists' only concern was being able to release a Beatles picture, any Beatles picture, before the group's stardom waned (which U.A. fully expected to happen before the fall of 1964), it allowed Lester absolute freedom. Lester saw this project as his chance to experiment indulgently without having to worry about damaging a film's commercial prospects. So he set about to make a picture by combining his own style as developed in live television and commercials with the multifarious styles of filmmakers he admired and always wanted to imitate.

Much of the film's anarchic quality—as personified by the Beatles—can be attributed to Lester's previously latent talent for serendipity. You'll see something distinctive to Lester, like the Beatles running, jumping, and standing still in a field, and then notice that he's pulled the camera high into the air and is filming them as if he were Busby Berkeley; he'll film the Beatles' concert as if he were doing one of his live television shows, then suddenly zoom in on screaming, crying fans in the audience ("George!" whimpers one female sobber) as if he were a documentarian, and then rush the Beatles outside and into a rising helicopter as if he were shooting the finale of Fellini's *La Dolce Vita* (1961). Moreover, there are traces of Antonioni, Sennett, Chaplin, Keaton, and others scattered about. One scene will be abstract, the next absurd, the next realistic, the next seemingly part of a cinéma vérité exercise. There are moments of parody, moments of satire, and moments of outright silliness. Alun Owen's semiplotless script, full of non sequiturs, is the perfect vehicle for Lester's mad method.

As Andrew Sarris wrote, when reviewing the film in 1964, "*A Hard Day's Night* is the *Citizen Kane* of jukebox musicals, the brilliant crystalization of such diverse cultural particles as the pop movie, rock 'n' roll, cinéma-vérité, the nouvelle vague, the affectedly hand-held camera, the cult of the sexless sub-adolescent, the semi-documentary, and studied spontaneity." It was only by bringing together so many dissimilar, yet familiar, "styles" and "cultural forms" that Lester was able to create his own style—one without form or restriction—that ironically seemed completely fresh.

Rock 'n' roll films typically have taken a defensive stance, whereby the singers and musicians spend the whole film trying to convince "squares" and older people that neither they nor their music is subversive. Lester chose to portray the Beatles as they really were, even allowing us to see their "vices": they play cards, drink (although their managers won't let them), smoke, chase schoolgirls, vainly look at themselves in the mirror, are thorns in the sides of authority figures, and prefer partying to answering fan mail. He neither glori-fied them, defended them and their music, nor was manipulative by having crotchety characters in the film suddenly "see the error of their ways" and convert into Beatles fans. Lester recognized the Beatles' natural appeal, placed them in familiar (though simulated) situations—press parties, interviews, rehearsals, etc.—and simply turned the camera on, often letting them dictate what would happen next. The Beatles come across as being extremely personable and good-natured, able to maintain their humor and remain tolerant despite being the only sane figures left in a Beatles-crazy world.

The Beatles, I suspect, must have thought it ludicrous to play themselves in a motion picture, so perhaps Lester's greatest achievement is getting engaging, insightful performances from them. In *Help!* (1965), Lester would mistakenly make the four Beatles interchangeable, but in *A Hard Day's Night* he gives them each a chance to display their singular personality traits. And they are a joy to watch. There's George shaving beardless Shake's mirror reflection; answering an interviewer's foolish "Has success changed your life?" with "Yes!" There's John going off with a buxom blonde "to examine," he says, "her stamp collection"; playing with

Causing trouble as usual, Paul's grandfather lets Ringo know that he's not keen on being removed from the casino.

*The final concert in
A Hard Day's Night—
a sequence we'll never tire of.*

a toy submarine in his bathtub; making Norm nervous by pretending to go down the drain. There's sulky Ringo taking a lonely walk across town while the instrumental of "This Boy" plays in the background; trying to pick up a girl who turns out to talk like a chipmunk; putting his coat over a puddle, like Sir Walter Raleigh, only to see the thankful maiden step on it and plunge into a manhole below it. And there's Paul, constantly worried about his rakish granddad; donning disguises to elude his fans but at the same time loving their attention.

Much of the film is about the Beatles trying to maintain their privacy in their fishbowl existence. Their loyalty to one another—more understated but as strong as the bond between Lester's Four Musketeers—has not so much to do with friendship as it has to do with them each being aware that only three other people in the world understand what they, as individuals, are going through. Some of the film's most revealing moments take place in the rock music club where the Beatles flee after escaping their hotel room. Particularly moving are close-ups of Paul, seemingly caught off guard, relaxing with a cigarette, occasionally smiling—as if he were actually enjoying time away from making the movie; and of George and Ringo dancing, punching the air like boxers, merrily jumping high into the air as if they were celebrating a chance to be in their own element, away from their fame and the infinite demands on their time and energy.

But soon it's back to work. The Beatles may balk at needless discipline, but they are neither lazy nor irresponsible. They realize they have obligations. They like their fans, though their adoration befuddles them; yet they realize that their fame dictates that they can't have much contact with them. When they do mingle in the outside world, they display not a touch of snobbery;

they never pull rank, even when ordered about by people who don't recognize them. They are apolitical, but they have decent, "common-folk" values; as Paul says, "We're working class and all that . . ." In a remarkably honest scene, Ringo comes upon a boy playing hooky. Being a truant from the Beatles himself —and not Spencer Tracy—Ringo makes no attempt to steer the boy on the "right" road (the one that supposedly, in films, at least, leads back to school). He gives him no advice at all. Lester realized that the Beatles were idols of millions and chose not to exploit that fact by making them inspirational figures, believing that would have been irresponsible on his part. He instead chose to be straightforward: to avoid words of wisdom, sentiment, and heroics (the Beatles don't rush into a burning orphanage or anything like that), at all costs.

If the Beatles are to be admired, it is because of their professional attitude toward their music. That is why Lester and Owen put so much emphasis on such a seemingly trivial thing as the Beatles showing up for a television appearance on time. The Beatles were very serious about their music, and Lester worked very hard to capture this on film. Over and over again, just when the pressures of their world are getting the better of them, the Beatles pick up their instruments, and before you know it, they are smiling again, and back in control, as if their batteries had been recharged. How exciting it still is to see them playing and singing together all those great Beatle songs: "I Should Have Known Better," "If I Fell," "And I Love Her," "I'm Happy Just to Dance with You," "Tell Me Why," and "She Loves You." Their happiness when they sing their songs and play their music truly is infectious. We are reminded that, while they were engaging movie personalities, they were first, and foremost, the most appealing pop music group the world has ever known.

The Harder They Come

Charismatic reggae singer Jimmy Cliff is electrifying as singer/revolutionary Ivan Martin in Jamaica's first feature film.

1973 New World release
of an International
Films production
Director: Perry Henzell
Producer: Perry Henzell
Screenplay: Perry Henzell and Trevor D. Rhone
Cinematography: Frank St. Juste, David McDonald, and Peter Jessop
Songs: "You Can Get It If You Really Want," "The Harder They Come," "Many Rivers to Cross," and "Sitting in Limbo" written and performed by Jimmy Cliff; "Draw Your Breaks" written by Derrick Harriot and D. Scott and performed by Scotty; "Rivers of Babylon" written by B. Dowe and F. McNaughton and performed by The Melodians; "Sweet and Dandy" and "Pressure Drop" written by F. Hibbert and performed by The Maytals; "Johnny Too Bad" written and performed by The Slickers; "Shanty Town" written and performed by Desmond Dekker
Editors: John Victor Smith, Seicland Anderson, and Richard White
Running Time: 98 minutes

Cast: Jimmy Cliff (Ivan), Carl Bradshaw (José), Janet Bartley (Elsa), Ras Daniel Hartman (Pedro), Basil Keane (preacher), Bobby Charlton (Hilton), Winston Stona (detective)

Synopsis: Ivan Martin, a young Jamaican from the country, arrives in Kingston. He hopes to enjoy the better life, make money, and become a recording star. That things will not come easy is forewarned when his belongings are stolen. Ivan finds it impossible to find work and has no luck begging for money. He ends up living in a wrecked car and working as a handyman for a preacher. The preacher fires him when he discovers Ivan has been seeing his ward Elsa behind his back. When Ivan goes to get his bicycle he finds that the other handyman is claiming it for himself. They fight and Ivan slashes him with a knife. Ivan is taken to prison and is whipped.

Out of jail and living with Elsa, Ivan gets Hilton, the island's top record producer, to let him record a song he wrote, "The Harder They Come." Hilton likes what he hears but only gives Ivan twenty dollars for all the rights. Believing Ivan to be a troublemaker because he complained about the low fee, Hilton releases the record but doesn't promote it.

Because Ivan needs money he agrees to work for José in the island's great ganja (marijuana) trade. The police let ganja business continue because they share in the profits. Ivan resents having to pay fifteen dollars each week to José, who acts as a middle man. When Ivan refuses to pay, José arranges for him to be set up. Against his Rastafarian friend Pedro's objections, Ivan had bought a gun, and when a policeman tries to arrest him when he is making his drug run, Ivan kills him. Ivan goes after José, who double-crossed him. He kills several more policemen and shoots José's girlfriend.

Ivan has become famous. His record is a smash hit and he is a folk hero, battling the corrupt police and drug dealers. The detective in charge of his case closes down the drug trade, hoping the dealers will help him find Ivan. Pedro arranges boat passage for Ivan to Cuba. Ivan waits two days on a beach for the boat to come.

The police beat Pedro to get him to tell them where Ivan is, but he won't talk. But Elsa, who is upset that Ivan was dealing drugs when he had told her he was making money fishing, returns to the preacher and he calls the police.

Ivan misses the boat. The police arrive en masse, on the beach. Ivan remembers a bloody western he saw during which the audience cheered a hero who gunned down many foes. He steps out of hiding and challenges the soldiers to a gunfight. He is shot down.

I find it peculiar that repertory theaters insist on double-billing *Black Orpheus* (1959), the famous Brazilian film, and *The Harder They Come*, Jamaica's stunning first feature. While they both take place in cities that attract American tourism—Rio de Janeiro and Kingston respectively—have all-black casts, a hero who dies in the end, and memorable musical scores,* *Black Orpheus* is an uncontroversial fairy tale held dear by the American (white) mass audience while the second is a hard-hitting, angry left-wing polemic that could only have "cult" appeal outside Jamaica. Just look at the films' two heroes and you can see why *Black Orpheus* is more "popular" in America. Bruno Mello looks like a Greek god, and in his carnival garb he even dresses the part. He is well built, straight-shouldered, smart but not surly, polite, and handsome in the Sidney Poitier mold—and as it is with Poitier, the average white moviegoer would be delighted to invite him home for dinner. Jimmy Cliff is a slightly built, gangly fellow who sports a goatee, stands stoop-shouldered with one knee bent, and struts as cockily as a "dirty" wrestler. He is charismatic, but his appeal is too sexual for most whites to feel comfortable with, especially when he sings: his eyes close, he dangles a cigarette in a half-closed hand that is constantly pumping, he sweats, his bottom lip curls under his teeth, he smacks his lips, he slowly shakes back and forth to the beat. As Ivan Martin, he wears loud clothes, slurs his words, speaks patois (the Rastafarian dialect), answers back, has a violent streak, carries weapons, is angry at being exploited and means to do something about it. No, he is not the hero that the white American middle class had been waiting for.

---

*The Harder They Come's reggae score is one of the best scores in movie history. Much of the film's cult is a result of the music; in fact, there are an astounding number of people who own the soundtrack album—the best reggae sampler—who have never seen the picture.

Rude boys: Jamaica's angry, unemployed black male population.

Recognizing that *The Harder They Come* would do poorly in first-run showcase theaters, New World, its American distributor, booked it primarily in black neighborhoods, hoping that black Americans would take to violent Rude Boy Ivan as they had to *Shaft* (1971) and *Superfly* (1972). At the time I thought New World's strategy correct: I had seen the picture with an all-white audience and during the scene in which Ivan uses his knife on the face of the big lug who tries to steal his bike, saying, "Don't [slash] mess [slash] with [slash] me [slash]!" the audience moaned in collective pain, taking on the part of the victim; also I had seen the picture with a predominantly black audience and after Ivan warned "Don't mess with me!" the audience cheered. Yet ultimately the film didn't catch on with those black Americans turned on by apolitical blaxploitation films. (The film's cult, however, consists of both politically inclined blacks and whites.) New World alibied that this failure had to do with the use of subtitles to help translate the patois—subtitles are the kiss of death in black neighborhood theaters—but in hindsight there seem to be much better reasons. Most crucial: I don't believe apolitical American blacks wish to identify with Ivan. While they probably like his music, his rebelliousness and his violent nature, and that he fights the police, I would guess they resent the fact that when Ivan emulates their heroes—the American black superstud stereotypes—director Perry Henzell is mocking the foolish, culturally corrupted, apolitical side of Ivan that contributes to his

downfall. Ivan is a product of his own singular environment, a *Jamaican* folk hero—part singer Jimmy Cliff—who when fourteen also sold his first song for a pittance—and part Rhygin (Rastafarian Ras Daniel Hartman), the legendary Kingston outlaw of the fifties also killed in a police shootout, who today is a symbol of Jamaican political insurrection. And the picture, while being neither elitist nor totally alien to Third World viewers around the globe, has a distinctly Jamaican sensibility. (I would even venture to say it has a "distinctly *black* Jamaican sensibility" if it weren't that Jamaican director-screenwriter Henzel is white.)

The Jamaica we see in *The Harder They Come* is a far cry from the Caribbean paradise presented in American-made travelogues. There is so little beautiful scenery in the film that it is probable that Henzell hoped his film would keep tourists away. The countryside looks barren and infertile; and Kingston, the tourist center, appears to be overcrowded, violent, seamy, and poverty-stricken—full of beggars, thieves, conmen, and hungry women and children rummaging through garbage for food. The only luxury hotel we see is the one from which Ivan is chased away; the only estate we see is the one owned by a rich racist white woman; the only golf course we see is the one Ivan contemptuously drives his stolen Cadillac across; the only sandy beach we see is the one on which Ivan yields his dying blood. Here is a former British colony that despite self-rule since 1959 is dominated economically and culturally by industrial powers, particularly the United States: there are Shell Oil signs, American-imported magazines, and movies (although the one Ivan sees is made in Italy, it is a western made in the American way). A black native disc jockey on a "Top 40" type radio show sounds like America's own Cousin Brucie. The shame of it all is that despite American, Canadian, and British investments, the great majority of blacks, who comprise 90 percent of the island's 2.1 million population, live in abject poverty.

At the film's beginning, Ivan leaves the countryside —pictured as peaceful and communal in Michael Thelwell's much-praised novel that is based and expands on the film. Ivan arrives in Kingston expecting to find, as the sign his bus passes reads, "the better life." But Ivan is disillusioned by the reality of the situation: there is no work for unskilled laborers. Ivan's predicament allows Henzell to bring him—an example of Jamaica's countless lumpen blacks—into contact with the island's major cultural influences: the Christian church, represented by the preacher; the record business, represented by Hilton; the ganja (marijuana) trade, represented by José; the Rastafarians, represented by Pedro; the government/police force, represented by the detective; outlaw mythology, represented by Johnny Too Bad (Rhygin?). In this way we come to understand what paths are available to the unemployed black Jamaicans.

Christianity. Like many black singers in America (as well as white singers, particularly in the South), Ivan thoroughly enjoys the Church's music, and his own music is influenced by it. One of the highlights of the film is the scene in which Ivan and the rest of a frenzied choir—standing in front of a sign on the church wall that, appropriately, reads "Behold I Come Quickly"— look as if they are bringing themselves to orgasms while singing a wild gospel song. But like the Rastafarians, Ivan rejects Christianity as a death-oriented religion meant to pacify rebellious poor folks. This refusal to accept having nothing in the present is at the center of Jimmy Cliff's personal philosophy expressed in his lyrics ("I'm gonna get my share *now* what's mine").

The record business. In America, young blacks dream of escaping the ghetto via sports or music. In Jamaica, poor blacks like Ivan dream of fame and fortune as singers—and if you sing and write as well as Jimmy Cliff there seems to be a good chance that you'll make it, because Jamaica releases more records per capita each week than any country in the world. Reggae (now called rockers) became the dominant musical force in Jamaica in the sixties. Influenced originally by New Orleans rhythm and blues, it has evolved with an almost distinctly Jamaican music by blending with the polka-like "ska" electronic sound and "rock steady," a shuffle-beat calypso. The music itself, distinguished by bass and guitar interplay and a steady drumbeat, has been a source of government scrutiny because it is a major part of the Rastafarian counterculture. The lyrics are in fact antigovernment. The music industry is as exploitative as everything else in Jamaica, and Hilton is based on real-life music producers who run their businesses like dictatorships.

For even non-Christians like Ivan, gospel music is inspirational.

The main contradiction is that Rastafarians, who abhor the practices of the music industry, are the main recruits for the industry.

The ganja trade. Ivan is the victim of a social system that will let people exploit and commit crimes against one another if those in power (the detective specifically) can profit by it. As in American ghettos, there is no work for young blacks in Jamaica other than in drug trafficking. The police don't interfere in the ganja business because (a) through spies in the trade they can keep tabs on the Rastafarians, who use ganja in their religious meditation, (b) they share profits from the trade, (c) by allowing Jamaicans to create a drug hierarchy, the police don't have to worry about a nation of blacks on the same economic scale uniting; those Jamaicans on the top of the hierarchy keep their thumbs on those on the bottom so there is repression without direct police involvement, and (d) ganja pacifies a great potentially hostile segment of the population.

The Rastafarians are the moral voice in the poor black community, the most influential force in the counterculture. Their origins are with Marcus Garvey and his "Back to Africa" movement in the 1920s and the communal practices of L. P. Howell in the 1930s, who introduced the use of ganja and the wearing of dreadlocks. They consider themselves citizens of Africa— Haile Selassie is their Messiah and Ethiopia is their Promised Land. It is the Rastafarians who evolved the patois to replace the Jamaican English they consider the language of slaves. The most notable characteristic of their patois is that "I" is used instead of the pronoun "me" associated with slavelike docility and objectification. It is also the Rastafarians who have politicized reggae music; the lyrics speak of universal love, the worth of the individual, peace, and an end to exploitation, neocolonialism, imperialism, and authoritarianism. Yet is is the Rastafarians who have kept the music upbeat, optimistic.

The police/government. Those in power in Jamaica are shown to be corrupt, brutal puppets for industrial powers, afraid that they are sitting on a powder keg. They count on the church, liquor, ganja, pinball ma-

chines, pool tables, dominoes, cards, and movies soothing the savage beast under their shaky hand. But it's just
a matter of time before rebellion. Seeing this film makes
one understand why violence was inevitable in 1972 if
Michael Manley's socialist People's National Party
didn't replace the conservative Jamaican Labor Party
which was for free enterprise and allowed foreign investors to exploit Jamaica's labor force and adapt its culture
to suit its own tastes. Also the film shows that there are
so many powerful forces at odds with one another on
the economically troubled island that violence would
break out no matter which party was in power—and it
did in 1980 when unemployment in urban areas reached
60 percent and Manley was forced to call for a new
election. (He lost and the Labor Party returned to
power.)

Outlaw mythology. As in most nations, the outlaw
in Jamaica is a folk hero, a recognizable symbol of
resistance for poor blacks who haven't been politically
indoctrinated but know (both instinctively and from
experience) that there's injustice when people must live
as they do while the men who control the repressive
police live in comfort. Early in the film Ivan is told that
he'd look like Johnny Too Bad if he carried a gun. Later
he picks up the gun and enjoys simultaneous fame as
both a recording star and an outlaw—a double hero.
Cheered on by his worshipers, he comes to believe in his
own invulnerability, that he has become a myth figure.
You hope he gets away but he is destined to die a martyr
(a *political* martyr though he is no longer political),
perhaps needlessly. But as the comforting words in the
theme song go, he'd rather be dead than be a "puppet
or a slave."

A great screen moment: Ivan sings the title song.

Harold and Maude

1971   Paramount
Director: Hal Ashby
Producers: Colin Higgins and Charles B. Mulvehill
Screenplay: Colin Higgins
Cinematography: John Alonzo
Music: Cat Stevens
Editors: William A. Sawyer and Edward Warschilka
Running Time: 90 minutes

Cast: Ruth Gordon (Maude), Bud Cort (Harold), Vivian Pickles
(Mrs. Chasen), Cyril Cusack (sculptor), Charles Tyner (Uncle
Victor), Ellen Geer (Sunshine), Eric Christmas (priest), G. Wood
(psychiatrist), Judy Engles (Candy), Shari Summers (Edith), M.
Borman (motorcycle cop)

Synopsis: Twenty-year-old Harold Chasen is a depressed, friendless
rich boy who lives in a big house with a mother who makes no
attempt to relate to him. He spends much of his time devising
intricate fake suicides—not for his mother's "benefit," as he tells his
psychiatrist, but to aggravate and punish her. She ignores his
antics, attributing them to his absurd sense of humor.

Infatuated with death, Harold drives a hearse and spends
afternoons attending funerals. At two funeral services he meets
Maude, a seventy-nine-year-old woman whose eccentricities are
even more pronounced than his own, though much healthier. Having
few inhibitions, no respect for foolish rules and moral standards,
and a great lust for life, Maude becomes Harold's one friend, telling
him to open himself up to all the opportunities life is presenting him
and to fight for his individuality. She gets him to dance and sing, and
she gives him a banjo.

Harold and Maude spend much time together, and Harold feels
happier and freer. One day they dig up a tree planted in a city
sidewalk, and after eluding police in their "stolen" car and speeding
through toll gates without paying, they return it to the forest. "I like to
watch things grow," says Maude, as they look at the liberated tree.
Maude seems happy with her new friend, but she cries when she
talks of her husband who is long dead. She does not speak of the
concentration camp number on her wrist.

Harold's mother decides her son should be married and arranges
for three computer dates to come for a visit. But Harold scares off
Sunshine, Candy, and Edith by pretending to immolate himself,
chop off his hand, and commit hara-kiri. Fed up with her son's lack
of discipline, Harold's mother decides that he should be enlisted into
the army by Uncle Victor, a career officer with a sadistic streak. But
with Maude's help—she pretends to drown when Harold chases her
with a shrunken head—Harold convinces Uncle Victor that he is *too*
bloodthirsty and insane to be in the army.

Harold and Maude reveal their love for one another and sleep
together. Harold tells his mother that he will marry Maude. Uncle
Victor, his psychiatrist, and his priest try to talk him out of the
relationship.

Harold helps Maude celebrate her eightieth birthday. Just before
he can propose, Maude tells Harold that she has taken poison—that
eighty is a good time to end one's life. Greatly upset, Harold drives
the woman he loves to the hospital. In the morning, she dies.
Tearfully, Harold drives his hearse over a cliff—but gets out in time.
Playing his banjo, Harold dances up a hill.

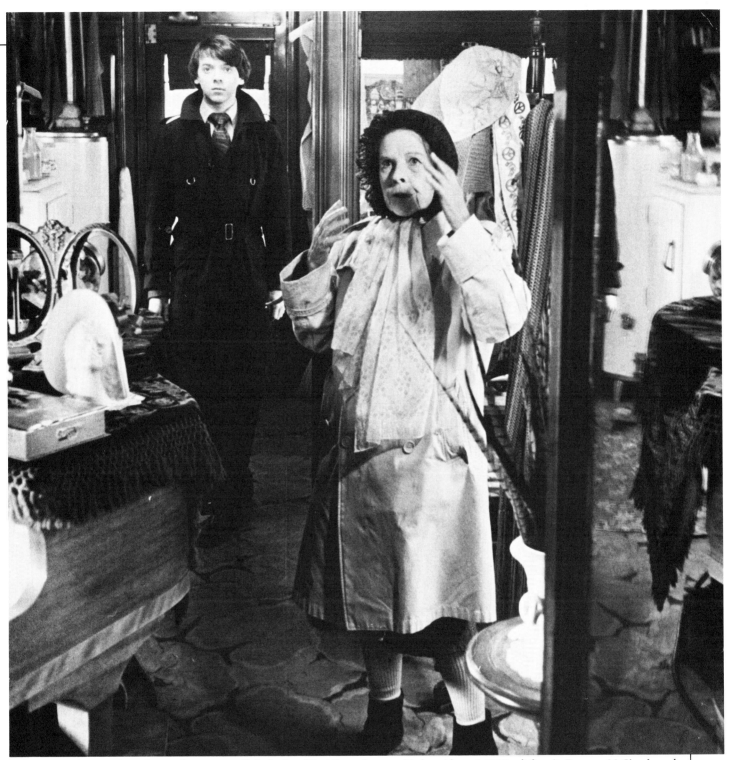

Inspired casting brought together young, tall, baby-faced Bud Cort, the star of Robert Altman's 1970 cult favorite Brewster McCloud, *and elderly dynamo Ruth Gordon, fresh from* Where's Poppa?, *another cult hit from 1970. At times Cort underplays his part; as often Gordon overacts. However, there is an odd, sweet chemistry between the two that makes the relationship of Harold and Maude special. Gordon is particularly effective at letting us glimpse sadness beneath the smiles.*

One of the runaway cult favorites of the seventies, *Harold and Maude* became a cause célèbre among college-age moviegoers throughout the United States and Canada, breaking longevity records in cities like Detroit, Montreal, and, most memorably, Minneapolis, where residents actually picketed the Westgate Theater trying to get management to replace the picture after a consecutive three-year run. Today the film is still going strong, packing repertory theaters, where it is often billed with *King of Hearts* (1967) or a second Hal Ashby film, and also doing exceptional business when Paramount periodically reissues it and books it into first-run theaters. Yet, as has been the case with many cult films, in 1971 Paramount

Harold's fake suicides highlight the film. (L-R) Mrs. Chasen swims past Harold who pretends that he has drowned in their pool; one of Harold's computer dates sees Harold pour gasoline all over himself; another date watches Harold thrust a dagger into his stomach—impressed, she will also fake a suicide with a knife; in front of his mother, Harold points a blank-filled gun at his head.

didn't anticipate *Harold and Maude's* phenomenal success; in fact, it feared that its little black comedy about the love affair between an eighty-year-old woman and a twenty-year-old manchild would repulse an entire nation of moviegoers. When a pre-release review in the influential *Variety*—"*Harold and Maude* has all the fun and gaiety of a burning orphanage," wrote Art Murphy—questioned the film's box office potential, Paramount was further convinced to just dump it into general release. Although the film failed as expected in most places—despite some scattered rave reviews—it became, after a brief time, an astronomical success in many college towns, with some viewers seeing it up to one hundred and fifty times. Consequently, the suddenly excited Paramount re-released the film—this time with a strong ad campaign aimed at the youth market—and *Harold and Maude* took off, its cult growing to mammoth proportions from coast to coast.

Harold and Maude holds up surprisingly well today, having perhaps even improved with time, whereas *King of Hearts*, a film with a similar cult history (its major success coming in Cambridge, Massachusetts), dates badly. Adapted by Colin Higgins from a twenty-minute film he made while a student at UCLA, *Harold and Maude* contains the self-gratuitous indulgences, puerile moments (the scenes with policemen), and caricatures (when there should be fully developed characters) that one has learned to expect in the script of a *young* first-time screenwriter (Higgins) and the film of a fairly *young* second-time director (Ashby); but there is a lilting, uplifting quality to this film, a spark, a breeziness, a spirit, a wonderful sense of successful rebellion that more than compensates for any shortcomings, pretentions, and misdirected flights of fancy.

While *Harold and Maude* is at best only intermittently funny, there are some brilliant comic moments, like when Harold announces to his mother that he is engaged and without forewarning her shows her eighty-year-old Maude's picture; or when Harold's mother fills out a questionnaire for Harold, stating that her son enjoyed his life as a child, while in response to her answers he points a pistol at her, then turns it on himself and fires. Harold's fake suicides come off particularly well, except for the swimming pool scene, which wrongly begins with an establishing shot of the entire pool. (Ashby shouldn't allow us to see the fully dressed Harold lying face down in the water until his mother nonchalantly swims past him and does her double take.) The other suicides are set up better and are more elaborate, usually ending with his mother saying something like "I suppose you think that's very funny, Harold." My favorite of these scenes is the one in which the robed Harold pours gasoline on himself while sitting in the garden, and his computer date inside the house watches him burst into flames. As the terrified girl jumps up, calling "Harold!" and looking at the ball of fire outside, Harold, in a suit, casually walks in behind her. As the now hysterical girl runs off, Harold gleefully turns to the camera, and only wipes off his self-satisfied, devilish grin when he realizes his mother, who is staring at her impossible child, doesn't think him as clever as he does himself. This is one of many revealing reaction shots between mother and child in which Harold must turn to *us* to express himself; when he is with Maude, he can react directly toward her and be understood.

Harold lives in a shell when he's with his mother: he is not forward enough to tell her not to choreograph his life—preferring instead to release his inner hostilities

toward her by inventively sabotaging her handiwork *after* she has gone through a great deal of trouble. With Maude, Harold opens up completely, verbally expressing his love, putting his arms around her, kissing her on the lips, and making love to her. (However, that all sexual activity takes place off screen is a valid source of criticism.)

Harold's mother is one of several characters in the film who represent society's repressive forces bent on making oddballs like Harold conform. Uncle Victor, who has portraits of Richard Nixon and Nathan "I regret I have but one life to give for my country" Hale on his wall, once was MacArthur's right-hand man, and coincidentally is missing his right hand. He teaches Harold racism, machoism, and jingoism. Harold's priest, who sits under a portrait of the Pope, teaches Harold morals, pointing out that the thought of Harold having intercourse with Maude "makes me want to vomit." Harold's psychiatrist, who has a portrait of Freud, wears the same clothes as Harold, "implying," as Beverle Huston and Marsha Kinder suggested in the short-lived *Women and Film,* "the power of therapy to create replicas." It is while feeling pressured by his mother, Victor, the priest, and the psychiatrist that Harold tells Maude that if he were a flower he'd want to be the dullest around, one like all the rest. Maude, being the renegade that she is, will not let Harold speak such nonsense. She tells him people are different, and, with seriousness evident on her face, stresses that people should be treated as individuals.

For Harold, Maude is a liberating force, the only thing in the world that keeps him from conforming. In Ashby's films there is usually such a character whose idealistic philosophical outlook is instrumental in getting other characters to drastically alter their previously limited, useless, conformist existences. Ruth Gordon's

Maude serves as a role model in the same way that some of Ashby's other characters do: Jack Nicholson in *The Last Detail* (1973), David Carradine (as Woody Guthrie) in *Bound for Glory* (1976), Jon Voight in *Coming Home* (1978), and Peter Sellers in *Being There* (1979). She tells Harold simple things: not to back away from life, to be an individual, to experiment, to take chances, to sing and dance, to play music. It is her optimistic nature, and her enjoyment of life to the fullest, that give her words meaning. "In the old fantasy," writes Huston and Kinder, "it is the fatherly man who offers stability and protection to a child-like woman. . . . Maude offers the stability of emotional engagement and full participation in life—the only stability present in the world of this film."

Maude reminds film historians Huston and Kinder of a fairy godmother. I think the fairy tale analogy is quite appropriate. The relationship between Harold and Maude makes me think of Val Lewton's *Curse of the Cat People* (1944), not a horror film as the title suggests, but a lovely fantasy (suggested by a Stevenson poem) originally titled *Aimée and Her Friend.* It is about a friendless, lonely little girl whose parents don't attempt to understand her need to fantasize. Seeking a friend, Aimée conjures up an invisible playmate, many years older than herself (Simone Simon). In the Lewton film, the playmate stays with the girl only until she is able to make it on her own—when her father offers to be her friend and give her support instead of lectures; in *Harold and Maude,* Maude leaves Harold when she, who professed to "like to see things grow," realizes that Harold has *grown* to be self-sufficient and no longer has a death wish. It would make perfect sense at this point if Maude turned out to be a figment of lonely Harold's imagination (or maybe the ghost of the "true" Maude who was a Nazi death camp victim). Unfortunately,

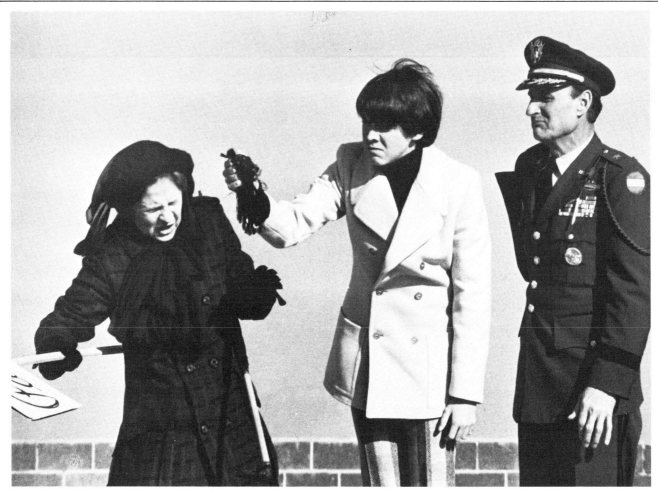

In a plot to keep Harold out of the army, Harold pretends to scare Maude with a shrunken head while Uncle Victor looks on, unaware that Harold and Maude know each other.

being a real person, Maude commits suicide—an unsatisfying, overly sentimental end for a film that has been purporting to be a celebration of life.

But I suppose Maude's suicide makes sense. Throughout the film we have witnessed moments where Maude cannot hide her inner misery. Whereas Harold's scenes with his mother are played almost entirely for laughs, there are scenes between him and Maude that catch you off guard because of their seriousness, that even manage to strike an emotional chord. It is during these tender, intimate scenes, happy scenes, that Maude cries while thinking of her long-dead husband; that we discover a concentration camp number on Maude's wrist, and surmise what happened to her husband—and also grasp Maude's heroic nature for the first time. That Maude is so outrageously optimistic most of the time makes these sad moments especially powerful, for we know that Maude's past must have been horribly painful for it to so affect this woman of indomitable spirit. (Ashby handles these scenes splendidly, never intruding upon Maude's privacy or exploiting her heartbreak.) From these glimpses into the tragic side of Maude, I would suspect that she wanted to die many years earlier—when her husband died, presumably in the death camps—but made a pact with herself to continue living and be a human monument to those who died in the camps and give meaning to a life (her own) that survived the Holocaust.

Harold and Maude is a film about death and resurrection, where death and life continuously overlap. (Maude considers death part of the life cycle.) The friendship of Harold and Maude begins in cemeteries and at funerals. They make love in Maude's antique-filled home, once a railroad car. Harold gets his hearse from a dead-car lot; when his mother gives him a brand-new car, he converts it into a hearse. When he sends his self-made hearse over a cliff, it symbolizes that his suicidal urges are over and he is a new person ready to mingle with life. Maude, of course, came out of a *death* camp to become, as Teena Webb writes, "a Life Goddess: externally young, wise, self-sufficient, and attuned to nature." But because of her tragic past part of Maude is still dead. When the last of life's energies seep out of Maude, they are transferred to Harold. Harold, once through mourning Maude's passing, walks over a hill playing the banjo Maude gave him, with Cat Stevens's great cheery theme song on the soundtrack: the manchild, determined never to conform, has blossomed into a man—wanting very much to live as Maude taught him.

The Honeymoon Killers

1970 Cinerama Releasing Corporation release of a Roxanne Production
Director: Leonard Kastle
Producer: Warren Steibel

Screenplay: Leonard Kastle
Cinematography: Oliver Wood
Music: Gustav Mahler
Editor: Stan Warnow
Running Time: 108 Minutes

Cast: Shirley Stoler (Martha Beck), Tony LoBianco (Ray Fernandez), Dortha Duckworth (Mrs. Beck), Doris Roberts (Bunny), Marilyn Chris (Myrtle Young), Mary Jane Higbee (Janet Fay), Kip McArdle (Delphine Downing), Mary Breen (Rainelle Downing), Barbara Cason (Evelyn Long), Ann Harris (Doris Acker), Guy Sorel (Mr. Dranoss)

Synopsis: Martha Beck, a two-hundred-pound head nurse at a Mobile, Alabama, hospital, lives a lonely life with her senile mother. Her friend Bunny convinces Martha to join a correspondence friendship club, and soon she is receiving torrid love letters from Ray Fernandez, a Spanish-born immigrant living in New York.

Ray visits Martha, who immediately falls deeply in love with him and thinks nothing of giving him some of her money. When Ray goes back to New York, the heartbroken, sex-starved Martha devises a plan whereby Ray ends up inviting her to come to New York. When she arrives, Ray confesses to being a gigolo who makes a living swindling lonely women he meets through lonely hearts' clubs. Rather than lose him, Martha says she will help him in his "profession," posing as his sister when he courts other women. Martha, fired from her job after her supervisor read Ray's letters to her, tells everyone that she and Ray have secretly married, places her tearful mother in a nursing home, and begins her life with Ray. Ray marries a Morristown, New Jersey, schoolteacher named Doris Acker. He and Martha steal her money and jewelry and head for Arkansas; there Ray marries pregnant Myrtle Young, who has agreed to pay him four thousand dollars for legitimizing her baby. When Myrtle tries to seduce Ray, jealous Martha gives her a lethal dose of sleeping pills. The next day Ray puts the dying Myrtle on a bus, and he and Martha drive off in Myrtle's car toward the Berkshire Hills in Massachusetts, where hearts' club correspondent Evelyn Long awaits Ray's arrival. When Ray pays too much attention to Evelyn, Martha is so upset she tries to drown herself. Ray saves her and swears that from that day forward he will be faithful to her.

Ray and Martha buy a home in Valley Stream, Long Island, and this is where they bring sixty-year-old Janet Fay, Ray's next wife. That first night Janet becomes suspicious of the couple's strange attachment for one another and their interest in her life savings. She threatens to call her children to let them know what is going on. At Ray's urging, Martha bludgeons her with a hammer, and he finishes her off by strangling her. After making love, they bury Janet in the basement.

Ray and Martha next go to Grand Rapids, Michigan, where Ray has promised to marry a patriotic widow named Delphine Downing and to become father to her young daughter Rainelle. Weeks pass by. When Delphine tells Martha that Ray has slept with her, the upset Martha feeds her some pills, putting her into a daze. When Ray returns, he shoots Delphine, who now knows too much, and Martha drowns Rainelle in the washing machine.

Realizing that Ray will never be true to her, Martha calls the police and they are arrested. In prison, awaiting trial for murder, Ray and Martha once again send love letters back and forth.

A lurid publicity shot that doesn't hint at the quality of the picture. Tony LoBianco holds Shirley Stoler.

Termed a "sleeper" when it was released in 1970, *The Honeymoon Killers* has never achieved the "classic" status many critics predicted for it back then. No doubt it is too sleazy, violent, low-brow, and crudely made to ever be accepted as a masterpiece by the average moviegoer, but there is little wonder why it has garnered a strong cult following. It is a chilling reenactment of the harrowing "Lonely Hearts (Club) Murders" which made headlines coast-to-coast during the late forties. It is also a fascinating, semi-comical examination of the true-life delirious romance between an ill-tempered, sexually frustrated two-hundred-pound ex-nurse named Martha Beck and her speciously charming and handsome, but not so smart, Spanish lover, gigolo Ray Fernandez: mercenary murderers whose amoral behavior went hand in hand with their mutual sexual attraction. It's the type of lurid tale that one finds in *True Detective* or *The Police Gazette*, but isn't likely to turn up on the screen. In fact, the

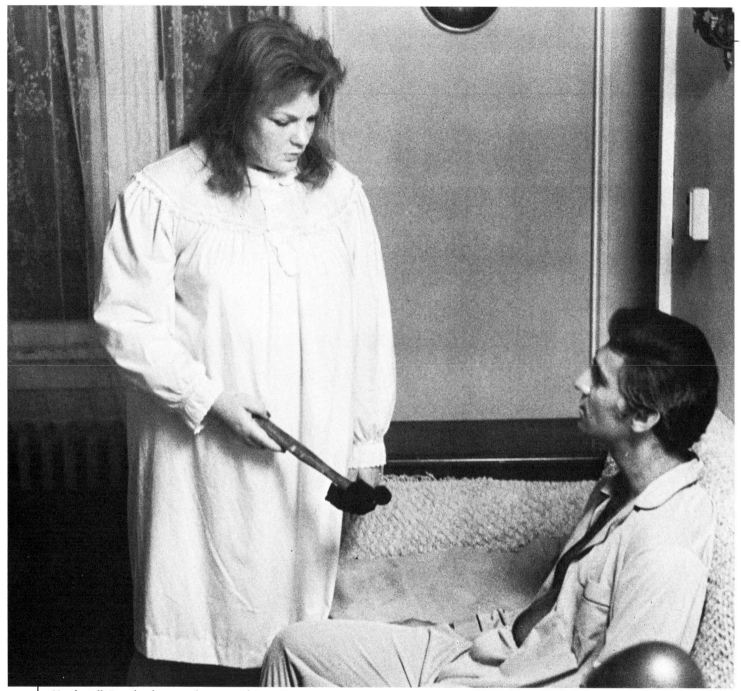

Martha tells Ray that he must do away with Janet Fay.

finished, independently financed picture was rejected sight unseen by all distributors until a rave in *Variety* convinced Cinerama Releasing to pick it up.

"It's such a terrible movie, I wouldn't recommend it to anyone," wrote Pauline Kael, usually the first major critic to discover a gem among the junk—but not this time. Luckily, her colleagues didn't agree with her (I am still amazed by how well mainstream critics received *The Honeymoon Killers*); and they did recommend it to *everyone*, helping it earn back its $200,000 in production costs in less than five days. These critics had much to cheer about in a dismal movie year, for here was a strangely captivating, cleverly scripted B-movie-like thriller full of odd yet interesting characters, all wonderfully acted; a black comedy—despite its subject matter,

there is a great deal of humor—that probes America's pathetic "lonely hearts"/gigolos subculture; and one of the few "criminal couple on the run" movies that neither romanticizes the crimes committed nor glamorizes the criminals.

Although Cinerama promoted *The Honeymoon Killers* as an exploitation movie, it was always the intention of director Leonard Kastle to make an "art" film. As the working title "Dear Martha"—which is how Ray begins his love letters to Martha—indicates, Kastle was more interested in Ray and Martha's bizarre relationship, which thrived because of the murders they committed, than on the murders themselves. An opera composer by profession, Kastle, not doing anything at the time, accepted an offer from a friend, producer

Warren Steibel, to research the Beck-Fernandez murder spree and to write a screenplay; when the director Steibel hired didn't work out, Kastle replaced him. Considering what a remarkable debut film *The Honeymoon Killers* is, it's startling that *nothing* more ever came from Kastle. (The last I heard of Kastle was in the early seventies, when he and Steibel were working on a movie about the Mafia's infiltration of the Catholic Church.)

In *The Honeymoon Killers* Kastle's lack of directorial experience is quite noticeable. There's shadowy lighting, microphones in the picture, grainy photography, and choppy editing that at times makes the story line nonsensical. But, inadvertently, because the film looks so unpolished by Hollywood standards—the small budget having dictated that retakes be kept to a minimum—it attains the realistic "documentary" look that Kastle was striving for. The stark black-and-white photography, on-location shooting in towns like Albany, New York, and Pittsfield, Massachusetts, the use of ready-made sets, and a cast of unknowns (as of 1970) also contribute to this end.

Though an amateur in moviemaking, Kastle exhibits much directorial flare. His handling of actors is truly outstanding, and this doesn't only pertain to his fine work with stars Shirley Stoler and Tony LoBianco, whose roles are strong to begin with. Significantly, his supporting actresses were given free reign to create very broad characters so their brief screen appearances could have greater impact than they normally would. As a result, in one American film, there are *several* powerful performances from actresses. Other directors probably would have kept these women low-keyed and as background characters one forgets as soon as their scenes are over. Equally noteworthy is Kastle's use of excerpts from the works of Gustav Mahler, thus accentuating the dramatic tension with music, much in the manner of Welles, Truffaut, and Chabrol. At times he will play overly "dramatic" soundtrack music outrageously loud to counterpoint the triviality of what is happening in the picture—for example, when the music blares as Martha swaggers down the street after having told off a nurse and an orderly for smooching in the hospital. More often the music is suspenseful or downright spooky, as when Martha sees Myrtle trying to seduce Ray and contemplates doing her in.

But it isn't only Kastle's use of music that once caused François Truffaut to hail *The Honeymoon Killers* as his favorite American film. For one thing, Kastle's impressive, properly motivated use of his camera is at times similar to Truffaut's. Like Truffaut, he uses tracking shots and pans to search for his characters, and in the process makes the viewer aware of the settings and the spatial relationships between the characters. One scene begins with a long shot of Delphine Downing spouting some nonsense about Abraham Lincoln's birthday (and why they will hold a party in his honor) to her daughter Rainelle. It is the first time we see the Downings, and throughout Delphine's long, foolish, intimate discourse about Lincoln, we are led to believe that she and her daughter are alone—when suddenly the long-stationary

In the film's grisliest scene, Janet Fay crawls across the floor, pleading with Ray not to kill her with a hammer. The real Martha Beck and Ray Fernandez were executed for killing Janet Fay.

camera pans to the other side of the living room where we discover Ray and Martha silently sitting on the couch.

At other times the camera remains stationary, as if it were a piece of furniture in a room. This is reminiscent of Truffaut's *Jules and Jim* (1961), when the characters pivot around a static camera in Catherine's living room, and often leave the frame, though they continue to say their lines and do bits of business required by the script. One always senses that something is happening off screen. The camera will remain on Martha and Ray in the hall, while they and we hear Doris singing and bathing in the bathroom; on Martha while she and we hear Myrtle trying to seduce Ray in the next room; or on Delphine's face while she and we hear Martha and Ray prepare to kill the semiconscious woman. It's always as if Kastle's frame has been extended and the actors who left the frame are still performing rather than being on their coffee break.

A sense of claustrophobia is meant to dominate the film. Kastle accomplishes this by placing his characters together indoors (or in cars) in small, restrictive spaces, where at least one character—usually Martha alone or Martha and one of the loud-mouthed women Ray is bilking—yaps and complains incessantly. In such an irritable environment, the worst qualities of all the individuals come out, they all get on each other's nerves and start snapping at one another. Much of the film's humor comes from watching the harassed Ray constantly trying to keep the jealous Martha, who is posing as his sister, from arguing with the women he is to marry, or has married, to such an extent that they will walk out before he can secure their money. These women never enjoy a moment's privacy with Ray; Kastle places them with Ray in a small room which would be an intimate setting except that he tosses the obese Martha in the room with them. It's almost like the crowded stateroom scene in *A Night at the Opera* (1935). Even at night, these women must share their beds and bedrooms, not with Ray but with Martha. It's no wonder that they become aggravated and start acting obnoxious. Unfortunately, it is because of their bad attitude, especially toward Martha, and not for their money that they are killed. Interestingly, the only woman Kastle places in an unclaustrophobic outdoor setting is Evelyn, who is the one genuinely nice, sympathetic person Ray and Martha come into contact with—and she is the only woman who escapes without the loss of her money or her life. All the other women are as useless, overbearing, fossilized, penurious, and unlovable as Chaplin's victims in *Monsieur Verdoux* (1947). Kastle wanted to get away from "presenting these wrongly harmed women as being overly virtuous."

Although none of the victims are like the "overly virtuous" Olivia de Havilland of *Hold Back the Dawn* (1941), Tony LoBianco, as Ray, does a splendid characterization of a sleazy, slimy Charles Boyer, who played the gigolo in that picture. His seduction of Martha is masterly: he does a hip-swinging rhumba in front of Martha's drugged mother, and when she falls asleep, dances over to Martha, takes her hand and places it over his fly while he continues to sway, coolly saying, "Don't be a shy nurse," with the voice intonation of a Spanish penny-ante confidence man. LoBianco is always amusing, whether complaining about having to live in Valley Stream, Long Island, or telling Martha straight-faced that he will not allow her to return to nursing because he doesn't want to live off a woman, or, after having offended Doris by referring to her as a spinster, covering up his faux pas by asking innocently, "Doesn't 'spinster' mean maaaiden?" He's just great.

Shirley Stoler, who would make another strong impression as a Nazi commandant in Lina Wertmuller's *Seven Beauties* (1976), is also fine as Martha Beck, a woman she greatly resembles. Her Martha is a cross between Divine, the Big Nurse, and an angry Godfrey Cambridge. She is strong when dishing out violence but turns to mush when Ray is untrue to her. It's totally believable that her Martha would attempt suicide if Ray rejected her, kill Janet Fay when he proves too weak to do it himself, and turn herself and Ray into the police when she realizes Ray can't be faithful to her. Martha is an awful person, but even so, we can empathize with her for being an unattractive woman who finally is loved by a handsome man and doesn't want to give him up. That is why we are moved when, at the film's conclusion, just *before* Martha is taken to the courthouse for trial, she receives a letter from Ray which swears his everlasting love. This couple has committed heinous crimes, but we must admire their deep love for one another; as Kastle said, "That was their one redeeming virtue."

Following a lengthy trial, the real Ray Fernandez and Martha Beck spent eighteen months in prison awaiting execution, having been convicted of murdering Janet Fay. As a last-ditch effort to save her lover from death, Martha offered to donate her body to science. She was turned down. The double execution took place as planned, in Sing Sing on March 7, 1951.

House of Wax

1953 Warner Bros.
Director: Andre de Toth
Producer: Byran Foy
Screenplay: Crane Wilbur
From a story by Charles Belden

Cinematography: Bert Glennon
Music: David Buttolph
Editor: Rudi Fehr
Running Time: 88 minutes

Cast: Vincent Price (Professor Henry Jarrod), Phyllis Kirk (Sue Allen), Frank Lovejoy (Lieutenant Tom Brennan), Paul Picerni (Scott Andrews), Carolyn Jones (Cathy Gray), Paul Cavanagh (Sidney Wallace), Roy Roberts (Matthew Burke), Dabbs Greer (Sergeant Jim Shane), Charles Buchinsky* (Igor), Angela Clarke (Mrs. Andrews), Ned Young (Leon Averill), Richard Benjamin (detective), Frank Ferguson (medical examiner), Reggie Rymal (barker)

Synopsis: In New York, in 1902, Professor Henry Jarrod, a master sculptor, runs a wax museum. His figures reveal his great love of beauty. His partner Matthew Burke wants him to create waxworks with macabre themes so they can make a profit on their enterprise, but he refuses. Art critic Sidney Wallace agrees to buy Burke out in three months, but Burke doesn't want to wait that long. To get $25,000 in insurance, he sets fire to the studio, destroying all the wax figures that Jarrod considered "his people," and leaving Jarrod for dead in the burning building. On the day Burke receives the money he agrees to marry flirtatious Cathy Gray, but at his office he is strangled by the horribly burned Jarrod, wearing a black cape, hat, and gloves.

Not too upset by Burke's death, Cathy tells her smart best friend, Sue Allen, who lives in the same boarding house, that she has a date with another man already. That night Sue goes into Cathy's room and finds she has been strangled, and her killer—a disfigured man dressed in black—is still in the room. He tries to kill Sue, but she escapes to the house of her boyfriend, Scott Andrews. That night, Jarrod steals Cathy's body from the morgue. Police officers Tom Brennan and Jim Shane note that the bodies of Matthew Burke and Patterson, an attorney, have also disappeared.

With money from Sidney Wallace, Jarrod opens up a wax museum that has a laboratory in the basement. As he is confined to a wheelchair and his hands have been burned beyond repair, two employees do his sculpting: Leon, an alcoholic, and Igor, a muscular mute. Jarrod says that he can no longer create beauty, and that explains why his new figures are arranged in violent tableaux.

Sue and Scott come to the House of Wax's grand opening. Sue is stunned to see how much Jarrod's Joan of Arc wax figure looks like Cathy. Jarrod convinces her that it is just a good reproduction of a face whose picture he saw in the newspaper. Jarrod offers a job to Scott, a striving sculptor, and gets Sue to agree to pose for his masterpiece, Marie Antoinette.

Spurred on by the still suspicious Sue, Brennan and Shane investigate Jarrod. They notice that the Edwin Booth wax figure looks much like Patterson. They question Leon, who they realize is an ex-con who has broken parole. When they find Patterson's watch in Leon's possession, they arrest him. They get him to admit that Jarrod has been murdering people and turning them into wax figures.

Sue comes to the wax museum after closing time to meet Scott, but Scott has been sent on an errand by Jarrod. She looks at the Joan of Arc wax figure and when she removes its wig discovers the real, blond Cathy underneath. Jarrod, no longer pretending to be crippled, appears and prevents her from leaving. She beats him on the chest, and his wax mask breaks. When she sees his disfigured face—the face of the man she saw in Cathy's room—she faints. Jarrod takes her to his laboratory and straps her beneath a giant cauldron full of hot wax. Just in time, Scott and the police arrive, Jarrod falls into the boiling wax, and as the liquid pours out, Brennan pulls Sue to safety.

*Charles Bronson

A 1953 publicity shot for House of Wax *featured stars Vincent Price, Phyllis Kirk, and Frank Lovejoy showcasing 3-D paraphernalia.*

In the early fifties, film studios panicked because television was cutting into their profits. To lure back its lost audience, they came up with 3-D, a process which added depth to the screen image and could not be duplicated on television. For about a year and a half, moviegoers flocked to theaters to see images that appeared to come right into the audience, and many producers believed 3-D (along with Cinema-Scope and Cinerama) was a permanent answer to their financial problems. But the 3-D craze quickly petered out, and 3-D films were considered box office poison. This is unfortunate, because filmmakers since then have been reluctant to give it another chance. (Perhaps the great increase in the number of uncut movies being made available to homebodies through video cassettes and pay television will convince filmmakers of the near future to revive 3-D.)

Some of those early 3-D films were quite entertaining and justified the stereoscopic process as an alternative cinema form. But you never would have known this by reading fifties' critics. They just couldn't take seriously films that required entire theater audiences to wear plastic green Polaroid glasses in cardboard frames. Those glasses cost ten cents and caused terrible headaches, not only because they were so dark that we wanted every screen character to carry a flashlight, but also because the glasses often couldn't eliminate the blurry double-vision effect caused by faulty camera-work (each scene was filmed simultaneously from two almost identical angles) or faulty projection (the two versions were projected simultaneously by two inter-locking projectors run by studio representatives). But audiences liked those glasses and kept them for souvenirs. And they truly enjoyed the films, no matter if they were bad, blurry, or boring. Years after the 3-D craze ended I still recall those films fondly, especially *House of Wax*, the most popular and commercially successful film that ever used the three-dimensional process.

House of Wax is by no means a great film, but even in the flat two-dimensional version shown on television it is great fun. I think one of the reasons the picture never got its due is because critics considered it inferior to Michael Curtiz's *Mystery of the Wax Museum* (1933), the film on which it was based. Unfortunately, for several decades the earlier picture was thought to be irretrievably lost, and 1950s critics assumed that it was a horror classic solely from what they had read—often material written by other critics who hadn't seen the picture since its release. The surprising discovery of a print of *Mystery of the Wax Museum* in the sixties embarrassed many film historians because the much-heralded film proved to be anything but extraordinary (except perhaps in its then experimental use of two-color Technicolor). There is some fine, moody photography

The spectacular burning of Jarrod's wax figures, particularly his beloved Marie Antoinette, gives Vincent Price a chance to ham it up.

in the Curtiz film, a solid performance from the venerable Lionell Atwill as the insane sculptor, and a chilling climax in which Fay Wray unmasks the disfigured Atwill and after a pregnant pause lets out a blood-curdling scream (in the remake Sue simply faints dead away). But the 1953 version, directed stylishly by Andre de Toth (ironically a one-eyed director who made a 3-D film) does not pale in comparison.

Vincent Price, starring in his first horror film, is not as good an actor as Atwill was, but he has more stature and better establishes a character—a man who is already a bit loony at the beginning (as is clear when he converses with his wax figures)—who would become a homicidal maniac when his life's work is destroyed and his hands are so crippled that he can never work again.

Of course, Price is a hammy actor and as always his overacting adds to the levity of the proceedings. In this case, it benefits the picture because he helps set up the proper atmosphere for the many comical inserts. (My favorite sight gag is when giddy young female visitors to Jarrod's Chamber of Horrors try to get a good look at the nude Marat wax figure in his bath.) On the other hand, the great quantity of humor in the Curtiz film seems out of whack with the somber atmosphere created by Atwill's no-nonsense performance.

House of Wax also has its share of exciting moments that compare favorably to those found in the 1933 film. The scene in which Sue discovers the ghoulish Jarrod in dead Cathy's room and is then chased by him through the dark, deserted streets is quite scary. So is the nocturnal scene in which Jarrod swings by a rope into the sleeping Sue's room; when she awakens and sits up, his shadow is cast on the wall behind her—a shot worthy of Curtiz, who used shadows as well as any director. Of course, the highlight of the film must be the early sequence when fire sweeps through Jarrod's studio and the wax figures melt. There is something both eerie and hypnotic about watching these figures in the fire: even when their eyes and cheeks start melting and we sadly imagine the figures to be in great pain, their expressions do not change, their smiles do not go away. This scene in the original is also chilling, but if *House of Wax* has an advantage over its predecessor, it is that 3-D makes such images more powerful by bringing them up close.

In *Bwana Devil* (1952), the first 3-D film, lions and other wild animals seemed to leap into our laps; in *Sign of the Pagan* (1954) it was charging horses that seemed to jump over our heads; in *It Came From Outer Space* (1953), a fiery meteor seemed to burst from the screen and zoom directly toward our seats. These are all powerful images, but the 3-D image that stayed with me longest after 3-D was outmoded is found in *House of Wax*. And it is not an image of one of the many props (chairs, weapons, bodies) that characters hurl our way to scare us, but of two little rubber balls attached to paddles with elastics that the barker in front of Jarrod's wax museum hits repeatedly toward the camera. The

3-D effect makes the balls seem to shoot from the screen toward our noses—crossing our eyes—return into the screen to the paddles and, hit again, come shooting back toward our noses once more. An acquaintance also remembers this image because it caused her right eye to turn in—not until after six months of wearing an eye patch did her eye muscles mend. But even if it was harmful to our eyes, it is evidence of the imagination put into the 3-D effects in *House of Wax*. And it also shows that those behind *House of Wax* were not embarrassed to admit that 3-D was a gimmick that they wanted to exploit to its fullest. Other filmmakers were reluctant to include effects that had nothing to do with the story, but de Toth was as interested in spectacle as plot. So, for instance, he felt no qualms about having Sue and Scott go to a café for no reason other than to show what 3-D can do with high-kicking can-can dancers.

This scene, where legs shoot out from the screen and we sneak glimpses under their dresses—de Toth's camera is located below the dancers to encourage us—goes on for some time and it is quite titillating. This is one of many times in the picture that the emphasis is on *sex* (which also could not be seen on television in 1953) rather than horror. Early on we see the shapely Cathy putting on a tight corset; at the end, the tied-up nude Sue lies under Jarrod's boiling wax (a classic "bondage" sequence). De Toth was probably the first to realize that the secret to good 3-D is a story having both horror and

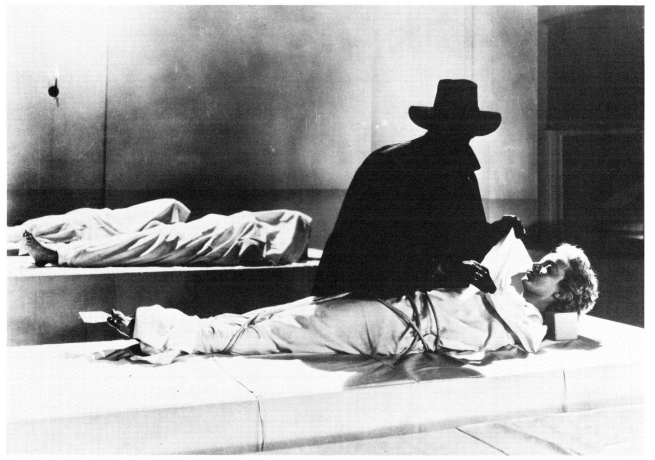

In his ghoul outfit, Jarrod abducts Cathy's corpse from the morgue.

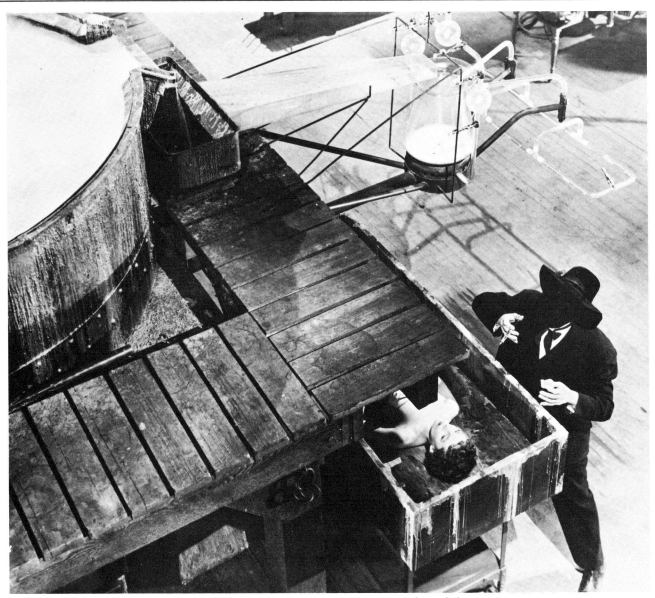

In the climactic scene in the film, Jarrod, in his lab outfit, tries to pour boiling wax on the nude but still-living Sue. In this publicity shot, Vincent Price wears Jarrod's ghoul costume.

sex—the elements 3-D certainly does the most justice to. As William Paul wrote in *The Village Voice* in the early seventies:

> This sense of things emerging from the screen has always been the most exploitable aspect of stereoscopy; it is the one element that ads for 3-D have always stressed the most. And it is this element which makes the process so suited to horror and pornography because it creates a kind of physical environment that plays on the passive—defenseless—nature of the audience.

More skillfully than any other 3-D film, *House of Wax* combines these elements. As the barker describes Jarrod's wax museum, *House of Wax* is full of "thrills, chills, and laughter." Plus sex.

A recent 3-D series at the 8th Street Playhouse in New York was cause for excitement because it featured the long-awaited 3-D print of Alfred Hitchcock's *Dial "M" for Murder* (1954) which until then had been commercially released only in a flat version. (The 3-D print had been shelved with the sudden demise of the 3-D craze.) But the Hitchcock film didn't live up to expectations. Unfortunately, Hitchcock proved too conservative in his use of the effect, probably because he didn't want to diminish the power of 3-D in the crucial scene in which Ray Milland's hired killer falls victim to Grace Kelly's pair of scissors. In this scene, Kelly, being strangled at the time, takes a long pair of scissors she finds on the desk, points them toward us, then stabs him in the back. The scissors protrude from his back, but with our new perspective we unfortunately realize that the scissors are actually as blunt as a pair of children's paper cutters. So once again, *House of Wax*, which was also shown in the series, emerged as the cream of the 3-D crop.

I Married a Monster from Outer Space

1958 Paramount
Director: Gene Fowler, Jr.
Producer: Gene Fowler, Jr.
Screenplay: Louis Vittes
Cinematography: Haskell Boggs
Special Effects: John P. Fulton
Editor: George Tomasini
Running Time: 78 minutes

Cast: Tom Tryon (Bill Farrell), Gloria Talbott (Marge Farrell), Ken Lynch (Dr. Wayne), John Eldredge (Collins), Valerie Allen (Francine), Alan Dexter (Sam Benson), Jean Carson (Helen), Maxie Rosenbloom (Grady), Peter Baldwin (Swanson)

Synopsis: Driving home from his bachelor party, Bill Farrell stops his car when he sees a body in the road. Getting out, he is startled to see a hideous space creature standing in front of him. Bill is engulfed by a vapor and his body disappears. "Bill," a creature in Bill's body, shows up at the wedding ceremony and marries Marge, who immediately notices his strange, cold behavior.

A year passes. During this time other men in town begin acting as strangely as Bill, without emotions of any kind. Many nights the men gather at a bar to have private conversations but don't taste their drinks—they are allergic to alcohol. They are waiting for their scientists' reports on chromosome alterations before they can mate with the earth women, their mission on earth. Following several strange occurances, suspicious Marge follows "Bill" into the woods late at night. She sees an alien creature leave Bill's body and enter a space ship. She now realizes that there is an invasion going on and that Bill has indeed been taken over.

Marge tries to contact Washington, but the operator tells her all lines are busy. When she tries to leave town, she is stopped by a police roadblock. Aliens in policemen's bodies tell her that a bridge has been washed out. She knows that they are lying. She tells her godfather, Police Chief Collins, what she has discovered—but he too has been replaced by an alien.

Marge tells "Bill" all she knows. He calmly explains that his planet, Andromeda, had lost all its women. The men from Andromeda had come to earth to propagate with the earth women. Their children would be creatures like him and eventually would conquer the world. As a last hope, Marge goes to see Dr. Wayne. He believes her story. He tells her that he will enlist the help of all men in town who have recently become fathers—evidence that they are not counterfeits.

Wayne and several men enter the woods where the spaceship is hidden. Several creatures come out of the ship. The men fire on them but their bullets have no effect. When several men are disintegrated by ray gun blasts, they let their trained German shepherds attack the creatures. The dogs rip open the creatures' exposed arteries and the creatures collapse, a gushy substance pouring from their bodies. Marge and "Bill" enter the forest. The townspeople go aboard the spaceship, where they find all the taken-over human beings attached to wires that feed the aliens their knowledge and memories. They unattach the wires, freeing the captives. At the same instant, their alien imposters turn into a gelatinous substance and die. A happy Marge and Bill unite. As "Collins" dies he sends a message to other aliens that the invasion has failed. Numerous spaceships flee from earth.

Wisely, the aliens decide that it will be easier to get earth women to agree to have babies by them if they take on the physical characteristics of earth men rather than look like this.

There were about half a dozen *outstanding* science fiction/horror films made in the fifties. *I Married a Monster from Outer Space* falls just below these in quality, but judging from how it has been neglected, one would think it was a total fiasco. In fact, even the most "complete" histories of science fiction and horror films don't bother to discuss it. Apparently, its title (in the scandal sheet exposé tradition), which in 1958 attracted huge crowds of juveniles to theaters and drive-ins (where it often played with *The Blob*) also had the adverse effect of turning away critics for years to come. Only in the last few years have horror and science fiction fans come to realize that the outrageous title is totally unsuited for what is basically an intelligent, atmospheric, subtly made sci-fi thriller.

I Married a Monster is part of an sf/horror film subgenre which includes all pictures about aliens taking over bodies of human beings as the first step in an all-out invasion. The two other significant films of the subgenre, *Invaders from Mars* (1953) and *Invasion of the Body Snatchers* (1955) are point-of-view films in which the camera records the stories almost exactly as they unfold in the eyes and minds of a boy (Jimmy Hunt) and a man (Kevin McCarthy) in the respective films. The suspense builds as they discover that more and more of their acquaintances have been replaced by counterfeits and as they futilely try to get someone to believe their incredible stories. *I Married a Monster* is structured just

Bride Marge Farrell is ecstatic, but she doesn't know that her groom Bill has been replaced by an alien duplicate (holding the door).

a bit differently so that the suspense builds from *two* directions at once. In part, it is a point-of-view film. We watch Marge as she picks up signs that things are amiss: "Bill" can see in the darkness, is allergic to alcohol, and has lost every *human* emotion; "Bill's" male friends are as cold as he; "Sam" dies when a doctor administers oxygen; the puppy she gives "Bill" tries to bite him—and it is later killed by "her husband," who has always been an animal lover. When Marge follows "Bill" through the woods and finds out that he is an alien, she tries to alert various individuals in the town, but because she is a woman she has an especially hard time getting men to take her story seriously. And she has the same difficulty Jimmy Hunt and Kevin McCarthy had telling the good guys from the bad. Even Police Chief Collins, her godfather, is one of *them*. Following in Kevin McCarthy's footsteps, she tries to make a long-distance call, but the operator tells her all lines are busy; she tries to send a telegram to the FBI but sees the telegraph operator toss her message into the garbage; she tries to leave town but is stopped by a police roadblock. All these signs of an invasion Marge is witness to. But unlike viewers of the other two films, we are not limited to the point of view of a single character. Unlike Marge, we see Bill taken over by "Bill"; an outer space creature walking the deserted streets late at night and killing the prostitute Francine when she mistakenly thinks he's a possible pickup; the hideous faces underneath the human visages of "Bill" and "Collins" when lightning flashes (a tremendous special effect); "Bill" intentionally strangling the puppy that has recognized his otherness; "Bill" telepathically communicating with two aliens who have replaced policemen; the two "policemen" withstanding bullets fired by a trespasser. And *we* overhear "Bill," "Sam," and the other aliens complaining about having to wear human disguises and discussing mating with earth women once their scientists give them the go-ahead. Because we are allowed to learn even more than Marge discovers through living with "Bill" for a year, we are able to see better than she just how cruel and powerful these aliens are. As a result of our knowl-edge we become nervous for Marge because she may be learning too much for her own welfare. Our extra fear would have been impossible if this were strictly a point-of-view film.

I Married a Monster was directed by Gene Fowler, Jr., who at one time was an editor for Fritz Lang. The Lang influence is very much in evidence, particularly in that Fowler skillfully creates a sense of paranoia—first in Marge, who fears she's alone in a town full of aliens, and then in the aliens themselves when they know that their presence has been revealed and that some of the towns-folk (recent fathers) have organized to destroy them. (Fowler's film has many scenes that are brightly lit or take place in the daylight, but at times when he wishes to heighten the paranoia his shadowy rooms and his bizarre camera angles remind one of Lang.) In Fowler's films, as in Lang's, people from a particular community always band together against aliens/intruders. In some of Lang's pictures, the aliens/intruders/loners are good guys and the townsfolk (especially in films set in Germany during World War II) are unfriendly. Fowler used this theme in his lone western, *Showdown at Boot Hill* (1958), in which our hero, a bounty hunter played by Charles Bronson, enters a hostile town where the people unite to protect the villain he is after. (At the end Bronson and the townspeople make peace.) But in Fowler's underrated *I Was a Teenage Werewolf* (1957), a conscientious, civic-minded posse tracks down a monster (Michael Landon) who is only sympathetic when in his human form. And in *I Married a Monster*, a heroic vigilante group tracks down monsters that aren't in the least bit sympathetic (although I wrongly suspected "Bill" would reform under Marge's influence). Interestingly, a German shepherd owned by a posse member is killed fighting the monster in *Teenage Werewolf*. In *I Married a Monster*, the German shepherds get their revenge.

There are two moments in the film which immediately recall Lang. Marge and "Bill" enter their hotel. The camera climbs upward along the front of the hotel and

Marge tells "Bill" that their marriage has left a lot to be desired.

One of the last aliens lies dead. The invasion is over.

settles on a balcony where (miraculously) Marge and "Bill" already stand in their night clothes. Of course Fowler had to stop his filming so actors Gloria Talbott and Tom Tryon could prepare themselves for the balcony scene, but he disguised his "cut" with some flashing lights as the camera reached the balcony. In Lang's *Fury* (1936), a cut is similarly disguised. In a night scene Spencer Tracy and Sylvia Sidney walk down the street and suddenly they are walking down another street and a great deal of time has passed—Lang moved the camera a little ahead of them to lose them, and when they walked back into frame it was much later. It's a nifty "invisible" editing technique, where we believe the camera runs continuously.

For me, the most jarring moment in *I Married a Monster* is not when the monster wearing a coat kills Francine. It is when this creature looks into a department store window and his monstrous reflection is superimposed over baby dolls in the window display—and we know he is thinking of propagation. I can't help but think of Lang's *M* (1931), when child-murderer

Peter Lorre looks into a window and his eyes triple in size when he sees the reflection of a little girl who passes by.

Mention should be made of the fine performance of Gloria Talbott as Marge. Talbott was not pretty in the "movie" heroine sense—she always reminded me of a sexier Roberta Shore—but she was a terrific heroine for science fiction and horror films because she projected a rare combination of strength and vulnerability. She was very believable playing the roles of women who were scared about what was happening to them but stood their ground and was truly an ideal choice to play the heroine who foils the alien invasion in *I Married a Monster*. Tom Tryon, years before he became a best-selling author, is less convincing although adequate as Bill/"Bill." Importantly, he is so handsome that we can understand Marge's unhappiness when someone with his looks acts like a robot. Tryon's "Bill" is more interesting than his human counterpoint; as Bill, Tryon plays a character with all sorts of emotions and doesn't quite pull it off.

I Walked with a Zombie

1943 RKO Radio
Director: Jacques Tourneur
Producer: Val Lewton
Screenplay: Curt Siodmak and
Ardel Wray

Based on a story by Inez Wallace
Cinematography: J. Roy Hunt
Music: Roy Webb
Editor: Mark Robson
Running Time: 68 minutes

Cast: Frances Dee (Betsy), Tom Conway (Paul Holland), James Ellison (Wesley Rand), Edith Barrett (Mrs. Rand), Christine Gordon (Jessica Holland), James Bell (Dr. Maxwell), Richard Abrams (Clement), Teresa Haris (Alma), Sir Lancelot (Calypso singer), Darby Jones (Carre-Four)

Synopsis: Betsy, an American nurse, is sent to Haiti to work for planter Paul Holland, taking care of his sick wife, Jessica. It does not take Betsy long to realize that Jessica's malady is most unusual.

Paul is convinced that his wife is insane. In fact, he is sure that he made her that way. The natives, however, are convinced that Jessica is a zombie, one of the walking dead, and her lifeless appearance, even during movement, seems to confirm their suspicions.

As time goes by, Betsy gets to know the other members of Paul's family. His mother is a woman caught between her strong belief in the church and a belief in the powers of voodoo. She, too, is tormented by her certainty that she turned Jessica into a zombie. Wesley, Paul's half-brother, has always loved Jessica, and hated Paul for having treated her so poorly. He seems intent on drinking himself to death.

All in all, the house is in a troubled state. Then to complicate matters, Paul and Betsy fall in love. They wish to marry, but cannot because Paul's wife is still alive, medically speaking, and he refuses to desert her in her sad state, for which he feels responsible. Although Betsy realizes she may lose Paul if Jessica returns to health, she sets out to cure her patient. But all fails, including shock treatments from Dr. Maxwell and taking her to a voodoo ceremony. It appears that nothing can rescue the Rand family from being in a permanent state of limbo.

Then Wesley arrives at a solution. He stabs Jessica and walks her into the ocean—before the voodoo priest can lay claim to her. He will be with her forever in death. Betsy and Paul unite in life.

A shot that illustrates the skill with which director Jacques Tourneur uses light, darkness, and shadows: Betsy is awakened by Carre-Four outside her bedroom.

In 1941, financially troubled RKO assigned Val Lewton, a former assistant to David O. Selznick, to produce a series of low-budget, escapist horror films. But Lewton—a historian, art expert, novelist, and nephew of legendary Russian actress Nazimova—was determined to please rather than exploit the wartime audience. He told his unit: "They may think I'm going to do the usual chiller stuff which will make a quick profit, be laughed at, and be forgotten, but I'm going to make the kind of suspense movie I like."

The nine horror-suspense movies Val Lewton made at RKO between 1942 and 1946 are distinguished by the intelligence and sensitivity that went into every aspect of production from music to characterization; as one critic of the time correctly noted, "There's a new kind of horror picture nowadays—snappy little spook shows full of beautiful girls and sharp dialogue, good food, and French lullabies." Lewton's films were made in direct opposition to horror classics of the past such as *Nosferatu* (1922), *Frankenstein* (1931), *The Mummy* (1932), *Dracula* (1931), and *King Kong* (1933), which scared people with frightening images; he relied on basic universal fears—darkness, sudden movements and sounds—to send chills through his audience. He was convinced that viewers could be scared to a far greater degree by what they *imagined* in the darkness, or just off screen, than by anything filmmakers could show them. The surprising financial and critical success that the Lewton series obtained is proof positive that his theories on horror, suspense, and terror were correct.

I Walked with a Zombie was the second Lewton horror film, and the second of three Lewton pictures directed by Jacques Tourneur. While its predecessor, *Cat People* (1942), has made the transition in recent years from "cult film" to "horror classic," and has become the prototype for countless films, *I Walked with a Zombie* has replaced it as the Lewton work that shows up most frequently at revival houses, the cult favorite of the Lewton films, a movie that defies imitation.

The reason no one has attempted to make a horror film along the lines of *I Walked with a Zombie* is that, in truth, it is not a horror film. True, there is some eerie photography, a few suspenseful, even scary, moments, a bit of voodoo, and some zombielike creatures on the screen, but basically this film is a domestic drama set in an exotic locale. (Lewton made it a point to mix the familiar with the exotic. In this film, an American goes to the West Indies. It is likely that had she been a West Indian native, Lewton would have brought her to America.)

The lurid title, which is also the first line of the film's (Betsy's) narration, came from a popular Hearst Sunday supplement article written by Inez Wallace. She wrote that she had been skeptical about the existence of zombies until she ran into one while walking across a Haitian plantation. These beings, she discovered, were not "dead," but their minds and vocal cords had been utterly destroyed from poison (or drugs). As they could understand simple orders, which they obediently carried out, they were put to work in the fields and lived in

Calypso singer Sir Lancelot, one of many nonactors Val Lewton cast in his films, is used like a Greek chorus, turning up every few scenes to explain in song what is going on in the story.

Betsy starts to fall for her employer Paul Holland. He loves her too but refuses to abandon his sick wife Jessica.

slavery. Lewton was stuck with the title RKO had purchased for him, but he ignored Wallace's text. "They may not recognize it," he told confidants, "but what I'm going to [make] is 'Jane Eyre in the West Indies.' " True to his word, the film does contain an essential Jane Eyre plot element: a young female in a house with a man and his insane wife.

Although the Lewton unit cared little about the zombie element of the film—Tourneur's attitude was "those things don't exist"—the film remains, along with Victor Halperin's *White Zombie* (1932), one of the few attempts to deal with the subject intelligently. Halperin

had tried to show what he believed to be the true nature of the zombie, and his work visualized the zombie of William Seabrook's *The Magic Island*, the same unfortunate creature about which Inez Wallace would later write. Halperin contended there are zombies. Lewton wanted viewers to make up their own minds. According to his film, a person can only become a zombie after death has occurred (which isn't the case in Halperin's film). We believe that Jessica's catatonic state is a direct result of her having become a zombie, yet we also know that she never actually died, making our basis for judgment invalid. Moreover, when Wesley "kills" Jes-

Nurse Betsy will try anything to cure Jessica of the strange malady —here she takes her through the woods to participate in a voodoo ceremony.

sica with a sword—a feat that was not possible earlier in the film—we must suspect that Jessica may have only been insane, after all. It is a mystery that is left unsolved.

Just as Lewton never insults those people in the world who do believe in the existence of the walking dead, he is careful not to criticize the superstitions of the black Haitians in the film. Even the most Christian of the white people in the film believe to a great extent in the powers of the voodoo priest. If anything, the picture shows that having faith in the magic of voodoo is well motivated.

The black characters in *I Walked with a Zombie* are treated with great respect. The rich whites have control of the economy of their island but the blacks have maintained control over everything that truly matters to them —their customs and religious practices—and they are the ones who understand what forces reign supreme on the island, while the whites wallow in confusion and terror. It is surprising that film historians who have traced the treatment of blacks in the movies have neglected to mention the entire Lewton series. While most Hollywood films of the time either had no blacks at all or used silly, familiar black stereotypes, the Lewton pictures were populated by black characters who possessed warmth, humor, and intelligence. For instance, one of the key roles in *I Walked with a Zombie* is that of a singer who wanders in and out of the film explaining the

plot in song, serving as a Greek chorus (one of several ideas Lewton borrowed from Greek tragedy evident in his films). This role was hauntingly played by a cherubic, Caribbean song improvisor named Sir Lancelot, a Lewton discovery making his film debut. He would return in Lewton's *Curse of the Cat People* (1944).

Likewise, feminist film historians have somehow neglected the entire Lewton horror catalog, despite the fact that nowhere in American films have there been women—working women, at that—more intelligent, responsible, resourceful, and courageous. There is not one instance, in *I Walked with a Zombie*, or any of the other eight horror films, in which there is male heroism at work—it is the woman, time after time, who accomplishes what has to be done, and gets herself out of her own misfortunes. Quite simply, this is extraordinary, considering that these pictures were made during the war years, when every other Hollywood movie was showcasing the gallantry of the American male. Frances Dee is part of the fine Lewton tradition that culminated in Anna Lee's dynamic social reformer of *Bedlam* (1946), his last film at RKO. Dee is strong, smart, independent, and brave. It is she who moves the story along, not the passive men around her. The men are brooders, she is a doer.

More than any other Lewton film, *I Walked with a Zombie* relies on atmosphere to transmit fright. There are few true moments of shock in the film, and those scenes that "promise" to shock—the one in which Betsy finds herself alone for the first time with Jessica, on a dark staircase, or the one in which the giant zombie (Darby Jones) threatens Betsy—are cut short before anything actually happens. Director Tourneur wanted his film to be fluid in nature, moving continuously forward, so he rejected any "shocks" that would abruptly halt his gentle pacing. He was attempting to create a "filmic poem."

Two sequences are among the best found in the Lewton series. The first has Betsy leading Jessica down an unfamiliar path through the cane fields, on the way to see the voodoo priest. Their walk, under the gray, ominous sky, their white flowing garments blowing gently in the wind, is dreamlike. Sounds fill the air: there is a rustling breeze; an owl hoots as if to signal the presence of intruders; voodoo drums beat louder with each step the women take. And a gargantuan black figure waits in their path, as if he were the angel of death.

The second sequence is the one in which Wesley carries Jessica into the ocean. Again, this is a long silent passage with a dreamlike quality. The walk of Wesley through the jungle, down the slopes, across the sandy beach, and deeper and deeper into the ocean until he and Jessica sink beneath the water, is truly moving, the vision of the giant zombie following them to the edge of the water, chilling. Both this segment and the first one capture the essence of the film. We are watching the ultimate "beautiful nightmare."

All the Lewton horror films are good—*Cat People, Curse of the Cat People,* and *The Body Snatcher* (1945) are masterpieces of the genre—but *I Walked with a Zombie* is the most impressive of the Lewton series from a visual standpoint. Most directors need dialogue—Jacques Tourneur did not. Tourneur obviously learned his lessons well from his father, Maurice Tourneur, one of the greatest directors of the silent era. The lyrical quality of the long silent passages, the shadows, the lighting, the music, the settings—all so important in his father's silent films—is what makes *I Walked With a Zombie* so fascinating, and so different from the typically brutal horror film. It is not surprising that *I Walked with a Zombie* is the film that made Tourneur proudest.

The Lewton series was received very enthusiastically in the forties by such influential critics as Manny Farber and James Agee, with Farber particularly excited about *The Leopard Man* (1943)—Tourneur's third film for Lewton—and Agee about *Curse of the Cat People* —which he said should have gotten an award for "the whole conception and performance of the family servant (played by Sir Lancelot), who is one of the most unpretentiously sympathetic, intelligent, antitraditional, and individualized Negro characters I have ever seen presented on the screen." Unfortunately, few moviegoers realized that Lewton's nine horror films were produced by the same man, and it wasn't until the mid-sixties—long after his death in 1951—that fans and critics recognized Lewton as the equal of James Whale and Tod Browning.

The islanders have retrieved the bodies of Jessica and Wesley from the ocean.

Invasion of the Body Snatchers

1956 Allied Artists
Director: Don Siegel
Producer: Walter Wanger
Screenplay: Daniel Mainwaring
From a Collier's magazine serial by Jack Finney
Cinematography: Ellsworth Fredericks
Music: Carmen Dragon
Editor: Robert S. Eisen
Running Time: 80 minutes

Cast: Kevin McCarthy (Miles Bennell), Dana Wynter (Becky Driscoll), King Donovan (Jack), Carolyn Jones (Theodora), Larry Gates (Dan Kaufman), Jean Willes (Sally), Virginia Christine (Wilma), Ralph Dumke (sheriff), Whitt Bissell (Dr. Hill), Richard Deacon (doctor), Dabbs Greer (gas station attendant), Sam Peckinpah

Synopsis: A doctor, arriving at a Los Angeles hospital, is directed to a hysterical man who was picked up on the highway shouting that the world is in danger. Everyone thinks Miles Bennell is insane, but the doctor agrees to listen to his story.

Miles says that he is a doctor, too, and that his practice is in the nearby town of Santa Mira. Several days ago, he returned home early from an out-of-town conference at the request of his nurse Sally. She told him that many of his patients were suffering from a mysterious malady; they believed that their friends and loved ones were imposters who looked exactly like those they replaced but lacked all traces of emotion. Miles saw this firsthand when little Jimmy Grimaldi insisted that his mother was not his mother; later Becky Driscoll, a longtime acquaintance with whom he has fallen in love, took Miles to visit her cousin Wilma, who insisted that her Uncle Ira was not Uncle Ira. Miles did not know how to explain this phenomenon, and not long afterwards Wilma and several others who had made appointments with him canceled their visits, assuring him that they were wrong in thinking people imposters.

Miles's friends Jack and Theodora found a half-formed body. It looked like Jack. When Jack napped, it took on more shape. They fled to Miles's house. Worried about Becky, Miles went to her house. In the basement he found a half-formed body resembling her. He got Becky from her bedroom and took her home. When he brought his friend Dan to show him the two half-formed bodies, they were gone.

Miles almost believed Dan when he said that they were imagining things, but the next night he found four pods, containing half-formed bodies of Becky, Jack, Theodora, and himself, growing in his greenhouse. He and the others destroyed the pods and decided to find help. They tried to call Washington but someone had taken control of the telephone. Taking separate cars, the two couples tried to make it out of town, but, after finding it impossible, Becky and Miles hid in Miles's office. In the morning they opened the door for Jack only to find out that he and Theodora had been taken over. They were trapped.

Dan, also taken over, and Jack offered them a life without pain, fears, or worries. But because it is a world that has no room for love, Becky and Miles rejected them. Dan and Jack put pods in the office—when Becky and Miles fell asleep they would be taken over.

Becky and Miles stabbed Dan and Jack with hypodermics and escaped. They were chased by the town's population into the mountains. When Becky fell asleep, she was taken over. She shouted for the other pod people to capture Miles. Miles ran onto the highway.

Miles finishes his story. The doctor doesn't know whether to believe him. A truck driver is wheeled in—his truck had crashed and he was buried under numerous pods. The truck was coming from Santa Mira. The doctor calls the FBI and the President.

During the first few minutes of Don Siegel's *Invasion of the Body Snatchers,* first-time viewers usually laugh raucously at Miles's breathless, sometimes overly dramatic and trite narration—often repeated verbatim in the dialogue—and lines like Miles's "Even these days, it's not as easy to go crazy as you think," and assume the superior attitude of people watching what they believe to be camp. They do not realize that Siegel has intentionally kept the beginning of the film light, even to the point of inserting silly lines to lull the audience into a false sense of complacency. Soon there is no more laughter, just a few nervous giggles. And from then on, as Siegel has sprung his trap, the theater is absolutely silent but for an occasional gasp or scream or yell to Miles and Becky "Run!" or "Don't fall asleep!" Afterward, the audience files out, still shaky, acknowledging that they have seen a genuine thriller.

For me, *Invasion of the Body Snatchers* rates at the top of fifties science fiction films, along with *The Thing* (1951), *The Day the Earth Stood Still* (1951), *Them!* (1954), and *The Incredible Shrinking Man* (1957), other pictures that make the fantastic seem perfectly credible. In fact, if it does have an advantage over these other films, it is because *everything* we see we believe—we may even have had similar nightmares. Philip Kaufman's 1977 remake of *Invasion of the Body Snatchers* cost about eight times what Siegel's 1956 picture did, it is in color, has fine special effects and much flashy hip-filmmaker pizzazz, yet, while it holds one's interest, about halfway through it stops being suspenseful. Where the original totally outshines the remake is in pacing—the excitement just keeps building. Siegel estab-

Discovering pods sprouting duplicates of themselves in Miles's greenhouse, Jack (with the pitchfork), Becky (L), Thea, and Miles figure that their time as the lone human beings alive in Santa Mira may be running out.

A publicity shot of Miles burning a pod that a garage attendant hid in his trunk.

lishes tension through a number of tricks: having characters in constant motion—moving from place to place, racing their cars, running; having characters peer at each other through windows and glass doors; having Miles and Becky hide from invaders in small spaces like closets and the hole beneath the boards in a cave; having characters leave their motors running when they get out of their cars; having many scenes take place in the dark or in shadows; having much activity take place in basements; and most effective of all, establishing that aliens have replaced Miles's friends in order to make us paranoid about everything that is ordinary and familiar. Interestingly, Siegel, a former special-effects expert, deliberately shied away from the special effects that most SF directors consider necessary to the genre. Instead he relied on diverse camera angles, penetrating close-ups of the characters mixed with mysterious long shots of large areas of Santa Mira, and sharp editing—all staples of the Hollywood action film Siegel knew so well—to create visual tension. By downplaying the special effects, Siegel would not make the mistake Kaufman made years later of having the science fiction elements of the story take precedence over the characters.

Invasion of the Body Snatchers is the best of an SF subgenre which deals with aliens taking over the bodies of everyone in a particular community. As in such films as *Invaders from Mars* (1953), *It Came from Outer Space* (1953), and *I Married a Monster From Outer Space* (1958), the alien takeovers in *Body Snatchers* take

on horrifying proportions smacking of totalitarianism when the police become part of the invasion. Even more terrifying is when a loved one—your security—becomes your enemy. In *Invaders From Mars*, young Jimmy Hunt, like Jimmy Grimaldi in *Body Snatchers*, realizes that his parents have been replaced; in *Monster from Outer Space*, bride Gloria Talbott notices a drastic change in the personality of her new husband; but

Miles and Jack bring Dan to Becky's basement where Miles swears he found a half-formed duplicate of Becky. But the proof is gone and Dan refuses to believe them. Is Dan one of the duplicates?

All the pod people of Santa Mira chase survivors Becky and Miles into the hills.

probably the most heartbreaking discovery is made by Miles in *Body Snatchers*. Early in the film, Miles jokingly implies that he will always be able to tell that Becky *is* Becky by her kiss. Later in the film, in the cave, he kisses her and pulls back in horror, looking into the cold eyes of the woman he knows is Becky's duplicate. In *An Illustrated History of the Horror Film* (Capricorn, 1968), Carlos Clarens makes this astute observation:

> The ultimate horror in science fiction is neither death nor destruction but dehumanization, a state in which emotional life is suspended, in which the individual is deprived of individual feelings, free will, and moral judgment. That the most successful SF films . . . seem to be concerned with dehumanization simply underlines the fact that this type of fiction hits the most exposed nerve of contemporary society: collective anxieties about the loss of individual identity, subliminal mind-bending, or downright scientific/ political brainwashing. (Not by accident the trend began to manifest itself after the Korean War and the well publicized reports coming out of it of brainwashing techniques.) We have come a long way from *Metropolis* [1921] and the encroachment of the ma-

chine. Nowadays man can become the machine himself. The automatoned slaves of modern times look perfectly efficient in their new painless state. From this aspect, they are like the zombies of old—only we never bothered to wonder if zombies were happy in their trance. Zombies, like vampires, seemed so incontrovertibly different; the human counterfeits of . . . *Invasion of the Body Snatchers* are those we love, our family and friends. The zombies are now among us, and we cannot tell them and the girl next door apart any longer.

Siegel's films often deal with men who must make enormous choices as to how they lead their lives—and these choices have to do with whether they are willing to relinquish their individuality. In *Riot in Cell Block 11* (1954), the prisoners choose not to toe the line, to revolt against what they consider to be dehumanizing prison conditions; in *Baby Face Nelson* (1957), Nelson rejects a life of anonymity as a law-biding citizen for fame as the FBI's "Most Wanted" criminal; in *Madigan* (1968), *Coogan's Bluff* (1968), and *Dirty Harry* (1971), hero cops choose to act according to their own devices and moral codes rather than follow the orders of their superiors. In *Invasion of the Body Snatchers* an individual chooses not to give in to his desire to conform like all those around him. To accept the aliens' offer to turn him into a pod person would have the same effect as taking a permanent pain-killer—and for Miles, who has suffered the loss of Becky and all of his friends, it is a brave act to reject such peace. Relinquishing his ability to love (which he rediscovered through Becky), laugh, and even cry—the emotions that distinguish one person from another—is too high a price to pay. When Donald Sutherland gives up his individuality by choice in Kaufman's remake and allows himself to go to sleep—knowing he will wake up a pod person—this is incredibly disturbing to us. (At least Becky tries to fight off sleep!) He has committed the ultimate sellout. But back in 1956, Siegel already believed that "the majority of people in the world unfortunately [have allowed themselves to become] pods, existing without any intellectual aspirations and incapable of love."

While Siegel contends that *Body Snatchers* was intended to be an "entertainment" film with the tepid message being that people were becoming podlike stereotypes, the film has long been subject of critical debate regarding its underlying political implications. Considering that it was made during the Cold War, during Eisenhower's presidency, a few years after Korea, when Joseph R. McCarthy was at his peak of power, it seems unlikely that Siegel's film was only meant to tell us that we were becoming identical to our neighbors. Much of the film's cult following is a result of the picture's ability to be interpreted in two quite contradictory ways: as being anti-McCarthy and an indictment of the red-scare American mentality; and as being an anticommunist allegory.

That the film is anticommunist is the more popular notion. Noel Carroll of the *Soho News* (Dec. 21, 1978) writes:

> The unraveling of the pod conspiracy has the flavor of an FBI exposé. The pod people represent a completely regimented society. Metaphorically, they are all alike as "two peas in a pod" because they have been sapped of their emotional individuality. The vegetarian metaphor literalizes Red-scare rhetoric of the "growth" of Communism as well as the idea that revolutions are made by planting seeds. There is a scene in which the pod people are assembled in the town square, where a loudspeaker reads off the day's orders; it is the quintessential Fifties image of socialism. And, of course, the simile that without freedom of thought people are . . . vegetables is a central theme of the narrative.

In *Invasion of the Body Snatchers,* that there are aliens in our midst taking over all phases of our lives and brainwashing our children is shown to be fact, not paranoia. That the takeover is accomplished through the movement of pods from the country into the towns may remind us that in the 1950s Russia was considered an agrarian society. While Siegel's villains are usually mad or emotionally unstable, the space aliens of *Body Snatchers* fit the mold that American schoolteachers describe as being characteristic of Russians: ice cold,

Exhausted after their escape from Santa Mira, Becky and Miles hide in a cave. It is here that Becky will fall asleep.

outwardly peaceful but very authoritarian, emotionless. Of course, most American schoolchildren of the fifties were taught that Communists had no feelings—especially concerning life and death—which is why, they were told, the Russians/Red Chinese would feel no qualms about going to war and losing much of their population. More than anything else I believe we kids were frightened of Communists because we were told they did not cry when people died. (In *Body Snatchers* it is upsetting when pod person Sally helps transform her child, saying "There'll be no more tears.") To dispel this indoctrination, in the antiwar documentary *Hearts and Minds* (1974), director Peter Davis included a long tragic scene in which a North Vietnamese mother and young son mourn the death of a family member, and directly following this incredible display of emotion is a bit with General Westmoreland, the commander of America's armed forces during the war, still spouting American rhetoric about how Americans are different from Communist peoples because *they* consider life cheap.

Those who argue that *Body Snatchers* is an anti-McCarthy polemic begin with the premise that Siegel establishes that the fascistic pod people *already* comprise the American majority, control the government, law enforcement agencies, and communications, and dictate the country's political line. In other words, Joseph R. McCarthy and his followers already control the country. In Santa Mira, a town where the Spanish must have pushed out the native Indian population, and subsequently English-speaking Americans must have pushed out the Spanish, the pod people are just one more in a long line of invaders who are bent on wiping out the previous culture. In *Body Snatchers,* the pod people,

Frantic, Miles runs onto the highway and tries to tell motorists heading toward Los Angeles what has happened in Santa Mira. No one will listen.

who, like McCarthy and the other red-baiters, look like typical, fine upstanding Americans, search out rebels like Miles who refuse to conform to what has been newly defined as the "American Way"—just as McCarthy and HUAC destroyed the lives of those who refused to knuckle under to their directives. The mob hysteria, the sense of paranoia, the fascist police, the witch hunt atmosphere of the picture certainly mirror the ills of McCarthy America.

The anti-McCarthy viewpoint comes across more clearly with the quicker ending Siegel originally intended, with Miles still on the highway yelling at the camera to us "You're next!" At this moment, Siegel tells us that if we're not careful, oppressive forces in our society will force us into submission and into conformity. With Miles's two words, Siegel reminds us of what Miles said earlier: "People allow their humanity to drain away and don't realize how precious it is until [they realize] it is directly threatened." Allied Artists made Siegel add the opening and closing scenes in the L.A. hospital because it thought Siegel's ending too downbeat. I agree. I find open endings terribly frustrating and unsatisfying, and resent sadistic directors who get pleasure from leaving viewers with monsters, killers, and maniacs lurking about. In *Body Snatchers,* I am relieved that there is still a chance to get rid of those damn pods as Miles does with fire in Jack Finney's story on which the film is based. I like the studio-imposed ending, I like the fact that Miles's story is believed, even if this means we might temporarily be placed under martial law. But, unfortunately, this studio-imposed ending blunts Siegel's original message expressed by Miles on the highway that we should fight off those Americans who wish to make us conform and delivers a new message: we are being infiltrated from the outside by alien forces (as McCarthy suggested) and we Americans must take action through an all-out joint effort by the President, the Congress, the military, and the FBI. This message, of course, is not anti-McCarthy but anticommunist.

It's a Gift

1934 Paramount
Director: Norman Z. McLeod
Producer: William LeBaron
Screenplay: Jack Cunningham
From a story by Charles Bogle
and J. P. McEvoy
Cinematography: Henry Sharp
Music: None
Editor: None credited
Running Time: 67 minutes

Cast: W. C. Fields (Harold Bissonette), Baby LeRoy (Baby Dunk), Kathleen Howard (Amelia Bissonette), Jean Rouveral (Mildred Bissonette), Tammany Young (Everett Ricks), Tom Bupp (Norman Z. Bissonette), Julian Madison (John Durston)

Synopsis: Harold Bissonette, a middle-aged store owner, lives an uncomfortable small-town life with his nagging, domineering wife Amelia, their young son Norman, and their daughter Mildred, who is about twenty. His daily life in the house and at his store is hectic and full of aggravations, and he can't even get a good night's sleep. His dream is to go to California and live on an orange grove like the one he has a picture of. When Uncle Bean dies from choking on an orange pit, Harold spends his entire five-thousand-dollar inheritance to buy a California orange grove sight unseen from John, Mildred's boyfriend. When John discovers that the land he has sold his future father-in-law is worthless and won't grow anything, he tries to give Harold back his money. But Harold refuses to give up his land.

Despite Amelia's loud complaints, Harold sells his store and takes his family by car to California. When they arrive, Amelia is so taken by the orange groves she sees, she admits that she may have been too hasty in disapproving Harold's scheme. But when she sees the barren land that Harold has bought and the dilapidated shack in which they are supposed to live, she takes the kids and starts to walk to a motel. Harold offers to drive them, but the car collapses. He believes his life is in ruins, when his neighbor comes to tell him that racetrack owners will be coming to buy his land because they need it desperately for a grandstand. He tells Harold he can hold out for any price he wants. Amelia comes back to Harold when she sees the racetrack men drive up. Harold keeps turning down their seemingly generous offers but finally agrees to sell the property for $44,000 plus the orange grove in his picture. Amelia faints from excitement at her husband's business acumen. "You're an old idiot," she tells him, "but I can't help but love you." He offers her a drink.

The Bissonettes move onto the orange grove Harold always wanted. He has his morning drink—mixed with orange juice—and smiles.

An aggravating day begins for Harold Bissonette when Mildred insists on using the mirror over the sink before he can finish shaving. Some people actually protested this scene because a father and daughter are shown together in a bathroom.

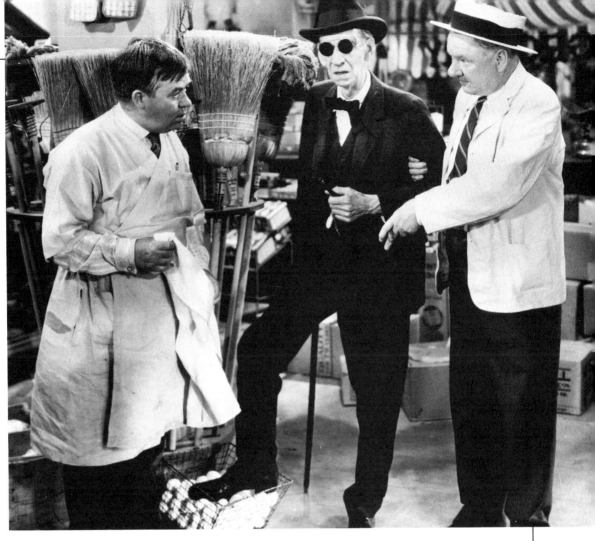

In the majority of his best feature films, W. C. Fields plays an unfriendly, cowardly, bumbling, larcenous mountebank who bluffs, boasts, and bullies his way through an absurd, surreal universe full of dishonest men, rich widows, imbeciles (whom he often employs) and annoying children—keeping a town ahead of an angry sheriff or some poor duped soul with a shotgun.

He is a boat captain in *Tillie and Gus* (1933) and *Mississippi* (1933), the leader of an itinerant acting troupe in *The Old-Fashioned Way* (1934), a vagabond medicine man in *My Little Chickadee* (1940), and runs traveling carnivals in *Sally of the Sawdust* (1926), its sound remake *Poppy* (1936), and *You Can't Cheat an Honest Man* (1939). He is so mean that in *Honest Man* he feeds Charlie McCarthy to the alligators and in *The Old-Fashioned Way* gives Baby LeRoy (who has dropped Fields's pocket watch into a bowl of soup) a stiff kick on the rear. He is so dishonest that he uses ventriloquism to sell a "talking dog" which, he then explains to the sucker who purchased it, is so offended at being sold that it will never speak again. Yet we find Fields lovable just the same—not only because he suffers indignities like leaning back in his chair and falling off a stage in *The Old-Fashioned Way*, being conked in the head with a croquet ball in *Poppy* and zapped in the face with snow obviously hurled by the propman in the short *The Fatal Glass of Beer* (1933), or because he has a soft spot

beneath his gruff exterior, or because his never-ending stream of tall tales breathes life into a mundane world, or because more than any other actor he reflects our cynicism toward a world that is corrupt and hostile, but also because his refusal to settle down makes him a renegade in our eyes. He is that rare individual with enough temerity and love of freedom to wage a continuous war against our terrifying oppressive world. He chooses jobs that take him far and wide to supply himself with an infinite number of people to swindle and to tell tall tales to without fear of contradiction; he knows that if he were to settle down and have a family and a typical job he would suffocate.

In Fields's few but outstanding white-collar comedies, *It's a Gift, The Man on the Flying Trapeze* (1935), and *The Bank Dick* 1940), he has in fact settled down and works in steady jobs (as a grocer, a memory expert with a reputable firm, and a bank guard, respectively), and the worst fears of Fields's other incarnation seem to have been realized. For this Fields has let himself be trapped in a world of nagging, browbeating wives, mothers-in-law, freeloaders, bosses, insurance salesmen, and children, always children—sometimes even his own. The rebellious Fields who burns a sheriff's subpoena in *The Old-Fashioned Way* and outraces the law across a state line in *Honest Man* now allows not one, not two, but three traffic cops to give him tickets in *Flying Trapeze;* the Fields without familial responsibili-

As always, Fields is unhappy to see his nemesis Baby LeRoy.

ties who spends most of his time drinking, swearing, smoking cigars, singing, and gambling now must continually sneak behind his wives' backs to partake in any of these pleasures that make his life worth living; where the bachelor Fields talks a blue streak to the women he meets and wishes something from, the married Fields's dialogue at home is reduced to "Yes, dear," a few incoherencies his wives pay no attention to, and another "Yes, dear" or two.

But we mustn't despair. While the domesticated Fields is indeed suffocating, he is simply too stubborn to give in entirely. He has only compromised himself. He allows his henpecking wives their martyrdom, criticisms, and rules because no matter what they say or do to him he still drinks on the sly and retains his other vices, and remains an iconoclast in a world of conformity. Ralph Kramden of TV's *The Honeymooners* may bellow that he is master of his house, but that is not the case. On the other hand, Fields may whisper, in *It's a Gift,* that he's master of his house so his wife can't hear him, but the fact is that he in this one instance speaks the truth: no matter how hard his wife tries to change him, he remains firm. He may swear to Amelia that he will go along with her wish to remain in New Jersey, but he uses their money to buy a California orange grove and sells his store without consulting her—and she must follow him to California or risk losing her man.

It's a Gift was considered one of Fields's lesser comedies when released at the end of 1934, but Fields cultists now consider it the equal of *The Bank Dick,* which has long been regarded as the great comedian's masterpiece. Its increase in stature can be attributed to its being recognized as the greatest showcase for Fields's unique brand of humor, based on characters annoying one another. It is these annoyances, piled one on top of another, that in Fields's eye summed up a day in the life of a married man in America.

Like most of Fields's films, *It's a Gift* doesn't bother much with plot. It is in fact a series of set pieces strung together to represent a typical day in the life of Harold Bissonette, husband, father of two children, and grocer. The first vignette takes place at home in the morning, during which time daughter Mildred interrupts Harold's shaving, son Norman leaves a roller skate for him to somersault over, and wife Amelia calls him an idiot and orders him to put out his cigar at the breakfast table (which is a reasonable request to be sure but not in the manner it is delivered). The second vignette shows a day at the grocery store, and the third shows Harold trying to get to sleep that night. The wild car trip to California—highlighted by the Bissonettes' picnic on a private estate which they leave garbage-strewn—is the fourth vignette, and the fifth is when they arrive on their California property, find it to be a desert, and then sell it to the racetrack men—as Harold unveils bartering abilities equal to that of other Fields characters in his carnival films.

Both the scene in the grocery and the one in which Fields tries to sleep have come to be regarded as classics. The grocery sequence begins with Harold arriving at the store and finding it impossible to fit his key into one of two glass doors. His moronic employee Everett Ricks opens one glass door for Harold but doesn't bother to tell him. Fields finally notices he can get in without a key, and walks in. A customer, Mr. Fitchmueller, is already inside when Harold arrives. Impatiently, he demands ten pounds of kumquats, which Harold won't admit to not having. Fitchmueller gets angrier and angrier at Harold's delaying tactics, especially when he has to spell "kumquats" one letter at a time for Harold. He screams repeatedly, "What about my kumquats?!" Harold spots a blind man coming toward the store. He shouts to Everett "Open the door for Mr. Muckle!" But Everett just stands there, and Mr. Muckle puts his cane through one of the glass doors. Then he walks in swinging his cane and knocks over boxes of glassware. He wants chewing gum. Harold sits him down and tells him not to move while he wraps up the gum. "Please!" But Mr. Muckle gets up and starts swinging his cane. Harold calls, "Sit down, Mr. Muckle, honey!" But Mr. Muckle knocks over about thirty light bulbs. Since Mr. Muckle doesn't want to lug the gum home, Harold sends Everett on his bike to deliver the gum. When Everett returns he runs the bike right into Harold, knocking him over the counter.

After Mr. Muckle, who naturally breaks the other glass door, and Fitchmueller have left, Mrs. Dunk drops off her baby Elwood for Harold and Everett to mind. Immediately Baby Dunk hits Harold in the elbow with a can. Harold looks at the can's label and adds insult to his injury: "I hate clams." Soon Elwood is totally covered with chocolate and soon after Harold is shocked to find that Elwood has opened a spigot on an enormous keg of molasses and that the floor is covered with the gooey substance. Harold asks Everett, who has been holding Elwood's hand the entire time, how he let the baby do such a thing, and Elwood replies, "I told him I wouldn't do it if I was him." Mrs. Dunk returns and, finding her baby's shoes covered with molasses, yells at Harold and doesn't buy the steak she ordered. Harold looks at Everett and says, "I hate you!" He then puts a sign on his door that reads: "Closed on account of molasses."

That night Amelia wakes Harold up from his nap on the couch: "Wake up and go to sleep." She acts like a martyr telling her husband, "You never think of me." At 4:30 A.M. she is still complaining about their twenty-year marriage and he still can't get to sleep. The phone rings and Harold crawls out of bed. It is a call *for* the maternity hospital. Amelia becomes very suspicious, and won't believe it's a wrong number. "Why would the maternity ward call *you*?" She asks. Harold goes onto the porch of their second-story apartment. He tries to sleep on a hanging swing. It crashes to the ground. Amelia moans from inside: "Please be quiet!" "Yes, dear," he mumbles. He balances the swing and tries to sleep. The milkman walks up the steps clanging bottles. Harold looks down below: "As a special favor, please stop playing with those sleigh bells." The milkman leaves, but a coconut he left for Mrs. Dunk upstairs rolls down three flights of stairs, one step at a time, and finally crashes into a garbage can. The swing falls again.

While Harold tries to adjust his swing, an obnoxious man in a suit calls from below, asking him if he knows "Carl LaFong! Capital 'L', small 'a', capital 'F', small 'o', small 'n', small 'g'. LaFong! Carl LaFong!" Harold replies angrily, "If I did know Carl LaFong—capital 'L', small 'a', capital 'F', small 'o', small 'n', small 'g'—I wouldn't admit it." Undeterred, the man runs up the stairs, telling Harold he is an insurance salesman who can sell him an annuity policy that will let Harold retire when he's ninety. Amelia comes out and complains about Harold having his friends over so early in the morning. Harold chases the man away with a meat cleaver. Harold lies back down on his swing. Elwood drops grapes through a hole in the porch above and they land in snoring Harold's mouth. Next, Elwood drops an ice pick into the wood an inch away from Harold's head. Minutes later, the Dunk's teen-age daughter bounces down the stairs and from below calls up to her mother. She is going on an errand and doesn't know what to buy or where to go. "It doesn't matter to me," says Mrs. Dunk. "It doesn't matter to me 'ither," drawls the girl. "I can tell you both where to go," mumbles Harold. Mrs. Dunk tells her daughter, "I can't hear a thing you're saying; a man on the second floor is shouting." Amelia comes out and demands to know what Harold and Mrs. Dunk were talking about. Harold tries to sleep. A neighbor hangs up her laundry on a squeaking wire which to Harold sounds like a mouse. Then a vegetable man comes by selling his wares below. Harold leaps to his feet and gets his shotgun. He calls sweetly "Vegetable man. Vegetable gentleman." Harold lies back on the swing. He drops the shotgun, which fires, and the swing crashes to the ground. Harold weakly swings at the gun with a fly swatter. End scene!*

These two scenes, which show off Fields's verbal and visual comic talents to best advantage, remarkably sustain hilarity throughout despite the fact that we are watching truly painful situations. From just these two scenes we understand that it is impossible to spend a day as Harold Bissonette does. No wonder he wants to go to California. Like Fields's other characters, Harold endures without self-pity or complaints. He accepts the absurdity of it all—it is he who points out matter-of-factly that Mr. Muckle is "the house detective over at the Grand Hotel"—and tolerates his predicament. No, Harold wouldn't complain, but Fields, the writer—under his Charles Bogle pseudonyms—and creator of each scene, allows us to see how Harold truly feels about his life under his expressionless facade. At the end, when Harold has his morning drink (mixed with orange juice) on his peaceful California orange grove, we know how free he must feel. That is why he smiles for the only time in the picture.

*This scene is a variation on the porch sequence in Fields's silent film *It's the Old Army Game* (1926).

It's a Wonderful Life

1946 RKO release of a Liberty Films production
Director: Frank Capra
Producer: Frank Capra
Screenplay: Frances Goodrich, Albert Hackett, and Frank Capra
Additional scenes: Jo Swerling

From a story by Philip Van Doren Stern
Cinematography: Joseph Walker and Joseph Biroc
Music: Dimitri Tiomkin
Editor: William Hornbeck
Running Time: 129 minutes

Cast: James Stewart (George Bailey), Donna Reed (Mary Hatch Bailey), Lionel Barrymore (Mr. Potter), Thomas Mitchell (Uncle Billy), Henry Travers (Clarence), Beulah Bondi (Mrs. Bailey), Frank Faylen (Ernie), Ward Bond (Bert), H. B. Warner (Mr. Gower), Gloria Grahame (Violet Bick), Todd Karns (Harry Bailey), Virginia Patton (Ruth), Samuel S. Hinds (Pa Bailey), Frank Albertson (Sam Wainwright), Mary Treen (Cousin Millie), Charles Williams (Cousin Eustace), Sarah Edwards (Mrs. Hatch), William Edmunds (Mr. Martini), Argentina Brunetti (Mrs. Martini), Bobbie Anderson (George, as a boy), Sheldon Leonard (Nick), Carol Coomes (Janie), Karolyn Grimes (Zuzu), Larry Simms (Pete), Jimmy Hawkins (Tommy)

Synopsis: Gentle angel Clarence Goodbody is given a chance to earn his wings by helping George Bailey, a man who is so discouraged that he contemplates suicide on Christmas Eve. The head angels tell Clarence George's life has been full of sacrifices and disappointments.

George has always lived in Bedford Falls although he had hoped to leave and explore the world. He was the oldest son of the owner of the Bailey Building and Loan, the only man who refused to sell out to greedy Mr. Potter, who owned everything else in town. As a boy, George saved his younger brother Harry from drowning and prevented Mr. Gower, the druggist for whom he worked, from accidentally filling a prescription with poison. Even then he was popular, and young Mary Hatch swore that she would love him all her life.

George planned on leaving town for college once Harry graduated from high school, but the death of their father necessitated his taking over the Building and Loan so Potter wouldn't get it. He gave his college money to Harry instead, and remained in Bedford Falls.

George married Mary. They planned a honeymoon but had to cancel it because they had to use their meager savings to ward off a run on the Building and Loan. George opened up Bailey Park for low-income families. Potter unsuccessfully tried to buy George out. Despite his low salary, George and Mary brought up three children.

World War II came and went. George's best friends Ernie, a cab driver, and Burt, a cop, went off to war, but his bad ear kept him home. He was proud of his brother for earning a medal by saving an American ship from being bombed.

On the day before Christmas, Uncle Billy misplaced the money he was depositing for the Building and Loan. Potter found and kept the money. The bank examiner arrived to look at their books, and George realized that because of the missing funds he could go to jail and the Building and Loan would be closed down. He asked Potter for a loan, but Potter turned him down and called the police to have him arrested. George panicked. Now he stands on a bridge determined to commit suicide because his insurance policy makes him worth more dead than alive. He believes everyone would be better off if he'd never been born. But before he can jump, Clarence flies past him into the water. George saves Clarence. Clarence convinces him that he is his guardian angel. He shows George what Bedford Falls would have been like if he had never existed. It is called Pottersville. Where Bedford Park was, a cemetery is instead. One grave is Harry's, who drowned when he was a boy and wasn't alive to save that ship from being bombed. The druggist had been sent to jail for poisoning a child accidentally. Mary is an old maid who screams when George tries to approach her. George asks Clarence to put it back the way it was; he does, and an ecstatic George runs through the streets yelling Merry Christmas. All his friends, and even the bank examiner, give George money with which to make up the deficit. George realizes that he is a rich man because he has so many friends. Clarence has earned his wings.

I t's a Wonderful Life originated as a short story called "The Greatest Gift" that writer Philip Van Doren Stern sent as a Christmas card to his friends. RKO bought Stern's story, but when scripts by Dalton Trumbo, Marc Connelly, and Clifford Odets all proved unsatisfactory, it was sold to Frank Capra, who was looking for the right property to inaugurate his independently run production company. RKO would then handle distribution. (The film proved to be the only project for the ill-fated Liberty Films.) Capra wrote in his fine autobiography, The Name Above the Title (Macmillan, 1971): "It was the story I'd been looking for all my life! Small town. A man. A good man, ambitious. But so busy helping others, life seems to pass him by. He wishes he'd never been born. He gets his wish. Wow! What an idea." So Capra turned the idea into a film. As for its quality, I agree with critic William S. Pechter: "It's a Wonderful Life is the kind of work that defies criticism; almost one might say, defies art. It is one of the funniest and one of the bleakest, as well as being one of the most technically adroit films ever made; it is a masterpiece." Frank Capra also agrees with this assessment; in his less-than-humble autobiography, he recalls how he felt after directing the film which he believed would be his ninth consecutive hit: "I thought it was the greatest film I had ever made. Better yet, I thought it was the greatest film anybody ever made." But in 1946 the mood of the country had changed from how it had been before the war during Capra's glory years, and the American public rejected "Capra-corn" in favor of less sentimental more cynical postwar themes; and It's a Wonderful Life disappointed at the box office. But today, more than thirty-five years later, it has received its due, and I believe that if a poll were taken it might rank just behind The Wizard of Oz (1939), Gone With the Wind (1939), Casablanca (1942), The Sound of Music (1965), and Star Wars (1977) as America's most popular film.

For many television viewers the film has become as much a tradition of a joyful Christmas season as Miracle on 34th Street (1947). The New Yorker ran a story in January 1979 about the eighth annual It's a Wonderful Life invitation party held by a group of dedicated East Siders and a second story in January 1981 after Frank Capra attended the tenth party. I suspect that there are many such gatherings across the country come Christmas time. Unfortunately, Marlo Thomas's unneeded TV-movie remake It Happened One Christmas has caused many stations to bump the Capra film from their schedules or move it to some non-Christmasy date, and some stations have substantially cut the lengthy film (it has been shown without the scenes of George as a boy and/or the flashback!). Cultists are often forced to seek it out in repertory theaters around December 25. Last Christmas I saw it in a packed theater and it was

Donna Reed and James Stewart, the appealing romantic leads of It's a Wonderful Life, *rehearse the film's Charleston number.*

immediately apparent that only the youngest children in the audience hadn't seen it several times. Wild applause and sighs greeted the titles. Afterwards, with their Christmas whole, people were cheerfully rattling off those many moments when they had been overcome by emotion.

There is no shame in crying while watching *It's a Wonderful Life*, admittedly one of the most sentimental

pictures of all time. Capra doesn't make us cry as do other directors when his characters die or are down on their luck. During those parts where George suffers most our eyes are dry. We cry when caught up in the happy emotions of characters who realize that life is indeed wonderful ("I want to live!" George discovers after Clarence shows him how miserable the world would have been if he had never been born); who

In the moonlight, George courts eighteen-year-old Mary.

kissing everyone in sight several times (in what is probably the most tear-causing scene in cinema history), thanking everyone for helping him out of his moral crisis and his financial difficulties; and Clarence leaves George his copy of *The Adventures of Tom Sawyer* and signs it "Love." *It's a Wonderful Life* is the most reassuring film: not only do you (whom George represents) have a family who loves you, a hometown sweetheart who loves you and marries you, a guardian angel who loves you and protects you, but also you have an entire town of people who love you and come to your aid when you are in trouble—in today's world when your next-door neighbor only comes to your door to tell you to keep the noise down, this is a wonderfully comforting image.

In Edgar G. Ulmer's *Ruthless* (1948), a nice young boy played by Bobbie Anderson saves another child from drowning. He never does another good deed and grows up to be a cad played by Zachary Scott who attempts to become the richest man on earth. In *It's a Wonderful Life*, a nice young boy played by Bobbie Anderson saves another child (his brother Harry) from drowning. He performs one good deed after another and grows up to be the truly generous George Bailey played by popular James Stewart, who, despite having little money, learns that he is "the richest man in the world," because he is rich with friends. Ulmer made gloomy melodramas about villains from *Bluebeard* (1944) to *The Amazing Transparent Man* (1957). Capra made comedy-dramas about heroes. While Capra's films are considered "populist" works (despite taking place in towns rather than in the country) because they typically deal with common folk who unite for a common cause, I think more accurately they are about individuals—one good (e.g., George) and the other bad (e.g., Potter)—who battle each other to see whose voice the masses will follow.

George Bailey follows in the footsteps of the other Capra heroes like Jefferson Smith, John Doe, and Longfellow Deeds. Like these other idealists with a tendency toward demagoguery ("George is always making a speech," observes Sam), he has both his faith in himself and his conservative values tested severely. But when he is at the brink of giving up (and like John Doe considers suicide on Christmas Eve), and releasing his "flock" to be swallowed up, (especially) financially speaking, by the Scrooge-like Potter, he has this faith restored by those very people he had spent a lifetime teaching through words and by example. By coming to his financial rescue, they prove to George that they have learned (while he has temporarily forgotten) his great lesson: people's most important investments are not in stocks and bonds or property but in each other.

The tear-jerking finale in which people come from all over to repay George and Mary for their kindnesses to them over the years—prefigured by the earlier joyous scene in which George and Mary dance off the gym floor and into a swimming pool and everyone else, instead of mocking them, jumps in with them—is similar to the finale of *Our Vines Have Tender Grapes* (1945), made a year earlier. In that picture, scripted by

overcome their problems (usually disillusionment), and who reward kindness with kindness. We are moved foremost by the affection these characters have for and are willing to show each other: Mr. Gower hugs young George when the boy prevents him from sending a prescription he accidentally had filled with poison instead of medicine; George ("I'll give you the moon") and Mary ("I'll take it") walk home from the dance at the high school harmonizing and, obviously in love, exchange their first kiss; George kisses his mother outside their house in a quietly played, very tender scene in which she expresses her understanding of his desire to leave Bedford Falls and her knowledge that George wants to see Mary although he declares otherwise; Ernie kisses Bert (a pre-Sesame Street Bert and Ernie) on the forehead after they have done such a good job of making George and Mary's wedding night romantic; George kisses his sick daughter Zuzu and "fixes" her flower by hiding the broken petals in his pocket ("Zuzu's petals!" he cries happily when he realizes Clarence has returned him to real life because the petals—missing in his nightmare—are back in his pocket); George runs through his house a few minutes after this discovery

Clarence (L) tells George that he is his guardian angel. Neither George nor the spooked bridgekeeper believes him although what he says is true.

Dalton Trumbo, who as mentioned wrote a rejected script for *It's a Wonderful Life*, the tear-jerking finale shows a group of poor farmers joining together to help save one of their lot from financial ruin. Trumbo, a left-winger who was later one of the blacklisted "Hollywood Ten," clearly saw this uniting of the farmers as a politically "progressive" act. On the other hand, the scene in which the folks of Bedford Falls unite to bail George out of trouble was meant by Capra to reflect his "conservatism"—his respect for America's founding fathers who—often inspired by leaders such as Washington, Jefferson, and Lincoln—stuck together through grave hardships and against corruptive influences and helped America persevere. This is that rare instance when differing political lines intersect.

It's a Wonderful Life was the first film James Stewart made after returning from active service during the war. He always has regarded "George Bailey" as his favorite part, and there is good reason for this: "George Bailey" blends his prewar persona with his postwar persona. For most of the picture he is the familiar "Jimmy Stewart": the boy next door; optimistic in an increasingly cynical, chaotic world; naive; a hick philosopher, talking slowly and making sense or talking so fast and exuberantly that his voice changes several octaves per sentence and you just know he'll have a sore throat in the morning. In order for George to talk he must move his hands about wildly; it is truly delightful when on his wedding night he comes to the Granville house and finds Mary waiting there in a romantic setting (posters from around the world line the walls, Hawaiian music plays on the record player), and is so stunned that he can't move his arms and thus remains speechless. Mary (played beautifully by beautiful Donna Reed) remains the steadying influence in the film,* while George changes completely into a character much like the ones he would play in the fifties in a series of

---

*In most early Capra films, cynical heroines do an about face under the heroes' good influences.

A publicity shot of the generous George lending money from his personal savings to the needy people of Bedford Falls as Uncle Billy looks on. In the film itself, Mary does not look distraught because George is giving away their honeymoon money—in fact, it is she who suggests he do this noble deed.

Interestingly, even at the film's end dishonest Mr. Potter continues to be an evil force in Bedford Falls.

Anthony Mann westerns and in Hitchcock's *Vertigo* (1958). He becomes pessimistic; tearful; violent; aware of the ways of the world and thinking the worst of it; and quite neurotic. It is brave of Capra, in fact, to let his hero degenerate so much that he even slaps bungling Uncle Billy. Never again would a picture offer Stewart a part with such a wide range of emotions. Stewart is a great movie actor, but this is the picture in which we can really see exactly how great he is.

Likewise, this film, which itself ranges from riotous comedy to dreadful nightmare, allows the rest of the wonderful cast (Capra's stock company) the same chance to show off their versatility. It is a disturbing series of images we see in the sequence in which George is shown Bedford Falls as it might have been if he weren't born. Particularly revealing are the faces of Beulah Bondi, Ward Bond, Frank Faylen, Sheldon Leonard, etc., faces that once had such warmth and suddenly are terrifying cold, like Potter's. (The only

unrealistic change is with Mary, whom Capra sees as an old maid who for some reason wears glasses—is this an indication that Potter with George out of the way would provide the town with inadequate lighting?)

The one face that glows in both the real world and in the nightmare world belongs to Clarence, played perfectly by Henry Travers, who Capra writes "was sent by heaven itself to play Stewart's pixy guardian." It is fitting that Travers be the one to help Stewart see clearly, for in the previous year's *Bells of St. Mary's* (1945), the film which is on the marquee of the one movie house in Bedford Falls, Travers plays the skinflint who becomes exceedingly generous under the prodding of nun Ingrid Bergman and *her* heavenly contacts.

Jason and the Argonauts

1963 Great Britain Columbia
Pictures release of a Morningside
Worldwide film
Director: Don Chaffey
Producer: Charles H. Schneer
Screenplay: Jan Read and

Beverley Cross
Cinematography: Wilkie Cooper
Special Effects: Ray Harryhausen
Music: Bernard Herrmann
Editor: Maurice Rootes
Running Time: 104 minutes

Cast: Todd Armstrong (Jason), Nancy Kovack (Medea), Gary
Raymond (Acostus), Laurence Naismith (Argus), Niall MacGinnis
(Zeus), Honor Blackman (Hera), Michael Gwynn (Hermes),
Douglas Wilmer (Pelias), Jack Gwillim (King Aeetes), John
Cairney (Hylas), Nigel Green (Hercules), Patrick Troughton
(Phineas), John Crawford (Polydeuces)

Synopsis: Pelias murders Aristo, the king of Thessaly, and takes his
throne. But he is unable to kill his baby son Jason (who has been
prophesied to retake the throne when an adult) because Hera,
queen of the gods, takes him under her protection. For twenty years
Pelias seeks Jason. At last they meet when Jason saves him from
drowning. Jason has come to claim his rightful throne, but, not
knowing who Pelias is, he follows his advice to first sail to the ends
of the earth to Colchis in search of the Golden Fleece, which will
bring peace and prosperity to the people of Thessaly. Pelias sends
Acostus to accompany Jason on his journey, telling him to kill Jason
if he should find the Fleece.

After Jason expresses a disbelief in the gods, Hermes transports
him to Mount Olympus. Hera tells Jason that she will grant him a
number of wishes in order to help him on his journey.

Jason assembles a crew of the finest physical specimens in
Greece. Even Hercules wants to go for the glory of such a trip. He
befriends a weak but clever young man named Hylas, whom Jason
allows on the journey. Their ship is the *Argo,* named after the master
builder Argus, and its distinctive feature is a figurehead of Hera on
the stern facing the ship's deck.

When the men run out of food and water, Hera directs them to
the Isle of Bronze, where they replenish themselves. But when
Hercules takes a gold shaft from a treasure trove of the gods, an
enormous statue of the titan Talos comes to life. It wrecks the ship
and attacks the men. Jason opens up a screw in Talos's foot, liquid
pours out, and it crashes to the ground. Hercules does not realize
that Talos fell on Hylos and vows to search the island until he finds
his friend. After rebuilding the ship, the others move on.

Because the blind Phineas disobeyed Zeus he was condemned to
be tormented daily by two harpies. Jason's men lock up the harpies,
and as a reward Phineas tells them how to get to Colchis: through
the "Clashing Rocks." He gives Jason a medallion of Neptune, the
god of the sea, for protection.

The Argonauts watch a ship pass through the Clashing Rocks
and be destroyed by falling rocks. The *Argo* attempts to go through.
When all seems lost, Jason throws his medallion in the water.
Triton, the son of Neptune, rises from the ocean and holds the
mountain while the men pass. In the water, Jason sees the pretty
Medea, the lone survivor from the other ship. She is the high
priestess of Colchis. Jason rescues her and they immediately
become attracted to each other. King Aeetes of Colchis has Jason
and his men arrested when Acostus tells him that they plan to steal
the Golden Fleece. But Medea drugs all Aeetes's guards and helps
Jason escape. She and Jason go in search of the Fleece. They find it
protected by a hydra, which has mortally wounded Acostus. After a
death-defying fight, Jason kills the hydra. He, Medea, Argus, and
two Argonauts take the Fleece and flee Aeetes and his soldiers.

Aeetes collects the hydra's teeth from its seven heads. He
confronts Jason high on a cliff. Argus takes Medea to the ship.
Jason and the two other men remain to fight. Seven sword-wielding
skeletons emerge from the soil where Aeetes throws the teeth. The
sword fight is long and brutal. Both Jason's companions are killed.
Jason escapes by jumping off the cliff into the ocean. He and Medea
sail off together on the *Argo,* with the Fleece. Hera is proud that she
outmaneuvered Zeus, making the events on earth transpire in
Jason's favor. Zeus warns her that he isn't through with Jason.

For those of us who thrill to fantasy-adventure
films in the *Thief of Bagdad* (1940) tradition,
there is no greater treat than the not-frequent-
enough release of a new spectacle featuring the
special effects of Ray Harryhausen. It is Harryhausen—not the actors, not the director—who is the
"star" of the pictures with which he is involved: he is the
attraction. With the exception of the much younger,
very talented Jim Danforth, there is no one who even
attempts the elaborate effects Harryhausen comes up
with (each of which may take several months to complete); and only Harryhausen is given film projects—
almost always produced by Charles H. Schneer—where
the budget is sufficient for anyone to spend time (up to
three years) and money on grand creations. With the
exception of his idol, Willis O'Brien, the special-effects
genius behind *King Kong* (1933), *One Million B.C.*
(1940), and *Mighty Joe Young* (1949), on which Harryhausen assisted him, Ray Harryhausen has done more
than anyone in the special-effects field. O'Brien was the
one who originated the use of stop-motion animation
photography whereby small models with movable parts
are used effectively in place of enormous creatures—
saving the studios great expense. The first to apply split-
screen techniques to stop-motion photography, Harryhausen also combines live action and model work, letting his performers and animated models appear on the
screen at the same time, often interacting. Directors of
these films have commented on how hard it is for actors
to interact with "invisible" creatures that later will be
placed in the shot through composite photography, but
the results have been dazzling. According to Dan Scap-
perotti of *Cinefantastique* (Winter 1980), Harryhausen
builds most of "the stop motion models himself, casting
the sculptures in foam rubber around articulated metal
armatures which serve as their skeletons, allowing them
to be repositioned to fit the desired action for each single
frame exposure." In his Dynamation process (also called
Superdynamation and Dynamation 90), Harryhausen
juxtaposes two 45-degree prisms to guarantee true regis-
tration of subjects from any given perspective. The system also involves a multiple exposure technique called
dyno-synchronization, which assures a realistic and accurate projection of images of varying sizes and proportions with maximum definition and depth of field vision.*

Harryhausen began his career in the forties working
on *Puppetoons*. Then he shared an Oscar with Willis
O'Brien for the terrific special effects in *Mighty Joe
Young*. But it is his remarkable achievements in such
science fiction and fantasy-adventure (his specialty)

---

*This information about Harryhausen's patented Dynamation 90
process was included in a Columbia Pictures publicity release in regard
to *Jason and the Argonauts,* which at the time was being filmed as
Jason and the Golden Fleece. This release was reprinted in the
magazine *Special Effects Created by Ray Harryhausen* (Summer 1971).

Holding the quaking rocks in place, Triton watches the Argo *sail into safe waters.*

films as *The Beast from 20,000 Fathoms* (1953), his first film as special effects coordinator, *It Came From Beneath the Sea* (1955), *Earth vs. the Flying Saucers* (1956), featuring a spectacularly destructive alien attack on Washington, the wondrous *The 7th Voyage of Sinbad* (1958), *The Three Worlds of Gulliver* (1960), *Mysterious Island* (1961), his masterpiece *Jason and the Argonauts, The First Men in the Moon* (1964), *Valley of Gwangi* (1969), *The Golden Voyage of Sinbad* (1974), *Sinbad and the Eye of the Tiger* (1977), and *Clash of the Titans* (1981) that have made Harryhausen a cause célèbre among special effects enthusiasts. Incredibly, in the early seventies there was even a fanzine called *Special Effects Created by Ray Harryhausen* filled with long articles about individual Harryhausen sequences and effects, a letters section in which fans from all over the world debated how Harryhausen accomplished his most sensational effects, and *several* "Harryhausen" editorials. An editorial by Sam Calvin (Summer 1971) is particularly revealing in terms of why Harryhausen is a cult figure and what is the singular nature of a hardcore Harryhausen cultist. An excerpt:

> Part of the appeal of Harryhausen's work comes from our knowledge of the scads of technical intricacies which animation and composite photography necessarily entail. As a result of every special effects fan's desire to figure out "how he did it," no effects shot in a Ray Harryhausen film ever escapes the closest scrutiny. . . . [But] Ray's films are designed to be enjoyed *once* by the theater patron eager to escape . . . into an expertly concocted world of fantasy—not for the super-animation-nut who sits through *Valley of Gwangi* five times straight (like me—and in Italian, no less!) in order to count the number of static matte foregrounds or cringe at some slightly less than perfect process shot. . . . But at least Mr. Harryhausen can take a little comfort . . . that as of right now, nuts like us are in the minority. And I must confess that I would not care to trade my "nuttiness" concerning Ray's work . . . for anything in the world.

Surprisingly, upon its release *Jason and the Argonauts*, a British production (although both Harryhausen and Schneer are American born), got extremely hostile reviews from the American press. Leo Mishkin of New York's *Morning Telegraph* wrote: "*Jason and the Argonauts* is strictly hot weather entertainment, suitable for keeping the children off the streets, perhaps, but hardly to be taken seriously by anybody beyond the age of puberty." And Mishkin was one of the kinder critics. The typical review lumped the picture with the numerous inferior Italian-made epics that flooded the country after the success of *Hercules* (1959) which also dealt with Jason's search for the Golden Fleece; and not one review I have come across mentioned either Harryhausen's name or the fact that the special visual effects were above the norm. But *Jason* has been vindicated as more and more critics have come to realize Harryhausen's amazing, unique talents and his importance to the industry. (Significantly, many of today's critics grew up with Harryhausen films.) And since Harryhausen has stated himself that *Jason* is his personal favorite among the films on which he has worked, it has slipped past *The 7th Voyage of Sinbad* to become the cult film of the Harryhausen collection.

There are a few minor problems with *Jason*. Medea, the love interest, is introduced too late in the film. Hera never gives Jason straight answers but her clues tell all just the same; for instance, before Jason battles Talos, she tells him to look "toward his ankle" in order to find his Achilles heel—when the screw on the back of Talos's foot is so obvious she might as well have said "Find a screw on the back of his foot." I also don't know why Hera sends Jason to Phineas to get directions to Colchis when *she* could tell him the way just as easily. Other problems: the Golden Fleece turns out to be far less interesting than the Maltese falcon; Harryhausen's hydra isn't threatening enough and puts up a terrible fight against Jason.

But forget the flaws. *Jason* is a truly glorious fantasy-adventure film. It is directed by Don Chaffey with equal proportions of wit and excitement. It is beautifully filmed by Wilkie Cooper (try to see a good print in a *theatre*)—and the mysterious blue ocean, white sandy beaches, and strange rock formations found around Palinuro, Italy (which is south of Naples) and the actual Greek temples found in Paestum give the picture historical authenticity. (Interiors were shot at a studio.) Bernard Herrmann's score gives grandeur to the production. Beverley Cross's fine script—he reworked Jan Read's screenplay—is both imaginative and literate. Even the acting is good. Todd Armstrong makes a fine Jason who, refreshingly, is not a musclebound hero but a man of average build who relies on his wits rather than his brawn. Hercules, too, is portrayed (well, I think, by Nigel Green) as a *man* of believable strength and physical proportions. Best of all are the squabbling Zeus, played by Niall MacGinnis, and Hera, played with self-assurance by Honor Blackman, destined for brief stardom as James Bond's "Pussy" Galore. (In *Clash of the Titans*, Laurence Olivier plays Zeus and Claire Bloom is Hera.)

Jason and the Argonauts contains many of Ray Harryhausen's most spectacular creations including (BL) the titan Talos who attacks Jason's men; (TR) the harpies that torment the blind Phineas; (TL) the hydra that protects the Golden Fleece from Jason; and (BR) the incredibly animated skeleton army brought to life by Aeetes.

And in *Jason*, despite the hydra scene, Harryhausen is at his peak. It's just amazing how believable the movements of his creatures are—the flying harpies that plague Phineas, the stiffly moving titan Talos, the miraculous sword-fighting skeletons—and how excellent the composite photography: I don't know how Harryhausen managed such visual tricks as having the animated harpies unravel Phineas's real belt. My favorite special-effects moments are the Clashing Rocks sequence when huge, bearded Triton, his fishtail flapping in the ocean, emerges from the water, holds the mountains apart, and watches the *Argo* as it sails under his arm; and, of course, the truly stupendous climactic skeleton-fighting scene—undoubtedly Harryhausen's ultimate achievement, and perhaps the best special-effects sequence of all time. In his book *Film Fantasy Scrapbook* (A. S. Barnes, 1972), Harryhausen writes:

The Skeleton Sequence was the most talked about part of *Jason*. Technically, it was unprecedented in the sphere of fantasy filming. When one pauses to think that there were seven skeletons fighting three men, with each skeleton having five appendages to move each frame of the film, and keeping them all in synchronization with the three actors' movements, one can readily see why it took four and a half months to record the sequence for the screen. Cer-

To the relief of Jason and Argus, the magical Golden Fleece brings Medea back to life.

tain other time-consuming technical "hocus-pocus" adjustments had to be done during the shooting to create the illusion of the animated figures in actual contact with the live actors.

Other than Harryhausen, I think the person chiefly responsible for Jason's *overall* quality is Beverley Cross, a Greek scholar and first-time scriptwriter, who kept the story and the dialogue on a high intellectual plane so adults could join juveniles in their appreciation of the film. There is an interesting theme that runs through the entire picture: man must fend for himself whether the gods exist or not. In times past, fate ruled men's lives completely; the gods were all-powerful and dominated men as a matter of course. Fate is still an important factor in Jason's time (e.g., he has been prophesied to be the future king of Thessaly), but more and more man chooses his own life's course (it is Jason who chooses to seek the Golden Fleece). Now the gods keep such a low profile, playing board (bored of human beings) games on Olympus, that man thinks the gods have deserted him. Zeus asks Jason what has taken the place of man's faith in the gods. "The hearts of men," he answers. Jason rebuffs Zeus's offer to supply him with a crew and is content to make the hazardous journey with only Hera's pledge to help him a few times. She helps with information and advice—not action. Jason has learned that prayers to the gods are not always answered; "The gods are best served by those who need their help least,"

Zeus alibis. When humans do get the help of the gods, they know they must still put themselves on the line. For instance, when Triton holds the quaking mountains, the Argonauts still must navigate their ship away from the few dangerous boulders that continue to fall. Phineas finds the gods petty ("I was a sinner, but I didn't sin every day. Why do they punish me every day?"); Jason thinks them cruel. One thing is clear: the gods can no longer frighten man into obedience. The Argonauts challenge Zeus when they kill Talos, who guards Zeus's treasures, and when they imprison the harpies, whom Zeus sent to torment Phineas. And they get away with it. "If I were to punish every blasphemy," Zeus concedes, "I would have no followers." Of the gods, Jason says, "In time all men will have to do without them." Such words frighten Zeus, and he admits as much to Hera; he thinks her "almost human" for staying with him despite such weakness. That is Cross's point: the pendulum has swung and the gods and the humans are fast becoming equals. But don't count Zeus out. He is not through giving insubordinates like Jason their comeuppance. At the picture's end he tells Hera that he will allow Jason and pretty Medea to sail away together ("I'm sentimental"), but he adds, "Let us continue with Jason another day." As legend has it, years later it was Zeus who refused to punish Medea for killing unfaithful Jason's children. Zeus was not one to forget.

1954 Republic
Director: Nicholas Ray
Producer: (uncredited)
Screenplay: Philip Yordan
Based on a novel by Roy Chanslor
Cinematography: Harry Stradling
Music: Victor Young
Theme song: Peggy Lee and Victor Young; sung by Peggy Lee
Editor: Richard L. Van Enger
Running Time: 111 minutes

Cast: Joan Crawford (Vienna), Sterling Hayden (Johnny Guitar), Mercedes McCambridge (Emma Small), Scott Brady (Dancin' Kid), Ward Bond (John McIvers), Ben Cooper (Turkey Ralston), Ernest Borgnine (Bart Lonergan), John Carradine (Old Tom), Royal Dano (Corey), Frank Ferguson (marshal), Paul Fix (Eddie), Rhys Williams (Mr. Andrews), Ian MacDonald (Pete)

Synopsis: Ex-gunslinger Johnny Logan, now calling himself Johnny Guitar, rides into a small town in post-Civil War Arizona. He has been hired to work as guitarist by Vienna, a beautiful, strong-willed saloon-casino owner. Five years earlier they had been lovers, but he walked out on her, too restless to settle down. Now Vienna insists that she has gotten over Johnny—just as he insists that he no longer has romantic designs on her—and is more interested in her business than in men. She has learned that the railroad will be passing through the area, and she stands to become rich once she sells it some of her land.

There is a stage robbery, and a banker is killed. Emma Small, the dead man's sister, comes to Vienna's accompanied by the town marshal, wealthy rancher John McIvers, and about a dozen townspeople. Emma and McIvers oppose the railroad because it will eliminate their control of the territory. Emma also despises Vienna because the man she loves, the Dancin' Kid, is attracted to her. She would rather see the Dancin' Kid dead than with Vienna, and tries to convince her companions that Vienna, the Kid, and the Kid's partners—mean Bart, sickly Corey, and young Turkey—are responsible for her brother's death and should be hanged. Neither the marshal nor McIvers will go along with Emma without real evidence, but McIvers orders Vienna and the Kid's gang to clear out of town. Vienna says that she is not leaving. Emma tells Vienna that she will kill her someday. Vienna replies, "I know—unless I kill you first."

That night, Vienna and Johnny admit they still love each other. They agree to start anew, but neither is sure the other can be depended upon. Vienna doesn't like Johnny's violent nature and Johnny is jealous that Vienna has had many lovers.

The Kid and his three companions decide to rob Emma's bank—figuring that as long as they are being forced to flee the area it might as well be for a genuine crime and not a stage robbery which they had no part in. The bank robbery takes place just as Vienna is withdrawing her money. Later Emma makes her bank teller swear that Vienna took part in the robbery. She, McIvers, and the marshal form a posse and ride hard to Vienna's. There they discover Vienna hiding Turkey, who had been injured while riding away from the bank. They scare him into swearing that Vienna helped with the robbery. Old Tom, the only employee whom Vienna was unable to send away in the face of impending danger (even Johnny had left), pulls a gun to help the marshal protect Vienna from the vigilantes who want to hang her. Emma shoots Tom, who accidentally kills the marshal with a stray bullet.

After burning down Vienna's, the mob hangs Turkey, but when Emma attempts to hang Vienna, Johnny, who has returned after seeing the fire, cuts the rope and helps Vienna escape. They go to the Kid's secret hideout, the mob close on their trail.

Neither the Kid nor Bart is happy to see Johnny, but Vienna keeps the men from fighting. Emma secretly meets Bart and tells him that he and Corey can go free if he helps arrange for the others to be caught. When Corey attempts to tell the Kid what Bart has planned with Emma, Bart kills him. Bart tries to kill the Kid, but Johnny shoots Bart first. The vigilantes decide that enough blood has been spilled, and stand back while Emma carries on her personal vendetta against Vienna. Both women wear guns and holsters, as Emma walks toward the shack where Vienna awaits her. They fire on one another and Emma kills the Kid. Although shot in the arm, Vienna kills Emma. Vienna and Johnny go off together.

Johnny Guitar

Italian director Bernardo Bertolucci calls Nicholas Ray's influential, legendary *Johnny Guitar* "the first of the baroque westerns." Others have questioned its being called a western at all. "It's not about horses and guns," argues French director François Truffaut, "it is about people and emotions." American film critic Michael Wilmington chooses a position of compromise, referring to it as "an impression of the present [America of the early fifties] filmed through the myths of the past." *Johnny Guitar* is in fact many things: an amusing parody of the "classic" western; high camp; a political satire; the visualization of a ballad much like "Frankie and Johnny"; a homage to *Rancho Notorious* (1952), the peculiar western made by Fritz Lang; a fifties youth gang picture with adults playing teen parts (Johnny Guitar being a violent motorcycle-leader type turned philosopher-poet-troubador); a hallucinatory venture into what Andrew Sarris calls "Freudian feminism." But paramountly, it is a serious indictment of McCarthyite mob hysteria and bigotry, controversial because Ray and screenwriters Philip Yordan dared attack the reactionary American political climate of 1954 by subverting what had always been a politically conservative genre.

Writing in *The Velvet Light Trap* (Spring 1974), Michael Wilmington pointed out that the characters in *Johnny Guitar* "can be schematized . . . from a purely political angle." According to Wilmington, the outlaws who live and work communally, who are blamed for every wrongdoing in town, whose "leader" is a lefty, "become symbolic Communists. Johnny, the ex-gunman, is the ex-Communists (now mere entertainers) called before HUAC. Vienna—consort of the outlaws—is a 'fellow traveler.' Emma . . . suggests those

Vienna finds it hard keeping the peace between the Dancin' Kid (L) and Johnny Guitar, the two men who love her.

vindictive witnesses and politicans who used the investigations to destroy the careers of their hated rivals. McIvers is big business. . . . The . . . marshal is the good man in government, caving in under McCarthy's bluster. And the townspeople are the American middle class—the film's audience."

It is easy to carry Wilmington's analogy further. Just as McCarthyites tried to link suspected Communists to alien governments and concerns, Emma constantly reminds the townspeople that Vienna (notice the name?) is a foreigner, having lived in the area only five years. Appealing to their bigotry, Emma warns them that if the railroad comes through as Vienna plans, dirt farmers will push the cattlemen out of the territory. Appealing to their warped "Americanism," she implies that Vienna wants the railroad because it will destroy their way of life: "You'd better wake up or you'll find your women and your kids will be squeezed between barbed wire and fence posts!"

Just as HUAC threatened witnesses to force them to testify against those HUAC had it in for, Emma bullies her bank teller into accusing Vienna of participating in the bank heist, and he complies so he won't lose his job. The posse Emma leads then gets Turkey to corroborate this testimony and point an accusatory finger at Vienna by promising him he can save himself by squealing. That Turkey turns in his mother figure indicates how low Ray considers those "friendly witnesses" that gave names to HUAC—to Ray, Turkey is as bad as those children who turned in their dissident parents to the Gestapo in Nazi Germany. The posse hangs the cowardly Turkey (he dresses in yellow and could have been called "chicken"), reminding us that many who were informers in front of HUAC didn't necessarily save their own necks.

Just as twentieth-century inquisitors assumed that a person might be a communist if his/her personal/social/sexual life deviated from the norm, Emma reminds the townspeople that ex-saloon girl Vienna has had many lovers—as if that were proof that she is capable of robbing banks and stages. In truth, Vienna has "reformed" in that she is no longer a "loose" woman, but as it was with suspected communists who had long since given up their left-wing affiliations, she finds it impossible to live down her past. Furthermore, she is guilty by association: Emma tries to convince the posse to arrest Vienna along with the Kid, not necessarily because she is guilty of the stage robbery but

Joan Crawford is at her best, and wittiest, in this scene where Vienna refuses to allow Emma and the ranchers to arrest her for the murder of Emma's brother.

With Bart lying dead in front of them, the posse looks toward the cabin where Vienna, Johnny, and the Kid are holed up. Emma will go up the embankment after Vienna, but McIvers (front row, R) will agree with the others that there has already been too much bloodshed.

because Emma considers her "the same as him." And Vienna is guilty by implication: since she hid Turkey, the posse concludes she was his accomplice when he robbed the bank.

As Michael Wilmington writes, Vienna is a "progressive." Her gambling establishment is located symbolically between the town and the outlaws' hideout— just as her "politics," though leaning toward that of the outlaws, lies somewhere between that of the two factions. She wants to remain neutral, and sit and wait for the railroad to come and make her rich. But when Vienna's is burned down, she must choose a side. Fleeing from the posse—the self-proclaimed law— Vienna enters an *underground* tunnel, a symbolic act that signifies she has become part of "the resistance." Before she and Johnny go off to join the Kid's gang and make a commitment to outright rebellion against the forces in control, she puts on a shirt and, fittingly, it is bright *red*.

This is a nineteenth-century witchhunt, but Ray makes Emma, the accuser—not Vienna, the accused— the witch, dressing her in a black funeral dress and having her ride her horse as if it were a broom. The witch image is clear when Emma shoots down the candelabra in Vienna's. As flames engulf the building, she spreads her arms and her shadow dominates the frame; then she comes outside into close-up, her face glowing happily—this is evil personified. Such a display of heartlessness is what one would expect from the woman Ray introduces during a violent windstorm—

much like the entrance of the wicked witch in *The Wizard of Oz* (1939).

In this rare western where *sexual drive* plays an integral part in the drama, it is intimated that Emma's madness/hysteria is a result of sexual repression. She detests Vienna, who has her choice of men, when the only man she can arouse herself is ugly Bart. And what is especially infuriating for Emma is that while she is desperate for the Kid's love, Vienna, who now has Johnny back, turns the Kid away and *still* he doesn't stop being faithful to her. Even before Johnny returned to her life, Vienna had gained control over her sexual desires; but Emma hasn't such will power. Michael Wilmington writes, "In light of Emma's sexual hangups, we can see why the Kid's robbery of her bank enrages her: not only does he have the gall to penetrate her vault, but he kisses her rival, Vienna, at the very entrance."

If we are to believe pistols are meant to be phallic symbols in the film, and this is implied when Turkey puts on a shooting demonstration to prove to Vienna he has become a man ("That's good shooting for a *boy*," she tells him), then we have clues about the psyche of Emma when she gingerly fondles her pistol; and of Vienna when she puts her hand over the drawn pistol of the excited Kid during the bank robbery—a gesture not meant to further excite him but to let him know she wants him to put it away. How they react to pistols tells us that Emma wants sex, Vienna can do without it. Similarly, Vienna stands at the top of the stairs and

It's like the Spanish Inquisition when the marshal can't prevent Emma, McIvers, and the other ranchers from forcing Turkey to incriminate himself and the innocent Vienna.

keeps a predominantly male posse at bay; stairs, of course, are a Freudian symbol signifying intercourse,* so what we are seeing is Vienna denying numerous, faceless men sexual entry when in years past she would have admitted them with a shrug of a shoulder. (The "male" part of her which wears pants and carries a gun thus protects her "female honor.")

Much praise has been given *Johnny Guitar* because of its radical reversal of traditional sex roles. Here a male dancer and male guitarist vie for the love of a gun-toting woman. As Michael Wilmington states, "Just as Vienna has become a 'Johnny' (she wears black and packs six-guns), Johnny has become a 'Vienna' (romantic and full of sentiment)." The film's title suggests that Johnny is the main character, but in truth it is Vienna who makes all the decisions, initiates the action, and takes the majority of heroic stands—privileges traditionally denied women in westerns. Johnny follows his boss Vienna's lead, just as the male posse follows Emma. (Like Vienna, Emma is referred to as a woman who wants to be a man, but Emma's "macho" bearing is not mitigated, as Vienna's is, by motherly instincts.) When Johnny tries to make Vienna feel guilty for having had many lovers, she rips into him for adhering to a double standard: "All a woman has to do is slip once and she's a tramp. A man can kill, lie, cheat . . ." Having been

---

*This film contains much Freudian symbolism. Vienna finds herself in a world of stairwells, pistols, vaults, caves, tunnels, mine shafts, streams, and waterfalls. Even the railroad must take on sexual meaning: Vienna knows it will *penetrate* her land because of "confidences" she had with the railroad's construction chief.

taught a lesson, Johnny makes no more attempts to deny Vienna the independence she has achieved from all men since he left her five years before. It is up to him to try to get Vienna back on new terms, where she won't have to answer to him for what *he* believes were/are indiscretions on her part. His first compromise: he admits *he* was wrong when he left her.

In Ray films, the lead characters strive to control hostile impulses: James Dean in *Rebel Without a Cause* (1955), James Mason, victim of a violence-inducing drug in *Bigger Than Life* (1956), Robert Wagner in *The True Story of Jesse James* (1957), et. al. There is a built-in nervous tension that causes viewers to wait anxiously for an *explosion of personality* (which may or may not come, depending on the character). *Johnny Guitar*, in fact, begins with a true explosion (dynamiting) that occurs when Johnny rides across the screen. Below him we see a stage robbery (the Old West), and above him construction (the New West); he rides a horse with a black tail (signifying Johnny's dark past which still haunts him) and a white body (signifying Johnny's current state of grace). We immediately suspect that here is a man with great internal conflict with a personality that is in a transition stage; and from this moment on we wait for someone or some series of events to detonate this (excuse the cliché) human time bomb. To make matters more exciting, Johnny comes into contact with a whole slew of *equally* volatile characters—all with clenched fists, sharp tongues, and itchy trigger fingers. A battle royal is unavoidable when such characters are thrown together into one arena (Vienna's), but Ray masterfully keeps up the suspense through a series of clever *stalling* tactics. Guns are pulled but not fired, threats are made but aren't carried out immediately. Ray's anxiety-building delays are reflected in the dialogue: after Johnny beats up Bart, the Kid warns him, "You've made a big mistake, mister. Bart's not a man to forget"; when the Kid robs Emma's bank, Vienna warns him, "Emma won't let you get away"; McIvers gives Vienna twenty-four hours to get out of town, and when she spitefully makes him pay for a bottle of liquor he breaks, he warns her, "I won't forget this." And then there's the double warning: "I'm going to kill you, Vienna," states Emma, who then must hear Vienna's unafraid response, "I know—if I don't kill you first." But here, too, the inevitable battle is postponed. Similarly, action where props are involved stops before completion: the Kid tosses a coin into the air, promising Johnny he'll kill him if it turns out "heads," but Vienna intercepts it in midair; a roulette wheel is stopped in midspin; a glass rolls off the bar but Johnny snares it before it breaks on the floor. Tension is built by repressing violence, symbolic and real. Significantly, when the candelabra crashes to the ground without someone stopping it in midair, we realize that the wait for violence is over.

Ray and Yordan didn't create a film where people become rivals simply because they don't like one another or feel jealousy. This work is so powerful because what they have presented us with—exposing their political intentions—is a series of *dialectically* opposed forces in confrontation. Thus the rivalries become: the future (civilization) versus the past (the untamed West represented by restless gunslingers like Johnny *Logan*); progressives (Vienna's visionaries who dream of a railroad and a new town) versus conservatives (those Arizonans who oppose a change in their way of life); dirt farmers (who will come into the area) versus wealthy ranchers (who now own all the land); the law (the marshal) versus mob rule (the vigilantes); female (Vienna) versus male (Johnny); righthanded (Johnny) versus lefthanded (the Kid); intellectuals (Corey, an outlaw who reads) versus nonintellectuals (Bart); the emotionally and sexually self-assured (Vienna) versus the unbalanced (Emma); persecutors (Emma and her followers) versus the persecuted (Vienna and her friends); and decency and goodness (what America really stands for) versus evil (Emma and those like her who represent the true threat to American ideals).

Even the dialogue reveals the contradictory nature of things: "Lie to me," Johnny tells Vienna while seeking the truth. A line is delivered and the next line fights it off. For example, when Johnny asks Vienna, "What's keeping you awake?" she answers, "Dreams, bad dreams." And when Johnny challenges her with "How many men have you forgotten?" she comes back with "As many as you've remembered."

The world of *Johnny Guitar* is one of conflict, where everyone and everything head toward a cataclysmic collision. Every bit of the film's energy takes us to the final climactic scene at the Kid's cabin. And the Vienna-Emma shootout lets no one down. "I'm coming up, Vienna!" "I'm waiting!"

The Killing

1956 United Artists
Director: Stanley Kubrick
Producer: James B. Harris
Screenplay: Stanley Kubrick
Additional dialogue: Jim
Thompson

From the novel *Clean Break* by Lionel White
Cinematography: Lucien Ballard
Music: Gerald Fried
Editor: Betty Steinberg
Running Time: 84 minutes

Cast: Sterling Hayden (Johnny Clay), Coleen Gray (Fay), Jay C. Flippen (Marvin Unger), Vince Edwards (Val Cannon), Marie Windsor (Sherry Peatty), Ted DeCorsia (Randy Kennan), Elisha Cook (George Peatty), Joe Sawyer (Mike O'Reilly), Tim Carey (Nikki Arane), Jay Adler (Leo), Joseph Turkel (Tiny), Maurice Oboukhoff (Kola Kwarian)

Synopsis: At the racetrack the seventh race is about to begin.

A week earlier, Johnny Clay and Fay were in his friend Marvin Unger's apartment. He told her that he and a few others were going to pull off a big job in a week's time. Clay was just out of prison after five years, and Fay, who has loved him since they were children, worried that he might end up back in jail. He told her that the risks were worth taking.

Later that night, the other men involved joined Johnny and Marvin to go over their plan to rob the track's two-million-dollar payroll. They were Randy Kennan, a policeman who needed money to pay off the mob; Mike O'Reilly, the track's bartender, who needed money to care for his sick wife; and Little George, a cashier at the track, who wanted money to buy luxuries for his wife Sherry. George was unaware that the sultry Sherry was having an affair with small-time mobster Val, whom she had told of the impending robbery in the hope that Val would take all the money from the robbers.

Johnny caught Sherry eavesdropping on their meeting. He knocked her out. Alone with her later, he told her to forget what she had heard or they would not attempt the robbery and she would not become rich. He could tell that she did not love her husband. But he did not know about Val. George told Sherry that he wanted to withdraw from the robbery, but she insisted that he participate. She told him that Johnny had tried to make love to her when they were alone.

Johnny hired part-time wrestler Kola Kwarian to cause a diversionary brawl during the seventh race; and Nikki to cause an equally great diversion by shooting the horse Red Lightning in the middle of the race.

The seventh race begins. Kola starts a brawl by Mike's bar. The track's guards subdue him. While they are occupied, George opens the door leading to the payroll office, and Johnny sneaks through. Johnny gets the machine gun Mike planted earlier in his locker and puts on a mask. He holds up the four men at the payroll office, fills up a huge laundry bag with two million dollars in bills, and tosses it out the window. Randy, waiting below, puts the money in his police car and drives to a motel, where he leaves it in a room Johnny has been renting. Meanwhile Johnny escapes from the track in the confusion caused when Nikki shoots Red Lightning with a high-powered rifle from a distant parking lot. Nikki is killed when a black cop whom he offended by calling him "nigger" shoots him as he attempts to flee.

Randy, Marvin, Mike, and George wait for Johnny to bring the money. Val charges in and there is a gunfight. Everyone is killed except George, who is fatally wounded. Realizing that Sherry had set him up with Val, George struggles to get home, where he kills Sherry and drops dead by her corpse.

Knowing that his accomplices have run into trouble, Johnny puts the money in a suitcase and joins Fay at the airport. He has purchased tickets for Boston. He has to check the suitcase, and watches in horror as it breaks open on the runway and the money all blows out. Johnny and Fay try to get out of the airport. They cannot get a taxi. "What's the difference?" says Johnny as he allows the approaching cops to arrest him.

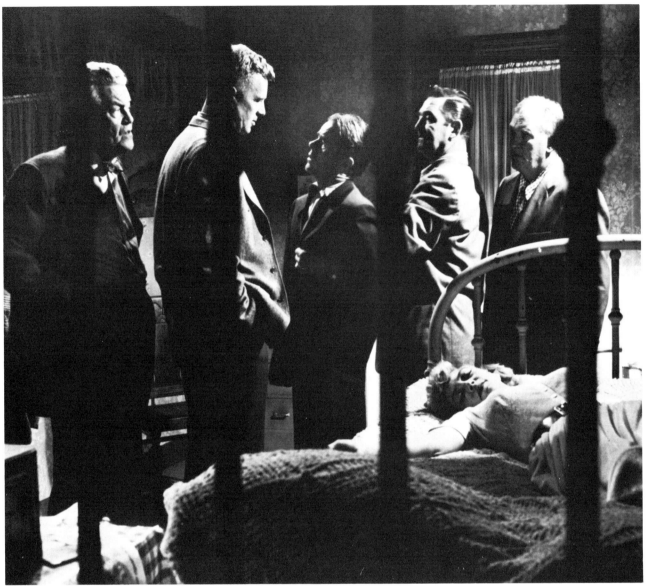

Johnny tells George that he knocked out his wife Sherry when he caught her eavesdropping on the heist plans. (L-R) Marvin, Randy, and Mike listen as George insists that Sherry won't interfere with their plans.

The works of Stanley Kubrick have long been sources for lively debate, but *The Killing*, made early in his career, is his one picture that causes few arguments. It is generally regarded by Kubrick's admirers and detractors alike as one of the best caper films: a taut, fast-paced thriller made by a clever director obviously in love with the filmmaking craft. He had made two films prior to *The Killing* that today remain obscure. *Fear and Desire* (1953) is a clumsy little picture for which Kubrick mistakenly post-dubbed the entire soundtrack. Better is *Killer's Kiss* (1955), an uneven yet interesting low-budget picture with some mismatched romantic leads (Jamie Smith and Irene Krane) who didn't go on to stardom, but some fine location footage of New York (back when a pizza slice was just ten cents), and a humdinger fight finale in a loft full of mannequins. While these pictures cost

$40,000 each, Kubrick made *The Killing* for $320,000, still small by Hollywood standards but a big jump for him, and the improvement in production values is staggering. Andrew Sarris, Kubrick's most vocal critic over the years, is one of many who consider *The Killing* the true beginning of Kubrick's career as a major director.

As is the case with most good low-budget films, directorial style triumphs over financial handicaps. The indoor sets are like shoeboxes—the motel room, the Peattys' one-room apartment, the payroll office, the track's locker room, etc.—but Kubrick doesn't hide this fact. He uses it to advantage. He moves his camera around these small sets, shooting from different angles and directions to impress upon us just how confining these spaces are, knowing that a sense of claustrophobia causes tension for viewers as well as for his characters.

Characters are further enveloped by darkness and shadows; when Johnny, Marvin, George, Randy, and Mike sit around the table plotting the robbery, the background is fairly dark, and we sense that Kubrick is hinting that their crime is doomed to failure. Planning a crime that will take place at a racetrack, as opposed to a bank or Tiffany's, is seedy in itself, but Kubrick strives to give the meeting an even more sleazy feel. He places the men so close together around the small cluttered table that we know they can smell the liquor on each other's breaths, their smoky clothes, and their sweat. Sitting so close, they can look each other in the eye and detect each others' uncertainties and weaknesses.

For such scenes of *intimacy*, Kubrick uses long, fairly static medium shots of his characters; but *The Killing* is memorable for his fluid camerawork, certainly influenced by French director Max Ophuls, a master of the mobile camera, to whom Kubrick acknowledges a debt. However, when Kubrick places his camera behind props and pans past a chair, a table, a lamp while following an actor who walks by, he creates a multiplane (the furniture, the "plane" on which the actor walks, the far part of the room, the far wall) effect that is reminiscent of Charles Laughton's *The Night of the Hunter* (1955) made one year earlier. In the Laughton film, when the canoe carrying the runaway children floats downstream, Laughton pans with a camera that is situated on land and picks up at least five different planes: animals in the foreground, a small stretch of land, the river with the canoe halfway across, the far bank, and finally, the horizon. Laughton used the multiplane technique, as Walt Disney did, to create a frame full of fantasy; Kubrick uses it to make his sets seem realistic.

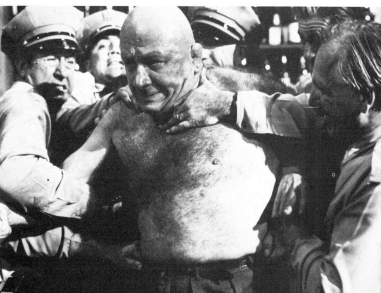

In an interview in Joseph Gelmis's *Film Director As Superstar* (Doubleday, 1970), Kubrick discussed editing:

> The most instructive book on film aesthetics I came across [when I was starting out] was [the Russian film theorist Vsevolod] Pudovkin's *Film Technique* which simply explained that editing was the aspect of the film art which was completely unique, and which separated it from all other art forms. The ability to show a simple action . . . from a number of angles . . . , to be able to see it in a special way not possible except through film—that is what it was all about. This is obvious, of course, but it's so important it cannot be too strongly stressed.

Not only is the rhythm of each sequence in *The Killing* established primarily by Kubrick's editing—his stringing together of diverse shots into a coherent series of images that make up a sequence—but also the narrative structure of the entire film is determined by the juxtaposition of the numerous *sequences*. *The Killing* might well have been told with all the sequences arranged chronologically to give the film continuity, but Kubrick decided that the conventional story would have more impact if it were told from several different viewpoints. So each time the race is about to begin and simultaneously the robbery plan is about to swing into action, Kubrick stops his film and moves back into time where

The plan swings into action. (T) Nikki gleefully shoots Red Lightning in the middle of the race. (M) Kola creates another diversion by pretending to be drunk and disorderly. (B) While track guards are kept busy by Nikki and Kola, Johnny, wearing a mask, robs the track's gate receipts.

As a result of a shootout, Val, Marvin, Randy, and Mike lie dead. Critically wounded George will live long enough to go home and kill Sherry for pulling a doublecross.

he will again approach the start of the race but from a new perspective. As a result, the tension builds as time seems to stand still; and viewers get to better understand the complexities of what is really an ingenious plot that depends on split-second timing and everyone involved carrying out his part of the plan to a T. By going back into time we are able to follow what the different men are doing in different locations at exactly the same time—and the pieces of a great puzzle fall into place.

The use of a narrator and of stock footage during the outdoor crowd and race segments at the track adds to the documentary nature of the film. The narrator, who sounds like someone involved in law enforcement rather than motion pictures, keeps taking us to different locales and moments in time, and his seriousness makes one think of those old quasi-documentaries like *The House on 92nd Street* (1945) which employed a narrator and news clips. When he tells us something happened at precisely 11:29 it builds suspense as effectively as Kubrick does with his increasingly fast cutting from scene to scene. The narrator also contributes to the feeling of impending disaster that pervades the film; on the morning of the robbery, the narrator comments, "Johnny Clay begins what may be the last day of his life."

If *The Killing* seems to come off second best to *The Asphalt Jungle* (1951), a picture which it resembles greatly, it may be because the criminals in the John Huston film are *professionals,* which in itself automatically gives added stature to their crime. Johnny's accomplices, he tells Fay, are not criminals in the usual sense. They are a sorry lot; it is the negative energy created by their vulnerability and weaknesses that contributes to their demise—not the police. Unlike the characters in the Huston film who *want* to pull off one more big job before retiring, these men are in *need* of money simply to escape unhappy financial situations. Mike has to pay for his wife's health care; Randy has to get a loan shark off his back; George thinks money will help him keep his bored wife from leaving him for someone who can offer her more; Marvin, the oldest of the group, wants a chance *to live.* Only Johnny, an ex-con, has a criminal streak, but, like the others, he no doubt realizes that he has no other way to acquire money. That his name is Clay and not something like "Stone" is further indication that he will fail. Greed does not motivate anybody (except Sherry, who is not directly involved in the crime); they all feel that they have been cheated by life and are trying to get their just rewards. Marvin tells

Johnny and Fay try to buy plane tickets and flee the city with the money. They won't get away.

Johnny that after he gets his share of the loot he wants "to go away and start over"; Fay hopes Johnny will settle down after he gets his share and, after being loyal to him for so many years, she will have him permanently by her side; Mike promises his wife that "things will be different"; Sherry promises George that "things will be better"—and she believes they will be better once she runs off with Val and everybody's money. When she is shot fatally by George without ever having enjoyed the good life, she voices Kubrick's cynicism: "It's not fair." Unlike Johnny, who resigns himself to his capture, saying "What's the difference?" she does not adhere to the maxim "Anytime you take a chance, make sure the risks are worth the payoff."* But like Johnny and the other characters (except for Nikki, a bigot, and Randy, a corrupt cop), Sherry is to be pitied. She is a manipulative shrew, but she, too, is a victim of a cold society, in which even a working man (George, Mike) cannot

*Johnny speaks of "risks" knowing that pulling off the robbery is a long shot at best. Ironically, the men do pull off the crime against incredible odds, but he is caught when his suitcase bursts open at the airport and two million dollars in cash goes flying about. What are the odds on that happening? Johnny realized that while everything was so well planned, success or failure depended on chance.

support his wife (Sherry, Ruth) in some semblance of dignity.

It is characteristic of Kubrick that he pays more attention to the George-Sherry relationship than the one between Johnny and Fay. Marie Windsor shows why she is considered the top female villain of fifties low-budget films, as underhanded as Barbara Stanwyck ever was. Elisha Cook, one of the all-time great character actors, his voice quivering uncertainly, his eyes blinking to hide his hurt feelings, plays a character (as usual) who tries to impress others by acting like a "big man" but hasn't the inner strength to carry it off. Since *Killer's Kiss*, Kubrick has always been uncomfortable showing couples who love one another, so he basically ignores Fay and Johnny. With George and Sherry, he can better show that he associates sexuality with perversity and evil—for a taste of this, watch Sherry seduce her husband to get him to commit the robbery. In Kubrick's cold, unromantic world, a *good* woman such as Fay is totally asexual, and the relationship between Johnny and Fay is undoubtedly platonic. Marie Windsor makes a great impression, but Coleen Gray, whom I have always liked, plays such an incidental character that I often forget she's in the film.

King Kong

(L-R) Carl Denham, Captain Englehorn, and Jack Driscoll chart a course to Skull Island.

1933 RKO Radio
Directors: Merian C. Cooper and Ernest B. Schoedsack
Executive Producer: David O. Selznick
Producers: Merian C. Cooper and Ernest B. Schoedsack
Screenplay: James Creelman and Ruth Rose
From an original sotry by Merian C. Cooper and Edgar Wallace
From an idea conceived by Merian C. Cooper
Cinematography: Edward Linden, Vernon L. Walker, and J. O. Taylor
Music: Max Steiner
Editor: Ted Cheesman
Running Time: 110 minutes

Cast: Robert Armstrong (Carl Denham), Fay Wray (Ann Darrow), Bruce Cabot (Jack Driscoll), Frank Reicher (Captain Englehorn), Victor Wong (Charley), Noble Johnson (native chief), Steve Clemento (witch king), James Flavin (second mate), Sam Hardy (Weston), Roscoe Ates (photographer), Dick Curtis (crewman), Paul Porcasi (fruit vendor), Leroy Mason (theater patron), Sandra Shaw (woman dropped by Kong)

Synopsis: Carl Denham has become famous making documentaries in unexplored regions all around the world. He tells Captain Englehorn of the ship *The Venture* and Jack Driscoll, the first mate, that critics and exhibitors demand that his next film be his first to feature a woman. As no actress will brave going with Denham into unexplored territory, he must search for his star. On the streets of Depression New York he discovers Ann Darrow, a pretty woman without work or money to buy food. He offers her "money, adventure, and fame" if she will come with him. She agrees.

The Venture travels through uncharted waters in search of Skull Island, which only Denham believes exists. On the journey, Ann and Driscoll fall in love. At last *The Venture* docks on Skull Island. Taking along their film equipment, the men and Ann explore the island. They discover a native village where a ceremony is taking place in honor of a god they call Kong. The natives plan to sacrifice one of their maidens to Kong, who lives on the other side of a great wall. When the natives spot the white intruders and take too much interest in the white-skinned Ann, everyone retreats to the boat.

That night the natives sneak on board *The Venture* and kidnap Ann. They tie her to two stakes on the other side of the great wall. She hears footsteps, branches breaking, and loud snapping. She screams as she sees that she is to be the bride of a fifty-foot gorilla—Kong. Kong unties her and, pleased with his bride, takes her toward his home. Driscoll, Denham, and several crew members pursue them. Realizing he is being followed, Kong attacks and kills all but Denham and Driscoll. Denham goes back to the boat and Driscoll continues to give chase. Kong rescues Ann from a tyrannosaur and is saving her from a pterodactyl when Driscoll sneaks into Kong's cave dwelling. Driscoll and Ann escape with a furious Kong at their heels. They make it back to the village, but Kong breaks through the door of the great wall and kills many natives. Denham and the remaining members of his crew finally knock him out with gas bombs. Denham decides to exhibit Kong in New York as "the Eighth Wonder of the World." Before a large formal gathering in a theater, Denham unveils the chained Kong. When photographers start taking pictures of Ann, Kong breaks his chains and attacks everyone in sight, causing a panic. Ann hides in her hotel across the street, but Kong finds her and carries her through the city, destroying everything and everyone in his path.

Kong carries Ann to the top of the Empire State Building. He is shot numerous times by machine guns in planes that fly around him. He lays Ann down in a safe place, lovingly looks at her one last time, and falls to his death far below. Denham is told that the airplanes killed Kong, but Denham disagrees: "It was beauty killed the beast."

With the exception of *The Birth of a Nation* (1915) and *Citizen Kane* (1941), no picture has been the subject of more critical writing than the original *King Kong*, an irreplaceable part of twentieth-century American culture, the greatest, most popular, most intriguing horror-fantasy film ever made. As *King Kong* is a testament for those who believe film is a *collaborative* art, the majority of articles have dealt with the various achievements of the numerous individuals who worked on the project, with the tremendous contributions of special-effects genius Willis O'Brien and composer Max Steiner (who understood that *Kong* should be scored like a silent picture) being singled out most often.* Because there is so much available material that documents the technical wizardry of *Kong*, I will confine myself to two other areas.

An Interpretation. Like most producers, Merian C. Cooper insisted that all his films, including *King Kong*, were strictly "entertaining pictures," but *Kong* is so rich in implication that few critics haven't read added significance into it. It has been interpreted as: a parable about an innocent, proud country boy (probably a muscular, uneducated black) who is humbled and finally destroyed when he comes to the cold, cruel city; an indictment of "bring 'em back alive" big-game hunters; a racist visualization of the fears a white woman has about being abducted by a black—or, as Harry Geduld and Ronald Gottesman suggest, "a white man's sick fantasy of the Negro's lust to ravish white women"; and a parable about the Great Depression, an interpretation I have never understood.

---

*For those interested in lengthy discussions about the people who contributed to *King Kong*, as well as articles offering various interpretations of the film and ones that explore the inspirational sources for the picture in literature and film, I recommend the anthology *The Girl in the Hairy Paw* (Avon, 1976); edited by Harry Geduld and Ronald Gottesman.

Numerous critics contend that *Kong* was intentionally filmed as if it were a nightmare. (If the picture is indeed a dream, this would explain the frequent changes in Kong's size, according to scale.) R C Dale writes:

> The film manages to bypass the critical, censorious level of the viewer's consciousness and to secure his suspension of disbelief with what appears to be great ease. A number of French critics have attributed this phenomenon to the film's oneiric qualities, its pervasive dreamlike control of some subconscious, uncritical part of the mind. Indeed it does succeed in dreaming for us.

I agree that *King Kong* is dreamlike—in fact, our first view of Skull Island is an exact reproduction of Arnold Böcklin's dreamlike painting "Isle of the Dead"—but I don't think that it is *our* dream we watch on the screen. The film begins in the *real* world, in dark, cold Depression New York where unemployed, hungry people stand in soup lines; but from the moment *The Venture* leaves port for uncharted regions, I believe we are on a journey through *Carl Denham's subconscious*. Just as Pauline Kael described the landscape of Altair-4 in the *Kong*-influenced *Forbidden Planet* (1956) as being "the caves, plains, and the towers of Dr. Morbius's mind," Skull (as in cerebral) Island's expressionistic landscape—fertile, overgrown, reptile-infested, watery, cave-filled—is Denham's fantasized sexual terrain.

And Kong, I believe, is a manifestation of Denham's subconscious. Much like Morbius's Id monster. Whereas Morbius conjures up his monster to kill off the men he fears will take away his daughter (likely his lover in his subconscious), Denham conjures up Kong as a surrogate to battle Driscoll for Ann's love and to perform sexually with her when he has never been willing (or able) to have a sexual encounter himself. Although young and virile, misogynist Denham has traveled to the far corners of the earth with an all-male crew to avoid intimate liaisons because he believes women will strip him of his masculinity ("Some hard-boiled egg gets a look at a pretty face and he cracks up and goes sappy"). Kong is Denham's female-lusting side—his alter ego, which he keeps in the dark recesses of his mind, as remotely located as Skull Island, behind a figurative great wall. Kong is evidence of Denham's desperate need to possess Ann; his birth is a result of Denham's continuing to suppress his sexual/romantic drive even after he meets, and immediately falls in love with, Ann.

In New York, Denham tells Ann, "Trust me and keep your chin up." A few seconds of screen time pass, and Ann, now on board *The Venture*, is struck accidentally by Driscoll—on the *chin*. This is a sign that Denham can't be trusted to protect Ann's physical well-being even if he wants to. As his secret (even from himself) love for Ann increases, his Kong side overcomes his desire to protect her. He betrays his lack of concern for her safety (from Kong): for her screen test aboard *The Venture*, he dresses Ann in white—with her bee-stung lips and hair style she looks like one of D. W. Griffith's virginal Victorian heroines—as if preparing her for sacrifice, or perhaps a sexual initiation rite; then he takes Ann onto Skull Island before he knows if it is safe. Just as Denham saved Ann in New York from jail (for stealing an apple), unemployment, and starvation, Kong continues Denham's gallantry toward Ann on Skull Island, saving her from a tyrannosaur and a pterodactyl. But the difference is clear: the civilized Denham (the man) believes his interest in Ann is

Fay Wray and Bruce Cabot in a publicity pose.

Kong saves Ann from the clutches of a pterodactyl, one of the masterful creations of special effects genius Willis O'Brien.

"strictly business," while the primitive Denham (Kong) has placed no such restrictions on himself.

Since Kong is a side of Denham, *Kong* needn't follow the movie formula of having Denham and Driscoll vie for Ann's affections. Denham can allow Driscoll free reign with her because, in truth, the schizophrenic Denham *is* moving in on Ann from his Kong side. Also, through Kong, Denham tries to eliminate Driscoll and all other men who "pursue" her. When Driscoll's kisses bring Ann to her height of sexual passion, and her breathing is heavy and her body is like jelly, he is conveniently (as far as Denham is concerned) called to a meeting with Denham and the captain. Suddenly natives, who to Denham probably represent the link between civilized man (himself) and his simian ancestors (apes), climb aboard *The Venture* at the very spot where Ann stands, at the first moment she is alone, and kidnap her to be Kong's bride. Is it the natives' lucky night? Or were things so easy for them—being part of Denham's dream—because Denham's subconscious orchestrated the whole thing in their favor?

That Denham and Kong are rarely in the same shot further gives one the impression that Kong is being directed by some external force, namely Denham's subconscious. At one time Kong is on one side of the tree-trunk bridge that holds Driscoll (who climbs off to safety) and several other men pursuing Ann (who fall to their deaths)—while Denham is *out of sight* on the other side of the bridge and only emerges after Kong has left. Not coincidentally, a later scene in New York shows Kong reaching into a hotel room (to which Denham's subconscious must have directed him), snatching Ann, and knocking down Driscoll—while Denham is *out of sight* in the hall and only appears after Kong has left.

Denham and Kong do confront each other (the visualization of Denham's internal struggle) when Kong breaks through the supposedly impenetrable door of the great wall (Denham's mental barricade)—just as the Id monster breaks through the supposedly impenetrable laboratory door in *Forbidden Planet.* Confronted with his bestial side, the civilized Denham—a model for Morbius, who at this point denies his Id monster, thereby making it cease to exist—puts it (Kong) to sleep with gas bombs. Back in New York, Denham still tries to control his sexual side by literally chaining up Kong. However, once Kong breaks out of his supposedly unbreakable chains, Denham's last barrier, we never see Kong and Denham together again until Kong lies dead.

Denham's words "It was beauty killed the beast" make sense only if the beast he's referring to was part of himself. It is an understatement to say that Kong is too big for Ann, but we could overlook this except for the fact that Kong's size prevents him from considering her a beauty. That he can't even recognize Ann by her looks is evident when he pulls the wrong woman from the hotel and can only tell she's not Ann by hair color and smell—not by beauty. That Kong reacts so violently when the photographers take pictures of Ann is not because he thinks they're trying to harm her—Kong probably doesn't recognize her—but because filmmaker Denham, a *voyeur* (as many critics have acknowledged), becomes filled with jealous rage because others are

Ann stolen from him, Kong breaks through the unbreakable village door and is about to wreak havoc on the natives.

With Jack and Ann at his side, Denham presents the humbled Kong to New York society.

taking pictures of his actress / woman / property / beauty; and it is *his* subconscious that wills Kong to intervene by breaking his bonds and chasing the photographers away. Once loose, Kong is out of the civilized Denham's control and goes all out to succeed in his mission of having sex with Ann. On Skull Island, a snake (a Freudian sex symbol) attacks Kong—a symbolic act that shows Denham is trying to suppress his sexual instincts; however, in New York, Kong attacks the snake—the Third Avenue El—making it clear that nothing will get in his way this time. Having no penis—is impotence the reason Denham avoids women?—Kong has symbolic intercourse with Ann when he takes her up the world's greatest phallic symbol: the Empire State Building. Once this sexual act has been carried out (consummated), Denham is no longer sexually repressed (or a virgin). As his sexual self can surface at last, he no longer has to enjoy sex vicariously through a surrogate—and Kong, now obsolete, can die. Therefore, it makes sense that in the Cooper–Ernest B. Schoedsack sequel, *Son of Kong* (1934), where Denham is the romantic lead and has a love affair with Helen Mack, the gorilla need not be and is not a sexual being.

Kong as Hero. That Kong is regarded as a hero rather than the prototype for all monster-villains is quite extraordinary, considering how many innocent people he kills and how much property he destroys, all done with the emotion of someone eating a melting ice cream cone. His hero status is even more unusual since the recent reinsertion of scenes censored in 1938 from all prints of the film. These scenes of Kong partially stripping Ann (touching her and smelling his finger), viciously trampling and chewing on helpless natives, and dropping the

woman he mistakes for Ann to her death from high above the city streets, make Kong's "beastliness" much more pronounced.

Kong is a hero, I suspect, because he is a great fighter, capable of beating Tunney or Dempsey with his pinky, or the entire United States Air Force if it fought fairly; he gallantly risks his life for his woman; black people see him as a black character who fights White America; the poor see him as their champion who wreaks havoc on New York City, home of Wall Street and the least popular city during the Great Depression and not much more popular since; women see that he doesn't hide his feelings as most men do. And Kong is certainly sympathetic. We feel sorry for grotesque characters whose love for someone beautiful is not returned—Fay Wray earned her reputation as the screen's top screamer by shrieking *every* time Kong came near her. He is taken forcibly from his homeland, where he was god, to be, as Denham tells the theater audience, "merely a captive to gratify your curiosity." He is destroyed by airplanes, something he can't understand, for reasons he can't comprehend. As his last act, he puts Ann in a safe place so she won't suffer his horrible fate—what is truly upsetting is that Ann doesn't verbally acknowledge the nobleness of this gesture. Kong dies so tragically and so theatrically (as a hammy silent movie star might) that we forgive and forget all that he has done. But for all this, as Robert Fiedel writes in *The Girl in the Hairy Paw* (Avon, 1976), "Most critics have always been at a loss to give adequate explanation for the great feeling of tragedy evoked by Kong's death." When the airplanes start firing on Kong we suddenly feel we are losing our best friend, when up

The heart-wrenching finale where Kong fights a losing battle against airplanes while atop the Empire State Building.

till now we have thought Kong our enemy. I believe Fiedel pinpoints the reason for our dramatic reversal:

> The answer lies, in fact, in the musical score. . . . Nowhere is the score more manipulative than in the death scene. As Kong realizes that his death is immediately impending, we hear a lamenting variation of the "Ann Darrow" motif played passionately by the strings. . . . Then as Kong finally dies and loses his hold atop the Empire State Building, his motif is resolved by rest chords . . . signifying his acceptance of defeat. . . . Kong's actual fall is accompanied by a sustained blaring dissonant chord, and finally resolved by an orchestral outburst. It is interesting that his fall is resolved only by the score, and not by the visuals. . . . The score serves the vital function of resolving the tension of the actual fall and denoting the precise moment to trigger our emotional responses. . . . As Denham muses philosophically over the body of Kong . . . a celestial statement of the "Ann Darrow" motif is played in the upper string register which makes a final tragic comment on the death of Kong. A final recapitulation of the resolved "Kong" motif ensues, concluding the film on a negative, disturbing theme.

King Kong is an institution, a folk hero, certainly more real to us today than the defunct studio that created him. Kong has been resurrected so many times—initially by major studio releases in 1938, 1942, 1946, 1952, and 1956, and then by impossible-to-miss television and repertory theater screenings—that he has become immortal. The King is dead!, etc., etc.

King of Hearts

(Le Roi de Cœur)

1967 France Lopert Productions release (later released in North America by United Artists) Director: Philippe de Broca Producer: Philippe de Broca Screenplay: Daniel Boulanger Cinematography: Pierre L'Homme Music: George Delerue Editor: François Javet Running Time: 101 minutes

Cast: Alan Bates (Private Charles Plumpick), Pierre Brasseur (General Geranium), Jean-Claude Brialy (The Duke), Genevieve Bujold (Coquelicot), Adolfo Celi (Colonel Alexander MacBibenbrook), Françoise Christophe (The Duchess), Julien Giomar (Bishop Daisy), Micheline Presle (Madame Eglantine), Michel Serrault (crazy barber), Marc Dudicourt (Lieutenant Hamburger), Daniel Boulanger (Colonel Helmut Von Krack)

Synopsis: In the final days of World War I the retreating German army marches out of Marville, the French town it had occupied. A member of the French resistance learns that the Germans have planted a bomb somewhere in the town that will explode at midnight. He informs a nearby British regiment of this fact and alerts the Marville citizens, who immediately desert the town.

Colonel MacBibenbrook chooses the nonviolent poetry-reading Scotsman Private Charles Plumpick to go into Marville and disconnect the bomb. When Charles arrives in town, he is chased by the few remaining Germans and takes refuge in the insane asylum. The inmates are convinced that he is the "King of Hearts," who has returned. After the Germans leave, Charles leaves the asylum but accidentally knocks himself out.

The inmates circulate through the empty town, returning to their former professions. One is a barber, another a general, another a bishop, another a madam; policemen mingle with soccer players. The Duke and Duchess spend an afternoon appreciating the wonders of nature; all the escaped inmates frolic about enjoying life.

Charles wakes up. At first he doesn't realize that the townspeople he sees are actually the people from the asylum and he tries unsuccessfully to get them to help him find out where the bomb is. But they have more important things on their minds, such as crowning him the King of Hearts. Several German soldiers return, but the loonies steal their tanks and chase them from the town. Several Scotsmen arrive but are so unnerved by the strange sights they see—wild animals mingling with strangely dressed people—that they go back to the colonel.

Now that Charles is the King of Hearts, he feels obligated to protect these people for whom he feels tremendous affection. He tries to get them to follow him out of the town, but they are too afraid.

He falls in love with Coquelicot, a virgin who works in Madame Eglantine's brothel. She has been assigned to provide the King comfort. It is for her especially that he wants to find the bomb. But like the others she refuses to be afraid of the imminent explosion.

Charles figures out that the bomb is planted in the town clock. He climbs up the clock tower and prevents the explosion at the stroke of midnight. The loonies congratulate him and decide to celebrate for three years. Charles and Coquelicot are about to make love when the British army arrives. The colonel doesn't realize that it is the loonies who greet his troops, and he happily allows his men to join in the festivities. He is attracted to Madame Eglantine.

In the morning, the regiment is about to pull out. Coquelicot is sad that Charles must go back to war. She and a few other escaped inmates pull him away from the others, tie him up and gag him. Charles and the inmates sit on a balcony as the men prepare to leave. Suddenly a German regiment marches into town. The two armies fight each other underneath the balcony and all the soldiers on both sides are killed.

The townspeople return. The inmates walk back to the asylum. Charles receives medals, but he is unhappy that he must return to fighting. He also misses his friends from the asylum. He strips off his clothes and goes to the asylum, where he voluntarily becomes one of the inmates.

Plumpick decides to give up the crazy outside world and move into the insane asylum with his friends.

A big hit with newspaper critics when it first appeared in America in 1967, Philippe de Broca's *King of Hearts* also became one of the most popular cult films of the late sixties and early seventies, attracting enormous audiences in cities like Austin, where it broke box office records, Los Angeles, San Francisco, Minneapolis, Milwaukee, and Detroit, and wherever there was a college campus. In 1971, in Cambridge, Massachusetts, it opened on the bottom half of a de Broca twin bill at the Central Square Theater and ended up playing five consecutive years as the headline attraction when students started coming in droves. Like *Singin' in the Rain* (1952), it was regarded as a guaranteed pick-me-up, a film with an infectious gaiety and charm. In 1975 Vincent Canby analyzed its mass appeal:

> In a certain kind of sentimental fiction, mental institutions are popular as metaphors for the world outside. The schizoids, the catatonics, the Napoleons and Josephines inside the hospital are the sanes, while all of us outside who have tried to adjust to a world that accepts war, hunger, poverty, and geno-cide are the real crazies. It's the appeal of this sappy

idea, I suspect, that keeps Philippe de Broca's *King of Hearts* playing almost continually around the country. In that film . . . Scots soldier (Alan Bates) seeks asylum among the certified lunatics while World War I rages nuttily outside. It's a comforting concept, and a little like believing in Santa Claus, to think that if we just give up, if we just throw in the towel, and stop thinking rationally while letting our wildest fantasies take hold, that we'll attain some kind of peace. No fear. No pain. No panic. The world becomes a garden of eccentric delights.

I admit liking *King of Hearts* when I first saw it in the sixties; it was a breezy film for a hot summer's day. But now I tend to agree with former *Esquire* critic Wilfrid Sheed, who wrote back then: "For a truly tiresome antiwar movie, the kind that makes you want to enlist and give Kaiser Bill a crack on the snout, I nominate *King of Hearts,* a smug little bonbon out of France." While it continues to be phenomenally popular, I find the film terribly dated, its delusions of importance, its triteness, and its lameness quite apparent, its humor and satiric bite somehow missing. Perhaps I am now seeing this film through jade(d)-colored-glasses, for I find it a film with themes that are

Plumpick and Coquelicot (wearing a crown) stop their smooching and watch Col. MacBibenbrook being entertained by women who, he doesn't realize, are escaped asylum inmates.

overly facile; have been used in one way or another in about half the films made during the last twenty years; and have the punch of a boxer without arms. How many times must we be told that: those people on the outside (of jails and asylums) should be the ones who are institutionalized; war is bad; war is crazy; and our beautiful landscapes have been contaminated by (warring) people? These are some of filmdom's greatest clichés. The picture may contain much fairy tale material—the inmates scurry out of the asylum as if they were mice, put on costumes of all types and colors (at which point de Broca films the top of the buildings as if the village had been transformed magically into Disneyland), and later return to the asylum minus their costumes as if they were Cinderella returning from the ball—but a simply told story need not be so simplistic; films dealing with war and insanity should have something new and constructive to say.

In years past, *King of Hearts* might very well have been a vehicle for Danny Kaye. It is quite similar in some ways to Kaye's *The Inspector General* (1949), in which he is a town dunce who pretends to be an important visiting official. It is very easy to picture Kaye as Plumpick, the harmless, French-speaking Scotsman who reads poetry to pigeons and finds companionship and equals among the loonies. But whereas Kaye would undoubtedly dominate the proceedings, Alan Bates

plays the role very passively and allows the loonies to carry the action and to create the ambience. This wouldn't be so bad if Bates, quite bad in this *one* picture, didn't come across as such a listless character. He does become heroic on account of the loonies, saving them from the bomb; but otherwise, none of his other (hidden) qualities are revealed. Like us, he just watches what is going on around him.

Even worse, the loonies, too, are characters of little dimension. Considering that they are "loonies," they should have great eccentricities, but they don't. De Broca seems more interested in the costumes they wear than in developing personalities for them. Every loony is exactly the same as the others; their mental illnesses are at exactly the same level and they look at the world in exactly the same manner. Watch the horribly directed crowd sequences in which none of the loonies is given any bits of "business" that might reveal singular character traits; Genevieve Bujold desperately looks for something to do and resorts to a series of silly curtsies. These characters are without subtlety, individuality, or *honest* emotions. It is most disturbing to see them so happy in their insanity; and it is terribly irritating that they don't care that their lives are in danger from the impending explosion. Since these are a people who have withdrawn to an asylum—their sanctuary—rather than participate in the cruel world, it makes sense that they should make

a real effort to keep that world from really infringing on them by taking their lives. They are defeatists despite their happy attitude, and they are *copping out* when they don't fight for survival.

The loonies accept no responsibility for improving the world that has driven them insane. They enjoy the good things life has to offer but they do not take living seriously—which is why they can tolerate their sorry state. "All life is a spectacle," contends the Duke. "You're on a stage." This life-is-a-play and everyone-plays-a-part attitude of the inmates is further confirmed by the loony General Geranium, who, when he sees the soldiers come into town, says, "More actors"; when the soldiers start killing each other, he asks Plumpick, "Don't you think those actors are going a little far for a game?" It is as Ellen Whitman wrote in *Montage* (Feb. 20, 1970): "[As] the Duke realizes, . . . the enjoyment of life lies in playing one's role as fully as possible while retaining the detachment which keeps one from taking it overly seriously. . . . The insanity which lies outside the institution is not men who kill each other but men who take their roles [as soldiers] so seriously that they kill."

The film's conclusion, which finds a naked Plumpick standing at the door of the asylum waiting to be let in, is *cute*. It is probably the highlight of the film. But wouldn't it be better if the loonies at this point changed their minds about spending the remainder of their lives in isolation and confinement and decided to join Plumpick outside? Their very presence *outside* the gates could certainly shake up a few things in a world that could stand a little improvement. Viewers usually find this final moment uplifting—I find it frustrating.

The bishop says: "To love this world, one must keep one's distance." That's the advice I give to viewers who remember *loving* this picture a few years back.

Plumpick watches a chess game between an escaped inmate and one of the zoo animals the loonies freed.

Kiss Me, Deadly

1955 United Artists release of a Parkline Productions film
Director: Robert Aldrich
Producer: Robert Aldrich
Screenplay: A. I. Bezzerides
Based on the novel by Mickey Spillane

Cinematography: Ernest Laszlo
Music: Frank Devol
"Rather Have the Blues" sung by Nat King Cole and Kitty White
Editor: Michael Luciano
Running Time: 105 minutes

Cast: Ralph Meeker (Mike Hammer), Albert Dekker (Dr. Soberin), Paul Stewart (Carl Evello), Juano Hernandez (Eddie Yeager), Wesley Addy (Pat Chambers), Marian Carr (Friday), Maxine Cooper (Velda), Cloris Leachman (Christina Bailey, a.k.a. Berga Torn), Gaby Rodgers (Lily Carver, a.k.a. Gabrielle), Nick Dennis (Nick), Jack Lambert (Sugar Smallhouse), Jack Elam (Charlie Max), Mort Marshall (Ray Diker), Jerry Zinneman (Sammy), Leigh Snowden (girl at Evello's pool), Percy Helton (morgue doctor), Madi Comfort (singer), Fortunio Bonanova (Trivaco), Strother Martin (Harvey Wallace)

Synopsis: Tough L.A. private eye Mike Hammer gives a ride to Christina Bailey, a frightened young woman he finds running along the road one night. The car is waylaid by unseen things. Hammer is knocked out and Christina is tortured in an unsuccessful attempt to get information from her. They are put back into Hammer's car, which then is forced off a cliff. Hammer wakes up in the hospital. Velda, his trusty, sexy secretary, informs him that Christina is dead. Her real name was Berga Torn. Pat Chambers, Mike's policeman friend, tells him to stay off the case, but Mike thinks it might be a big story—meaning big money for him—because the FBI is interested. He, Velda, and Nick, his garage mechanic friend, start investigating in hopes of finding out why Christina was killed.

Hammer forces ex-science reporter Ray Diker, whom he has learned the FBI has talked to, to give him Christina's address. He goes there and finds a poetry book written by *Christina* Rosetti. It contains a sonnet with the title "Remember Me"—the two words Christina had said to Mike before their abduction. Hammer finds out where Lily Carver, Christina's roommate, has fled. He finds her in a tenement with a gun—she says she is hiding out from gangsters.

Hammer kills a thug who is following him. He also finds the explosive devices in the car some unknown man has given him to replace the one he sent over the cliff.

Diker gives Hammer the names of two men whom Christina knew who have met recent mysterious deaths: Raymond and ex-boxer Kowalsky. Eddie, Kowalsky's manager, won't talk to Hammer because he has been strong-armed by two thugs, Sugar and Charlie Max, into keeping quiet. Pat tells Mike that these two men work for rich gangster Carl Evello. Mike goes to Evello's mansion, kisses Evello's half-sister Friday, beats up Sugar and Charlie Max, and tries to get information from Evello, who likewise wants Hammer to talk. Mike realizes that Evello and his men are carrying out someone else's orders.

Nick is killed and Velda is kidnaped when she goes to keep a date with Dr. Soberin, a man who Diker said was involved in the case. Evello's men grab Mike and take him to a beachhouse, where they torture him. Mike breaks free, and soon Evello and Sugar lie dead.

Having figured out what "Remember Me" means, Mike and Lily go to the morgue, where by force Mike gets the medical examiner to give him the key that Christina had swallowed. It is to Raymond's locker at the Hollywood Athletic Club. Mike finds a case inside the locker, but when he opens it an inch, he burns his hands. He thinks it wise to put it back in the locker. Meanwhile Lily has disappeared.

Contemptuously, Pat tells Mike that he has gotten mixed up in things too big for him—that the contents of the case have something to do with "Manhattan Project. Los Alamos. Trinity." He tells Mike that the real Lily Carver was drowned two weeks before. Gabrielle, who was pretending to be Lily, has taken the case from the locker.

Hammer discovers that Dr. Soberin owns the beachhouse and goes there in hopes of finding Velda. At the beachhouse, Gabrielle and Dr. Soberin prepare for a trip during which they will make a fortune selling the case's contents. Gabrielle insists that Dr. Soberin reveal what is inside. Warning her of dangers, he refuses. Wanting the contents for herself, she kills him. Mike walks in just as she is about to look inside the case. She shoots him in the stomach. She opens the case. There is a bright light. She screams and catches fire. The building shakes as Mike crawls to a locked hallway door and frees Velda. They leave just as there is an enormous explosion.

A major influence on the French New Wave because of its audacious utilization of wild camera angles and abrupt, jarring editing to symbolize a world out of its orbit, Robert Aldrich's *Kiss Me, Deadly* remains one of the most dazzling works of the fifties, as swiftly paced, thrilling, precipitous, and jolting to the senses as a ride on a broken roller coaster. It has always been controversial because of its great brutality, and prior to its release Aldrich was so concerned about public response that he wrote an article for the *New York Herald-Tribune* explaining and defending his scenes of violence and torture. Still the public was not prepared. For here is a picture where the very rhythm seems to come from the slaps and punches Mike Hammer dishes out; where (hysterical) high points are represented by horrific screams (by Christina, Nick, Sugar, and Gabrielle); and the scenes usually end with Hammer being knocked out—no less than six times does he lapse into unconsciousness—and begin with Hammer awakening but still feeling the effects of blows received. The main motif of this picture seems to be pain: the film opens with Christina running along the highway, her bare feet slapping on the concrete; soon Hammer is beaten by thugs; Christina is tortured to death with pliers (only the dangling legs of the screaming woman are visible); Hammer is driven over a cliff; the thug tailing Hammer is caught in the act and Hammer smashes him in the face, slams his head repeatedly against the side of a brick building, and tosses him to certain death down a long flight of stone stairs; Sugar and Charlie Max are viciously punched out by Hammer (mostly off screen); Nick is killed when a car is lowered on him; Hammer is knocked out by a blackjack, beaten up on the beach, strapped belly-down on a bed and worked over by Sugar and Charlie Max (off screen), and given the needle (containing truth serum) by Evello (off screen); Evello is stabbed to death by Sugar; Sugar is brutally killed by Hammer (off screen); the medical examiner has his fingers smashed in a drawer by Hammer (a tactic employed often by Darren McGavin in the *Mike Hammer* TV series of the fifties); the health club attendant is slapped around by Hammer; Diker is slapped around by Hammer; Hammer burns his hand when opening up the lead case slightly; Dr. Soberin is shot by Gabrielle; Hammer is shot by Gabrielle; and in the final scene, Gabrielle opens the lead case all the way and suffers indescribable terror and pain as she is exposed to great heat and catches fire. Such goings-on certainly could use a defense.

Aldrich concluded his aforementioned article: "We think we have kept faith with the sixty million Mickey Spillane readers. We also think we have made a movie of action, violence, and suspense in good taste." But if *Kiss Me, Deadly* is in "good taste"—which seems impossible

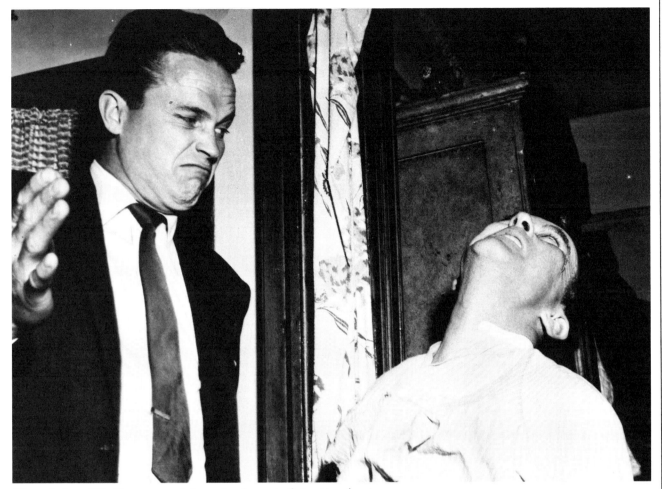

The typical way Mike Hammer gets information. It was perfect casting choosing
Ralph Meeker, always good at playing unlikable characters, to play the brutal Hammer.

considering the ferocious plot elements—then it is because Aldrich greatly altered the point of view of Spillane's work, turning the decidedly fascist novel into a sardonic overview of a sick society, or as critic David Thomson suggests, "a glittering allegory of violence, fascism, and corruption in America."

Aldrich's Mike Hammer is as much of a fascist as Spillane's protagonist, minus a touch of sentimentality and a moral code. Cruel, coldblooded, and emotionless (his lovemaking indicates his mechanical nature), Hammer's joy comes from systematically terrorizing people and running roughshod over them. He delights equally in bringing physical discomfort to the medical examiner for demanding a bribe and the health club attendant for refusing one. He smiles smugly after brutally killing the thug who was trailing him. Hammer's power is based on the fist and gun. But while the two Hammers are basically the same, there is a big difference in how the men are handled, specifically in how they are meant to be regarded by readers / viewers.

We identify with Spillane's fascist hero. As the book is written in the first person it is simple for Spillane to manipulate his prose so Hammer's point of view (his judgments, his way of handling things) becomes ours. We cheer his violence toward people because we believe

they deserve the treatment (punishment) Hammer feels they deserve. The end justifies his fascist means.

But A. I. Bezzerides's script doesn't contain the first-person narration that is found in many private-eye pictures. This is indicative of the fact that we are *not* meant to identify with the movie Hammer, but merely observe him. Before long we realize that we are not even expected to like him or in any way respect him. In the novel, Hammer always comments about foul odors in rooms inhabited by scoundrels; but in the film, after *Hammer* leaves an interrogation with members of a crime commission, they open the window to air out the room. "All right," Hammer admits to these men, who know all about him, "I'm a stinker." And we agree. Hammer is a "bedroom dick"—a detective who specializes in divorce cases, the lowest, seediest form of detective work. He uses his loyal, loving secretary Velda (who embodies sleaziness) to set up sexual traps for men whose wives want evidence of their infidelity—and he later plays back the tapes for his own amusement. While Spillane's Hammer investigates the death of Christina in hopes of paying her torturers back in kind, Aldrich's Hammer is unmoved by Christina's grisly manner of death and only proceeds with his investigation because he smells big bucks. Only when Nick is killed does

If there were ever a picture so sleazy that one would suspect a casting couch was used to pick the film's actresses, this would be it. All the women in this film had lurid publicity shots taken with Ralph Meeker on this couch including (L) Maxine Cooper who plays Velda and (R) Gaby Rodgers who plays Gabrielle.

Hammer think in terms of revenge. Nick's death, Velda's admonishment ("All your friends will get it one of these days"), and Velda's kidnaping serve as a long overdue lesson to Mike—learned too late—that his self-serving way of life will eventually bring harm to those loyal to him. We cannot condone the crude, uncaring manner in which Hammer pulls off his investigation, stepping on anyone who gets in his way. We don't like that he sends Velda against her wishes to date Dr. Soberin so he can get information; we despise him when he gets Trivaco to talk by breaking the comical "poor man's Caruso's" irreplaceable opera records—much like the teen hoods breaking the priceless swing records of the mathematics teacher in *The Blackboard Jungle* (1955). We can appreciate the rugged individualism of Spillane's hero, but this Hammer is pure lowlife. Even the fact that his friends are members of minorities—Greeks and blacks—is meant more to show his seedy life-style than to indicate he has decency.*

The novel is about the Mafia searching for two to four million dollars in narcotics which murdered Ray-

*Filmmakers have traditionally (and exploitatively) used Indians (in westerns), blacks, the handicapped (especially blind newsdealers), children, and animals as friends of white heroes to quickly (and supposedly subtly) establish that the white fellow is a regular joe. Notice, for instance, how we are manipulated into liking Clint Eastwood in *Escape from Alcatraz* (1979) solely by being shown that black characters consider him their soul brothers—when in truth they would probably hate the guy.

mond hid in his health club locker. With the complicity of his good friend Pat Chambers, Hammer works to bring to task those responsible for Christina's death. His methods are rough, but they result in his retrieving the narcotics, the arrest of many Mafia kingpins, and the "justified" deaths of those directly responsible for killing Christina—including Gabrielle, whom he kills by setting her scar-tissue-covered body on fire with his cigarette lighter, thus preventing her escape. As in such fascist films as *Dirty Harry* (1971), the Hammer of the novel is proven justified—RIGHT—in using fascist tactics.

The film is about Evello's gangsters helping a mercenary (Dr. Soberin) track down the radioactive bomb Raymond hid so he can sell it to some foreign nation. Without Pat's support, Hammer unwittingly does Soberin's work for him. He finds the bomb, but before he can turn it over to the police, Gabrielle, whom he had wrongly trusted, snatches it and takes it to Soberin. No Mafia kingpins are arrested; and she'd get away if Hammer were all that she had to cope with. She blows herself up—Hammer has nothing to do with it. At the film's conclusion, Hammer does nothing to prevent the ultimate disaster Pat warned him about—the explosion of an atomic bomb. Aldrich's Mike Hammer is no hero: as Pat realizes, Hammer has gotten involved in something he is not smart enough to comprehend and his brutal methods are not enough to help him get the upper hand; he has, in fact, quite possibly contributed to the

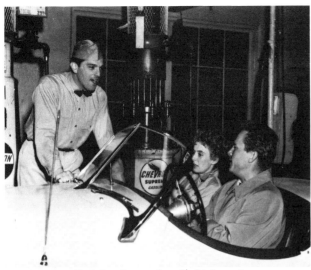

Young actress Cloris Leachman plays the frightened young woman Hammer picks up on a deserted highway.

destruction of the world (or, at very least, a major section of California).* Hammer's fascist tactics are proven to be futile—WRONG—only a calm, rational approach might have prevailed.

To Aldrich, Hammer is part of the villainy of the world. (That is why villain-type Ralph Meeker is so effective in the role.) He in fact draws a strong parallel between Hammer and Gabrielle. As part of the film's "Pandora's box" motif, Hammer is repeatedly warned to stay out of the Christina murder *case:* "What you don't know won't hurt you," Christina tells him before she is killed. "Step aside," Pat tells him. Likewise, Soberin warns Gabrielle not to open the case. He actually speaks of it as a Pandora's box, and reminds her of Lot's wife, who turned to stone for looking where she wasn't supposed to. Neither Hammer nor Gabrielle heed the good advice given them and, driven by greed, open their respective "cases"—and evil is set free on the world.

Aldrich switched the setting from New York City to Los Angeles, Chandler country. In L.A., Hammer becomes more dependent on the automobile than he'd be in New York, and this gives the picture a surge of souped-up power and speed ("Va-va-voom!" says Nick) that the film might otherwise be lacking. But more significantly, the film is set in a locale in which paranoia reigned supreme in the fifties, especially to those working in the movie industry being investigated by HUAC. And this film is about paranoia. The long dark stairways, the shadowy rooms, and the sounds of the street coming through the open tenement window are meant

---

*While the studio synopsis states that Hammer and Velda get out of the house before the explosion and watch it go up in flames from the beach, I have never seen such a print of the film. All I have seen is the two rushing toward the door when the house explodes and the film ends. But even if they make it to the shore, it is likely that this bomb is so powerful that anyone within an enormous radius would be killed. It is not a bomb which only has power to destroy the beachhouse. That is why Soberin, though dying, tells Gabrielle not to open the case. It is possible that Hammer is already dying from the burn on his hand.

to create a somber atmosphere in *film noir*, but here they are meant to convey the fear felt by individuals who expect someone lurking about to jump them. The danger is not imagined. Hammer is followed by unknown assailants; both the police and gangsters are after him; his car is booby-trapped; he is trailed; strangers call him on the phone and threaten him. Hammer is no better than the others; in his work he acts as a spy, even taping bedroom conversations. Inquisitions mean *torture* to someone, even when Hammer is asking the questions.

This is no longer a free America. Brutes (who like jazz and the blues!) and gangsters (who listen to horse races and boxing matches) are in charge and rule by muscle. Culture is on the way out as these barbarians take over: Trivaco, who sings opera (badly), is beaten; Velda, who practices ballet exercises (badly), is used by the man she loves as if she were a hooker and he were her pimp; Christina (the most likable character in the film), who appreciates poetry, classical music, and art, is eliminated. Intellectuals (Soberin) are killed, and the fate of the world rests on the shoulders of stupid Gabrielle. It is relevant that Aldrich did away with the narcotics angle of the book and replaced it with a radioactive bomb. It is much more unnerving because the seeds of our destruction have been planted by our government, who built the bomb. The men in charge of America's security, Aldrich believes, are in reality leading us to an apocalypse.

Dr. Soberin warns Gabrielle not to open the box, because in this instance curiosity could kill all the cats in the world.

La Cage aux Folles

(Birds of a Feather)

1979 France-Italy   United Artists release of a Les Productions Artistes Associes–Da Ma Produzione SPA, film
Director: Edouard Molinaro
Producer: Marcello Danon
Screenplay: Franis Veber, Edouard Molinaro, Marcello Danon, and Jean Poiret
From a play by Jean Poiret
Cinematography: Armando Mannuzzi
Music: Ennio Morricone
Editors: Robert and Monique Isnardon
Running Time: 99 minutes

Cast: Ugo Tognazzi (Renato), Michel Serrault (Albin, a.k.a. Zaza), Michel Galabru (Charrier), Claire Maurier (Simone), Remy Laurent (Laurent), Benny Luke (Jacob), Carmen Scarpitta (Madame Charrier), Luisa Maneri (Andrea)

Synopsis: Albin and Renato have been lovers for twenty years. They own La Cage aux Folles, a scandalous nightclub where transvestites perform. Albin, under his stage name, Zaza, is the star attraction. Renato's son Laurent returns home from college. He tells his father that he is engaged to Andrea, the daughter of Charrier, the secretary for the Union of Moral Order. Andrea has lied to her parents that Renato, Laurent's father, is a cultural attaché and his mother a housewife, the mother of six. When the president of the Union of Moral Order dies while making love to a thirteen-year-old black prostitute, Charrier worries about his own reputation. His wife convinces him that Andrea's marriage into such a reputable family will raise him above the scandal.

Laurent invites Andrea and her parents home to meet his family. He gets Renato to change the decor of his apartment, making it more conservative. Renato visits Laurent's mother, Simone, whom he hasn't seen since she seduced him twenty years ago. He asks her to make an appearance at the dinner for her son's sake. She accepts the offer. She also tries to seduce him. Albin interrupts them and is very upset. He walks out on Renato, but Renato finds him at the train station and convinces him that he loves him only.

The guests arrive. Albin dresses as a woman and pretends to be Laurent's mother while Laurent tries to head off his real mother. Charrier thinks things are very odd. Jacob, the butler, acts very strangely, laughing at Albin and shrieking when a champagne cork flies through the air. Charrier suspects Jacob is gay. Dinner proceeds and Albin's wig is knocked askew. Then Simone shows up. The transvestites from the nightclub enter the apartment to congratulate Renato and Albin on their twentieth anniversary. Charrier is beside himself. He tries to leave but reporters are outside waiting to snap his picture. Albin dresses Charrier in drag so he can escape without being noticed by reporters.

Laurent and Andrea get married. At the ceremony Albin is jealous that Simone is in attendance, sitting next to Andrea's parents. Renato and Albin hold hands.

Director Edouard Molinaro, miffed that fans flocked to La Cage aux Folles *while ignoring the scores of films he made in the past, wasn't too happy with the end result. He blamed stars Michel Serrault and Ugo Tognazzi, neither gay, for feeling so uncomfortable playing gays that they hopelessly overplayed their parts. That Serrault would be uncomfortable is unlikely considering he had starred in the long-running play from which the film was adapted.*

Nominated for Best Director and Best Screenplay at 1979's Academy Awards, *La Cage aux Folles*, a French-Italian coproduction, has been a surprise box office hit in the United States, the most successful foreign film ever, raking in more than $40 million in limited engagements and playing in some theaters for more than a year. (No wonder *La Cage aux Folles II,* 1981, went into production.) Considering all the excitement it has caused among lovers of the picture and among those, in equal number, who despise it, I am stunned that it is such an innocuous film. After all the word-of-mouth, I didn't necessarily expect it to be a great film, but I thought it would be inventive, outrageous to the point of hysteria, with gags flying in all directions nonstop, and I thought our viewing sensibilities would be severely tested. But in reality this is a family comedy that never rises above a level of mediocrity. It is as rollicksome as the most tired French bedroom farce but not as risqué, as stupid as a Laura Antonelli sex comedy but not as arousing, and as "controversial" and "relevant" as *Guess Who's Coming to Dinner?* (1967) is today.

Of course, what is supposed to be so different, so brave, about *La Cage aux Folles* is that it dares tell a story in which the romantic leads are two men: the urbane Renato and the high-strung Albin, who works as a transvestite named Zaza. But this dishonest picture is so timid that it suggests that this couple would raise a heterosexual son—and a boring son at that. And it plays it so safe that the closest we come to a lovemaking scene is one between a male (Renato) and a female (Simone). Renato and Albin may hold hands and peck each other on the cheek so we think there is some sexual intimacy between them, but where is a long, loving embrace? Or, more important, where's the bed they share? The only time director Edouard Molinaro leads us to believe he will be brave enough to show meaningful physical contact between men it turns out that the two men who we think are lovers are actually father (Renato) and son (Laurent). This deception is reminiscent of Robert Red-

Renato isn't startled by many people—but his butler Jacob is an exception.

ford ordering Katharine Ross to disrobe in *Butch Cassidy and the Sundance Kid* (1969) before the audience learns that they know each other intimately—the deception in *Folles* is equally needless and more embarrassing. When it turns out that the slightly built Laurent, who in his first scene looks like he has white powder on his face and could be someone who dresses in drag, is not only Renato's son but heterosexual as well, we feel we were unduly manipulated.

La Cage aux Folles has done great business with straight audiences, and this is not surprising. It is clear that this is who the picture was made for. Much of the film's humor comes at the gay characters' expense; repeatedly we are supposed to laugh at how effeminate Albin and butler Jacob are, at how exaggerated their mannerisms are, at how physically awkward they are when walking or gesturing, at how affected their voices are (laughs come not from what they say, but how they say it), and at how silly they are as they whine or scream excitedly in surprise over *everything* that happens, from Albin's toast breaking to the cork in a champagne bottle flying off. Molinaro never bothers to explore the subtleties of his characters or accentuate the idiosyncracies and fine traits that their friends and lovers find so endearing. We never get a hold on these supposedly unusual men because Molinaro treats them so shallowly. Therefore, when Albin gets upset or riled up over everything under

the sun, we don't know whether to take him seriously or shrug off his antics to frequent temper tantrums. Renato tells Albin he loves him because he makes him laugh—but Molinaro forgets to include any moments in the film where Albin even makes Renato smile broadly. I sense no warmth or affection between the two men—and I

The most sensual scene, for some reason, is between Renato and Simone.

believe it stems from Molinaro having no such feelings for the men either. Albin comes across as so silly, weak, fussy, irrational, self-pitying, cloying, annoying, and temperamental that it is a wonder Renato puts up with him. Worse is that Renato tolerates Albin in a conventional movie way—like a husband who accepts the childish activities and personality of his wife for the simple reasons that she is female and is supposed to be that way. Renato, himself, is no winner. He is expressionless and tired. And mean too. He has the cruel nerve to allow Simone to seduce him while poor jealous Albin waits anxiously for him outside her office. We are expected to see the sweet, responsible, noble side of Renato and Albin when they sacrifice their pride to help Laurent deceive Andrea's conservative parents into thinking he comes from a respectable family. (What an overused movie plot!) What they should do is put the kid over their knees and spank him for being so presumptuous as to ask them to clean up their act.

At least there are several amusing moments in the picture: when Renato toasts Andrea over the phone by breaking a glass on the receiver; when Renato instructs Albin how to butter his toast and stir his tea in a masculine manner (without a pinky in the air); when Renato defends Albin's honor by challenging a short fellow he thinks called Albin a "queer" only to find out it was a muscleman who insulted him (Ennio Morricone's twangy western music fits in this bar scene as it does nowhere else in the picture); when Charrier overreacts to the circumstances surrounding the president's death; and when Charrier and Albin quibble over whether the nude figures on the dinner dishes are all boys, as Charrier insists, or are male and female, as Albin fibs. But most of the humor is predictable and comes in trickles rather than waves. Molinaro has no flare for comedy and never lets a scene run long enough for the gags to develop sufficiently. Numerous scenes are too short, often ending before the punch line. For instance, I would like to see more of the rehearsal with Albin and the leather-jacketed, bubble-gum-blowing young gay dancer, but Molinaro only keeps the camera on them until it starts to get interesting—and then he moves elsewhere. And I would like to see more of the seduction scene between Renato and Simone—not because it is so funny, but because it is never made clear what happens between them (consequently, we don't know how mad Albin has a right to be). Even the climactic dinner sequence starts out as if it is going to develop into something hilarious only to be cut short. We want it to get wilder and wilder, especially with the appearance of Laurent's real mother and the numerous transvestites from the club, but the scene just dribbles to a conclusion before it really gets started. Then the finale with Charrier looking hideous in drag to escape the reporters and saying the film's funniest line—"White makes me look fat"—ends lamely, with Charrier and his chauffeur engaging in fisticuffs and arguing over something or other. As trite as the premise is there is much potential for terrific humor in these sequences but Molinaro isn't inventive enough to carry it off. He doesn't even take advantage of the fact that the jealous Albin and Simone both appear at the dinner. (If nothing is to happen between them, then better Albin show up as Laurent's uncle as first planned.) As Chekhov stressed: if you bring a gun onto the stage, shoot it. Unfortunately, in *La Cage aux Folles*, there are intimations that there will be fireworks but Molinaro forgot the matches.

Land of the Pharaohs

Egyptian President Nasser allowed Howard Hawks to use 10,000 men, including 5,000 soldiers, as extras in the extravagant pyramid-building scenes.

1955   Warner Bros. release of a Continental Productions film
Director: Howard Hawks
Producer: Howard Hawks
Screenplay: William Faulkner, Harry Kurnitz, and Harold Jack Bloom
Cinematography: Lee Garmes and Russell Harlan
Music: Dimitri Tiomkin
Editor: V. Sagovsky
Running Time: 106 minutes

Cast: Jack Hawkins (pharaoh), Joan Collins (Princess Nellifer), Dewey Martin (Senta), Alexis Minotis (Hamar), James Robertson Justice (Vashtar), Louise Boni (Kyra), Sydney Chaplin (Treneh), Kerima (Queen Nailla), James Hayter (Vashtar's servant), Piero Giaghoni (Pharaoh's son)

Synopsis: The pharaoh returns home after months in the desert, having fought his fifth war in six years. During his victorious escapades he has accumulated an enormous quantity of gold. He tells his lifelong friend Hamar, the high priest, that he wants two things: a son by his queen, Nailla, and an enormous tomb where he, Hamar, his servants, his priests, and his gold will be buried for eternity. Because he wants the tomb to be impregnable, he assigns the slave Vashtar, an architect far superior to any Egyptian, to design it. Vashtar agrees to help the pharaoh on the condition that once the pyramid-tomb is constructed, the slaves will be freed. Only Vashtar, who will know the secret to entering the tomb, will have to die. Work on the pyramid goes on for years. Both slaves and Egyptians, who were promised "a place in the land to come" through their labors, help in the construction of the massive tomb. As time passes the life of everyone in the country begins to evolve more and more around the pyramid. During this time the queen bears the pharaoh a son, and Vashtar's son Senta grows into manhood.

The pharaoh asks every nation to send him a tribute in gold. But Cyprus sends him a beautiful young woman named Nellifer instead. Although her refusal to bow to his demands angers him, she also excites him. She becomes his second wife.

While the pharaoh is distracted by the progress on his pyramid, Nellifer schemes to become heir to his throne and to his enormous wealth. She wins the heart of Treneh, a palace guard, and together they plot to kill the pharaoh and his son. Both murder attempts fail, although Queen Nailla is killed while saving her son, and the pharaoh is injured.

The sly Nellifer convinces the pharaoh that it was Treneh alone who tried to kill him and his son. The pharaoh kills Treneh but is mortally wounded himself. Instead of calling for aid, Nellifer watches him die. At the last moment, the pharaoh realizes that it was she behind his downfall.

Nellifer discovers that the pharaoh's gold is in the tomb. She goes inside with the pharaoh's funeral procession, intending to order the gold brought out the moment she becomes queen. However, Hamar informs her that she will be buried alive with the rest of them: "This is your kingdom." She falls to the ground, crying hysterically. Outside, Vashtar and Senta, whom Hamar has freed, lead their people from bondage.

There were three films I saw repeatedly as a child in the mid-fifties: John Ford's *The Searchers* (1956), Nicholas Ray's *Rebel Without a Cause* (1955), and Howard Hawks's *Land of the Pharaohs*. They impressed me equally. One had John Wayne, another had James Dean, and the third had a bunch of bald, tongueless priests who allowed themselves to be buried alive, some cowards who get thrown into an alligator pit, and a statuesque beauty with a bare midriff. Over the years I stored away virtually every scene and image from the Ford and Ray films, but all that I could recall from *Land of the Pharaohs* were the priests, the alligators, and the midriff. When, after a great many years, I saw it again, I understood why I had forgotten so much: other than the breathtaking (pun intended) climax when those bald priests and the sexy Nellifer meet their doom sealed in the tomb, amidst pouring sand and sliding stone blocks, and perhaps the alligator-pit scene (which is too short and not graphic enough), *Land of the Pharaohs* is quite forgettable. It is a movie that appeals more to children than to adults, as children tend to be more tolerant of stilted acting and pointless dialogue as long as there are a few moments of color and spectacle; so it is not surprising that the film's loyal cult seems to be made up almost entirely of people who saw it as kids and distinctly remember what an exciting movie it was. These cultists acknowledge that the late French film archivist Henri Langois was more than charitable when he declared *Land of the Pharaohs* to be "the only epic which has style, rigor, and plastic beauty." They realize that it is just as silly as all those other epics, with just as little historical value. But for

The pharaoh is madly in love with Nellifer who, in turn, is madly in love with his riches.

them, it has a bit more charm than the rest of the lot—plus the priests, the alligators, etc.

Land of the Pharaohs is Howard Hawks's odd film out, a mediocre entry in an otherwise brilliant career, a major departure in terms of time and place, subject, and themes. A fictional account of the building of the Great Pyramid of Khufu the Cheops (circa 3000 B.C.), it is Hawks's most ambitious project conceptually—requiring some 10,000 extras, fifty days' filming in Egypt, and the simulated construction of the base of the Great Pyramid.* Unfortunately it is also one of his biggest critical and commercial failures, a project that squandered time, talent, and money.

Although a great deal was spent on production, little is evident on the screen. While there are expensive crowd scenes, there are no complicated (expensive) battle sequences that would have taken great advantage of the wide screen (Hawks's first attempt with Cinema-Scope); the cast is second-rate, especially the supporting players; even the makeup is bad, with all the actors over fifty looking as if someone had thrown white flour in their hair. But the picture suffers not so much from the

---

*Since no one knows how the Great Pyramid was built, Hawks came up with his own theory: that the 2.5 million 2.5-ton stone blocks were floated down the Nile and brought close to the construction site each flood season for many years.

misuse of a large budget as from a lackluster script by William Faulkner and Harry Kurnitz (and possibly Harold Jack Bloom, who receives screen credit). The plot borrows heavily from Greek tragedy, but as a film it lacks intrigue, suspense, and imaginative visual elements (action, for one thing). In addition to the script problems, the movie's major problems are related to Hawks's lazy direction. Hawks's usual comment on *Land of the Pharaohs* was "we had fun doing it," and we can assume from that statement that work on this film wasn't all business. Directors have been known to make films in foreign locales in order to avoid studio pressure and to have a working vacation.

The picture has characters quite foreign to other Hawks films. For instance, the vain, greedy Nellifer is the only true-blue female villain in the entire Hawks collection, his only female without warmth or wit. It appears that Hawks disliked this character so much that he didn't take the time to explore what was going on inside her, thus stranding Joan Collins, not an accomplished actress to begin with, in a very underdeveloped (no pun intended) role. There is male bonding, which is very central to Hawks's work: the pharaoh, his best friend Hamar, Vashtar, and his son Senta, four men who respect one another, *jointly* try to get the pyramid built; when the pharaoh is killed, Hamar takes over his work

Senta wins the pharaoh's favor by saving him from one of the devices meant to discourage tomb-robbing.

(as if he were his wrestling tag team partner), and when Vashtar goes blind, Senta takes his place. But the men in this film are unlike those exciting Hawksian heroes who fly bombers, ride horses, and race cars. These fellows wear togas and lead a life of leisure. A typical day: the pharaoh visits his gold and chats; Hamar writes in his chronicle and addresses Moonie-like gatherings; Vashtar oversees the building of the pyramid but never gets his own hands dirty; and Senta helps pop. It is a sign of things to come when the film opens, as in *Agamemnon*, with the pharaoh *returning* from the battle rather than going off to battle, wanting to bathe and rest. As the film progresses, the pharaoh, like the other men, only gets wearier and wearier. Why is this pharaoh so dull? At the 1970 Chicago Film Festival, Hawks gave us a hint:

> We started to work . . . and Faulkner said, "I don't know how a pharaoh talks. . . . Is it all right if I write him like a Kentucky colonel?" And Kurnitz, a very fine playright, said, "I can't do it like a Kentucky colonel, but I'm a student of Shakespeare. I think I could do it as though it were *King Lear*." So I said, "Well, you fellows go ahead and I'll rewrite your stuff." They did it, and I messed it up. . . . [We] didn't know what a pharaoh *did*.*

---

*From an interview transcribed and edited by Joseph McBride and Michael Wilmington. First published as "Do I Get to Play the Drunk This Time?: An Encounter with Howard Hawks," in *Sight and Sound*, (Spring 1971).

So the pharaoh does little. Perhaps Laughton or Olivier could have given the pharaoh some dimension through their presence alone, but workmanlike actor Jack Hawkins can only be up the Nile with such a part. Part of the problem is that the audience doesn't know whether he is a tyrant or basically a good person who just has an unnatural lust for gold. Even the pharaoh's obsession for gold seems more of a plot device than a real sickness. There is a major flaw in the script: neither the slaves nor the Egyptian workers ever rebel against the pharaoh. Such a scene is essential, for only by seeing how the pharaoh deals with dissidents can we decide if he has decency. Strangely, this revolution scene is set up in the script, when Hamar narrates that the workers have grown disheartened after so many years of drudgery and that they are being subjected to the whip to make them continue working—but nothing actually transpires! All we end up feeling for the pharaoh is pity, because while he was so preoccupied with the construction of his pyramid, he didn't see what was happening in his own house, between the scheming Nellifer and the guard Treneh, that would ultimately lead to his downfall. (As in *Rio Bravo* [1959], Hawks's men have trouble concentrating on their work when there is a woman around.)

Much current interest in *Land of the Pharaohs* is due to its being the last picture on which William Faulkner was involved. His disappointing career in Hollywood, during which time he did rewrites for

Hamar brings Nellifer into the dead pharaoh's tomb. He didn't bother to tell her yet that he, she, and the monks behind them are about to be sealed in the tomb for eternity.

several scriptwriters but was mostly rewritten himself, was at least sparked by several collaborations with his great friend Howard Hawks. Among their projects which actually came to fruition were *Today We Live* (1933), based on Faulkner's story "Turn About," for which Faulkner received *dialogue* and *story* screen credit; *The Road to Glory* (1936), for which Faulkner received *co-screenplay* credit with Joel Sayre; *Air Force* (1943), for which Faulkner received no screen credit but worked on two scenes; *To Have and Have Not* (1944), for which he received *co-screenplay* credit with Jules Furthman; and *The Big Sleep* (1946), for which he received *co-screenplay* credit with Leigh Brackett. In addition, Hawks and Faulkner worked on many unrealized projects which were either abandoned or were taken over by other directors and / or screenwriters.

Exactly how much of a contribution Faulkner made to *Land of the Pharaohs* is unknown, although one suspects that the sultry vamp Nellifer is akin to Faulkner's wayward southern belles and the slaves of the pharaoh could have been transplanted from a Faulkner plantation. In *Faulkner and Film* (Ungar, 1977), Bruce F. Kerwin made these further observations:

> Faulkner described the story as another *Red River* [1948], with the Pharaoh amassing treasure and constructing his tomb in the same spirit as John Wayne had built up his cattle herd and driven it to market. It is just as easy, however, to note the similarities between *Land of the Pharaohs* and *Absalom, Ab-*

salom!: Pharaoh's plans for the great pyramid obsess him precisely as Sutpen's "design" does him, and in both cases the overreachers are destroyed by their compulsions. The evil [Nellifer] . . . arose more from Faulkner's nightmare of "abomination and bitchery" *(Light in August)* than from Hawks's view of women. As in *Absolution,* the hero gives up everything "for a woman who was not worth it." Even the lifelong friendship between Pharaoh and the priest Hamar . . . is introduced by a scene that could have come from "Turn About" . . . Pharaoh's central compulsion, which originates in a childhood fight [between the two], determines the entire tragedy. . . . Although Hawks mainly remember[ed] the fun he and Faulkner had in devising a system of hydraulics to seal the pyramid, it is clear that the two men were engaged as well in an intimate thematic collaboration.

Howard Hawks was one of the most accessible directors in Hollywood, particularly in his later years, when he was continually granting interviews and appearing at "Howard Hawks" symposiums. Shamelessly, he would repeat the same anecdotes over and over again. One of his favorites, about Faulkner, was heard by everyone in Hollywood at one time or another. It had to do with the time in the forties when he introduced Faulkner to Clark Gable:

GABLE: I hear you're a writer, Mr. Faulkner.
FAULKNER: That's right, Mr. Gable. And what do you do?

Laura

1944 20th Century-Fox
Director: Otto Preminger
Producer: Otto Preminger
Screenplay: Jay Dratler, Samuel Hoffenstein, and Betty Reinhardt
Based on a novel by Vera Caspary
Cinematography: Joseph La Shelle
Music: David Raksin
"Laura" theme: Johnny Mercer and David Raksin
Editor: Louis Loeffler
Running Time: 88 minutes

Cast: Gene Tierney (Laura), Dana Andrews (Mark McPherson), Clifton Webb (Waldo Lydecker), Vincent Price (Shelby Carpenter), Judith Anderson (Ann Treadwell), Dorothy Adams (Bessie Clary), James Flavin (McAvity), Clyde Fillmore (Bullitt), Ralph Dunn (Fred Callahan), Grant Mitchell (Corey)

Synopsis: On Friday night, Laura Hunt, a beautiful advertising executive, has been reported murdered in her apartment—shot in the face by a shotgun blast. The body was identified by the clothes. The murder weapon is missing. Police detective Mark McPherson investigates several suspects: Waldo Lydecker, snide intellectual newspaper columnist who was Laura's friend and companion: Shelby Carpenter, her good-for-nothing money-hungry fiancé; and Ann Treadwell, Laura's rich, unscrupulous aunt, who loves Shelby. Waldo says he thinks Shelby committed the crime because Laura had decided to break off the engagement.

McPherson becomes infatuated with Laura when he sees her portrait in her apartment. Waldo, having little respect for the detective, who has more brawn than brains and calls women "dames," tells him about Laura. Waldo had been having lunch at the Algonquin when she had been bold enough to introduce herself and ask for his endorsement for a pen account her firm was handling. He declined, snapping at her for interrupting his lunch. Later, unable to get her out of his mind, Waldo apologized, agreed to the pen endorsement, and asked her out for dinner. They became constant, platonic companions. He introduced her to many important clients, and "her talent and imagination led her to the top of her profession and kept her there." He became very disturbed when she started breaking their dates to see other men, but all her affairs proved insignificant and impermanent until she met Shelby. Eventually they became engaged. Jealous, Waldo told Laura of Shelby's shady past and that he was having an affair with model Diane Redfern. Laura decided to go away for the weekend to work things out regarding Shelby. But that Friday she was shot.

McPherson falls asleep while sitting in front of Laura's portrait. When he wakes up, he finds Laura standing in her doorway, very much alive. They figure that the woman killed Friday night was actually Diane Redfern. When Waldo enters and sees Laura he faints. But Shelby already knows that Diane Redfern was the murder victim. He confesses to McPherson that he brought her to Laura's apartment to break off with her. When the doorbell rang, Diane, wearing Laura's robe, had answered the door and had been shot. Shelby thinks Laura killed Diane in a fit of jealous rage. Laura is insulted by this insinuation and breaks off completely from Shelby.

McPherson and Laura express their love for one another. Believing Laura to be innocent, McPherson searches Waldo's apartment. He discovers a hiding place in a clock. Realizing it is big enough to hide the missing murder weapon, he goes to Laura's apartment and looks in the identical clock that Waldo had given Laura as a present. He finds the shotgun. He removes the bullets and puts it back. He goes to arrest Waldo, who he thinks is doing a radio show, not knowing the show has been taped. Waldo sneaks into Laura's apartment and reloads the gun. He tells Laura that he can't bear to think of her loving McPherson and tries to kill her. His shot misses when she pushes the gun. McPherson and other policemen charge into the apartment and gun Waldo down.

A strange obsession: McPherson falls in love with the supposedly dead Laura by looking at her portrait.

Rouben Mamoulian claims that he is the true director of *Laura*, that he filmed three quarters of the release print and prepared the remaining scenes. And Lucien Ballard, Mamoulian's cameraman on the film, concurs. But it was Otto Preminger who brought Vera Caspary's novel to the attention of Twentieth's studio head Darryl F. Zanuck, convinced Zanuck to let him produce the picture (though not direct it), and took over as director (bringing in cameraman Joseph La Shelle) when Zanuck pulled Mamoulian off the project. And it was Preminger (who claims to have reshot everything done by Mamoulian) who accepted sole directorial screen credit for *Laura*, the cult classic and revival house favorite which elevated him from minor director to one of the giants in the industry.

Mamoulian may have directed most of *Laura*, but the picture seems to fit better into Preminger's oeuvre than his own. Over the next few years, in fact, Preminger would direct several films that bear remarkable similarity to *Laura*: *Fallen Angel* (1945) with Dana Andrews; *Whirlpool* (1949) with Gene Tierney; *Where the Sidewalk Ends* (1950), reuniting Andrews and Tierney; and *Angel Face* (1953). These are all somber excursions in psychological melodrama, with brutal intonations but that deal primarily with the perversity of the mind. Repeatedly, elegance mixes with decadence, wit with cruelty, and the conflict comes from Preminger mixing together people who don't match. Even stylistically, *Laura* resembles Preminger's later films: fluid camerawork and long static shots blend together; emphasis is on settings, including carpets, curtains, shelves, books, artifacts—anything that helps the viewer determine the cultural, financial, and intellectual standing of his characters; characters and plot elements common to *film noir* are taken out of dark rooms, alleys, and tenements and brought into lush settings, all brightly lit, where in the background we can hear melodious music rather than the jazz riffs played in a *film noir* speakeasy. This is *All About Eve* (1950) with a mystery.

Throughout his career Preminger has been preoccupied with characters that are in some way "flawed." Eventually the flaws would manifest themselves as actual physical infirmities, as in *Tell Me That You Love Me, Junie Moon* (1970); but early in his career, beginning with *Laura*, Preminger was more concerned with his characters' psychological makeup. "For an intelligent woman, you surround yourself with dopes," McPherson tells Laura. But they aren't so much dopes as they are good-for-nothings and losers with peculiar personality traits. Shelby, once Laura's fiancé, is a slimy, money-hungry two-timer. If you shook hands with him you would find your palm sweaty and your ring on his finger. The key is that you *would* find the ring on his finger because he wouldn't think of hiding it. Time and again Shelby is caught in some lie—first by Waldo, who investigates his past, then by Laura, who discovers him dining with Ann when he said he'd be elsewhere, and finally by McPherson, who discovers an enormous hole in his alibi on the night of the murder and untruths everytime Shelby opens his mouth thereafter. He can't help lying, as he believes that anyone would drop him like a hot potato if they knew the truth about him. And anyone would drop him except for Ann Treadwell. While Shelby pretends to have dignity, Ann's one redeeming quality is that she doesn't deceive herself into thinking she has any other redeeming qualities. "Shelby's no good," she admits, "but he's what I want. We belong together because we're weak and can't seem to help it." It is fitting that the last we see of this pitiful couple is at Laura's welcome-home party: Shelby sits slumped in a chair holding his stomach, which McPherson has punched, wetly kissing the palm of Ann's comforting hand.

Mark McPherson may think poorly of those people who populate Laura's world, but he is no prize himself. He has neither the self-confidence nor the devil-may-care attitude of other superhero detectives with alliterated names, like Bogart's Sam Spade. He's a crude fellow, quite brutal, who is in control in the gutter, his usual beat, but is on shaky new ground with people who dine at "21," the Colony, and the Algonquin. His insecurity is evident: he calms his nerves by playing with a handheld baseball game, much like Bogart's insane Captain Queeg, who jiggles those metal balls in *The Caine Mutiny* (1954). His immaturity is evident: he plays this kid's game, he snoops through Laura's love letters, he punches Shelby simply because he doesn't like him. Women totally baffle him, and he apparently has had little experience with them although he admits to Waldo that he once was taken for a fox fur by "a dame from Washington Heights." When he first sees the portrait of Laura, he is oblivious that the people around him may be upset by her supposed death; like the caveman he is, he looks at her portrait and tells them, "Not bad."

Rarely has a hero been shown to sink so low as McPherson, who develops an obsessive love for Laura, whom he believes to be dead. There is an astonishing

McPherson questions Waldo while he bathes.

*Waldo and Laura watch McPherson slug Shelby in the stomach. In the background
is Laura's portrait that, along with the theme music, dominates the proceedings.*

scene in which McPherson is alone in Laura's apartment. Immediately, there is suspenseful music, indicating the smoldering sexuality that dominates the scene. Alone, smoking a cigarette, he stares at Laura's portrait. He strips off his jacket and loosens his tie as the music keeps pace. He sits on the chair and stares at the portrait, but is too worked up to remain seated. He nervously puts out his cigarette, and as the camera watches from the living room, he goes into the bedroom, where he rummages through her closet and drawers and smells her perfume. He then returns to the living room and, perhaps feeling a tinge of guilt, pours himself a drink. Again he stares at the portrait. Waldo recognizes the perverted nature of McPherson's visits to Laura's apartment: "Ever strike you that you're acting crazy? . . . You'll end up in a psycho ward. I don't think they've ever had a patient who fell in love with a corpse." And the movies have never had a hero caught up in necrophilia.

Waldo Lydecker is a much more interesting character than McPherson. And Waldo knows this. That is why he can't tolerate the thought of Laura dumping him

for McPherson. He accuses Laura of falling for any man who has a strong body—and he has a point. Why else would she fall for McPherson so quickly?

In *From Reverence to Rape* (Holt, Rinehart & Winston, 1974), Molly Haskell writes about the relationship of Waldo and Laura:

> The sexually unthreatening male, whether as romantic lover or friend, crops up repeatedly in fiction written by women. The character of Waldo Lydecker, the acid-tongued columnist, is a perfect example. In Preminger's coolly perverse melodrama . . . the beautiful self-possessed heroine has evaded marriage largely through the ritual savaging of her beaux by Clifton Webb's brilliant Lydecker. They make a dazzling team—Gene Tierney's career woman and the epicene, knife-blade lean New York intellectual. Lydecker has a hold on Laura that cannot be explained merely by her indebtedness to him.

Yes, Waldo and Laura are the best couple imaginable, considering all the participants in this drama. Waldo is conceited ("In my case self-absorption is justified") and

Again in front of the portrait of the "illusionary" Laura, the tough Laura tells Waldo that she prefers brutish McPherson to him.

thinks himself incomparably callous ("I would be sincerely sorry to see my neighbor's children devoured by wolves"). But under Laura's influence he is as gentle, generous, and civil as she wants him to be. And importantly, he respects her need to be independent, and her professional skills. He is everything to Laura except the dumb hunk of man she desires. In the novel, Waldo keeps his rifle in his cane rather than inside the clock. According to Vera Caspary, this rifle-in-cane is the telltale Freudian symbol of Waldo's impotence, and suggests the reason for Waldo's sexual frustration when Laura turns to other men to satisfy her sexual needs. The fact that Waldo is sexually attracted to Laura is not really dealt with in the film; instead, Waldo's attraction for her seems to be based on her being a companion who, among other things, is an "eloquent listener."

Laura doesn't turn up in the film until it is exactly half over. By this time McPherson is madly in love with her. Everyone has spoken of her so highly that to him she is an angel. McPherson looks at her picture, smells her perfume, and everywhere he goes hears the haunting Laura theme song (on the radio, on her record player). She becomes his dream lady/dame. When she finally appears in front of him, the camera is purposely out of focus as if to give the impression that McPherson thinks he is still dreaming.

The dreamlike quality of the film can be attributed in part to the fact that Zanuck originally wanted a final scene in which everything turns out to be a dream. Preminger shot the sequence but it didn't work and was excised from the final print. Even with Laura in the film, the portrait still dominates the frame and the music still plays, meaning the dream continues—McPherson still loves the woman he dreamed about. He doesn't seem to realize what we do: the real Laura is disappointing. She is not the warm, wide-eyed innocent we were told about by Waldo. As played by Tierney, she is hard and angry, swearing "No man will ever hurt me again" and "I'll never do anything that isn't of my own free will." Has she changed so much? Not really—her falling for Mark McPherson clearly intimates that to her, it is still as Waldo once said: "A long, strong body is the measure of a man." The movie ends in chaos when Waldo is shot and dying, but the real eruption will come later, when Laura and her new man get married—just wait till the old-fashioned McPherson tells Laura that he doesn't like having a wife who makes more money than he does. Then she'll miss Waldo.

The Little Shop of Horrors

1960 Filmgroup
Director: Roger Corman
Producer: Roger Corman
Screenplay: Charles B. Griffith
Cinematography: Archie Dalzell
Music: Fred Katz
Editor: Marshall Neilan, Jr.
Running Time: 70 minutes

Cast: Jonathan Haze (Seymour Krelboin), Jackie Joseph (Audrey), Mel Welles (Gravis Mushnik*), Jack Nicholson (Wilbur Force), Dick Miller (Fouch), Myrtle Vail (Winifred Krelboin), Leola Wendorff (Mrs. Shiva)

Synopsis: Seymour Krelboin lives with his always sick, always complaining mother and works as a clerk in Gravis Mushnik's florist shop in Skid Row. Mushnik blames Seymour for losing what business he has and would fire him if his daughter Audrey didn't love him.

Seymour invents a new plant by combining a butterworth and a Venus's-flytrap. Audrey is touched when Seymour names it Audrey, Jr. But the plant looks sickly and Seymour decides to stay at the shop and nurse it back to health. At sunset Audrey, Jr., opens up. Seymour accidentally pricks himself and his blood drips into Audrey, Jr. The plant claps.

The next day, Mushnik treats Seymour like a son. Seymour looks at Audrey, Jr., and sees why. It has grown incredibly. Mushnik has put a sign on his window announcing the existence of the plant, and representatives of the Rose Bowl Float Committee say that because of Audrey, Jr., they might order two thousand dollars' worth of flowers from Mushnik. But suddenly, Audrey, Jr., looks dead. Mushnik tells Seymour that if he doesn't bring the plant back to life, he will be fired.

That night Seymour pricks all his fingers and feeds Audrey, Jr., his blood. But the plant isn't satisfied and keeps screaming "Feeed me!!!" Discouraged, Seymour takes a walk by the railroad tracks. He throws a rock at a bottle and accidentally strikes a drunk who stumbles under a train and is killed. Seymour puts him in a sack and feeds him to Audrey, Jr. Mushnik walks in when Seymour is feeding the plant the dead man's foot. He is disgusted, but decides not to tell the police when crowds line up the next morning to get a look at the even bigger plant. Mushnik has never made so much money.

Seymour goes to Dr. Forbes, a dentist, who insists on treating Seymour without Novocaine. Seymour ends up killing him. He feeds Dr. Forbes to the insatiable plant. Now that two men have been killed, detectives Frank Fink and Joe Smith begin investigations.

Seymour is thrilled with his new notoriety. Even the Society of Silent Flower Observers of Southern California wants to give him a trophy. He takes Audrey home to meet his mother and they eat cod liver oil soup. They announce their engagement. A thief tries to rob Mushnik. Mushnik tells him he keeps his money in Audrey, Jr. The thief reaches inside the plant and is eaten alive.

Seymour and Audrey have a picnic in the store. Everytime Audrey wants to kiss him, the plant says "Feeed me!" Seymour tells her he is a ventriloquist. She gets annoyed and walks out. Audrey, Jr., hypnotizes Seymour and sends him out for food. He accidentally kills a prostitute who is trying to pick him up.

Fink and Smith, Mushnik, Audrey, Mrs. Krelboin, and several customers enter the store. Audrey Jr.'s buds open and they can see the faces of the plant's victims. They chase Seymour through a tire factory and a toilet accessories warehouse. He hides in a toilet and gets away. Seymour returns to the store. Intending to do away with his creation, he climbs into Audrey, Jr., with a knife. Everyone returns to the store. One bloom opens. They see Seymour's face. "I didn't mean it!" are his last words. The bloom falls over.

*The character is listed as Mushnik in the end titles, but his shop is called "Mushnick's."

Ironically, both American films that were invited to be shown "out-of-competition" at Cannes in 1960 were about Jewish people. Otto Preminger's *Exodus* (1960) was about Jewish refugees and freedom fighters trying to establish a Jewish homeland. Roger Corman's *The Little Shop of Horrors* dealt with a miserly Yiddish businessman, his slow-thinking Jewish princess daughter, his schlemiel employee, the schlemiel's possessive, hypochondriac mother ("You promised you wouldn't marry until you bought me an iron lung"), a Jewish lady with a funeral obsession, and a sadistic Jewish dentist who has a business arrangement with the undertaker. Preminger's film was set in Israel and was seen all over the world; Corman's was set on Skid Row and played on Skid Row (or within walking distance). Today *Exodus* is considered an overblown spectacle; *The Little Shop of Horrors* is considered one of the most efficient pieces of filmmaking ever accomplished.

The story Corman tells is that he made *Little Shop* because he had the opportunity to utilize sets left standing, temporarily, from another film—worth gold to the low-budget producer—and was excited by the challenge of trying to make a picture before the sets were torn down. This meant working around the clock, but filming took only two days to complete, breaking Corman's personal five-day shooting record set with *Bucket of Blood* (1959). What is remarkable is that despite the minuscule shooting schedule and budget (estimates range from $22,000 to $100,000), *Little Shop* is inventively written (by Corman alumnus Charles B. Griffith), spiritedly played, and professionally made. It is not sloppy at all, and, unlike *Bucket of Blood*, it is consistently amusing. In fact, along with John Landis's minor cult favorite *Schlock!* (1973) and *Abbott and Costello Meet Frankenstein* (1948), *Little Shop* is the best comedy-horror film around, regardless of budgetary considerations.

A film in which the romantic leads are Jonathan Haze, of *Stakeout on Dope Street* (1958)—and nothing else—nonfame, and Jackie Joseph, a quirky, likable lass whose best work since 1960 has been helping Doris Day save homeless animals in Hollywood, can't be taking itself too seriously. Nor can a film that has characters named Gravis Mushnik, Seymour Krelboin, Mrs. Shiva, and Sergeant Frank Fink, and which contains a flower-eating man and a man-eating flower. *Little Shop* is a send-up without pretensions of relevance or artistic merit; if it had turned out to be a disaster, Corman likely would have released it anyway. Fortunately, everything on this film clicked, due to a combination of good writing and energetic direction and performances, and, while it is no masterpiece, *Little Shop* is a low-budget gem.

The most romantic moment in the film: Seymour and Audrey pucker up while having an indoor picnic.

Little Shop is a spoof of both every mad-scientist picture in which blood is needed to keep some experimental creature alive and of every fifties science fiction film in which the emphasis is on giant mutations. There are also numerous traces of past *horror* films. When the hypnotized Seymour goes out to bring back victims for his blood-drinking plant, it is like a Dracula film. When the obnoxious plant keeps screaming "Feed me!" one recalls the minute part-man, part-fly screaming "Help me!" as a hungry spider approaches at the end of *The Fly* (1958). The man-eating Audrey, Jr., reminds me of several giant carnivorous plants in cinema history, including George Coulouris's in an abomination called *Woman Eater* (1959). Corman's film also deals with a true horror: a trip to the dentist ("Now you're going to get it!" Dr. Forbes tells his frightened patient).

Little Shop is in a way a takeoff on Jerry Lewis comedies, with Seymour Krelboin as the Lewis-like character with an IQ of seven, a good heart, a lousy personality, and work habits that drive his boss crazy. It is also a takeoff on fifties television comedies, and most of the scenes are staged with the characters facing forward as if they were playing to a live audience. (I truly think the picture might be even funnier if at times a laugh track were used.) The scenes with Smith and Fink are filmed with a little more speed, intensity, and varied angles, as befitting a *Dragnet* parody. Some of the terse unemotional Jack Webb–like dialogue is hilarious.

SMITH: How are your kids?
FINK: I lost one yesterday.
SMITH: How did it happen?
FINK: Playing with matches.
SMITH: Those are the breaks.

Or, when Winifred tells Fink he has trenchmouth:

FINK: Have me look into that, Joe.
SMITH: Whatever you say, Frank.

And *Little Shop* is a parody of low-budget films. For instance, in most inexpensively produced films where producers can't afford to take everyone out on location, the director will try to build up the visceral excitement with close-ups as characters run through makeshift jungles or wade through fake streams. The close-up is used because a long shot would reveal that the character could easily walk *next* to the water. In *Little Shop* there is a *long shot* of a small puddle surrounded by dry ground on all sides. Corman has every character plopping through the puddle. It's funny.

Little Shop can also be considered satire. The use of Jewish stereotypes may offend some. But they're so ridiculous, I doubt if anyone can take them seriously. The plant itself can be seen as a metaphor for the vicissitudes of fame. Seymour sees how fame is fleeting—each time Audrey, Jr., looks dead, Mushnik, who loves Seymour when the plant grows, wants to fire him. Seymour learns that one must keep feeding success—

A thief demands to know where Mushnik keeps his money. He lies that it is in Audrey, Jr., and watches the thief as he is gobbled up while trying to retrieve it.

you're only as successful as your last picture—although it means destroying all those around him and finally himself. Even for a nobody like Seymour, life was better before he had recognition and a two-dollar raise.

Importantly, *Little Shop* works on its own terms as a good, straight comedy. The cast is marvelous. They might be a Yiddish repertory company who had been working with this script for years instead of doing it while it was being written. Particularly memorable are Mel Welles as the petulant Yiddish florist, Corman-regular Dick Miller as the low-keyed flower-eater ("I like to eat in small, out-of-the-way places"), Jackie Joseph ("I could eat a hearse"), whom I've always liked although I can't remember what else I've seen her in, and the then little-known Jack Nicholson as the masochistic Wilbur Force, a hero for anyone who goes to the dentist more often than every six months. The picture is filled with funny vignettes, but Wilbur's is the most popular. A young man with a bow tie, hair parted down the middle, and a squeaky voice like the one Richard Crenna used on TV's *Our Miss Brooks*, puts down *Pain* magazine and joyously enters Dr. Forbes's office. Since Seymour has killed Dr. Forbes, Seymour pretends to be the dentist and removes several of Wilbur's teeth, as Wilbur seems to work toward an orgasm. Wilbur leaves saying: "I never enjoyed myself so much." This scene isn't for all tastes, but neither is the rest of this often morbid black comedy.

But if you do like Wilbur, you can't help but appreciate Audrey, Jr. It looks like an ugly egg when Seymour first brings it to the store in a small box. And it grows to be a despicable creature that burps and spits out things it can't digest. You'll probably leave the theater imitating his (Audrey, Jr., has a male voice) call to be fed. But even better than "Feeeed me!!" are his ad libs: "I'm hungry!"; "I'm starved!"; "More!"; and, my favorite, "I want some chow!"

Mushnik and Audrey look approvingly at Audrey, Jr. But Seymour realizes the plant has grown so much because it has feasted on blood.

Lola Montès

Also known as *The Sins of Lola Montès*

1955 France Gamma Films–Florida and Oska Films
Director: Max Ophuls
Screenplay: Max Ophuls, Annette Wademant, and Franz Geiger
Based on the novel *La Vie Extraordinaire de Lola Montès*, by Cecil St. Laurent
Cinematography: Christian Matras
Music: Georges Auric
Editor: Madeleine Gug
Running Time: 110 minutes (uncut); 90 minutes in standard cut version

Cast: Martine Carol (Lola Montès), Peter Ustinov (circus master), Anton Walbrook (Louis I, King of Bavaria), Ivan Desny (James), Will Quadflieg (Liszt), Oskar Werner (student).

Synopsis: The ringmaster for a circus in New Orleans introduces his star attraction: Lola Montès, the most scandalous woman in the world. He tells the predominantly male audience that she is a wild animal who has broken hearts, caused suicides and losses of fortune, and was lover to many of the most powerful men in Europe. Past her prime, Lola looks very ill, but reenacts her life in pantomime and answers very personal questions from the audience for twenty-five cents apiece.

The ringmaster tells her story, beginning with her brief affair with the composer Liszt, and then going back in time to when she was a teen-ager on board a ship with her mother, who ignored her and spent much time in the company of Lieutenant James. In Paris, while her mother was arranging her marriage to a baron, Lola and Lieutenant James eloped. But James drank and had mistresses, and Lola left him. She wanted to be a great dancer, made her debut in Madrid in 1841, and then danced in Rome. She had affairs with men from Poland, France, and Russia.

The doctor examines Lola and tells the ringmaster that her heart is weak and that she should not continue with the grueling show, which involves dancing, tightrope walking, and a jump from a high platform.

The ringmaster mentions more of Lola's affairs. She was the first woman to smoke a cigar; and when she discovered her conductor-lover was married she told his wife in public of his infidelity. She began to get a reputation along the Riviera. The ringmaster visited her there and asked her to sign a contract with him so he could star her in America. Not wanting to be part of his seedy show, she refused, but he told her that he was keeping his offer open.

Lola gets ready to jump from the high platform. She looks very ill and dizzy and the ringmaster worries. Meanwhile he tells her greatest adventure. Lost in Bavaria, she met a student on the road. He took her to Munich, her destination, and they were lovers for one night. She auditioned for a dance theater, but they didn't like her doing a Spanish dance and rejected her. In time her money ran out, so she sought an audience with Louis I, the king of Bavaria. He was charmed by her. He arranged for her to do her Spanish dances in a theater and for her portrait to be painted. He hired the artist who would take the longest time to complete the portrait. The king and Lola fell in love and she taught him about art. But the people of Bavaria resented their king being so profoundly influenced by a foreigner. There was a revolt. Though she loved the king, she told him to return to his family and avoid a civil war. The student helped her flee the country. He proposed to her, offering her a simple life, but she turned him down because after losing the man she loved she had no more feelings. "I'm empty," she said.

Lola refuses to use a net in her dangerous act. Her jump is successful—much to the relief of the ringmaster, who loves her and tells her he can't live without her. Thousands of men line up to give Lola a dollar apiece to kiss her hand.

In both Gustav Machaty's fine, controversial Czech film *Ecstasy* (1933) and Max Ophuls's *Le Plaisir* (1952), there is a beautiful scene in which a woman stands alone—one on a balcony, the other by an open window—smoking a cigarette, looking out into the night and thinking about a man. Neither scene has dialogue, but it's not hard to tell that Machaty's Hedy Lamarr—the cigarette smoke escaping her wide-open mouth as if a fire were burning inside her—is at the mercy of her *libido;* while Ophuls's Danielle Darrieux, more composed than Lamarr, is being guided by her *heart.* Lamarr needs sex and Darrieux desires love—the difference between the two women is the difference between lust and passion, sin and romance. Ophuls's women in all his films certainly are willing to make love to men they aren't married to and even have their children, but he thinks too highly of them to equate their actions with wrongdoing. Lamarr will fall in love with the man who gives her sexual pleasure; Ophuls's women love the men they sleep with before they have sex—even if they met them only minutes before. Machaty considers Lamarr a sinner when she yields to her sexual urges and searches out her man for *sex;* he may sympathize with her, but he still feels she deserves punishment and must sacrifice all (the man she now loves) at the end of the picture. But a line from a song in *Lola Montès,* directed at Lola, reveals that Ophuls doesn't consider his women sinners: "You give your body but you keep your soul."

Max Ophuls's illustrious career spanned twenty-five years. He made films in Vienna (from where he, a German-born Jew, fled with the rise of Hitler), Italy, France, Hollywood (where he made four films in the forties), and France again, where in the fifties he made four films that have received critical acclaim: *La Ronde* (1950), *Le Plaisir* (1952) *The Earrings of Madame de . . .* (1953), and the legendary *Lola Montès.* Wherever he went, he made films about women. Beautiful women. Smart women. At first young, naive, and overwhelmed by a large world; but later mature and wise to the ways of that world. Independent women. Moral women. Their names often begin with the letter "L"—Lola, Lisa, Leonora—like the word *love,* which plays such an important part in their lives. These are passionate ladies who strive to achieve their heart's desires—like Garbo without the guilt and suffering, or Dietrich without the cynicism, or Jennifer Jones without the greed. They live in ordered societies but stubbornly refuse to adhere to social conventions that dictate whom a woman can and cannot love and marry: in Ophuls's American masterpiece, *Letter from an Unknown Woman* (1948), Lisa (Joan Fontaine) turns down a proposal of marriage from a career soldier of whom her parents approve and pursues her unrequited love for pianist Stefan (Louis Jourdan); in *Lola Montès,* young Lola walks out on her mother, who is arranging the girl's marriage with someone she doesn't know—a common social practice—and elopes with Lieutenant James, her mother's suitor.

Ophuls treats his women reverently. They are not merely human. For instance, Leonora (Barbara Bel

The circus master presents the world's most famous lover and courtesan to her male admirers.

Geddes) of *Caught* (1949) is an ideal: a smart, unassuming, warmhearted woman who can do anything but type and even learns to do that. Lisa of *Letter from an Unknown Woman* is dead when the picture begins (which we learn late in the film) but Ophuls lets her "live" behind the grave through her letter to Stefan, which serves as the narration for the film's flashbacks. As Molly Haskell contends, Madame de becomes "the shadow of a saint," even before her death. Lola Montès is a living legend. The screen's greatest ornamentalist places his women in marvelously composed shots amidst sumptuous decor, "to reveal," as British film historian John Kobal points out, "things of beauty about the people within it." So his women are often found in great rooms that contain a dazzling array of statues, gilt-edged mirrors, paintings, plants, draped brass beds, winding staircases, cozy loveseats, luxurious couches, curtains, crystal, candles, chandeliers, and plush carpets; as often as possible, he dresses them in majestic gowns and jewelry. Ophuls's works are tasteful, graceful, and quite elegant, and it is his women who benefit. Even Leonora, who has no money at the beginning of *Caught*, is introduced with such opulent music of many violins that when the camera concludes its dolly we expect to find someone at a grand ball waltzing away—but instead we find her in her modest apartment soaking her feet after having pounded the pavement that day in search of work. This is hardly an act that other directors would think justifies such glorious music; but Ophuls treats his women in a manner more befitting their hearts and souls than their bank accounts. As Molly Haskell writes in *From Reverence to Rape* (Holt, 1974): "Ophuls is one of the few directors, indeed few artists, of any nationality to treat woman, in Simone de Beauvoir's terminology, as 'subject' rather than 'object,' as an absolute rather than a contingent being."

It is as the student (Oskar Werner, young and already terrific) contends: Lola Montès, the heroine of

Ophuls's final film, "represents love and liberty." She epitomizes Ophuls's intelligent, free-willed, free-spirited, brave ("I'm not afraid of any man") woman who stands in defiance of social rules. She is not necessarily a rebel by intention, but her rebellious actions that mock society's norms make her an example for other repressed women. "I'm not looking for scandal," she insists, "I just do what I want." What she wants is what her heart wants, and it is not surprising that when we come upon her long past her prime she is suffering from a weak *heart*—it has worn out after so many liaisons over her life's course. She has always understood that love is a balm to the senses as is nothing else, but too much of anything, she learns ("I lived too long and too intensely") drains life's energies. Love has the power to consume an individual, and she feels a great loss each time one of her love affairs comes to an end, as it must in Ophuls's predetermined world ("Events always occur at their prescribed times," Louis tells Lola as he reluctantly ends their relationship and returns to affairs of state). She refuses to protect herself from heartache because she believes in living and loving with intensity.

Like all of Ophuls's women, Lola exists in a world of impermanence, of transition. "For me, life is move-

Young Lola's relationship with Lt. James, whom she married, was always full of misery.

Lola's one desire was to be a famous dancer, and she danced all over Europe, picking up lovers along the way.

ment," she says, and appropriately Ophuls's camera is in constant motion to emphasize the shifts and uncertainties in her life, as well as the numerous changes in locale. Life is determined by little things: the road you follow, even the mode of transportation you use—for in Ophuls's universe, trains, boats, carriages, and cars are meant to lead characters to their destinies. It isn't just the camera that moves but the characters within the frame as well, and moreover there are continual shifts back and forth across time. Time is Lola's emotional domain. She is in fact a product of her past (which explains the abundance of flashbacks). Her memories are bittersweet at best, but they remain an integral part of her, the part that smiles but is damaged. Lola remembers every affair she has had—unlike Stefan in *Letter from an Unknown Woman*, who doesn't recognize Lisa years after their brief romance which resulted in her pregnancy—and she suffers because each man took something of her with him. When she loses Louis, she acknowledges that her many losses have taken their toll. "Now it's over," she laments. "I'm empty."

Max Ophuls is recognized as the cinema's master of the mobile camera, and he characteristically begins *Lola*

In Bavaria, Lola had a brief fling with a student, played by a young Oskar Werner.

Montès with an incredible shot that begins high in the circus rafters and ends three flights below, on the ground. We may think that this is a high-class extrava-

Lola's one true love was Louis I, the king of Bavaria, who became excited by her a minute after their meeting when she began to disrobe for him.

ganza to which Ophuls so dramatically brings us, featuring Lola as the star in her own life's story. But we can understand from Lola's "Life is motion" quote that the camera *descended* for the express purpose of showing us to what *depths* Lola has fallen since she was mistress to many of Europe's most important men. She is in fact accepting donations from the audience for the Society of Fallen Women. Her conversation with the ringmaster in a flashback confirms that she is at the nadir of her existence. Having once booked a three-headed woman and a musical elephant in his circus, he offers her a contract. She turns down his offer to be presented as "The World's Most Scandalous Woman." As he leaves, he tells her, "You know where to find me for better or worse." "It'll be 'worse,'" she acknowledges. She must have been without any self-respect years later to have accepted the ringmaster's offer. Lola is ill at the film's beginning, but she does not die of her heart condition. Just when it appears that she is about to pass out and plummet to her death off the high platform, she learns that there is a whole audience of men willing to pay a dollar each just to kiss her hand. She completes her jump without misfortune. She has been revived even in so degrading a setting as this circus, and I believe that the self-satisfied smile is a genuine expression of her feelings as thousands of male admirers line up for the privilege of paying her tribute. It is her final victory. She would spend her last days in New York saving souls of other lost women. She died penniless.

Lola Montès is a rich, beautifully designed, scored, and photographed work by a master stylist. But there are lapses in the script and with characters. The Ustinov ringmaster does not compare to the one played by Anton Walbrook in *La Ronde*. He is as uninteresting as Ralph Edwards emceeing *This Is Your Life*. Martine Carol is exciting at rare moments, as in the scene when she seduces Franz Liszt, but mostly she is bland and unable to project the inner beauty that the men Lola meets always sense in her; and in a terribly silly scene where she seduces Louis by stripping for him, Carol may as well be Maria Montez. Carol was famous in the fifties as a sex goddess of sorts and for taking nude baths in a series of French historical dramas, but, an actress of limited means, she is unable to convey the subtleties of Lola's character. In fact, when late in the film she tells the student, "Bavaria was my last chance," it is the first time we realize the extent of Lola's inner suffering.

Max Ophuls died in 1957, two years after the European release of *Lola Montès*. It would take another dozen years before the picture would come to America in an uncut version and be championed by Andrew Sarris and other critics as one of the cinema's true masterpieces. Already a cult film in Europe among cinéastes, it would attract a following among critics and film historians who had long been curious about Ophuls's last film. I don't agree with the high assessment given the film by Sarris and others, but *Lola Montès* does reveal Ophuls's genius with the camera and for set design, and gives insight into his unique vision of women. These are reasons enough for it to be seen several times.

The Long Goodbye

1973 United Artists
Director: Robert Altman
Producer: Jerry Bick
Screenplay: Leigh Brackett
From the novel by Raymond Chandler
Cinematography: Vilmos Zsigmond
Music: John Williams
Editor: Lou Lombardo
Running Time: 112 minutes

Cast: Elliott Gould (Philip Marlowe), Nina van Pallandt (Eileen Wade), Sterling Hayden (Roger Wade), Mark Rydell (Marty Augustine), Henry Gibson (Dr. Verringer), David Arkin (Harry), Jim Bouton (Terry Lennox), Warren Berlinger (Morgan), Jo Ann Brody (Jo Ann Eggenweiler), David Carradine (prisoner)

Synopsis: Private eye Philip Marlowe wakes up in the middle of the night. His cat wants to be fed. He goes to an all-night Los Angeles supermarket, but can only buy a brand his cat hates. His cat runs out on him.

Marlowe's friend Terry Lennox comes by. He gets Marlowe to drive him to Tijuana. In the morning, the L.A. police arrest Marlowe for helping Terry escape. They say that Terry Lennox beat up and killed his wife Sylvia. Marlowe doesn't believe his friend is capable of such a crime. The next morning, Marlowe is freed and the case has been closed. According to Mexican newspapers, Terry Lennox committed suicide.

Marlowe is hired by Terry's ex-neighbor, Eileen Wade, to find her husband, author Roger Wade. He tracks Wade to a sanitorium where he is being treated for alcoholism by Dr. Verringer, a money-hungry quack. Marlowe brings Wade home. He observes that the Wades are at odds with each other. She has a bruise on her face to prove it. Wade is full of self-pity and has writer's block. Marlowe wonders if Wade, a big, powerful, violent, depressed man, might have known Sylvia Lennox.

Gangster Marty Augustine threatens Marlowe, telling him to return the money Terry was running for him but took to Mexico. Marlowe knows nothing about the money. Marty tells him to find it. Marlowe follows Marty's car to the Wades' house. The next day, Wade tells Marlowe that Marty owes him a lot of money.

The Wades throw a party. Dr. Verringer shows up and demands Wade pay him the money he owes him. He slaps Wade, greatly embarrassing him. The party ends. Eileen makes dinner for Marlowe. She tells him she doesn't believe Terry was violent enough to have killed Sylvia. Wade walks into the ocean and commits suicide. The tearful Eileen tells Marlowe that Wade and Sylvia were having an affair and she thinks he killed her. Marty's men pick up Marlowe. Marty threatens to beat him up. But when the money Terry owed turns up, they let Marlowe go.

Marlowe is accidentally run down by a car while following Eileen's car on foot. When he gets out of the hospital, he discovers Eileen has moved.

He takes the five thousand dollars he received in the mail from Terry on the day Terry went to Mexico and goes back to Mexico himself. There he bribes the coroner and learns that Terry's funeral was a fake, that Terry is still alive.

Terry is not surprised to see Marlowe. He admits that he killed his wife because she was going to squeal on him for running money for Marty. "No one cares," he tells Marlowe. But Marlowe says he cares. Upset that Terry would brutally kill his wife and that Terry would play him for a fool, Marlowe pulls out a gun and shoots Terry.

He dances back up the road, passing Eileen, who has been living with her lover, Terry.

Marlowe and Eileen watch Roger Wade become unnerved when Dr. Verringer (R) demands a check from him at a party.

I n 1977, I did a career interview with Elliott Gould for the short-lived *Bijou*. The picture he was most eager to talk about was *The Long Goodbye*, Robert Altman's fine, quirky detective film parody based on Raymond Chandler's 1953 Philip Marlowe novel:

I don't have favorites, but *The Long Goodbye* is my favorite. David Picker at United Artists sent me the script. I loved the ending in which Marlowe pulls the trigger on Terry Lennox in order to get on with his own life. I thought it was so brave. It was Leigh Brackett's conception—in the book, Terry just walks away. Other than that ending, the reasons I wanted to do the picture were that I needed a job and I wanted to create an original Chandler character based on the one I remembered Bogart and Dick Powell playing. I played the traditional classic hero in a world that he has no understanding of—modern L.A.—and that couldn't care less about him. . . . I chose my wardrobe: the white socks, the jacket, the pants, the shoes . . . you never saw my tie too closely because it had small American flags on it. And we tested Nina van Pallandt, of Clifford Irving fame, who Altman wanted to use. I interviewed her from behind the camera and we talked about *Freaks* [1932], and she got the part. I was really impressed with her performance. I suggested using Jim Bouton, the ex-ballplayer and writer, and Altman brought

him in. And I loved working with the cat—actually two cats . . . I loved Sterling Hayden. I never met anyone like him before. He was a father figure to me. I almost drowned going after him—really trying to save him (in my mind)—during a take of the Roger Wade suicide scene.

As always, Altman gave me a lot of space. He let me put all that black stuff on my face in the police station and say "I've got a big game coming up against Notre Dame," and do Jolson. . . . Altman told me that I scared him a lot in the film because I really punctured myself and penetrated inside.

I'm really crazy about *The Long Goodbye*, and I'm really upset that it didn't do well. We wanted a big, big hit, and I needed to reestablish myself as a commercial entity. They made the mistake of opening it in Los Angeles and it was destroyed in the papers. It's an *art film* that should have opened in New York. Luckily, Altman pulled it, redesigned it, and reopened it a few months later in New York. It got great reviews and we got something back on it.

The Long Goodbye, Chandler's next-to-last Philip Marlowe book, was published after the demise of *film noir*, the dark, cynical, tough, atmospheric film style that was ideal for Marlowe and other forties detectives. Consequently, studios bypassed it as possible movie fare (although I believe there was a television adaptation circa 1954). Bill Richards's excellent *Farewell, My*

Popeye—who Altman liked enough to make a movie about, and who Gould, I happen to know, has been fanatical about since a kid. Gould considers himself a "jazz actor," and in *The Long Goodbye* Altman allows him to improvise repeatedly. Gould ad-libbed those optimistic seventies lines to his cellmate ("You're not in here—it's only your body") and hospital roommate ("It don't hurt to die") that seem a long way from Marlowe's postwar pessimism. But Gould is not as far away as some critics contend from Chandler's Marlowe, the one a bullying detective mocked in the novel:

> Tarzan on a big scooter. A tough guy. Lets me come in here and walk all over him. A guy that gets hired for nickels and dimes and gets pushed around by everybody. No dough. No family. No prospects.

Critics objected that Gould's Marlowe seems characterized by his passivity, his willingness to take insults and physical abuse without fighting back. "It's okay with me" is his catchphrase, but it is only okay with him up to a point. Throughout most of the picture, we don't know if he carries a gun or is even capable of throwing a punch. But when he pulls out his gun at the end and blows a hole in Terry's stomach, we suddenly understand what makes this character tick. We know from this one gesture that he wasn't out of his league when being roughed up by brutal cops or Marty Augustine's thugs. He was capable of taking care of himself—he was just biding his time. He is as tough as Bogart, Powell, or Mitchum. Only Roger Wade senses there is more to this

Throughout The Long Goodbye, *Marlowe is harassed by every animal and human being whose path he crosses.*

Lovely brought Marlowe to the screen in 1975 in the person of Robert Mitchum. But whereas Richards set his picture in the forties, dressed Marlowe in a trench-coat, and made the film in *noir* style, United Artists chose to update *The Long Goodbye* to modern, sun-drenched, washed-out, neon-lit L.A. with its all-night supermarkets and Laundromats, physical-fitness nuts, nude sunbathers, medical quacks, and various movie types. This updating annoyed the Marlowe faithful among California movie critics, but what they couldn't tolerate was that their hero had suddenly become a Jew from the East. On the other hand, New York critics sensed that the picture is about an old-fashioned character with old-fashioned views on loyalty and morality who can't find his niche in a seventies me-generation playground and they thought no one could be more out of place than a New York Jew in Hollywood—therefore they considered the casting of Elliott Gould inspired.

I, too, think Gould makes an interesting Marlowe. Slovenly dressed and in need of a shave, he drives along in his '48 Lincoln, or struts down a street with his legs slightly apart and his knees rising high and at odd angles as if he were one of Ingmar Bergman's Swedish actors entering a cold lake in his long johns. He always has a lit cigarette in his mouth and mutters to himself, recalling both Jean-Paul Belmondo impersonating Bogart in *Breathless* (1959) and the top mutterer of them all—

Terry Lennox was played by ex-baseball pitcher Jim Bouton, one of several odd choices Altman made when selecting his cast.

Robert Altman directs tyro actress Nina Van Pallandt and Elliott Gould, who had starred in Altman's 1970 breakthrough film M*A*S*H. *The beautiful Van Pallandt surprised many viewers with her stirring performance.*

Marlowe than first meets the eye: "You've been around more than it looks," he tells Gould after examining his face, Gould's gentle eyes and all.

In an interview with Steve Swires for *Films in Review* (August-September 1976), the late Leigh Brackett, who also co-wrote *The Big Sleep* (1946), in which Bogart created the definitive movie Marlowe, commented on *The Long Goodbye*'s controversial ending:

> The ending of the book was totally inconclusive. . . . You feel that Marlowe has been wounded in his most sensitive heart as it were—he's trusted this man as his friend, the friend has betrayed him, what do we do? We said let's just face up to it. He kills him. In the time we made *The Big Sleep* you couldn't do that because of censorship, had you wanted to. We stuck very closely to Chandler's own estimate of Marlowe as a loser, so we made him a real loser—he loses everything. Here is the totally honest man in a dishonest world, and it suddenly rears up and kicks him in the face, and he says: "The hell with you." Bang!

In *Take One* (January 1974), Brackett wrote:

> It seemed that the only satisfactory ending was for the cruelly-diddled Marlowe to blow Terry's guts out, partly to keep Terry from getting away with it all, partly out of sheer human rage. Something the old Marlowe would never have done. He would have

set Terry up somehow, got somebody else to pull the trigger. At least one critic went into a frothing fit over this blasphemy. But it seemed right, and honest. Chandler's Marlowe operated in his own peculiar world. Bogart's Marlowe perforce operated within both Chandler's world and the restrictions of the Code then governing motion picture morality. Being free of both in the seventies, we felt that we could be bold.

I think it interesting that in the above quote, Brackett uses the term "human rage" to describe Marlowe's motivation. Critics who didn't like Gould's interpretation thought his Marlowe lacked this inner fury until the very last scene, that until then he was completely stoical. But this is simply not true—his anger mounts; in our interview Gould told me: "Having been blacklisted for two years prior to *The Long Goodbye*, and working now for a quarter of my previous fee just to pay off debts, I was so enraged at the disposition of the business toward me and at my lack of knowledge about the business that I was always dealing with that *rage*—which was also basic in the Marlowe character."

Characteristically, Altman keeps his camera moving in *The Long Goodbye*. There are a number of long takes and several interesting shots in which people speak in the foreground while action takes place in the distance, sometimes through glass. The camera is especially inti-

mate during scenes with two people—Marlowe and Eileen, Eileen and Roger—and Altman frequently uses revealing close-ups of characters at their height of emotion. Roger Wade says he likes faces—so does Altman. Because of Altman's peculiar style, the picture is on one level comedic. There is a great deal to laugh at: Marlowe's interplay with his fussy cat, who runs away when Marlowe tries to feed him a cheap brand of cat food (and this detective has it so bad, he never is able to track down the cat); the way the theme song reappears throughout the film, sung and played in diverse styles by sundry singers and musicians; Marlowe's spaced-out female neighbors who are always outside doing yoga in the nude; Dr. Verringer's way of running-hopping after Marlowe; the Malibu Colony guard who does impersonations; Marlowe's trouble with dogs; Marlowe's teasing of Harry, who tries to learn the ropes to be a good gangster; and Marlowe's many ad libs. The improvisational feel to the film, the references to *The Third Man* (1949), the Chandler-scripted *Double Indemnity* (1944), *A Star Is Born* (1954), *The Thin Man* (1934), Walter Brennan, and Cary Grant (who Chandler considered the ideal choice for Marlowe), and the offbeat casting of Van Pallandt, Bouton, Henry Gibson, and movie director Mark Rydell further contribute to the picture's frivolous air. But the world Gould's Marlowe inhabits is as corrupt and menacing as the ones once roamed by the other movie Marlowes. For one thing, Vilmos Zsigmond's spellbinding night photography evokes such a spooky, surreal L.A. it would take a stout heart to venture there. The film doesn't have all that much violence—just an occasional punch, slap, or loud shout—but what we witness, we realize, is only the tip of the iceberg. The three couples in the film—the

Wades, the Lennoxes, Marty and mistress Jo Ann—have violence (toward women) in their relationships in common. We don't actually see Roger slap Eileen, but her face is bruised. We don't see Terry hit Sylvia, but he beats her to death off screen before the picture begins. And, in one of the screen's most brutal moments, Marty breaks a Coke bottle across Jo Ann's face. Just as Marlowe's shooting of Terry is enough to show that he has a violent nature when pushed too far, the Coke bottle scene is enough to impress upon us that these are incredibly violent people we are dealing with—and Altman needn't show any more violent incidents because this scene is unforgettable (as well as unbelievable, because Coke bottles won't break that easily).

Chandler contended that a character like Marlowe who *cares* enough to stand alone against a corrupt world was bound to wind up looking foolish and sentimental. Gould's Marlowe realizes he is foolish when he confronts the smug Terry in Mexico and is told "Nobody cares." "Yeah, nobody cares but me," he acknowledges. "You're a born loser," Terry shrugs. "Yeah, I even lost my cat." Out with the gun. Bang! Now Marlowe takes out his miniature harmonica and dances down the road as "Hooray for Hollywood" plays on the soundtrack. He knows he looks silly kicking up his heels, but for once others look sillier: Terry, who lies dead in his swimming pool, and Eileen who rides home to rendezvous with Terry, her lover. Sentimentalist that he is, he is not really happy that his one friend is dead—as Chandler wrote, "To say goodbye is to die a little"—but unlike the Marlowe in the book, he has refused to play the sap for anybody (Sam Spade's old axiom). Now if he can just find his cat, things will at least be satisfactory—Marlowe never asked for anything more.

Mad Max

A car flies through a trailer during one of the many spectacular highway scenes in Mad Max, *a film for lovers of great stunts.*

1979 Australia American International
Director: George Miller
Producer: Byron Kennedy
Screenplay: James McCausland and George Miller
Cinematography: David Eggby
Music: Brian May
Editors: Tom Paterson and Cliff Hayes
Running Time: 89 minutes

Cast: Mel Gibson (Max), Joanne Samuel (Jessie), Toecutter (Hugh Keays-Byrne), Roger Ward (Fiffi), Tim Burns (Johnny), Steve Bisley (Jim Goose), Geoff Parry (Bubba Zanetti)

Synopsis: It is five years in the future. It looks as if there has been a nuclear war. On Australia's highways there is an ongoing battle between a ruthless gang of cyclists and the Bronze, the main police force. The Bronze ride in cars that are marked "Pursuit" or "Interceptor." Max and his partner, the Goose, are interceptors. During a high-speed chase, the Nightrider, the leader of the cycle gang, is killed in a violent crash. Now led by Toecutter and Bubba, the vengeful cyclists ride into a town on their motorcycles and for sport beat up some of the people there. They drive after a young couple and break their car apart with axes. Then they rape them both. The Goose arrests Johnny, a demented cyclist who was too high to leave the scene. Lawyers get Johnny out of jail, which infuriates the Goose.

On the road alone, the Goose is waylaid by gang members and crashes, ending up hanging upside down in his car. Toecutter makes Johnny prove himself by setting fire to the car. When he finds the Goose in the hospital with his body burned beyond recognition, Max tells his commander Fifi that he wants to quit the force because, except for the bronze badge, he has become no better than the cyclists. Max, his wife Jessie, and their baby drive into the country toward her mother's house by the sea. On the way, Jessie and Max separate for a few minutes while Jessie drives to get ice cream. Surrounded by the cyclists, Jessie knees Toecutter in the groin and pushes an ice cream cone into his face. One cyclist tries to hook a chain on the back of her car and jump on but she gets away. Later Jessie finds the chain and his hand still attached. Max and Jessie arrive at May's farm. Feeling safe, Jessie walks through the woods to the beach. After a swim, as she returns she realizes that she is being followed by cyclists. She runs safely back to Max, who goes out after them. Meanwhile, Jessie discovers that the cyclists have taken the baby. With a shotgun, May makes them give Jessie back her baby and the three of them get into the car and try to drive away. When the car stalls on the highway, Jessie tries to run with the baby. The cyclists ride them down, killing the baby and mortally injuring Jessie.

Mad Max puts his uniform back on and gets into his souped-up police car. He goes after the cyclists and by driving through their formation knocks most of them off a bridge. Further along, he is shot during an ambush. Although badly injured, he speeds after Toecutter, who loses control of his cycle, rides into an oncoming truck, and is killed. Max finds Johnny, the last of the bikers, alongside the road by a wrecked car trying to rob the driver's corpse. Seeing that the car is leaking fuel, Max handcuffs Johnny's leg to the car. He hands him a small saw and tells him that the car will explode in ten minutes but he can saw through his ankle in five minutes and get away. Max drives off. There is an explosion.

While America's art house crowd has been paying top dollar to see Australia's *My Brilliant Career* (1979), another film from Down Under has been causing equal excitement in America's grind houses at bargain prices. *Mad Max*. George Miller's first film was a hit at Cannes in 1978, and since then has been a big moneymaker in countries outside of Australia with the major exceptions of the United States and France, where it was banned. It is true that it has done well wherever it has played here due to good word-of-mouth, but it is equally true that its United States distributor, American International, which took the trouble of dubbing the dialogue with American voices, hasn't considered getting the picture first-class bookings a top priority. For instance it wasn't until late 1980 that it played in the major New York City market and then it was on the lower half of a twin bill on Forty-second Street; a month later it was already showing on pay TV, indicating that AIP had no plans for giving it a theatrical release of consequence. This is unfortunate, for whatever *Mad Max*'s thematic failings, from a visual standpoint it is a thrilling picture that should be seen on the *big* wide screen.

Mad Max stands alone, the first and only film of a genre that surely could be explored and exploited, with interesting results, by action-oriented filmmakers. It is extremely probable, I believe, that if Australian filmmakers began churning out similar violent, futuristic car-motorcycle films full of spectacular chases and crashes—films in which the stuntmen are the stars—it could be the start of an international craze equal to that caused by Italian westerns and Chinese kung fu movies a few years back. Miller might then be induced to make more films in this vein. His striking visual style—his use of a fender-level camera, sweeping pans, breakneck-speed trucking shots, and "shock" editing—corresponds

perfectly to the powerful images he shoots, specifically the speeding and crashing cars and cycles. While you'll certainly like Max and Jessie, a terrific married couple played by handsome Mel Gibson (who looks like a cross between Brad Davis and Fabian with a haircut) and pretty, frizzy-haired Joanne Samuel, and you'll like the cocky, high-strung Goose, you'll find *Mad Max* less interesting as a story about "people" than as a marriage between a filmmaker's machines (his camera, his editing tools) and the motor-powered machines that he films.

Early on, we see that it is Miller's intention to dehumanize his post-apocalyptic gladiators and make them part of the machinery, part of the hardware. By dressing the Bronze (named after their badges) in leather gear and putting helmets on the cycle gang, Miller succeeds in making them all look like robots akin to *Star Wars'* Darth Vadar, physical extensions of their cars and bikes. Moreover, their personalities are functions of their vehicles: they must constantly shout to be heard over their blaring engines; impersonal voices shoot back and forth over the cars' intercoms (other machines). That man and machine are interchangeable is made clear when the speed-crazy Nightrider declares on his way toward his own collision, "I'm a fuel-injected suicide machine!" It has come to a point when doctors discuss their patients in terms of being "salvageable," and the man who does the best transplants in the world is the guy who works in the Bronze's garage and puts cars together by combining parts from old wrecks.

About halfway through the film, Max rejects the way of life that has been draining away his humanity—a rare commodity since the apocalypse. "I'm scared," he tells Fifi. "It's a rat circus out there and I'm beginning to enjoy it." So he takes off his uniform and puts on a T-shirt, checks in his superpowered police car (with the last of the V-8 engines and 600 horsepower) and climbs into his family van, and goes off with Jessie and their baby on holiday. Except for a brief time at Max and

Jessie's isolated, rustic house, we spend the first part of the picture on the speedways outside of town and the bombed-out Halls of Justice. It is their trip through a lovely rural Australia and visit to the elderly May's seaside / country house that gives us the false impression that there can be an idyllic, Eden-like life and the birth of a compassionate people—beginning with Max, Jessie, and their child—after an apocalypse. But this comforting vision is shattered when Jessie is mortally injured and the baby is killed—symbolizing the true death of the human race; and Max, who has become desensitized by his great loss, puts his uniform back on, gets into his police car, and rejoins the rat circus.

While the cult fascination for *Mad Max* has a lot to do with its apartness from other contemporary films, there is much in it that suggests certain familiar influences on Miller. One film that may have caught his eye is *A Boy and His Dog* (1975), a picture based on Harlan Ellison's novella that is set in a post-apocalyptic age when brigands search civilization's ruins for women to rape and murder. AIP's biker films of the sixties likely had impact on Miller as the cyclists menacing demeanor and slovenly appearance recalls the Hell's Angels types of the AIP drive-in pix. However, the scene in which the cyclists ride into a small town to spread terror among the townspeople, and line up their motorcycles as if they were a paramilitary outfit, is more reminiscent of *The Wild One* (1954), the original gang picture. But the conventional beat jargon of Marlon Brando's leatherjackets has evolved into the cryptic beat jargon of Toecutter's gang. The cyclists also have kinship with the futuristic gang in Stanley Kubrick's *A Clockwork Orange* (1971). Not only do both groups speak a similar descriptive language—in Kubrick, intercourse is "in-out, in-out"; in Miller, fighting is "push me–shove you"—but they also vent their hostilities, boredom, and disrespect for law and order through sadistic rapes and thrill killings. That the cyclists and the

A brief respite from the turmoil: Jessie and Max, a very likable screen couple.

main police force are distinguished from one another more by dress than by morality reminds me less of other cop-versus-gang films than it does of *Quadrophenia* (1979), an English film with a growing cult about the often violent sixties rivalry between the Mods and the Rockers. (One thing that strikes me is that the individual members of the cyclists seem to have come from opposite cultural backgrounds, as is indicated by their dress and overall appearance.) The red-streaked hair of Nightrider's girlfriend and Bubba's short-cropped hair aren't the result of cinematic influence but show that Miller has incorporated *punk* into his pop art.

The first part of the film, which is dominated by the Goose, is a straight motorcycle gang picture. But from the point where Max looks at the Goose's charred body to where Jessie realizes that the cyclists have snatched her baby is directed alternately as a bike picture and an atmospheric horror film. (In fact, posters for *Mad Max* promise that it is a "terrifying" film.) The horror begins when Max approaches the Goose in the hospital bed and his partner's burned-black hand falls out from beneath the sheets. It resembles a monster's claw. Jessie's confrontation with the cyclists while getting ice cream is typical gang picture fare, but when she later discovers the severed hand of one of the bikers attached to her car, we are once more in the horror picture domain. The horror elements take over completely as Jessie walks alone through the woods, swims in the ocean, and

sunbathes on the beach far away from Max's protection. Suddenly, above her on the rocks, a motorcycle wheel rolls into the frame. Miller builds the suspense by not showing us who is on the bike. Now Jessie, feeling a bit paranoid because her dog has run off, walks back toward the house through the woods. Looking behind her, she sees shadowy figures dart back and forth between the trees. (How many horror movies have had identical scenes?) Terrified, she begins to run. A bird flies into her face. Then she is face level with her dead dog, hanging upside down from a tree. Then she runs into a huge, toothless man (not a gang member and harmless) who starts laughing when she starts screaming. Once at the house, May, an old lady with leg braces, takes her inside, and while she phones the police and Max searches the woods for the gang members, Jessie is left alone in the living room, draped in a blanket, shivering from fear. From across the room at knee level, the camera creeps toward her. She is indoors but we don't think she is "out of the woods" and expect someone to attack her or appear at the window directly behind her. But at this moment the horror-movie portion of the film ends and Jessie jumps up and races from the house to look for her baby.

What has been a stunningly well-photographed and edited film reaches new heights a few minutes later. Fleeing with May and her baby, Jessie is horrified when the car breaks down. After futilely banging her hands on

At film's end, Max threatens Johnny, the last of the cyclists.

the driving wheel, she grabs her child and runs down the middle of the highway, the bikers in pursuit. May gets out of the car and aims her shotgun at the bikers as they approach in military formation. She misses as they whiz by. Now there is nothing between them and Jessie. We see her running scared. Then we see the bikers. Then there is a dramatic shot of a cycle's speedometer, which suddenly registers a great increase in speed, surprising in that we had expected the bikers to slow down to attack Jessie. There is a blur as the cycles zoom past Jessie (who looks over her shoulder) and the baby and without slowing down head down the road. At this moment the camera is focused on a part of the road (in the foreground) which the running Jessie should then pass if she is all right, but all that comes into frame is her shoe and the baby's bouncing ball. Next Max runs up to the car, hesitates, spots Jessie and the baby crumpled farther up the road, and races toward them. There are several shots of him running. Then from behind, in a long shot, we see him fall on his knees by their bodies and throw his arms about in a manner that leaves little doubt that what he has discovered is catastrophic. We cut to a nightmarish scene in a hospital where doctors and nurses discuss the death of Max's baby and the terrible condition of Jessie. They decide not to tell Max the severity of her state, but Miller's camera pulls back to reveal that Max, standing against a wall in the next room, has overheard them. By his tormented expression we see that he has gone slightly mad: now he is *Mad* Max. All this action on the highway and the hospital which contains so much information and produces so much visual excitement takes place in a matter of seconds. Obviously, a master cinematic storyteller is at work.

What follows is the third consecutive thrilling sequence in a row. (You'll be hard pressed to find any recent film so consistently exciting in the second half). Here Max becomes the latest in the long line of vengeance-bent fascist superheroes as he kills off all the cyclists in brutal fashion. The death of Toecutter is the most shocking: eluding Max, he rides his cycle smack into and under an enormous truck which we then see bounce over him a few times. This is one of several unbelievable stunts in the film. (Another is a guy being struck in the head by a flying motorcycle.) With the gang members dead, Mad Max drives off. Where to? Maybe to an equally well-made sequel.

The Maltese Falcon

1941 Warner Bros.–First National
Director: John Huston
Producer: Hal B. Wallis
Screenplay: John Huston
From the novel by Dashiell Hammett
Cinematography: Arthur Edeson
Music: Adolph Deutsch
Editor: Thomas Richards
Running Time: 100 minutes

Cast: Humphrey Bogart (Sam Spade), Mary Astor (Brigid O'Shaughnessy), Gladys George (Iva Archer), Peter Lorre (Joel Cairo), Sydney Greenstreet (Casper Gutman), Barton MacLane (Lieutenant Dundy), Lee Patrick (Effie Perine), Elisha Cook, Jr. (Wilmer Cook), Ward Bond (Detective Tom Polhaus), Jerome Cowan (Miles Archer), James Burke (Luke), Murray Alper (Frank Richman), John Hamilton (District Attorney Bryan), Walter Huston (Captain Jacobi).

Synopsis: Sam Spade is partner of a San Francisco detective agency with Miles Archer. Spade doesn't like Archer and at one time had an affair with his wife, Iva, whom he has tired of and is trying to get off his back. A beautiful woman named Miss Wonderly hires the firm to save her sister from getting too deeply involved with a man named Floyd Thursby. Miles goes out on the case and is murdered. Soon after this Floyd Thursby is discovered murdered. The police think that Spade might have killed his partner because he loves Iva.

Spade visits Miss Wonderly, whose real name turns out to be Brigid O'Shaughnessy. She has no sister and admits to being a compulsive liar. She tells him Thursby killed Miles, but she doesn't know who killed Thursby. Spade and Brigid begin a romance.

After his loyal secretary Effie goes home, Spade is visited in his office by Joel Cairo, a strange little man with curly hair and an aroma of gardenias about him. He tells Spade that the man he works for is prepared to offer him five thousand dollars for his help. He then points a gun at Spade in order to search his office. Spade takes away the gun and slaps him, then knocks him out. When Cairo wakes up, he repeats the offer and again points a gun at Spade. Laughingly, Spade lets him search the office.

Spade is followed around by a young punk named Wilmer, who is a gun-for-hire for Casper Gutman, "the fat man," Cairo's partner. Spade enjoys making a fool of him. When Wilmer takes him at gunpoint to meet Gutman, Spade takes his gun away from him to embarrass him in front of his boss. The very knowledgeable Gutman tells Spade that he and Cairo are willing to make him a partner in their venture: to get hold of a priceless antique, the Maltese falcon. They think that he might be in cahoots with Brigid, their former partner, who also wants the bird. Spade accepts their deal. Spade discovers that everyone interested in the black bird is paying special attention to the arrival of the ship *La Paloma* from Hong Kong, where Brigid has recently been. The ship catches fire in port. Its captain, Jacobi, comes to Spade's office. He has been shot and dies. However, he has brought the Maltese falcon. Spade hides it in a locker at the bus depot.

Eventually, Spade, Brigid, whom he has fallen in love with, Cairo, Gutman, and Wilmer gather in Spade's apartment. Spade says he has the black bird but they must decide on someone to take the rap for the murders of Miles, Thursby, and Jacobi so he will get off the hook. Spade suggests they turn in Wilmer. Although reluctant to depart with someone he thinks of as a son, Gutman agrees to turn in Wilmer in order to get the falcon. Gutman tells Spade that Wilmer killed Thursby, Brigid's partner, and Jacobi. Wilmer runs away.

Effie brings the falcon. It turns out to be a fake. Everyone is terribly upset, but Gutman and Cairo decide to continue their search. They go outside, where they are arrested. Wilmer is also arrested.

Spade tells Brigid that he may love her but that he is going to turn her in for murdering his partner Miles. "I won't play the sap for you." She admits she killed Miles but pleads with him to let her go free. But he doesn't want someone around who might plug him for knowing too much. Brigid is taken to prison.

The boy looked at Gutman. Gutman smiled benignly at him and said: "Well, Wilmer, I'm sorry indeed to lose you, and I want you to know that I couldn't be any fonder of you if you were my own son; but—well, by Gad!—if you lose a son it's possible to get another—and there's only one Maltese falcon."

As Dashiell Hammett wrote in his classic 1930 detective novel, there were worthless imitations but only *one* priceless—forever elusive—black bird. But Warner Bros. wasn't content to make just one film about it, and within a ten-year period the studio adapted Hammett's *The Maltese Falcon* three times, ending up with that rare imitation (made in 1941) that is more impressive than the original (made in 1931).

The second *Falcon* adaptation, *Satan Met a Lady*, made in 1936 by William Dieterle, is a thinly disguised telling of the Hammett tale, with the infamous black bird being replaced by Roland's legendary trumpet (filled with jewels), and all the characters' names being changed. While this low-budget programmer is not as bad as its reputation, its star, Warren William, is simply ghastly as Ted Shane, a smirking, giggling, conceited, distorted version of Sam Spade. Shane is so obnoxious that villain Valerie Purvis, the film's Brigid O'Shaughnessy character, pays someone to turn her over to the police so Shane won't have the satisfaction of capturing her or getting the reward money for her arrest. Not yet a star, Bette Davis gives a spirited performance playing the genre's most famous femme fatale in a highly unusual manner. Valerie is chipper,

The cinema's supreme detective: Sam Spade, as played by Humphrey Bogart in The Maltese Falcon.

As in the novel, Effie (L) feels a bond toward Brigid. It is based on her realization that the course of events is dictated by men and that women like herself and Brigid understandably use whatever means or talents possible to give significance to their lives.

confidant, and witty; and rather than waste her energy pretending to Shane that she isn't constantly lying and playacting around him, she simply does it as a matter of course—not caring if he sees through her or not. Valerie is likable and such a good sport that she even smiles on her way to prison.

Far superior to *Satan Met a Lady*, Roy Del Ruth's *The Maltese Falcon* (also called *Dangerous Female*), the first (1931) film version of Hammett's book, is a first-rate detective yarn that has never received adequate recognition. With one exception, having the female lead go under the name Ruth Wonderly for the entire film, instead of really turning out to be Brigid O'Shaughnessy, the content in this *Falcon* is the most faithful to the book. While not as charismatic as Bogart, Ricardo Cortez is excellent as Sam Spade: part cavalier, part crumb; part hero, part heel; part smooth, part slimy. Unlike Humphrey Bogart's Spade, but like Hammett's character, Cortez's private eye actually does detective work. One of the best scenes in the film (also found in the novel) is when he examines Ruth's hotel room and, the professional that he is, leaves no stone unturned: he even looks into her garbage and cold cream. Whereas Bogart is a detective because he enjoys mingling with the odd, entertaining brand of people who inhabit the world of crime, spiffy Cortez seems to be in the profession because it gives him the opportunity to meet women who are in trouble and willing to do anything for his help. This is why his loyal secretary Effie is so happy whenever she can tell him that his new client is a "knockout." The picture of actress Louise Brooks on Cortez's wall suggests what is on his mind; Bogart has a picture of a horse and rider. I really like Bebe Daniels, a blonde here, as the jittery, sexy, cheating, confused, deceptive, dangerous Ruth Wonderly. Ruth is the only one of the three movie "Brigids" who uses both her femininity and her body to win over Spade. Unlike Davis and Astor's women, Ruth realizes that feigning to be a *lady*, instead of the dame without morals that she is, will only hurt her efforts to get a man like him. (As

Bogart tells Astor: "I'm glad you're not as innocent as you pretend to be.") And how seductive Ruth is in this pre-Code film: stripping, bathing, lounging in her underwear, or just moving about or posing in a suggestive manner! Even though Bogart's Spade shows he has poor taste in women by having an affair with the floozy Iva (Gladys George), I have never believed he could fall for the beautiful but too prim Brigid (as portrayed by classy Mary Astor)—especially since their brief acquaintance doesn't include spending a night together like Cortez and Daniels have. However, I can see how seedy gigolo Cortez would fall for loose woman Daniels, who is as amoral as he—they are indeed a perfect match.

As an adaptation of the Hammett novel, the fine Roy Del Ruth film didn't leave much room for improvement; and it's a wonder that this picture was remade even once. But then came *Satan Met a Lady*, and after that screenwriter John Huston convinced Jack Warner that he could write and direct (his debut) the definitive *The Maltese Falcon*. Given the go-ahead, Huston proved himself correct.

What is surprising about the Huston film is how little of the dialogue (which Huston is known for) or plot elements are original; almost everything can be found in the book or in one or both of the two earlier *Falcon* films. What makes the Huston picture so special, a true masterpiece, is the style, the impeccable casting, and the stressing of the various characters' peculiarities. The first difference you notice between the Huston film and the other two *Falcons* is its incredible pacing. This is accomplished by Huston's rapid-fire editing within scenes (a succession of shots taken from diverse angles mixed with many close-ups of characters' reactions) and dialogue that shoots back and forth so quickly that it excites you even though you might not understand what is being said. (I am sure that part of the reason this film has such a strong cult is that the story is so muddled that you can't remember from one viewing to the next exactly what happens—so it's always like new.) The low-key camerawork in the picture is especially noteworthy because it helped make *film noir* the dominant style for detective films of the forties. There are several scenes where rooms are lit only by light filtering in through a window or where the only light in a dark room is that which shines on a white door—shadows will soon appear on that door. Yet compared to future *film noir* detective films like *Out of the Past* (1947), *The Maltese Falcon* seems brightly lit. (For one thing, there are no rainswept streets lit by a single street lamp—almost obligatory in *noir* photography.) Arthur Edeson's atmospheric photography is outstanding. I particularly like the way he films menacing Sydney Greenstreet from below to give him even more size than he has; and in the scene in Brigid's hotel room where she wears striped pajamas, the furniture is striped also, and the whole room looks striped because Edeson photographs it as if light were coming in through venetian blinds.

The Maltese Falcon is a landmark film not only because it set the style and tone for the hardboiled detective genre but also because it established screen

In his too large coat, Wilmer threatens Spade. Notice how Huston uses Greenstreet/Gutman to balance the frame: if Gutman stood up, Huston would have Wilmer join Spade and Brigid on the right side of the frame.

personas for most of its players. Making his screen debut at age sixty-two, Sydney Greenstreet found the character which would serve as the basis for most of his future roles. His Gutman is a brilliant conversationalist ("I'm a man who likes talking to a man who likes to talk"), erudite (while waiting for Effie to deliver the "falcon," others sleep, he reads), corrupt, power-hungry, sinister, ruthless, and of course, fat (although he is as quick as a cat). Huston, in fact, repeatedly uses his bulky frame to lend "balance" to the frame; for instance, if Greenstreet is on the right, Huston will move three characters to the left—wherever he sits, he is at the *center* of the action, and all the others just gather around. Although Gutman is as intelligent and civilized as a history professor at Oxford, like most Greenstreet characters he is greedy enough to get involved in wild, foolish schemes with such off-their-rocker characters as Cairo, Wilmer, and Brigid. And as usual he is doomed to failure. Notice the way this calm fellow starts to sweat profusely as his downfall nears. The incomparable Peter Lorre is magnificent as the neurotic, fussy ("Look what you did to my shirt," he complains to Spade after being roughed up), effeminate, emotional Joel Cairo. One second he is threatening someone, the next he is crying. He straightens his clothing as if he were Rodney Dangerfield—angry he gets no respect. A truly funny man with the most expressive eyes in Hollywood, Lorre delivers one of his first quirky comedic roles and finds

the perfect partner in Greenstreet. Together they make villainy endearing. Elisha Cook, Jr., one of the truly great character actors, is splendid as Wilmer, the "gunsel" who wants to be a "tough guy" ("They're gonna be pickin' iron out of your liver!" he warns Spade) but is destined to be the fall guy. As he would do so well for years to come, Cook plays a character who can't back his verbal threats with physical action. His too-big overcoat is symbolic of how foolish this slight figure is trying to be a big shot. *The Maltese Falcon* depends on characterizations more than anything else, and the presence of Greenstreet, Lorre, and Cook—it's impossible to put together a better ensemble—is as responsible as Bogart for making this picture so memorable. Mary Astor is also fine as Brigid (a.k.a. Miss Wonderly). But I can't stand her hair style, which I think makes her look matronly—and a bad visual match for Bogart. I also think that the breathless, "helpless," pleading character Huston conceived for her is a bit much. As she comes up with one fabrication after another ("I've always been a liar"), Spade tells her, "You're good, you're *very* good." (Cortez also said this to Daniels.) But in truth Brigid is so bad at playacting that anyone can see through her.

As in *High Sierra*, released earlier in 1941, Bogart got the chance to play a "tough guy" whose redeeming quality is a strict moral code. And this is the persona that Bogart would be known for from then on. Signifi-

Another example of Huston's frame in balance. *Spade, Cairo, and Brigid watch Gutman unwrap the falcon, only to discover it is a forgery.*

cantly, Bogart, whose roles would include Roy Earle, Rick Blane, and Fred C. Dobbs, plays the *only* character whose first *and* last names have only one syllable; yet, simple name and all, he is the film's most complex figure, a man who is characterized by his ambiguity and contradictions. Bogart's Sam Spade is patient (he rolls his cigarettes), sadistic ("When you're slapped, you'll take it and like it," he tells Cairo after slapping him), glib ("You always have a smooth answer ready," Cairo tells him), witty ("You want me to learn how to stutter?" he retorts to Cairo), and cynical (he looks as if the ugliness of the world is etched into his face). He realizes that his evil, seedy world calls for everyone to put up a strong front in order to survive; and he enjoys pulling off his "tough guy" act with cops and thugs. After telling off Gutman, he storms out in the hall to the elevator, where he breaks into a smile when he sees that his hand is shaking. Like Philip Marlowe, when alone this Spade mocks his own "tough guy" image.

Unlike Cortez's Spade, Bogart's enjoys his work. He manipulates all the characters he finds in his world as if they were pieces in a chess game—often playing them off against each other. And this *is* a game (albeit deadly) that he's involved in, where he must make the correct "moves" in order to (a) get the falcon; (b) get the money; and (c) get Miles's murderer. Also, this is a nonscientific experiment—a challenge to Spade because *every* test specimen (character) has a variable: they all lie. Undeniably Spade is a louse. See how quickly he has his dead partner's name removed from the office door. The only person he is on *friendly* terms with is Effie, whom he trusts and respects because like him she relies more on intuition than facts to make judgments. (She

proves wrong in regard to Brigid, who she thinks is "all right.") Spade treats the other women in his life, Iva and Brigid, shabbily. Even though they might deserve and be asking for it, it's still hard to admire him for his callousness. "If you get a break," Spade tells Brigid, "You'll get twenty years. If they hang you, I'll always remember you." Some consolation. Spade cites two *major* reasons to Brigid for turning her in for killing Archer: "When your partner is killed, you have to do something about it"; and more important (Spade repeats this *four* times in the novel), "I won't play the sap for you"—a statement that will become a catchphrase for all future moral detectives.

On first viewing, it seems honorable that our hero sacrifices the woman he loves (although Effie is appalled by his actions in the novel) because she committed a crime. This is what a man of high moral standards should do, right? Well, the contradiction comes from Spade admitting to Brigid that if the falcon had turned out to be real and he had a chance to make a great deal of money, he might not have turned her in (and I assume he would have quit his nickel-and-dime job). So much for morality—everyone (except Philip Marlowe), even Spade, has his price. Does Huston sympathize with Spade and pardon his actions? One must look at the last scene for the answer. The police take Brigid into an elevator that looks like a prison cell because of its bars. She goes *down* as if she were on her way to meet the devil. (We recall the title *Satan Met a Lady.*) Huston doesn't have Spade walk back into his apartment, but has him *walk down the staircase.* Sam Spade won't end up in hell as quickly as Brigid will, but he will get there eventually.

Man of the West

1958 United Artists release of an Ashton production
Director: Anthony Mann
Producer: Walter M. Mirisch
Screenplay: Reginald Rose
From the novel *The Border Jumpers,* by Will C. Brown
Cinematography: Ernest Haller
Music: Leigh Harline
Title song: Bobby Troup
Editor: Richard Heermance
Running Time: 100 minutes

Cast: Gary Cooper (Link Jones), Julie London (Billie Ellis), Lee J. Cobb (Dock Tobin), Arthur O'Connell (Sam Beasley), Jack Lord (Coaley), John Dehner (Claude), Royal Dano (Trout), Robert Wilke (Ponch), Frank Ferguson.

Synopsis: In Crosscut, Texas, Link Jones, a seemingly naive, timid man buys a train ticket to Fort Worth. He carries money entrusted to him by the people of the town where he lives with his wife and two children. He is supposed to use it to hire a schoolteacher.

Also on the train is Sam Beasley, a cowardly but friendly swindler, who tries to gyp Link out of his money. He tells Link that Billie Ellis, a pretty saloon singer on the train, is a teacher. Billie, who left Crosscut because she tired of indecent proposals, is not comfortable going along with the deception.

The scheme is forgotten when the train is robbed by the notorious Tobin gang, and Link, Billie, and Sam are stranded in the wilderness when the train takes off without them. They walk to a house Link knows of from his youth. He is unhappy to find that his uncle, Dock Tobin, and his cousins, the violent Coaley, the crazy, speechless Trout, and the unintelligent Ponch, are holed up in the cabin. Tobin is thrilled to see Link, whom he raised and loves dearly and who used to commit crimes alongside him, and he is happy to believe Link when he lies that he wants to rejoin the gang. The other men don't like Link or trust him, but Tobin's word goes.

Coaley holds a knife to Link's throat and orders Billie to strip. When she is down to her undergarments, Tobin intervenes and yells at Coaley for botching the train robbery. Link tells Tobin that Billie is his woman and Tobin says he will make sure his gang respects this fact. He takes Link's money but allows Link and Billie to stay together in the barn. Billie starts to fall in love with Link and envy his wife. Claude, Link's cousin, arrives. He is much smarter than the other gang members and has been Tobin's righthand man since Link walked out. Claude tells Link that he knows he is fooling Tobin and will see that he doesn't get away with it.

Everyone heads toward Lassoo, where there is a bank Tobin wishes to rob. Along the way, Link and Coaley have a brutal fight. Link beats Coaley up and strips off his clothes. Humiliated, Coaley tries to shoot Link. Sam steps in the way of the bullet and is killed. Tobin guns down Coaley.

Link convinces Tobin to let him be the one to ride into Lassoo to look over the bank. Trout goes with him. Lassoo has become a ghost town, deserted but for a harmless Mexican woman in the empty bank. Trout kills her for no reason, and Link shoots him. When Link doesn't return, Claude and Ponch go to Lassoo, where they find Trout's body. Link kills Ponch, and after a hard fought gun battle during which both men are wounded, Link kills Claude. He is unhappy he had to do it because he realizes Claude is the person he might have been if he hadn't left Tobin. He feels like he shot himself.

Link returns to camp and discovers Tobin has raped Billie. He finds Tobin in the mountains and tells him that he has killed Claude, Ponch, and Trout. Miserable over what has happened to his family, Tobin shoots wildly in the air. Link shoots him dead. He takes his money off the corpse.

Link and Billie ride toward town. Although Link will be returning to his wife, Billie is thankful she has finally learned what loving a man is like.

The television revolution of the late forties and early fifties brought about the quick curtailment in production of most "B" movies, including the "cheapie" westerns that had long been an endearing staple of the industry. In order to provide alternatives to the studio-shot kiddie westerns on TV like *The Gene Autry Show, The Roy Rogers Show, Hopalong Cassidy* (featuring clips from Hoppy's "B" westerns), *The Lone Ranger,* and *The Cisco Kid,* movie studios began producing big-budget westerns, often in color and using a wide-screen process, made by top directors and boasting big-name stars, on-location shooting, and, most important of all, "adult" themes. As a result, this was an era of remarkable achievement in theatrical westerns.

Among the most impressive westerns of the period were five directed by Anthony Mann which starred James Stewart. *Winchester 73* (1950), *Bend of the River* (1952), *The Naked Spur* (1953), *The Far Country* (1955), and *The Man From Laramie* (1955) are all first-rate "adult" westerns that today have separate cult followings. One characteristic that made them so refreshingly different from the television fare of the day was their magnificent outdoor settings (filming took place in the most scenic regions of the West and Northwest), which give the pictures authenticity and provide the characters with the appropriate environment for their uncivilized behavior. Not merely backdrops, the vast, beautiful Mann landscapes serve to comment on the intrusion of civilization; men torn between their civilized "training" and their primitive natures, and the ugly actions of man within a god-made world. Equally remarkable about Mann's films in relation to early fifties television westerns are their flawed heroes, whose moral codes are not in accord with their society's/civilization's/church's doctrines on law and justice. Stewart's sadistic, vengeance-bent heroes are akin (and sometimes kin) to the villains they chase; as Mann stated: "I always tried to build my films on opposition of characters. By putting the accent on the common points of the two characters—the good guy and the bad—then making them collide, the story acquires much more strength and . . . intensity." While Stewart's tarnished heroes would not have been acceptable role models for children back then, grateful adults found them more fascinating than the pure-blooded, simple TV westerners. Mann's pictures did extremely good business and helped elevate James Stewart to the box office Top Ten. (However, Anthony Mann gained little fame as a result.)

Between 1955 and 1958, the so-called adult western came to television with such series as *Gunsmoke, Cheyenne, Maverick,* and the very brutal *The Rifleman,* for which Sam Peckinpah directed several episodes. Although Mann's heroes were still too morally corrupt and obsessive (to the point of near insanity) to be television

Link (L) takes cover when Claude and Ponch arrive in Lassoo to kill him. He will kill them instead. Typical of Anthony Mann westerns, the landscape dominates the frame.

series leads, television westerns had, for the average fan not aware of such things as directoral skills and production values, caught up with theatrical westerns. ("Adult" westerns would dominate the television ratings into the early sixties.) In fact, Mann's tepid *The Tin Star* (1957), starring Henry Fonda, would serve as the basis for the Henry Fonda TV series *The Deputy.* But in 1958 Mann made *Man of the West,* a western so "adult" that it could never be adapted to the TV medium. One of the cinema's harshest portraits of the West, it contains psychotic killers who are the total opposites of the romanticized badmen of countless westerns, a morally ambiguous hero who yields to his long-held-in-check violent nature in order to do in his brutal kin, and a very liberal dose of sex, an ingredient never found in television westerns.

Man of the West is a beautifully filmed, bloody, unsparing western, replete with interesting, complex characters and exciting situations. If it has a major flaw it comes at the beginning. Perhaps it is Mann's view that civilization emasculates men that causes Gary Cooper to play the scenes in Crosscut and on the train to Fort Worth as if he were Longfellow Deeds once again.

Having him come across as being so gullible and innocent that Sam and Billie would attempt to wheedle him out of the money he has to pay for a schoolteacher is completely deceptive on Mann's part. If this naive-chump bit were an act by Link to cover up his identity, it would make sense, but it's for real, and when we discover that Link used to be a hardened criminal, these early scenes come across as ridiculous. Mann might have been trying to get us to believe Link a weakling so we would be pleasantly surprised later in the film when we see him do heroic deeds—just like we are when James Stewart turns out to be a brave sharpshooter in *Destry Rides Again* (1939). But the change here is too drastic; and anyway, Sam is the film's coward-who-turns-hero. Rather than have Cooper do a bumbling act similar to Stewart's at the beginning of George Marshall's *Destry,* I would prefer him to emulate the Stewart of Mann's *Winchester 73,* whose gun is blazing from the moment he hits the screen.

Once Link, Billie, and Sam fall into the clutches of Dock Tobin and his gang, the picture shifts from half-comedy to tense melodrama: in fact, Mann likened the cabin scenes to those in *Key Largo* (1948). Link

(L) As Coaley prevents Link from interfering, Billie begins the famous strip that gave Man of the West instant notoriety in 1958. (TR) Billie's strip in front of Dock's men is cut short when Dock chastizes them for messing up the train robbery. (MR) Link pays Coaley back for humiliating Billie, stripping him in front of (L-R) Sam, Trout, Billie, and (not seen) Dock, Claude, and Ponch. (BR) Fighting back his tears, Coaley tries to shoot Link. But Sam steps in the way and is killed. Meanwhile, Dock guns down Coaley, while Claude (L) and Ponch can only look on.

stops being a hick and starts acting serious and clever. "You've changed," Sam observes. "You act like you belong with these people." For Dock also to believe Link could fit in with his gang means that he must have seen Link engage in many heinous crimes in the past, before Link deserted him and went off to get married and raise two kids. Having been raised by Dock, his uncle, to rob and kill, Link is indeed capable of being as brutal as Dock and his cousins Claude, Coaley, Ponch, and Trout. And this disturbs him greatly. He pulls away before he strangles Coaley to death, not because he wants Coaley to live, but because he doesn't want to be as coldblooded as Coaley. But there is a great difference between Link and his depraved relatives, and it comes across in the way they treat Billie. Except for the intelligent Claude, the members of Tobin's gang are characterized by *machismo*, a pride in masculinity that has them bullying other men to prove their own worth and treating women with contempt and as playthings. (Tobin himself regards both men and women as property; he speaks of "*my* outfit," and of Link being "mine" in the old days; Link believes Dock will leave Billie alone if he tells him "She's mine.") Most western heroes distrust women, but Link, who grew up with males and likely equates women with the civilized world he loves being part of, respects at least two: his wife and Billie. It makes no difference to him that in Billie's shady past she has probably taken off her clothes for many men and gone much farther than that; when Coaley forces Billie to disrobe, Link realizes her humiliation. After beating up Coaley Link makes him cry by stripping off his

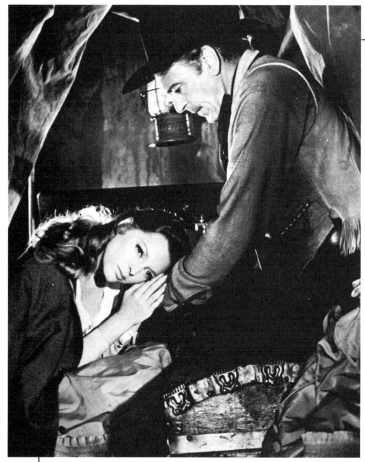

Billie admits her feelings for Link— he is tempted, but...

clothes in front of Billie, reminding him of how he insulted Billie: "How does it feel??!!" Billie is no virgin, but Link feels that her rape by Dock must be avenged just the same because it was, as Dock meant it to be, an act of unparalleled degradation. Interestingly, the two men see the rape differently: Dock raped Billie because he thought it *humiliating to Link*, to whom Dock thinks she belongs; but Link knows better than to take it as an affront to his masculinity—he knows that Billie is the one who suffered the outrage.

Billie is one of the few women in the history of movie westerns (a conservative genre) who is raped and doesn't die off before the end of the picture. In the cinema's twisted moral code, a raped woman is unworthy of the hero. He can only marry a virgin or a widow. In *Hondo* (1953), when John Wayne proposes to a widow with a child, living proof she had intercourse with her husband, it was somewhat groundbreaking.* A sinner himself, Link doesn't judge Billie's past harshly. And after she is raped, he doesn't think any less of her—which seems perfectly reasonable except that during the fifties movie heroes were rarely understanding where rape was concerned. But the question remains: was Link given a wife in the story just so no decision would have to be made about him marrying a victim of rape?

---

*In Budd Boetticher's *The Tall T* (1957), to which *Man of the West* bears great similarity in plot and tone, Randolph Scott ends up with Maureen O'Sullivan, a widow whose husband was killed on their wedding day—*before* the marriage was consummated.

Man of the West gained instant notoriety in 1958 because of the scene in which Billie strips for the Tobin gang. As I pointed out, the strip scene does have thematic function and is not just of prurient interest. (Happily, the rape takes place entirely off screen, and because a sympathetic female has been ravished by a lunatic it doesn't make viewers fantasize arousing images.) A scene with far greater sexual intensity than the striptease is the one in which Link crouches over Billie, lying in the barn in her undergarments, and oddly enough tells her about his wife—if you turned off the dialogue, you'd swear that the film was about to become X-rated. Another "sexy" scene takes place in the wagon when Billie puts her hand and then her face on Link's hands and tells him how much she loves him and loves touching him. "I've found what I want," she says, "and I can't keep it, can I?" "You don't have to ask me that, do you?" he says as the sexual tension builds. He almost puts his hand on her head to soothe her but stops himself, knowing that he will be unable to hold back his passions. And in the final scene, as they ride off toward town, where they will have to part, Billie again tells Link she loves him. They look each other in the eyes as they ride close. Will they kiss? Or will Link remain faithful—for no reason other than the movie convention that he should go back to his family rather than remain with a raped woman? Mann quickly cuts to a long shot, and the question is not answered. But I hope Link and the worthy Billie took the money meant for the schoolteacher and bought a ranch in Laramie.

Link must take part in two gun battles at the end of *Man of the West*. The first takes place in Lassoo, a ghost town which symbolizes the life Link left behind. Here, Link reveals the dreadful talents Dock taught him. After disposing of Trout and Ponch, he kills Claude after a brutal fight. Having respect for his cousin who didn't desert Dock as he did, and who he sees as being the person he might have been if he hadn't reformed, Link pounds the ground in disgust. As is true of many of Mann's heroes, when Link kills his counterpart, he destroys a part of himself. In Mann films, killing someone is difficult and not to be taken lightly.

After finding Billie has been raped, Link goes off to find Dock. Most filmmakers stage their final showdowns between hero and villain in the middle of town at high noon so the entire population can watch the hero, suddenly a standard-bearer for civilization, win a fair fight. But Mann typically sets his final gun battles far away from civilization, off in the wilderness, away from all eyes, where both men can fight as unfairly as possible to win—life and death battles need not be fairly fought. In the mountains, Dock, ranting like King Lear, meets his death and rolls unceremoniously down an incline. It isn't the type of kingly death Dock would have thought he deserved, but it is the one he is worthy of. When Claude died, Link folded his arms over his chest so that his corpse could look dignified. When Dock dies, Link takes the money Dock stole from him, and leaves him sprawled out on the ground. . . . In his treatment of the two bodies, Link has made the ultimate comment on his own life.

Night of the Living Dead

1968 Walter Reade Organization release, through Continental
Distributing, of an Image 10 production
Director: George A. Romero
Producers: Russell Streinger and Karl Hardman
Screenplay: John A. Russo
Cinematography: George A. Romero
Music: No credit
Editor: George A. Romero
Running Time: 90 minutes

Cast: Judith O'Dea (Barbara), Russell Streinger (Johnny), Duane
Jones (Ben), Karl Hardman (Harry Cooper), Keith Wayne (Tom),
Judith Ridley (Judy), Marilyn Eastman (Helen Cooper), Kyra
Schon (Karen)

Synopsis: Barbara and her brother Johnny drive to an abandoned
cemetery in western Pennsylvania to visit their father's grave.
Suddenly, a zombielike man attacks Barbara. Johnny defends her
and is killed when his head strikes a tombstone. Barbara flees to an
abandoned farmhouse. Exploring the house, she discovers a half-
eaten body at the top of the staircase. She panics and is about to run
out of the house when a stranger named Ben comes in, having been
chased inside by several zombielike creatures. Barbara helps Ben
barricade the windows and doors. Meanwhile the house is surrounded. Barbara slowly withdraws into a catatonic state, having
endured more than she can stand.

It turns out that Ben and Barbara are not alone in the house. Judy
and Tom, a young couple, and Helen and Harry Cooper have been
hiding in the basement with the Coopers' daughter Karen, who is
very ill after having been bitten by a ghoul. Ben and Harry don't get
along at all because Harry is domineering, insisting that Ben and
Barbara come down to the basement when Ben thinks it wiser to stay
above. When Helen finds out that there is a television upstairs, she
yells at her husband for being so stubborn and goes to join the
others.

Everyone watches television. Reports say that due to the release
of a freak molecular mutation brought back by a Venus space probe,
the dead have been rising, killing people and eating them. Reports
also state that recently killed people will turn into ghouls as well. The
police are scouring the country shooting zombies in the head. TV
commentators tell people to try to make their way to local national
defense stations.

Ben and Tom go outside, hoping to drive a truck to some gas
tanks a few hundred yards away, so everyone can then escape. Judy
follows them outside. They use torches to keep the zombies away,
but the zombies follow them. Gasoline accidentally pours from the
tank and catches fire. The truck blows up with Tom and Judy inside.
Ben makes his way back into the house. When the terrified Harry
won't let him in, he beats Harry up. Outside, the zombies eat Judy
and Tom. Harry tries to get Ben's rifle away from him so he can be
the one to give orders. Ben shoots him, and he stumbles into the
basement to die. Helen goes downstairs and finds Karen, who has
died and become a zombie, eating Harry. Karen kills Helen and
begins to eat her, too.

Upstairs, the zombies' attack continues. Barbara is pulled
outside by Johnny, now a zombie. Karen attacks Ben, but he
sidesteps her. He locks himself in the basement and puts bullets in
the heads of Helen and Harry so they won't become zombies. The
ghouls cannot get into the basement.

In the morning, the police have things under control. They shoot
anything that moves. They kill all the zombies around the farmhouse. When they see Ben come upstairs and stand near a window,
they think him a zombie and shoot him in the head. Ben and all the
dead zombies are thrown into a great fire.

Seeing *Night of the Living Dead* today, one can
hardly believe that it scared the living daylights
out of moviegoers some dozen years ago. Not
that it isn't still lots of fun (it is) or doesn't have
moments that are still quite spooky (it does),
but it is tame compared to all those gruesome low-
budget horror films it has spawned, including its more
brutal but less satisfying sequel *Dawn of the Dead*
(1978). Today one is more likely to laugh at the picture's
considerable wit than hide under a chair.

One of the most successful independently made
films ever, *Night of the Living Dead* was produced by a
small Pittsburgh production company which had specialized in making industrial films, political spots, and
commercials and had never been involved in entertainment films. Likewise, George Romero (now a major
"cult director") had never made a feature before, his
only experience in that area having come when he was a
nineteen-year-old grip on Hitchcock's *North by Northwest* (1959). Romero had written the original story—"an
allegory," he told *Filmmakers Newsletter*, "meant to
draw a parallel between what people are becoming and
the idea that people are operating on many levels of
insanity that are only clear to themselves"—and he and
nine other frustrated filmmakers invested six hundred
dollars apiece to convert it into a film. Romero cast the
picture with unknowns and amateurs (with townspeople
playing the ghouls), and production began—although
Romero and John Russo were still working on the
script. Production was forced to stop cold on several
occasions while Romero found additional financing; in
time he came up with another hundred thousand dollars
by showing potential investors completed footage and
selling them stock in the picture. And after thirty
shooting days, staggered over a seven-month period, the
film was completed.

Columbia turned the picture down because it wasn't
in color, and AIP rejected it because it has no romance
and has a downbeat ending; but the Walter Reade

*Hysterical Barbara, Ben (with the gun), and Tom attempt to keep
cool inside the house while ghouls walk about outside.*

(L) Ghouls attempt to break into the house where Barbara, Ben, Tom, Judy, and the Coopers have barricaded themselves. (TR) Some of the ghouls that are visible from the house. (MR) The burial tag on the ghoul on the left seems to indicate that the supply of potential ghouls is endless. (BR) Ghouls that have been killed for the second time.

Organization agreed to distribute it, and soon it was playing on the bottom of the bill in drive-ins and neighborhood theaters showing triple features. If ever a picture became a hit because of favorable word-of-mouth, this is it. Horror aficionados stumbled upon it in run-down theaters on New York's Forty-second Street or in drive-ins in the sticks, and soon spread the word that they had "discovered a masterpiece of the genre." Critics started tracking down prints, and their reaction was equally enthusiastic. *Living Dead* had risen out of its coffin and was suddenly in demand all over the country. Lines formed around the block, and the picture quickly made back its cost thirty times over. Art houses booked it, and film societies, and then the Museum of Modern Art. When people had seen it several times, *Night of the Living Dead* moved to the midnight movie circuit (way back in 1969!), where it attracted a new audience as well as repeaters. Still today, it remains one of the most popular midnight movies.

Just as many films have been influenced by *Living Dead*, it likewise is a derivative film. Romero himself cites those lurid, pre-comic-code EC comics (especially *Tales From the Crypt*) as inspiration, as well as Richard Matheson's *I Am Legend*, the exciting novel about the sole human survivor in a world of mutants that has been the basis of several dull pictures. Among the films with which *Living Dead* has most in common are: *The Invisible Invaders* (1953), in which a group of scientists are trapped in a house that is under siege from ghouls that like those in the Romero work seem to be sleepwalking; *Carnival of Souls* (1960), an excellent, eerie independent feature (made in Lawrence, Kansas) about a blonde who refuses to acknowledge that she is already dead and is terrified by the ghouls around her; and

Hitchcock's *The Birds* (1963), in which a group of people barricade themselves in a house to protect themselves from creatures (birds) that are *inexplicably* killing human beings. Hitchcock's influence on Romero is quite evident: the silent passages, the collision montage (rapid-fire, rhythmic editing of powerful images), the series of (character) reaction shots, filmed from below at sharp angles—just as Hitchcock framed his characters in *The Birds* when they were fearfully listening to the birds hammer away at the house. When Barbara climbs the stairs and discovers the face of a half-eaten cadaver, we must think of *Psycho;* as we do when Karen stabs Helen many times with a trowel and the camera aims high to the peak point where Karen lifts the weapon—much like how the camera concentrates on the knife that kills Martin Balsam in the Hitchcock film.

Pessimistic and unsentimental, *Living Dead* is so effective because it is totally without pretension. It works on basic fears: unrelenting terror, monsters, darkness, claustrophobia. "Aliens" attack us on American soil; protectors, even *blood* relations, turn on one another (it was wise on Romero's part to have Johnny be Barbara's brother instead of her boyfriend because when he "eats" her it becomes strictly an image of horror—and not sexual in any way).

The black-and-white photography, necessitated by the low budget, contributes to the nightmarish look of the film. It starts out as Barbara's nightmare but it swiftly becomes ours too—especially if we identify with Barbara—and we wish someone was capable of answering her oft-asked question, "What's happening?"

In other films in which people are holed up in a house while threatening monsters lurk outside, the people are there for shelter, to protect their house, to

plan strategy to battle the monster(s), or to give themselves logistical advantage (the house becomes a fort) in the fight. *The Birds* and *Living Dead* are exceptional in that the people congregate in the house for one reason only: fear. These people don't know what to do or where to go. They only know that they want to get out of the area as quickly as possible—they are not interested in fighting with ghouls, just saving themselves. The realization that they are incapable of battling these monsters—their undisguised terror—is one of the major reasons, I believe, *Living Dead* succeeds in scaring audiences. What also scares them is that they don't feel that anyone—including Ben (the hero) and Barbara (the heroine)—will survive, especially since the performers are all unknowns and thus are, in movie terms, expendable.

Along the way there are several scary moments. I particularly like the opening sequence. Johnny starts to frighten Barbara, using a Boris Karloff voice, jokingly telling her that the strange-looking man stumbling toward them is "coming to get you." When the man (being a ghoul) does in fact grab her despite Johnny's presence and without being the least bit sneaky about it, we are startled. When Barbara flees the ghoul, who has killed Johnny, she finds "safety" in a car. We remember all those horror films in which the guy tells the girl to stay locked inside the car where she'll be safe while he goes off to find out what is making the noises in the bushes. But, as we suspected and Romero knew, "the girl" isn't safe at all—and the ghoul starts to pound away at the car, rocking it back and forth and smashing the window with a large stone. Barbara sits inside, helpless and in definite jeopardy. I don't find anything that happens later as scary as this opening sequence, but it has the lasting effect of letting viewers know that nothing in this film is predictable—even to those who know the horror genre inside out.

Throughout the film there are nice horror touches. I like it when Barbara looks at the face of a dead ghoul lying on the floor and the camera studies (in close-up) its bloody head, which suddenly moves. . . . We jump. . . . Luckily, it turns out that the ghoul is not moving by itself but only because Ben is pulling it out of the house. Also I like it when the catatonic Barbara—one of the few movie heroines who is not required by cinematic convention to get over the loss of a loved one in five minutes of screen time—sits alone in the living room, the camera alternately making a slow zoom toward her face and toward the radio, on which a newscaster (who wrote his own copy, incidentally) speaks of ghouls on murder sprees across the country. This isn't meant to build toward a shock moment, and nothing happens, but this scene adds greatly to the film's tension. The one true "jump-out-of-your-seats" moment comes when Ben walks close to a wall and hands suddenly come through the windows and grab him— much like the asylum patients shooting their hands through the bars in *Bedlam* (1946).

"The zombies are us," says Romero. "We create them so we can kill them off, justifying ourselves—it's a kind of penance, self-exorcism." Unfortunately,

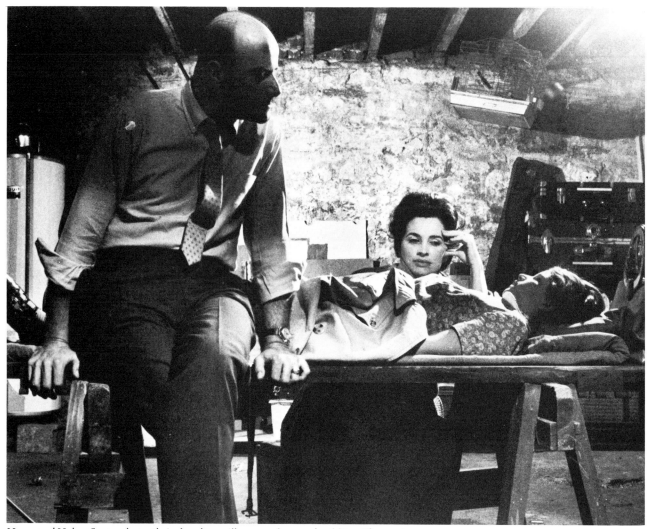

Harry and Helen Cooper hope their daughter will recover from a ghoul bite. She won't.

Romero's zombies aren't very frightening. In fact, they're kind of silly, wearing dumpy clothes and walking around as if they'd just downed a fifth of bourbon. (You wouldn't even have wanted to associate with these people when they were alive.) As for the scenes in which they eat the innards (donated by an investor who was a butcher) of their victims, I think Romero mistakenly lets us see the feast up close. It is much ghastlier when we just hear slurping noises.

Of course, the ghouls are, in a way, meant to contribute to the picture's absurd humor. Why else have one ghoul eat a worm off a tree, or a nude ghoul walk by with a morgue ticket still on her, or so many participate in what seems to be an Indian war dance around the truck? They definitely contribute to the film's intentional campiness. So do the amateurish performances of the lead actors and the overly dramatic internecine squabbling of their characters.

Most interesting is the ongoing rivalry between Ben and Harry. This is played mostly for laughs ("Shut up," Ben tells Harry to end every conversation), but it also serves to complement the ghouls' attack from outside with some in-the-house hostilities. Much praise has

been given the film because the lead, Duane Jones, is black and no mention is made of this in the script. If Romero was, in fact, thinking in terms of color when he cast Jones, he would have certainly made the scowling, clench-fisted, loudmouthed Harry a *bigot* who would spit racial slurs at Ben—this would have been perfectly believable considering what we already know about Harry.

Harry is a cowardly bully who cares only about himself, and Ben is brave and concerned about the welfare of the others in his house; so whatever our race, we side with Ben. Yet, if we were in the house with these two men, maybe we should think again. It took me many years to realize this, but Ben, our hero, turns out to be terribly *wrong* when he adamantly tells everyone that they have a better chance for survival if they remain *upstairs* with him instead of following Harry's advice and locking themselves in the basement. Everyone dies as a result of following Ben's lead and coming upstairs—and ironically, Ben alone survives the night and keeps away from the ghouls by locking himself in the basement. Has anyone else noticed this?

The Nutty Professor

1963 Paramount
Director: Jerry Lewis
Producers: Jerry Lewis and
Ernest D. Glucksman
Screenplay: Jerry Lewis and Bill
Richmond

Cinematography: Wallace Kelley
Music: Walter Scharf
Editor: John Woodcock
Special Effects: Paul K. Lerpae
Running Time: 107 min.

Cast: Jerry Lewis (Julius F. Kelp/Buddy Love), Stella Stevens (Stella Purdy), Del Moore (Doctor Warfield), Kathleen Freeman (Millie Lemmon), Howard Morris (Elmer Kelp), Elvia Allman (Edwina Kelp), Buddy Lester, Julie Parrish, Milton Frome, Norman Alden, Henry Gibson, Les Brown and his Band of Renown, Bill Richmond

Synopsis: Intelligent but clumsy, weak, buck-toothed, and myopic, Julius Kelp teaches chemistry at Mathews College. He continually gets in trouble with the dean, Doctor Warfield, because his science experiments inevitably end up with buildings collapsing and students winding up in the hospital.

Julius is greatly attracted to one of his students, Stella Purdy, a beautiful, sexy blonde who hangs out with the football players at the Purple Pit nightclub. Julius is too shy and self-conscious to let Stella know his feelings toward her. He decides to win her affections by taking a muscle-building course at Vic Tanny's. When that doesn't work, he elects to resort to science to change himself, to approach his problem "from the chemistry standpoint."

One night in his lab, Julius drinks a vial containing a mixture of potent chemicals. His body undergoes a tremendous physical transformation: he becomes a dashing, irresistible fellow, completely the opposite of Julius. Buddy Love, as he calls himself, is the most conceited person in the universe.

Buddy goes to the Purple Pit, where he becomes the idol of the college students when he sings and plays the piano for them. He also sweeps Stella off her feet. While she cannot stand his narcissistic attitude, she finds herself uncontrollably attracted to him.

Buddy's love life seems to be going well, but—always at the wrong time—the formula wears off and he reverts to being Julius, and he has to run off so Stella won't discover his secret. But on the night of the prom, when Buddy is supposed to perform, he changes back to Julius right in front of the entire student body's eyes. There is nothing for Julius to do but apologize to all the students he deceived, to tell them that he didn't want to hurt anybody, and that he learned a valuable lesson: "You may as well like yourself; if you don't think too much of yourself, how do you expect others to?"

Just when he thinks his whole life is ruined, Stella comes to Julius and assures him that it is he—the good inner side of Buddy—whom she loves. They will be married.

Mention the name Jerry Lewis in critics' circles and an argument is only minutes away. It is well known that Lewis has been hailed in Europe as the equal of the great silent comedians (in France, in the mid-sixties even the feuding *Positif* and *Cahiers du Cinema* joined hands to sing his praise) but that home in America, critics resentful of his great popular success have made a personal crusade of "putting Lewis in his place"—far down on their sacred ladder of cinema clowns/comedians. Lewis, hurt by the poor treatment given him by the very people he thinks should be championing his films, hasn't tried to cloak his bitterness. In Larry Wild's *The Great Comedians Talk About Comedy*, Lewis leveled a typical blast at his detractors: "We don't have American critics. We have American denouncers. They like to denounce things, 'cause if they didn't they'd be part of the masses that like it."

Actually, Lewis has never been entirely without defenders among American movie critics. There have always been a few brave souls willing to stick their necks out, to voice support for the only screen comedian who hasn't ever been afraid to make a fool of himself, who has time and again fallen flat on his face in his comedic experiments, pulling his supporters with him into the pits of embarrassment. Back in 1964, for instance, Stuart Byron wrote a glowing tribute to Lewis's comedy: "Lewis has really made his view of life into a true comic vision that can be discussed on par with Chaplin's, Keaton's, and Laurel and Hardy's." And a year earlier, Howard Thompson, writing for *The New York Times*, no less, was laudatory in his review of *The Nutty Professor:* "Credit the effervescent Mr. Lewis for trying something different—a comical study, with an edge of

*Stella helps Julius
remove his sleeve
from the punch bowl.*

Jerry's a mousey chemistry prof who invents the greatest new drink since Dracula discovered bloody marys.

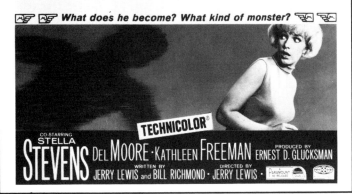

PARAMOUNT PICTURES presents **JERRY LEWIS** as "**THE NUTTY PROFESSOR**" (A Jerry Lewis Production)

What does he become? What kind of monster?

TECHNICOLOR®

CO-STARRING **STELLA STEVENS** · DEL MOORE · KATHLEEN FREEMAN · PRODUCED BY ERNEST D. GLUCKSMAN

WRITTEN BY JERRY LEWIS and BILL RICHMOND · DIRECTED BY JERRY LEWIS · PARAMOUNT

The Jekyll-and-Hyde poster for what most Lewis fans consider his best film; a film Stella Stevens fanatics consider one of her few good showcases.

pathos. The surprising, rather disturbing result is less a showcase for a clown than the revelation of a superb actor. . . . Attaboy, Jerry." Over the years, the films of Jerry Lewis have divided critics into two warring factions: the anti-Lewis forces who contend that anyone who takes Lewis's comedy seriously knows nothing about comedy, and the Lewis cultists.

I am a Jerry Lewis fan. Sure, I too cringe while watching his sanctimonious behavior on his annual muscular-dystrophy telethon; and I dislike *all* his non-self-directed pictures made after Frank Tashlin's *The Disorderly Orderly* (1964), agree with those who say that Lewis has never directed a masterpiece, and would be the first to suggest that Lewis work with a codirector who would tell him "enough is enough!" when his humor becomes tasteless (or unfunny) and when his moments of pathos become long scenes of self-pity and martyrdom. Yet, at the same time, I go along with Lewis cultists who are in awe of his talent (which unfortunately goes astray too often) and energy; who claim that the Martin and Lewis films come off quite well in retrospect, and that the skinny, frantic Lewis, under control, was truly hilarious back in his primitive Elvis-Presley-at-Sun Records-like period; and who insist that even the lesser of the Lewis-directed films are

wildly inventive from both an actor's and a director's standpoint. (Witness the magnificent transformation scene in *The Nutty Professor* and the subsequent P.O.V. sequence when the "new" Julius Kelp—Buddy Love— walks toward the Purple Pit. This is all done to honor, or perhaps parody, the Fredric March version of *Dr. Jekyll and Mr. Hyde* (1932), but Lewis is easily the equal of both actor March during the transformation and director Rouben Mamoulian, once considered the most inventive filmmaker in Hollywood.)

Jerry Lewis's mass appeal, like that of Lou Costello, is with children, and you'll find that most Lewis cultists were youngsters during his prime and have remained loyal. Lewis played a character who was an adult as far as age was concerned but in all other ways was the "kid." He was a nice guy, a nobody, whose mental capacities were that of a preteener, and who was too simple and innocent to understand the hard, complicated world around him. He was funny-looking, weak (he made sure that he was *always* the weakest character, male or female, in his films), unappreciated (especially by Dean Martin), pushed around, lonely (pretty women ignored him though animals adored him), and so awkward that one would think he'd sprouted up about ten inches while in summer camp. Lewis was someone any child in the audience could identify with or be happy to call friend. So children swarmed to his films.

If *The Nutty Professor* is Lewis's best film, and I believe it is, it is not so much because it is his funniest as because it is his most daring. It is daring in the sense that Lewis, who begs for love in all his other films, knew he was making a picture to which his greatest fans, children, would probably react negatively. In a 1965 interview with Axel Madsen, Lewis remembered:

> It was a real Jekyll-Hyde situation at home as well as on the set. When I played the scientist everything was O.K. but when I played the other character things would get chillier at home. And to this day, my children have not seen the film. It's the only film my wife won't permit them to see. And I said to her, "Don't you want them to see my transformation, my best performance?" And she said, "No. . . . I don't want them to see Buddy Love." And this kind of shook me up and I said, "You're telling me I did a very good job." And she said, "You did a marvelous job playing the worst human being I've ever seen in my life."

It has often been written that Buddy Love, Kelp's alter ego, represents Lewis's ex-partner Dean Martin, cocky, romantic, singing, boozing. It certainly is similar to the character Martin played in the Martin and Lewis films, only taken to the nth degree. But what struck me the last time I saw the film, for the first time in several years, is how similar Buddy Love is to the *Jerry Lewis* we see each year on the telethon: that angry older fellow who tries, unsuccessfully at times, to keep the "kid" character bottled up inside him (the "kid" breaks out in emergencies to get Lewis off the hook when the proceedings become too gloomy); that conceited fellow with the slicked-back hair who is either (you can't tell which) good-naturedly teasing his guests or insulting

Freudian flashback shows young Julius in his crib watching his mother dominate his docile father.

them, singing songs he is sure his captive audience is eager to hear (he considers himself a singer), and, as in the film, giving the bandleader a hard time. It's scary, but it now appears that Buddy Love was actually the alter ego of Jerry Lewis, the part of himself he once tried to suppress.

Many critics have complained that Jerry Lewis has added nothing original to screen comedy. This is a fallacy. Jerry Lewis is the only comic in cinema history (with the possible exception of Jacques Tati) who has devised routines in which pantomime or a series of quick sight gags is used in conjunction with the *music* and *noises* he has placed on the *sound*track. For instance, there is his classic no-dialogue sequence in *The Errand Boy* (1962) where Lewis lip-synchs to a blaring musical composition while pretending to be a bossy executive barking out orders to his (invisible) staff. The musical notes replace the words Lewis would speak. In *The Nutty Professor*, Lewis carries his peculiar art further; there are several instances when he uses the soundtrack to make his "silent" humor work. In one great bit, Kelp sneaks down a dark hallway. When he notices the loud squeaking noises he is making, he removes his shoes before continuing his walking—only to discover that his feet, and not the shoes, are what is squeaking. In

another sequence, Kelp comes to class with the worst hangover of all times. Every sound he hears—pencils clicking, chalk squeaking, gum being chewed—is magnified a thousand times, as if cannonballs were going off in his head, and the humor is in watching his face contort in reaction to the booming soundtrack.

And there is a brilliant bit where *Lewis* speaks dialogue but it isn't the words that have importance, but the *sound* of the voice. It's late at night and everyone has left the Purple Pit except for Buddy Love and Stella. For several moments (one camera position, one take), Buddy plays the piano, and Stella patiently watches. The setting is romantic, the smoke in the air making the atmosphere intense. At last, Buddy says, "I'm tired." Now this could be interpreted as an invitation to Stella to hop into the nearest bed—except that Buddy's words came out in Kelp's funny nasal voice, and the incongruous *sound* of that silly voice coming from handsome Buddy completely shatters the seductive mood.

There are other memorable moments: the camera pulls back from the love-struck Kelp, in white tuxedo, talking to Stella, and we find his arm deep in the punch bowl; Kelp drops his musical pocket watch into Dean Warfield's fishtank and we hear a garbled "Stars and Stripes Forever"; Kelp reports that his six-month Vic

Tanny course resulted in his losing two pounds; and at the prom Kelp does one of Jerry Lewis's patented "spastic" dances, arms and legs flailing about.

Perhaps the funniest sight gag is in the Vic Tanny sequence. The Scrawny Kelp is handed an incredibly heavy dumbbell. But it doesn't knock him over. Instead it falls to the floor. Trouble is he forgets to let go, and though he continues to stand straight up, his arms stretch like taffy until his hands are at feet level. (That night, we see him scratch the bottoms of his feet without bending his back or his legs.) This gag, in which Kelp's body functions like an elastic band, is reminiscent of gags found in cartoons where all characters are contortionists. It was obviously influenced by Lewis's mentor, Frank Tashlin, who directed *Looney Tunes* before switching to live-action features. We also must look to Tashlin for the scene in which Kelp imagines the gorgeous Stella in several tantalizing outfits. Tashlin did the same thing with Tom Ewell and Julie London in *The Girl Can't Help It* (1956). And finally, it's to honor Tashlin that Lewis, at one point, interjects the title card, "That's *Not* All, Folks!"—a twist on the *Looney Tunes* signoff.

Lewis claims that he wrote the story for *The Nutty Professor* ten years before he felt he was ready to attempt it. It is his most difficult undertaking—and his most experimental—from technique to plot to character. That he was able to pull off his entry into the world of black comedy is a compliment to his maturity (at the time) as both a filmmaker and an actor. *The Nutty Professor* did cause many of the masses who adored Lewis to reject him until he returned to making films about the "kid," but, as Lewis suspected, it caused many impressed critics to join his cult.

Lewis does his patented "spastic" act: Julius dances for an unimpressed Doctor Warfield and Miss Lemmon.

Once upon a Time in the West

1969 Italy Paramount release of a Rafran–San Marco production
Director: Sergio Leone
Producer: Sergio Leone
Screenplay: Sergio Leone and Sergio Donati
From a story by Dario Argento, Bernardo Bertolucci, and Sergio Leone
Cinematography: Tonino Delli Colli
Music: Ennio Morricone
Editor: Nin Baragli
Running Time: 140 minutes in most U.S. 35-mm release prints; 165 minutes in 16 mm. (The shortened version does not contain the first meeting between Jill, The Man, and Cheyenne, or Cheyenne's death.)

Cast: Claudia Cardinale (Jill McBain), Henry Fonda (Frank), Jason Robards (Cheyenne), Charles Bronson (The Man), Frank Wolff (Brett McBain) Gabriele Ferzetti (Morton), Keenan Wynn (sheriff), Paolo Stoppa (Sam), Lionel Stander (bartender in 16-mm version), Woody Strode, Jack Elam

Synopsis: The Man arrives by train at a station outside Flagstone. He has an appointment with gunslinger Frank, but Frank has sent three men to kill him. The Man shoots all three.

Meanwhile, Frank and more of his men are in the desert at Sweetwater—the name Brett McBain has given his land. Brett awaits the arrival of his bride from New Orleans, but before he can send his son to meet her, he and his children are massacred by Frank and his men, who leave evidence to implicate the outlaw Cheyenne.

Jill, a former prostitute in New Orleans, arrives in town and learns of the tragedy. She tells the townspeople that she and McBain had been married a month before, and moves into McBain's house. Among her belongings she finds miniatures of various buildings. She doesn't know what they signify. Cheyenne arrives. He tells her he didn't kill her husband and doesn't know why he was killed. Cheyenne rides away but keeps an eye on her house from a distance.

The Man arrives at Jill's house. Two of Frank's men gallop toward him and Jill, and he guns them down before they can fire. With Jill's help, The Man traces Frank to the private three-car train of his boss, Morton, a crippled railroad baron. Frank captures The Man, who is a stranger to him. He tries to find out why The Man wants to kill him, but The Man won't tell him. Frank goes off to try to secure Jill's land for Morton, leaving his men to guard The Man. Cheyenne kills the guards and rescues The Man.

Frank seduces Jill and decides not to kill her. To save herself, she agrees to sell her land at public auction. Frank's men scare others from bidding. They offer a paltry five hundred dollars. At the last minute, The Man offers five thousand dollars (the bounty for turning in Cheyenne to the law) and he gets the land. He knows that Morton wants the land because it has water. McBain had wanted to build a town there, because he knew the railroad would have to pass it. The Man gives the land back to Jill.

Morton buys off several of Frank's men and tries to have Frank killed because he had been trying to take over his business. The Man helps Frank kill his assassins; he wants to kill Frank himself. Frank returns to Morton's train. He finds his men and Cheyenne's men, who attacked the train after Cheyenne's escape from the law, all dead. Frank watches Morton die.

Cheyenne arrives at Jill's house. Outside, The Man and Frank have a gun battle. The Man wins and tells Frank at the point of death that many years earlier Frank killed his brother.

Cheyenne and The Man leave the disappointed Jill behind. She will stay, watch her town grow, and treat the railroad workers well. When the two men ride over a hill, Cheyenne dies of wounds suffered while attacking Morton's train. The Man rides off leading Cheyenne's horse, which has Cheyenne draped over its back.

That Leone utilizes every section of his wide frame is evident in this beautifully composed deep-focus shot. Frank tells The Man that he will agree to their fated gun battle if The Man will reveal the reason he wants to kill him.

Sergio Leone, probably the contemporary cinema's greatest stylist, didn't invent the Italian-made Western, but there are none better than the five he directed, produced, and co-wrote: *A Fistful of Dollars* (1966); with Clint Eastwood and Gian Marie Volonte; *For a Few Dollars More* (1967), with Eastwood, Volonte, and Lee Van Cleef; *The Good, the Bad, and the Ugly* (1968), with Eastwood, Van Cleef, and Eli Wallach; *Once upon a Time in the West;* and *Duck, You Sucker!* (1972), with Rod Steiger and James Coburn. A cut above *The Good, the Bad, and the Ugly, Once upon a Time in the West* is Leone's masterpiece and certainly one of the all-time great westerns. It is beautifully shot, incredibly ambitious, compelling, erotic, humorous, perfectly cast, and wonderfully scored by Leone's regular composer Ennio Morricone, whose haunting melodies, musical motifs, theme songs, simple tunes, and choral numbers are just as important as the sparse dialogue in commenting on the action and moving the plot forward. Although obviously influenced by John Ford's *The Searchers* (1956), Nicholas Ray's *Johnny Guitar* (1954), and countless other Hollywood westerns, as well as Italian epics, it can best be appreciated when looked at in context of the entire Leone oeuvre.

I believe that Leone works from the fairy tale premise that "once upon a time," before there was history, there was a mythical American West much like Homer's mythical Greece but for the cowboy garb, guns, holsters, nooses and lingo. During this violent, timeless period, which might well have extended from biblical times to the 1850s, several warriors were blessed with divine powers to help them in their never-ending combat: to be able to outdraw and outshoot anyone in the world (except each other); to have no fear of death, although not invulnerable; to be able to withstand terrible physical punishment; to sense impending danger and have the cunning to get out of it. These warriors were like Hercules, the protagonist of several popular Italian-made epics: supermen who lived among mortals. However, most of these men were probably killed off by one another or while performing dangerous tasks for their godly benefactors. Leone's three films with Clint Eastwood (the "*Dollars* trilogy") and *Once upon a Time in the West* are about the few survivors of this mythological race during the epoch when civilization and recorded history emerge and eventually replace the mythical age. When Eastwood's "The Man With No Name"—the character that made him an international star—rides his donkey onto the screen like the archangel

Gabriel at the beginning of *A Fistful of Dollars*, we see that these mythical men still exist; when Charles Bronson's "The Man"—the character that made him an international star—rides toward the horizon at the end of *Once Upon a Time*—with other superwarriors Frank and Cheyenne already dead—we witness the death of "an ancient race" (as The Man defines it to Frank) of MAN. Leone considers *Once upon a Time* his one pessimistic film—not only is it his one film where a woman is more than a peripheral character, it is a woman who is the lone survivor come the advent of civilization. As he told Noel Simsolo of *Take One* (May 1973): "You had there the end of the world; the birth of matriarchy [embodied by Jill] and the beginning of a world without balls."

In *A Fistful of Dollars*, civilization doesn't exist; in *For a Few Dollars More*, it serves as background. In *The Good, the Bad, and the Ugly*, the mythological and historical worlds overlap, but "The Man with No Name" is still able to literally send history/the Civil War elsewhere by blowing up a strategic bridge so he can carry on his own greedy activities. But Bronson's "The Man" is forced to move elsewhere when he realizes that post-Civil War civilization—signaled by the laying down of railroad tracks going toward the Pacific Ocean; the building of Sweetwater; and ex-whore Jill becoming a lady, a businesswoman, a maker of coffee, a bearer of water—cannot be denied. He won't even try to fit into the civilized West as Frank did before realizing the futility of it. Mythological warriors are passé. This is clear when Morton repeatedly proves money is more influential than the gun in the New West, and when Leone replaces a shot of a smoking gun with a shot of a smoking train. Like "The Man with No Name," "The Man" rides off into western folklore.

The link between Eastwood's and Bronson's super-warriors is more than their anonymity. It is also their taciturnity, their lack of emotions, their quicker-than-the-eye draws, their disinterest in women, their air of mystery, their macabre sense of humor. But what the two have most in common is that they are likely the most ruthless heroes in movie history. They aren't *heroes* because they do good deeds or help anyone but themselves, but simply because they kill so many wicked people in the cruel manner audiences feel they deserve. They are truly monsters but could be nothing else in their brutal world and survive. It's just lucky that they have so much potential for cruelty.

It could very well be that "The Man with No Name" and "The Man" are the same character, especially since the number of years Charles Bronson is older than Clint Eastwood could be the exact number of years that lapsed between the Civil War in *The Good, the Bad, and the Ugly* and the coming of the railroad in *Once upon a Time*. But there are two important differences. "The Man with No Name" has no past whatsoever— although he tells a woman in his first picture that he knew someone like her once—while a revealing flashback shows "The Man" when he was a boy at the time Frank hanged his older brother. (The mystical setting in the flashback confirms that both "The Man" and Frank come from a prehistoric age.) "The Man" is motivated by *revenge,* his need to kill Frank for having killed his brother; but we never understand why Eastwood's character puts his life on the line repeatedly (a fistful of dollars isn't a good enough reason) if it is not that he might be performing some "holy" mission.

In Leone's eyes, "The Man With No Name" and "The Man" (as well as Van Cleef's Mortimer in *For a Few Dollars More* and Coburn's international revolu-

Jill, The Man, and the bartender turn to see Cheyenne enter the roadside saloon. This is the first time Jill, The Man, and Cheyenne meet one another, yet this scene is missing in the short (35mm) version of the film that was released in America.

A scene of immense erotic power: Lustful Jill can't resist the sexual advances of Frank even though she knows he murdered her husband.

Cheyenne is a frequent visitor to Jill's home. It is he who contributes most of the picture's dialogue.

tionary in *Duck, You Sucker!*) are classified as "good" by default. It's all relative; at least they confine themselves to rubbing out villains while the "bad" guys of the world don't make any such distinction when they pull their triggers. Perhaps it is because they are doing a (pagan?) god's work that their ruthless measures can be tolerated; and it is because they purge the land of evildoers whom their god wants out of the way that, by this god's standards, they are considered "good" angels. It is the fallen angels that are "the bad" in Leone's world: Volonte's Indio in *For a Few Dollars More*, who talks to his vicious gang while standing behind a church pulpit; Van Cleef's monstrous Angeleyes in *The Good, the Bad, and the Ugly*, who profits from the Civil War; and Henry Fonda's despicable Frank in *Once upon a Time*, whose baby-blue eyes belie that like the other two men he is a child killer, which Cheyenne tells Jill is the same as being a priest killer.

There is only a thin line between Leone's "the good" and "the bad." In *Once upon a Time*, the line is so thin that though Frank has a much more trustworthy face than "The Man," Frank is the villain. Frank even has the only heroic theme tune in the film—Cheyenne has a comical, banjo-plucking theme; the tuneless harmonica motif Leone gives "The Man" is fitting for a rat. Frank is even introduced ceremoniously, like a king, with a low angle shot of him emerging from the bushes, the dust swirling, his men moving aside to let him pass, with loud glorious music (mixed with discordant harmonica riffs) on the soundtrack—all this, right after he has massacred most of the McBain family and is about to shoot the youngest son. It is quite consistent that Leone lets Frank be the only one who gets to make love to the beautiful Jill, in an incredibly perverse erotic sequence. (Such favoritism is understandable considering that

Henry Fonda is Leone's favorite actor, his first choice for "The Man with No Name" in *A Fistful of Dollars*.)

In Leone's triadic struggle, there is one other type of superwarrior who falls between Leone's "good" and "bad." Jason Robards's Cheyenne in *Once upon a Time*, Eli Wallach's Tuco in *The Good, the Bad, and the Ugly*, and Rod Steiger's Mexican peasant bandito in *Duck, You Sucker!* fall into "the ugly" category. I don't think the term "ugly" has anything to do with looks (although a fly seems to live on Tuco's cheek) but refers to the fact that they are "flawed" superwarriors. They talk too much, are funny, have emotions, are arrested often, always have posses on their trail, and are blamed for every crime committed in the West. (Still, they are cunning fighters: Tuco kills a villain with a gun he hides in his bath water, Cheyenne kills a villain with a gun he hides in a boot.) I suspect that they are hybrids, the products of marriages between superheroes and mortal women. (In fact, Cheyenne's mother, he says, was a whore.) "The good" and "the bad" are the last of the pureblooded superheroes—the last to receive divine powers directly from a god and not through birth, when powers received are diluted. Both Cheyenne and Tuco have pasts, and experience touches of guilt (unlike Leone's "good" and "bad," they seem to know the difference between right and wrong) that is founded in their (subconscious) attachment to or fear of a god. This lifts them above Leone's evil, god-denying men.

As in every Leone film, in *Once upon a Time* "the good" and "the ugly" form an uneasy alliance (friendship) against "the bad," and take turns helping each other out of jams—though "the good" usually takes advantage of "the ugly" and gets the best of the deal. At the end of the film, however, "the ugly" must step aside (oddly Cheyenne and Frank are never seen together) so that the final confrontation is between "the good" and

The beautiful
Claudia Cardinale,
the first
actress given
star billing
by Leone.

"the bad"—just as it was in ancient times. Neither avoids this gunfight. It is as Frank says when he comes to meet "The Man" for their final showdown: "Nothing [else] matters—not the land, not the money, not the woman." It is fated for Frank and "The Man" to meet like this and for one of them to die. It is part of the divine plan, the reason the two combatants in all Leone films make such a ritual of it. In accordance with the ceremonious aspect of these duels Leone often stages them in circular areas, corridas, where you expect the men either to sing opera or to fight bulls. In *Once upon a Time* Leone builds up tension by slowly circling Frank and "The Man" with his camera, and interspersing tight shots of the men's eyes and hands in relation to their guns. Also, the level of the music is raised and the conflicting musical themes of the two men intermingle. (Morricone's music in *Once upon a Time* shifts easily from dramatic to ethereal to ironic to comical; importantly *for Leone*, even when the film becomes dominated by historical elements, the music still sounds like music from a mystical, mythical age.)*

The sheer audacity of Leone's staging of his gun battles—particularly in the elaborate title sequence where Frank's men await "The Man" at a train station only to be gunned down by him—lends to the comedic effect of *Once upon a Time*. The violence is further tempered by the fact that all gunplay in Leone has comic twists; the manner in which villains die is always filled with irony. The blood, the violence, the humor, the many gunfights, and the final showdown in *Once upon a Time* have been constants in Leone's works since *A Fistful of Dollars*. So is his unerring eye for faces (particularly male faces, although there are numerous stunning close-ups of gorgeous Claudia Cardinale), setting, detail, color, and movement. There is no one better than Leone at using the frame. What wonderful shots he gives us of the landscape (some exteriors were shot in Monument Valley, John Ford's favorite locale), and how overwhelming is the visual when the camera cranes up and over the Flagstone train station office to reveal a sprawling town on the other side, where countless townsfolk go about their business. (I think Leone directs extras better than anyone!)

Unlike most directors who use a wide screen, Leone doesn't do away with extreme close-ups to concentrate on spectacle. In fact, he characteristically uses close-ups instead of dialogue to reveal what a character is thinking. In *The Good, the Bad, and the Ugly*, he blocks out a beautiful landscape and blue sky by having a hideous visage of a scarred, scraggly bearded minor villain suddenly fill the entire frame. In *Once upon a Time*, extreme close-ups of Jack Elam, Woody Strode, and Lionel Stander, who only have brief roles, are just as memorable as those dramatic close-ups of Bronson, Fonda, Robards, and Cardinale, who all have fascinating faces.

Perhaps Leone's most striking use of the extreme close-up comes in the final shootout of *Once upon a Time in the West*. In a medium-long shot, Frank moves into the frame from right to left. We expect "The Man" to then come in from the left with his back toward us—as most western directors would have him do. But "The Man" also moves into the frame from the right, not facing Frank but looking toward the left part of the frame with his profile in extreme close-up and filling the right half of the frame, his hat rim stretching across the frame, and with both him and Frank in focus despite their distance apart. (Leone is known for his wide-angle, deep-focus photography.) This is a brave, marvelous stroke, powerful and amusing at the same time—the essence of Sergio Leone.

---

*As critic Robert C. Cumbow suggests, "Leone and Morricone are that rare combination of film director and film composer whose work together unerringly builds to a total integration of film and score."

Out of the Past

1947 RKO Radio
Director: Jacques Tourneur
Producer: Warren Duff
Screenplay: Geoffrey Homes (Daniel Mainwaring)
Based on his novel *Build My*

Gallows High
Cinematography: Nicholas Musuraca
Music: Mischa Bakaleinikoff
Editor: Samuel E. Beetley
Running Time: 97 minutes

Cast: Robert Mitchum (Jeff Markham, a.k.a. Jeff Bailey), Jane Greer (Kathie Moffat), Kirk Douglas (Whit Sterling), Rhonda Fleming (Meta Carson), Richard Webb (Jim), Steve Brodie (Fisher), Virginia Huston (Ann), Paul Valentine (Joe Stefanos), Dickie Moore (mute boy), Ken Niles (Leonard Eels)

Synopsis: Jeff Bailey has recently come to Bridgeport, California, where he has opened up a filling station, befriended a mute boy, and become intimate with Ann, whom he hopes to marry. By chance, hood Joe Stefanos passes through Bridgeport and notices Jeff's garage sign. His intuition tells him that Jeff Bailey may be Jeff Markham, for whom his boss Whit Sterling, a big-time gambler, has been searching for a year. He tracks Jeff down and finds out that he has guessed correctly. He tells Jeff that he must see Whit in Lake Tahoe. Ann goes with Jeff to Lake Tahoe. As they drive along, he tells her of his past. As Jeff Markham, he was a New York private investigator. He and his partner Fisher were hired by Whit to find Whit's mistress, Kathie Moffat, who shot him and fled with forty thousand dollars of his money. Jeff tracked her down in Acapulco. He and Kathie began a torrid love affair and he decided not to inform Whit of her whereabouts. She told him that she hated Whit but that she had not taken his money. Jeff decided that it didn't matter one way or the other about the money. He and Kathie fled to San Francisco, where they led the lives of fugitives.

Fisher spotted Jeff at the racetrack and later tracked Jeff and Kathie to a mountain cabin. He told them that Whit had hired him to find Jeff and that he now wanted to be paid to keep his mouth shut. Jeff and Fisher struggled, and Kathie killed Fisher. She then jumped in her car and fled. Jeff found her bankbook, which showed she had deposited forty thousand dollars. Feeling disillusioned and like a chump, Jeff buried Fisher and, changing his name to Bailey, came to Bridgeport.

At Lake Tahoe, Ann takes the car to go back while Jeff visits with Whit. Whit wants him to retrieve some tax records of his from Eels, a San Francisco lawyer, who is threatening to turn them over to the IRS. By doing this, he says, Jeff can make up for botching his previous assignment. Jeff agrees. He is surprised to find that Kathie is again Whit's mistress. She tells Jeff that she still loves him, but has returned to Whit out of fear.

In San Francisco, Jeff is set up for the murder of Eels, actually committed by Stefanos. Jeff also learns from Kathie that Whit had forced her to sign an affidavit saying he killed Fisher. Wanted for two murders, Jeff flees town and hides out near Bridgeport. Kathie sends Stefanos to kill him, but the mute boy kills Stefanos.

Rather than go to jail for tax evasion, Whit agrees to buy Jeff's silence by giving him fifty thousand dollars and a way out of the country, and to turn Kathie over to the police as the murderer of Fisher.

Jeff says good-bye to Ann, whom he knows he can never be with. He returns to Whit's house and finds that Kathie has killed him. When she says that they should go to Mexico City together, he agrees. But while she is packing he calls the police, who set up a roadblock. When Kathie sees the police she kills Jeff, and then dies herself from police bullets. The mute boy lies to Ann that Jeff intended to go off with Kathie, making his death easier for her to take.

If you're looking for the picture that best exemplifies good *film noir*, the fascinating albeit cynical style/genre that was a dominant form in Hollywood in the forties, start with *Out of the Past*. Here you'll find all the ingredients: tainted characters; entangled relationships; large sums of money; murder; a tough, morally ambiguous hero with a gun in his trenchcoat, a dark hat on his head, and a cigarette in his mouth; a lying, cheating, chameleon-like femme fatale (when Ann says that Kathie can't be all bad, Jeff replies, "She's the closest thing to it")—a corruptive influence who leads an essentially good guy down the wayward path ("Nothing mattered except I had her," Jeff says of Kathie); and ultimately betrayal, frame-ups and fall guys, and double- and triple-crosses. ("The sum of deceitful complications that occur in *Out of the Past*," wrote Bosley Crowther in *The New York Times*, "must be reckoned by logarithmic tables, so numerous and involved do they become.") In *film noir* fashion, *Out of the Past* takes place mostly at night—when evil elements function best. Director Jacques Tourneur and his cameraman Nicholas Musuraca use low-key lighting for these night scenes, and single-source illumination that has the effect of placing spooky shadows on the faces of the characters and across entire sets. This, plus the fact that no picture in memory has the camera stationed so many times *behind* characters' backs and shoulders (further blocking out the source light), establishes a tremendous sense of paranoia—essential to *film noir*. In addition to creating a forbidding atmosphere for the characters, the darkness is used metaphorically to express the malignant evil that spreads from character to character. A powerful example of this comes when Jeff and Kathie kiss and, by bringing their faces together, block out the one light behind them and make the screen black—like their fate. And chainsmoker Jeff lights matches over and over again, not only to jar himself into action as if he were self-winding, but to give us a sign (from director Tourneur) that "goodness"—a white flame in the blackness—still flickers within the evil world that tries to devour him.

Daniel Mainwaring (Geoffrey Homes), who would take paranoia to new heights in his script for *Invasion of the Body Snatchers* (1956), adapted *Out of the Past* from his novel *Build My Gallows High*. He took his script to Bogart who, noting its similarities to *The Maltese Falcon*, wanted to play the part of Jeff Bailey. If Warners had let Bogart do it, the chances are that, through his presence alone, it would have been regarded as an instant classic of the *film noir*. But Warners refused, and Robert Mitchum, a hit in *The Story of G. I. Joe* (1944) but not nearly as well known as Bogart, got the part on the rebound. Since Mitchum, Jane Greer, and Kirk Douglas weren't "name" stars at the time, RKO regarded *Out of the Past* as a "B" picture and it suffered the fate of most pictures so designated: critical indifference. Only in the last dozen years, since the new wave of critics has taken an interest in the career of Jacques Tourneur and has elevated Robert Mitchum to his rightful place as one of the few *great* movie actors, has *Out of the Past* been reappraised and discovered to be up

Among the few scenes in which the frame is full of light are those in which Jeff is with Ann, the good woman in his life.

there with John Huston's *The Maltese Falcon* (1941), Billy Wilder's *Double Indemnity* (1944), Edward Dmytryk's *Murder, My Sweet* (1944), Howard Hawks's *The Big Sleep* (1946), and the works of Fritz Lang and Robert Siodmak, as the gems of the *film noir*.

As it turns out, Mitchum is a better choice than Bogart to play Jeff Bailey. For one thing, Mitchum's reserved style is more in keeping with the way Tourneur directs his actors. All through his career Tourneur strove for realism by having his performers speak in low tones, with little change in their voice level or pitch or facial expressions when angry or joking. (While a humanist director, he rarely had his characters laugh or express happiness.) In *Out of the Past*, the quiet, hollow-sounding conversations contribute to the menacing atmosphere (especially in cold outdoor settings when the characters' breaths are seen) and helps build tension, as we know this group of characters can't stay calm forever. (Even Kirk Douglas plays his part coolly.) Bogart is at his best when talking fast and furiously, using his hands, salivating, laughing at the ironies of life, and, unlike Jeff, enjoying the intrigues of his detective profession.

Also what makes Mitchum preferable to Bogart is their eighteen-year age difference. The Bogart who plays detectives Sam Spade and Philip Marlowe (the one *film noir* hero who has a *strict* moral code from which he doesn't waver) may get himself in trouble from trusting women, even falling in love, but he has been around enough of them through the years to know that he must

leave himself an out in case of betrayal. He is too smart, as Sam Spade says, "to play the sap" for any double-dealing femme fatale. Jeff is a smart guy too, which is why Whit wants him in his employ and as company, but as Meta, Eels's secretary, says to him, "For someone who may be clever, you can act like an idiot." Jeff's excuse for acting like an idiot, a chump, is his youth; he is just thirty, while Spade and the world-weary Marlowe are played by an actor in his forties. Jeff hasn't experienced woman as Spade and Marlowe have, so it is understandable that he is unprepared for the likes of Kathie and welcomes her with open arms. When she asks Jeff to believe that she didn't steal Whit's forty grand, he replies, "Baby, I don't care." But it turns out he does care after all when she kills Fisher and leaves him to take the rap and he finds she deposited forty grand in her bank account. The next time he meets a femme fatale, Meta, Jeff has wised up and, as shrewdly as Spade or Marlowe, refuses to let her play him for a fool, too. Having been burned once is all that it takes to teach a smart fellow like Jeff the ways of the world—and it will never happen to him again. Unfortunately, it is already *too* late: he is a doomed hero.

The question of who should receive the most credit for the excellence of *Out of the Past* was subject of a 1974 debate in the pages of *The Velvet Light Trap* (volumes 10 and 11) between Tom Flinn, a regular contributor to the Wisconsin-based magazine, and Richard Jameson, the editor of Seattle's *Movietone News*. Prefacing an interview with Daniel Mainwaring, Flinn wrote: "He alone is responsible for the thematic density of the film in which such ultimate *noir* elements as betrayal, the femme fatale, and the 'frame-up' are combined with reckless abandon."

Jameson responded: "My experience of the Jacques Tourneur films leaves me in little doubt that the film is largely the director's. It is his impeccably civilized style that translates this gangster story of revenge and double-dealing into such an emotionally ambiguous, eerily beautiful experience. The fluid opening movements, the delicately stressed yet uninsistent measurements of character revelation and interaction, the soft-spoken, almost contemplative delivery of the generic patter—all powerfully recall the quiet poetry and decorous intuitions of the magical in the best parts of [his] *The Cat People* [1942], *I Walked with a Zombie* [1943], and even *Canyon Passage* [1946]."

Flinn came back with: "I do not see how it is possible to deny thematic credit to a writer who receives sole screen credit for adapting his own novel. . . . *Out of the Past* was a project initiated by Producer Warren Duff, who convinced the studio to buy the book and supervised the writing of the screenplay which was completed by the time Tourneur came to the film. As a result, Tourneur's contribution . . . is primarily stylistic."

Whatever Tourneur's contribution, *Out of the Past* couldn't have been a more ideal picture for *him* to direct. For one thing, in his work with Val Lewton's horror unit at RKO, he had become accustomed to using the single-source lighting, shadows, silhouettes, and total darkness that became part of the *noir* style, not only to scare viewers but to cover up the fact that Lewton's minimal budgets required studio sets that would have looked tacky if revealed by high-key lighting. As in his Lewton films, in *Out of the Past* a major theme is that beside or within peaceful, prosaic, everyday environments there lurk evil people and forces.

Jeff's ex-partner Fisher tracks Jeff and Kathie to a mountain cabin.

Much was implied rather than shown: both Kathie's killing of Whit and Jeff's telephone call to the police are kept off screen. And as in various of his Lewton films, Tourneur uses nonstereotypical blacks, a mute character, and puts major emphasis on exotic locales. (For a "B" picture, *Out of the Past* almost reaches "epic" proportions: it takes place in such places as Bridgeport,

In San Francisco, Jeff rendezvouses with Meta Carson, another woman who can't be trusted.

California; Los Angeles; San Francisco; Lake Tahoe; New York; Mexico City [briefly]; and Acapulco. Unusual for Tourneur, he was allowed to do much location footage.)

Mainwaring borrowed greatly from Dashiell Hammett and Raymond Chandler, and it is definitely he who is responsible for the narrative structure, the sexual intensity, and a tough male hero—none of which was characteristic of Tourneur's previous films. But in the films and books of Hammett and Chandler, the heroes (Spade, the Continental Op, Marlowe), are in control of their own destinies, while in *Out of the Past*, as in the films of Lang and Siodmak, the destinies of the characters are predetermined—fatalism, predestination, had indeed been a trait of Tourneur's earlier films. For instance, in Tourneur's *The Leopard Man* (1943), in which Margo's death is sealed by a bad reading from a fortune teller, James Bell compares man's state in the universe to a ball that is permanently kept airborne by water from a fountain. Similarly, in *Out of the Past*, in which Jeff's breaking a glass symbolizes that his easy, honest life has been shattered, a roulette wheel becomes a metaphor for life. "Is there a way to win?" asks Kathie, who is betting large sums on each turn of the wheel. "There's a way to lose more slowly," answers Jeff. *Out of the Past* repeatedly suggests that lives are determined by chance: Stefanos notices Jeff's garage sign

*Always plotting, Kathie listens coolly while
Whit and Jeff discuss business.*

as he drives along the highway and is able to track him down; the Acapulco telegraph office is closed for siesta so Jeff can't wire Whit that he found Kathie; Fisher spots Jeff at the racetrack; the car starts, after the motor failed to turn over a few times, and is able to carry Jeff and Kathie to their deaths at the police roadblock. And once Jeff decides to throw his lot in with Kathie, his dismal end is assured.

In the Mainwaring interview mentioned earlier, he noted that James M. Cain worked on a version of the script that was totally abandoned. Nevertheless, I suspect that Cain may have been the major influence on the last scenes between Jeff and Kathie. (Mainwaring's novel has Jeff being killed by Whit's men, instead of being killed by Kathie before she herself is mowed down by police guns.) In Cain's novel *Double Indemnity*, Phyllis and Walter, with nowhere to go and tortured by inner demons, agree to commit double suicide by ritualistically jumping off a ship. Similarly, in *Out of the Past*, Jeff and Kathie are destined to die together for their sins. Kathie tells Jeff why they must go off together: "I'm no good and neither are you." After having packed for him (while he called the police), she adds, "Jeff, we've been wrong a lot and unlucky. I think we deserve a lucky break." He answers simply and fatalistically, "We deserve each other." Like Cain's sinners.

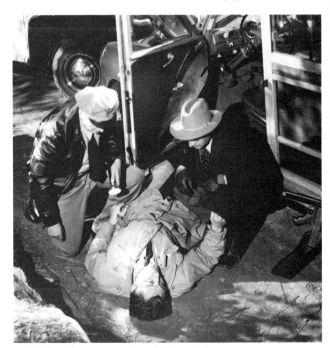

Jeff suffers the common fate of film noir *heroes
who fall for evil women.*

Outrageous!

1977 Canada A Herbert R. Steinmann–Billy Baxter presentation financed in part by the Film Consortium of Canada
Director: Richard Benner
Producers: William Marshall and Henk Van Der Kolk
Screenplay: Richard Benner
Based on a story from *Butterfly Ward*, by Margaret Gibson
Cinematography: James B. Kelly
Music: Paul Hoffert
Editor: George Appleby
Running Time: 96 minutes

Cast: Craig Russell (Robin Turner), Hollis McLaren (Liza Connors), Richard Easley (Perry), Allan Moyle (Martin), David Meilwraith (Bob), Jerry Salzberg (Jason), Andree Pelletier (Anne), Helen Shaver (Jo)

Synopsis: Robin Turner, a young gay hairdresser, watches a female impersonator perform in a Toronto nightclub. "I'm not that desperate for attention," he says. "Not yet." Liza, Robin's best friend, walks out of a home for the insane where her mother had her committed because she always cried. Robin lets Liza stay in his apartment. She suffers because she believes "the bonecrusher," an imaginary being, won't leave her alone. "We'll lick it together," Robin tells her. Liza's psychiatrist allows Liza to stay with Robin when she assures him that their relationship is not of a sexual nature. He insists that she not become pregnant in her state and prescribes pills for her. But Liza sleeps with a guy and doesn't take her pills.

Robin is unhappy with his job and his sexual relationships with "normal" gay men. Liza tells him to get out of his rut by doing something "dazzling." She convinces him to enter a drag queen contest with his friend Perry. Robin dresses as Tallulah Bankhead and is offered a club date at no pay doing female impersonations. Liza tells him "Do your act for all us crazies." Robin nervously does the club act and is a big hit as Bette Davis.

Liza is thrilled to learn she is pregnant: "It proves I'm alive." Robin's gay boss fires him because their clients have learned that Robin does female impersonations. But Robin gets an offer to do his act at the Jack Rabbit in New York—for pay. He is afraid to take it because it means leaving Liza behind while she has her baby. Liza and her friend Martin, whom she knew from the mental hospital, accompany Robin to the train. As soon as Robin leaves, Liza feels the presence of "the bonecrusher."

Bob, the New York cabdriver who takes Robin to the Jack Rabbit, turns out to be gay and an agent. He agrees to represent Robin. Robin debuts at the gay club and does well impersonating Mae West. Eventually Bob gets Robin a tryout at an uptown middle-class nightclub. Robin is a hit performing for this mixed audience and Bob arranges a good contract for him there. Although he can afford better, Robin rents an apartment in a freaky neighborhood so Liza will feel comfortable staying with him. Martin stabs someone and is put in jail. Liza is lonely although she keeps writing her short stories in a book she always carries with her. She stays with her friend Jo, an editor who tells her she'll try to help get her stories published. But Jo finds Liza too hysterical to take care of her. Liza's baby is born dead. Liza becomes catatonic. Her lesbian friend Anne takes her home but can't help her.

Robin and Bob drive to Canada. Anne and Robin have always fought, but she lets Robin take Liza to New York because she realizes he is Liza's only hope. Once in New York, Liza starts to come out of her daze. She goes to the Jack Rabbit, where Robin puts on a show. In his dressing room, she tells him that among all the friendly gay men there she no longer feels the presence of "the bonecrusher." "He'll show up," jokes Robin, "everyone does." He tells her that she is not dead inside like she thinks but very much alive; he tells her that she'll never be "normal," but she is *special* and can have fun among the eight million other crazies in New York. Robin and the smiling Liza join all the male customers in the nightclub. They all dance.

Although a Canadian film, *Outrageous!* had its world theatrical premiere at New York City's Cinema II, the same theater where 1977's Oscar-winning *Rocky* had done fantastic business. Everyone was surprised when the lines outside the theater grew to equal those for *Rocky;* and this spurred on several critics to compare the two films, seemingly so different, in terms of their appeal to the movie audience of 1977. This comparison has validity, for the people who came to see *Outrageous!* were not just gays, but also "straight" people who found *Rocky* uplifting and wanted other pictures to raise their spirits. In *Rocky,* you have a guy who everyone, including himself, thinks a bum; but he is motivated to pull himself out of the lower depths and he becomes *a somebody,* not the champion of *Rocky* II (1979) but someone who can be proud/happy that he has brought meaning to his life. It is the same in *Outrageous!,* where two people at the bottom of the social register—Liza, a schizophrenic, and Robin, a depressed gay hairdresser —pick themselves up, move out of an oppressive city, and make the best of their potential ("You have a healthy brand of craziness," Robin tells Liza. "Make it work for you"). They don't become champions or overcome all their problems, but by finding a satisfying level of self-fulfillment they can no longer be termed *losers.* Both *Rocky* and *Outrageous!* are *success stories* wherein the characters' successes are according to their own standards. Going the distance (Rocky), earning a living as a female impersonator (Robin), and no longer being tormented by "the bonecrusher" (Liza) are the achievements of these characters. Few of us would think them successes for ourselves; but we can relate to these characters' triumphs because we all have small, personal goals and ambitions that only have meaning for us. Therein lies the popularity of both films.

In his review of *Outrageous!* for *The New York Times,* Frank Rich wrote: "It's moving for once to see a film about crazies that doesn't end with the character either lobotomized, locked up in a padded cell, transformed into a 'normal' zombie or killed." I agree with

Three "crazies"—(L-R) Martin, Robin, and Liza—together on a Toronto bus.

Bob is happy to be Robin's agent because by hanging out with a "star" (here made up as Mae West), Bob gets to score with a lot of gay customers.

Rich's comment about the happy ending, but more important is his assertion that *Outrageous!* is about *two* crazies more than it is about one homosexual man and one crazy young woman. Because of the terrible image of homosexuals in Hollywood films, some gays faulted *Outrageous!* for not attempting to be the first commercial picture that defines what it is like to be gay in a nongay world; but, in terms of Robin, the picture is *not* about being gay but about being an outcast (a crazy) among people (gays) who are already outcasts. As Robin's gay boss says: "Being gay is one thing but going in drag is something else." Robin has long come out of the proverbial closet; his depression comes from trying to conform to a "normal" gay life, which he finds restrictive and boring. When Robin has to pay *The Advocate*'s (a gay newspaper) back-cover boy for a night of sex, he must think that he is playing out the sad, sordid Hollywood cliché about sexual relationships between gays.* This is the gay life he wants to get away from. That Robin is gay is not the issue for him. The issue is that he wants to break down the barriers that gays have set up for themselves: he wants to be a female impersonator and become part of the more adventuresome and dazzling element of the gay community that many gays shun.

As the film's gay director, Richard Benner, states: "The story is of two people who are so fringe or so strange that they can't fit in anyplace except with each other." *Outrageous!* is foremost a story about friendship, about a man and woman who "sleep in two different worlds," as Liza tells her psychiatrist, but provide each other with comfort, companionship, advice, and support. As much as *Outrageous!* is a breakthrough film because it features a gay lead character who is played by a gay actor and makes the important statement that gays aren't necessarily depressed by their homosexuality,* it is equally noteworthy for being a commercial film with a relationship between a young man and a young woman that is based on friendship rather than romance. And what a friendship theirs is. Liza kicks her lover out of her bed after he makes a disparaging remark about Robin, her "best friend," and breaks out of the grasp of her militant feminist friends after they blame Robin for her unhappiness. For his part, Robin drives all the way from New York to Toronto to rescue Liza from a mental relapse after her baby is born dead. Liza is the one who gets Robin out of his depression by convincing him to pursue a career as a

---

*Perhaps *Outrageous!* would have avoided criticism among some gays if Robin were shown having at least one rewarding sexual experience.

*In William Friedkin's *Boys in the Band* (1970), one gay laments: "Show me a happy homosexual and I'll show you a gay corpse." It's movies like *Boys*, which project homosexuals as tormented, that have infuriated gay activists.

female impersonator; he gets her out of her funk, at picture's end, with words of wisdom: "You're not dead inside, honey. You're alive and sick and living in New York, like eight million other people. You're never gonna be normal, but you're *special,* and you can have a hell of a lot of fun." It is as Robin tells Liza the first night she sleeps in his Toronto apartment and is tormented by "the bonecrusher": "We'll lick this together." What I find most appealing about *Outrageous!* is that the characters care for and look after one another. And not only Robin and Liza. It's really touching when Bob keeps a protective eye on Liza in the Jack Rabbit, and when Anne forgets her differences with Robin and becomes friendly to him (letting him take Liza with him to New York) when she understands that he really is a healthy influence on Liza.

At times, *Outrageous!* is a sloppy film, poorly lit and edited in a manner which causes you to lose all track of time; but the characters are so likable and believably played and the direction is so spirited and tender that you are more than willing to forgive it for not being as polished as a big-budget Hollywood film. In fact, several Hollywood directors had offered Richard Benner deals to adapt his script. Benner refused, as he wanted to make the picture (then called *Looney Tunes*) himself despite having no directorial experience whatsoever. Benner based his script on a story by Margaret Gibson, who had lived for a time with Craig Russell. Called "Making It" (later published in a collection called *Butterfly Ward*), it is a series of letters between Liza, a character based on Gibson herself and other women she knew, and Robin, a character influenced by but unlike Russell. "When people read *Butterfly Ward,*" Benner

said to *Soho News* writer Rob Baker, "and think of that character as Craig Russell, it's almost libelous, practically, because Margaret sees the world in a depressed fashion. . . . [Her Robin was] depressive, suicidal—and that didn't match up with my perception of the people I knew. I've known a lot of these kids, and they're not any more suicidal than I am, or anybody."

Craig Russell was voted Best Actor at the Berlin Film Festival for his performance as Robin, and he is truly winning in the role. His Robin has great range: he is kind-hearted, angry, witty, philosophical, moody, weak to criticism, strong when he has to be, even heroic, extremely sarcastic, and harmlessly bitchy (Lisa thinks Robin has Tallulah Bankhead living inside him). And when Robin does his impersonations (written by Benner) of Streisand, Channing, Garland, Bankhead, Davis, West, et al, he accomplishes what he wants: he is *dazzling.*

At the end of *Outrageous!,* Robin works two clubs, the all-gay Jack Rabbit and an exclusive uptown night spot where he performs a less bawdy act for a mixed, middle-class audience. But just because Robin has "made it" by getting the uptown engagement, it does not mean he will sell out. He insists on living in a "freaky" neighborhood where someone of his financial resources need not live, and he continues to perform at the Jack Rabbit. In fact, Benner stages the *finale* in the Jack Rabbit, where both Robin and Liza can be the most comfortable. Here among their peers and friends, they will continue their struggle to retain their "healthy brand of craziness" in a dehumanized world and still have fun. Perhaps the film's title shouldn't be *Outrageous!* but *Courageous!*

Pandora's Box

Also known as *Lulu*

1929   Germany   Nero Film A.G.
Director: G. W. Pabst
Producer: George C. Hosetzky
Screenplay: Ladislaus Vajda
From two plays, *Erdgeist* and *Die Büchse der Pandora*, by Frank Wedekind
Cinematography: Günther Krampf
Editor: Joseph R. Fliesler
Running Time: 131 minutes

Cast: Louise Brooks (Lulu), Fritz Kortner (Dr. Peter Schön), Franz Lederer (Alwa Schön), Carl Götz (Schigolch, a.k.a. Papa Brommer), Alice Roberts (Countess Anna Geschwitz), Daisy d'Ora (Marie de Zarniko), Krafft Raschig (Rodrigo Quast), Michael von Newlinsky (Marquis Casti-Piani), Siegfried Arno (the stage manager), Gustav Diessl (Jack the Ripper)

Synopsis: Lulu owns her own apartment. She is the mistress of noted editor Dr. Peter Schön. She is happy with her life, she tells her former sugar daddy, Schigolch, when he visits her. He is angry that Lulu hasn't kept up with her dancing but is pacified when Lulu gives him money and alcohol. She loves him and calls him Poppa Brommer.

Schön tells Lulu that he is going to marry Charlotte Marie Adelaide, the daughter of a minister. Lulu doesn't mind as long as he continues to love her. When Schön finds Schigolch in her apartment, he becomes jealous and rushes out. She laughs. Schigolch introduces Lulu to muscleman Rodrigo Quast, who wants to do a variety act with her. Schön's son Alwa is Lulu's best friend. He tries to get his father to marry Lulu, but Schön doesn't want to ruin his career. Alwa puts on a revue for which Countess Geschwitz, who loves Lulu, does the costume design. His father tells him to let Lulu do her act in the revue and Schön's newspaper will make sure she gets great notices.

Lulu refuses to do her number once Schön comes backstage with his fiancé Marie. Schön pretends not to recognize her and they argue. She seduces him in the property room. Alwa and Marie find them clutching one another. The happy Lulu does her act. She will marry Schön.

At the wedding reception, the drunk Schigolch and Rodrigo go into Lulu and Schön's bedroom to put flowers on the bed. Lulu finds them there and kisses Schigolch. Schön enters the room and thinks Lulu and these men have been having a romantic interlude. He chases the men from the apartment with a revolver. He tries to force Lulu to kill herself, but in the struggle for the gun he is killed.

Lulu is sentenced to five years in prison for manslaughter even though Alwa, who now loves her, speaks in her defense. Her friends arrange her escape from the courthouse. She seduces Alwa and they flee the country together. Geschwitz lends her a passport.

On a train, Lulu is recognized by the money-hungry Marquis Casti-Piani. He forces Alwa to pay him so he won't turn in Lulu for a reward. He convinces them to go with him to a gambling boat. Schigolch and Rodrigo go with them.

Three months later, Alwa has lost all his money gambling. Rodrigo demands money from Lulu because he wants to get married. Casti-Piani sells Lulu to an Egyptian cabaret owner. If she and Alwa can't match the Egyptian's offer she will have to go with him. Geschwitz comes on board. Schigolch, trying to help Lulu, tells Rodrigo that Geschwitz loves him and will give him the money he needs. Lulu asks Geschwitz to help her. The countess gives Lulu money so Alwa can once again try his luck at cards; and she goes with Rodrigo to a cabin on deck although he repulses her. Rodrigo forces himself on her. Alwa borrows marked cards from Schigolch. He begins to win but then is caught cheating. There is pandemonium on the boat. Police arrive. They discover that Rodrigo has been killed. Lulu escapes by exchanging clothes with a cabin boy. She, Schigolch, and Alwa row a boat to London. There they live in an ice-cold garret. Alwa is sick. They have no money or food. Lulu decides to make money by being a prostitute. Alwa protests, but Schigolch won't let him interfere. On Christmas Eve she brings her first customer back to the garret, not knowing he is Jack the Ripper. She lets him come with her although he says he hasn't any money. He truly likes her for her kindness but he can't stop himself from killing her. Alwa follows a Salvation Army band off into the night. Schigolch is given food at a pub. Neither knows what has happened to Lulu.

By the time one becomes expert on film history, s/he has seen almost every movie "classic" (and *The Late Late Show*) several times. In fact, after many thousands of screenings, it becomes so infrequent to see a gem from the past for the *first* time that film authorities tend to envy movie viewers who have years of cinematic discoveries ahead of them. So it is that for American film scholars and critics the recent availability of a restored print of German director G. W. Pabst's *Pandora's Box*, which has turned out to be a *masterpiece* of the silent era, has been a wonderful revelation.

Adapted from *The Earth's Spirit* and *Lulu*, two once-controversial plays by German dramatist/poet Frank Wedekind, *Pandora's Box* was received harshly by many critics in its native Germany. As Wedekind's *Lulu*—a source of national pride by 1929—had been mistreated in the 1890s, Pabst's film was condemned as being immoral and scandalous. Its unveiled sexual content caused such a stir that for foreign (and I believe domestic) distribution the picture was heavily censored. (In England, for instance, all scenes with Countess Geschwitz, the cinema's first lesbian, were excised.) The same fate lay in store for *Diary of a Lost Girl* (1930), the other sexually explicit Pabst film which starred beautiful

Trouble free and happy, Lulu does her novelty dance in Alwa's show.

Countess Geschwitz, probably the screen's first lesbian, sadly hugs Lulu on her wedding night.

Pabst's two films. Certainly they were superior to Pabst's certified classics: *Joyless Street* (1925) and *The Threepenny Opera* (1931). Many more years passed before uncut prints of *Pandora's Box* got widespread distribution in America and it became the most prestigious film on repertory theater schedules. (Unfortunately, *Diary of a Lost Girl* remains nearly impossible to see in America.) There is no doubt about it: *Pandora's Box* is a *great*, important film, a tremendous discovery. Not only is it fascinatingly unorthodox in its treatment of what would normally be a classic version vamp/femme fatale and in its daringly uncompromising presentation of sexual themes, but also, and most significant, it allows viewers the rare chance to see the brilliant Louise Brooks.

In *Close-Ups* (Workman, 1978), her friend, film publicist John Springer, writes about the pre-Pabst Brooks:

> Certainly she was a beauty. Anyone with a memory going back to the 1920s knows that. They remember her as a Scandals and Follies girl who had not only beauty but individuality. They remember how her short, square, black patent-leather bob created a coiffure trend: they may remember that she had a reputation for devastating wit, and was considered an intellectual—a strange tag for someone with such a breezy, flapper personality. She never took movies seriously. . . . When, as in *Love 'em and Leave 'em* (1926) and *Beggars of Life* (1928) she had a role that called for more than mere prettiness or peppiness, she worked at it, but for the most part moviemaking was something to get through the day so she could experience the life of a Hollywood star at night. This ex-chorus girl from Kansas was a darling of what today we'd call the jet set. Rich and powerful men courted her. The most publicized playboys sought her out. . . . But in Hollywood movies, Louise Brooks was always second-string.

It was in fact in a second-string role as a circus highdiver in Howard Hawks's *A Girl in Every Port* (1928) that Brooks caught Pabst's eye. Just as humorist

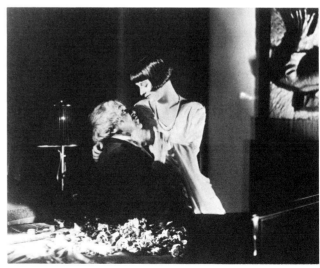

Lulu innocently sits on Schigolch's knee. This is the pose in which Dr. Schön will find his bride when he enters their bedroom.

American actress Louise Brooks. In America, where by 1929 most films with subtitles were no longer imported, the Pabst films were known primarily by reputation. (*Pandora's Box* played only briefly in America in late 1929.) Although Brooks became more famous and a genuine sex symbol as a result of her appearance in what were reputed to be two notorious films, few in America thought they were missing out in not seeing pictures that were generally lambasted in the European press. Soon the Pabst films were stored away without ever having attained fair critical evaluation, and original, uncut versions were lost forever. Although it is possible that he never saw the picture, Siegfried Kracauer confirmed *Pandora's Box* to be a failure in *From Caligari to Hitler* (Princeton University Press, 1947), which for years was mistakenly regarded as the bible on the German cinema. Fortunately, newly restored prints of the Pabst films surfaced in the fifties at film festivals and Louise Brooks retrospectives throughout Europe, and word spread to the United States that both European critics circa 1929–1930 and Kracauer had grossly underestimated

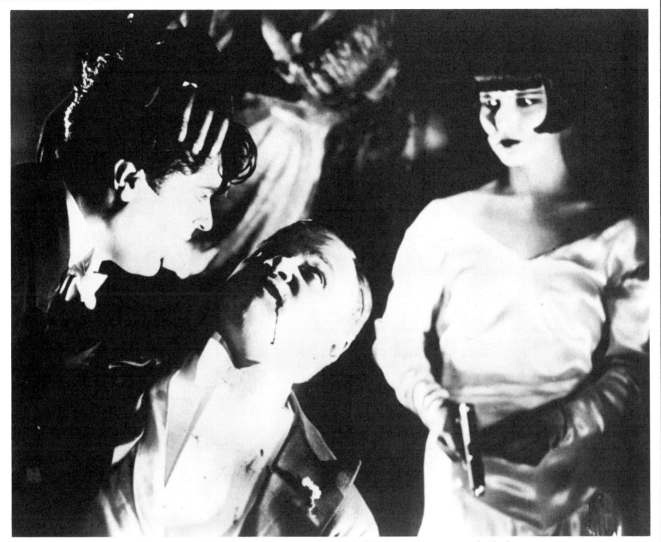

Alwa holds his dying father, Dr. Schön, who warns him about Lulu. She holds the smoking gun with which she accidentally shot her husband when he tried to force her to commit suicide.

J. P. McEvoy would find his "Dixie Dugan" in Louise Brooks, Pabst sensed that Brooks was his Lulu. (He rejected a young Marlene Dietrich.) Her contract with Paramount terminated, she accepted Pabst's offer and immediately left for Germany. Because she refused to stay long enough to dub the voice for her last Paramount role in *The Canary Murder Case* (1929), she would find herself virtually blacklisted when she returned to Holly-wood in 1930.*

In *The Haunted Screen—Expressionism in the German Cinema and the Influence of Max Reinhardt*

---

*After working with Pabst, Brooks starred in her last major film, *Prix de Beauté* (1930), by French director René Clair. Then she came back to Hollywood but could only find parts in minor films. Her fame disappeared as the stars of the sound era emerged. She left Hollywood and drifted off into obscurity. As a result of the birth of a Louise Brooks cult in Europe in the mid-fifties, James Card, curator of motion pictures for the Eastman House in Rochester, New York, tracked her down—she was living in New York City. He convinced her to come to Rochester to look at films. Eventually she moved there, where she attended screenings every day. She became an astute film critic and chronologer and contributed pieces on film to several magazines.

(Secker & Warburg, 1969), Lotte Eisner writes about the unveiling of a great actress:

> In *Pandora's Box* and *Diary of a Lost Girl*, we have the miracle of Louise Brooks. Her gifts of profound intuition may seem purely passive to an inexperienced audience, yet she succeeded in stimulating an otherwise unequal director's talent to the extreme. Pabst's remarkable evolution must thus be seen as an encounter with an actress who needed no direction, but could move across the screen causing works of art to be born by her mere presence. Louise Brooks, always enigmatically impassive, overwhelmingly exists throughout these two films. We know now that Louise Brooks is a remarkable actress endowed with uncommon intelligence, and not merely a dazzlingly beautiful woman.

Brooks is stunning in *Pandora's Box*. She lights up the screen just as Lulu is supposed to provide the brightest light in the dreary lives of the men she loves. She is not just going through the motions—in her eyes and her subtle expressions we see that she understands the sexual drives and needs that Lulu feels and her desire

A fine example of German expressionism. Now a prostitute, Lulu asks her first customer to come with her to her London garret. She doesn't realize he is Jack the Ripper.

to make her world a sexual playground. (Brooks had, after all, been part of Hollywood's wild scene in the twenties.) She betrays her sympathy for her character by playing her with aloofness and recklessness but without a trace of meanness. Her Lulu doesn't try to control her sexual impulses—she thinks they cause no damage—but she knows that others will try to condemn her for them. She protects herself from accusers through laughter, although sometimes Brooks lets the pain show through. And the anger. But *never* self-pity. Lulu is a passive character, but Brooks has the intelligence to realize that passivity does not rule out a character having substance. We read a lot into Lulu's character and that's not because we are *imagining* Brooks is transmitting Lulu's deepest thoughts to us, all Lulu's motivations—Brooks really is doing this. She is one of the few actresses whose movements express feelings. When first we see Lulu she is zipping around her room, bouncing, twirling. She will never be so happy again. We watch Brooks's speed, her energy level, for an indication of how she feels at any given moment. How erotically she slithers across a bed and how beautifully she glides across a room—like the

dancer she was. But when she stops being bubbly and stands half-frozen in the London streets, wrapped only in a thin shawl, she—the actress and character—is incredibly soulful and captures your heart. There is dignity in her debasement.

Brooks is Wedekind's conception of Lulu: a young, vivacious innocent with animal beauty and no moral sense. She doesn't want to harm anyone but her very existence causes the weak men around her to self-destruct.* Her looks and sparkling personality are reasons enough for a man to give up his respectability and are the reasons everyone she comes into contact with (except money-hungry Casti-Piani) falls for her, including a cabin boy and Countess Geschwitz. Brooks plays Lulu as if she were a spoiled but not malicious schoolgirl who forgets she is no longer ten years old when she sits in men's laps; repeatedly admires herself in the mirror;

---

*In this sense, Lulu prefigures the teen-age girl with the sexy knee in Eric Rohmer's *Claire's Knee* (1970) and the beautiful schoolteacher in Claude Chabrol's *Le Boucher* (1970) whose mere presence causes the male leads of the respective films to act irrationally.

stubbornly refuses to do her variety act when Schön offends her, and even cries and kicks her feet in mock anger; hangs from Rodrigo's muscular arm and swings from the curtain rail in front of the turned-on Alwa; looks through a fashion magazine only minutes after eluding police; and cries and faints one moment and laughs and dances the next.

While Lotte Eisner champions Brooks, she downplays Pabst's contribution to *Pandora's Box.* But it is he who creates the expressionistic atmosphere so conducive to the sexual delirium that prevails. And Pabst is the one responsible for satirizing upper-class German morality and painting a despairing picture of the poverty-stricken who live in London's slums. (Wedekind and screenwriter Ladislaus Vajda must share this credit.) He is also to be commended for making Lulu the *victim* of the weak men around her rather than the traditional femme fatale/vamp who causes (with pleasure) their downfall. Lulu is a scapegoat who gets blamed for Schön's death and who is sold to the Egyptian because her man Alwa loses all their money gambling. That Pabst is aware of her scapegoat role is clear in that several times he films Lulu straight on while the camera is behind a male character's back: this visually conveys that the man, in a pose of an accuser, is condemning her for some wrongdoing, although we know that she is without sin. The men suffer but *they* are responsible. Lulu suffers because Schön can't control his jealousy, Alwa can't control his gambling urges or self-pity, Schigolch can't control his alcoholism, Rodrigo and Casti-Piani can't control their greed, and Jack the Ripper can't control his psychosis.

Lulu is very likable, a very warmhearted free spirit without worries or inhibitions, that rare bird without jealousy. She only asks to be loved and can't bear rejection. When Schön tells her he's engaged, she laughs with relief, "And is that why you don't kiss me, because you want to get married?" Likewise, when Jack the Ripper balks at following her because he has no money she is relieved his hesitancy isn't because he doesn't want to make love to her. At the beginning we learn that Lulu left Schigolch because she didn't want to live with him in an attic. ("You've made a lot of progress," he admits when he sees her flat.) But poor Lulu winds up in a freezing London garret with both Schigolch and Alwa—it is the low point of her life. Lulu has always been free with her body but, as she tells Casti-Piani, "I cannot sell myself. That would be worse than prison." But poor Lulu winds up a streetwalker, willing to sell herself so she and the two men can eat. Indeed a victim, she is—with the possible exception of the tormented Jack the Ripper—the film's one sympathetic character.

Scene after scene, *Pandora's Box* is incredibly erotic. These characters could not live without constant physical contact and rarely a moment goes by without characters embracing or kissing. While never vulgar, the picture seems to drip with sex. Lulu, in fact, embodies sex; she is, as Wedekind wrote, "the personification of primitive sexuality who inspires evil unaware." So it is fated that at the story's end "primitive sexuality" (Lulu) attracts "evil" (Jack the Ripper). Both suffering victims of a world that feeds their amorality, each enjoys a

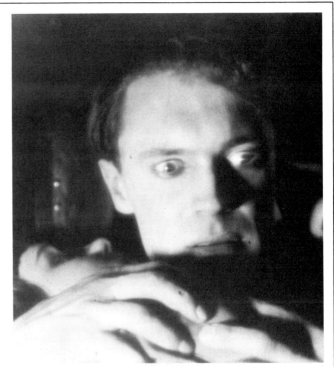

In a heated embrace, Lulu and Jack the Ripper. His mounting sexual fever only can be subdued by stabbing her with the knife he spots nearby.

moment of peace together with the *only* other companion who shares the same anguish. In the garret, the sexual tension is tremendous. Lulu is now loving, not flirtatious. Perhaps she realizes how meaningful the act of love is and is telling herself that she will reserve giving her body to only special people she loves—like Jack. The sexual intensity builds toward a climax—their sexual climax—as she sits in his lap, in his arms, her smooth, peaceful face glowing in the candlelight. His eyes are ablaze as he inserts the knife into her body (symbolic intercourse). She doesn't scream. Her hand falls gently, her eyes close peacefully. Her death near mistletoe suggests that she has been redeemed and forgiven—by God or Pabst. She is out of her misery and on her way to heaven, having been rewarded with the salvation that Alwa desires and the Ripper (perhaps an angel of God or death) knows he can never have. In *Sight and Sound* (Summer 1965) Brooks wrote:

> I did not realize until I saw *Pandora's Box* in 1956 how marvelously Mr. Pabst's perfect costume sense symbolized Lulu's character and her destruction. There is not a single spot of blood on the pure white bridal satin in which she kills her husband. Making love to her wearing a white peignor, Alwa asks, "Do you love me, Lulu?" "I? Never a soul!" It is in the worn and filthy garments of the streetwalker that she feels passion for the first time—comes to life so that she may die. When she picks up Jack the Ripper on the foggy London street and he tells her he has no money to pay her, she says "Never mind, I like you." It is Christmas Eve and she is about to receive the gift which has been her dream since childhood. Death by a sexual maniac.

Peeping Tom

1960 Great Britain   Anglo Amalgamated (released in the U.S. in 1962 by Astor; re-released in 1979 by Corinth)
Director: Michael Powell
Producer: Michael Powell
Screenplay: Leo Marks
Cinematography: Otto Heller
Music: Brian Easdale
Editor: Norman Ackland
Running time: 103 minutes

Cast: Carl Boehm (Mark Lewis), Moira Shearer (Vivian), Anna Massey (Helen Stephens), Maxine Audley (Mrs. Stephens), Esmond Knight (Arthur Baden), Bartlet Mullins (Mr. Peters), Brenda Bruce (Dora), Martin Miller (Dr. Rosen), Pamela Green (Millie), Michael Powell (Professor Lewis), Shirley Ann Field, Michael Goodliffe, Jack Watson, Nigel Davenport

Synopsis: With his 16-mm camera turned on and hidden from sight, Mark Lewis approaches a prostitute on the street. She takes him back to her room, where she looks toward him and becomes terribly frightened. That night in his flat, Mark views the film he took of her murder. The next morning, he films the police investigation of her murder for the documentary he is making.

Mark works as a focus puller at a film studio, but for extra money he takes girlie pictures above a corner cigar store. At his house he meets Helen Stephens, a young woman who lives with her blind mother in a downstairs flat. She visits his flat, which has a projection room and a photographic lab. He tells her he wants to be a director.

Mark shows Helen black-and-white films that were taken of him when he was a child. She is horrified to see that his scientist father used him as a guinea pig in various experiments, taking movies of him crying while watching a couple make love nearby and screaming when his father wakes him up by throwing a lizard on his bed. Mark tells Helen that his whole childhood was filmed; that his father was interested in the reactions of fear to the nervous system.

After work at the film studio, understudy Vivian stays behind for a secret rendezvous with Mark, who has promised to give her a screen test. Mark turns on his 16-mm camera. A blade extended from the tripod is aimed directly at her throat. She screams. The next day her body is discovered. Mark films the police investigation. Mark promises Helen he will take pictures for a children's book she is writing. They go on a date. She makes him leave his camera behind and for the first time he seems at ease and to be enjoying himself. Afterward, Helen kisses him goodnight. He goes upstairs to his flat and turns on the projector, not knowing that Mrs. Stephens is there. He is disappointed that Vivian's face does not have the right expression of terror he is seeking. Mrs. Stephens startles him with her presence. Being blind, she doesn't know what Mark was screening, but she is suspicious of him nevertheless. He knows that there is no use in trying to con her. He promises that he will never film Helen and put her in danger. She tells him to get psychological help.

At the studio, Mark speaks to Dr. Rosen, a psychiatrist who knew his father. He finds out that the cure for a scoptophiliac (one who obtains sexual pleasure by looking at erotic objects or pictures, nude women, etc.) will take two years, far too long. The detectives investigating the murders of the prostitute and Vivian become suspicious of this conversation. They tail Mark. He knows that he is being followed, but still goes to take pictures of the model Millie above the cigar store. Later, detectives find her dead. Helen enters Mark's flat. She turns on the projector and sees Vivian's murder. Mark returns and confesses his crimes. He shows her the blade on the camera and an attached mirror so victims can see themselves being killed. Police arrive. Mark films them. Then he turns the camera on himself and runs into the blade, seeing his own scared face in the mirror.

Upon its 1960 release, *Peeping Tom* was damned by British newspaper critics like no film in memory. This picture about a filmmaker who murders his subjects as he films them was not merely judged trashy or amoral but was called Sadian, necrophilic, perverted, destructive, a blight on the British cinema. (The most famous quote is Derek Hill's in the *Tribune:* "The only really satisfactory way to dispose of *Peeping Tom* would be to shovel it up and flush it swiftly down the nearest sewer. Even then the stench would remain.") Ironically, director Michael Powell had done more than anyone to establish the proud British film tradition, but suddenly critics were forgetting about such noteworthy achievements as *The Thief of Baghdad* (1940), *The 49th Parallel* (1941), *One of Our Aircraft Is Missing* (1942), *The Life and Death of Colonel Blimp* (1943), *Black Narcissus* (1947), *The Red Shoes* (1948), *The Small Black Room* (1949) and *The Tales of Hoffmann* (1951). Instead, they pointed out what they believed was the first sign of Powell's perversity: when Eric Portman pours glue in a girl's hair in *A Canterbury Tale* (1944). After thirty years as a writer and director, Powell was an outcast in his own country as a result of *Peeping Tom*, and considered unbankable by studio heads. Because of the harsh press, the picture failed miserably, although its backers made a last-ditch effort to make it more "presentable" by excising scenes the critics found objectionable. Unfortunately, it was this badly butchered version that briefly played in United States grind houses in 1962, and for years we Americans waited to see the notorious full-length version that had created such a furor across the Atlantic. Finally, in 1979, chiefly through the efforts of Martin Scorsese, a beautiful uncut 35-mm print was screened at the New York Film Festival and on the art-house circuit. As a result, impressed American critics joined the French and Italians in vindicating a fascinating film that was too far ahead of its time to be appreciated by the British in 1960. (To set the record straight: it was Britain's daily press which, reflecting the attitudes of its readership, lambasted it; trade reviews were much kinder.) It is certainly worth seeing, especially by film devotees. It is full of *cinema* in-jokes,* "looks" more like a "cult film" than any cult film around, and raises some interesting questions about the nature of filmgoers and filmmakers. It's unique and great subject matter for an argument. And it's part of film history.

There are numerous reasons why *Peeping Tom* was greeted with such hostility in England. For one thing it fell under the broad classification of "horror movie,"

---

*While Michael Powell insists that screenwriter Leo Marks (whose name is certainly quite similar to Mark Lewis, the main character) was solely responsible for the thematic content in *Peeping Tom*, film scholars sense Powell's strong personal attachment to the project. He plays Mark's father in the home movies and ran the 16-mm projector himself. Powell's son plays Mark as a child. Characteristically Powell populates his film with red-headed women, including Moira Shearer, the great ballerina who starred in his *The Red Shoes* and *The Tales of Hoffmann*—here she does an odd high-kicking jazz dance. Another Powell favorite, Esmond Knight, plays the director at Mark's studio —strange casting (in a film about voyeurism) since Knight was almost completely blind.

Mark and one of his victims. That Powell strived for a sleazy look to the proceedings is quite evident.

and horror movies had always been in disfavor in that country: horror movies come from a *German* cinema-theater tradition, and Britons have never been keen on letting the genre become part of their culture. In the late fifties a few British-made horror films were released—Jacques Tourneur's *Curse of the Demon* (1958) and Hammer Studios' initial horror efforts, *The Curse of Frankenstein* (1958) and *Horror of Dracula* (1959)—to be given the tag of disrespectability by the daily press (which would become quite receptive to Hammer films a few years later); but prior to this—other than *Dead of Night* (1946)—you will find few British horror films. (Even horror films that were imported from America often were given an "X" certificate, which meant they couldn't be seen by children, and this consequently

limited their bookings.) Of all England's directors, Michael Powell, whose hatred of Nazis is quite visible in his numerous war films, was the only one who allowed German art to enter his work, particularly in his staging, design, and lighting. While no one felt uncomfortable with his quick flights of expressionism in his fantasy films *The Thief of Baghdad, A Matter of Life and Death* (1946), *The Red Shoes,* and *Black Narcissus,* they were disturbed by Powell's nightmarish *Peeping Tom,* which not only looks like a film in the German horror tradition but features a lead character not unlike Peter Lorre in Fritz Lang's German classic *M* (1931).

Equally unsettling in 1959 was that *Peeping Tom* is a *psychological* horror film. Even in America, where horror films had been mass-produced since the twenties,

Mark shows Helen the documentary that his father made of him when he was a child. She is horrified.

only a few dealt with psychological disorders as the basis of murders. Karl Freund's remarkable *Mad Love* (1935), with Peter Lorre, naturally, and the Val Lewton films of the forties are the only pictures that come to mind in which the reasons for the insanity and the process of losing one's mind are more important to the story than the murders the insane men commit. Then, of course, there is a nonhorror movie, Hitchcock's *Strangers on a Train* (1949). But it took his *Psycho* (1960) to really start the wave of psychological thrillers which, twenty years later, is still the dominant type of horror film. But back when *Peeping Tom* was released, critics (especially in England) considered it perverse to have a lead character who is insane. (As in *M*.)

Also making the English critics uneasy was that prior to *Peeping Tom* only a few films in cinema history had dared make the correlation between a person's violent acts and his/her sexual gratification/satisfaction. This was a touchy theme that rarely got by the censors. Powell doesn't try to be subtle in showing that Mark is sexually excited by the murders he commits. Mark may be outwardly calm, but the long, sharp knife that emerges from hiding right before the act of murder immediately "exposes" Mark's sexual frenzy.

In Mark's peculiar case, the murder of a woman does not by itself give him sexual satisfaction. The insertion of the blade into her is a necessary step, but his onanistic "climax" takes place back in his room when he projects her dying expression on his wall. And only when his camera has captured in her face the absolute expression of fear (he is always disappointed/frustrated) can he truly be sexually satisfied. Mark's need to achieve sexual fulfillment through a process which includes murdering young women was hard enough for 1960 British critics to tolerate, but what made it even more difficult was that unlike the other sexual deviants—even the sympathetic Jack the Ripper in *Pandora's Box* and Peter Lorre in *M*—Mark is not presented as a villain. The villain of the piece is Mark's dead father, who used the young Mark as a guinea pig in his mad experiments.

Not only does Powell not condemn Mark for his grisly crimes, but he gets us to like him, even root for him. When there is a point-of-view shot we are Mark's accomplices. But Powell's film is even more jarring to our sensibilities because at times we even *identify* with Mark. By having Mark's "sexual act" take place in two stages—the murder and the screening of the murder—Powell makes the distinction between participation (count us out) and voyeurism (count us in). Both have their own erotic appeal: for instance, one can enjoy active sex and still derive a different pleasure from watching sexual acts from a distance. To Mark, *seeing* is even more exciting than participating. We can relate to Mark's voyeuristic tendencies because like him we moviegoers become entranced by horrible images on the screen. Murders, rapes, even mutilation. This is usually fiction, true, but we even have paid money to see *documentaries* in which real people are killed. (I recall the scandal a few years back when it was rumored that filmmakers on one of those "Mondo" documentaries may have paid off some African natives to kill a man on screen.) Voyeurs like us are in compliance with filmmakers who place brutal pornographic images on the screen for our gratification. Powell won't let us plead innocent.

Powell has several "peeping toms" in his films: in a couple of his thirties pictures there are newspapermen who are snoopers by profession (Mark tells detectives in *Peeping Tom* that he's with the *Observer*); in *A Matter of Life and Death*, friendly Dr. Reeves has a telescopic device which lets him spy on a whole town; in *The Red Shoes,* the Contessa uses binoculars to look at the people watching a ballet performance. Powell equates voyeurism with the violation of another's privacy; he believes that everyone is, by nature, a "peeping tom"/voyeur of sorts. This is only dangerous when voyeurism becomes an obsession, as it does with Mark. And it is particularly dangerous in his case because for him to enjoy his voyeurism to the fullest he must create exciting images to observe. This is where Mark the filmmaker comes in.

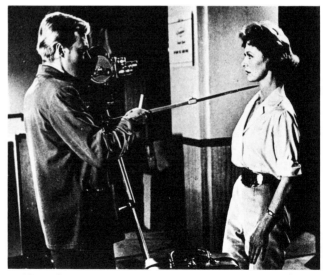

Publicity shot of Mark about to kill Vivian, played by Moira Shearer, the star of Powell's The Red Shoes.

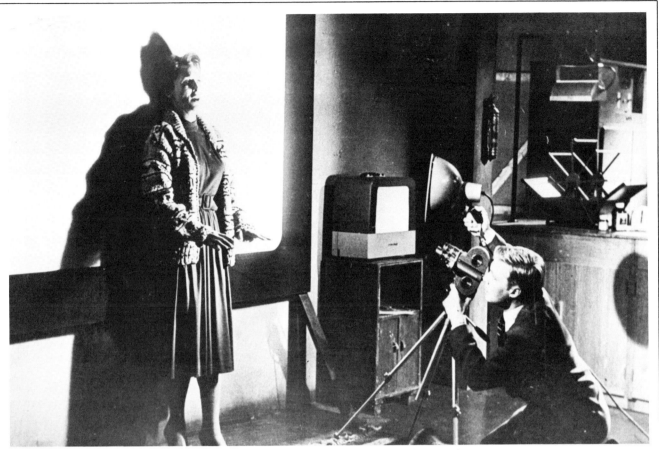

Mark films the Blind Mrs. Stevens, the only person who realizes the seriousness of Mark's mental state.

If the voyeur is guilty of *violating* one's privacy, then Powell sees the filmmaker as being guilty of *rape*. Filming/photographing someone is an aggressive act whereby you capture on film a moment in time (and personal emotions) that the filmed person can never have back. Mark believes that the camera is a lethal weapon. In fact, he promises not to photograph Helen because by doing so he thinks it means he'll kill her. He could kill his victims in countless ways, but he does so with a *knife attached to the camera.* He knows that his father's camera, which deprived him of privacy when he was a child and was always present when his father scared him, is what drove him crazy and what has destroyed him. His death is recorded in his father's films—it is only a matter of time until he is buried.

Powell sees the filmmaker as scientist. With a camera in his hands he is no longer a human being: the only time Mark's father seems kindly is in the home movie which his new wife is shooting; the only time Mark seems like a real person is when he goes out with Helen and leaves his camera home (at her suggestion). Both the filmmaker and the scientist are destructive artists. Both are outcasts. Both are experimenters. Both seek perfection, and to them the end justifies the means. The trouble is that both this filmmaker and this scientist need human guinea pigs. And Mark figures that since his scientist-filmmaker father in effect murdered his "guinea pig," then he, a filmmaker-scientist, has the right to do the same thing when continuing the experiments.

Mark realizes that his father is responsible for his insanity, but he bears him no grudge. The victims he chooses—the prostitute, the actress-dancer, and the nude model—all remind him of the one person he hates: the woman his father married six months after his mother's death. He calls her his "surrogate female," and it is my guess that her presence interfered with the relationship Mark and his father were developing as partners in his father's noxious experiment. All the movies of Mark as a child were perfectly photographed —except for the one out-of-focus moment when *she* stepped behind the camera to film Mark and his father. I think it is more than coincidence that Mark earns his living as a *focus puller* and that when he films his victims he strives for photographic impeccability ("so even *he* will think it perfect"). By having everything in focus, he can prove to his father that he is a better partner than the woman who didn't know how to use a camera. This is why Mark is so upset when Viv's murder is not as well photographed as he had hoped. Of course, Mark's anger is misdirected. Killing women will never satisfy him. Subconsciously, he wants to punish his father. Only through suicide can Mark complete his father's experiment and at the same time show the world that his father was a murderer *in fact*. He is glad he looks frightened when he looks in the mirror attached to the camera. Only now, at the moment of his own death, does he get a glimpse of true fear—an image even his father was unable to capture.

Performance

1970 Great Britain   Warner Bros. release of a Goodtimes Enterprises production.
Directors: Donald Cammell and Nicolas Roeg
Producer: Sanford Lieberson
Screenplay: Donald Cammell
Cinematography: Nicolas Roeg
Music: Jack Nitzsche
Editors: Anthony Gibbs and Brian Smedley-Ashton
Running Time: 106 minutes

Cast: James Fox (Chas), Mick Jagger (Turner), Anita Pallenberg (Pherber), Michele Breton (Lucy), Johnny Shannon (Harry Flowers), Anthony Valentine (Joey Maddocks), Ken Colley (Tony Farrell)

Synopsis: Chas considers his sex life normal although he would just as soon strangle a woman as make love to her. As for his work as a London protection-rackets hood—he performs it with great enthusiasm, beating, terrorizing, humiliating, and killing anyone who puts up any resistance. When Joey Maddocks, a personal enemy, whom he is supposed to be protecting, beats him up, Chas kills him. This does not set too well with Chas's boss Harry Flowers, who sends his men out to kill Chas. Wearing dark glasses, and having dyed his blond hair red, Chas flees the pursuers.

While Chas's friend Tony tries to arrange his safe passage out of the country, Chas finds refuge in a town house owned by Turner, an ex-rock star who has retired and gone into seclusion to find himself. Also living in this house of physical pleasures are Turner's two lovemates, Pherber and Lucy. Turner and the two women become fascinated by the gangster, his gun, and his whip marks, and turn him on to their way of living. In time they have him eating hallucinogenic mushrooms, wearing outlandish wigs and costumes, and willing to make love with each of them. Meanwhile Turner becomes more and more fascinated with Chas, wanting to enter his brain to see what makes him tick, perhaps becoming a gangster like him. As time goes on, the four characters start to mingle, becoming interchangeable.

Eventually Harry Flowers traces Chas to the town house. When Chas realizes that he is trapped and will be taken away and assassinated, he excuses himself for a minute, goes upstairs, and shoots Turner through the brain. Harry's men now take Chas away. Although they don't seem to notice it, Chas now looks exactly like Turner.

Often a movie will leave a viewer with a bitter aftertaste, but *Performance* makes you feel from frame one that someone is resting his dirtiest finger in the back of your throat. For 106 minutes, directors Donald Cammell and Nicolas Roeg bombard you with brutal images—a forced head-shaving that resembles an amputation, a whipping, a beating, a bullet entering a skull—and you feel like gagging, as if somehow you have become Malcolm McDowell strapped to a movie seat in *A Clockwork Orange* (1971), being forced to watch violent images that consequently will nauseate you. *Performance* is an arrogant, needless slap at our viewing sensibilities, an odious, amoral work, its oozing decadence as manifest behind the camera as it is on the screen. That it is a personally successful rendering of a personal vision is probably true, but it certainly is no labor of love.

With the possible exceptions of the best-forgotten *Scent of Mystery* (1960), during which audiences were subjected through Smell-O-Vision to peculiar scents at certain moments in the film; *Beyond the Great Wall* (1959), which treated audiences to AromaRama; and John Waters's *Polyester* (1981), which introduced the audience-participation gimmick Odorama, *Performance* is likely the only picture in history which can be, and has been, discussed in terms of stench. Not surprisingly, it was John Simon who, in his blistering attack on the picture, "The Most Loathsome Film of All," first called attention to the fact that the theaters in which *Performance* was initially shown constantly smelled from viewers' throwing up. And it was Andrew Sarris who, upon having difficulty describing the "feel" of the film, clutched for new cinematic reference points: "If movies had odors, *Performance* would stink, but in a different way." Correct. Aesthetics aside, *Performance* still stinks.

Perhaps by design, each screen image in *Performance* stimulates the viewers sense of smell as much as it

James Fox and Mick Jagger are the stars in this film about decadence.

does his/her senses of sight and hearing. Almost every object (prop) that catches our attention and each setting into which we are taken has the remarkable effect of causing us to recall a familiar odor. So it is that while watching *Performance,* we feel as if we are sniffing, at one time or another, such things as the liquor fumes in the saloon where Harry yells at Chas; the stale air of Chas's underworld of seedy garages, back rooms, and windowless offices; the antiseptic odors of Chas's super-clean, superorderly bachelor apartment; the plants and vegetables in Turner's greenhouse; the ever-accumulating aromatic mixture of sex, sweat, and soap that obviously permeates Turner's large stuffy house as thoroughly as if it were a brothel; and the characteristic smells of the sulfuric acid eating into the body of the Rolls-Royce, the hallucinogenic mushrooms Chas eats, the uneasy red paint-Bryl Cream combination with which Chas dyes his hair, and, for some, the constant smell of blood and death, even perversion. And of course once Chas arrives at Turner's house, we sense the overpowering fragrance of drugs in the air, doubtless a real treat for those viewers who like to burn incense every night. For once, the marijuana we smell in the theater seems to originate on the screen rather than in the audience, and that in itself illustrates the infinite power of the Motion Picture.

Performance was released during the summer of 1970, well over a year after its completion. It had been shelved by Ken Hyman, the head of Warners, when he concluded that no amount of editing, relooping, rescheduling would cover up the fact that the picture ultimately made no sense. However, Ted Ashley, Hyman's successor at Warners, thought *Performance* salvageable—he assumed that any film with rock idol Mick Jagger in various states of undress would have some camp appeal. Ashley was wrong in guessing that the picture would be considered campy—the violence is too strong, the absurd humor too disguised, and Jagger too introverted. But coming at a time when young audiences were into heady, ambitious projects with blaring soundtracks and antisocial characters who turn on to dope and sex at the drop of a director's hat, and into anything Jagger did, *Performance* quickly gained a cult following. This cult has grown with the increased interest in the works of Nicolas Roeg.

The critics were not kind to *Performance,** generally agreeing that without the presence of Jagger and James Fox it would have been unendurable. In 1970, we were curious to see if Jagger's dynamism would transfer to the screen; today, seeing *Performance* (as well as *Ned Kelly,* 1970), we better understand why he didn't click as a movie star. He is withdrawn, awkward, restricted so much that he sings his only song while behind a desk, and is forced to spit out through his swollen red lips such inanities as "I don't like music!" and "The only 'Performance' is one that achieves madness." Fox comes off better, especially in the beginning, when he exhibits a kind of Michael Caine blue-collar toughness, but later,

---

*Among the better critics who have written strong defenses of *Performance* are Roger Greenspun and Bill Nichols.

Vicious Chas delights in turning the tables on the men who beat him up.

when he reaches Turner's town house, he looks stranded among amateurs. It's one thing to have pros Dirk Bogarde and Sarah Miles emasculate Fox in *The Servant* (1963), but he is too strong to succumb to neophytes Jagger and Pallenberg.

Oddly, it is the two women who are the most interesting performers to watch today. The flat-chested Michele Breton may look like the androgynous Jagger, but she may remind some of an early version of Marie Schneider, spunky and sexy. Anita Pallenberg is now a curiosity. Today she is the overweight (in the Diana Dors sense) ex-girl friend of Rolling Stones guitarist Keith Richard, and is known best for being charged for illegal gun possession after a teen-age boy committed suicide in her bed in 1979. But in *Performance* she is beautiful, and probably the film's most energetic performer. Who can forget the scene when the fur-coated Pherber lies down on a bed while talking to Chas, whom she has just met, and begins to fondle the fur just over her otherwise naked crotch? This is definitely one of the most erotic moments in cinema history.

There is much wrong with *Performance:* The unpleasant array of characters, the offensive violence which seems too joyfully orchestrated, and particularly the absence of a comprehensive dramatic structure (often it seems like we are watching the stars backstage, having an orgy between camera setups). The tendency has been to throw the first stone at writer–codirector Donald Cammell for all the problems, and to absolve his highly respected codirector and cinematographer Nicolas Roeg from all blame. But we shouldn't be so quick, for there is much in the film that is definitely characteristic of Roeg. The look of the film with its trick shots, wild crosscutting, quick transitions, great sexual

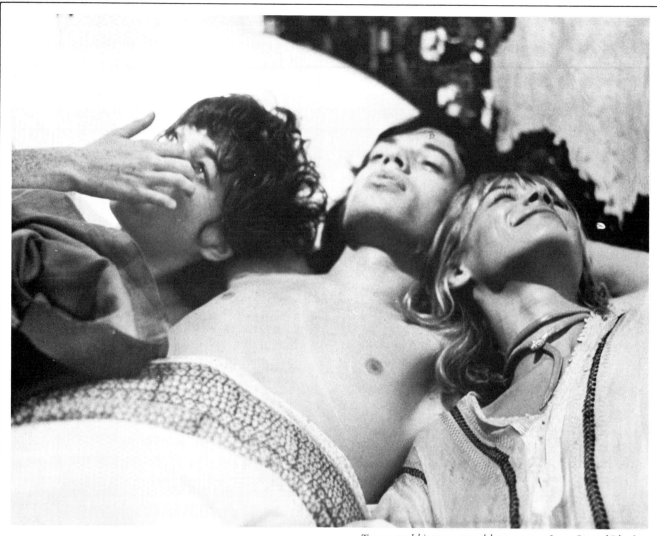

Turner and his two sensual housemates, Lucy (L) and Pherber.

activity, especially around water, and strong emphasis on color (more somber here than in other Roeg films), particularly red, is pure Roeg. In fact, the two major themes of the film are very central to the films Roeg would solo direct, the magnificent, incomparably shot *Walkabout* (1970), *Don't Look Now* (1973), *The Man Who Fell to Earth* (1976), and *Bad Timing* (1980). The first theme is that in today's world the savage (Chas's world) and the gentle (Turner's world) exist side by side. From this theme we arrive at Roeg's second, more important, theme: man must be able to uncover and activate previously latent aspects of his personality (e. g. Chas's homosexuality), thereby discovering his true, complete self, in order to adapt to a new environment.

In *Performance* the only way for Chas and Turner, on the surface as opposite as Attila the Hun and Ravi Shankar, to emerge from their respective funks is by literally *merging*—there is no takeover of one person by the other—in mind and body. Such a merger is possible because, according to the men who made this film, everyone is part violent and part gentle; part male and part female; part "normal" and part "perverted"; part of each other. Such metaphysical concepts can be confusing, even unfilmable, and in the case of *Performance*, they are muddled beyond belief, and repair.

Chas's appearance has begun to change from straight to weird as a result of staying in Turner's house. Pherber and her hallucinogenic mushrooms have much to do with it.

Petulia

1968 Warner Bros.–Seven Arts
Director: Richard Lester
Producer: Raymond Wagner
Screenplay: Lawrence B. Marcus
From the novel *Me and the Arch Kook Petulia,* by John Haase
Cinematography: Nicolas Roeg
Music: John Barry
Editor: Anthony Gibbs
Running Time: 105 minutes

Cast: George C. Scott (Archie Bollen), Julie Christie (Petulia), Richard Chamberlain (David), Arthur Hill (Barney), Shirley Knight (Polo), Pippa Scott (May), Kathleen Widdoes (Wilma), Joseph Cotten (Mr. Danner), Roger Bowen (Warren), The Grateful Dead, Big Brother and the Holding Company, members of The Committee, members of the A.T.C. Company

Synopsis: Archie Bollen is a bored, middle-aged surgeon trying to adjust to single life after a lengthy marriage. He feels guilty about having walked out on his wife Polo and their two sons; and a bit jealous of Warren, the man Polo wants to marry. At a party, Archie meets a screwed-up young married woman named Petulia, who convinces him to have an affair with her. Although she changes her mind about having sex with him that night, she tells Archie that in time she will marry him. Archie and Petulia do have an intense affair, although very little time is spent in bed. He is fascinated by her unpredictability and feels she has pumped new life into him; he can't stop thinking about her. Unbeknownst to Archie, Petulia had planned to "accidentally" meet him. She had seen him perform a successful operation on Oliver, a young Mexican boy for whom she secretly provides. Petulia loves Archie because of his gentle surgeon's hands.

Petulia's husband David once had gentle hands also. But since their marriage six months earlier, he has taken to beating her up. He is frustrated because Petulia has refused to attempt lovemaking with him since he was impotent on their wedding night. He orders her to throw Oliver out of the house, screaming at her, "He's not mine!" When David finds Petulia in Archie's apartment, he brutally beats her. Archie, returning home, finds the badly injured Petulia, bloody and broken. He has her taken to the hospital and watches over her during her long recovery. One day he is horrified to find that she has checked out and gone home with David. He goes to their mansion, but Petulia will not leave with him. Angry and worried about Petulia's welfare, Archie charges off. That night, David promises Petulia that he will never beat her again. Tearfully, he asks her not to expect too much of him, as she did when she married him. Petulia comforts him.

Nine months pass. Polo has married Warren. Petulia is about to have David's baby. In the hospital Archie asks her to come away with him. She says she will, but, as she expected, he changes his mind. Archie leaves the hospital just as the flower-carrying David enters. As another doctor's gentle hand touches her face, she asks hopefully, "Archie?" A mask covers her face, and Petulia is put to sleep for the delivery.

Their affair almost begins when Archie and Petulia slip away from a party and check into a motel.

Petulia is expatriate Richard Lester's shattering vision of America in the late sixties. Despite the presence of George C. Scott and Julie Christie, two of the period's most formidable movie stars, it was sadly neglected, except by cultists who recognized it as one of the only pictures to offer an incisive, though certainly subjective, portrait of a turbulent, important transitional time in American history.* Fortunately, *Petulia*'s critical reputation has improved dramatically to a point where it is rightly considered one of the best American films of the last fifteen years.†

Petulia is a brilliant film, inspiringly cast and beautifully acted, so rich in character and visual and aural detail that it takes several viewings to absorb it all. Lester makes the viewer work to grasp the meaning of his film. The rapid-fire editing is deliberately oblique, with flashbacks—of events which didn't necessarily happen at all—and flashforwards interjected at odd intervals. (This fragmentary filmmaking is characteristic of both Lester, who had his roots in commercials, and cinematographer Nicolas Roeg, who later would use similar editing devices when he became a director.) Lester fills his busy frame and soundtrack with a copious amount of peripheral material—incidental characters, sight gags, throwaway lines—so that on one level his picture comes across as a comical essay on a world gone haywire; but at heart it is something much more: a tragic look at the individuals who must fight a (losing) battle for survival in this zany world. Lester is the baffled, sympathetic outsider examining a culture that has somehow gone awry and which exists solely on the momentum of its own death trip.

To Lester the great American tragedy is that a country founded by a resourceful, enterprising, responsible people of high values and ideals has become so

---

*Renata Adler of *The New York Times* was one of the few major critics to review *Petulia* favorably and include it on 1968's "Ten Best" list.
†In a poll conducted by James Monaco for *Take One* (July 1978), critics voted it the third best American film of 1968–78.

Archie can't totally relax when ex-wife Polo brings Warren to his apartment.

utterly wasteful of money, time, human life, and human potential. On Archie's always-blaring-but-never-watched television, we see that American soldiers fight on endlessly in Vietnam while on the homefront a desensitized nation no longer pays any attention. Patients in anarchic American hospitals are subjected to doctors—Archie is the rare caring doctor—and nurses who have little regard for their welfare. Americans spend their leisure time, and entertainment dollar, going to see roller derbies, trained penguins performing tricks, and a closed-down prison (Alcatraz) that incredulously has been declared a national shrine. The affluent, who *only* have leisure time, buy expensive knickknacks: flashy sports cars, houseboats, private swimming pools, costly clothing, jewelry, and furs— even private, electronic, moving footbridges. Rampant consumerism and ultracommercialism are the signs of the times: we see Porsches raced by uniformed nuns; hideous assembly-line apartment buildings that stretch from the foreground to the horizon; hospital rooms with false-front TV sets meant to stimulate bored, bed-ridden patients into renting the real things; hospital corridors filled with salesmen and film crews; a fresh-air park used as a setting for a cigarette commercial; all-night supermarkets; motel room doors that signal when a guest approaches with the key, so even stoned people can find their way; restaurants that attract male customers by having topless waitresses.

Even people have become commodities. Petulia tells David that the first time she saw him, she decided, "I want one." So when she discovers that David isn't the Ideal (as in toy) man, after all, she wants the "perfect" Archie as a replacement. Characteristically, Petulia takes Oliver out of Mexico as if he were a tourist's souvenir, a Kewpie doll. Then there's Mr. Danner, who voluntarily goes along with the dehumanization, at one point equating himself with the *money* he donates to the hospital. People are defined by their wealth or lack of it, their occupations, and their power.

America's institutions—the army, hospitals, prisons—are shown to be as impotent as David is in bed.

Even the sacred institution of marriage is a casualty of the modern age. In years past, *boredom* would not have been a satisfactory reason for Archie to walk out on his wife and children. In the past, a battered wife was expected to stay with her husband, but Petulia desperately tries to break that tradition and, like Archie, tries to come to terms with the guilt she feels for breaking marital vows, whatever the reasons. Ironically, this modern age requires a *man* to please his female sexual partner, and it is this requirement that resulted in the intimidated David's impotency—and a chain reaction which inadvertently led David from frustration to the sadism that caused Petulia to desire an exit from their marriage.

It is as if the globe were spinning too fast and America fell off, and when someone put it back, it ended up a little off center. There is a sense that everything is out of whack, that there is no equilibrium, no solid footing, no foundation. (It is proper that *Petulia* was filmed in San Francisco, near the San Andreas fault, where everyone nervously waits for the inevitable earthquake.) And there stands Petulia, a symbol of the shaky times: miniskirted, on wobbly legs. She is that proverbial moth drawn to a flame, aware of its doom but too weary of life to resist. Her face is stoical, but her sad eyes give one the impression that she has lost something irretrievable, as if she were a boxer who blew that one chance for the crown and sees ahead a downhill road to oblivion. Perhaps it is her innocence that she wants back—but it is not an innocence that has to do with youth or virginity: her "innocence" refers to a time when she wasn't capable of hurting anyone, to the moment before she and David climbed into bed on their wedding night. Like everyone else in the film, she looks hopelessly dazed, or in her case, punchdrunk, as if she suddenly woke up to find that her life had inexplicably changed. Six months ago she entered her marriage with

Whereas Polo was predictable, Petulia is so unpredictable that she wakes up Archie by bringing him a tuba.

Archie cannot convince Petulia to leave David for him.

great optimism, but her gentle husband has become brutal, and now she wants out of the marriage, to marry Archie, whom she has just met, and to adopt Oliver.

Likewise, Archie's world is changing too swiftly for him to get his bearings. A little while ago, he was living an ordered, happy life with his wife and children. There has been no fight between him and Polo, and they still have much love for each other; yet here he is living alone and lonely, in a bachelor apartment, while Warren has taken his place with Polo and his kids. And as if that weren't enough to sort out, the middle-aged Archie finds himself already deeply involved with Petulia, from the "Pepsi generation," whom he has just met, and who insists, convincingly, that she will marry him once both she and he get their divorces. Even Archie's supposedly happily married friends Barney and Wilma contemplate a separation. Nothing makes sense.

The characters in *Petulia* are all in the process of reworking their lives, while being subjected to many discordant pressures that take their toll. Their marriages are all breaking up or are in jeopardy, but they don't have the time or breathing space to figure out which direction their lives should take, and with whom. They try not to confuse love and loyalty, love and desire. No scene better illustrates the overpowering *disorientation* the characters feel than the magnificent sequence when Polo visits Archie's apartment for the first time. It is remarkable for how many times, and how quickly, the two characters switch roles with each other: from being an aggressor to a human target, manipulator to manipu-

lated, bitch/bastard to comforter, mother/father to child. Every time one of them lets his/her defenses down, the other delivers a low blow; every time one of them makes a concession to the other, he/she gets burned. This scene is shot with many close-ups, including some gems of the bewildered Shirley Knight and of the intruded-upon George C. Scott, about to lose his temper and hurl Polo's cookies at her back. In a few minutes, much is revealed about their relationship, past and present; most importantly, we are witness to the vulnerability each has, and see that each is aware that the other person can damage him or her severely. Even nice people like Archie and Polo can be insensitive, and cruel; thus their defensive attitudes, and their quick retreats once one of them has favorably responded to the other's love baiting. Their feelings for each other are always in conflict. It is the same with Archie and Petulia. At the beginning, Petulia seduces Archie but backs off once Archie is ready to make love. At the conclusion, Archie tells Petulia that they can always be together if she gives him the word, but he changes his mind when she agrees to this proposal, and he bids her a final farewell (a rare instance when a film doesn't go along with a book's happy ending).

The characters in *Petulia* are afraid of commitment, and with good reason. They have been that route before, and know that with commitment comes pain. Lester intentionally keeps the Vietnam War in the background as a reminder that American violence is everywhere, but his film is about the "casual violence," as he termed it,

The picture's strange final shot: Petulia, who loved Archie because of his gentle hands, holds the hand of the doctor who is about to put her to sleep prior to her baby being delivered. "Archie?" she asks hopefully.

that invariably occurs when two people enter a relationship in our topsy-turvy society. Every character in *Petulia* is hurt at one time or another by one of the other characters. This is bad enough, but what really damages them is that they themselves cause others anguish. All these characters share one trait: guilt. Petulia blames David neither for being sexually impotent nor for beating her up; instead, she blames herself for ruining him, correctly believing that she put so much pressure on him to be a perfect sexual partner that he was unable to perform in bed, wrongly believing that her subsequent mishandling of their sexual problems justified his beating her up. The only reason she decides against leaving David for Archie is that she doesn't want any more guilt. She tells David, "You were the gentlest man I ever knew. . . . I would have turned his [Archie's] hands into fists."

In the novel Petulia tells Archie, "I'd hate to have an affair with an unmarried man. I think there ought to be some equality of guilt." She needn't have worried—there is enough guilt to go around. Archie feels guilty for walking out on his wife and kids; Polo, for remarrying and still asking Archie for alimony; Archie's sons, for having a good time with Warren; David, for beating up Petulia; Barney and Wilma, for considering a divorce. Lester sees the whole of America as decadent, but his characters feel remorse because they are *moral* people.

Archie and Petulia constantly test each other and themselves by engaging in fast, convoluted conversations. When Myrna Loy and William Powell trade quips, each is confident that the other will have a comeback line ready. They have fun with their witty chatter. Archie and Petulia, on the other hand, are not so at ease with their sophisticated dialogue; in fact, they seem to be treading a highwire which has room for only one. Still, it is vital that they impress one another. Petulia realizes that what Archie needs is an unpredictable woman; someone quite unlike Polo. So she brings him a tuba, which, according to the novel, the predictable Polo definitely would have made into a flower pot. Archie considers himself a predator, so Petulia keeps him off balance by constantly ambushing him. She is a liar, and a sexual tease, and the confusion she causes the genteel Archie drives him to distraction and keeps him hopelessly interested in her. Petulia, to win Archie, must make herself seem more exciting than she really is. This is very integral to Lester's characters: they all are their own rivals. When Archie finds out that Petulia will only have an affair with a married man, he quickly reassures her that his divorce isn't final yet. Polo tells Archie that they were a perfect couple *because they never fought*—only to have him respond that "not fighting" has nothing to do with being compatible. Here being *too good* is bad.

Nobody in this film is able to realize his or her potential because they all try to meet the expectations of those people whom they love. David's pleaful words to Petulia, said just before their initial attempt at lovemaking on their wedding night, is the lesson that all the characters in *Petulia* must learn: "I can't compete with myself."

Pink Flamingos

1973   New Line Cinema
release of Saliva Films
Production
Director: John Waters
Producer: John Waters

Screenplay: John Waters
Cinematography: John Waters
Music: Not original
Editor: John Waters
Running Time: 95 minutes

Cast: Divine (Divine, a.k.a. Babs Johnson), David Lochary (Raymond Marble), Mink Stole (Connie Marble), Mary Vivian Pearce (Cotton), Edith Massey (Mama Edie), Danny Mills (Crackers), Channing Wilroy (Channing), Cookie Mueller (Cookie), Paul Swift (eggman), Susan Walsh (first kidnaped woman), Linda Olgeirson (second kidnaped woman)

Synopsis: Three-hundred-pound Divine, a.k.a. Babs Johnson, lives in a trailer with her demented Mama Edie, who has an egg fixation, her moronic son Crackers, and the pretty Cotton, who tells Edie stories about eggs and watches Crackers have perverse sex in the shed out back. Divine is popularly acknowledged as "the filthiest person in the world," which makes Raymond and Connie Marble jealous. They think they deserve the title because they invest in pornography, sell heroin in elementary schools, and kidnap young women, have their butler Channing forcibly impregnate them, and sell their babies—while Divine is simply a whore and a murderer. The Marbles hire Cookie to spy on Divine by allowing Crackers to have sex with her. She screams and cries while Crackers makes love to her with a live chicken placed between their two bodies, but learns that Divine will be having a birthday party. The Marbles send Divine a birthday present: a one-year-old turd with a card that says that they are the filthiest people in the world. Horrified, Divine swears that she will out-filthy the Marbles and then murder them.

Divine has a birthday party, during which Edie marries the eggman, who promises to feed her one hundred eggs a day. The Marbles inform the police that a truly disgusting party is taking place, but when the police arrive they are ambushed and eaten by Divine's guests.

Divine and Crackers go to the Marbles' house and curse it by licking all the furniture and spitting and rubbing themselves all over everything. They find Channing in a closet, where the Marbles have locked him for dressing in Connie's clothes. They turn Channing over to the two pregnant women they find in the basement, who then castrate him.

The Marbles burn down Divine's trailer. They return home to find that their furniture has rejected them. Divine and Crackers, angry that their home is just ashes, capture the Marbles. In front of reporters, Divine ties up the Marbles, who have already been tarred and feathered. She answers questions about herself and shoots her captives.

Divine, Crackers, and Cotton decide to move to Boise, Idaho. Divine eats dog excrement and proves herself to be the world's filthiest person.

As a high school student, director John Waters—"the King of Sleaze"—used to see Divine standing on a Baltimore street corner, having a different hair color every day. Naturally when he started making movies with odd types from Baltimore, Waters picked Divine to be his star. He is unforgettable as Babs Johnson in Pink Flamingos.

Sometime back John Waters—an NYU film school dropout who lives in Baltimore—must have gotten the notion that he'd like to make films that are so disgusting and sexually perverse that critics couldn't write about them without seeming like absolute perverts to their readers for having sat through them. And he accomplished just that. Influenced perhaps by Warhol, Buñuel, Dali, and the funny side of Rasputin, Waters wrote, directed, produced, filmed, and edited a series of outrageous no-holds-barred 16-mm and 35-mm "comedies" full of repulsive images, abominable behavior, and grotesque characters that are unique in cinema history. No doubt the most despicable and famous of Waters's stock company is a round-headed, three-hundred-pound bald loudmouth in drag who uses the name "Divine," compliments of Waters. It is safe to say that the cults for Waters and Divine—consisting of college kids, dropouts from both school and society, and connoisseurs of decadence wherever it might be found—have developed simultaneously with each release of their many collaborations: *Eat Your Make-Up* (1968), *Multiple Maniacs* (1970), *The Diane Linkletter Story* (c. 1971), *Mondo Trasho* (1969), *Female Trouble* (1974), and *Polyester* (1981).

Waters and Divine made it to the big time with *Pink Flamingos*. Waters's first color film was made in Baltimore for twelve thousand dollars and has since grossed several million dollars as an underground favorite and a blockbuster hit on the Midnight Movie circuit. Waters termed this film "a trip through decadence" and promoted it as "the most disgusting picture of all time," a claim that is confirmed in the final moments when Divine proves she is indeed the "world's filthiest person" by really truly eating dog excrement on the screen (and smiling yet). In a weird interview with Lisa Hoffman for the short-lived media newspaper *Image* (Spring 1977), Divine talked in part about his/her role in *Pink Flamingos*. To provide special insight into something or other, that section is excerpted (and edited) here:

LISA HOFFMAN: You have a reputation . . . of being the filthiest person.

DIVINE: No, I just play the part in *Pink Flamingos.* . . . I think I'm the furthest person from that image.

L.H.: What you did in it . . . rather shocked me. . . . Couldn't you refuse to do it?

D.: I'm not into being difficult or bitching or any of those things, I like to be easygoing.

L.H.: But it's not being bitchy, refusing to eat dog shit!

D.: Well, I thought about it and checked with doctors and things and they said it really wouldn't hurt me or do anything to me. It was strictly done for shock value. I threw up afterward, and then I used mouth-wash and brushed my teeth. There was no aftertaste of anything. I just forgot about it as quickly as I could.

L.H.: Would you mind telling me a little about yourself, beginning with your early childhood.

D.: Well, I grew up in the suburbs of Maryland, in an upper middle class family, an only child.

L.H.: What was your name?

D.: Glenn . . .

Actually, Divine is not bad as an actress or, better, a comedienne. And she's certainly no more disgusting than the egg-eating Edith Massey as Mama Edie. Now Edith Massey, who is equally obnoxious as the per-verted queen in Waters's *Desperate Living* (1977), is one actress who, I have to admit, makes me sick. As for the other stars of *Pink Flamingos:* they're not bad; they can't act, of course, but they can overact, and this contributes to the intentional campiness of the whole affair. They are a strange conglomeration of characters, to say the least, the type Warhol's Superstars and flies (and lice) would look on as genuine trash.

The film is imaginative and at times witty. It's so ridiculous and crude that you laugh despite yourself. The premise, itself, is kind of intriguing. Divine and her family versus the Marbles in a battle to prove who is indeed worthy of the title "The World's Filthiest." Waters lets us decide as he switches back and forth between two camps as if he were at a Ping-Pong match, not cutting away until the participants do something mean or act like pigs.

At the beginning, in the trailer, Edie wakes up in her crib and demands eggs; Babs appears in a hideous dress that emphasizes her obesity, wearing bright red lipstick and blue eye makeup. Switch to the Marbles' home. Connie Marble turns down a job applicant who gave up her job because Connie promised her a position; when the upset girl asks her what she's supposed to do now that she has no job, Connie tells her "You can eat shit for all I care" and philosophizes, "There are two

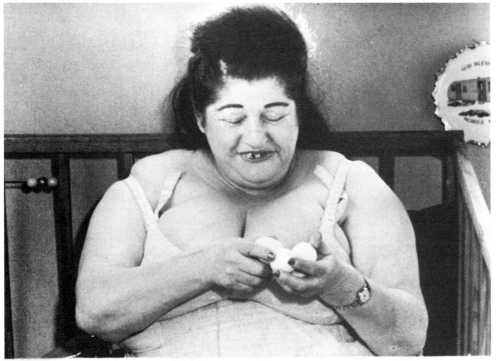

Baltimore legend Edith Massey, a Waters regular, is revolting as the egg-loving Mama Edie.

Raymond and Connie Marble claim to be "the world's filthiest people." But Divine will prove them wrong.

kinds of people: my kind and assholes." Switch. Babs and Crackers drive to town; they laugh as they almost run over a jogger and fool a hitch-hiking soldier into thinking they are giving him a lift. Switch. Connie sells two women a baby named Noodles; we learn that she kidnaps young women and locks them in the basement, has her butler Channing impregnate them, and sells their babies after the sometimes-fatal childbirth. Switch.

In a grocery store, Babs steals a slab of meat and puts it in her crotch; she then struts to the ritzy part of town and defecates on a lawn. Switch. Raymond, who has blue hair, exposes himself to two young women in a park; when they see a wiener dangling from his penis, they run off and he steals the purses they leave behind. Switch. Cookie, the Marbles' spy, meets Edie, who is asleep and snoring with egg all over her face; then she degrades herself by allowing Crackers to make love to her with a chicken dying between their two bodies and Cotton watching through a window. Switch. Raymond kidnaps a new girl and throws her into the basement, where Channing masturbates and inserts his sperm into the screaming girl's vagina while the pregnant girl already there vomits; upstairs the Marbles (she in men's underwear) suck on each other's toes and say they love each other more than original sin itself. Switch.

Babs cooks the meat she stole and Edie eats eggs when the mailman arrives and Babs threatens to break his neck; Babs opens up her birthday present and utters one of the funniest lines in cinema history, "Someone has sent me a bowel movement," whereupon Crackers

tells her, "Mama, no one sends you a turd and expects to live!" Switch. The Marbles lock Channing in a closet after discovering him wearing Connie's clothes and imitating her. Switch. Edie and the eggman, who has steam coming from his mouth, kiss and discuss marriage—this is, I think, the scene that audiences find hardest to watch. Babs has a birthday party and gets a meat cleaver, and the guests act like the degenerates they are: the police arrive but the guests kill them and eat them. Switch. Raymond exposes himself to a woman in the park but she turns out to be a hermaphrodite and he runs away in disgust. Switch.

In what I think is the most hilarious scene in the film (actually the only *hilarious* scene), Babs and Crackers come to the Marbles house and curse it by rubbing their bodies all over the furniture and licking and spitting on everything they see, getting special pleasure performing their ritual in the room in which the Marbles eat: they become so excited that Babs performs fellatio on her son, who says "Do my balls, Mama" but is upset when she stops before he's climaxed. They discover Channing and the kidnaped women in the basement, and allow them to castrate him. Switch. The Marbles burn down Divine's trailer. Finally the Marbles and Divine come together. Angry that their trailer has been burned down, Divine and Crackers take the Marbles prisoners and, in front of representatives from *The Tattler*, *Confidential*, and *Midnight*, execute them. The rivalry is over, and all that remains is for Divine to eat dog-doo.

As I have said, I think Waters and Company are funny. But there is something about Waters's work I don't trust. I find Waters awfully fascinated by castrations, torture, rape, horrible executions, pain, perversion, foul language, blood, meanness, and fire (on which his camera lingers in *Pink Flamingos*). I don't believe any of this is included in his work solely for shock value but rather to amuse those in the audience with sick fantasies. I don't think Waters is a perverted fascist, but I believe his trying-to-be-funny style calls for him to make films as if he *were* a perverted fascist with a camera. There is something scary about the *Saturday Night Live*–"Mr. Bill" mentality that equates anything shocking, rude, or considered offensive by the average citizen with *hip humor*—especially scenes that depict pain, destruction of property, and extreme violence. "Filth are my politics," Divine ("I am God") tells reporters. "Killing and blood make me come." This fascist attitude is meant to be outrageous, but it's not funny; it is as revolting as Crackers bloodying the chicken during sex with Cookie and as disturbing as Divine's party guest wearing a Nazi insignia on her jacket. During a time when youth violence for kicks is on the upswing, when many young people equate being against the system with admiring Hitler—witness the increase in Nazi graffiti and cross burnings—whom they know nothing about except that their elders despise him, much of the cinema of John Waters is irresponsible.

Divine assassinates the Marbles and proclaims herself God. As Waters contends, his films are popular with the "hate generation."

Plan 9 from Outer Space

Also known as *Grave Robbers from Outer Space*

1956 DCA (Distributors Corporation of America)
Director: Edward D. Wood, Jr.
Producer: Edward D. Wood, Jr.
Screenplay: Edward D. Wood, Jr.
Cinematography: William C. Thompson
Music: Gordon Zahler
Running Time: 79 minutes

Cast: Bela Lugosi (The Ghoul Man), Vampira (The Ghoul Woman), Tor Johnson (Police Inspector Clay), Criswell (himself), Gregory Walcott (Jeff Trent), Mona McKinnon (Paula Trent), Lyle Talbot (General Roberts), Tom Keene (Colonel Tom Edwards), Dudley Manlove (Eros), Joanna Lee (Tanna), John Breckinridge (The Ruler)

Synopsis: An old man attends his wife's funeral. Afterward, when the mourners have gone home, a flash from an electrode gun from a passing flying saucer brings her back to life as The Ghoul Woman. She attacks the gravediggers. The grieving old man is run over by a car. At his funeral, a woman notices the dead bodies of the gravediggers. The police come to the cemetery. Inspector Clay investigates. The Ghoul Woman kills him. Meanwhile the dead old man has risen from his grave as The Ghoul Man. Clay is buried. "The bell has rung upon his great career."

Flying saucers travel over Hollywood Boulevard. Others attack Washington. Colonel Tom Edwards repels an invading force. He visits General Roberts at the Pentagon, who admits that, despite government statements, the existence of UFOs has been substantiated. Edwards is sent to the San Fernando Valley, where saucers have been spotted.

Commercial airlines pilot Jeff Trent is disturbed because he was ordered by the government to hush up the fact he spotted a flying saucer. Back home in San Fernando, where he lives with his wife Paula near the cemetery, he tells Paula what he saw. He then goes off on a trip.

The leader of the aliens tells Eros and Tanna that earthlings have failed to acknowledge their existence. They are to begin Plan 9 and revive the dead on earth to attack the living. They speed back toward earth. The Ghoul Man enters Paula's bedroom. To escape she runs through the cemetery. The Ghoul Woman and Clay, who has risen from his grave, attack her. She reaches the highway and is safe.

Edwards and a police lieutenant visit Jeff and Paula on their patio to discuss flying saucers. The Ghoul Man attacks policeman Calvin, but dies when a light flashes in the distance. Everyone decides to investigate the light. They drive to the cemetery. Paula remains in the car. Eros and Tanna send Clay to get her. He knocks out a policeman and snatches her from the car. She faints.

Eros opens up the spaceship door so Jeff, Edwards, and the lieutenant can enter. He tells them that earth must be destroyed because its people are so stupid, headstrong, and violent that they will build a solarite bomb that will blow up the entire universe. Jeff slaps him. Eros shows them a television monitor which reveals Clay holding Paula. He threatens that Paula will be killed on his command. But two policemen sneak up behind Clay and knock him out. Eros tries to revive him by turning on the ship's electrode device but Jeff prevents him from doing so. They fight and Jeff beats up Eros. The ship catches fire. The earthlings escape, the ship explodes in the air, and Eros and Tanna are killed.

Paula is revived. Clay is "dead" and the men expect to find The Ghoul Woman "dead" elsewhere.

Narrator Criswell swears he has presented a true story. "God help us in the future!"

As if there were a foul odor in the air, everyone looks at one another to determine who is responsible. Colonel Edwards (L), the Lieutenant (with a gun pointed at his foot), and Paula and Jeff Trent are among those standing awkwardly in the graveyard, perhaps waiting for the director to return to the set.

How bad is it? Well, *Plan 9 from Outer Space* has the distinction of being elected, by an overwhelming margin, "The Worst Film of All Time" in a recent reader's poll conducted by Harry and Michael Medved for their book *The Golden Turkey Awards* (Perigee, 1980). If you see it, it's unlikely you will argue that any film is worse—although I seem to recall a film about a six-foot-six eleven-year-old with a beard . . . In an era when bad-film freaks have come out of the woodwork and really awful films are looked on with affection, *Plan 9* is revered by a large and growing cult who note that it has moved beyond camp—a category reserved for films so bad they make you laugh smugly—to legend status. How bad is it? (It's inspired title should give you some clue.) Well, it's so bad that it borders on the ludicrous. To think that such an inept, *berserk* picture exists truly boggles the mind.

Plan 9 was directed by the idiosyncratic Edward "Eddie" D. Wood, Jr., a legend in his own right, who was selected "The Worst Director of All Time" in the Medved book. According to the Medveds, Wood was a transvestite who characteristically wore women's pantsuits, high heels, panty hose, and angora sweaters on the set; and who, as a World War II marine, landed on an enemy beach wearing a bra and panties under his uniform. In fact, one of his films deals with a transvestite theme: *Glen or Glenda* (1952), also titled *I Changed My Sex*, a picture that is now earning a cult of its own. Other Wood films include *Bride of the Monster* (1953), *Jail Bait* (1954), *Night of the Ghouls* (1960), and several 8-mm hard-core "educational" sex films. (He also earned a living in his later years writing pornography.) The only thing that distinguishes his films, besides their shameless cheapness in subject matter and production values, is that Wood's good, loyal friend Bela Lugosi—by this time a recovered drug addict mocked by Hollywood—made some of his last appearances in them. They were working on another film, called *Tomb of the Vampire*, when Lugosi died, but a couple of years later Wood took the two minutes of Lugosi footage and used it in *Plan 9*, hiring his wife's chiropractor to be Lugosi's double. Since there were no lines to be spoken, the chiropractor didn't have to worry that he was the only person in Hollywood who couldn't do Lugosi's accent, but since he looked nothing like Lugosi, he was required to hold a cape over his face whenever he appeared on the screen (and maybe whenever he appeared on the set). As for Lugosi: he appears

Director Wood has Tor Johnson and Vampira walk through the woods numerous times in their roles as the dead Inspector Clay and the Ghoul Woman.

at his wife's funeral scene at the beginning of *Plan 9;* then we see him stumbling out of the house he once shared with his wife and looking around (probably for the director) while narrator Criswell bemoans "the sky to which he once looked was only a covering to *her* dead body" and "the flowers were nothing more than the lost roses of her cheeks." Lugosi then walks out of the frame and we hear him being run over—it should've been Criswell. The real Lugosi also appears in footage used later in the film: in his Dracula cape for the last time, he sneaks into what is supposed to be the Trents' home and, in a scene repeated at least five times (to make it seem Lugosi has a substantial part), he emerges from the woods, walks to a tombstone, spreads his cape for the camera, and goes back into the woods. The cape scenes seem to come from the scuttled vampire movie—the two earlier scenes do not. (Were Wood and Lugosi actually making *two* films at the time of Lugosi's death?)

Famous, but inaccurate, television psychic Criswell, another good friend of Wood's, serves as narrator of the early non-dialogue scenes containing Lugosi and, equally important, speaks directly to us in a prologue and epilogue. With all the conviction of a Billy Graham, he tells us that *Plan 9* is based on the "sworn testimony" of "miserable souls who survived the ordeal of . . . graverobbers from outer space." ("Can you prove it didn't happen?" he asks us.) After telling us the film story already happened, he adds: "Future events like these will affect you in the future." At the end of the film, he rises: "God help us in the future!" This man belongs in a booby hatch.

Another Wood friend, four-hundred-pound (and ugly) Tor Johnson, a Swedish ex-wrestler, plays Inspector Clay. He appeared in several cheapie horror films in the fifties—and an exciting *Peter Gunn* television episode I still remember—but this is the only time I recall where he was trusted with dialogue. He is no Leslie Howard. My favorite moments with Tor are when he rises from his grave and has trouble lifting his heavy

frame off the ground, and when he starts strangling Eros for no reason—as if he had misread the script.

Vampira, a long-haired beatnik with no waist, is a fine addition to Wood's acting stable. She was the popular hostess of a late-night-horror-movie series on Los Angeles television in the fifties, and her looks remind me a great deal of Carol Borland, Lugosi's costar in Tod Browning's *Mark of the Vampire* (1935)—except that Borland has screen presence and Vampira just looks like she has anorexia. Vampira has no dialogue in the picture and is required to do nothing but walk around the woods and cemetery with her arms outstretched like a sleepwalker. She murders Clay and the gravediggers off screen and Wood doesn't even have her die on screen—I guess the budget didn't allow her a death scene, so she just disappears. It may interest her fans to know that at a 1980 screening of *Plan 9* at a Los Angeles theater (which sold *Plan 9* T-shirts in the lobby) Vampira made a personal appearance.

Other members of the cast are not so distinguished, with the exception of veteran character actor Lyle Talbot, who has a minor part, and Joanna Lee, who is now one of television's best scriptwriters. Their performances are adequate, but otherwise the acting is atrocious—although, for some reason, the actors seem to be inspired.

As bad as it is, *Plan 9* is, except for about a hundred dull spots, a lot of fun. Nowhere have you seen such terrible, cheap sets: the cemetery with cardboard tombstones (including one which topples over); the airplane cockpit that doesn't have a control panel or steering equipment, just two chairs and a blanket across a doorway (the type of set used by improv groups); and the Trent house, where the same flimsy furniture is found in the bedroom and on the patio (where it is blown down by passing saucers). You want laughs? Notice how police cars always zoom across the screen from right to left; how in one shot it's night and in the next shot it's day; how the flying saucers look like chinaware flung into the air (they are actually *paper* plates!); how the saucers, for some reason, fly past NBC, ABC, and CBS; how Jeff goes off on a several-day trip with a teeny overnight bag; how "Plan 9" swings into action (at the alien leader's command) when, in actuality, this plan to revive the dead has already been completed; how everyone fails to respond while The Ghoul Man (the chiropractor) strangles Officer Calvin in front of their eyes; how the dead Clay, who carries Paula, walks and walks and walks to the spaceship but never arrives, although it took Trent, the lieutenant, and Edwards a matter of seconds to get there; how Eros and Tanna allow the earthlings into their spaceship although they have no defense against them. More laughs? Try

the incomparable dialogue. After a battle with flying saucers, a soldier asks Colonel Edwards: "Are you worried about them, sir?" When Clay is found murdered, quick-thinking detectives deduce: "Inspector Clay's dead. Murdered. And somebody's responsible!" The Medveds quote much of the dialogue in their book, but they missed one of my favorite exchanges; two men discuss how brash Paula wants to go with them to investigate the aliens:

> "Modern women!"
> "Yeah, they've been like that through the ages . . . especially in a spot like this."

Plan 9 is a delirious movie, but perhaps we are missing the point. Could it be that putting up a crazy facade is the only way that Wood can get away with making a *subversive* movie? Remember: this is the radical, iconoclastic director who promoted transvestism beneath the sensationalism of *Glen or Glenda* and

Horror icon Bela Lugosi, in his last role.

protested the arms race (when other directors kept silent) by ending *Bride of the Monster* with a nuclear explosion. All through *Plan 9* there are inferences that the United States government is wrongly keeping facts from the American public in regard to UFOs when what the aliens have to say may be beneficial to mankind. Jeff is upset he can't report the flying saucer he sighted. Likewise, Colonel Edwards is peeved that the destruction of an entire town has been covered up (how does one cover up such a thing?) and that there is a government directive stating flying saucers are just a rumor—despite the fact that the government has received radio messages ("How can a race be so stupid?" the aliens ask politely) from space. The really peculiar thing about *Plan 9* which film historians have overlooked completely is that, when Eros confronts earthlings Trent, Edwards, and the lieutenant, only the fact that he has a diabolical laugh and a lot of conceit covers up that what he says to them makes sense. Eros is concerned with the future of the universe and his message to the earthlings is that they should get off their destructive course, which will lead them to blow up that universe. Eventually earthlings will learn how to harness sun particles and build solarite bombs that, when detonated, will start a chain reaction and destroy all the sun's planets. After the atom and hydrogen bombs, Eros says, this is the logical course. Eros is for peace, and women like Tanna are

meant "to advance [a] race," he says, "not destroy it." When Eros calls earthlings stupid, headstrong, and violent, Jeff is so insulted that he—characteristically—reacts in a stupid, headstrong, and violent way (although he doesn't realize he proves Eros's point): he slaps Eros, who responds that earthlings "make no use of the mind that God gave you." The fact that these aliens believe in God is further proof that Eros is Wood's spokesman—the film's one voice of reason/logic—and Jeff and Edwards, whom we mistakenly accept as heroes, turn out to be brutish jerks who rely on the fist and the gun. Don't let the fact that Eros is a maniac throw you off—at rare moments, he is as sound a visionary as is Preacher Casey in *The Grapes of Wrath* (1940). Wood just had to make Eros crazy to camouflage his political message so that he wouldn't have trouble with censors. I believe that in this one scene (in the spaceship), in this one godawful, terribly made, poor excuse for a picture, Edward D. Wood is more critical of America's government and military strategy (that calls for an arms build-up and further nuclear experiments) than any other director dared to be. (Better directors who made pictures that made sense couldn't get away with such pointed criticism of American institutions.) *Plan 9*, dreadful as it is, is something far more significant, and therefore better, than "The Worst Film of All Time" could possibly be.

Eros wipes away the blood trickling from his mouth while the Lieutenant keeps him at bay. Joanna Lee, who plays Tanna, has climbed up from these depths to become one of the top writers of TV movies.

Pretty Poison

1968 20th Century-Fox
Director: Noel Black
Producers: Marshal Backler and Noel Black
Screenplay: Lorenzo Semple, Jr.
From a novel by Stephen Geller
Cinematography: David Quaid
Music: Johnny Mandel
Editor: William Ziegler
Running Time: 89 minutes

Cast: Anthony Perkins (Dennis Pitt), Tuesday Weld (Sue Ann Stepanek), Beverly Garland (Mrs. Stepanek), John Randolph (Azenauer), Dick O'Neill (Mr. Munsch), Clarice Blackburn (Mrs. Bronson), Joseph Bova (Pete), Ken Kercheval (Harry).

Synopsis: When he was a young boy, Dennis Pitt was caught by his aunt playing "doctor" with a little girl. She beat him with sticks. He later set fire to those sticks and burned down her house, not knowing she was in it at the time (he claimed). After many years in an institution and much therapy, Dennis is placed on probation. Azenauer, his probation officer, gets him a job with a lumber company.

Dennis lives in a trailer by Bronson's Garage. He works at the lumber company and takes many pictures of the operation with his "spy-like" camera. He is attracted to a pretty high school majorette named Sue Ann Stepanek. She becomes interested in him when he tells her he is with the CIA and that he is investigating the lumber company, which is being used by a foreign power to pollute the water supply. Sue Ann agrees to help Dennis, which he tells her means she must make love to him to prove her loyalty. She gladly does so.

Sue Ann tells Dennis that she feels trapped by her strict mother, who won't let her go out most nights. When Mrs. Stepanek meets Dennis and catches him lying about who he is, she won't allow Sue Ann to date him. But Sue Ann defies her mother.

Dennis and Sue Ann go to the lumber mill—from where Dennis has been fired. They start to unscrew the bridge supports from which the pollutants flow into the water. The guard discovers them. Dennis becomes terrified, but Sue Ann is calm. She kills the guard by striking him many times with a pair of large pliers. Then she places his body under the bridge.

While investigation of the guard's death takes place, and Dennis is placed under suspicion, Sue Ann and Dennis make plans to flee to Mexico and get married. They go to Sue Ann's house so she can pack. Her mother comes home. Sue Ann tells Dennis to kill her with the gun she stole from the guard. Dennis can't do it and becomes sick. Sue Ann gleefully shoots her mother herself and sends Dennis to dump the corpse in the river.

Dennis drives to the river, but instead of throwing in the body, he calls the police and turns himself in. When the angry policemen bring him to the station, Sue Ann is there telling other cops that Dennis had led her on and had killed the guard and her mother. They believe her. Dennis doesn't protest her lies. He shouts to her that he still loves her.

A year later, Azenauer visits Dennis in prison. He does not believe Dennis is guilty of the crimes. Dennis tells him that no one would have believed him if he told the true story. He speaks of a pretty poison that will soon spread so even the blindest person can see it—he tells Azenauer to keep his eye on Sue Ann.

Sue Ann meets Harry, a young worker at the lumber company. She tells him that the people she lives with don't let her out at night. They start planning how to rectify this situation. Azenauer sits in his car watching them.

Dennis gets Sue Ann to become interested in him by pretending to be a government agent. Here he secretly gives her a vial containing damaging evidence against the lumber company—or so he says.

One of the few still-sparkling gems of the late sixties, *Pretty Poison* boasts not only a clever, thought-provoking script by Lorenzo Semple, Jr., and a most impressive, unpretentious debut effort by director Noel Black (who hasn't made as good a film since), but also the definitive performance of the inimitable Tuesday Weld, who otherwise has been totally misused in films.

Perhaps the antiviolence mood of the country in 1968—brought about by the assassinations of Robert Kennedy and Martin Luther King—was partly responsible for its box office failure; more likely the major fault lay with Twentieth Century-Fox, which had such little faith in the picture that it held few (if any) advance screenings for reviewers and, other than some misleading ads which likened the picture to a cross between *Psycho* (1960) and *Bonnie and Clyde* (1967), did little to promote it. *Pretty Poison* opened quietly, got unflattering reviews in the daily press, and closed quickly. Luckily, it was rescued from obscurity by magazine critics, like Pauline Kael of *The New Yorker:*

> I rushed to see it, because a movie that makes the movie companies so nervous they're afraid to show it to the critics stands an awfully good chance of being an interesting movie. Mediocrity and stupidity certainly don't scare them; talent does. . . .

Having the time of her life, Sue Ann kills the lumber company guard who caught her and Dennis trespassing.

Pretty Poison is a good little movie, and I use "little" not in a pejorative sense but as a form of protection and also a term of affection.

Pretty Poison is for specialized audiences and belongs in art houses, but Twentieth didn't recognize this and gave up on it entirely once it failed to fill large theaters. Yet as a result of critics hailing it as a sleeper it has survived—having been booked on college campuses in the late sixties and early seventies and in selective repertory theaters ever since.

Pretty Poison is a sometimes violent black comedy with occasional glances of sharp humor scattered throughout its serious framework. Its style reminds me a great deal of William Marsh's novel *The Bad Seed;* in fact, seventeen-year-old Sue Ann Stepanek might well be diabolical eight-year-old Rhoda Penmark grown up. Rhoda was *born* evil—a source of Marsh's novel's controversy—and like Sue Ann hid this characteristic well. Sue Ann has refined her evil with age so that it now corresponds with her sexual amorality. As she brutally kills the guard at the lumber company by slugging him numerous times with a pair of enormous pliers, she straddles his back to hold him down in the river water and allows her dress to ride up, looking as if she were bucking herself to an orgasm. Afterwards, the deliriously excited Sue Ann asks Dennis to "make out" with her. Likewise, after Sue Ann kills her mother— whose death is particularly coldblooded because at the moment she is being nice to Sue Ann for the only time in the picture—she lies down on her bed and laughs, and asks Dennis: "What do people do when they get married?"

Sex without violence means nothing to her. The first time Dennis kisses her, she complains about being jabbed by the car's gear shift; after they make love for the first (and only?) time she asks, "When do we do anything exciting?"

Sue Ann is a strange character. It isn't exactly clear when she stops believing that she is helping Dennis with CIA activities or if she believes his story in the first place. The only hint that she thinks him a true CIA agent is at the chilling moment after she first knocks out the guard (before tossing him in the water and killing him) and she reports to Dennis as if she were an operative talking to her commanding officer: "I hit him *twice*. When he fell, I hit him on the back of his head." She is very clinical at this moment, and this gives the impression that she is serious about her "espionage" work. However, her speech seems to be equally coldhearted at other times. When Dennis tells her he's sorry her father died, she responds, "That's life." After killing her mother, she calmly analyzes, "She wasn't the least bit frightened. Just a little surprised." What becomes increasingly evident is that it is Sue Ann who is leading Dennis on instead of the other way around. (The film's working title? *She Let Him Continue.*) She tells Dennis they will run off to Mexico and get married, yet she rushes off to school each day to keep herself on the honor role, letting us know that she has no intention of going anywhere. Soon her reasons for leading Dennis on are clear. She gets him to come to her house under the pretense that her mother has gone away for the weekend. While she stalls with her packing, her mother drives up with groceries. Sue Ann was setting a trap, for both a victim (her mother) and a fall guy (Dennis). Clever girl.

Sue Ann gets away with her lie that Dennis—an outsider to this town—killed the guard and her mother. But how could it be different? She comes across as the archetypical American innocent, a pretty, high-spirited blonde who is on the honor roll, takes hygiene classes, and carries the American flag while marching with her school band. Noel Black's theme, as reflected in his paradoxical title and as embodied by Sue Ann, is that paranoid America is not so much in danger from foreigners as it is from evil, epidemiclike forces that have given birth in America's heartland. Black sees this small, peaceful Massachusetts town as a microcosm of a sick, self-destructive America: a lumber company dumps pretty-looking capsules of chemical waste into the river, which may have the effect of polluting the drinking supply (Dennis had told Sue Ann the ludicrous story that foreign powers were trying to poison the water); pretty Sue Ann commits murders—blames an outsider for the crimes—and plans on doing it again. The point Black seems to be making is that we should stop blaming foreigners for all our country's ills and turn a suspicious, prudent eye at ourselves and look beyond the "pretty" facades that exist to where we can really find the root of many of America's problems.

Anthony Perkins properly plays Dennis as a man who, institutionalized since his youth, is very much a boy. (Of course the boyish-looking Perkins perfectly

While Dennis throws up in the bathroom, Sue Ann calmly kills her mother.

fits the part.) Dennis is dominated by fantasies that he acts out to put some excitement into his boring life, living in a small town in a trailer, eating at a hot dog stand, working in an office for a lumber company. His whole character reminds me of the scene in *Psycho* (1960) in which Perkins, as Norman Bates, loses his cockiness when the car containing Janet Leigh's body momentarily fails to sink in the lake. At this moment, Norman realizes that he can be caught and his sick look reflects that he thinks this a ridiculous way for him to lose his freedom. Well, Dennis, who always gets into predicaments over his head, is *caught* repeatedly: by his aunt while playing "doctor" with a little girl; by Mrs. Stepanek when he lies that he is the son of one of her acquaintances; by Mr. Munsch, who discovers that Dennis, an ex-arsonist, works in his lumber company and fires him; by the guard at the lumber company who Dennis knows will send him back to prison for a harmless prank (unscrewing the bridge) meant to impress Sue Ann; by the police who find him in "Make-Out Lane" with Sue Ann; by a stranger making love to his girl inside a car Dennis stumbles past, who thinks Dennis a "Peeping Tom" and beats him up; and by Sue Ann in her trap. Dennis thinks himself clever, but he is a jerk, a loser with a capital "L." Only at the end does he

realize his life is jinxed and turn himself in—thereby avoiding the inevitable moment he will be caught.

Like such actresses as Stella Stevens, Blythe Danner, and Lee Remick, Tuesday Weld has never reached the movie stardom critics believe she deserves. She is at her peak as the young girl who turns the tables on the adult who was leading her on; who enjoys guilt; who is turned on by evil for its own sake. It is a part which allows Weld to be energetic, and this spark is what makes her so appealing—and the lack of it in Weld's characters in *Play It As It Lays* (1975) and *A Safe Place* (1975) is why those films work so miserably. Her true admirers still remember her as Thalia Menninger in the classic television comedy series *The Many Loves of Dobie Gillis* in the late fifties. Much of Sue Ann comes from Thalia, Dobie's fantasy girlfriend whom he can only have if he becomes rich. Like Thalia, Sue Ann needs excitement—and if you want her, you have to keep feeding it to her. She is sexy, but it has less to do with her body than her manner. Her sexiness lies in a cherubic face with eyes that sparkle with wickedness, her conceit, the nervous edge in her voice. And what a date she is: she is a lot of fun, amusing, bright, and begs you to please her. She is the manipulative dream girl for masochists like Dennis Pitt.

The Producers

1968 Embassy Pictures
Director: Mel Brooks
Producer: Sidney Glazier
Screenplay: Mel Brooks
Cinematography: Joe Coffey
Music: John Morris
Songs: "The Producers" by John Morris and Mort Goode; "Love Power" by Norman Blagman and Herb Hartig; "Springtime for Hitler" and "Prisoners of Love" by Mel Brooks
Editor: Ralph Rosenbloom
Running Time: 88 minutes

Cast: Zero Mostel (Max Bialystock), Gene Wilder (Leo Bloom), Dick Shawn (Lorenzo St. Du Bois/LSD), Kenneth Mars (Franz Liebkind), Estelle Winwood (old lady), Christopher Hewett (Roger De Bris), Andreas Voutsinas (Carmen Giya), Lee Meredith (Ulla), Renée Taylor ("Eva Braun"), Michael Davis (tenor)

Synopsis: Max Bialystock is a washed-up Broadway producer who makes money by fulfilling the sexual fantasies of a number of old ladies. Timid accountant Leo Bloom comes to investigate Max's books and discovers Max has juggled the numbers. Feeling sorry for him, Leo agrees to move a couple of decimal points to help him out. Leo figures out that a Broadway producer could become rich if he collected a lot of money from investors for a play that would fail immediately and that he only put a *little* of the money into. Max loves the idea and convinces Leo to quit his job and join him in producing a show. Not just any show, but one that is bound to close after one performance: the worst play ever written. Leo agrees to join Max, and for the first time in his life he is happy. But he still carries his baby blanket for security.

After delving through countless scripts, Max comes upon the one that he thinks will make them a fortune because it is so terrible: *Springtime for Hitler*. They visit Franz Liebkind, the author, who at first thinks they are there to arrest him for war crimes. "I was just following orders!" he tells them. He is thrilled that his play will be produced and that the world will get to see the Hitler he loved, who was a much better dancer and handsomer than Winston Churchill. Max and Leo realize he is crazy, but that is unimportant. They get him to sign a contract. Max and Leo convince Roger De Bris, a transvestite who is the world's worst director, to direct their show. Sure of having an absolute failure, Max goes out and gets money from all his old-lady acquaintances. He sells 25,000 percent of the show, counting on the play's failure to guarantee he won't have to pay anyone royalties.

Auditions for Hitler ("No experience needed") are held. Max gives the part to the worst of the lot, a middle-aged hippie named LSD.

Springtime for Hitler has its premiere, which Max and Leo also figure will be its closing performance. The play starts out as they had hoped. There is a big production number which glorifies Hitler and Nazi Germany. The dancers include women who wear Nazi regalia. Other women wear very little. The entire audience reacts with surprise and disgust. People walk out. The only person who applauds is beaten. But when LSD appears as a hippie Hitler the crowd returns to their seats. He gives such a weird interpretation of the script that the audience believes the play is a brilliant satire on Hitler. They laugh and laugh, and it is clear that *Springtime for Hitler* will play on Broadway for years.

Franz comes to Max and Leo's office to kill them for distorting his play and making fun of Hitler. The three of them decide that the only way to end the play is by blowing up the theater. They do so and are arrested. Leo puts up a fine defense and they promise never to participate in such a scheme again.

Max, Leo, and Franz are sent to jail. They begin rehearsals for a prison production called *Prisoners of Love*. They sell shares to the other prisoners and to the warden until way more than 100 percent of the play has been sold.

Mel Brooks started out in the early fifties as an anonymous writer on *Your Show of Shows*, the classic live television series starring Sid Caesar and Imogene Coca. He eventually demanded a place in the credits on the basis of having created such characters as Caesar's "The Professor" and finally became known throughout the business as the show's most gifted writer. When the last of numerous incarnations of the Caesar show went off the air, Brooks achieved some *public* recognition for the first time as "The 2000-Year-Old Man" (in a routine he did with actor-writer Carl Reiner, a more famous Caesar alumnus), as the director-writer-voice of *The Critic* (a prize-winning animated short), and as the cocreator (with Buck Henry) of the very popular *Get Smart*, the most consistently funny television series of the sixties. Still he was not widely known by the public—which is what this man with an enormous ego no doubt wanted.

That Brooks was tired of his half-fame perhaps can be deduced from his giving in jest four of the five major characters in *The Producers*, his first movie, last names that, like his own, begin with the letter "B": Bialystock (whom Brooks based on a producer he worked for as a boy), Bloom (whom Zero Mostel played in a theatrical production of Joyce's *Ulysses*), (Du) Bois, and (De) Bris. By telling viewers that what was coming out of the characters' mouths was written by him he was reminding them, informing them, re-reminding them that he, Mel Brooks, director and screenwriter, was responsible, solely, for what they were seeing on the screen. Why hadn't he given the fifth character, Franz Liebkind, a name beginning with a "B"? Because Brooks wrote the part thinking he'd play it himself.

Well, *The Producers* caught on and, sure enough, as Brooks had hoped, his name was soon known across America. But there are many of us who believe that Brooks's accomplishments in films are not as great as what he did before he became really famous. *The Producers*, like his second film, *The Twelve Chairs* (1970), showed that he had tremendous promise to become a topflight comedy director once he learned the intricacies of filmmaking. (In his first two films he shows no understanding of movie staging, why a camera should be placed in one place instead of another, when to cut, or how to make directorial statements with the camera.) Brooks's career since *Chairs* has been disappointing—although he has been a box office winner. The problem is that Brooks equates innovation with simply breaking taboos—cursing, grossness, sex, bawdy humor—in existing generic forms (the horror film, the western, the silent movie, the Hitchcock-like suspense film); and has been content to make spoofs rather than original comedies. He could make introspective pictures as fascinating as those Woody Allen has given us since

So they really feel like big-time Broadway producers, Max and Leo hire Ulla to be their secretary.

he chucked the "movie-spoof" route, but Brooks thinks it safer to gear his pictures for the mass movie audience. As a result, his films are filled with infantile, often vulgar, collegiate humor that is unworthy of a man with such unique, *mature* talents.

The major strength of *The Producers* is its clever premise. Brooks claimed that it is based on fact, that there really were old-time Broadway producers who made a living by finding backers for shows they knew would flop so they could pocket the investment. Even so, critic Andrew Sarris has questioned whether Jews would be so desperate for money that for their surefire flop they would choose to produce a *Nazi* play. It has been documented that Jewish owners of adult bookstores—some on Forty-second Street, off Broadway— stock large quantities of pornography with Nazi themes (even those taking place in concentration camps), so one can't assume all Jewish producers have too much integrity to back such a tasteless production: one doesn't

need the devil's prodding to sell one's soul. The question is, would *these* Jews, Max and Leo, be willing to be associated with the infamous *Springtime for Hitler: a Gay Romp with Adolf and Eva in Berchtesgarten*? Probably not. These are sweet men. Even Max, who has been reduced to wearing a cardboard belt and making love to old ladies (for their money) who "are on their way to the cemetery," doesn't seem obsessive enough in his quest for fortune and fame to corrupt himself in such a manner. (Undoubtedly, among the plays sent to *him*, Max could find other losers comparable in quality to *Springtime* that aren't homages to Hitler.) Just as it is implausible that Franz, as crazy as he is, wouldn't recognize Max and Leo as Jews and refuse to associate with them, it is farfetched that Max and Leo would sing "Deutschland über Alles" with Franz, or, especially, wear Nazi armbands while walking down the street. At least Brooks attempts to show that Max and Leo find their actions objectionable; they are embarrassed while

On a rooftop, Max and Leo visit Franz Liebkind, the author of Springtime for Hitler.

singing, and rip off the armbands once they are out of Franz's sight and throw them in the garbage where Leo spits on them.

Brooks, of course, is satirizing the theater world when he shows to what lengths producers will go to make a buck, but, as I said, I think he is unable to convince us that such despicable enterprises take place, because likable Max isn't sinister enough and likable Leo isn't corruptible enough. (Two who would have been ideal as Max and Leo as they undertake a mad, foolish scheme having to do with money and status are Sydney Greenstreet and Peter Lorre.) Moreover, the satire fails in the climactic *Springtime* scene. The production number spoof "Springtime for Hitler" works beautifully (although I can't understand how De Bris was able to find such good dancers), but I don't believe the crowd that starts to walk out on the play would return to their seats when LSD appears. Those people who find *Springtime* an offensive play and choose to walk out wouldn't think a hippie Hitler funny. Those people who think unfunny LSD is funny might also find *Springtime* offensive but would like it for just that reason.

Conceived as a play, *The Producers* would seem to be an ideal vehicle for stage great Zero Mostel. But it is one more film failure for Mostel, whose best movie appearance turned out to be as himself singing with the retarded Philly in the documentary *Best Boy* (1979). Not that Mostel doesn't have his moments in *The Producers*. I like the weird scene at the beginning when he "plays" with Estelle Winwood and she almost breaks his neck, scratches him like a cat across the face, and climbs on him and knees him in the crotch. Especially good is when he courts a woman (I don't remember if it's Winwood again) in the Blue Gypsy for money ("a checkie") and Brooks lets the camera run while Mostel does a whole lot of business, including pouring a bottle of wine on an annoying violinist's pants. Mostel is best when he's at center stage, but he looks uncomfortable whenever anyone else is dominating the scene. Like the most unskilled performer, he resorts to mugging in absence of dialogue to try to get the viewer's attention away from the person with the lines. Over and over Mostel's eyes bulge and he gets a weird look on his face. But perhaps Mostel knew something: once Max and Leo

Springtime for Hitler *has its Broadway debut. (TL) LSD plays a hip Hitler who reads to a swinging Eva Braun. (TR and B) The big tasteless musical number that leaves the audience stunned.*

start recruiting people for the production, Wilder (unlike Mostel) stops battling to be noticed on the screen and his character sort of drifts into the background (until the trial sequence). Mostel and Wilder are wonderful actors and some of their time together on screen is great—but Mostel is better making asides to the audience ("How do they all find me?" he asks after Leo has one of his crazy spells) then he is playing Wilder's straight man. It's unfortunate Brooks won't let Wilder be more prominent than Mostel, because the wilder Wilder is, the better the picture. Most of Brooks's films are about the "love" relationship between two men (Brooks's women are nonpeople). Usually the paternal member of the two will teach the simpler character all there is to know about dealing with an evil world. *The Producers* starts out this way, and there are some nice bits where Leo runs around the fountain at Lincoln Center celebrating his corruption and sits with Max in a canoe in Central Park saying "I'm happy." I wish Brooks had carried this father-son relationship through the rest of the film instead of dropping it once the business with the play begins.

Once Max and Leo become producers, the film's humor takes on a lowbrow burlesque air. The scene in which they meet transvestite Roger De Bris, wearing a dress, and his obviously gay companion (lover?) Carmen Giya* has a familiar ring to it as if it were a companion piece to all those bawdy "Doctor and Nurse" burlesque routines. Sexy, miniskirted, big-chested secretary Ulla is, of course, the very epitome of those burlesque "Nurses." The female dancers in the "Springtime" number who wear little on their breasts and do a lot of high kicking are much more suitable for a burlesque house than the Broadway stage. And, as in burlesque houses, there is much "Jewish" humor in the picture. Most of it has to do with "Jewish greed." "How can you take the last penny out of a poor man's hand?" Max asks his Jewish landlord. "I have to. I'm a landlord."

As in all Mel Brooks films there are enough funny moments to make the abundance of awful gags almost palatable. I laughed out loud when Franz becomes excited that his play is about to be produced and turns to tell the birds he keeps on the roof the good news. Likewise, when stingy Max tells the bartender the drinks are on him and there is only one other person in the joint; and when Max waits and waits while an old lady he courts opens up all the locks on her door (we never see her). But my favorite bit in the film is when LSD auditions for the Hitler role and sings "Love Power" which begins as a love song about flowers and ends up with lyrics about him being clubbed on the head by a cop, his girlfriend being stuffed in the garbage can by the garbage man, and his landlord flushing his flower down the toilet, where it goes "in the sewer with the yuck running through'er" and ends up in the "water that we drink." *This* song *deserves* Mostel's bulging eyes.

---

*Some contend that Brooks adds scenes to his films that mock homosexuals so viewers won't mistakenly conclude his male leads are gay.

The Rain People

1969   Warner Bros.–Seven Arts
Director: Francis Ford Coppola
Producers: Bart Patton and
Ronald Colby
Screenplay: Francis Ford Coppola
Cinematography: Wilmer Butler
Music: Ronald Stein
Editor: Blackie Malkin
Running Time: 102 minutes

Cast: Shirley Knight (Natalie), James Caan (Kilgannon), Robert Duvall (Gordon), Marya Zimmet (Rosalie), Tom Aldredge (Mr. Alfred), Laurie Crewes (Ellen), Andrew Duncan (Artie), Margaret Fairchild (Marion), Sally Gracie (Beth), Alan Manson (Lou), Robert Modica (Vinny)

Synopsis: Early one rainy morning, Natalie Ravenna, a childless Long Island housewife, decides to leave her husband, Vinny, while he sleeps. She climbs into her station wagon and embarks on a long journey along America's turnpikes. Although she has left her husband, she does not believe it will be permanently. She calls him often during her journey, assuring him that she is safe, telling him that she was not much of a wife. She also tells Vinny that she is pregnant, and is not sure that she wants to have the baby. At first Vinny is furious with her, threatening her if she has an abortion, but in time he says that he will okay the abortion if she returns to him.

On her trip, Natalie picks up a hitchhiker, hoping for a sexual experience with someone other than her husband. But "Killer" Kilgannon turns out to be an injured ex-football player who is retarded and wears a plate in his head. Natalie winds up feeling responsible for him and resents his intrusion in her life. "Killer" believes that he loves Natalie. Natalie unsuccessfully tries to leave "Killer" behind on several occasions, once at the house of his old girlfriend Ellen, who will now have nothing to do with him, and another time at Mr. Alfred's Reptile Ranch, where she has found him an awful job. But "Killer" always ends up back with her.

One night Natalie tries to have an affair with Gordon, a motorcycle cop, in his trailer. She changes her mind at the last minute and Gordon becomes furious. They struggle. "Killer" breaks in on them and unmercifully beats up Gordon, whose terrified young daughter Rosalie looks on. Rosalie picks up Gordon's gun and shoots "Killer." Natalie tells "Killer" that she and Vinny will always take care of him, but he can't hear her—he is dead.

Natalie, who contemplates an abortion, spends the entire film trying to rid herself of Kilgannon, a retarded, childlike hitchhiker she picks up.

In the sixties, Francis Ford Coppola was recognized more for being the first film school (UCLA) graduate to make commercial Hollywood pictures than for the pictures themselves. It is nearly impossible to find anyone who sought out *The Rain People* during its initial run in 1969 other than a few disgruntled reviewers who complained about the film's depressing tone and summarily dismissed it. Most of the *The Rain People's* admirers didn't see it until a few years later, when *The Godfather* (1972) and Coppola's subsequent productions spurred their interest in his earlier works. What they discovered is probably Coppola's most personally felt film, and certainly his most honest one, neither as calculated for audience response or as intellectually pretentious as *The Godfather, Part II* (1974), *The Conversation* (1974), or *Apocalypse Now* (1979).

More important, they found a Hollywood film which actually attempted to deal with a genuine situation facing many American women. While the film's shaky resolution is far from satisfactory, it is hard not to commend its brave premise: a woman who loves her husband may not want his child, and may conceivably want out of the marriage. (It is a premise that could scare away a lot of married male studio execs from financing such a picture.) Made in an industry which itself proclaimed an embarrassment, *Stand Up and Be Counted,* to be its first film dealing specifically with the women's movement in 1972, and which hailed *An Unmarried Woman* as being a breakthrough film as late as 1978, *The Rain People* was obviously way ahead of its time.

A publicity shot: Robert Duvall and Shirley Knight.

Not yet realizing that Kilgannon has a metal plate in his head, Natalie orders him to make love to her. His blind obedience confuses her until she realizes he has the mind of a child.

Coppola starts Natalie on her cross-country odyssey with two strikes against her: she is leaving a nice husband; she wants an abortion. Traditionally, the cinema has been populated with self-sacrificing heroines who give up everything including their dignity to preserve their families. When their marriages suffer, these women find solace—actually a reason for living—in their children, as did Marlene Dietrich in *Blonde Venus* (1932) and Maureen O'Hara in *The Foxes of Harrow* (1947), to name just two of many. If a woman becomes pregnant, she dutifully has the child. Coppola did not expect audiences brought up on these movie heroines to share his sympathy for Natalie; he anticipated that they would find her actions as irresponsible and selfish as Natalie did herself. Coppola's task was to present *her* case and to show us that Natalie was, in her own haphazard way, doing what was best for her.

For *Kramer vs. Kramer* (1979), director-screenwriter Robert Benton did away with the first part of Avery Corman's novel, which deals with the wife's reasons for walking out on her husband and child, automatically making Meryl Streep a villain, and putting the audience in Dustin Hoffman's corner. Coppola did not do Natalie such a disservice. Instead of beginning the film at the moment Natalie calls Vinny from the turnpike phone booth to say she isn't returning to him, Coppola allows us a glimpse of Natalie prior to her departure that

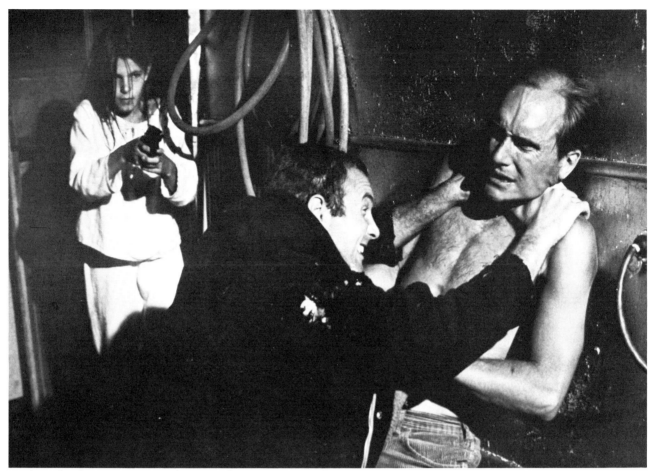

Gordon's daughter aims a gun at Kilgannon, who is trying to strangle Gordon for forcing himself on Natalie.

morning. There is no dialogue, but through a series of images we get a pretty good idea of how miserable Natalie has become.

The first time we see Natalie she is lying flat on her back in bed. It is very early in the morning but she is awake, her sleeping husband's heavy arm locked around her body. From this image, we get the distinct impression that he is holding her down—not just here in bed, but in life—and is, in fact, smothering her. Next, Natalie takes a shower. It appears that the shower stall is the only place where she has sanctuary, where she can be nude and feel comfortable; and it appears that she takes the shower to wash away some kind of sticky marital web that has formed around her. Finally, we see that Natalie is so overly conditioned to trying to be the "perfect wife," that before she walks out on her still-sleeping husband, she sets out the silverware for his breakfast. After Natalie talks to her husband over the phone—"[Before our marriage] I used to wake up in the morning and the day was mine. Now it's yours"— we see just how liberating leaving her husband is. In the motel the first night, she sleeps nude—with her husband she wore a nightgown; moreover, she makes *herself* a cup of coffee, a small kindness that she probably never would have granted herself back home.

Natalie is correct in that she needs to get away from Vinny, at least temporarily, so she can sort things out and attempt to get back her own identity. She is also correct when she tells Vinny: "I have a hunch I'm not ready to be a mother." The key word is "ready." At this point in her life, a child would only trap her deeper in a marriage relationship she says is "getting desperate." It would also deprive her of the time she needs to establish her own strength and independence. Natalie's maturation was abruptly halted on her wedding day, and we see that she is still a child at times: she refers to herself in the third person; takes on an alias for no reason with "Killer"; and puts on makeup like a teen-ager before going out with Gordon, bragging to "Killer" about the "heavy date" she is about to have. The irresponsible manner in which she cares for the retarded childlike "Killer"—her surrogate baby—only serves to further prove her point: she is not fit, at this time in her life, to be a mother.

Coppola sets himself up for feminist outrage by (a) having Natalie want to make it with every man she sees once she hits the road, and (b) giving one the impression that a woman on her own will ultimately lead herself and others to a bad end. But there is a defense for Coppola. Natalie goes after men as soon as she has left Vinny because she falsely believes that is what a woman who has left her husband most desires. It is the only explanation she can comprehend for why she left Vinny; the only one that makes any sense to *her*. Natalie is a confused woman who doesn't know what is expected of her now that she is on her own: such a woman who is headed on a lonesome, treacherous path could conceivably be destructive to herself and those she meets along the way. The reason she gives herself to a man such as Gordon, the reason she is so hard on herself, is that she is *punishing* herself for not being like the heroines in all those movies. Most of all, *The Rain People* is about Natalie's shame for not fulfilling what she believes to be her wifely obligations. Her words to her husband are always apologetic when they should be self-assertive: "You married an incompetent. I'm irresponsible, cruel, and aimless. I hate to cook and I'm sloppy. If you really knew me, you'd hate me." Natalie considers herself a failure, a freak, the only woman in the world with her problems. Of course, the fledgling women's movement could tell her otherwise, that the misgivings she is having about her marriage and about having a child are quite common and certainly nothing to feel ashamed about. Her trip across America needn't be lonesome, for there are women everywhere who share her concerns—real women, not those up on movie screens.

The Rain People was Coppola's last film to feature a female lead. It's hard to believe that the same man who would create such domineering male characters as Patton, the Corleone clan, and Kurtz in the seventies could have shifted gears so completely. In *The Rain People*, all the men are easily manipulated by women: Artie, the drive-in theater owner, by his daughter Ellen; "Killer" by Natalie and Ellen; Gordon by his young daughter Rosalie; and finally Vinny by Natalie when he reverses his stubborn stance and totally gives in to her ("I'll do anything you want. I'll change. I'll quit my job. If you want to lose the baby, it'll be all right. It'll be on your terms"). This is certainly a long way from Al Pacino slamming the door in wife Diane Keaton's face in *The Godfather, Part II*.

George Lucas's documentary about the making of *The Rain People* includes much footage of tearful arguments between Coppola and his star, Shirley Knight, for whom he had written the script. (He based it on "Echoes," a story he wrote in college about three women who leave their husbands). Despite their conflicts, Knight, as always, gives a great performance. She is able to project the disorientation so integral to Natalie, her confusion, her loneliness, her self-hatred. She is one minute a young girl trying to be sexy like the big girls are, and the next a woman legitimately trying to care for "Killer" as if she were his mother. Natalie is as interesting as she is because she is ever changing. The audience is not alone in trying to define her—both Knight and her character are doing the same thing.

As the rain pours down, a desperate Natalie tries to raise Kilgannon to his feet. But he is dead. The film ends at this time, but it was originally intended for there to be another scene in which Natalie is picked up by her husband the following morning.

Rebel Without a Cause

1955   Warner Bros.
Director: Nicholas Ray
Producer: David Weisbart
Screenplay: Stewart Stern
Adaptation by Irving Shulman

From a story by Nicholas Ray
Cinematography: Ernest Haller
Music: Leonard Rosenman
Editor: William Ziegler
Running time: 111 minutes

Cast: James Dean (Jim), Natalie Wood (Judy), Sal Mineo (Plato), Corey Allen (Buzz), Jim Backus (Jim's father), Ann Doran (Jim's mother), William Hopper (Judy's father), Rochelle Hudson (Judy's mother), Dennis Hopper (Goon), Edward C. Platt (Ray), Steffi Sidney (Mil), Marietta Canty (housekeeper), Frank Mazzola (Crunch)

Synopsis: Teen-ager Jim Stark has been in trouble often, causing his family to move from one town to another. New to Los Angeles, Jim is brought into Juvenile Hall on drunk and disorderly charges. He tells an officer named Ray that his home is like a zoo, that his mother and father smother him with love but never listen to him or give him sound advice, and that his mother eats his weak father alive. Jim wishes that he'd have one day in which he didn't feel ashamed of himself or confused. Before Jim's parents arrive from their posh club to take him home, Jim notices two other teen-agers who have been picked up that night. Plato is an emotionally disturbed boy who has killed some puppies. He is without friends, and his rich parents, now divorced, are never in Los Angeles. The only person who cares about him is the housekeeper. Judy is a pretty girl who was picked up for walking the streets long after dark.

The next morning, Jim goes to his new school for the first time. He offers neighbor Judy a ride, but she rudely turns him down and goes with her boyfriend Buzz and their wild friends. That afternoon, the students go to the planetarium. Jim and Plato become friends but Buzz and his leather-jacketed gang decide to give Jim the business. After slashing the tires on Jim's car, Buzz coaxes Jim into a knife fight by calling him chicken. Jim wins the fight but, not wanting trouble, throws his knife away. He agrees to meet Buzz that night for a "chickie run"—although he doesn't know what it is. Without telling his father exactly what is expected of him, Jim asks him if he should do something dangerous to save his honor. His father tells Jim not to rush into anything.

That night, Buzz decides he likes Jim but they go ahead with the "chickie run" anyway. While many teen-agers, including Plato and Judy, look on nervously, Buzz and Jim race their stolen cars toward the edge of a cliff. Whoever jumps first is "chicken," although just participating proves one has guts. Jim jumps out of the car safely, but Buzz's sleeve gets caught on the door handle and he plunges to his death. Jim takes the stunned Judy home.

When Jim tells his parents what happened, they tell him he mustn't call the police as he wants to do. His mother wants to go away. There is a family argument, and Jim knocks down his father for not standing up for him against his mother and rushes out. He goes to the police station to speak to Ray but Ray is not there. Buzz's friends Crunch, Goon, and another boy see Jim there and decide to shut him up before he squeals.

Jim picks up Judy and they go to a deserted mansion Plato told Jim about. Knowing Buzz's friends are after Jim, Plato arrives at the mansion carrying a gun. They act like a family: Plato at last has parents and Jim and Judy have found in each other someone to love and be loved by. Plato falls asleep and Judy and Jim explore the mansion. Meanwhile, Crunch, Goon, and the other boy break into the mansion. They terrorize Plato, who shoots and wounds Crunch. Feeling deserted by Jim and Judy, Plato goes berserk and shoots at policemen investigating the break-in. Plato runs to the planetarium and locks himself inside. Ray, Jim's parents, and Plato's house-keeper arrive at the scene with many policemen. Jim and Judy go into the planetarium and convince Plato to come outside where he has friends. Jim removes the cartridge from Plato's gun. When he sees the police, Plato panics and runs, and a policeman, thinking Plato's gun is loaded, shoots him down. As Jim cries over his friend, his father tells him that they will face things together. Jim and Judy embrace.

At the beginning of *Rebel Without a Cause*, teen-agers Jim, Judy, and Plato are picked up by police and brought to Juvenile Hall. They aren't introduced but observe each other through the windowed walls that separate the individual offices from each other and from the waiting room. At times the viewer can also see the three of them within the same frame, which is meaningful because director Nicholas Ray, in order to show the division between kids and adults, rarely will have an adult and a teen-ager in the same shot, even when they are in the same room. Because the windowed walls allow Ray maneuverability with his framing, he is able to visually establish the bond that unites all of America's troubled, troublesome, alienated middle-class teen-agers, who, with little variation, are mirror images of one another.

This window-as-mirror analogy becomes important later in the picture when, preceding the "chickie run" that claims Buzz's life, Jim looks out his car's (rolled

Nicholas Ray has James Dean and Corey Allen (today a director himself) rehearse Jim and Buzz's scuffle in the planetarium driveway. Among the actors gathered around is Nick Adams (in the hat).

Judy, Goon, and Jim look over the cliff from which the dead Buzz's car plunged.

down) passenger side window *at Buzz*, who is sitting in a car parked parallel to his own. Through his window frame, Jim sees Judy standing next to Buzz's door, kissing Buzz and giving him dirt to rub on his hands for the upcoming race. At this moment, Jim most definitely wishes he were Buzz, who has two things he wants: many friends and Judy for a girlfriend. That he is seeing himself in Buzz's place is clear when he calls Judy to stand by his door and says, "Me, too." Judy now hands dirt to *Jim* and, except for there being no kiss between Jim and Judy—it is deferred until later that night when Jim replaces the dead Buzz as Judy's boyfriend, fulfilling a great part of his wish—the image Jim saw through his window frame is duplicated; only Jim has taken Buzz's place in the setup.

So that we are able to perceive what monumental effect Buzz's imminent death will have on Jim, director Ray makes us aware that when Jim looks at Buzz prior to the "chickie run" Jim already senses that whatever may happen to Buzz—his "mirror image" in this sequence—might very well happen to him, because he leads the same dangerous life Buzz does. Because James Dean was killed in a car crash on September 5, 1955, less than two months before *Rebel*'s release, this scene has *always* had greater impact than Ray anticipated. I find it devastating, and a bit eerie, because not only are we watching Jim Stark looking at a character who is about to show him how he could end up (dead), but also we are watching actor James Dean look at another actor (Corey Allen) playing someone who is about to be killed in a manner strikingly similar to how Dean would be killed a few months after shooting this scene. Strong

images such as these in *Rebel* firmly plant in our minds that James Dean and Jim Stark were as close to being the same person as an actor and his character can possibly be. Critics such as David Thomson contend that the real Dean was no rebel. Thomson also contends that Dean was more a brooding romantic than a renegade, only exploiting his misfit persona to gain notoriety, and that "the vividness of his performances lies in the calculated mannerisms of an actor pretending to be ill at ease." Dean's cultists, however, as well as many of his closest acquaintances, insist that Dean greatly resembled the vulnerable, sensitive, self-destructive loner of *Rebel*. So it is that while everyone acknowledges Dean's greatness in interpreting Steinbeck's Cal Trask in *East of Eden* (1955), released six months before Dean's death, it is *Rebel Without a Cause* that the Dean legions watch over and over again for "true" insight into the legendary actor.

Jim Stark is a lonely kid who supposedly hasn't a friend in the world when we first see him lying drunk in an L.A. gutter, but his personality is such that within a twenty-four-hour period he makes friends with Plato, Buzz, and Judy, three teen-agers completely different from each other and himself. (Of course, their differences, according to Ray, are not as strong as their common problems.) Likewise, the immense popularity for outcast James Dean resulted from his rare ability to appeal to the entire spectrum of America's youth. I believe that females take to Dean as Jim Stark for the same reasons Judy falls in love with Jim: "A girl wants a man who's gentle and sweet and who doesn't run away." Jim's other appealing characteristics are his

The volatile homelife of Jim, characterized by his always being at odds with parents who come at him from two different directions (T) stands in marked contrast to the warm, peaceful, idealized family life set up by "parents" Jim and Judy and "son" Plato in the deserted mansion (B).

sincerity, his warmth toward Judy, his concern for his friend Plato—whom no one else likes, his protectiveness, his shyness, his bravery, his (Dean's) good looks, his tender way of kissing ("Your lips are soft," Judy tells him), and (appealing to some females) his desperate need to be loved. (Judy's desperate need to be loved has the same attraction for some males.) And Jim is the rare male who is not only willing to tell stranger Ray that he loves his father, but also has the capacity to cry—which he does often. His one bad characteristic is his violent nature, but at least his violence is not directed at Judy or his friends. And most appealing is that his girlfriend Judy blossoms in his presence rather than being stifled. As Cal has the same effect on Abra in *East of Eden* and Dean's Jett has the same effect on Elizabeth Taylor in *Giant* (1956), James Dean comes across as one male star whose characters consistently were good influences on the women they loved.

Every teen-age boy who considers himself "misunderstood" can readily identify with Jim Stark. Jim is the friendless, confused, aimless outcast that even the most popular teen-age boy thinks himself to be. Actually *hopes to be;* it's a high school truism that the friendless, confused, aimless outcast always gets the girl. When we saw *Rebel* ten to fifteen times in our youth, we, martyrs all, fantasized ourselves sitting on the floor and smashing our fists into Ray's desk out of frustration. And as teen-agers we liked being called "rebels." (It's better than "squares" or "dorks".) At that age we weren't out to destroy the system, we weren't revolutionaries; but we romanticized that like Jim we were rebelling inside. (In *Rebel*, director Ray dealt with his primary concern: inner violence.) As teen-agers, we wanted the "system" to become more sensitive to our needs, to apologize (that'll be the day) for being negligent in the past, and to make us part of the existing order. Even the most timid of us saw ourselves hellbent when teen-agers; we related to Jim because while we felt we had a self-destructive streak we also had Jim's strong feelings for self-preservation—potential suicides who call everyone (several times) in hopes of being talked out of it. (Dean, on the other hand, seemed to have a death wish similar to Montgomery Clift's.) We recognized Jim's inability to communicate with his parents and other adults; and the way he mumbled when he thought no one was listening and started his sentences over, louder and clearer, when he discovered with surprise that he *was* being heard. But we responded even more to how well Jim seemed to relate to his peer group. He was our ideal: everything he said was so right, so clever, so "cool." When the unfriendly Judy calls him a yoyo and runs off to join her friends, he says softly, "I love you, too" (my favorite line); when the now friendly Judy asks Jim why he kissed her on the forehead, he says simply and directly, "I felt like it"; when Buzz asks Jim if he knows what a "chickie run" is, Jim fibs, "That's all I ever do"; when Plato asks Jim if he can keep Jim's jacket, Jim asks rhetorically, "Well, what do you think?" All short lines that look lame in print, but that are as memorable to me as Dean's incredible histrionics. And I also remember Dean's/Jim's "perfect" movements: the way he shuffles when he walks to show his uncertainty; and how he is often in a half-crouch like a boxer ready to come out punching; the way he smiles after getting garbled directions to school from Buzz and Judy's friends, and, half-shrugging, slowly turns back toward his steering wheel; the way he tumbles out of his car during the "chickie run"—displaying the athletic ability that made Dean a several-letter man in high school; the way he signifies to Buzz that he's listening to him as they sit in different cars by simply taking his lit cigarette from his mouth; the way he extends his comforting hand to Judy (their fingertips touch) on top of the cliff following Buzz's death. I don't consider myself as fanatical about James Dean as are true-blood Dean cultists, although I am fanatical about *Rebel*, which I've seen countless times since 1955, but almost everything Dean does and says in this film elicits bursts of emotion (some nostalgia-related) from me—and I'm not alone.

Amidst all the pain and confusion, Jim and Judy fall in love.

In the police station at the beginning of *Rebel* we see a March of Dimes poster on a pole. This is a film about juvenile delinquency, but from this poster we see immediately that director Ray is on the side of all kids—who have all sorts of problems to contend with (including diseases that usually strike the young). More than any other film, in fact, *Rebel* sympathizes with youth. Getting money isn't the problem of teen-agers in *Rebel* as it is with the poverty-stricken John Derek in Ray's *Knock on Any Door* (1949). These middle-class teen-agers have more complex problems. As the title states, their causes are impossible to define. But at the heart of the matter is their need to win acceptance from their peers, which too often requires they take part in dangerous, illegal rituals, and their need to get their parents' attention and understanding. Interestingly, in Ray's film there are no classroom scenes, which leads us to believe that Ray and screenwriter Stewart Stern considered a teacher's influence on a teen-ager negligible. The *two* influential factors on a youth are parents and peers. Ray is critical of parents who refuse to deal with the modern world of a teen-ager. Judy's mother is the only one who has any conception of what kids are going through ("She's at that age when nothing seems to fit") but even she doesn't conceive how terribly different (more dangerous) is the decade Judy lives in than the time when she grew up. Jim's parents love him but they respond to his problems as poorly as Judy's and Plato's parents. Jim's father is afraid of a serious conversation with his son, so he jokes all the time, always calling his son "Jimbo." Like many parents of delinquents, Jim's mother blames her son for their inadequacies as parents. The only person who understands these kids is Ray (the

policeman named after the film's director), but he realizes he is not important enough to the kids to help them—it is the parents who must come around.

Ray's teen-agers are hopelessly confused, seeking advice and getting no answers. Their confusion is symbolized by Plato's mismatched socks; both Jim and Judy look at them but instead of laughing at him admit that they have done the same thing. Jim, Judy, and John (Plato's real name) pretend to be a family so they can do things right. But Jim and Judy come to the conclusion that being parents in this day and age is harder than they thought. They are unsuccessful as Plato's "surrogate parents"—doing even less for his welfare than his own parents, whom he never sees. In fact, it is because Plato thinks Jim and Judy neglectful parents that he goes berserk and ends up shot by police.

Rebel Without a Cause isn't a very didactic, moralistic film. It is in some ways strongly pessimistic: the dawn that brings on a new better life (hopefully) for Jim and Judy signals Plato's death. In a hard world where there are no solutions to problems we can only look for painkillers; people can survive only if supported by others in the same situation. Watch the film—see how essential it is for each character to be touched, hugged, and kissed by his/her lovers, friends, and family members. At the end, tearful Jim is lifted to his feet by his father, who holds him and assures him he will stand by him as he has never done before. When his father is through holding Jim, Judy takes over. In order for the characters in *Rebel* to have strength enough to make it through another day, they must revive themselves through physical contact. That is why *Rebel Without a Cause* is the most emotional of films.

The Red Shoes

1948   Great Britain   Eagle-Lion release of a J. Arthur Rank
presentation of an Archers production
Directors: Michael Powell and Emeric Pressburger
Producers: Michael Powell and Emeric Pressburger
Screenplay: Emeric Pressburger
Additional dialogue: Keith Winter
Cinematography: Jack Cardiff
Music: Brian Easdale
Choreography: Robert Helpmann
Editor: Reginald Mills
Running time: 133 minutes

Cast: Anton Walbrook (Boris Lermontov), Marius Goring (Julian
Craster), Moira Shearer (Victoria Page), Robert Helpmann (Ivan
Boleslawsky), Leonide Massine (Ljubov), Albert Basserman
(Ratov), Ludmilla Tcherina (Boronskaja), Esmond Knight (Livy),
Jean Short (Terry), Gordon Littman (Ike), Austin Trevor (Pro-
fessor Palmer), Eric Berry (Dimitri), Irene Brown (Lady Nelson)

Synopsis: Following a performance of the "Heart of Fire" ballet,
impressario Boris Lermontov accepts an invitation to the party of a
contessa. He doesn't want to watch her niece, Vicky, perform for
him—"I hate amateurs"—but when he meets the beautiful young
woman he becomes interested in her. She tells him that dancing is
more important to her than life itself. He invites her to audition for
the National Ballet Theatre. Student Julian Craster sends a note to
Boris saying that his teacher, Professor Palmer, stole his music to
score the "Heart of Fire." Realizing Julian's talent, Boris hires him to
be orchestra coach.

Boris attends a recital given by Vicky. He is impressed by her
ability and love of dance and offers her a position with the ballet
company. He is also impressed by Julian's work and gives him more
freedom with arrangements. The ballet company goes on tour. Irena
Boronskaja, the prima ballerina, quits to get married. Boris thinks it
wasteful for a great dancer to throw away her art for love. He assigns
Julian the task of composing the score for a ballet based on Hans
Christian Andersen's children's story "The Red Shoes." It is about a
girl devoured by her obsessive need to dance in a pair of red shoes.
Life and love pass her by. Julian asks what happens at the end. Boris
shrugs. "She dies."

Boris gives the excited Vicky the opportunity to dance the lead in
"The Ballet of the Red Shoes." She and Julian spend much time
together rehearsing (and arguing). Her dancing and his score
complement each other beautifully and the ballet is a big success.
Boris promises them both more and more work, but becomes
terribly upset when he learns that Vicky and Julian have fallen in
love. He starts being critical of their work. When he criticizes one of
Julian's scores that everyone else concedes is excellent, Julian
quits. Vicky, deciding her allegiance is to Julian, also quits and
marries Julian. Boris acts as if her leaving doesn't bother him.
But he tells her that she will never become a great dancer if she is
with Julian.

Boris owns the rights to the "Red Shoes" ballet and makes sure
that Vicky can't dance it for any other company. Vicky can find little
dancing work and little satisfaction.

Time passes. Boris misses Vicky terribly. He learns that she is
coming to Paris and meets her at the train station. He asks her to
give one concert performance of "The Red Shoes." She cannot
resist, although it will mean she will miss Julian's new score being
performed at Covent Garden in London.

In the dressing room, Vicky puts on her dance costume and her
red shoes. Julian arrives. He has relinquished conducting his own
score that night to try to convince Vicky not to dance for Boris,
whom he hates. Boris joins the argument. As Vicky tries to decide
between Julian and dancing, the red shoes take on a will of their
own. They lead her to a balcony. She seems to fly off as if pulled off
by a strange force. She is struck by a passing train underneath. At
her request, Julian removes the red shoes. Then she dies. Tearful
Boris announces that the ballet will go on as planned. Throughout
the performance, a lone spotlight shines on the space on the stage
where Vicky would have danced.

"Why do you want to dance?"
"Why do you want to live?"
"I don't know exactly why but I must."
"That's my answer too."

In the mid-thirties, Emeric Pressburger, a Hun-
garian-born expatriate from Germany living in England, wrote a script of *The Red Shoes* for producer-
director Alexander Korda, who was looking for a
vehicle for his wife Merle Oberon. Korda didn't
pursue the project, and a decade later Pressburger and
Michael Powell, who had emerged as England's most
respected directing-producing-screenwriting team during the war years, bought back the property. They
reworked the story of a woman torn between dancing
and "living" for the beautiful, extraordinarily gifted
Sadler's Wells ballet star Moira Shearer. (What do you
want from life, to live?" asks Boris. "To dance," Vicky
replies.) When the 133-minute film went 200,000
pounds over budget, British backer J. Arthur Rank
thought he had a disaster on his hands. Studio executives
at Universal Studios, the picture's American distributor,
privately screened the picture and made the same bleak
prediction. Of course, *The Red Shoes* went on to
become one of Great Britain's all-time top money-
makers, win several Academy Awards, earn raves from
critics worldwide, attract highbrow viewers who cate-
gorically snubbed their noses at movies, take its place as
a movie classic and the best-ever ballet film, and inspire
generation after generation of young girls into becoming
dancers. So glorious are the visuals—movement, color,
elegant decor, lavish costumes, all surrounded by
music—and so strong is the identifiable career versus
marriage conflict which Vicky (unsuccessfully) tries to
resolve that I would guess that if American females
selected the film for which they have the most emotional
attachment (i.e., their favorite picture), *The Red Shoes*
would be at the top.

The common characteristic of *The Red Shoes* and
the three other films which seem to appeal particularly
to females, *The Wizard of Oz* (1939), *Beauty and the
Beast* (1946), and *Black Orpheus* (1960), is their blend of
realism and fantasy, the two ingredients that distinguish
a great many of Powell and Pressburger's works.
(Powell, in particular, has been interested in exploring
the method of cinematic storytelling which combines
these two seemingly opposing forms.) *The Red Shoes* is
simultaneously romantic and expressionistic, a day-
dream and a nightmare, a psychological drama and a
fairy tale. As Thomas Elsessor wrote of Powell and
Pressburger's other expressionistic dance film, *The Tales
of Hoffmann* (1951), *The Red Shoes* is "a pure meditation on the cinema, in its dual aspects of intimate art and
mass-medium, of emotional reality and perverse illusion."

Except for the opulent sets and wealthy characters,

Lermontov (R) instructs Julian to play "The Red Shoes" score for Vicky at all times, including when she dines. He doesn't expect that as a result of spending so much time together, Julian and Vicky will fall in love.

The Red Shoes starts out like a typical Hollywood backstage musical. In fact, plotwise it is reminiscent of Busby Berkeley's *Gold Diggers of 1935*, but since we are dealing with a high art (ballet) and not a low, popular art (Broadway musicals) the aspiring songwriter (Dick Powell) becomes an aspiring composer (Marius Goring as Julian Craster) and the songwriter's hoofer girlfriend (Ruby Keeler) becomes the composer's ballerina girlfriend (Moira Shearer as Victoria Page). But into this familiar, believable (if not realistic) backstage milieu, directors Powell and Pressburger inject fantasy. Our early glimpse of impresario Boris (wonderfully played by Anton Walbrook) is so mysterious—he sits in the darkness, peeking out from behind the curtains of his opera box, then shows his hand but not his face—that he might well be "the phantom of the opera." This "surrealistic" horror-movie-like introduction is most suitable for the standard wicked character ("a cruel monster," Vicky writes of him) of a fairy tale. And we have hints that this picture is, in part, a fairy tale. While realism dominates the early proceedings, there is an unmistakable "Cinderella" feeling surrounding Vicky's "discovery" by Boris and her winning the right to put on the ballet company's slippers.

At the moment Boris tells Vicky she has won a place in the company, we hear a train whistle on the soundtrack. This is our signal that fate, important to fairy tales, fantasies, and horror stories, will be a determining factor in Vicky's life ("I believe in destiny," Vicky tells Julian). Trains will be used throughout the film as symbols of fate to remind us that a sad end awaits Vicky: Ludmilla, Vicky's predecessor, leaves in a train to get married—angry Boris will not kiss her good-bye; too excited by their "Red Shoes" assignments to sleep, Vicky and Julian stand on a balcony as a train passes

underneath and shoots ominous steam into the air; with steam billowing outside the window, Vicky sits with the unfriendly Boris in his train compartment telling him that like Ludmilla she has chosen marriage over a career; Boris meets Vicky's train in Paris and convinces her to dance "The Red Shoes" once more; Julian tells Vicky that she mustn't dance "The Red Shoes" for Boris because it will signify that dance is more important to her than their marriage, and pleads with her to get on the eight o'clock train; controlled by her red shoes, Vicky jumps off a balcony and is killed by the passing train below.

Where fairy tale becomes tantamount to realism is in Monte Carlo, a real-life fantasy world where the scenery is *unbelievable* but real. But Powell and Pressburger heighten the fantasy created by the natural beauty of this magical land by having Vicky look like a princess in a flowing gown and tiara. Dressed this way, she ascends a seemingly endless staircase—similar to the one going toward heaven in the directors' *A Matter of Life and Death* (1946)—leading to a magnificent palace somewhere in the vicinity, no doubt, of Mount Olympus. There's opera in the background, and serenity in the air. Vicky enters the palace, where a hectic story conference is taking place. We are jolted back to reality—but just for a moment. "King" Boris tells Vicky that she will dance the lead in "The Ballet of the Red Shoes." *A dream come true.*

The rehearsal scenes that follow, filled with enjoyable byplay among the ballet company's fascinating members, and the preballet "opening-night jitters" bits cap off what I believe is a masterful first half of the film. However, the authenticity of these scenes may be a drawback, because we are totally unprepared for the ballet itself. The twenty-minute "Ballet of the Red

Lermontov visits Vicky in her dressing room prior to her debut in "The Red Shoes." Also readying himself is Ljobov, played by the extraordinary dancer Leonide Massine.

Shoes" sequence (the film's highlight, according to *Red Shoes* cultists) is highly stylized. Use is made of a myriad of camera tricks, including having the audience behind conductor Julian become a roaring ocean, and having the ballet take place on enormous sets that couldn't possibly fit on a stage. Moira Shearer does stun you with her dancing—and she may be the most beautiful performer ever on a movie screen in her white chiffon ballet costume with a blue-trimmed white bodice, a blue ribbon in her flaming red hair, and those "living" red shoes on her feet; and Powell and Pressburger's expressionistic vision does capture the nightmarish spirit of Hans Christian Andersen's fairy tale ("You shall dance in your red shoes till you are pale and cold; till your skin shrivels up and you are a skeleton!"). But I much prefer Vicky's earlier, simpler performance at the Mercury. My main objection is not that the "Red Shoes" sequence is poorly done—it is a visual delight—but that it does not fit. Remember: this ballet was staged by Boris—not by Powell and Pressburger. And not by those stage directors found in the Busby Berkeley movies, philistines who, if they had a camera, would take it up in the rafters. But by a non-innovator, Boris, the ultimate ballet purist who says "Ballet is a religion" and that he won't tolerate ballet being performed in the wrong atmosphere. If Boris would "lower himself" to allowing someone to film the ballet he conceived, he would insist on a stationary camera. And *no* special effects! (As for the music: he would certainly object to the jazzy interludes.)

Because of the cinematic liberties and excesses taken during the ballet sequence, it is impossible to readjust to those realistic sequences that follow. The intrusive camera has permanently fixed in our mind that we are watching a *movie* and our magical trance has been disrupted. The only moments that stylistically fit in the picture after the ballet are those that continue to work in the ballet's fantasy vein: the dreamlike sequence when Vicky and Julian wake up in the middle of the night in their expressionistically designed bedroom (there doesn't seem to be a ceiling or four walls); and the final sequence in which the red shoes take Vicky to her death. For me the picture goes downhill after the ballet and it's not the fault of the performers.

Admittedly, my disenchantment with the second half of *The Red Shoes* comes in part from the fact that it is naturally more enjoyable seeing characters strive for and achieve their goals than it is to see their happy lives destroyed. The second part of the picture almost wipes out the first half. It is disheartening to watch three characters constantly tormented: Vicky, who is consumed by her *need* to dance; Julian, whose selfishness prevents him from realizing that Vicky can never be happy if she doesn't dance; and Boris, who is consumed by his jealousy because Julian possesses Vicky's heart, and this keeps her from concentrating fully on dance. ("A dancer who falls in love will never be a great dancer," Boris contends.) Sadly, there is no happy medium that will satisfy all three. There is no way for Vicky to compromise: she must give up either dance or

"The Ballet of the Red Shoes." (R) Powell and Pressburger dabble in expressionism as the red shoes lead Vicky onward and onward. (B) The townspeople (including Robert Helpmann, in center of the front row) reject the girl who can do nothing but dance.

Julian (on his knees) and the crowd grieve over Vicky, who was driven to her death by the red shoes.

Julian. It is a decision that she can't make and her confusion so weakens her that the red shoes she wears can control her.

After Vicky's triumph in "The Ballet of the Red Shoes," Boris tells her that he will arrange for her to dance all the great ballets. There is a close-up of his face as he says that he'll do all the talking and she'll do all the dancing, followed by a quick cut to a close-up of Vicky's face, not standing by Boris but dancing on a stage. She is smiling broadly and we realize that she can never be as happy as she is when dancing. Boris is correct in thinking Vicky can't achieve the artistic greatness she is capable of if distracted by Julian—unfortunately, a person only has so much energy to spend. We could reconcile Vicky's giving up Julian for dance *if* we didn't equate dance with Boris. It is a shame that Boris comes across so cruelly—unlike the kindly ballet impressario Ralph Bellamy plays in *Dance, Girl, Dance* (1940) who takes ballerina Maureen O'Hara under his wing once she willingly gives up boyfriend Louis Hayward for her dance career. Because Boris is so spiteful, petty, and jealous, we assume what he expects in the way of sacrifices from Vicky (and Julian) is unfair; but it is probable that what he wants for Vicky is what is best for her, and what she truly wants for herself. When he spoke of the character in the ballet dancing herself to death while life and love passed her by, Boris was emotionless and we despised his cold heart; but when Vicky dies because she can't give up dancing, Boris cries. If we had seen this sensitive side of Boris earlier, we might not have minded Vicky taking his advice and choosing a career over marriage. But we have been manipulated into not liking Boris. So at the time Vicky chooses dancing over Julian and follows the advice of someone we think wicked, we tend to go along with Powell and Pressburger's decision to punish her for making the *wrong* (seemingly selfish) decision. That the directors-writers consider her decision to be wrong is confirmed when the dying Vicky tells Julian to *remove* her red shoes, which she blames for her misfortune. Pressburger and particularly Powell are fine directors, but I have never liked the endings of their films. The finale to this picture is too melodramatic and is so disappointing. Why not let Vicky commit herself to Julian or dance? Why kill her off? Fairy tales, even Andersen's otherwise gruesome "The Red Shoes," traditionally have uplifting endings, and I would have preferred such an ending to this picture.

Reefer Madness

Also known as *Tell Your Children, The Burning Question, Dope Addict, Doped Youth,* and *Love Madness*

1936 Motion Pictures Ventures release of a G & H production, currently distributed by New Line Films
Director: Louis Gasnier
Producer: George A. Hirliman
Screenplay: Arthur Hoerl, from an original story by Lawrence Meade
Additional Dialogue: Paul Franklin
Cinematography: Jack Greenhalgh
Musical Director: Abe Meyer
Editor: Carl Pierson
Running Time: 67 minutes

Cast: Dorothy Short (Mary), Kenneth Craig (Bill), Lillian Miles (Blanche), Dave O'Brien (Ralph), Thelma White (Mae), Carleton Young (Jimmy), Pat Royale (Agnes), Josef Forte (Dr. Carroll)

Synopsis: High school principal Dr. Carroll tells parents at a PTA meeting that they must stamp out the menace of marijuana—the number-one assassin of youth. He relates a story that illustrates the dangers of marijuana.

Mae Coleman had an apartment near the high school. Jack, her accomplice in crime, would bring high school students there for wild parties during which the kids would smoke marijuana. One of the older boys Jack had hooked was Ralph, who had an eye on the innocent Mary, Bill's girlfriend and Jimmy's sister. Ralph and Jack brought Jimmy to Mae's, where he willingly joined in the wild scene, smoking marijuana, dancing, and necking with the girls there. Later, Bill came with Jimmy to Mae's, and he too succumbed to the power of marijuana. He stopped doing well in school and spending time with Mary; each night he would go to Mae's and smoke marijuana and party with Blanche, Ralph's older girlfriend.

Jimmy drove Jack to see Jack's boss. Jack placed a big order for marijuana; meanwhile, in the car, Jimmy smoked marijuana. When they drove back to Mae's, Jimmy lost control of the car. He struck a pedestrian and sped away.

Already upset that Bill had been avoiding her, Mary began to notice that Jimmy acted suspiciously. She tracked him to Mae's. Jimmy was not there, but the superhigh Ralph, who was getting increasingly addicted to marijuana, invited her in. He got her to smoke a joint by making her believe it was a normal cigarette. When she was high, Ralph tried to rape her. She resisted. Bill, who had spent the night in Mae's bedroom with Blanche, came into the living room. Still under the influence of marijuana, he believed that Mary was allowing Ralph to make love to her. He jealously charged Ralph and the two boys struggled. Wanting to stop the noise, Jack tried to conk Bill on the head with his gun. The gun went off and killed Mary. Bill had passed out, but when he woke up, Jack and Mae convinced the grieving boy that he had killed Mary. Bill went on trial. Meanwhile, Ralph and Blanche, who knew what really happened, were holed up at Mae's constantly smoking marijuana. Ralph felt guilty about letting Bill take the rap for Mary's death, and Jack began to worry that he would squeal. Jack got permission from his boss to rub out Ralph. But when Jack tried to kill Ralph, Ralph killed him instead. The police raided Mae's.

Bill was convicted for Mary's killing, but Blanche and Mae later told the police what happened. The judge reversed his decision and let Bill go free with a strong reprimand.

Mae went to prison along with many drug kingpins in the city whom she ratted on. A remorseful Blanche jumped from a high window to her death. Bill watched Ralph's brief trial, during which it was determined that Ralph was so addicted to marijuana that he should be committed for life to a mental hospital. Bill swore he would never smoke the evil weed again.

Dr. Carroll tells the PTA members that they must enlighten their kids on the menace of marijuana or the next tragedy might be theirs.

Reefer Madness, also commonly titled *Tell Your Children* and *The Burning Question*, is an incredibly silly quasi-documentary that was supposedly designed to stimulate PTA groups and civic organizations into taking steps to halt the spread of marijuana, which was "destroying the youth of America in alarmingly increasing numbers" in 1936. But its sleazy visuals, which include many minutes of Mae putting on her stockings, sweet Mary in a skintight sweater for a game of tennis, passionate kissing among high school students, close dancing, wild orgies, Bill and the older Blanche retreating into Mae's bedroom where they give in to their physical desires, and Ralph unzipping Mary's dress and attempting to rape her, give one the impression that the film was really intended to stimulate the sexual impulses of its viewers, much in the way those early moralistic potboilers on "white slavery" and prostitution used their subjects as an excuse for the inclusion of crowd-drawing nudity and sex. This film may purport to be a vehemently anti-marijuana work, but its exploitation plot is so formulized that it would not surprise me if the script were used intact to churn out other potboilers like *VD Madness, Gambling Madness, Drinking Madness, Juvenile Delinquency Madness,* or *Wild Party Madness.* Such films may indeed be hidden in some studio's vaults.

Reefer Madness has come to be regarded as the ultimate camp film: a poorly made, sensationalized account of a subject its filmmakers obviously knew

While Jack (L, standing) and Ralph look on approvingly, Blanche (L) and Mae try to turn Bill into another dope-crazed youth by offering him a reefer.

Jack won't even let Jimmy alone when he's with friends at his favorite high school hangout.

nothing about. It is a preposterous film that reenforces every falsehood you've ever heard about marijuana—it is violence-inducing, as bad as heroin, and ends *often* in one's "*inevitable* insanity." It was distributed in the early seventies by the National Organization for the Repeal of Marijuana Laws to make money for its lobbying efforts. Since then it has been a big hit on campuses and at midnight screenings where dope-smoking audiences sit and laugh at the naivete of the older generations who wrote up today's antimarijuana laws. (And when it is revealed in documentary footage that marijuana is impossible to stamp out because it grows wildly here in America, audiences cheer.)

Reefer Madness's foreword asserts that "Marihuana [sic] is . . . a violent narcotic—an unspeakable scourge —THE REAL PUBLIC ENEMY NUMBER ONE!!" It is clearly shown to be addictive, even to a newcomer to the drug such as Jimmy, who nervously asks Jack for a joint before he can drive. And it is a hallucinogenic, as shown when Bill imagines Mary is unzipping her own dress for Ralph instead of him forcing her to strip.

Director Louis Gasnier doesn't think it necessary for his characters to *inhale* in order to be overcome by marijuana's power, and his players sit around puffing like steamboats, immediately feeling its effects and acting like speed freaks. Clearly, like many Americans, Gasnier associates marijuana addiction with people who either dance wildly or play hip music. (The fast-playing pianist at the malt shop is the first we see who goes insane from the drug.)

The violent nature of the drug is emphasized. After relating the case of a marijuana-influenced boy who axed his parents to death, Dr. Carroll is *then* told a really vicious tale of someone addicted to the drug. Too much marijuana, according to the film, will lead to insanity just as too much masturbation will. By the end of the film, Ralph is in worse shape than the pianist. Surrounding his eyes are hideous black marks, and we can only agree when looking at his mindless expression that he should be sent to a mental hospital for life. We understand just how harmful marijuana is because Jack and Mae, who both drink, don't use the stuff—they just give it to the kids. (Incidentally, why doesn't Gasnier ever deal with the issue of money? The kids are never shown paying Jack or Mae for the joints.) One big gangster quits the operation rather than give kids marijuana—since he's the type of thug who would kill without guilt, we think marijuana must be harmful for *him* to back out.

The personal tragedy we witness is the ruination of the relationship between Mary and Bill, both nice kids who drink hot chocolate, are good students who study together, recite *Romeo and Juliet*, and play tennis. They are a healthy couple, as "straight" as two kids can be. Bill even wears a bow tie, and his mother says he doesn't ever lie. He fixes his brother's toy airplane and calls Mary a "swell girl," just like Dick Powell was doing at the time in Busby Berkeley musicals. If Bill can get involved with marijuana, Dr. Carroll seems to be telling the constantly nodding members of the PTA, then any kid can fall under the influence of the evil weed. And even if their kids don't get directly involved in smoking marijuana they can still be victims to its consequences —as Mary certainly was. No wonder Dr. Carroll slams his fist on the desk so many times.

So in *Reefer Madness*, we see Mary and Jack killed, Blanche driven to suicide, Mae (as immoral as bluenoses in 1936 believed her namesake Mae West to be) sent to prison, Ralph sent permanently to the mental hospital, a pedestrian run down, families broken up, hearts torn apart, and kids who will suffer guilt and bad memories until the day they die—all because kids couldn't resist a few kicks! Certainly this tale is strong enough for anyone who believes the film's premise that marijuana causes violence and insanity to make them refrain from using it. Or is it? The great time the marijuana smokers have—drinking free liquor, partying, meeting friendly people like Jack and Mae (villains from the TV Superman school), having sex, loose women, and lots of laughs—*before* facing the tragic circumstances—makes me think of a famous anti-VD film once shown to American soldiers. In that simulated-action short, several GI's are picked up by a beautiful brunette who gives them syphillis; the army stopped showing the film when soldiers reported they would gladly accept VD for a few minutes in bed with such a gorgeous woman. If anything, the wild life depicted in *Reefer Madness* would make high schoolers keen on joining the drug scene.

The expressions of Blanche, Mae, and the permanently stoned Ralph tell us that the jig is up in this den of mad dope fiends.

Rio Bravo

1959 Warner Bros. release of an Armada production
Director: Howard Hawks
Producer: Howard Hawks
Screenplay: Jules Furthman and Leigh Brackett
From a short story by B. H. McCampbell
Cinematography: Russell Harlan
Music: Dimitri Tiomkin
Editor: Folmar Blangsted
Running Time: 140 minutes

Cast: John Wayne (John T. Chance), Dean Martin (Dude), Ricky Nelson (Colorado), Angie Dickinson (Feathers), Walter Brennan (Stumpy), Ward Bond (Pat Wheeler), John Russell (Nathan Burdette), Pedro Gonzalez (Carlos), Estelita Rodriguez (Consuela), Claude Akins (Joe Burdette), Malcolm Atterbury (Jake), Harry Carey, Jr. (Harold), Bob Steele (Matt Harris)

Synopsis: John T. Chance is sheriff of a Texas border town. His ex-deputy, Dude, has become a drunk because the woman he loved turned out to be no good. When Joe Burdette throws a coin into a spittoon, Dude is so desperate for a drink that he goes after it. Chance kicks the spittoon away. Joe brutally beats Chance while his men hold him. Then he kills a bystander who tried to stop him. With Dude's help, Chance arrests Joe. They want to hold him for a United States marshal who will be coming through Rio Bravo in a few days. They worry that Joe's brother, Nathan Burdette, will try to break Joe out. Since Burdette has thirty or forty men in his employ, Chance knows that Burdette has a good chance for success. All Chance has to help him keep his prisoner in jail is Dude, who doesn't know if he has what it takes to be a lawman any more, and Stumpy, an old man with a limp, a cantankerous demeanor, and great loyalty to Chance and Dude. Chance turns down offers of help from Pat Wheeler and his men because he doesn't want amateurs. However, he would like Wheeler's top gun, Colorado, a young, cocky man with a quick draw, to join him. But Colorado says it's not his business. During this confusion, Chance tries to force Feathers, a beautiful gambling lady who has a bad reputation, to leave town. Feathers decides she wants to stay because she likes Chance. Contrary to what he believed, he learns that she is on the up-and-up. He finds himself attracted to her but has a hard time admitting it to himself.

Pat is shot in the back by a Burdette man. Dude chases the wounded killer into a saloon and kills him. Chance congratulates him.

Dude stands on the edge of town collecting guns from men who ride in. He is jumped and one of Burdette's hired killers puts on his outfit. Several of Burdette's men approach Chance, who stands in front of the hotel. Thinking they have been disarmed by the man in Dude's clothes, Chance is taken by surprise. They make him drop his holster. Colorado comes onto the street. Following Colorado's instructions, Feathers tosses a flower pot through the window and gets the bad guys' attention. Colorado tosses Chance a gun and the two men kill the villains and revive Dude. Chance accepts Colorado's help in fighting Burdette.

Dude and Chance are captured by Burdette while in the hotel. Two men take Chance toward the jail. Chance calls to Stumpy and tells him to let Joe go free. As both Dude and Joe expected, Stumpy pays no heed to this directive and shoots down the men guarding Chance.

Chance and Colorado set up an exchange: Joe for Dude. While all the others on both sides are under cover, Joe and Dude start walking toward their own sides. But as they pass, Dude jumps him and Joe is again their prisoner. There is a huge gun battle. Burdette and his men are holed up in a building. Stumpy suggests that Chance throw dynamite from Wheeler's wagons toward the building and try to shoot each stick. They blow up the building. Burdette is defeated. Dude is cured of his alcoholism. He will stay on as deputy.

Chance visits Feathers in her hotel room. She is wearing the skimpy outfit that will be her costume if she works for Carlos in his hotel. Chance tells her he'll arrest her if she wears the outfit in public. Feathers realizes that he loves her. Chance throws the outfit out the window.

If I were asked to choose a film that would justify the existence of Hollywood, I think it would be Rio Bravo.

—Robin Wood

For the armchair film critic who wants to explain the *auteur* theory to the person in the next seat, the films of Howard Hawks are still the ideal subjects for study. In his uncomplicated, thoroughly comprehensible body of work, it is truly simple to find Hawksian themes, characters, and plot elements that appear in film after film—regardless of the pictures' eras, casts, screenwriters, or genres. Hawks even boasted that he stole from himself, that he took a character from one film and put him/her in another film and that he repeated bits of action in several different films. ("If it worked once, it can work again.") *Rio Bravo* crosses genres to borrow heavily from both the Hawks-directed *To Have and Have Not* (1944) and the Hawks-produced and supervised *The Thing* (1951); and in turn serves as the prototype for *El Dorado* (1967) and *Rio Lobo* (1970), the other two westerns in Hawks's so-called *Rio Bravo* trilogy.

A slam-bang, exciting, truly funny western, *Rio Bravo* is quintessential Hawks. It is unabashedly commercial yet personal (which is why Hawks is revered by today's money-hungry young philistine directors); is about a group of heroic men of action who work

John Wayne and his unlikely partners in Rio Bravo: *Dean Martin and Ricky Nelson, actors and singers popular with entirely different generations.*

Chance arrests Joe Burdette, who, it's easy to tell, has made him extremely angry.

together for a common moral purpose; expresses a masculine code of conduct based on courage, loyalty, perseverance, and expertise; has a female lead that impresses the male lead by having what *he* believes are (positive) *masculine* traits (i.e., independence, loyalty, inner fortitude) and at the same time excites him with her femininity; contains action, humor, and large doses of dialogue (Hawks loves chatter); is filmed with a functional, unobtrusive camera—typically set at waist or eye level (he is an unpretentious filmmaker to say the least); and ends happily—which, especially during Hawks's later, genial years, is very characteristic of his films: if *any* of his major characters were to die, then the group's mission would be unsuccessful. Hawks's age may have something to do with why, beginning with *Rio Bravo*, his westerns took place, not in the great outdoors as did his *Red River* (1948) and *The Big Sky* (1952), but in (stylized, movie-set type) towns, and why almost all of *Rio Lobo* and *El Dorado*, too, take place in cloistered settings.

Probably the pivotal scene in *Rio Bravo* in terms of expressing Hawksian philosophy is when Pat Wheeler's killer runs into a saloon where a dozen of Burdette's men will give him protection. Dude knows that it is

now-or-never to see if he has recovered from his two-year drunk and regained his nerves and confidence. He tells Chance that he wants to be the one who will go through the saloon's batwing doors and instigate the action inside and that Chance should enter through the back door and assume the less dangerous role of backing him up. Chance asks: "Do you think you're good enough?" "I'd like to find out." "So would I."

Like most Hawks films, *Rio Bravo* is about men who *willingly* face a test of courage in order to prove that they are worthy men to themselves and their male friends (who, like Chance, often set the standards for male conduct). In Hawks, a man is not defined by how well he relates to women—quite obviously he is mystified by them ("You don't know women," Carlos tells Chance; "I don't know anything about women," admits Dude); he is defined by how well he handles pressure and how he reacts to danger. It is perfectly acceptable for Dude to be afraid—when a mule suddenly appears in front of Chance, the brave man jumps in fright; when the clean-shaven, spiffily-dressed Dude approaches the jail, jittery Stumpy, though reliable when the going gets tough, mistakes him for an outlaw and almost kills him. It is also acceptable for Dude to want assistance from his

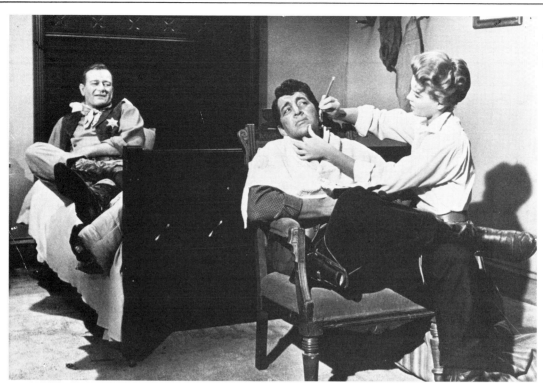

friends—if Chance didn't get help from Dude, Stumpy, Feathers, and Colorado, he would be killed several times over. But when the chips are down and other men need *his* assistance, Dude must be *dependable*, which along with the word *proficient* is how Hawks defines "good"—the highest rating a person can have.

In Hawks a man must prove himself "good" or he gets no respect. This is reflected in dialogue throughout the film: when Pat denigrates Dude, Chance replies, "He's been doing a good job taking care of me"; of self-assured Colorado, Chance comments, "I feel he's so good, he doesn't have to prove it"; when Dude starts wallowing in self-pity, Chance tells him, "Maybe you're right, and you aren't good anymore"; a bit jealous that Colorado is taking his place in Chance's eyes, Dude asks, "Is he as good as I used to be?"; when Stumpy thinks of the dynamite plan, he jokingly asks Chance, "Do you shoot as *well* [Stumpy doesn't use "good" English] as you think?" The only way Dude—it is *his* film, Hawks claimed—can earn the valued "good" distinction is by going into the saloon after Pat's killer. He must try to make it on his own, no matter what the odds. That is the mark of the professional. Well, Dude goes into the saloon, guns down Pat's killer, and bullies many of Burdette's hirelings. He doesn't get a raise in salary, but he gets something he'd much rather have: Chance tells him, "You were good in there."

In fact, Howard Hawks made *Rio Bravo* in reaction to *High Noon* (1952), in which lawman Gary Cooper spends more than an hour's worth of screen time pleading with townspeople to help him fight off a band of outlaws. Hawks was convinced that the professional Cooper was supposed to be would have tried to handle the situation himself rather than risking the lives of the people he was hired to protect. In *Rio Bravo*, Pat asks

sheriff Chance if he wants to use any of his men as deputies in fighting Burdette's men. Chance turns down Pat's offer because Pat's men are all amateurs. Chance will "chance" it with the help of Dude and Stumpy. "That's all you've got?" asks Pat with a touch of disbelief. "That *what* I've got," Chance responds, knowing that Dude and Stumpy (who must have been something in his heyday) at least have had experience in similar situations. They will be doing their *job*.

In *The Man Who Shot Liberty Valance* (1962), John Ford mocks his friend Howard Hawks's propensity for having his male characters never back down from a fight even when it means they are initiating the fight themselves. In *Rio Bravo*'s famous wordless opening, villain Joe Burdette throws a coin in a spittoon to see if drunkard Dude will stoop so low as to retrieve it in order to buy himself a drink. Before Dude can put his hand into the spittoon, Chance kicks it away. Dude looks up at his friend. The point-of-view camera angle emphasizes how far beneath the standards set by Chance Dude realizes he has fallen. Now Chance is willing to confront Joe, to fight him in all probability and maybe die, because of how Joe has humiliated Dude. And Dude, though gunless, is willing to fight the whole world. The same scene in *Liberty Valance*: villain Valance (Lee Marvin) trips gunless Jimmy Stewart as he carries a steak dinner to a customer he is serving in the restaurant where he works. He stumbles and the steak falls to the ground. Stewart has been humiliated and Valance, who calls Stewart "Dude," is not through with him. Suddenly John Wayne enters the frame next to the crouched Stewart. He comes in right to left as in the Hawks film. He reveals his gunbelt as he faces Valance and is ready to draw on him and maybe die because of what Valance has done to Stewart. He orders Valance to

Stumpy gives Chance the support he needs to subdue Burdette's men. Walter Brennan is wonderful in many films. Rio Bravo *is one of them.*

pick up the steak. But Stewart realizes how stupid this whole episode is and gets to his feet, yells at the two men for being willing to risk their lives over someone else's honor which wasn't damaged badly in the first place, and slaps the steak he picked off the ground back on the plate. There is no fight and no one gets killed (including an innocent bystander like the one killed in *Rio Bravo*).

Like his friend Ford, Hawks realized that his heroes often toss away common sense while trying to prove themselves in battle. He loved his characters because they were a little bit crazy, and childish to boot. "We're all fools," acknowledges Feathers after examining the desperate situation the characters find they are in but make no attempt to get out of. When Colorado decides not to put himself on the line by fighting Burdette's men, Chance approves: "He made sense. I'd like to have him." When Colorado does join the lawman, Stumpy articulates Hawks's feelings when he addresses Chance: "You've found yourself another knucklehead." As if to reward his characters for living with reckless abandon, Hawks will find a way to let them survive their ordeal. In *Rio Bravo* the men win out primarily because they fight *together*. But Hawks helps them by having the outlaws mistakenly play the "cutthroat" song with which Santa Anna tried to intimidate the Texans under siege in the Alamo back in 1836. They unwittingly have equated these four men holed up in the jail with those gallant Texans, and by doing this they inadvertently have elevated them from men to heroes. And they will fight like heroes. As the music plays, Dude puts down his glass untouched and sees that his hands no longer shake. He knows he has his confidence back. "All because of a piece of music," he says.

As in most Hawks films there is a woman on the fringe of the male group who, as critic David Thomson suggests, has the "ability to inhabit a man's world without asking concessions and without needing to rock the conventions." Feathers does indeed have what Chance considers masculine traits: she gambles, drinks

Chance spends much time in doorways when talking with Feathers—an indication that he is confused by her and isn't sure whether he should stay or leave.

herself drunk, participates in a gun battle (albeit in a feminine way—throwing a flower pot through a window), and even sits outside Chance's door while he sleeps to protect him from intruders (a traditional masculine duty for sleeping females in jeopardy). She is Chance's equal, he realizes, because of her brave deeds and because she refuses to be intimidated by this giant of a man. And through it all Feathers—played by a young, beautiful Angie Dickinson back when her legs were insured for a million dollars—remains feminine. As in most films, the male and female lead impress each other by trading jibes and by having the ability (at least on the female's part) of reading each others' minds. There is a lot of play and sparring, but under it all there is tenderness (how wonderful is the wordless scene when Chance comes down the stairs of the hotel while in his socks, picks up and cradles the sleeping Feathers in his arms, and carries her back up the stairs to her bed), and maturity: as Molly Haskell has often written, more than any other actor, Wayne could carry on mature, adult, mutually respectful relationships with women. Probably the distinguishing characteristic of the relationship between Chance and Feathers is how much time is spent in doorways, indicating how wary each is of getting into a relationship that might restrict his or her independence and which might end with one or both of them making absolute fools of themselves. But Chance and Feathers are willing to put themselves on the line. In *Take One* (October 1972), the late Leigh Brackett, who wrote or co-wrote the screenplays for Hawks's *The Big Sleep* (1946), *Rio Bravo* (1959), *Hatari!* (1962), *El Dorado* (1967), and *Rio Lobo* (1970), commented:

> Your own self is the only person you can always be certain of having around. I think Howard Hawks knows this, too, and that is why there is so little of the living-happily-ever-after in his films. His heroes and heroines are what he calls "grown up." They don't expect the moon with a string around it, they do not expect or desire to own each other. They are content with what they have, for as long as they have it, and this is possible because the Hawksian woman is not husband-hunting or looking for "security." She is secure in herself, and she is giving her love as a free person, with open hands.

This is an action western, but what makes *Rio Bravo* so special are the relationships between the individual characters. Not just Feathers and Chance, and Dude and Chance, but also Stumpy and Chance (I'll bet prankster Hawks had Wayne retake the scene many times where he kisses Walter Brennan's forehead); Stumpy and Dude, whom Stumpy seems to idolize even more than he does Chance; and Dude and Colorado. It is a highlight of the film when Ricky Nelson and Dean Martin join each other for some singing and guitar picking, and the great Walter Brennan joins in with his harmonica and scratchy but energetic singing. It is as if a few of the Seven Dwarfs got together for some merriment. Stumpy's voice takes away from the musical harmony, but Hawks's masculine harmony rings through loud and clear; and Chance understandably looks on with a smile of approval.

Rock 'n' Roll High School

1979 New World
Director: Allan Arkush
Producer: Michael Finnell
Screenplay: Richard Whitley,
Russ Dvonch, and Joseph McBride
From a story by Allan Arkush

and Joe Dante
Cinematography: Dean Cundey
Music: The Ramones
Editors: Larry Bock and Gail Werbin
Running time: 93 minutes

Cast: P. J. Soles (Riff Randell), Vincent Van Patten (Tom Roberts), Clint Howard (Eaglebauer), Dey Young (Kate Rambeau), Mary Woronov (Evelyn Togar), Dick Miller (Police Chief Klein), Paul Bartel (Mr. McGree), Alix Elias (Coach Steroid), Don Steele (Screamin' Steve Stevens), Loren Lester (Fritz Hansel), Daniel Davies (Fritz Gretel), Lynn Farrell (Angel Dust), Grady Sutton (school board president), The Ramones: Joey, Johnny, Dee Dee, and Marky Ramone (themselves)

Synopsis: Vince Lombardi High has the worst academic standing in California. Three principals in a row have suffered breakdowns because the student body cares about nothing but rock 'n' roll. Tough new principal Miss Togar promises to bring an end to the music craze. She sends two monitors, Fritz Hansel and Fritz Gretel, through the halls to spy on the students.

Cheerleader Riff Randall is the girl Miss Togar blames for the trouble in the school. Riff doesn't care about studies, just her favorite music group, The Ramones. She writes a song called "Rock 'n' Roll High School" which she hopes to sell to the group. She skips school so she can be the first in line to buy tickets for an upcoming Ramones concert.

Football player Tom Roberts has a crush on Riff, but he can't make a good impression on her—she thinks him handsome but a dork. In fact, every girl in school except brainy virgin Kate Rambeau, who has a crush on him, thinks Tom unbearably square. He pays a visit to Eaglebauer, a student who has an office in the boys' room and promises students that he can get them anything they want. Eaglebauer says he can get Tom a date with Riff and eventually get him to score with her.

Kate asks Eaglebauer to help her have an affair with Tom. Eaglebauer arranges it so Tom thinks Kate is the girl he will practice with before braving a date with Riff. Riff buys tickets to the Ramones for herself and the whole student body. But Miss Togar is so angry at her for skipping classes that she sends Hansel and Gretel to take the tickets away. Having nothing else to do, Riff agrees to go out with Tom in his new van, but she doesn't tell him that she will be bringing Kate along as his date. Riff and Kate cancel the date when Riff wins a radio contest prize of tickets to the Ramones concert. They attend the concert and meet the Ramones. Angel Dust, a groupie, steals Riff's song and tries to run away with the package it's in. Tom, who has come to the concert, gives chase and knocks the package from Angel Dust's arms. Riff thanks him and runs off to see Joey Ramone, whom she has a great crush on. Tom sees that only Kate really cares about him and they agree to be friends. The Ramones agree to play Riff's song on their next album.

Miss Togar and several concerned parents try to burn Ramones records in front of the school. Riff and Tom prevent them from doing so. All the students rush into the school and take it over, renaming it Rock 'n' Roll High School. The Ramones arrive and become honorary members of the student body. There is wild dancing and partying. Even kindly music teacher Mr. McGree joins in the festivities. Square Kate and square Tom dance with the others and hug and kiss each other.

Miss Togar calls the police and orders the students out of the school. Kate and Eaglebauer devise a bomb. All the students file out of the school. Then they resume their party and the school explodes. Miss Togar is taken off to a mental hospital.

For viewers who aren't crazy about the Ramones, the picture's musical highlight is when Riff (center) and other members of the gym class sing and dance to the title song.

Rock 'n' Roll High School is the prime example of a picture that became a "cult" favorite by design. In most locations, New World Pictures chose not to open it in neighborhood theaters and drive-ins, as is standard practice with its new pictures, but premiered it as a Midnight Movie, hoping that it would *immediately* become an "event picture" among Ramones fanatics on the order of *The Rocky Horror Picture Show* (1977). Because of the unusual distribution stratagem whereby it was publicized to be a "cult film" before it had earned that distinction, it attracted many curious moviegoers who (knowing nothing of the Ramones) might have bypassed it otherwise; as a result it developed a small but genuine cult following among film enthusiasts, especially in college towns.

The best thing *Rock 'n' Roll High School* has going for it is a high-spirited young cast headed by *Carrie* (1976) and *Halloween* (1978) alumnus P. J. Soles, bebopping and high-kicking nonstop, drooling over how Joey Ramone "slithers pizza into his mouth," and repeatedly injecting life into the picture when the humor has gone limp. Also quite good are pretty Dey Young (the sister of Leigh Taylor-Young) and handsome Vincent Van Patten (the tennis pro son of Dick Van Patten), and former Warhol Superstar Mary Woronov,

who is so deglamorized that her Miss Togar comes across as an evil Eve Arden. I am less impressed with Clint Howard (the brother of Ron Howard), who has the other major role: he is too laid-back (the director's fault) as the Sergeant Bilko-like Eaglebauer. And then there are The Ramones, one of the least attractive punk rock groups (which is saying a lot). I am not a fan of their high-powered music (Joey composes songs while using a one-string guitar), but they're amusing in this film and fun to watch when performing. Certainly one of the highlights occurs when there is a line outside the theater at which they will perform, and the Ramones, in black leather jackets and jeans ripped at the knees, walk past slowly, their legs and backs bent, their bodies crooked; playing their instruments, singing, and shooting their clenched fists into the air to get a response from their fans. The funniest moment also involves the Ramones: they come onto the school grounds and one of them rudely sticks Miss Togar in the rear with the arm of his guitar, prompting her to ask the group, "Does your mother know you're Ramones?"

The film was scripted by Richard Whitley and Russ Dvonch of the *National Lampoon* (with an assist from Joseph McBride), and the humor is so inconsistent, with a good gag/joke being followed by a dud, that I wouldn't be surprised if they took turns writing lines—

Riff looks into Joey Ramone's eyes as he performs at the big concert. Directly behind her are (L-R) Tom, Eaglebauer, and Kate. The extra holding up his arm is one of numerous Ramones fans allowed at the free concert. They were so unruly that P.J. Soles was terrified while filming this entire sequence.

or if one of them is funny and the other came along for the ride. Someone must be held responsible for unimaginative one-liners like "(Tom's) brother thinks he's an only child"; "I sold (Tom) his first touchdown"; "I don't want to have fun, I want to be with Tom"; "I once played nurse with the boy next door and got sued for malpractice"; and (I admit I snickered) "I only use my math book on special equations." On the other hand someone must take credit for the scream of gags having to do with mice (some of which are giants that walk on two legs and wear headsets) and how they are affected by rock 'n' roll; and the three-day gag during which Kate delivers Riff's excuses to Miss Toger, saying she is absent from school because of the deaths of her mother, her father, and her goldfish. That in itself isn't so funny, but it all leads up to a good punch line: when Fritz Hansel and Fritz Gretel bring Riff's still active goldfish to Miss Togar, the upset principal concludes: "I'm sure her parents are alive, too."

While the film is full of nonsensical humor, I think it lacks diabolically conceived outrageousness. It needs more bawdiness, or better, downright *filthiness* in spots. This is the *one* film that cries out for the "sick" humor found in *National Lampoon's Animal House* (1978), but the filmmakers have for some reason kept the picture quite wholesome. It's a shame that a major part of the film has to do with Tom and Kate's efforts to get "laid" (their expression), yet the whole thing is treated in PG fashion, like a picture about the making of an X-rated film that has no nudity. I would have much preferred it if what Tom wanted was a kiss or date from Riff and Kate wanted the same from Tom. If the final solution is going to be so innocent—Tom and Kate kiss—then we don't want to be teased by hints of a more exciting finale (on screen or off).

Probably the worst mistake the filmmakers made was in not exploiting the fact that everyone hates high school. Only on occasion is our memory of high school jolted: when the monitors stop a guy in the hall and demand his pass—when he doesn't have it they laugh at the picture on his I.D., give him demerits for looking ugly, and push a beany into his face; when the rebelling students throw "Tuesday Surprise" at the cooks who made it; and when Miss Togar gets mad at Riff for punching her and gives her "detention for life!" I love all of this, but regrettably, not much more of the film's humor comes out of its setting in a high school.

The finale in which the school is blown up reminds me of a serious Dolly Parton musical composition called "Evening Shade," about a group of kids who set fire to their orphanage with the evil proprietor still inside, and it burns to the ground "just like the hell it was." I always found the Parton song remarkable because there is no standard final verse where the children get retribution for killing someone and destroying property.

The song is subversive because it has revolutionaries (young as they are) who are in the right. I think the filmmakers wanted their final scene to have the same effect. This may be a silly comedy but there is no other commercial American film in which an American institution is destroyed and no one is punished for the deed. The only trouble is that because the filmmakers didn't take the time to establish Vince Lombardi High as a "prison" no matter who the principal is, the act of blowing it up seems a foolish gesture (only there so the special effects crew could do their stuff). Education isn't

You'll find their counterparts in your high school yearbook. (L-R) Miss Togar, Mr. McGree (played by Paul Bartel, who has directed New World productions), and Coach Steroid.

the enemy—Miss Togar is—so leave the school up. The film should have ended minutes earlier when the students and the more liberal teachers take over the school from Togar and rename it Rock 'n' Roll High School, turning Vince Lombardi's picture to the wall. Only with the school in their hands can they claim victory over the likes of Miss Togar. With no school, neither they nor Miss Togar can enjoy the spoils of victory.

Riff leads the Ramones, (L-R) Johnny, Marky, Joey, and Dee Dee, through the halls of the liberated high school, now called Rock 'n' Roll High School.

The Rocky Horror Picture Show

1975 Great Britain 20th Century-Fox release of a Lou Adler– Michael White production
Director: Jim Sharman
Producer: Michael White
Screenplay: Jim Sharman and Richard O'Brien
From the play *The Rocky Horror Show,* by Richard O'Brien
Cinematography: Peter Suschitzky
Music and lyrics: Richard O'Brien
Editor: Graeme Clifford
Running time: 100 minutes

Cast: Tim Curry (Dr. Frank-N-Furter), Susan Sarandon (Janet Weiss), Barry Bostwick (Brad Majors), Richard O'Brien (Riff Raff), Patricia Quinn (Magenta), Little Nell (Columbia), Jonathan Adams (Dr. Everett V. Scott), Peter Hinwood (Rocky Horror), Meatloaf (Eddie), Charles Gray (Criminologist), Jeremy Newson (Ralph Hapschatt), Hilary Labow (Betty Munroe)

Synopsis: The Criminologist narrates this story. After the wedding of Ralph and Betty Hapschatt, Brad Majors proposes to Janet Weiss. She accepts. They will have a night to remember. After leaving Denton, Ohio, they get lost in the rain. They visit a castle, where they are let in by Riff Raff, a strange butler. They meet the equally strange maid, Magenta. It turns out that at Dr. Frank-N-Furter's castle, on this very night, the annual convention of visitors from the planet Transsexual in the galaxy Transylvania is being held. Brad and Janet are stripped down to their underwear, although they would rather go home. Janet faints because of the excitement.

Dr. Frank-N-Furter, wearing high heels, lipstick, eye makeup, and sexy female underwear, appears. He is about to complete an experiment—bringing Rocky Horror, a handsome, muscular young man, to life. But when Rocky comes to life, he is scared of Frank and runs away. Eddie arrives on his motorcycle. Groupie Columbia almost swoons every time she sees him. Frank locks Rocky up and kills Eddie with an ice pick.

Frank seduces Janet and then Brad. Each makes him promise not to tell the other. However, Janet sees Frank and Brad together on a television monitor. She weeps. Then she sings for Rocky to make love to her.

Dr. Everett Scott, Brad's science teacher from Denton High, arrives at the castle. Frank knows Scott has a government contract to investigate UFOs and he suspects that Brad and Janet are his accomplices. In truth, Scott has come to the castle to find out what has happened to his nephew, Eddie, who sent a note saying strange things were happening in the castle. Frank serves everyone dinner—and then reveals they are eating Eddie. Columbia is upset, and Scott isn't too happy either. Frank turns Scott, Brad, Janet, and Columbia into statues. He tells Riff Raff and Magenta that they will be rewarded for helping him discover the plot.

Frank, Brad, Janet, Scott (in his wheelchair), and Rocky dance for the conventioneers in front of the RKO tower and sing about old horror movies. Frank says he will be going home to Transylvania, but Riff Raff and Magenta, wearing space outfits, tell him to say hello to oblivion. Riff Raff kills him with an antimatter laser blast. A sad Rocky picks him up and they climb up the RKO tower. Magenta dies from a blast. Riff Raff says he will transport the whole castle back to Transylvania. Scott, Brad, and Janet escape as the castle explodes and becomes, as the Criminologist says, lost in time, and space, and meaning.

The dynamic Tim Curry is Dr. Frank-N-Furter, the queen *of the cinema.*

The undisputed king . . . no . . . *queen* of the Midnight Movie circuit, *The Rocky Horror Picture Show* has become the very definition of the term "cult picture." It is the *one* film that cannot even be discussed without mentioning its fans—for they have changed it from being an undistinguished campy movie to an entertaining multimedia show. Every Friday and Saturday night for the last few years *Rocky Horror* fanatics—members of the National Rocky Horror Fan Club, participants in local *Rocky Horror* actalongs that accompany the film, or just viewers who see the film every week—show up at approximately two hundred theaters around the United States and Canada, many dressed in the outrageous costumes and makeup worn in the picture by the various characters. They hawk *Rocky Horror* T-shirts, buttons, dolls, magazines, books, and newsletters, announce birthdays of club members and other special events, welcome "virgins" (newcomers) to the screenings and encourage them to actively participate in the proceedings, and then watch the picture for what may be their three hundredth time or more. But "watch" isn't the correct word. Only the most timid "virgins" watch. This is the ultimate audience participation film: the cultists recite the dialogue en masse, shout out their own additions to the script, which vary slightly around the country ("How do you spell urine?" they yell at "asshole" Brad just before he asks, "You are?"), and, under a spotlight, put on a singing-dancing-mime performance that half duplicates, half parodies the action taking place simultaneously on the screen above them. Participants also run up and down the aisles throughout the picture. When rice is thrown by the screen actors during the wedding scene, the cultists reach into their prop bags and heave rice into the audience. When Brad and Janet step out into the rain, the cultists shoot their water pistols. However, the regulars come prepared—they whip out umbrellas while the "virgins" get wet. The crowd activities are zany, boisterous, sometimes vulgar, and nonstop. In *Fame* (1980), there is a scene that is set at a *Rocky Horror Picture Show* screening where a "virgin" tells the fanatics to sit down so he can watch the show. Their angry reply is that they *are* the show and that *he* should sit down or go home. Truly, they are the show, what elevates an evening at *Rocky Horror* into an event, what raises the entertainment level one hundred percent. In fact, I believe that your enjoyment is totally dependent on how funny, creative, and unified the *Rocky Horror* fanatics are on the night you attend the show. If they are "on" there is a chance you will have such a good time that you will become one of the regulars, and show up again the following weekend. It is like no other show around, neither intimidating nor smug under the right circumstances, almost a throwback to when cheering small-town audiences filled theaters on Main Streets and movies were community get-togethers. As Jonathan Rosenbaum suggested in *Sight and Sound*

(Spring 1980), "this audience, rather than allow itself to be used as an empty vessel to be filled with a filmmaker's grand mythic meanings, has been learning how to use a film chiefly as a means of communicating with itself." When the shy teen-age girl in *Fame* jumps out of her seat and joins the *Rocky Horror* regulars dancing "The Time Warp," she finds it a liberating experience—and that's really the way it is for all those shy people who go wild and become entertainers/stars at *Rocky Horror* Fridays and Saturdays at midnight. Who needs parties?

What became the cinema's greatest phenomenon outside of *Star Wars* (1977) began as a rock opera written by English actor Richard O'Brien with the memorable title of *They Came from Denton High*. It later became *The Rock Horroar Show* and finally *The Rocky Horror Show*, the title used when it opened at the London Royal Court's sixty-seat Theatre Upstairs. Produced by Michael White, directed by Australian Jim Sharman, and starring Tim Curry, O'Brien, Patricia Quinn, Little Nell, Jonathan Adams, and Meatloaf—who would all participate in the film version—it proved so popular that it moved to the five-hundred-seat King's Road Theatre . . . where it is still playing.

In 1974, American producer Lou Adler convinced White to bring his show to America, and it did spectacular business at Adler's Roxy Theater on the Sunset Strip in Hollywood. Adler next convinced Twentieth

The excitement is too much for Janet, dammit, and she faints into the arms of Brad. Neither Riff Raff (played by the creator of The Rocky Horror Show, *Richard O'Brien) nor Magenta is overly concerned.*

Columbia unravels Rocky's bandages. He sings "The Sword of Damocies" for the onlookers.

Century-Fox to finance a movie version, and filming was completed in London in the spring of 1975 for about $1.5 million. Before the release of *The Rocky Horror Picture Show*, Adler opened the play on Broadway, where it flopped and closed after only forty-five performances. The movie also proved to be a disaster when first released in September 1975. But because it quickly developed an underground reputation, Adler and Fox publicist Tim Deegan didn't give up on it. Instead, they looked for new ways to push it. On April Fool's Day in 1976, *The Rocky Horror Picture Show* made its debut as a Midnight Movie at the Waverly in New York's Greenwich Village. Soon after, it opened midnights in theaters around the country. This strategy was determined by the simple fact that Adler and Deegan couldn't get the picture regular bookings and "Midnights" was their only alternative. Of course the picture caught on at the Waverly and in cities and towns throughout the country, and its incredible cult has refused to let it die. At first, in some cities, homosexuals, transvestites, and cyclists who like to harass homosexuals and transvestites were the chief audiences, but today's audiences are very diverse. In one row you're likely to find gays, transvestites, psychology students from the university, punk rockers, comic-book addicts, science fiction nuts, stoned-out viewers from the film that ended at midnight, high school students out on dates, a man in a raincoat, a woman in a man's raincoat, a tattooed marine, a prim lady who appropriately calls Brad "asshole" (his designation throughout the world) every time he shows his face, and people who wonder what they're doing there. This film has definite appeal to people who consider themselves outsiders but also to straitlaced Brads and Janets. No film attracts such a mixed crowd.

After a long stay at the Waverly, *Rocky Horror* changed theaters, following a few outbreaks of violence against gays. The Waverly *Rocky* cultists, considered the number-one group in America, moved with the film, and it was at the 8th Street Playhouse that I saw them and the picture for the only time. I was wary of attending the show (at such a late hour in New York) because of all the bad press about theater violence, but I found the reports exaggerated. It was a totally comfortable performance with no troublemakers in the audience, and supposedly that is the way it always is. Although I can't say I will ever see it again, for one evening I found it both entertaining and fascinating; it

Janet, dammit, finds the hiding Rocky and, sexually aroused, sings "Touch-a Touch-a Touch-a Touch Me" to him.

Transylvanian conventioneers do "The Time Warp" again.

was certainly better than I expected and I felt I got my money's worth. Go! It is just a little wearying—and I think that is the fault of the picture rather than the live show. The cast isn't always funny or clever but they are full of spirit and give their all.

I don't find the picture well made or particularly amusing, but there are a few things I like. When the stodgy criminologist suddenly demonstrates the "Time Warp" and shows the dance steps on a chart, I can't help thinking how funny it would have been if Dr. Frank Baxter had danced during all those high school science films the Criminologist's scene seems to be spoofing. The "Time Warp" number is a lot of fun, as is Meat Loaf's wild rock number "Whatever Happened to Saturday Night?" which he sings after zooming in on a motorcycle. I am less impressed with the other songs. The concept of having the doctor in the Frankenstein tale be the monster is novel and clever, but Rocky Horror seems too dull a creature for the flamboyant Dr. Frank-N-Furter to fall so deeply in love with. Tim Curry is dynamic as Frank and, importantly, is the cinema's one masculine-acting (sweet) transvestite! It's odd seeing this muscular actor in drag. I wish the film were a bit sexier—although Tim Curry does his bit to help, and the "Touch-a Touch-a Touch-a Touch Me" dirty-lyrics number Janet sings to Rocky while moving his hands over her breasts is not something one would find in a PG-rated picture. No doubt the most jarring (and humorous) "sexual" encounter is when Frank seduces Janet by pretending to be Brad and then seduces Brad by pretending to be Janet. The script should have other against-the-norm, brave moments like these. Unfortunately, this send-up of horror pictures and teen pictures is trite and trivial. The picture peters out (and, to a first-time viewer, becomes a bit confusing) and by

the time Frank-N-Furter was killed, I wished the film had ended twenty minutes earlier. The hectic pace was too much to maintain.

In a world of impermanence, it is reassuring to know that every Friday and Saturday night, at midnight, many weirdly dressed, friendly people get together to enjoy themselves and entertain others. I have a good feeling toward these *Rocky Horror Picture Show* cultists and hope they will continue their good work. (I am glad Twentieth has made a sequel for them.) Let there always be lips.

The Rocky Horror Picture Show *has gone haywire by the time (L-R) Rocky, Columbia, Frank-N-Furter, Janet, dammit, and Brad (out of picture) sing and dance a tribute to RKO Radio Pictures, the makers of* King Kong.

The Scarlet Empress

1934 Paramount
Director: Josef von Sternberg
Screenplay: Manuel Komroff
Adapted from a diary of Catherine the Great
Cinematography: Bert Glennon
Music: Mendelssohn and Tchaikovsky
Musical arrangement: John M. Leopold, W. Frank Harling, and Milan Roder.
Running Time: 110 minutes

Cast: Marlene Dietrich (Sophia Frederica, later Catherine II of Russia), Sam Jaffe (Grand Duke Peter), John Lodge (Count Alexei), Louise Dresser (Empress Elizabeth), Maria Sieber (Sophia as a child), C. Aubrey Smith (Prince August), Ruthelma Stevens (Countess Elisabeth), Olive Tell (Princess Johanna), Gavin Gordon (Gregory Orloff), Jameson Thomas (Lieutenant Ovtsyn), Erville Alderson (Chancellor Beatuchef), Marie Wells (Marie), Edward Van Sloan (Herr Wagner), Hans von Twardowski (Ivan Shuvolov), Davison Clark (Archimandrite Simeon Tevedovsky), Jane Darwell (Mlle. Cardell)

Synopsis: As a child in Germany, Princess Sophia Frederica has her toys taken away from her and is told that she must begin preparing for life in some royal house. Several years later the teen-age Sophia is informed that she has been chosen by Empress Elizabeth of Russia to marry Grand Duke Peter, the heir to her throne. So the shy, innocent—but a little spoiled—Sophia travels with her mother, Princess Johanna, to Russia, a nation Sophia knows to be educationally backward, uncultured, and brutal. She becomes attracted to her handsome escort Count Alexei, who steals kisses from her when Johanna is not watching. He tells Sophia that Peter is magnificent looking, and though Alexei appeals to her, she cannot wait to see the man she will marry.

When Sophia arrives in the Russian court, she is overwhelmed by the immense surroundings. She is taken to see Empress Elizabeth, a tough, ill-mannered, illiterate woman who immediately changes Sophia's name to Catherine and orders her to give birth to a male heir. Already having trouble adapting to the drastic changes in her life, Catherine is upset to discover that Peter is a cruel, cowardly half-wit, whom Elizabeth orders about as if he were a dumb animal. Catherine and Peter are married, but the marriage is never consummated. Peter develops a great hatred for his bride, preferring the company of his lover, Countess Elisabeth. Catherine doesn't mind Peter spending time with Elisabeth so long as he doesn't interfere with her affairs.

Catherine continues to be attracted to Count Alexei, but when she discovers him to be one of Empress Elizabeth's many lovers, she becomes disillusioned, swearing that she will no longer be pushed around and used. Immediately, she begins a romance with the captain of the guards. She gives birth to a son, which pleases Empress Elizabeth but embarrasses Peter because he and everyone else in the country knows that he is not the boy's father. His hatred of Catherine increases, but she pays little attention to his threats and insults.

Empress Elizabeth dies, and Peter becomes emperor. While his men terrorize the countryside, Peter insults Russia and its church. He threatens to have Catherine executed and to replace her on the throne with Countess Elisabeth. Realizing she has no choice but to act quickly in order to save herself, Catherine approves a plan by the army, among whom she has many intimate contacts, and the ministers to overthrow Peter. In the coup d'état, Peter is strangled. Catherine becomes the empress of Russia.

Josef von Sternberg's *The Scarlet Empress*, the great director's self-expressed "relentless excursion in style," is certainly among the most bewildering and bizarre films ever to emerge from a major Hollywood studio. The sixth and most idiosyncratic of the seven Sternberg-Dietrich collaborations stimulates the senses with provocative sexual imagery, often of a perverse nature; breathtaking montages of barbaric torture, some nightmarish, some realistic; mammoth palace chambers, heatless and sparsely furnished, with heavy, fifteen-foot-high doors that groups of nameless scurrying ladies of the court struggle to open, and large, weirdly sculptured gargoyles, saints, and martyrs supporting mirrors and candelabra, their faces and bodies twisted into attitudes of great suffering; an eighteenth-century Russian court full of oddball characters one would more expect to find in Alice's Wonderland, with Sam Jaffe's unforgettable Grand Duke Peter a genuine mad Mad Hatter; and strangely amusing tête-à-têtes—so familiar to Dietrich throughout her career, but especially in her Sternberg films—where what's implied by voice fluctuations, hand and shoulder gestures, and subtle facial and eye movements is far more meaningful than what is actually said.

At times we seem to be watching a silent movie, as parts of Sternberg's drama unfolds, not with dialogue but with only music and sound effects to heighten the impact of the extraordinary images. There are many such passages, but among the most astonishing, I think, are: the wedding ceremony in the magnificent cathedral, with Rubenstein's lovely "Kameni Ostraw" sung in the background, while the camera moves back and forth between extreme close-ups of the gloating Peter, obviously looking forward to the night ahead with Catherine in his bed, eyes wide and teeth bared, his head moving incessantly from side to side as he chomps on a ceremonial wafer as if it were a wad of tobacco, and the beautiful, overwhelmed Catherine, tearful and gasping for breath—so close to the flickering, bright flame of a candle that her sad face appears to be melting as if it were part of a burning doll; the wedding banquet, during which a solo violinist plays a Sternberg composition while the camera moves over the cadaverous remains of a feast obviously wolfed down by gluttonous barbarians, and then rises to reveal those around the table, all looking too bloated to move or speak (Peter, however, continues to eat); and the sweeping finale, with the music soaring to a feverish pitch, bells clanging, and horses clomping across wooden palace floors and up wooden stairs, as Catherine takes power, her "rapturous ride up the palace steps," suggests Andrew Sarris, "the visual correlative of soaring sexual ecstasy."

Visually, *The Scarlet Empress* is dazzling, the most imaginative film of the sound era prior to *Citizen Kane* (1941). Every frame is masterfully composed, with light and shadow perfectly balanced, and the players, in their makeup and period costumes, part of the decor. In trying to achieve the exact "look" he desired, Sternberg worked closely with Paramount's resident costume designer Travis Banton; with imported Swiss artist Peter Balbush, Hans Drier, and Richard Kollorsz on the

Young Catherine looks at Prince August, part of her old, strict life in Germany. On her left is Count Alexei,
a much younger companion for Catherine, part of her new romance-filled life in Russia.

incredible Byzantine sets (that were meant to be "re-creations" of the Russian court, not replicas); and with cinematographer Bert Glennon on camera placement and movement, and lighting. His insistence on controlling every facet of the production was not always appreciated; in an interview I did with Sam Jaffe in 1977, he complained:

> He was a strange kind of director. He imposed himself upon his actors and technicians more than anybody with any individuality could stand. He had some brilliant men design the gargoyles and stair-wells, and then he'd take out a pencil and "fix up" their drawings. If you had to fix one of those cuckoo clocks, he was there. He was always there. In fact, he shot the whole thing—he was always down on the floor, forgetting he had a cameraman getting paid by Paramount. He was a "wonderful" character, all right. . . . We didn't get along at all because he allowed me no freedom to act. He tried to absorb me. As for Marlene, when she couldn't get the dialogue the way he wanted it, he'd have her raise her skirt a little. That's the kind of treatment she was subjected to.

Although there was discontent on the set—Jaffe even temporarily quit when he had to do fifty takes of the tremendous scene in which Peter screams at the dead aunt he loathed—as critic John Baxter writes: "There is no scene, no set, no shot that is not an emotional experience."

Writing in the historical journal *Mankind* (October 1968), Kate Holliday made this assessment: "If there is one constant in history's appraisal of Catherine II of Russia, it is that no two historians agree about her and her reign." Nevertheless, Sternberg has been accused of distorting history in his telling of Catherine's tale. Sam Jaffe was one of many to voice disapproval: "Sternberg was very careful about the buttons on the clothes we'd wear, and hired historians to make sure the period setting was correct—but he had no respect for historical accuracy whatsoever."

Sternberg did indeed take liberties with the facts, mostly by combining characters, condensing what really happened over many years into what at least seems to be a brief time span (although Dietrich's face ages/matures because of makeup modification, as the film progresses), and omitting certain details that would have complicated the story. But I would not say that Sternberg's discrepencies "distort" history. In fact, the "excesses" Sternberg supposedly took to make his characters seem outrageous—the main reason for critical complaint—were based entirely on fact. Peter really did drill spy-holes through chamber walls, and as an adult he played with toy soldiers (which Catherine helped him hide from Elizabeth)—even lynching a rat he caught chewing on some. Elizabeth could speak several languages, but, like Louise Dresser's ignorant hussy, truly could not read or write, and was as carnal, ill-mannered, uncouth, egocentric, and dictatorial as a madam in a cheap

With Alexei at her side, Catherine waits while her mother kisses the ring of Empress Elizabeth on the day Catherine arrives in Russia.

brothel; and Catherine does not wear military uniforms in the film simply to satisfy Sternberg's urge to dress Dietrich once again in men's clothing, as his detractors have claimed, but because the real Catherine often dressed that way.

In fact, Elizabeth also loved to wear men's clothing, and, to give herself ample opportunities, held a weekly ball, at which, by ukase, women dressed in pants and men dressed in hoopskirts. If Sternberg really wanted to be "excessive," he might have tried to slip a scene of such a ball past the studio chiefs. Moreover, he could have lengthened his film to include scenes from Catherine's thirty-four-year reign, which was characterized as much by her extreme libertinage as by the "enlightened" despot's opening of the cultural "window to the West." (As it is, Sternberg ends the film with a not so subtle ironic touch, forecasting the sexual depravity of Catherine later on: Catherine, straight-spined and smiling, is not shown in extreme close-up as is Garbo at the end of the same year's *Queen Christina*, but in a two-shot with a horse—it has, after all, been fairly well substantiated by most historians that the healthy sixty-seven-year-old Catherine's sudden death occurred while she was attempting intercourse with a mighty, and mighty heavy, steed.)

Sternberg's film is about a woman who rejects her fate, and through self-determinism achieves self-preservation. "Be obedient, and be worthy of a glorious destiny," is the awful advice given Sophia by Prince August, and for many years she naively follows it. At age seven she is deprived of her toys, and preparation begins for a royal marriage. At fifteen she is whisked from Germany to Russia and forced to marry an absolute idiot. Her parents are lost to her forever, not being allowed in Elizabeth's court. Her religion and name are changed, and she is *ordered* to have a *male* baby. Time and again, she is publicly humiliated by Elizabeth and Peter but does not question the life others have set out for her.

However, once she dutifully gives birth to a male heir, and is hurt by Alexei in romance, she is through being pushed around, and goes on the offensive to realize her personal ambitions, using what she acknowledges to be her own special "weapons." As the titles say, "Catherine has no more ideals." In Zoé Oldenbourg's biography, *Catherine the Great* (Pantheon, 1965), the turning point for Catherine comes at precisely the same time, when she had given birth and was upset by Saltykov's wavering affections: "She harbored herself against love and in the future, she would not be any man's plaything. She had had enough of figuring permanently in the light of a victim. . . . She made up her mind that in the future, she would be hard, acid, and mocking, and she succeeded, avenging herself on . . . the whole world." Oldenbourg saw this "self-enforced hardness" as "having an air of childish rebellion." But Sternberg's Catherine, at this point, is 100 percent woman—specifically, Marlene Dietrich.

Until Catherine rejects Alexei as he had rejected her earlier, we have seen Dietrich as she has never been in Sternberg's films, without her absolute control, her sense of irony, her air of superiority, her mystery, and her indifference. But now, thank goodness, *Dietrich* is back, living by her wit, her own code and logic, manipulating men who once thought they were controlling her. And how nonchalantly she reacts to Peter's cruelty and indulgences, all but ignoring the mock firing squad he surrounds her with and the return to court of his lover and comrade in perversity, Countess Elisabeth; the real Catherine cried when Peter called her a fool, and ordered her to drink a toast to his lover who, he swore, would soon replace Catherine as his queen—Dietrich takes it all in stride.

Film historian Tom Flinn writes, "As in Sternberg's *Shanghai Express* (1932) and *Blonde Venus* (1932), Dietrich manages to turn the tables on her male lover-adversary [Count Alexei] and still win his respect. In this reversal of conventional sex roles and the frank depiction of the sexual basis of power as well as the power of sex, *The Scarlet Empress* is easily thirty years ahead of its time." Sternberg was one of the few directors to recognize and explore the direct link be-

Catherine becomes empress when Peter is deposed. By her is a mighty steed, very much part of her legendary future.

tween sexual politics and political power. As it had been with Elizabeth, Catherine's coup d'état would not have been possible, according to Sternberg, if she hadn't won over the members of the Russian court and the military (from top to bottom) through sexual means.

Ugly until she reached her early twenties, and until then love-starved by her parents as well as boys and men, the real Catherine's desire for sexual satisfaction, once she had her first affair, became insatiable, as her memoirs attest: "It is my misfortune that my heart cannot rest content, even for an hour, without love." Yet, significantly, Catherine was still choosey (at least, before she became ruler) about to whom she gave her affections and sexual favors; as Zoé Oldenbourg points out, Catherine "had the faculty for making her amours coincide with the interests of her ambition." Dietrich is wonderful as Catherine, witty, ambitious, playful, and sexy, but I have one misgiving about casting her in the part: we cannot explore the real *reasons* so many men pursued the not very pretty Catherine, because with Dietrich in the role, her beauty alone is more than enough reason.

Now generally considered one of Sternberg's best films (though most mainstream critics are not convinced), *The Scarlet Empress* got terrible notices in 1934, and consequently did poorly at the box office with a public already tiring of Sternberg-Dietrich films. Meanwhile, Paul Czinner's stilted, conventionally made English production, *Catherine the Great*, received fine reviews in America and did well commercially. In Sternberg's next, and final, film with Dietrich, *The Devil Is a Woman* (1935), a character reflects what must have been Sternberg's attitude toward the unjustly harsh treatment *The Scarlet Empress* was subjected to: "Critics don't value genius."

Catherine is less than thrilled that her husband, Grand Duke Peter, is demented. Here he holds one of his treasured toy soldiers.

1956 Warner Bros.
Director: John Ford
Producers: C. V. Whitney and
Merian C. Cooper
Screenplay: Frank S. Nugent
From the novel by Alan Le May

Cinematography: Winton C. Hoch
Music: Max Steiner
Title Song: Stan Jones
Editor: Jack Murray
Running Time: 119 minutes

Cast: John Wayne (Ethan Edwards), Jeffrey Hunter (Martin Pawley), Vera Miles (Laurie Jorgensen), Ward Bond (Captain Reverend Samuel Clayton), Natalie Wood (Debbie Edwards), John Qualen (Lars Jorgensen), Olive Carey (Mrs. Jorgensen), Henry Brandon (Scar), Ken Curtis (Charlie McCorry), Harry Carey, Jr. (Brad Jorgensen), Antonio Moreno (Emilio Figueroa), Hank Wordon (Mose Harper), Lana Wood (Debbie as a child), Walter Coy (Aaron Edwards), Dorothy Jordan (Martha Edwards), Pippa Scott (Lucy Edwards), Robert Lyden (Ben Edwards), Pat Wayne (Lieutenant Greenhill), Beulah Archuletta (Look), Jack Pennick (private), Peter Mamakos (Futterman), Frank McGrath, Terry Wilson, Mae Marsh

Synopsis: In 1868, Ethan Edwards returns to Texas. No one has seen him in the three years since the Civil War ended. His brother Aaron welcomes him into his home, an isolated cabin where he lives with his wife Martha, son Ben, and two daughters, Lucy and young Debbie. Their adopted son is the almost-grown Marty, who is part Cherokee, which keeps Indian-hater Ethan from considering him a relative. But it was Ethan who saved him from Indians after his parents were killed. Lucy is being courted by Brad Jorgensen; Laurie Jorgensen has had a lifelong crush on Marty.

Captain Reverend Samuel Clayton arrives with his Rangers. Indians have driven some cattle off Lars Jorgensen's ranch and he needs men to hunt them down. Marty and Ethan agree to join him, although Ethan and Sam don't see eye to eye on anything. The Rangers find the cattle have been killed, and realize they were stolen to lure the men away from the ranches. Ethan, Marty, and old Indian scout Mose Harper rush back to the Edwards ranch, too late. Martha, Aaron, and Ben have been killed and mutilated. Lucy and Debbie have been taken away. When the Rangers must retreat, Ethan, Marty, and Brad follow the Comanche's trail. Ethan discovers Lucy has been killed and raped. Brad goes crazy and rides into an Indian camp firing his gun. He is killed. Ethan and Marty continue the search, hoping to find Comanche under a chief named Scar. Marty worries that when Ethan finds Debbie he will kill her because she has been forced to have sex with Indians. The search goes on for a year. They return temporarily to the Jorgensens'. Laurie wants Marty to stay, but when Ethan follows a new lead, Marty follows. They buy a piece of cloth that came from Debbie's dress from a crooked trader named Futterman. Futterman and two others try to ambush Ethan and Marty, and Ethan shoots them all in the back. The search goes on for another four years.

Marty writes Laurie that when he thought he was bartering for a blanket with an Indian chief he ended up with his daughter, Look, for a bride. When they asked her about Scar, she got scared and ran away. They later found her dead in a Comanche camp that had been wiped out by the cavalry. In New Mexico they run into Mose Harper. Mose introduces them to a Mexican horsetrader who has seen Debbie. They are taken to Scar's camp and smoke with him. They see Debbie, now one of Scar's brides. When alone with Marty she tells him that he and Ethan should go and leave her with her people. Ethan tries to kill her but Marty prevents it. Then an arrow hits Ethan. The two men flee.

Ethan and Marty return home, having once again lost Debbie's trail. They arrive on the day Laurie is supposed to marry Charlie McCorry. Marty tells Laurie he has always loved her. He and Charlie have a fistfight. Neither wins, but the wedding is called off. They learn that Scar is camped nearby. Sam organizes his Rangers—he tells Ethan that he will have to arrest him for suspicion of murdering Futterman when their mission is done.

Marty sneaks into the Indian camp. He arouses Debbie. Scar walks into the tent. Marty shoots him. The Rangers ride into the camp and drive off the Indians' horses. The victory is theirs. Ethan rides past Marty, knocking him down. He chases Debbie up an embankment. She falls. She expects Ethan to kill her. But he picks her up: "Let's go home, Debbie." Ethan brings Debbie to the Jorgensens. They take her into their home. Marty and Laurie follow them inside. Ethan turns and walks away.

The Searchers

"You want to quit, Ethan?"
"That'll be the day."

I probably saw *The Searchers* twenty times in the fifties, but unfortunately it was out of circulation during much of the sixties at the time interest in John Ford peaked among film critics and buffs. I remember that many of us who had seen *The Searchers* insisted that it was Ford's masterpiece despite its having received less than rave reviews when released in 1956 and having been virtually ignored in film texts thereafter. Luckily, beautiful 35-mm prints of *The Searchers* appeared circa 1970 and our high claims were shown to be valid. It has yet to become widely known to the general movie audience, but it has emerged as the "Super-Cult Movie of the New Hollywood"—as Stuart Byron termed it in his article on the film for *New York* (March 5, 1979)—and has served as inspiration for material in such diverse films as *Dirty Harry* (1971), which John Wayne turned down; *Ulzana's Raid* (1972); *Taxi Driver* (1976); *The Wind and the Lion* (1975); *Hardcore* (1979); and *Dillinger* (1973) and the Italian-made *Once Upon a Time in the West* (1969), which both borrow from Ford's beautifully filmed, incredibly terrifying family massacre scene. In addition, it has come to be regarded by today's critics as the best western of all time; for instance, in a 1974 critics' poll conducted by *The Velvet Light Trap*, it tied *Johnny Guitar* (1954) for first place, beating out other Ford-Wayne classics *Stagecoach* (1939), *Fort Apache* (1948), *She Wore a Yellow Ribbon* (1949), and *The Man Who Shot Liberty Valance* (1962) as well as the four Hawks-Wayne westerns.

The lengthy search for the kidnapped Debbie begins with (L-R) Brad, Martin, and Ethan following Scar's trail.

Ethan assumes the father role in his brother Aaron's home. While Martha looks over his shoulder, Ethan gives presents to Lucy and the young Debbie. Aaron sits away from the scene.

(Significantly, unlike in Hawks's *Rio Bravo* trilogy Wayne's characters in Ford films are flawed and fallible —in *The Searchers* and *Liberty Valance*, they are even wrong-headed; in Hawks, Wayne's men may grow old and "comfortable," but they will not, as in Ford, become obsolete with the coming of civilization to a West they helped tame.)

What I hadn't noticed back in the fifties is that *The Searchers* has some minor flaws: there are clumsy jump cuts in action sequences; some outdoor scenes were obviously shot on a soundstage; the light in the sky changes too drastically from shot to shot during the attack on Scar's camp; because Ford didn't hire enough Indians for the attack scene it looks like they, and not Sam's Rangers, are the ones who are badly outnumbered; the harsh treatment of Look by Marty and Ethan is meant to be comical, but when she is kicked down an incline, it is too disturbing. But regardless of the flaws, *The Searchers* is a *great* film, one that has a fascinating, epic story, complex, psychologically motivated (and troubled) characters (Wayne is superb as Ethan Edwards, his favorite role), enormous scope, and breathtaking physical beauty—this was the ninth time Ford shot footage in red-clayed Monument Valley, where the stunning rock formations are both gorgeous and eerie. Scene after scene, image after image, evokes an emotional response: the wind sweeping across a landscape or through a woman's hair; a lone rider set against the blue sky; white men riding scared through a valley while painted Indians ride on both sides of them; dignified women in simple yet colorful dresses, their white aprons half covering them; men dancing, or standing with pipes in their mouths and pride on their faces; families gathered together in the houses they built with their own hands; old Mose Harper sitting in his rocking chair; the numerous reunions, which mean so much to these Texans who live in near isolation; the sad look of the women as their men ride off to perform some task, perhaps never to return; Martha folding Ethan's coat in a manner that betrays her love for him; the lonely Ethan sitting on the porch while his brother Aaron goes into the bedroom with Martha, the woman Ethan obviously loves; Laurie beaming while watching Marty and Charlie fighting over her; the anguish on Ethan's face as he scrubs down his horse, knowing that he can't prevent the murder raid about to take place at Martha's house; his anguished expression (he's thinking of Debbie) when he visits the insane white girls who had been held by the Comanche; Lucy screaming in terror as Ford's camera zooms into a close-up, when she realizes why her parents are acting nervously; Debbie running down a sandy hill toward Marty for their first hug in five years; and, of course, Ethan lifting the scared Debbie into his arms and saying "Let's go home, Debbie."

The Searchers was my favorite movie as a kid. But oddly, considering I liked westerns that had a lot of fighting, the two images that had the most impact on me had nothing to do with action: Scar standing over little

Brad becomes uncontrollable when he learns that his fiancée has been raped and killed by the Comanches. In the background is one of Monument Valley's stunning rock formations that helped make it John Ford's favorite western locale.

Debbie who is crouched by a family tombstone (we see Scar's shadow covering the girl before we see him); and Ethan standing over the older but again scared Debbie five years later, and, instead of killing her as he had planned, picking her up into his arms as if she were a kid once more, as he did when she *was* a kid in the reunion scene, as if he wants to yank her out of a nightmare she's lived in since being snatched from her family. Even in 1956, I think I realized that these two scenes—both with an adult male standing over a young girl who expects him to kill her when what he actually will do is take her away from those she considers her people and bring her to his "home"—were meant to show the strong bond between Ethan and Scar, to impress upon us that Scar is Ethan's alter ego. Further parallels abound: Ethan's family was killed by Indians, Scar's sons were killed by whites. As a result, both men are vengeance-bent, each determined to make the other's race pay. They are racists but have learned each other's tongues—which surprises, impresses, and annoys them both. Both men are rejected by the white society and are considered outlaws. Both are nomads. The Ethan-accompanied attack on Scar's village, which wipes out the Indians, is meant to parallel the Scar-led massacre of the Edwards home, and serve as adequate retribution. The only difference we see between the two men is that Ethan pets a dog and Scar throws a rock at one.

That Scar is Ethan's alter ego is important when looking at the opening scene. Ethan rides bareback (Indian-style) out of the desert, a dot on an immense landscape, more a myth figure than a man. Since he comes from out of the blue after having been gone without explanation for three years and arrives right before his family is massacred, it is possible that he has been sent, or called, on a divine mission of some sort. His mission is surely to rescue Debbie, but it is also to purge *himself* of the racism and savagery that is embodied by Scar. The five-year search is meaningless as far as the story goes because Star eventually brings Debbie back to the area from which he took her anyway, and moreover it is Mose, not Ethan or Marty, who discovers Debbie's presence in the vicinity. The search has significance on a different plane: it is Ethan's search for himself, his way of finding internal tranquility. It is proper that Marty kills Scar because he does so for the right, "moral" reasons and not because Scar is an Indian. But, importantly, *once Scar is dead,* Ethan no longer feels the urge to kill Debbie. With the death of the savage, Ethan's evil instincts have been expelled from his body and mind.

The cleansing of Ethan's soul is central to a picture that is obsessed with the concepts *pure* and *impure.* The glorious virgin land was pure before the coming of the white man. Now it has been "penetrated"—raped like the white women taken hostage by the Comanche. The Comanche we see are nomadic, so they take their homes (tents) with them, never marring the landscape with permanent structures. But the white man—with no harm intended—cuts down trees and builds homes, forts, trading posts. Where once all killed animals were eaten, the friction between the races results in *uneaten* carcasses of cattle, horses (food for Indians), and buffalo rotting on the otherwise beautiful terrain. And now murdered men and women are buried in the once-untouched soil. As Laurie says, Texas has become a "godforsaken land"—God has left while the people clumsily try to get things together. In turn the people put God on hold: Ethan interrupts a funeral service; Reverend Sam puts away his Bible and shoots Indians; Laurie, in a white bridal gown that symbolizes her purity of body, tells Marty that because Debbie probably slept with numerous bucks she would be better off dead. Miscegenation is what most of these people (but not part-Indian Marty) dread more than anything else. When Ethan tells Brad that he found Lucy's body, Brad doesn't ask if she suffered, but is more specific, "Was she . . .?" To Ethan, Scar's name signifies that he continuously defiles the once-pure Debbie, and, by having intercourse with her (she becomes one of his wives so that their having sex is to be taken for granted), he puts a blemish (a "scar") on the name of the pureblooded Edwards family. By killing Debbie, not Scar, Ethan feels he can end the family's and particularly Martha's disgrace. (Ethan's knightly quest for revenge is thus marred by *impure* motives.) Ethan's feelings toward a mixing of the bloods—symbolically conveyed when he almost dies from a poison arrow—dominates his life. But through his odyssey, while his racism doesn't vanish, he comes to realize that it is wrong. He comes to realize that anyone who harbors racist feelings doesn't belong in this new thing called civilization, where the races *must* mix, where everyone *must* live in harmony.

But during the transitional period in which *The Searchers* takes place, the antagonism between the races creates chaos. The country's disarray is characterized in part by the continuous breakup of families and the formation of new families. Marty lost his natural parents; he then loses his adopted parents (the Edwardses) and ends up with the Jorgensens. Debbie loses her parents, becomes part of the Indian family ("These are my people"), and also ends up with the Jorgensens. The Jorgensens lose their son Brad; they add a son (Marty) and daughter (Debbie). The disruption of the family—also prevalent during the Civil War—is further emphasized with the coming of Ethan into Aaron's home. Not only does Ethan cause a rift between Aaron and Martha (subtly conveyed), but also between Aaron and his children, who idolize their uncle.

Director Ford stresses the fragility of not only family life but life in general, by time and again *intruding* upon life's rituals. The arrival of Sam's Rangers interrupts Ethan's *homecoming;* Ethan refuses to take an *oath of allegiance* to the Rangers—just as he refused to be at the South's *surrender* in 1865; the Indians attack the Edwards' home just before *dinner;* Ethan cuts short the Edwards' *funeral* to begin the pursuit of the kidnapers; Ethan shoots out a dead Comanche's eyes to make his *burial* meaningless, end his rest in peace, and doom his soul to wander forever; the death of Lucy ends the *courtship* by Brad; likewise the pursuit precludes there being any *engagement* for Marty and Laurie; the "marriage" of Marty and Look ends with her death before the *marriage is consummated;* the *peace pipe-smoking ceremony* between Scar, Ethan, Marty, and Emilio ends prematurely due to the hostility of the participants; the *gunfight* between Ethan and Marty (who protects Debbie from him) is broken off when Ethan is struck by an arrow; Marty's return results in Laurie and Charlie calling off their *wedding;* Ethan stops himself from performing what he wrongly believes is the *mercy killing* of Debbie; and Ethan doesn't enter the Jorgensens' home during the final *homecoming,* choosing instead to walk away. By cutting off the completion of rituals, Ford builds tension and hastens pacing; most importantly, he gives us an idea of how tentative things were during a time when living a long life was quite rare.

Ethan's obsession with killing Debbie is mostly the

Men like Martin are always coming and going in the Texas of The Searchers, *while women like Mrs. Jorgensen and her daughter Laurie must remain at home.*

After many hard years of searching, Ethan and Martin discover Debbie in Scar's lodge. Here she displays Scar's many scalps.

result of his not being able to bear the daughter of Martha being treated so badly. (We discover years later that Debbie seems perfectly fine.) That he sees Martha for the last time standing alone with Debbie suggests that he might even equate Debbie with Martha, which would further help define his blind anger toward Scar. In a studio synopsis containing material not included in the script or the film itself, the Debbie-Martha parallel is confirmed. Ethan is just about to shoot her—"I'm sorry, girl. Shut your eyes"—when "Debbie's eyes gaze fearlessly, innocently into Ethan's face. He knows that his worst fears are unjustified, and lowers his gun. 'You sure favor your mother,' he says softly."

This Warner Bros. synopsis contains several other interesting items. In it, Scar kills Look for trying to free Debbie; by having Look killed by the cavalry instead, Ford reveals a disenchantment for soldiers that he didn't have in his earlier cavalry films. When Marty comes into Debbie's tent, she doesn't hug him but fights and screams so she can remain with the Indians; Ford had to change this so Ethan and Marty don't have to strap her down to make her come home. Also, in the synopsis Ethan hands Debbie to the Jorgensens and "rides off alone, mission accomplished." It is so much more effective that Ford has Ethan walk up to the front door of the Jorgensen house (the camera is inside facing out, Wayne's large body is framed by the doorway) before realizing that he doesn't belong.* He doesn't ride away

triumphantly, but walks off (toward his horse), sadly rejected by family and time. And the door closes, making the screen black, signifying that Ethan has missed his one opportunity to integrate himself into a country moving toward civilization.

Ethan brings Debbie home.

---

*The famous ending of *The Searchers* bears striking similarity to the ending of Ford's friend Henry Hathaway's *Call Northside 777* (1948). In that film, reporter James Stewart returns the man (Richard Conte) he got out of prison to his family. After being part of all their lives for so long, he must stand back and watch the reunion. The camera pans away from the group to find Stewart standing by himself, forgotten and looking rejected.

Shock Corridor

1963 Allied Artists
Director: Samuel Fuller
Producer: Samuel Fuller
Screenplay: Samuel Fuller
Cinematography: Stanley Cortez
Music: Paul Dunlap
Editor: Jerome Thoms
Running Time: 101 minutes

Cast: Peter Breck (Johnny Barratt), Constance Towers (Cathy), Gene Evans (Boden), James Best (Stuart), Hari Rhodes (Trent), Larry Tucker (Pagliacci), William Zuckert (Swanee), Philip Ahn (Dr. Fong), Meyle Morrow (psycho), Paul Dubov (Dr. Menkin), Chuck Roberson (Wilkes), John Mathews (Dr. Cristo)

Synopsis: Crime reporter Johnny Barratt wants to win the Pulitzer prize. He convinces his editor, Swanee, to let him try to get it by solving the murder of a man named Sloane in the mental hospital. With the guidance of Swanee's psychiatrist friend Dr. Fong, Johnny learns how to pass himself off as insane enough to be committed to the hospital. His stripper girlfriend Cathy thinks Johnny's plan is absurd, but agrees to help him when he threatens to break off with her. She tells the police she is Johnny's sister and that he has been making incestuous advances toward her. Johnny is arrested and questioned by Dr. Cristo. He asks exactly what Dr. Fong predicted and Johnny has the answers waiting. Cristo is convinced Johnny needs sexual therapy.

Johnny is admitted to the hospital. The two attendants in the men's ward are Wilkes, a seemingly nice guy, and Lloyd, who is mean out of frustration—he doesn't think the patients can be cured. Johnny talks to Stuart, one of three patients (the others are Trent and Boden) who were witness to Sloane's murder. Stuart thinks he is a Confederate soldier. In fact, he was an American soldier who was a turncoat in Korea. When he came back to America, he was hounded by reporters and branded a traitor—and he cracked. During a rare sane moment, Stuart tells Johnny an attendant killed Sloane.

Johnny tries to talk to Trent. He had gone insane trying to be the first black student to integrate an all-white southern college. He now thinks he is white, and a member of the KKK. Trent is too mentally crippled to tell Johnny anything.

Even before he speaks to Boden, Johnny's mind starts to snap. Each night he has nightmares about Cathy wanting to see other men. He is often woken up by the enormous Pagliacci, who holds him down while he sings opera or sticks gum into Johnny's mouth. He is attacked by nymphomaniacs. He is given shock treatments. He is strapped down next to Trent while he shouts white supremacist rhetoric all night long. When he begins to believe that Cathy is truly his sister, Cathy gives Cristo permission to give him more shock treatments in hopes he will reveal himself and Cristo will throw him out. All that happens is that Johnny temporarily loses his voice.

Boden was once a genius who helped create the atomic bomb. Now he has the mind of a six-year-old. Johnny coaxes him back to sanity by allowing him to paint his portrait. Boden reveals that Wilkes killed Sloane to cover up that he was taking sexual advantage of patients in the women's ward. Johnny sees Boden's portrait of him and like a baby becomes so angry that he beats Boden up. Boden reverts to being six. Johnny is too insane to remember the murderer's name.

After imagining a thunderstorm in the hall, Johnny remembers Wilkes killed Sloane. He beats up Wilkes and gets him to confess to the murder in front of Cristo.

Johnny will get his Pulitzer prize. But he has gone totally insane. He can't even feel Cathy's desperate hug.

After twelve lean years during which he made only one picture, not released in America, Sam Fuller completed *The Big Red One* (1980), a war film that received nationwide distribution and garnered more critical attention than any picture in his illustrious thirty-year directing career. It's not a bad film, but unfortunately it's neither top-grade Fuller nor very representative of his work, which is odd since it is undoubtedly his most personal project. It is simply too self-consciously artsy (even dreamlike) for this director who gained a cult by virtue of his unpretentious pictures for the working-class audience: and too emotionless for someone whose pictures were typically characterized by incredible intensity, ferocity, even madness. Nonetheless, *The Big Red One*, which put the likable, cigar-smoking Fuller on the talk show circuit, gave one of America's great cinematic talents the public recognition he had long deserved. (France has long treated him as the equal of John Ford, but American critics have traditionally spurned low-budget filmmakers like Fuller.)

By the time *Shock Corridor* came out in 1963, Fuller had already directed many excellent, visually dynamic films—although his best, *The Naked Kiss*, wouldn't come out until 1965. I had liked *The Steel Helmet* (1951), one of the favorite films of my youth, *Fixed Bayonets* (1951), *Pickup on South Street* (1953), *House of Bamboo* (1955), *The Crimson Kimono* (1959), and

The last shot of the picture reveals a corridor in the mental hospital full of overachievers. (R-L) Stuart, an unknown patient, Trent, Boden, Johnny, and Pagliacci.

There are many incidents that contribute to Johnny's going crazy including (B) his being attacked by patients in the nympho ward and (R) his being awakened each night by heavyset murderer Pagliacci, who conducts an opera score he imagines hearing for Johnny's pleasure.

Merrill's Marauders (1961)—the only Fuller films I had seen as of 1963—but I don't think I knew Fuller's name or attributed these pictures to the same man. (The *auteur* theory, which just started to make inroads in America in 1963 through two Andrew Sarris articles in *Film Culture,* would eventually make Fuller's name well known among film scholars.) I went to see *Shock Corridor* because a Forty-second Street theater presented it on its marquee as if it were a horror film. (Even today, because of its title, it turns up on TV as part of horror movie series.) Needless to say, I was confused—and felt gypped. Not only wasn't it scary, but I thought it one of the most preposterous films of all time. In general, newspaper critics had an even worse reaction. One review:

> [*Shock Corridor*] is not only outright trash, but stands also as one of the most vicious and irresponsible pieces of film-making that the screen has given us in years! . . . Why any film producer should have made it, or why any theater, in this day and age, should show it, is beyond understanding.

Indeed, more than any other film, *Shock Corridor* treads a fine line between art and trash. Like Fuller's other "tabloid" films, which have stories befitting *True Confessions, Police Gazette,* and the old-style New York *Daily News, Shock Corridor* thrives on sensationalism. But the inclusion of sexual content, integral to Fuller's other pictures, here seems solely intended to make the picture appear lurid. From a story standpoint, it works that Cathy is a stripper: her particular occupation is certainly a bona fide reason for the extreme jealousy boyfriend Johnny suffers when confined to the asylum. Yet it is overdoing it when on his *first* night alone

Johnny imagines Cathy (superimposed in miniature) in her strip outfit, expressing her need for a man and mentioning another reporter who told her that her "mouth is a tunnel" and her "movements evoke the most inflammatory passions." That Johnny pretends to be guilty of incestuous behavior in order to get into the mental hospital, that Johnny is attacked by nymphomaniacs in the asylum, and that Wilkes is guilty of having taken sexual advantage of patients in the women's ward contribute to the picture's intended sleaziness. But since the picture, when reduced to its basic plotline, has nothing at all to do with sex, all this comes across as laughable window dressing thought up by a director desperate for an audience grabber.

I have other objections as well. Almost every line spoken, especially by Cathy, is quotable as if taken from Bartlett's. The sets are terribly cheap, even by low-budget film standards. Fuller's use of color home-movie footage which he himself took in Japan and in Africa is totally inappropriate as visual accompaniment to Stuart's recollections of Korea and Trent's of the South and being terrorized by the KKK, respectively. (What could he have been thinking?) But after several viewings since 1963, I have come around to liking *Shock Corridor.* I still think it preposterous, but as it is with the characters in the asylum, there is temporary sanity amidst the confusion, and every once in a while someone—Pagliacci, Stuart, Trent, Boden—will say something more honest and moving and brave than we are used to in the American cinema.

Many critics used to think Fuller's films fascist because his lead characters—soldiers, cops, bigots—often have fascistic tendencies. But Fuller is one of the few directors who doesn't treat his lead characters as heroes or people viewers should identify with. On the contrary. Johnny Barratt, a crime reporter like Fuller once was, is an immature, dishonest, self-promoting protagonist. Cathy, who is too good for him, realizes how foolish he is in his pursuit of "who killed Sloane in the kitchen with a knife?" He is as juvenile as a youngster playing Clue. "Why don't you sneak on a rocketship and do the *Memoirs of an Astronaut?*" she teases him. "Don't be Moses leading lunatics to the Pulitzer prize." Johnny will suffer throughout the film, but the suffering is of his own doing (except when a desperate Cathy gives Cristo the go-ahead for shock treatments). The real victim is Cathy, the smartest character in the film and the one character with whom we can identify. First she must humiliate herself by telling the desk sergeant, who looks down on her from his lofty seat, that her brother has made incestuous advances toward her. Later she suffers further indignities when Cristo suggests that she, a stripper, may have provoked her brother's sexual advances. She is the most loyal of girlfriends, but Johnny dreams nightly of her infidelity. The worst rebuff: when Johnny believes that she is his sister and won't kiss her. Cathy ends up with an insane, catatonic mute for a boyfriend. No, it isn't Johnny who has had it the roughest.

Fuller originally wanted to make a film that exposed the conditions in America's mental hospitals. However, he abandoned that idea to tell a modern version of the Nellie Bly story. Except for the brutal shock treatments, Wilkes using his position for sexual favors from women prisoners, and Cristo's incompetence—admitting the sane Johnny and later telling the broken-down Johnny "I think you're making real progress"—there is very little in the film that seems to have any relation to real mental hospitals.

Shock Corridor is most importantly a sad-eyed view of America, where people are encouraged to strive beyond their capacity for accomplishment and to do their country proud even if they can't accept responsibility and fame. Stuart let down his country when he failed to be a good soldier; Trent let down his race when he couldn't withstand the pressures of being a James Meredith-like guinea pig integrating an all-white southern college; pacifist Boden felt he had the burden of mankind on his shoulders when he worked on the atomic bomb. It's no wonder they are now in an asylum—their one escape from the public eye. And now they are joined by Johnny, whose road to insanity was more selfish than theirs. He once said, "Ever since my voice changed I wanted to be in the company of the journalistic greats." Fittingly, he loses his voice entirely —and his mind as well—as he wins the most prestigious award in his profession, the Pulitzer prize. If his goal hadn't been so lofty, chances are he'd still be able to talk.

Poor Cathy cannot get the hopelessly insane Johnny out of his catatonic state.

A mysterious woman (played by fifties super-starlet Millie Perkins) hires Grashade (R) and Coley to escort her on her secret mission.

1967* Walter Reade Organization release of a Proteus film (It also has been handled in the U.S. by Jack H. Harris Enterprises.)
Director: Monte Hellman
Producers: Jack Nicholson and Monte Hellman
Screenplay: Adrien Joyce
Cinematography: Gregory Sandor
Music: Richard Markowitz
Editor: Monte Hellman
Running Time: 82 minutes

Cast: Warren Oates (Willet Grashade), Millie Perkins (woman), Jack Nicholson (Billy Spear), Will Hutchins (Coley)

Synopsis: Bounty hunter Willet Grashade returns to camp. His not very smart friend Coley tells him that he has been holed up for two days. Coin, Grashade's brother, had gotten drunk in Winslow and had run down a small boy. Coin's partner, Leland Drum, had been shot in the back by an unknown assailant. Coley lets Grashade have his gun so he won't get into trouble. Both men are paranoid.

The next day, a shot rings out. The men discover a mysterious woman outside of camp. She has killed her horse although Grashade sees nothing was wrong with it. She offers Grashade a thousand dollars to take her to Kingsley. Although he doesn't like her, he accepts the offer. He hopes to find out what happened to Coin.

Grashade, Coley, and the woman, who refuses to give her name, travel toward Crosstree. They squabble the entire time. After leaving Crosstree, where Grashade learns Coin has been seen, the three travelers move through the desert. The woman flirts with Coley. Grashade tells her to leave his friend alone. He can tell that she is sending signals to someone following them. Finally gunslinger Billy Spear emerges from hiding. He joins the group. Billy and Coley are constantly threatening each other. Grashade tells Coley not to rile Billy because Billy would love the opportunity to kill him.

The woman's horse dies. Coley gives his to her and rides with Grashade. But Billy orders Coley to dismount. Coley is left behind. They come upon an acquaintance of the woman who is stranded in the desert with a broken leg. He tells her her prey is only a day away. She leaves him water and goes on. Coley snares the man's horse and charges Billy. Billy guns him down. The woman is upset that Billy did this. Grashade sadly buries his friend. The journey winds down. The horses die. They all run out of water. Grashade and Billy fight brutally in the sand. Grashade beats Billy up and crushes his gun hand with a large rock.

Grashade follows the woman into the rocks. There they spot the man who killed her child. He turns around. He looks exactly like Grashade. It is Coin. Coin shoots and kills Grashade and the woman while they shoot at him.† Billy walks around aimlessly in the desert.

---

*This is the date usually given for *The Shooting*.
†I have only seen the picture on television, where it is hard to tell if Coin is also killed.

The Shooting

Monte Hellman directed *The Shooting* in the Utah desert during the summer of 1965, filming it back-to-back with a companion western, *Ride the Whirlwind*, over a six-week period. Both films were produced on shoestring budgets by Hellman and Jack Nicholson, with Roger Corman serving as (uncredited) executive producer. Both were photographed by Gregory Sandor, whose striking evocation of an unfriendly western landscape might have convinced Horace Greeley to keep his mouth shut. Each film has four lead players: Nicholson, Millie Perkins, Warren Oates, and Will Hutchins are in *The Shooting;* Nicholson, Perkins, Cameron Mitchell, and Tom Filer are in *Whirlwind.* Although Nicholson wrote *Whirlwind* and Adrien Joyce (who would write Nicholson's 1970 film *Five Easy Pieces*) scripted *The Shooting*, the pictures are so similar in dialogue style, in the way characters relate to one another, and in how the West is depicted, that they seem to have been written by the same person. Considering how much the pictures have in common, it is not surprising that they shared the same sorry fate in terms of distribution. In his article "Vanishing Films" for *Show* (February 1970), Ralph Blasi wrote:

> Hellman spent almost a year editing the two films, and then *The Shooting* was shown in Montreal [at the Festival]. Later at the Cannes Film Festival it was screened out of competition where it was received with great enthusiasm. *Ride the Whirlwind* was shown in several festivals including San Francisco, Vancouver, and Pesaro. At the latter festival it came in second in the popular vote. Nicholson . . . sold the foreign distribution rights to a French producer, thinking it would make the film's reputation. However, the producer went bankrupt and . . . the prints of both films remained in bond at the Paris airport for almost two years. Following considerable legal maneuvering, Hellman and Nicholson had the rights revert back to them. In 1968, both films finally opened in Paris, without a distributor.

As Blasi later pointed out, "Domestically, the films fared less well." The Walter Reade Organization bought the United States rights to the pictures but instead of placing them in Reade theaters sold them directly to television. This wouldn't be so bad if they were shown on television with regularity, but I have seen each film only once—on *The Late Late Show.* In Canada and Europe, these two American westerns, among the best made in the last twenty years, have become cult favorites through rare screenings, but in America their reputations are more the result of word of mouth than of actual viewings.

A long way from such majestic cinema locales as John Ford's Monument Valley and Anthony Mann's Mount Hood, Hellman's West is an ugly, barren,

Grashade is upset that Billy Spear has killed his good friend Coley.

godforsaken land full of rocks, infertile soil, and sage-brush. It is a lonely, cruel world where one's nearest neighbor lives a day's ride away; where women are almost as scarce as the wildlife; where a few men have families but most live with male companions/work partners. Those who live here are a hard, violent people strong enough to fend for themselves, possessive of their property and reputations, and, if they're smart, distrust-ful of strangers, to whom they speak with well-chosen words and shotguns in readiness. They aren't particu-larly sociable even amongst friends; their conversations are typically lacking in substance and humor. These are a poor, uneducated people who wear the same dust-ridden clothes every day, rarely bathe, sleep several to a room or tent, and who might have to give it all up if someone swiped their horses, cows, or rifles. Their lives are fixed to a work routine that varies little from day to day. For 365 days a year, from dusk till dawn, they toil under a hot, glaring sun while the wind whistles through their ears and kicks up thick dust around their eyes and into their mouths. Without conversation to interrupt the daily routine, it is little wonder that many of these people seem to have lost some of their faculties.

It is a "realistic" West Hellman presents, yet the situations he places his characters in are existential in nature. In both *The Shooting* and *Whirlwind*, the good guys suddenly find themselves thrust into predicaments that are beyond their understanding. In *Whirlwind*, cowpokes Wes (Nicholson), Verne (Mitchell), and Otis (Filer) are mistaken for thieves by a hang-'em-first-ask-questions-later posse, and realize that for no reason at all their lives have been placed in great danger. ("We weren't doing anything, dammit!" Wes complains.) In *The Shooting*, neither Grashade nor the simple-minded Coley understands why the Perkins character refuses to give her name or why she hires *them*. Just like the driver and the mechanic in Hellman's modern-day "road" film *Two-Lane Blacktop* (1971), the men in these two films end up taking part in journeys that go nowhere. In *Whirlwind*, Wes and Verne buy nothing but time climb-ing a mountain that leads straight up. ("It's a shame to do all this walking for nothing," Wes remarks.) In *The Shooting*, the woman orders Grashade and Coley to lead her on trails which Grashade has told her might cause them to become hopelessly lost; and then into the desert from which there can be no return. Grashade goes along

because he knows he is fated to complete this journey. ("It's a feeling I have to see through," he explains to Coley.) Before he met the woman, he spotted a buzzard in the sky circling the horse she had killed; already he figured that *her* arrival signified that death awaited them all. And eventually they are all dead except for Billy Spear. At the end of *Whirlwind*, only Wes rides off to safety. But neither he nor we know exactly where he is heading. Similarly, Hellman's quite interesting recent western, *China 9, Liberty 37* (1980), ends with the various survivors heading down roads to parts unknown. (This is also Jack Nicholson's fate in *Five Easy Pieces*.) As in *Whirlwind*, the Nicholson character in *The Shooting* is the only one around at the end, but his death is assured. Without a horse or a canteen, Billy Spear stumbles aimlessly through the vast desert clutching his painfully crushed gun hand. He will suffer what he hoped his nemesis Coley would when he stranded Coley in the desert a while back: "Your brain's going to fry out here." Billy's fate is similar to *Blacktop*'s driver's (James Taylor), whose brain seems to symbolically explode and disintegrate.

Both *The Shooting* and *Whirlwind* are gritty, gripping westerns featuring offbeat characters and odd bits of dialogue. (Verne: "It's peculiar sitting here playing checkers while a bunch of men wait to string us up." Wes: "Why don't you put a tune to it?") The pictures are thoroughly absorbing and never predictable. If *The Shooting* is a trifle better than *Whirlwind*, it is probably because the presence of a villain and a female *on the* journey with the good guys heightens the picture's intensity. (In *Whirlwind*, the good guys are *chased* the

entire film by the villainous posse; they only meet Perkins during a brief rest at a cabin.) Moreover, the cast for *The Shooting* is slightly stronger. Will Hutchins, television's Sugarfoot in the late fifties, never appeared in much else, but he is ideal as the simple, nice guy who falls for the woman and who gets on Billy Spear's nerves. Cameron Mitchell has never been better than in *Whirlwind*, but Warren Oates is one of the great American actors (which is why Hellman has always used him since). Billy Spear is a villain in the mold of Jack Palance in *Shane* (1953), and Oates's atypical hero Grashade makes a fascinating, disarming foe for him. He is no fast draw, but his intriguing face reveals he has enough intelligence and determination to help him defeat Billy if it ever comes to a fight to the death. Oates projects authenticity; Perkins and Nicholson are strongest when the characters they portray are almost mystical—the more you learn about them, the more human they are, the weaker they become.

Whereas *Whirlwind* is a very straightforwardly-told picture, *The Shooting* is somewhat puzzling. While you can guess the surprise climax in which Grashade's brother turns out to be the killer of the woman's child, you'll be hard pressed to explain why it is significant that Grashade and Coin (the other side of the coin) are twins. (I'm surprised the woman didn't mistakenly kill Grashade, thinking him to be Coin.) But while the end may ask more questions than it answers, the exciting journey that brings us to this point is one of the most rewarding sequences in the history of westerns. *The Shooting* is a unique film that deserves theatrical distribution even if just in repertory cinemas.

Singin' in the Rain

1952 MGM
Directors: Gene Kelly and Stanley Donen
Producer: Arthur Freed
Screenplay: Adolph Green and Betty Comden
Cinematography: Harold Rosson
Musical Director: Lennie Hayton
Songs: Arthur Freed and Nacio Herb Brown; "Moses" by Betty
Comden, Adolph Green, and Roger Edens
Editor: Adrienne Fazan
Running Time: 103 minutes

Cast: Gene Kelly (Don Lockwood), Debbie Reynolds (Kathy
Selden), Donald O'Connor (Cosmo Brown), Jean Hagen (Lina
Lamont), Millard Mitchell (R. F. Simpson), Rita Moreno (Zelda
Zanders), Douglas Fowley (Roscoe Dexter), King Donovan
(Rod), Cyd Charisse (dancer), Madge Blake (Dora Bailey),
Kathleen Freeman (Phoebe Dinsmore), Mae Clarke (hairdresser),
Dawn Addams, Elaine Stewart, Joi Lansing, Russ Saunders

Synopsis: At the 1927 Hollywood premiere of the latest Don
Lockwood–Lina Lamont silent romantic swashbuckler, gossip
columnist Dora Bailey interviews Don and Lina, who has such a silly
voice that Don won't let her open her mouth lest her fans hear her.
Don tells Dora that during his rise to the top he had a motto:
"Dignity—always dignity."

In truth, Don and his partner Cosmo Brown used to sing and
dance in burlesque houses. Then they came to Hollywood, where
they were stuntmen in Lina Lamont's silent pictures. When Don
approached her, she snubbed him. But Don was such an impressive
performer that producer R. F. Simpson agreed to give him a chance
to star in films with Lina. Then Lina tried to sweeten up to Don, but
he told her that they would only be romantically involved in the
newspapers to sell movie tickets. In real life, he wanted nothing to
do with her. Don and Lina became the biggest romantic leads of the
silent era. The newest Lockwood-Lamont film is a hit. Don must
elude fans afterwards and he jumps into the car being driven by
Kathy Selden, a pretty young girl who tells Don that she doesn't
consider him much of an actor and that she wants to be a serious
actress. They squabble—each thinks the other is conceited.

R. F. throws a party to celebrate the film's success. A chorus girl
jumps out of a cake. It is Kathy and Don laughs. She throws a cake
at him but it lands on Lina's face. Lina has her fired. Don would like
to see Kathy again but doesn't know where to find her.

During production of *The Dueling Cavalier*, R. F. shuts down the
studio because SOUND has come to the motion pictures and he
wants to make the picture as a sound musical, *The Dancing Cavalier*.
The major problem: Lina Lamont has a terrible talking voice, and
can't sing.

When Don and Cosmo find out that Kathy has a job at the studio,
they come up with the idea of having Kathy sing and talk for Lina,
who would only have to lip-synch. R. F. goes along with the plan.

Don and Kathy fall in love. Lina is jealous and is determined to
ruin their relationship. She puts pressure on R. F. to write it into her
contract that Kathy can never be more than her ghost singer, thus
forcing R. F. to cancel his plans to star Kathy in a picture with Don.
Kathy is heartbroken.

The Dancing Cavalier has its premiere. It is wildly received. Lina
walks onto the stage to *talk* to the crowd. Everyone decides to let her
make a fool of herself. The audience is confused by her terribly
squeaky voice. They tell her to sing. R. F. orders Kathy to stand
behind the curtain and sing while Lina mouths the words. While she
reluctantly sings "Singin' in the Rain," R. F. and Cosmo pull up the
curtain so the audience can see that Kathy is the one who is singing
and that she is the real talent. Lina's star days are over. Don and
Kathy will appear in a new musical called *Singin' in the Rain*.

*Gene Kelly and Debbie Reynolds, the stars of what many people
think is the cinema's greatest musical.*

A s fresh as it was thirty years and as many
viewings ago, *Singin' in the Rain* is truly one of
the great joys of the cinema, the most uplifting
of films ("I'm laughing at clouds so dark up
above, there's a song in my heart . . ."), the
best movie musical, in my opinion, of all time. The
Astaire-Rogers films are terrific, surely, but fans of that
series aren't necessarily *movie* buffs. *Singin' in the Rain*
is the ultimate musical for lovers of the film medium.
Not only do innovative directors Gene Kelly and Stanley Donen use "film" (i.e. color, lighting, editing,
special effects, camera placement, camera movement,
and sound) to enhance the fabulous songs and dances
but, as scripted by Adolph Green and Betty Comden,
this is also the best, most perceptive, most informative
picture ever made about the movie industry. (It is no
surprise that film director/scholar/critic François Truffaut, who also satirized filmmaking in 1972's *Day for
Night*, is one of the countless millions who consider
Singin' in the Rain a genuine masterpiece.)

The person responsible for initiating the *Singin' in
the Rain* project was Arthur Freed, the legendary MGM
producer whose credits already included such classic
musicals as *Meet Me in St. Louis* (1944), *Easter Parade*
(1948), *Words and Music* (1948), and *On the Town*
(1949). The last was the first picture directed by the
Kelly and Donen team, the first musical that went out
on location, and the first success for writers Green and
Comden, formerly performers with a four-person revue

The classic "Singin' in the Rain" number in which Don/Kelly sings and dances with "a smile on my face."

Kathy emerges from a cake during a party for Don and Lola. Much of the film's tremendous energy can be attributed to the vital Debbie Reynolds.

(including Judy Holliday) in New York. For *Singin' in the Rain*, Freed assigned Green and Comden to come up with a story that could utilize some of the song hits—including the title song—that he and his partner Nacio Herb Brown had composed in the twenties and thirties. Disappointed that they wouldn't be allowed to write an original score, Green and Comden reluctantly went to work. The first major decision they made was to set the picture during the era Freed and Brown wrote their songs rather than try to adapt tunes with an old-timey flavor to a modern milieu. Being movie fans interested in the industry's history, they chose to construct a story that was set, specifically, in 1927–28, when Jolson and *The Jazz Singer* (1927) turned Hollywood upside down and made *music* vital to the medium's survival. Importantly from a dramatic standpoint, the coming of sound to pictures, signaling the end of many stars' careers and the birth of stardom for many others, especially those who could sing and dance, immediately gave the picture its necessary "conflict" (a town in turmoil). The characters' personal stories and conflicts reflect what is happening around them on a larger scale.

Green and Comden wanted Kelly to star in their film, but since he was busy making *An American in Paris* (1951), they believed they were writing a vehicle for Howard Keel. Their initial story wasn't about a romantic idol in costume pictures but about a bit player

in silent westerns who makes it big as a "singing cowboy" during the sound era. Of course, the premise changed once Kelly and Donen read the script and insisted that it be their second joint project. Today Kelly remembers that once he became involved in the project, he, Green, and Comden collected anecdotes from old-timers on the MGM lot who had been around when the studios went bananas making the quick switch to sound —before they were expert about the technical problems involved. So all the funny moments in the picture where actors have trouble speaking into microphones that are hidden in flower arrangements or in their costumes, and pick up their heartbeats better than their voices, are based on true incidents. So is the plight of Lina Lamont, whose squeaky, outlandish voice makes her totally unsuitable to be a romantic lead in the sound era. Lina reminds one of John Gilbert, the silent screen's top romantic idol, whose career came to an abrupt end because of his high-pitched voice. (Early on, Green and Comden considered giving the *male* lead the voice problems.) In *Singin' in the Rain* there is a scene in which a sneak preview audience laughs at Lina because, with her limited vocabulary, all she can think of to say to Don during a romantic interlude is "I love you" over and over and over again. This was based on an embarrassing sneak preview of a Gilbert film when he also repeated "I love you" numerous times—not realizing

Don, with a cocky smile for his fans, and Lola turn up for a premiere of their latest movie.

that he couldn't get away with the limited dialogues he recited during silent movie love scenes. For Gilbert it was tragic—Lina gets her just desserts.

Green and Comden are accurate in depicting the flapper era when stars were more famous than presidents. They also beautifully spoof numerous Hollywood types: suicidal stuntmen (Don, Cosmo) who take *any* insulting, unrewarding, dangerous assignment to earn a buck and get into pictures; starlets (Kathy) with pretentions of being serious thespians but who are willing to jump out of cakes to be part of show business; brainless gossip columnists (Dora) who believe anything that stars tell them; tough directors (Roscoe) who think they are on the battlefield; stuffy, smug diction coaches who must work with wild, uneducated stars; confused producers (R. F.) who use initials instead of names and are torn between doing their jobs and satisfying their fussy actors; flaky music coordinators (Cosmo) who are a different breed—outsiders—from the rest of the people at the studio; cocky actors (Don) who know the importance of "image" to stardom ("Dignity—always dignity," Don fibs, has been the secret of his rise to the top); and the stupid, conceited actresses (Lina) who believe their own press ("Don't be ridiculous," Lina tells Don when he says he loves Kathy. "Everyone knows you're in love with me").

Singin' in the Rain overflows with wit, gaiety, energy, and class. The musical numbers are *all* outstanding; Kelly, Debbie Reynolds (already an old trouper at

The athletic feet-flying, high-kicking dancing of the earlier numbers gives way to elegance when Kelly and Cyd Charisse team up.

Donald O'Connor matches Kelly step-for-step and jump-for-jump in the ''Moses'' number, one of many show-stopping numbers.

age twenty), and Donald O'Connor display the most amazing athletic dancing skills seen anywhere outside of the house-building number in Donen's *Seven Brides for Seven Brothers* (1954). There are wonderful, memorable moments within the dances themselves: Don and Cosmo playing each other's fiddles and climbing on each other during "Fit As a Fiddle and Ready for Love," a snappy, catchy, terrifically danced (and underrated) vaudeville number; Kathy jumping out of the cake and joining the other chorus girls for the nifty ditty "All I Do Is Dream of You"; Don and Cosmo bewildering their diction teacher with some tongue twisters and flying feet in the "Moses" number; the camera looking down the singer's throat in the lavish Busby Berkeley parody; Don, Kathy, and Cosmo, in perfect step with each other, dancing on Kathy's furniture and singing the infectious "Good Mornin'"; Cosmo stopping the show by dancing up walls and doing flips in his incredible "Make 'em Laugh" solo (the one newly written Freed-Brown composition); almost everything in the ambi-

tious "Broadway Rhythm" number, especially Kelly and Cyd Charisse dancing a dreamlike ballet, and Kelly singing out several times "Gotta dance! Gotta dance!"—quieter —"Gotta dance"; and of course, Don happily dancing through puddles while singing the title song. (Once it was raining after a screening I attended and everyone who filed out of the theater automatically burst into the song and proceeded to dance through the puddles—a strange sight.) The great moment in the film? During the "Singin' in the Rain" number when the camera cranes over Kelly's beaming face for a close-up just as he sings "There's a smile on my face."

Even the scenes without music are great. I love Don's hilarious movie stunts which somehow he survives; the knife-in-the-back squabbling between Don and Lina; Lina's unsuccessful diction lessons, where she can't learn to properly pronounce the letter *a* in the phrase "I can't stand it"; the fascinating film at R. F.'s party in which a weird man explains the "sound film"; the many humorous incidents with microphones; the finale where Cosmo, R. F., and Rod mischievously pull up the stage curtain so the audience can see that Kathy is singing instead of Lina. It's all delightful movie fare.

I believe that the secret to the picture's greatness is that Kelly, the star, the codirector, willingly shared his picture with his costars. It is not by mere chance that Reynolds, O'Connor, and Hagen have *never* been better. True, Kelly takes many moments in the limelight, dancing up a storm and turning in a fine, self-parodying (hammy, conceited, smiling) comedic performance. Yet he allows Jean Hagen ample opportunity to walk away with acting honors. Best known for playing Danny Thomas's wife in the TV series *Make Room for Daddy,* Hagen turns in a gem of a performance, almost of the level of Judy Holliday. From this picture, we see that Hagen was never allowed the chance to be the fine comedienne (on TV she was Thomas's straight man) she was obviously capable of being. And Kelly allows Donald O'Connor to show off his rare, remarkable talents—especially in the "Make 'em Laugh" number. Take a look at all of O'Connor's other films and you'd

never know that he was such a gifted song-and-dance man. Thank Kelly for lifting him up to join other dance immortals. Former "Miss Burbank" Debbie Reynolds had only done one musical number prior to appearing in *Singin' in the Rain.* It was in *Three Little Words* (1950) and, ironically, she mouthed the lyrics while Helen Kane sang in her Betty Boop voice—just as Kathy Selden would sing while Lina, who has a Betty Boop voice but sillier, lip-synched. I don't think Kelly wanted Reynolds for the picture, but once he had her he gave her ample time in the spotlight and her first chance in the movies to sing and dance—and how absolutely great, how bubbly, how vivacious she is! Astaire used to keep the dance solos for himself—but Kelly shows no signs of jealousy toward Reynolds. Kelly doesn't foolishly worry that his performance will be diminished by the brilliance of the other musical stars—Reynolds, O'Conner, and Charisse. No one suffers because the others are at their peaks—and the picture, full of solos, duets, threesomes, and huge production numbers (as well as bright comedy) just keeps getting better and better.

Cosmo, Kathy, and Don begin the catchy ''Good Mornin' '' number.

Sunset Boulevard

1950 Paramount
Director: Billy Wilder
Producer: Charles Brackett
Screenplay: Charles Brackett,
Billy Wilder, and D. M.

Marshman, Jr.
Cinematography: John F. Seitz
Music: Franz Waxman
Editor: Arthur Schmidt
Running Time: 110 minutes

Cast: William Holden (Joe Gillis), Gloria Swanson (Norma Desmond), Erich von Stroheim (Max Von Mayerling), Nancy Olson (Betty Schaefer), Fred Clark (Sheldrake), Cecil B. De Mille (himself), Lloyd Gough (Morino), Jack Webb (Artie Green), Hedda Hopper (herself), Franklyn Farnum (the undertaker), Buster Keaton, Anna Q. Nilsson, H. B. Warner, Ray Evans, and Jay Livingston (themselves)

Synopsis: Joe Gillis lies shot and dead in a swimming pool by an old mansion on Sunset Boulevard in Beverly Hills, California. He narrates the events that led to his death.

Joe was a down-and-out writer, behind on his rent and car payments. He went to Paramount to see what producer Sheldrake thought of his baseball script. He overheard reader Betty Schaefer tell Sheldrake that Joe's script was "flat and trite." Sheldrake turned it down. MGM did the same. Having no prospects, Joe decided to drive home to Dayton, Ohio. Eluding finance men, Joe pulled into a driveway on Sunset Boulevard. The deteriorating mansion belonged to Norma Desmond, Paramount's greatest star during the silent era, but forgotten for twenty years. Thinking Joe to be the undertaker for her dead chimpanzee, Norma invited him in. Resenting anyone who had anything to do with sound pictures, she tried to kick him out when she discovered him to be a screenwriter, but changed her mind and asked him to read a script she wrote: *Salome*. She hoped it would be the film that would mark her *return* to motion pictures for the fans who still wrote her letters. He thought the script was terrible, but sensing a chance to make money, he told her that it just needed a little polishing. As he hoped, she hired him to fix it. Her Prussian-like chauffeur-butler Max set Joe up in a room over the garage. Eventually, Joe moved into a room in the house where Norma's three husbands had once lived. With Norma looking over his shoulder, Joe worked on her script every day. At night, they usually watched Norma's old films. On occasion some of Norma's friends—long-forgotten stars—came to the house to play bridge, and Joe would stand behind Norma with an ashtray in his hand. He began doing other services for her and resented it. On New Year's Eve he walked out on her and went to his friend Artie Green's party. He discovered that Betty Schaefer was Artie's fiancée. She told him that she had found a few pages of his scripts she liked and thought he should develop those into a script. He wasn't interested. Finding out that Norma had attempted suicide, a frequent practice of hers in the past, Joe returned to her. "You're the only person in this stinking town who's been kind to me," he told her, and they became lovers.

Norma sent *Salome* to Paramount. When the studio called, hoping to borrow her car for a picture, she thought they were interested in her. She drove to the studio to visit her old-time director Cecil B. De Mille. He didn't have the heart to tell her that everyone considered her script dreadful. Meanwhile, Joe and Betty worked on a script together. They fell in love. She wanted to break off with Artie so they could get married. Norma called up Betty and told her Joe was a gigolo having a love affair with her (not just living at her house as Joe had told her). Trying to do one decent thing—keep Betty from getting badly hurt by being mixed up with him—Joe told Betty that he would always stay with Norma: "I have a lifetime contract with no options." Extremely upset and confused, Betty went back to Artie. But Joe decided to leave Norma just the same. He told her that Max wrote all her fan mail and that De Mille didn't want to work with her again. Hysterically, she shot him in the back and he fell dead in the pool.

The police and photographers fill Norma's house. Norma prepares for her final scene. Max, her first husband and her greatest director, tells her how to walk down the stairs. She is thrilled to be making films again. She descends her stairway and moves into an out-of-focus close-up.

A woman from a long-forgotten age resides in self-imposed exile in a gloomy mansion in the hills. She still moves about although those who know of her insist she is dead. She is strong-willed, intelligent, and artistically gifted. She is alternately vain and self-despising; proud of her strength and capabilities but ashamed that she can't control her weaknesses: her destructive tendencies, her refusal to accept anyone not doing her bidding, and her jealousy toward "normal" women. It is her touch of melancholy and her woeful loneliness—no one is as out of place in the world—that makes her sympathetic despite her selfish, often cruel attitude and conduct. The only person who understands her is her peculiar manservant (played by an actor-director) who provides services for her without her having to ask, constantly reminds her of her past when her ventures into the present world prove unrewarding to her, and brings her "lovers" / "victims." She asks the help of a man whose singular professional skills, she hopes, will help her enter the modern world, which she feels she has avoided for far too long. But he can't help her because the modern world is as hostile to her as she is alien to it. She is much older than he, but she falls in love with him and wants him to live with her. He is intrigued by her strangeness but loves a woman his own age. She becomes jealous and tries to bring about an end to the relationship between him and the younger woman. Fearing harm will come to the younger woman just from knowing him, he agrees to do what the older woman wants and move into her mansion permanently. But this is just a ruse on his part; he has no intention of staying with her and letting her possess him. When she realizes she has been deluded, the older woman tries to kill him. . . . The story I have just told is, of course, a skeletal outline for Billy Wilder's *Sunset Boulevard*, a brilliantly scripted film about a silent-movie queen living in Beverly Hills with only her past for a companion until a young "script doctor" stumbles along. It is also a skeletal outline for *Dracula's Daughter* (1936), a fine horror film about a female vampire who has lived for centuries in the Transylvanian mountains (hills) and who falls in love with a young English doctor.*

---

*Gloria Holden (no relation to William) plays the lead in *Dracula's Daughter*, a sympathetic vampire who would rather paint and play the piano than drink blood. Otto Kruger is the psychiatrist who tries to help her adjust to the modern world by altering her mental state—just as Joe Gillis alters Norma's script in preparation for her coming out of exile. Actor-director Irving Pichel is the servant who continuously reminds his mistress about her lust for blood (which she wants to ignore) and brings her lovers (some female—there is a definite trace of lesbianism in the scenes where she seduces and kills females) who become her victims; this prefigures Max making the room above Norma's garage into Joe's bedroom and bringing his belongings from town. Marguerite Chapman is the innocent victim of a selfish woman's love for a man, not just years but eras younger than herself. (However, Chapman and Kruger are united in the end.)

A publicity shot in which Nancy Olson, William Holden, and Erich von Stroheim circle around the star of Sunset Boulevard: *Gloria Swanson.*

As Richard Corliss contends in *Talking Pictures* (Overlook, 1974), *Sunset Boulevard* is, above all else, "the definitive Hollywood horror movie." Not only does its morbid, death-obsessed plot parallel the one for *Dracula's Daughter*, but also the film abounds in horror movie references and imagery (the burial services for Norma's dead chimpanzee; the rats in the long-empty swimming pool). Although von Stroheim's Prussian-like butler Max is more sympathetic and intelligent (and loquacious) than the standard horror movie butler, he is in the tradition of Boris Karloff's butler in James Whale's *The Old Dark House* (1932); Norma's ghost-like bridge guests (silent stars Buster Keaton, Anna Q. Nilsson, and H. B. Warner) are referred to as "waxworks," by movie buff Joe, who likely is thinking of Paul Leni's silent horror movie classic of that name; and Norma is called a "sleepwalker" by Joe, evoking thoughts of vampires and zombies from pre-1950 horror films. Norma Desmond anticipates by twelve years Bette Davis's warped ex-star obsessed by her past in *What Ever Happened to Baby Jane?* (1962), and, living as she does in a relic-filled tomblike mansion, she also predates the tetched Vincent Price characters in Roger Corman's psychologically oriented Edgar Allan Poe movie adaptations of the fifties and early sixties. Speaking of Poe, *Sunset Boulevard* is another conception of the horror of *premature burial.* As Gloria Swanson wrote about silent movie stars in *Close-Ups* (Workman, 1977): "It has become difficult to prove you're not dead. So many of us are."

What better locale for a "ghost" story than Hollywood, a town built on illusions and delusions, where people grow old but remain young on celluloid, where people become has-beens often before they've made it. ("I heard he had talent," Betty says of Joe. "That was last year," Joe declares.) Thirty years after its release, *Sunset Boulevard* is still rightly considered the harshest indictment of Hollywood on film. Director Billy Wilder and his writing partner Charles Brackett attack agents, producers, directors, and studio heads. Their gripe is with the Hollywood product of 1950: filmmakers are more likely to use a great veteran actress's antique car than the actress herself; an Alan Ladd hardball picture can only be made if it is turned into a Betty Hutton softball picture (as Sheldrake suggests). More than just an assault on the people who made Hollywood a place where talent and integrity have little meaning, *Sunset Boulevard* is, in fact, a funeral elegy to the old-style Hollywood films. And it is not just a homage to the (then) out-of-fashion horror film but also a reminder of those elegant, romantic silent films we recall during the screenings in Norma's home ("They don't make *faces* like that anymore!" she says as she looks at her own

Norma's possessive streak is very much in evidence when she refuses to let Joe leave. In another couple of minutes she will kill him.

face*); of those great silent comedies we recall when Norma does a remarkable Chaplin impersonation; of those naive backlot romances of the late twenties and early thirties (when sound came to films) we recall when Joe and Betty walk around the Paramount lot and he kisses her on the nose; and of those brooding gothic-novel adaptations like *Wuthering Heights* (1939), *Rebecca* (1940), and *Dragonwyck* (1946) we recall each minute we are in Norma's stuffy mansion.

But other than the horror film, *Sunset Boulevard* is most indebted to the *film noir.* Andrew Sarris suggests that the reason *All About Eve* (1950) swept 1950's Academy Awards is that its chief rival, *Sunset Boulevard,* was made in the already outmoded *noir* style of the forties. I think the picture was made in this style *purposely* to lament its passing. It is from the *film noir* tradition that *Sunset Boulevard's* fatalism comes; its Los Angeles (Chandler country) backdrop and the importance of the automobile; its weak hero and his destruction from romantic entanglement with a strong, manipulative, also doomed woman; and its first-person narration, recalling memories of such *noir* classics as Wilder's *Double Indemnity* (1944).

Sunset Boulevard has been criticized for being too wordy. I think this is unjustified because a film *about* there being too much talk in films ("You made a rope of words and strangled this business," silent queen Norma tells screenwriter Joe) should be a case in point. The narration has received the brunt of the criticism for being overly descriptive and hyperbolic. I think it is precisely how a hack two-story-a-week writer like Joe would talk: Joe's "B" film style narration—in 1950 when "B" films are outdated—tells us that Joe, like Norma, is obsolete in Hollywood. He realizes this, and

Bored Joe spends many nights watching Norma play cards with other forgotten stars of the silent era such as Buster Keaton (in shadows) and Anna Q. Nilsson.

*We see clips from Gloria Swanson's *Queen Kelly* (1928), which the star also produced. During filming Swanson had great battles with its director—Erich von Stroheim.

that is why he is so cynical: "I talked to a couple of yes men at Metro—they said no to me"; "I wrote a script about Okies in the Dust Bowl—it played on a torpedo boat"; "I took an inventory of my prospects—zero." It is his cynicism that makes him a standard *noir* "hero." No wonder no one wants Joe in 1950's Hollywood.

Joe Gillis fits into the line of Wilder and Brackett's tarnished heroes: Fred MacMurray in *Double Indemnity*, Ray Milland in *The Lost Weekend* (1945), Kirk Douglas in *Ace in the Hole* (1951), William Holden in *Stalag 17* (1953). He is most reminiscent of the gigolo (Charles Boyer) in the Mitchell Leisen-directed *Hold Back the Dawn* (1941) who winds up selling his woeful tale to Hollywood.

At first glance *Sunset Boulevard* appears to be a film about how pathetic Norma Desmond is and how unfortunate it is for Joe to have fallen into her clutches. But this is only the story if we are to go along with Joe's perspective (his narration). Joe only speaks of Norma in pitiful terms. Her handwriting he calls childlike. While reading her script of *Salome*, he comments, "It's sometimes interesting how bad *bad writing* can be." He calls her a "sleepwalker" and says she is a "poor devil, still waving at a parade that has gone by." When she descends the stairs to face the photographers and policemen, he wryly comments, "Life had taken pity." He is even rude to her face, "You used to be big." To this Norma responds, "I am big, it's the pictures that got small." And we're inclined to believe she's right. Joe tries to get our sympathy by telling us how low he has fallen by getting hooked up with Norma, but it is the other way around. When they dance, she says that Valentino, another gigolo, told her "there's nothing like tile for a tango." She once was intimate with the world's most renowned lover but now she has Joe—it's clear that she is the one who has lowered herself. Joe main-

The final shot of the picture: Norma walks toward the newsman's camera, imagining herself in front of DeMille's camera again.

tains his superior attitude throughout, failing to acknowledge that Norma was a great star and is still talented, as her Chaplin imitation confirms, while he has never accomplished anything in his life. If his narration is any indication of his writing talent, and I believe it is, then perhaps his pictures should indeed be limited to screenings on torpedo boats. He may laugh at Norma's writing deficiencies but writing is not her skill—acting is. He is the writer, and he should be the one to suffer the insults of the Paramount brass directed at the *Salome* script—after all, he spent many months revising it. He is just one more person of the sound era who has refused to give Norma her due, one more of the many Hollywood men who have knifed her in the back. It is fitting that she should end up shooting *him* in the back. Talk about pathetic: that's Joe lying dead in the pool, a human rat. In *On the Verge of Revolt* (Ungar, 1978), Brandon French writes: "At the end of *Sunset Boulevard,* Norma finally manages to turn her aggression outward, onto someone else; and in a dreadful sense, that is a triumph, just as her brief comeback before the newsreel cameras is a victory, however feeble and ironic."

Unlike Norma Desmond, Gloria Swanson left Hollywood in 1938, having never had a fondness for the town or the people there. But like Norma, she understood what it was to have enormous fame and then, because of the advent of sound, nothing. She knew better than to wait in Hollywood for her fame to be recaptured. Wilder originally tried to get Mary Pickford to play Norma, and then Pola Negri—but there is no better choice than Swanson. She is dynamic. Her Norma perfectly complements and eventually dwarfs Joe Gillis: she not only delivers lines with the power of Bette Davis, but she has the added capacity of being able to transmit emotions with the tricks of a consummate silent screen actress. On the other hand, Holden's bland Joe (by design) can only get his thoughts across verbally and never with the help of facial expressions and gestures. *Sunset Boulevard* broke new ground with its conception of a love affair between a woman and much younger man; and Joe acts as revolted by it as many hostile viewers were in 1950. But Norma suffers none of the middle-aged anxiety of Bette Davis in *All About Eve;* unlike Margo Channing, Norma is aware that she is still beautiful (though someone else should do her makeup) and talented. Joe may not be attracted to her but she is more desirable in her own way than he is: she is vital and is looking toward the future when she can return to the screen and appease the fans she feels she deserted; Joe is dead, literally and figuratively, too cynical and lazy to make a real go of it, even with the ambitious Betty's prodding. Like many *noir* heels, Joe only has the energy and cleverness to try to milk someone he thinks beneath him. But what happens to most of these men is that the tables are turned on them by women who turn out to be wiser than they thought. Joe thinks he is giving Norma a break by staying with her as her lover after her New Year's Eve suicide attempt, but Norma's no fool: she knows he's a gigolo (as she tells Betty) and that it is she who is using him.

Sylvia Scarlett

1936 RKO Radio
Director: George Cukor
Producer: Pandro S. Berman
Screenplay: Gladys Unger, John Collier, and Mortimer Offner
From the novel *The Early Life and Adventures of Sylvia Scarlett* by Compton MacKenzie
Cinematography: John August
Music: Roy Webb
Editor: Jane Loring
Running Time: 97 minutes

Cast: Katharine Hepburn (Sylvia Scarlett), Cary Grant (Jimmy Monkley), Brian Aherne (Michael Fane), Edmund Gwenn (Henry Scarlett), Natalie Paley (Lily), Dennie Moore (Maudie Tilt)

Synopsis: Sylvia Scarlett's mother has just died. Her father Henry is in despair because he has lost his money gambling. He decides to leave France for England, where he hopes to sell lace he will smuggle in. Sylvia wants to go with him, but since he stole the lace he is afraid her presence will alert the authorities. Sylvia cuts her hair and puts on boy's clothes and calls herself Sylvester.

On the boat Henry gets drunk and tells a cockney Englishman named Jimmy Monkley about the lace. Monkley tells the customs officials about the lace to divert their attention away from him, as he is smuggling gems in his shoe. Henry is arrested and pays the authorities all the money he has as duty. When "Sylvester" sees Jimmy on a train, she slugs him. But Jimmy makes it up to both "Sylvester" and Henry by giving them money. Jimmy gives a speech about some people being sparrows and others, like him, being hawks. He convinces them to become hawks as well and join him in swindling people. Sylvia does not let on that she is a female. After several schemes for making money fail, Henry and Jimmy go to a Buckingham Gate home where Jimmy's acquaintance Maudie works as a maid for a rich family that is out of the country. They convince her to put on her mistress's jewelry, which they steal. But "Sylvester" arrives and gets the men to return the jewelry so Maudie won't get in trouble. Maudie wants to be a singer. "Sylvester" convinces her to quit her job and invest her money in a Pierrot show. The four of them will put on song and dance shows. Henry and Maudie get married.

Near the sea as they are putting on a show, they are taunted by Michael Fane, a rich artist who lives in the area. "Sylvester" scolds him for being so rude, and he apologizes. He asks the acting troupe to come to his house and join a party. Sylvia becomes interested in Fane, while Jimmy takes a liking to Fane's mean stuck-up Russian girlfriend Lily. And Fane can't understand his attraction to "Sylvester." Jimmy sees "Sylvester" steal a dress on the beach. At last he realizes that his companion is a girl. Sylvia visits Fane and he is happy to see that it is a female he was attracted to. He immediately tries to steal a kiss from her, and he tells the naive, awkward girl that she will become like all other women: devious. Lily arrives and Fane affirms his love for her, telling her that Sylvia is just a child.

Maudie runs off with another man. Drunk and insane from worrying about his wife, Henry walks off into the night during a violent thunderstorm. The next morning, Jimmy and Sylvia find him dead. Jimmy and Sylvia decide to go off together, but Jimmy misses Lily and Sylvia misses Fane.

To get Fane's attention Lily tries to commit suicide by drowning in the ocean. Sylvia saves her. She leaves her with Jimmy while she informs Fane. Fane is impressed by Sylvia's daring in rescuing Lily. They go to get Lily only to discover she has taken off with Jimmy. They give chase and all end up on the same train. Sylvia and Fane finally reveal their love for one another and jump off. Jimmy and Lily, meanwhile, are having the first of countless arguments they will have during their lifetime together.

*Jimmy foresees trouble ahead when "Sylvester" convinces Maudie to invest her money in a Pierrot show.
Already in love with Maudie, Henry is happy that she will become part of the troupe.*

ollowing a disastrous preview of *Sylvia Scarlett*, both director George Cukor and star Katharine Hepburn (it has been said) offered to make another picture for RKO without pay if the studio decided to shelve it. Unwilling to lose production costs, RKO chose to release the picture anyway. And sure enough: it fared miserably at the box office. For years after this, Cukor would say that *Sylvia Scarlett* was the one embarrassing blot on his and Hepburn's otherwise illustrious careers. No one expressed more shock than Cukor when, in the mid-sixties, the picture began turning up with increasing frequency on college campuses and in repertory theaters, and a cult for the film took root.

It was hard to find critics in 1935 who didn't detest *Sylvia Scarlett*, but their anger was directed at the picture and not at the stars. Most agreed that Hepburn as the awkward, rambunctious, petulant, high-spirited, too-wise-for-her-own-good, athletic, quick-thinking, quixotic Sylvia was as fine as she had been in her triumphant *Alice Adams* (1935) playing the small-town wallflower. But while her notices were excellent, many critics tended to downplay her acting and allude to the fact that her role required that she spend almost the entire picture with short hair and dressed like a boy. *Time:* "*Sylvia Scarlett* reveals the interesting fact that Katharine Hepburn is better-looking as a boy than as a woman"; the *New York Herald-Tribune:* "The dynamic Miss Hepburn is the handsomest boy of the season"; the New York *Post:* "Her achievement is an accident of looks rather than a creative effort, and as such belongs among those museum pieces which are ordinarily found under a glass case." Some critics were nicer than others.

The critical praise for Hepburn in *Sylvia Scarlett* did little to help her stardom. RKO knew she was a great actress, but it didn't know if she could pull in an audience no matter what the vehicle; *Sylvia Scarlett* was one of several Hepburn flops in the thirties that convinced RKO that she was box office poison. On the other hand, *Sylvia Scarlett* gave Cary Grant's career a needed boost. He was warmly received as the disreputable cockney Jimmy Monkley, the role that proved he could play parts more complex than the handsome-but-stiff leading men he'd been relegated to in the past. This was the first picture that let Grant loosen up, and for the first time he reveals his remarkable comedic talents. Considering that Cukor and producer Pandro S. Berman (who would use Grant again, most memorably in the 1939 adventure classic *Gunga Din)* borrowed Grant from Paramount for a role unlike anything he had done before, this was a true case of inspired casting.

While Hepburn devotees seek out *Sylvia Scarlett*

"Sylvester" is always the one to step forward when the company suffers verbal abuse.

because it contains what is perhaps her most animated performance—if the boy she were playing were *Peter Pan*, it's likely she could fly without wires—the cult for the film is equally the result of both the unique style of the picture and the unconventional presentation of sex roles.

Numerous Cukor films deal with actors / performers on stage (screen) and off. A few titles are: *What Price Hollywood?* (1932), *Zaza* (1938), *A Double Life* (1948), *The Actress* (1953), *A Star Is Born* (1954), *Heller in Pink Tights* (1960), and *Let's Make Love* (1960). But no film of Cukor's—or anyone else's, for that matter—is more concerned with "acting" as a method (rather than a profession) for living one's life. *Sylvia Scarlett* is populated with characters whose lives revolve around disguise and deception, pretense and playacting.

Sylvia cuts her hair and *disguises* herself as a boy, *deceiving* everyone but Henry, her father, into thinking she's Sylvester. She and Henry cross the Channel from France to England *pretending* to be law-abiding citizens when they are actually smuggling in lace without paying the tariff. Jimmy Monkley sees Sylvia but thinks her a boy because of her *costume*. Jimmy *deceives* the drunk Henry into trusting him enough to show him the lace. Then Jimmy, who is smuggling gems in his shoe, *fools*

the police into thinking him honest by ratting on Henry. Once "Sylvester," Henry, and Jimmy have joined forces, Sylvia does an *act* in a public park *pretending* to be a French boy who has been brought to England without any money. Henry and Jimmy help her out by *pretending* to be English citizens moved by the boy's plight into passing the hat around. In another scheme, Henry and Jimmy *pretend* they are interested in the maid Maudie's singing career, when they are actually trying to steal her mistress's jewelry. As part of the game, Henry *dresses up* in the master of the house's "Little Lord Fauntleroy" garb, and Maudie *puts on* her mistress's best gown and jewelry, which the men steal though they *pretend* innocence. Once "Sylvester" had made the men return the jewelry, the four of them break out *singing and dancing* to celebrate their entry into show business. They set off in a Pierrot show during which all of them wear clown *costumes* and are *in white face*. But the offstage deception, playacting, etc., doesn't come to a halt. Sylvia already dresses as a *boy*, but Maudie draws a Ronald Colman *mustache* on her to make "Sylvester" more of a man. Maudie *pretends* to love Henry, to whom she is married, but she is having an affair. When she runs away, Henry, in his clown *costume* and *playing* the fool, drunkenly and deliriously

An awkward moment: Fane asks "Sylvester" to spend the night, not realizing that "the boy" is really a female.

walks off a cliff to his death. Sylvia *fools* Fane into thinking her a boy. When she later comes to him in a dress—the first time she's been out of costume—their male-female relationship gets off on the wrong foot. So they back things up a few minutes and they *pretend* Sylvia is arriving for the first time. They go into *playacting*, repeating lines which they had recited on the first visit, which they now treat as a *rehearsal*. When they realize that Jimmy has run off with Lily, each *pretends* to be concerned for the other's benefit. Only at the last minute do Sylvia and Fane admit they've been deceiving each other and that they love each other. They jump off the train. Jimmy sees this but *pretends* otherwise for his own amusement (at Lily's expense), letting Lily blab on about how much Fane wants her back. She knows this is not the case and so does Jimmy, but neither of them will let on. There is *deception* until the very end.

Stylistically speaking, I can think of few pictures so rooted in theater. But this is a *film,* and Cukor didn't make the mistake of directing it as if it were part of the grand theater tradition. You will more likely be reminded of street theater, improvisational theater, theater-in-the-round, and traveling French Pierrot troupes such as the one in the film. And you'll be reminded of Shakespeare—not Shakespeare as performed at a university but "Shakespeare in the Park." There is an incredibly relaxed, breezy feeling to this film, an open-air quality that makes you feel like you're watching fine, amusing, dramatic (with the right touch of hamminess) performances while sitting on the grass.

Critics in the thirties never mentioned the sexual implications in *Sylvia Scarlett.* It is quite remarkable that during a period when such things as transvestism and bisexuality were taboo no one even mentioned the strange sights found in this picture. We actually see Katharine Hepburn kissed on the lips by another woman, when Maudie thinks Sylvia is a boy and starts to seduce "him." And we have Michael Fane inviting "Sylvester" to sleep with him. Fane's intentions may be innocent, but how many men in their thirties are such good friends with teen-age boys? Then, of course, there is Fane's famous line to "Sylvester": "I don't know what it is that gives me a *queer* feeling when I look at you." When Sylvia reveals to Fane that she is a female, his love for her is so quick in coming that we have to believe he felt more than simple friendship for "Sylvester." Of course he doesn't have to change his thinking: there is little personality difference between "Sylvester" and the tomboyish Sylvia.

It is fun to figure out but is of trivial importance who in *Sylvia Scarlett* is bisexual (judging by contemporary standards). What is more significant to cultists is the unique (in film history) sexual role played by Hepburn. When Henry says at the beginning of the film "I have nothing," Sylvia objects: "You have me." When Sylvia dresses as a boy, and thus becomes a man in her father's eyes, she becomes *everything* to him, including his partner who makes all the decisions. When Sylvia cuts off her hair, she gains stature in his eyes and gains independence—only as a boy can she accompany Henry to England. By dressing in men's clothes, she is able to free that latent part of herself previously kept hidden by convention; not only can she start being athletic— jumping fences, climbing up the sides of buildings, hanging upside down on the rings (which she does to stop herself from revealing to Fane she is female), and punching Jimmy—but she can also speak her mind for the first time and be listened to by men like Jimmy and Fane who think women silly. And she can be privy to antifemale speeches by Jimmy and Fane that they would hold back if they knew her to be female. ("If I were a girl," she tells Jimmy, "I wouldn't want to get hooked up with you"; "I hate women too," "Sylvester" tells Fane.) So only by pretending to be a male can Sylvia open up the world for herself and bring out her real self. And only as a male can Sylvia control her own destiny and make her own rules. *Sylvia Scarlett* is probably the first film that calls for the elimination of sexual barriers which keep women from exploring their own personalities. "Sylvester" is not the alter ego of Sylvia but is *more* of Sylvia.

Sylvia Scarlett is far from being a great film. Cukor wasn't able to decide whether he was filming a comedy or a drama. It is dull at times. There are too many moments when characters display cruelty that is sadistic and hard to watch. And I think it a letdown that Sylvia goes off with the conceited, sexist Fane instead of the cocky, sexist Jimmy (who is at least more fun); Fane comes into the picture so late we already have been convinced that Jimmy and Sylvia are falling in love—and it's hard to adjust our thinking, especially when we don't like Fane as much as Jimmy. But having Sylvia go off with the wrong man—Grant is even listed ahead of Brian Aherne in the credits—is another of many instances in the film where movie conventions are broken, and this contributes to making *Sylvia Scarlett*, whatever its faults, one of the most interesting films of the thirties.

A publicity shot from final sequence. In the film, Fane and Sylvia pretend that they don't know Jimmy and Lily are on the same train, and vice versa.

The Tall T

1957   Columbia release of a Scott-Brown Productions film
Director: Budd Boetticher
Producer: Harry Joe Brown
Screenplay: Burt Kennedy
From a story by Elmore Leonard
Cinematography: Charles Lawton, Jr.
Music: Heinz Roemheld
Editor: Al Clark
Running Time: 77 minutes

Cast: Randolph Scott (Pat Brennan), Richard Boone (Frank Usher), Maureen O'Sullivan (Doretta Mims), Arthur Hunnicut (Ed Rintoon), Skip Homeier (Billy Jack), Henry Silva (Chink), John Hubbard (Willard Mims), Robert Burton (Tenvoorde), Robert Anderson (Jace), Fred E. Sherman (Hank Parker), Chris Olsen (Jeff)

Synopsis: Pat Brennan, now long past his prime, has worked many years as ramrod for Mr. Tenvoorde, saving his money to buy a spread. He rides onto Tenvoorde's ranch hoping he can buy a bull. Tenvoorde is reluctant to sell. Jace, the new ramrod, challenges Pat to ride the bull—if Pat rides it to a standstill, he will win it from Tenvoorde, but if he is thrown off he will lose his horse to him. Pat loses his horse.

Pat walks home through the desert. He is given a lift by Rintoon, the driver of the mail stage. There are two passengers on the stage, middle-aged newlyweds Willard and Doretta Mims. The stage pulls into the station in the middle of the desert. Two outlaws step out. Frank is an intelligent man in his middle years; Billy Jack is a teen-ager. They have killed the station owner and his son. Rintoon goes for his rifle and is gunned down by the murderous Chink, who is hiding in the shadows. Afraid to die, Willard tells Frank, the leader, that Doretta is the daughter of a wealthy copper mine owner. He says that he can arrange for a fifty-thousand-dollar ransom to be paid for her. Frank sends Willard and Chink off to make arrangements for a payoff, and plans to rendezvous with them in the mountains. Meanwhile, Pat and Doretta are kept hostage. Frank gets to like Pat, who is very much like him except that Pat is honest and decent. He envies Pat and wants a spread like his. He advises Pat to get married.

Chink and Willard ride into camp. Plans have been made for the money to be delivered near the camp the following day. Frank tells Willard that he can leave. Although this means leaving his wife behind, Willard happily rides away. But before he gets out of sight, Frank orders Chink to kill him. Doretta is upset by her husband's death. But Frank tells her Willard sold her out.

Alone in the cave with Pat, Doretta says that she is no longer upset that Willard was killed—just that she is alone, and unloved. They kiss.

Frank rides off to pick up the ransom. Knowing he and Doretta are to be killed, Pat thinks of a plan. He convinces Chink that Frank intends to take all the money and go to Mexico. Chink decides to ride after Frank to keep an eye on him. Pat tells Doretta to open her blouse in order to look seductive to Billy Jack. When Billy Jack sees her like this, he grabs her and tries to kiss her. Pat catches him off guard and they struggle for Billy Jack's shotgun. Pat shoots him in the face.

Chink hears the shot and heads back toward camp. Pat tells Doretta to take Billy Jack's horse and to ride toward his spread to safety. But she insists on staying with him. When Chink arrives, she keeps him holed up by shooting bullets in his direction, allowing Pat time to move into an advantageous position. Pat calls to him. Chink turns and draws. Pat kills him.

Frank returns with the money. Pat gets the drop on him, but Frank refuses to turn around to face him. Knowing Pat won't shoot him in the back, Frank walks toward his horse, climbs up, and rides out of camp. However, once out of sight, he pulls out his rifle and charges back into camp. Pat shoots him in the face. Frank is momentarily blinded, then he falls dead.

Pat and Doretta start out toward Pat's ranch, where they will make a new life for themselves.

Pat realizes there is trouble brewing at the stage station.

Howard Hawks used to say it was foolhardy to attempt to make a popular western without John Wayne in the lead role. Naturally, it *was* reassuring for a director to have as his star the tall, powerful Wayne, who embodied the vast, rugged western landscape and had come to represent the qualities moviegoers associate with western heroes: bravery, loyalty, integrity, determination, independence, and resourcefulness. The Duke was the king of the movie western, but there have been other charismatic male stars whose mere presence/look/attitude lent the authenticity, strength, and physical dimension so necessary to the masculine western genre. Today Clint Eastwood rides alone, but he follows a movie trail blazed by such luminaries as William S. Hart, Tom Mix, Tim McCoy, Gary Cooper, John Wayne, "Wild Bill" Elliott, Joel McCrea, and Randolph Scott, all believable when dressed in cowboy gear, shooting six-shooters, and sitting tall in the saddle, all part of the land, all icons of "the West" moviegoers consider the real West.

Frank grows fond of his captive because he considers Pat civilized, like himself.

In the fifties, when the theatrical western flourished, despite the decline of the "B" western, almost every big star strapped on a gunbelt. Cagney, Peck, Power, Lancaster, Douglas, Holden, Newman, Mitchum, Ford, Widmark, even Joan Crawford and Barbara Stanwyck. But certainly many of the most memorable westerns of the period starred veterans of the genre. Wayne worked for both Hawks and John Ford; Joel McCrea made two excellent oaters for Jacques Tourneur. Gary Cooper won an Oscar for Fred Zinnemann's *High Noon* (1952), but cultists think him better in *Man of the West* (1958), directed by Anthony Mann, who also made five classic westerns with James Stewart.* The Mann-Stewart series came to an end in 1955, but the huge gap it left was quickly filled by an equally remarkable series of second-feature outdoor westerns starring Randolph Scott, directed by Budd Boetticher, a cult favorite of *auteur* critics, and produced by Harry Joe Brown.† The long, lanky, deep-voiced Scott had

appeared in westerns since 1928 and was considered a reliable, sturdy hero, but nothing more significant. It was the Boetticher series—*Seven Men From Now* (1956), *The Tall T, Decision at Sundown* (1957), *Buchanan Rides Alone* (1958), *Ride Lonesome* (1959), *Westbound* (1959), and *Comanche Station* (1960)—that established Scott's most interesting persona—a man who, if not as complex or introspective as Stewart's characters, at least has subtleties, meaning, and value—and finally secured for him, in his mid-fifties, his rightful place alongside the cinema's other great western stars.

An obvious influence on many westerns, including Mann's *Man of the West,** *The Tall T* is probably the quintessential Scott-Boetticher film, beautifully shot, strongly yet straightforwardly written (by Burt Kennedy, who scripted four films of the series), and dealing with Boetticher's primary concerns: pride and honor (there is a distinction between the two), and how people choose to lead their lives in a West that is becoming increasingly civilized yet, paradoxically, more violent and amoral. America is growing, and, not surprisingly, almost everyone in *The Tall T* wants something. Pat thinks he's satisfied now that he owns a small spread, but he learns what others, including Frank, already know: that he desires female companionship. Frank, on the other hand, would be satisfied with a ranch like Pat's ("A man should have something that belongs to him").

---

*I excluded James Stewart from the "luminary" list although he was a fine hero in scores of westerns. I did this because Stewart usually, particularly in the Mann films, played men whose modern-day concerns and obsessions make them more complex than the traditional westerners, who were completely rooted to their time.

†*Seven Men From Now* was a Batjac production, but subsequent films in the series were made by Scott and Brown's production company Ranown.

Doretta wants someone to love her ("I couldn't stand being alone anymore"), thinking that will raise her opinion of herself. Willard Mims, far less sympathetic than the three villains, wants wealth and position, which is why he married a rich man's daughter, but he is willing to sacrifice her to save his own neck. Chink wants to add notches to his gunbelt—he's up to seven and counting. Billy Jack wants to be a man. The most backward-looking characters in the picture are the station owner, who mourns for his dead wife and wants to move into town, and Rintoon, an old-timer, who is the last mule skinner on "the last mail line in the territory." The quick deaths of these two men immediately indicates that the picture will be about American progress, and not about returning to the past or maintaining the status quo. Mims is the next character to be killed; Boetticher and Kennedy want to downplay the growth of America in terms of opportunists and moneymen: hardworking men and women like Pat and Doretta are the foundation for America's growth. The next characters eliminated are Billy Jack and Chink, the wild, lawless elements that ran amuck before civilization and law and order came to America. Whereas Boetticher shows Mims killed in long shot, conveying that his death is insignificant, he allows Billy Jack and then Chink to be killed close-up, thereby encouraging audience empathy. They are villains, but Billy Jack is too young and immature to know much better, and Chink's background—when twelve, he killed his father for beating his mother—partly explains his hateful nature. At the end, Pat and Frank are the only men left. Both are survivors of the Old West and are intrigued by the possibility of starting a new life. Both men can make it in the civilized world, only Frank is unwilling to try peacefully, the hard way. "I like you," Frank tells Pat, but adds that if he has to choose between him and Chink and Billy Jack "I ride with them."

Pat lets us know verbally only two things about himself: that he is scared of dying (which he admits to both Frank and Doretta), and that his honor prevents him from running away from responsibility ("There are some things a man can't ride around"). But we learn more about him by observing his actions: he is true to his word; treats women with honesty and politeness, if not with a great deal of respect—and he doesn't argue

with Doretta when she insists on staying with him intead of fleeing to safety; is human enough to fall off a bull and bang his head when walking out of a cave; is prideful enough to accept Jace's challenge ("You've gone gentle, Brennan") to ride the bull but humble and smart enough to jump into a water trough so it won't run him through; and, though scared, he won't cower to Frank, Chink, or Billy Jack. In addition, Pat is defined by others. The most significant remark is made by Tenvoorde, who tells Pat, "A guy can turn his back when you're around." Even enemies can turn their backs when Pat is around. Before Pat fires at Chink, he calls to him so that they will be face to face when they shoot at one another. In fact, Frank is so sure Pat won't shoot him in the back, he simply walks out of camp. And Doretta, even when she doesn't like Pat, feels comfortable enough to sleep with her back toward him while she is alone with him in the cave.

Likewise, Frank doesn't take advantage of the sleeping Doretta when he is alone with her in the cave; nor does he circle around Pat at the film's end so he can shoot him in the back—instead he chooses to charge him while in plain sight. Pat and Frank are *mirror* images/inversions of one another; their clash results from Pat being a moral man with violent tendencies and Frank being a violent man with moral tendencies. Boetticher told Eric Sherman and Martin Rubin, editors of *The Director's Event* (Atheneum, 1969):

> I felt that [Frank] really loved [Pat] in the picture, to the point of being terribly attracted to him physically. He would have liked to have been [Pat]. . . . In every one of the Scott pictures, I felt that I could have traded Randy's part with the villain's.

The tragedy of *The Tall T* is that Pat and Frank are on opposite sides of the law when they should ride together. Frank likes Pat so much that he doesn't let

---

*Both *The Tall T* and *Man of the West* begin as comedies but quickly become harsh melodramas. In each film, two men and a woman are held hostage by a violent gang that plans a robbery. The second man is killed off in both; in both, the hero and the woman are forced to share sleeping quarters although they aren't married. In both, the hero is kept alive by a member of the gang who likes him better than the vile group he travels with—until the end, when hero and villain must fight to the death. In both films, the hero leaves all the villains dead and unburied and goes off with the woman in the film's final shot. Just as Frank is Pat's mirror image, in *Man of the West* Claude is Link's mirror image, which is why both heroes are upset when they kill the villain. (In fact, if Dock Tobin didn't exist in *Man of the West*, and Claude were in charge of the gang, the two films would be virtually identical.) Chink is the precursor to *Man*'s Coaley; Doretta is just as unfulfilled and self-deprecating as Billie. Yes, *Man of the West* bears too many similarities to *The Tall T* for it to be called coincidental, but to be fair, *The Tall T* has almost the same premise as Henry Hathaway's 1951 western, *Rawhide*.

Falling into Pat's trap, Billy Jack tries to have his way with Doretta.

Chink kill him although his death would make things much simpler. He even admits he likes Pat's company much more than the "animals" he rides with. While Frank lets Pat know that likely he will be killed eventually, at the same time he talks to him about his spread as if Pat will be returning to it unharmed. He tells Pat he should have a wife and, as if he were Pat's kin, starts playing matchmaker between Pat and Doretta. What more could any matchmaker do for Pat than kill Doretta's husband ("What's the matter with her?" he asks in surprise when she is upset by Willard's death), make Pat and Doretta sleep together in the dark cave, order Doretta to pour Pat's coffee, and talk to Pat about her plainness so Pat will not only stick up for her but continually think about her. Frank, who calls Doretta "lady," and Pat, who calls her "ma'am," both realize Doretta's great potential, tell her to be prideful, and coax her into allowing herself to be pretty—which she becomes when she lets her hair down and stands with her hair and clothing blowing gently in the wind. Frank would like her, as much as Pat, to be *his* companion on the spread he dreams about—but since he can't have her, he wants Pat to be the lucky one. The similarity between the two men is seen in how they go about realizing their dreams. Pat puts down Frank for trying to acquire a spread, his dream, with stolen money; yet Pat, who has a spread, tries to acquire a woman, his dream, by following his own philosophy: "Sometimes you have to walk up to something and take what you want."

Budd Boetticher was a former bullfighter, and made three films on the subject during his career. His fascina-tion with bullfighting even comes into play in his westerns, including *The Tall T.* Pat is successful in his battle against the odds because he has a strong sense of himself and the self-discipline not to let fear intrude on his mental capacities. He never wavers from his plan of escape or takes unnecessary chances that might shorten the ordeal. Like a bullfighter, he bluffs, parries, uses his intelligence, physical talents, and patience. Importantly, he doesn't strike at the strong point (Frank) of the gang first, but undermines the whole by doing away with the weak links (Billy Jack and Chink). The final battle is not between two enemies (Pat calls him "Frank" for the first time), as far as Pat is concerned, but between two combatants who respect one another. On his horse, Frank charges Pat as if he were a bull attacking a matador. (Like Pat, Frank has too much honor to avoid this inevitable confrontation.) Pat stands his ground, and when he can almost touch Frank, or insert a matador's sword if he had one, he guns Frank down. But there are no "olés."

"It ain't right for a woman to be alone," Frank said. And, to Boetticher, the growth of America was the result of loners like Pat settling down with a good woman like Doretta. (They fought together and now they can work the land together.) The stability of the country was dependent on marriage, family, and property. Many people are dead, but it is with optimism (some critics think—wrongly I believe—the ending to be ironic and pessimistic) that Pat tells Doretta, "Come on—it's going to be a nice day." They are going to help build the New West. Better them than Willard or Frank.

Targets

1968 Paramount release of a Saticoy Productions film
Director: Peter Bogdanovich
Producer: Peter Bogdanovich
Screenplay: Peter Bogdanovich
From an original story by Polly Platt and Peter Bogdanovich
Cinematography: Laszlo Kovacs
Running Time: 90 minutes

Cast: Boris Karloff (Byron Orlok), Tim O'Kelly (Bobby Thompson),
Nancy Hsueh (Jenny), Peter Bogdanovich (Sammy Michaels),
James Brown (Robert Thompson, Sr.), Sandy Baron (Kip
Larkin), Arthur Peterson (Ed Laughlin), Mary Jackson (Charlotte
Thompson), Tanya Morgan (Ilene Thompson), Monty Landis
(Marshall Smith)

Synopsis: In Hollywood, Byron Orlok, veteran star of horror movies,
decides to retire from pictures. He considers himself an anachron-
ism because people no longer are frightened by horror pictures. He
contends that real life is more terrifying because every day someone
goes berserk and starts shooting down innocent people. Director
Sammy Michaels, who is in love with Orlok's secretary, Jenny, tries
to convince Orlok to make a picture he wrote that will cast him as a
real-life person rather than a bogeyman; but Orlok is fed up with the
whole movie business and refuses to even read Sammy's script. But
at Jenny's and Sammy's urging he agrees to make a final,
promotional appearance at the drive-in that is debuting *The Terror,*
his latest film, which Sammy directed.

Bobby Thompson is a young man with a pretty wife named Ilene,
a flashy convertible, and a keen talent for shooting rifles and pistols.
He learned his shooting skills from Robert Senior, and since Bobby
and Ilene live with Bobby's parents, it is convenient for the two men
to practice and go hunting together. On the shooting range, Bobby
points his rifle at his father, who orders him to put it down—because
pointing a gun at a human being goes against everything he has
taught his son. That night, Bobby tells Ilene that he has been getting
strange thoughts in his head and is perplexed. Since she has to work
the nightshift at the telephone company, she hasn't the time to hear
him out. When she returns late that night, he no longer wants to
talk.

In the morning, when his father is at work, Bobby shoots Ilene,
his mother, and a delivery boy. He leaves behind a note that says he
will continue his killing spree until he is apprehended. After
purchasing many rounds of ammunition, he climbs on top of an oil
storage tank and lays out many long-range rifles and pistols he has
brought with him. He kills many people as they drive along the
freeway, and an oil company attendant who investigates the shooting. When he hears police sirens, Bobby collects most of his guns
and runs back to his car. A police car gives chase, but he eludes it by
driving into the very drive-in that is showing *The Terror.* He gets
out of his car, and, carrying his rifles in a pouch, he climbs in back of the
screen. When it gets dark and the movie goes on, he begins to shoot
viewers through a small hole in the screen. He even kills the
projectionist.

Orlok arrives for his special appearance and parks close to the
screen. Meanwhile, many viewers start to leave because they realize
there is a sniper present. A traffic jam ensues. Some male viewers
take guns from their trunks and walk toward the screen. Panicking,
Bobby climbs down and runs to an area at the side of the screen. He
shoots wildly, and one bullet slightly injures Jenny. Orlok angrily
walks toward Bobby, who is confused because on the screen the
Orlok character seems to be walking toward him as well. He shoots
at the wrong Orlok and this gives the real Orlok the chance to knock
the gun from his hand with a cane. The police arrest Bobby.

Bobby and his father spend
an afternoon shooting at cans.
These targets start to bore Bobby.

Just after Bobby has murdered his wife, his
mother, and a delivery boy and has left behind a
note that promises he will kill people at random
until he is caught, he walks into a gun shop and
orders several boxes of ammunition. We all have
seen this type of scene before and are positive that
Bobby will have trouble. We expect that the clerk will
be suspicious because Bobby has ordered so much
ammunition and seems a bit jittery, and will stall for
time to make sure things are on the up-and-up. So we
settle back nervously to wait for the suspense to build.
Will the clerk call the police? Will Bobby realize he is
doing this and shoot him? What actually transpires is a
complete shock. There is no suspense at all: the ammunition is sold without question, and Bobby, fully
equipped for his deadly endeavor, walks out on the
street to kill again. We, the viewers, are the "targets"
referred to in the film's title—the people Bobby will
indiscriminately shoot at on the highway and in the
drive-in; and as we can tell from this scene in the gun
shop, the society that doesn't care that lethal weapons
are accessible to anybody is the *target* of Peter Bogdanovich's picture.

Targets is a remarkable debut film—many consider
it Bogdanovich's best picture—not only because of the
sophisticated camerawork (particularly in the scenes
along the highway and in Bobby's house) and overall
technical expertise but because it is a Hollywood picture
daring enough to have both an anti-Hollywood bias
(Orlok even complains that the town itself has become
ugly) and a strong social message as well. In *The Harder
They Fall* (1956), Humphrey Bogart makes a plea for
boxing to be outlawed even if it takes an act of Congress
for this to happen. In wishy-washy Hollywood, no film
other than this tried to strike at a specific root of the
violence in our country—until *Targets.* This picture is
such a strong indictment of the proliferation of guns in
America's private sector that it is obvious that Bogdanovich is calling for more than gun control—he would like
a constitutional amendment to repeal our *right* to bear
arms.

Bogdanovich doesn't contend that Bobby's actions
are those of the average man on the street—although
murder sprees are becoming commonplace occurrences

Orlok tells Sammy that he wants to retire because horror films are no longer as frightening as real life.

—but he sees the average man as a potential Bobby. He uses a clever tactic to show the similarity between the mentalities of certain members of our society and that of Bobby *before* he went berserk. As Bobby fires upon people in the drive-in, an all-male vigilante committee forms among the spectators. Car trunks open, and so many guns are exposed that it looks as if these men have been preparing for war. Earlier in the film we had gasped when Bobby had opened his trunk and we saw it filled with numerous rifles and pistols—we had thought this gun craze to be peculiar to him, but, to our dismay, we now see that Bobby is not alone. These men at the drive-in are an unnecessary danger to *us;* from them and others who consider guns an important part of their lives will come our future snipers, our future mass murderers. In our country, many violence-prone individuals go insane—no one can dispute this; what is terrifyingly true is that many of these people whose minds snap own guns and know how to shoot them. How many times already have there been true stories about characters like Bobby? Too many, thinks Bogdanovich.

In a world where headlines speak of nuclear bombs and antiballistic missiles, it is quite easy for America's powerful gun lobby to make antiviolence advocates believe that handguns and rifles aren't so much weapons as the harmless possessions of hobbyists and sportsmen. Bogdanovich attempts to show us just how lethal weapons are (just as Budd Schulberg wanted to show that boxing isn't just another *sport*). He forces us to look through the gun sights with Bobby and help him line up his victim. It is frustrating—we want Bobby to miss but each time we see that his aim is true. It is bad enough when unidentified people fall dead, but often Bogdanovich will have Bobby take aim at someone and pull the trigger only to find himself out of bullets. While he reloads we have time to get to know and suffer with the intended prey. We want to yell "Get the hell out of here!" But each time we must watch helplessly as he is gunned down. And again we have been denied the chance of saving someone. These sniper scenes are so realistic that they give me chills. There is no letup: Bobby shoots often, and, when he misses, he gets a second chance. And it looks so easy to kill with Bobby's long-range equipment that we fear that anyone, with just a *little* practice, could be almost as accurate as Bobby.

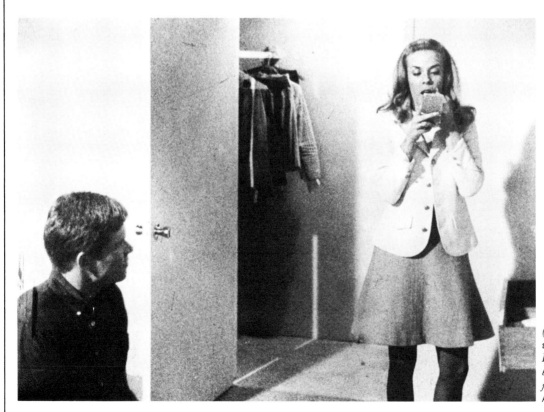

(L) Frustrated Bobby watches his pretty wife, Ilene, make herself up before going to her night job. (R) The next day, he kills her.

The gun lobbyist's argument that proper gun instruction will prevent abuse is strongly denounced. Since Bobby was a small boy, his outdoorsman father has raised him on a diet of guns, making Bobby his practice partner and taking him hunting. Robert Senior has taught Bobby so well that the pupil has become the better marksman; and he has been a good supervisor, telling Bobby all the rules of safety and emphasizing that shooting is a sport. Why then does Bobby move his gun sights away from the practice cans and toward his father's face? The question arises: how long does it take someone to get bored shooting at cans, or limiting hunting to killing animals? To Bobby, people represent a far more exciting challenge. One realizes that Bogdanovich thinks Bobby sees his snipering as an extension of his previous "games." As he is being taken off to jail by gun-toting police at the end, he boasts to those he thinks might be interested in his prowess: "I didn't miss much, did I?" Bobby now makes his own rules.

Bogdanovich refrains from explaining exactly why Bobby goes crazy and starts shooting people. No specific reason would be satisfactory; suffice it to say that people really do go crazy and want to start shooting people and that we must make sure no guns are available to them. I believe Bobby's actions are meant to be a direct result of his immaturity. (Bogdanovich thinks men who carry guns are subconsciously trying to compensate for their arrested sexual, psychological, emotional, or intellectual development.) In an era when young people wear wild clothes and have long hair, Bobby does his father proud by wearing a suit and keeping his hair trim. He eats Baby Ruths; speeds along the freeway in his flashy convertible, changing lanes without signaling, his radio blaring Top 40 rock; tinkers with his car; and practices shooting. He even addresses his note about his projected killing spree "To Whom It May Concern," as if he were applying for his first job.

We see that Bobby's immaturity is not all of his own doing, but stems from a stifling family life. He and his pretty wife Ilene live with his parents. He still calls his authoritarian father sir, and his father calls him Bobby Boy (never Bob); his well-meaning mother calls him dear and says things to him such as "That's a good boy." Bobby never acts hostilely to any of this, but how can it not be eating him up? Bogdanovich emphasizes the *ordinariness* of this family, for many mass killers come from "ordinary" home lives. Robert says "dammit," Ilene says "darn"; Ilene and Bobby's mother cook together and have dinner waiting when Robert Senior comes come and says "Hello, group. Is dinner ready?";

Reminding one of crazed gunman Charles Whitman, who killed and wounded a total of forty-six people while stationed in a University of Texas bell tower in 1966, Bobby takes out a whole arsenal—and a typical American lunch—before firing on cars passing on the highway near the oil tank on which he sits.

before dinner there is prayer, and during dinner there is idle chatter; at night the family watches *The Joey Bishop Show,* the old TV talk show for those who found Johnny Carson too erudite; then Robert says "I'm bushed" and goes off to bed, telling his wife to follow. The house is spotless and has no signs of culture—no bookcases, and the walls are quite bare except for one family portrait, some hunting pictures and certificates, and some antlers. The house has a blue exterior, a blue interior, blue lamps, blue bedspreads, blue dish racks, blue cloth towels, blue paper towels, and even a blue flower in the kitchen. What isn't blue is a purplish gray or off-white. This house was not decorated by creative people—but their effect on Bobby is obvious, as he wears a gray suit and a white shirt.

Bobby, I believe, is jobless; his wife dolls herself up at night and goes out to work as a telephone operator. Bobby asks her if she thinks him a failure, and she replies with a cliché: "You can do anything you set your mind to." Bobby's world is without sexual or intellectual stimulation. A great sense of vacancy exists: there is no dirt in the house, no pictures on the wall, and worse, no wife in bed at night. Guns are Bobby's only companion, his only security.

Bobby doesn't know what causes him to want to kill people ("pigs," he tells the gun shop attendant when asked what he's going to be hunting). "I don't know what's happening to me," he remarks to his wife when she has no time to hear him out. "I get funny ideas." Later I think he understands where to lay the blame: when he buys the ammunition, instead of writing a check as he did earlier, he charges the purchase to the account of his father. His father is not a bad man—he is kind and generous, allowing his son and daughter-in-law to share his house—but he has always been such an intimidating figure to Bobby that Bobby now believes he was the one who made him into a weakling. That he is still scared of his father despite being willing to take on the whole L.A. police department is clear when he waits until his father is off to work before he shoots Ilene and his mother (the only moment in the picture that is in slow motion).

As this was his first film, former film critic Bogdanovich took the opportunity to pay homage to some of his idols. The scene in which Bobby tries to retrieve his dropped weapon behind the movie screen is reminiscent of Bruno (Robert Walker) reaching into a drain for the dropped cigarette lighter in Hitchcock's *Strangers on a Train* (1951). When the camera moves through the house, it's Hitchcock. Hitchcock used scenes of dialogue immediately following shock sequences in *Psycho* (1960): that is one of the main purposes for the amusing scenes with Byron Orlok and Sammy Michaels. When Orlok and Sammy watch television, the movie playing on it is Howard Hawks's *The Criminal Code* (1931), which was Karloff's first major film; Sammy takes the opportunity to say how Hawks could "really tell a story." When Orlok and Sammy both get drunk and fall asleep side by side in Orlok's bed, it might very well have been directed by another Bogdanovich favorite, John Ford. And of course the whole film is a tribute to Karloff, one of the greats.

The Byron Orlok story is woven into the film quite well. The scenes between Sammy and Orlok are entertaining and provide levity in an otherwise unrelentingly bleak film. The highlights occur when Orlok tells a brief ghost story and when Orlok looks at himself in the mirror and jumps with fright. The serious script Sammy wants Orlok to do is *Targets,* although the title is never used, and it is so nice that Karloff, if not Orlok, agreed to do a picture which allowed him to play a real character rather than his one millionth bogeyman in succession. It was fitting that a year before Karloff died, he at last played a hero! That the unarmed Orlok is the one to capture Bobby—who goes into a crouch, after Orlok slaps him, like a child caught stealing—while dozens of armed men scurry about is Bogdanovich's final statement about the need of guns in our society.

The scenes in which Orlok complains that real life is so horrifying that horror films have lost their ability to scare anyone remind us that we are watching a movie. While Bogdanovich places the sniper in a screen where *The Terror* (1963), a not-very-scary Roger Corman horror film starring the real Boris Karloff, is being projected, to prove that Orlok is correct in thinking "real" life more frightening than horror films, he is also reminding *us* that no matter how terrifying we find Bobby's actions in *Targets,* it is only a movie we are watching and doesn't compare to the *real* real thing.

Tarzan and His Mate

1934 MGM
Director: Cedric Gibbons (and Jack Conway, uncredited)
Producer: Orman K. Hyman
Screenplay: Howard Emmett Rogers and Leon Gordon
From a story by J. Kevin McGuinness
Based on Edgar Rice Burroughs's characters
Cinematography: Charles Clarke and Clyde De Vinna
Editor: Tom Held
Running Time: 92 minutes

Cast: Johnny Weissmuller (Tarzan), Maureen O'Sullivan (Jane Parker*), Neil Hamilton (Harry Holt), Paul Cavanagh (Martin Arlington), Forrester Harvey (Beamish), Nathan Curry (Saidi)

Synopsis: Englishmen Harry Holt and Martin Arlington head a safari into the African jungles in search of ivory. They are accompanied by black bearers under the supervision of Saidi. A year earlier, while on another expedition, Harry had seen Jane, the woman he loved, leave him for Tarzan, a man who had lived in the jungles and grown up with the apes. Harry has brought along presents for Jane in hopes that she will return with him to civilization. He tells Arlington that perhaps Tarzan will lead them to an elephant burial ground near which Jane's father is buried. They will need Tarzan's help, because men from another safari stole their maps.

Deep in the jungle, Harry and Arlington discover that the other safari has been massacred by a savage tribe that now attacks them. They escape by climbing a mountain the natives think taboo and won't go near. But the safari is made the target of some huge boulder-hurling gorillas. Several bearers are killed before the gorillas stop at the order of Tarzan, who comes flying through the trees. He is soon joined by Jane, who has learned to swing through the trees and has become accustomed to jungle life. Both Tarzan and Jane are happy to be reunited with Harry.

That night, Jane tries on a beautiful dress that Harry has brought her. But she insists that she has no intention of going back to England. Harry gives up trying to win her back. However, Arlington makes a play for her affections. Jane says that Tarzan is her man.

Tarzan refuses to lead Harry and Arlington to the elephant burial ground. Arlington mortally wounds Timba, Tarzan's favorite elephant, knowing that it will walk back to the burial ground.

Holt and Arlington arrive at the burial ground, where Timba dies. They start loading ivory when Tarzan and Jane appear. Tarzan won't allow them to steal the ivory. Much to everyone's surprise, Arlington agrees to leave the ivory there. Jane visits her father's grave and gives Tarzan her father's watch, which he promises to wear always. The next morning Arlington shoots Tarzan, who is fishing alone. He thinks he has killed him but doesn't see a hippo take the injured Tarzan from the water and deliver him to the apes and chimps, who then take him to a tree house and begin to nurse him back to health. Arlington tells Jane that he saw Tarzan killed by a crocodile. When her father's watch is found in the river, she believes Tarzan dead and agrees to leave the jungle with Arlington and Harry, who also take along the ivory.

Cheetah, Tarzan's chimp, intercepts the departing safari and "tells" Jane that Tarzan is still alive. The safari is attacked by a savage tribe of natives. Jane, Arlington, and Harry take refuge in the rocks, while Cheetah runs to Tarzan for help. The bearers are all killed and Saidi is taken prisoner. The savages, "Men Who Eat Lions," use drums to call lions into the area. The lions eat the bearers and Saidi, and kill Harry when he tries to save Saidi. The lions go after Jane and Arlington. He is killed protecting her. Tarzan arrives with a herd of elephants that kill the lions. Chimps knock the savages from trees to be eaten by other lions. Tarzan saves Jane.

---

*Although MGM often listed this character as Jane Parker, in the Burroughs books she is Jane Porter.

The best Tarzan/Jane combination was at its most appealing when wearing daring costumes in Tarzan and His Mate. *A platonic relationship this was not.*

Like many boys addicted to *The Early Show* in the fifties and early sixties, I wanted to be the Tarzan played by Johnny Weissmuller. Not only could he dive off the Brooklyn Bridge without being harmed, as he does in *Tarzan's New York Adventure* (1942), swim like an Olympic and world champion (which Weissmuller was), swing from vine to vine with the chimps, converse with animals, be a pacifist and at the same time win fight after fight with wild animals and villains, and let out a cry that simultaneously rallied all the friendly creatures of his domain to his defense and struck terror in the hearts of every savage* in the jungle, but he also spent his time with Maureen O'Sullivan, the prettiest, most appealing Jane there ever has been or will be. Usually boys like their heroes to remain romantically unattached (at least until the very end of a picture), but we all had crushes on O'Sullivan and welcomed *her* into Tarzan's arms. Most

---

*While the Tarzan films are degrading to blacks and at times downright racist, Tarzan and Jane were not bigots and treated *peaceful* blacks with friendship and respect. Remarkably, in *Tarzan's Secret Treasure* (1941), they adopt a black orphan boy as one of the family. However, although he is with them at the end of the last frame, he is nowhere to be seen come the next picture in the series.

Injured by Arlington's bullet, Tarzan is rescued by his friends the apes. Fans of the series have actually expressed the belief that these weren't real apes, but actors in costumes.

of Tarzan's mighty legion of fans will agree that the Tarzan films with other actresses playing Jane are the least interesting of the series. The main appeal of the Tarzan story, I believe, is not that there is a superhero who lives in the African jungles, but that a male and a female live together in a primitive natural environment—we can't help but fantasize about the sexual nature of their relationship. Without Jane, the essential eroticism of Burroughs's original tale is missing.

American Weissmuller and Englishwoman O'Sullivan complement each other beautifully. He is brawny and powerful and she is small and delicate, but they both move gracefully and are splendid physical specimens. She is a trained actress and has perfect diction, but surprisingly the unschooled Weissmuller, despite a noticeable awkwardness with dialogue, is the more expressive of the two during silent passages. O'Sullivan, in fact, often responded to critics who laughed at Weissmuller's acting ability by declaring that he could have been a *great* silent actor because his gestures were so natural and his face and eyes were so sensitive and sincere. Proof of his skill in pantomime can be found in *Tarzan Escapes* (1936), when Tarzan doesn't know which way to turn when he thinks Jane has deserted him and Weissmuller falls limp on the ground and cries. It's a truly moving scene. Weissmuller's Tarzan is very masculine, with a great deal of emphasis placed on his physique and physical prowess (which is why he became a top sex symbol of his day); O'Sullivan represents femininity—she is the ideal lady for a true lord of the jungle. Burroughs resented MGM turning his erudite multilingual Tarzan—John Clayton, a.k.a. Lord Greystoke—who moves through the civilized and savage

worlds with equal facility, into the monosyllabic Weissmuller character who refers to New York City as "Stone Jungle"; but I much prefer the alteration because it allows Jane to have equal intellectual status with her mate. In the books, Tarzan is so smart and worldly that Jane can offer him nothing but a son. In the movies, there is ample give-and-take between the two. He is her protector, she is his nurse. He teaches her the ways of the jungle, she teaches him the ways of the world. They are playmates, friends, lovers. They scold each other when bad—as he becomes a father figure after her real father dies in the first film, and she becomes his mother, telling him in *Tarzan and His Mate* "You're a bad boy," after he has been acting too childish—but both are forgiving. Both are considerate, strong, faithful. And both are extremely stubborn, which creates a natural, interesting conflict between them: her superior knowledge of civilization and his superior knowledge of the jungle environment, his primitive instincts and her woman's intuition. To a great extent the films are about how two people from totally different cultures adapt to one another. In later films from the series, which were meant for family audiences, Tarzan becomes increasingly civilized and domesticated under Jane's influence (even building her a permanent jungle home). But in *Tarzan, the Ape Man* (1932) and *Tarzan and His Mate*, which were both made for adults, it is the lady Jane who reverts to her primitive nature and "goes native." Both films begin with safaris venturing into darkest Africa. It is only after several sequences that Tarzan makes his appearance in the first film; and that Jane and Tarzan appear in the sequel. These films begin in this way so that the audience feels that it is making a discovery: in

When Tarzan and Jane are on the screen together in this film, they are invariably touching.

the original, Jane and the audience learn all about Tarzan; in the second film we are not so much interested in Tarzan as we are about how Jane has taken to jungle life after a year with Tarzan. (We immediately find out when we see her flying through the trees in a scandalously skimpy outfit.) *Tarzan and His Mate* is unique among the six Weissmuller–O'Sullivan collaborations made at MGM between 1932 and 1942 primarily because it is more about Jane than about the wild man of Borneo.

In *Tarzan and His Mate*, there is a great deal of action: Harry and Martin's safari is attacked by headhunters; gorillas hurling huge boulders kill several bear-ers; Tarzan rescues Jane by engaging in life-and-death fights with a lion, an eighteen-foot crocodile, a wild rhino (on which Weissmuller actually rode) and a lion; and as usual in Tarzan finales (which always made me teary as a boy), a herd of elephants rushes to its master's aid. But the reason for this film's cult status is not only the abundance of exciting action sequences nor just that Jane is featured more prominently than in other Tarzan films; as cultists will readily admit, most of its popularity—especially among males—is a direct result of Maureen O'Sullivan wearing one of the most revealing costumes in screen history. In the previous film, Jane was a member of a safari, so O'Sullivan wore pants, a shirt, boots, and even a safari hat. For her final four films as Jane—*Tarzan Escapes, Tarzan Finds a Son* (1939), *Tarzan's Secret Treasure* (1941), and *Tarzan's New York Adventure*—the newly formed Hays Office ordered her to wear a very concealing one-piece outfit that wouldn't offend or excite various family members. But for just this one film, O'Sullivan donned a tiny halter top and a loin cloth which left her midriff bare, her thighs and hips exposed, and little to the imagination. (As Jane says, "Woman's greatest weapon is man's imagination.") Because Jane is a *lady* from England (not Baltimore as in the books)—with perfect diction, etc.— her wearing such an outfit, symbolic of her sexual freedom, is particularly exciting.

Jane's brief costume and other characteristics as well might well be traced to *Bird of Paradise* (1932), another film about a couple living together out of wedlock in an exotic setting. In that box office blockbuster, lovely Dolores Del Rio, as native girl Luana, wears a feathery hula skirt, a flower wreath that (just barely) covers the front, but not the sides, of her breasts, and nothing else. Del Rio also has a cry to hail Joel McCrea when in

Tarzan arrives in the nick of time to save Jane from lions.

Living in sin: the (probably) unmarried Tarzan and Jane and their "housemate" Cheetah. In compliance with the newly formed Hays Office, in future films, geared for a family audience, Tarzan and Jane would wear more concealing clothing, live in a large tree house with walls, floors, and a roof, and be parents to an adopted son named Boy.

danger that is similar to Jane's when calling Tarzan; and she takes a nude swim, as does Jane in *Tarzan and His Mate*—although Jane's scene is excised from television prints. The reason that Jane borrows so much from Luana is that Cedric Gibbons, the director of *Tarzan and His Mate,* was married to Del Rio.

That O'Sullivan swims in the nude with Weissmuller in *Tarzan and His Mate* is indicative that the picture was made with adults in mind. (There was no nude swim in *Tarzan, the Ape Man,* the other adult film of the series, but O'Sullivan was pawed consistently by Weissmuller and was placed in very sexual poses, even on her back with the scantily clad Weissmuller leaning over her.) In *Tarzan's Secret Treasure* Tarzan and Jane again swim in the river, but as this film is geared for children as well as adults, O'Sullivan is fully clothed and the couple is joined in the water by their adopted son Boy (Johnny Sheffield), a turtle, and an elephant.

Throughout *Tarzan and His Mate* O'Sullivan is presented provocatively. In addition to wearing her famous loin cloth, Jane is shown sleeping in the nude; she only puts on a dress when cavorting through the jungle so that Arlington and Harry "won't think me immodest"; after Cheetah playfully steals her dress, she is like Hedy Lamarr in *Ecstasy* (1933), stranded in the jungle without a stitch of clothing on her body. Jane's casual dress around Tarzan and the fact that she and he sleep together is all the more startling by Hollywood standards because they are not married. In *The Return*

of *Tarzan,* the second Tarzan novel, Jane Porter becomes Jane Clayton, Mrs. Tarzan, when they are married by her minister father.* But in the movies there is no wedding ceremony. Rather than gloss over this fact, MGM obviously played it up; in the cast credits the studio submitted to newspapers to include with printed reviews, Jane is referred to as "Jane Parker" (strange since her name was Porter) to remind us that she is still single. MGM knew it was more titillating that they were living "in sin."

With the exception of *Tarzan's Greatest Adventure* (1960) with Gordon Scott, I consider *Tarzan and His Mate* the finest Tarzan film ever made. One of the things I find fascinating about it is the strange "movie" morality that it contains. I believe that the filmmakers kill off Arlington in the end not because he is a villain (he redeems himself in this respect when he bravely gives his life to save Jane's) but because he saw Jane's very revealing nude silhouette when she changed inside a well-lit tent; because she sucked arrow poison from his arm (while he smiled sensually); because she danced with him; and because he stole a kiss from her. Jane is Tarzan's woman, even if not his wife, and no man can live who has enjoyed what should be solely Tarzan's "husbandly" pleasures.

---

*Because Jane's father was a minister from Baltimore, he probably had no license to perform marital rites in Africa. Some libraries, claiming the Tarzan-Jane marriage to be invalid, kept Tarzan books off their shelves.

The Texas Chain Saw Massacre

Cast: Marilyn Burns (Sally), Allen Danziger (Jerry), Paul A. Partain (Franklyn), William Vail (Kirk), Teri McMinn (Pam), Edwin Neal (hitchhiker), Jim Siedow (old man), Gunnar Hansen (Leatherface), John Dugan (Grandfather), Jerry Lorenz (truck driver)

Synopsis: Having heard that vandals have violated the graveyard where her grandfather is buried, Sally wants to check out the family plot. With her fat, wheelchair-confined brother Franklyn, her boyfriend Jerry, her friend Pam and Pam's boyfriend, Kirk, Sally makes the trip by van into a part of Texas she hasn't seen since she was a child. Sally and the ill-tempered, sadistic Franklyn decide they should all visit their grandfather's deserted farm. On the way there they pass a slaughterhouse and Franklyn graphically explains how cattle used to be slaughtered with a sledgehammer. Now they use an air gun. They pick up a skinny, maniacal-looking hitchhiker. He says the slaughterhouse fired many men who used the old methods. He invites them all home for dinner. They decline. He takes pictures of them with a Polaroid and demands money for the awful results. He then carves the palm of his hand with a knife, and tries to slash Franklyn. They manage to push him out of the van.

The van stops at a Gulf station. The strange attendant tells them he is waiting for the gas tanker. But he invites them to sample some of his tasty meats inside. Franklyn really enjoys the "sausage." They arrive at the deserted house. Pam and Kirk go off in search of a swimming hole Franklyn remembers from his childhood. They come to another house. There is a buzzing noise inside. Numerous automobiles are hidden on the property. While Pam waits outside, Kirk goes into the house to inquire about gasoline. As soon as he steps inside the door and calls, the buzzing stops. Suddenly a huge man wearing a mask made out of a human face charges Kirk and knocks his head in with a mighty stroke of a sledgehammer. A few minutes later, Pam goes into the house to investigate what has happened to Kirk. She walks into a room filled with skeletons and human debris. She vomits. Leatherface scoops her up and carries her into the room used for carving meat. He puts the screaming girl onto a meat hook and resumes carving up the dead Kirk with a chain saw. Brought to the area by the sound of a gas generator, Jerry enters the house looking for his friends. He comes into the room where there is the carving table and the meat hooks. No one is in sight. He opens up a Deepfreeze and finds Pam, all blue, but still alive. But he can't help her because Leatherface kills him.

At night, Sally wheels Franklyn through the woods in search of the others. Leatherface charges out of the woods and puts his chain saw through Franklyn's stomach. Sally runs in terror with Leatherface hot on her trail. She runs into a house that unfortunately is Leatherface's house. She runs upstairs and dives out the window. She hobbles to the Gulf station and asks the attendant for help. Instead he beats her and stuffs her in a bag and takes her home.

The attendant, Leatherface, and the hitchhiker come from the same family. They kill people who pass through the area, eat their flesh, and sell the remains for sausage. They tie Sally to an armchair which has human arms for arms. They present grandpa, who looks like a corpse. He drinks Sally's blood, and tries to kill her by beating her on the head with a hammer. He is too weak. Sally escapes. She runs upstairs and dives out the window again. Leatherface with his chain saw and the knife-wielding hitchhiker give chase. She makes it to the highway. A gas truck runs over the hitchhiker. A truckdriver stops to help Sally. They drive away as Leatherface holds the chain saw high in the air.

1974 Bryanston Pictures release of a Vortex/Henkel/Hooper film
Director: Tobe Hooper
Producer: Tobe Hooper
Screenplay: Kim Henkel and Tobe Hooper
Cinematography: Daniel Pearl
Music: Tobe Hooper and Wayne Bell
Songs: Roger Bartlett & Friends, Timberline Rose, Arkey Blue, and Los Cyclones
Editors: Sallye Richardson and Larry Carroll
Running Time: 87 Minutes

I first heard of *The Texas Chain Saw Massacre*, Tobe Hooper's well-made but excruciatingly unpleasant horror film, in the fall of 1974, just prior to its national release. Nationwide news accounts stated that it had been sneak-previewed at San Francisco's Empire Theater with the Walter Matthau suspense thriller *The Taking of Pelham One, Two, Three* (1974), and that prior to the lights being dimmed the audience had no knowledge of the film's violent, stomach-turning content or even its forbidding title. It only knew that, like *Pelham*, it was rated R. Soon unsuspecting viewers were seeing a huge man with a chain saw in a mask made out of what once was a human face, making mincemeat out of a bunch of college-age kids. Some viewers threw up; others stormed the lobby to protest what they (and their children) were being subjected to—when no money was refunded, punches were thrown; two city officials in attendance that night threatened to sue the theater on behalf of themselves and other irate viewers. So began the bizarre history of the seventies' most controversial cult horror film.

Soon after the San Francisco preview, *Chain Saw* went into general release. It quickly appeared on *Variety*'s list of top-grossing films although Hooper and others who helped raise the $100,000–$200,000 production costs for the independent picture weren't getting much money back: the picture's original releasing company had disbanded and millions of dollars worth of ticket receipts mysteriously disappeared.* But the picture kept doing great business wherever it played. Horror fans were attracted to the movie because of its newspaper slogan ("Who will survive—and what will be left of them?"), which defied viewers to try to sit through a picture with so much gore, and because it got surprisingly favorable critical response. As its cult grew, so did its reputation for quality: the Museum of Modern Art added a print to its permanent film collection; it was screened during the prestigious Directors' Fortnight at the Cannes Film Festival; it won the Grand Prize at the 1976 Avoriaz Film Festival. But it has never gained "respectability" despite the obvious talent behind the project; for instance, it has been banned *twice* in France for being an "incitement to violence." I really detest some of the content in *Chain Saw*, particularly the scene in which captive Sally is tortured by the depraved villains Leatherface, the hitchhiker, the old man, and the

---

*Officers were convicted on obscenity charges in the famous *Deep Throat* (1972) case.

Much of the blood on actress Marilyn Burns is real when Sally crawls away from the murderers' house.

grandfather. But I don't go along with the French charge against the film. Importantly, we are never manipulated into wanting to see the villains do away with their victims—we always are on the side of the kids. Not so with absolute trash like *The Last House on the Left* (1972)—which, too, has a cult following. In that picture the filmmakers seem to get great pleasure from the torture, sexual humiliation, and killing of two truly sweet teen-age girls by a bunch of unwashed perverts. That is the one film where I felt embarrassed to be in the audience and the one film in which I felt paranoid leaving the theater because audience members had been cheering the girls' misfortune. What saves *Chain Saw* from being a film that deserves to be banned is that it is made (skillfully) for viewers who see themselves as being the villains' potential prey—like the young people in the film—and not for those who see themselves as being the killers. *Chain Saw* is meant to be a nightmare; *Last House* (and many films like it) is a sick sexual fantasy for predators that is indeed an "incitement to violence."

The *Texas Chain Saw Massacre* claims to be a true story, and I would guess that it is based loosely on the ghoulish exploits of one of America's worst fiends, Ed Gein. I don't know much about Gein (who now resides for life, hopefully, in a mental hospital) other than that he was a Plainfield, Wisconsin, handyman who, in the fifties, killed young women and wore their skins—his partner in crime was even more disgusting, wearing the skins only after Gein got tired of them. As stories about Gein are contradictory, I don't know if he ate human flesh, or dug up bodies from graveyards, or kept his dead mother's corpse around the house as did the villains of two other films based on the Gein case: Alfred Hitchcock's *Psycho* (1960), starring Anthony Perkins, and an obscure, not very good bloodbath called *Deranged* (1974), which has a surprisingly effective performance by Roberts Blossom in the "Gein" role. In *Chain Saw*, the villains live with the corpses of their grandmother and the family dog, plus bits and pieces of other people and animals that are scattered about or are part of the furniture (e.g., an armchair has real arms); they eat human flesh; and, I'm sure, they commit every

Terrified and sick Pam realizes that she has stumbled into an evil house when she finds a living room full of human bones.

Leatherface temporarily interrupts his carving up of Kirk to hang Pam on a meat hook. The dimness and graininess of the scene can be attributed to the use of high-speed film.

crime against nature that is possible (although they don't seem to have any sexual urges). The main differences between *Chain Saw* and both *Psycho* and *Deranged* is that its villains are *completely* unsympathetic, and that it is more about cannibalism than necrophilia.

Since the days of the Greek tragedians, cannibalism has been an acceptable theme in the arts, although it hasn't always been handled "tastefully." My favorite picture from the cannibalism subgenre is *The Folks at Red Wolf Inn* (1973), a nifty little black comedy that recalls the works of Roald Dahl. The "humor" and the horror come from watching characters unwittingly wolf down "meat" which they don't know was carved from the corpses of the latest victims. But *Chain Saw*, even more so than *The Demon Barber of Fleet Street* (1936) and the suitably titled *The Bloodthirsty Butchers* (1969), is the most striking example of a picture about cannibalism that emphasizes the *slaughter* of human beings for their "meat," rather than the feast. It can be suggested that *Chain Saw* was made by vegetarians and animal lovers, making viewers identify with poor animals in a slaughterhouse that have their heads crushed by sledgehammers (like Kirk), are hung on meat hooks (like Pam), are put into freezers (like the-alive-but-no-longer-kicking Pam), and are sliced up into little chunks by chain saws in preparation for human consumption.

Ed Gein was born and bred in Wisconsin, but Texan Hooper transported the setting of his film to his own home state. Inadvertently his film reenforces the nonsoutherner's paranoia about the Deep off-the-main-highway South partly established by the murders of three northern civil rights workers in the early sixties

and by such antiredneck films as *Easy Rider* (1969). In fact, *Chain Saw* closely resembles what is probably the most anti-South film in cinema history: Herschell Gordon Lewis's legendary horror film *Two Thousand Maniacs* (1964), a picture that tells northerners to change their license plates when driving through the South. In the Lewis picture, six northerners accidentally drive into a small town after following purposely misleading road signs. The always cheerful townsfolk treat them royally and get them to participate in their one-hundredth anniversary celebration, not telling them that their sacrifices are to be part of the festivities. Like the villains in *Chain Saw*, they have a great time as they torture and kill the visitors one by one.*

I think *Chain Saw* is much superior to *Maniacs*, but it is effective for the same reason: it perfectly reproduces our worst nightmare—being in a strange locale where we are attacked for no reason at all by homicidal maniacs we have never seen before. In his article on *Chain Saw*

---

*It can be deduced that *Two Thousand Maniacs* influenced *Chain Saw* because of the similarity between the grisly events that take place in the two films. In *Maniacs* a victim is killed by an ax blow that severs her arm—much like Kirk being killed by a blow of a sledgehammer; another is rolled down a hill in a spike-studded barrel—much like Pam being hung on a meat hook that pierces her back; another is drawn and quartered—much like Leatherface's victims being chopped up by his chain saw. The fourth victim in *Maniacs* is crushed by a giant boulder: various townspeople throw at a target which when hit will release the boulder that hangs over the unwilling female victim, and the suspense builds as the first few jolly contestants miss the target; we are similarly teased in *Chain Saw* when the grandfather keeps trying to kill Sally by hitting her on the head with a hammer—this scene is unwatchable—but only manages to injure her repeatedly because his blows are too feeble.

The chilling last shot of the film: Leatherface twirls round and round at the edge of the highway, his chain saw's buzzing drowning out his squealing.

for *The Village Voice* (February 9, 1976), titled "A Real Nightmare Makes a Great Horror Film," Michael Goodwin writes:

> *Chain Saw* captures the syntax and structure of a nightmare with astonishing fidelity. The quality of the images, the texture of the sound, the illogic by which one incident follows another—all conform to the way we dream. No one's done that before, at least not in a commercial, mass market movie.
>
> There have been nightmare films . . . but even in these films the filmmakers seemed unable or unwilling to cross an "acceptable" perimeter of terror. This may have less to do with studio censorship than with inborn psychic defense mechanisms; when a real nightmare becomes unbearable, we wake up.
>
> What makes *Chain Saw* interesting is that since we are watching it with our eyes open, it's a nightmare from which we can't wake up.

As Goodwin points out in his article (by far the best piece written on *Chain Saw*), the picture is extremely well acted and crafted for a low-budget film. Tobe Hooper (whose main *Hollywood* success has been the 1979 TV movie adaptation of *Salem's Lot*) credits Alfred Hitchcock with being an influence on his work, but *Chain Saw* is totally different from anything Hitchcock. (One similarity, however, is that in both directors' films viewers *imagine* there is more blood on the screen than is actually shown.) Hitchcock inserted expository sequences between shock moments so his audience could catch its breath. In this way, over and over he could *build* suspense—the key to his films. Hooper prefers having one shock after another (giving his audience its money's worth)—he strives for *terror;* for him, suspense is secondary. Hitchcock built tension, Hooper totally unnerves us. (Both deliver a wallop.) Hitchcock constantly reminded us that we were watching a *movie,* Hooper strives for and achieves realism. Hitchcock believed in giving the audience information his characters do not have. For instance, in *Psycho,* when Martin Balsam sneaks up the stairs in the Bates house, Hitchcock cuts to a shot of a door opening on the second floor. When Kirk enters the house in *Chain Saw,* neither he nor we are prepared when Leatherface appears. His sudden appearance—when we were expecting to be forewarned by a shadow on a wall or a foot showing from behind a curtain—startles us (particularly when we see what he looks like for the first time); when he charges the rooted-to-the-spot Kirk and smashes his brains in with a sledgehammer we are even more shocked than when "Mrs. Bates," instead of sneaking up on Balsam, charges out of her room with her knife held high. For one thing, "Mrs. Bates" had reason to kill Balsam (self-protection), but Leatherface kills Kirk without any provocation. That Leatherface and his zany relatives, unlike Anthony Perkins, have no fear of the law or intruders or anything at all makes them absolutely terrifying. If they see you, they kill you.

"All the characters in *Chain Saw* are horrible," writes Michael Goodwin, no doubt thinking what a despicable person even "good guy" Franklyn is. "People are constantly hurting themselves and others—sometimes emotionally, sometimes physically. Pain, given and received, is the only medium of communication." Interestingly, Goodwin interviewed many of the technicians and cast members responsible for *Chain Saw* and arrived at the conclusion that the film is full of pain because the people working on it were in agony. Not only could no one sleep more than a couple of hours a night while working on the film, but actors Paul Partain and Marilyn Burns, who play feuding siblings, couldn't stand each other, actor Edwin Neal hated director Hooper ("If I ever meet Hooper again I'm gonna kill him"), art director Bob Burns claimed Hooper made the film "by lying and cheating and selling his friends down the river," Hooper claimed Burns was "crazy" and a "blackmailer." In addition, there was the physical discomfort of the actors. Of the dinner table sequence, Neal told Goodwin: "The animals on the table were filled with formaldehyde, and they were literally rotting under the lights. . . . As soon as they'd yell 'Cut,' we'd run to the windows and throw up. For thirty-six hours straight!" Of the scene in which Sally runs into the gas station, Hooper said, "Marilyn had busted both knees up, she was bleeding badly, she was . . . pretty badly injured. It was terrible, but it played very well." Of the graphic scene in which Pam is hung on a meat hook, Bob Burns commented, "When she was screaming in pain, she was screaming in *pain.* All they had to hold her up was a strip of nylon stocking, and it was cutting her in two." "Everyone was injured at one time or another," Hooper told Goodwin. "Everyone got sliced, or cut, or was bleeding. Leatherface got hurt a lot of times, falling with the chain saw. His mask had no peripheral vision, so he'd run into doorstalls and crack his head."

"There's something about *Chain Saw,*" writes Goodwin, "that goes beyond technique, some mysterious quality in the texture of the film itself that won't let go." I believe Goodwin guessed right that the mysterious ingredient was realism transferred from the set to the screen: "a real nightmare inside a filmed nightmare." Unfortunately, I think *Chain Saw* is too realistic for its own good.

Top Hat

1935 RKO Radio
Director: Mark Sandrich
Producer: Pandro S. Berman
Screenplay: Dwight Taylor
and Allan Scott
Cinematography: David Abel

Music and lyrics: Irving Berlin
Musical direction: Max Steiner
Choreography: Hermes Pan
Editor: William Hamilton
Running Time: 101 minutes

Cast: Fred Astaire (Jerry Travers), Ginger Rogers (Dale Tremont), Edward Everett Horton (Horace Hardwick), Erik Rhodes (Alberto Beddini), Eric Blore (Bates), Helen Broderick (Madge Hardwick), Lucille Ball (flower clerk).

Synopsis: In London, wealthy Horace Hardwick hires American entertainer Jerry Travers to headline a musical show. Jerry stays in Horace's hotel suite and his dancing at night wakes up pretty Dale Tremont in the suite below. When she comes to Horace's suite to tell Jerry not to disturb her, he falls in love with her. He follows her the next day. He sings to her and then they dance and she falls in love with him. However, she doesn't learn his name. She mistakenly believes that he is Horace, whom she has never met. She knows Horace is married to her friend Madge, who has written her that he is in the hotel. Thinking Jerry is two-timing Madge, she slaps him and leaves London with her dress designer, Alberto Beddini. They go to Venice to visit Madge in a hotel. Madge secretly wants to arrange a meeting between Dale and Jerry. Meanwhile, Horace is suspicious of Dale's intentions. He doesn't know she is Madge's friend and wrongly suspects she is trying to cause a scandal that could ruin his show. He sends his invaluable butler Bates to follow her. Bates uses a number of disguises.

The show is a success. Jerry learns Madge has invited Dale to Venice. He and Horace fly there for the weekend. Again Jerry courts Dale, who still thinks he is Horace, Madge's husband. When Dale tells Madge that her husband is flirting with her, Madge gives the real Horace a black eye. After dancing with Dale, Jerry proposes to her. Thinking he's already married, Dale slaps him again. In order to forget him, Dale marries Alberto, who keeps threatening the real Horace. At last, Jerry, Horace, and Madge figure out the identity mix-up. While Madge and Horace keep Alberto occupied on his wedding night, Jerry takes Dale on a romantic gondola ride. He explains to her who he is. They try to talk to Alberto. Luckily it turns out that Dale and Beddini were married by Bates when he was disguised as a priest. Dale and Alberto aren't really married. A happy Jerry and Dale dance away together.

There was a Great Depression going on, but you would never know it by watching them. Astaire wore a top hat, white tie, and tails, and Rogers, a Busby Berkeley alumna who should have been more sensitive, slipped into one lavish gown after another. They tripped the light fantastic from New York to Paris, from London to Venice, staying in the fanciest hotels, dining in the most extravagant nightspots, associating with the richest people. They weren't concerned with employment opportunities, where their next meal was coming from, or the dismal state of the world, but with romance, the proper way to say "tomato", and answers to such relevant questions as "Shall we dance?" and "Isn't it a lovely day?" They were as frivolous a pair as ever lit up a movie screen, but we can forgive them. They provided escapist entertainment for countless millions during that Depression and after, brought the musical in the cinema to new peaks, and have been the ideals for generations of moviegoers excited by grace, elegance, and talent.

Theirs was as fine a romance as there has ever been in the movies. Ginger Rogers was young, beautiful, and alluring. And witty, too, although until *Carefree* (1938), for some reason *he* got the funny lines and comic bits. On the other hand, Fred Astaire was small and skinny, weighing in at only 140 pounds, had the strangest, ugliest short hair, which looked like it belonged to a ventriloquist's dummy, and had a face that, as Bosley Crowther suggested, resembled that of a happy Stan Laurel. For picture after picture, Astaire courted Rogers, refusing to take no for an answer. He was as brash as—and more irritating than—Errol Flynn in his flirtations with Olivia de Havilland, and like Flynn gave male viewers the awful impression that if you chase a woman long enough she will always give in. Rogers put up resistance each film, but it wasn't with much conviction. Ginger looked sternly at Fred, but smiled in our direction to let us know that she was in fact charmed by

The "Top Hat, White Tie, and Tails" number. As usual, Astaire takes several solos, while Rogers only dances with Astaire.

Bates explains to (L-R) a delighted Horace, Madge, Dale, and Jerry, and a very upset Beddini that he was the one who married Dale and Beddini; since Bates is a butler, the marriage isn't legal.

his attention. And when the music came on, Astaire suddenly was as handsome as any man ever on the screen—a perfect physical match for her. He smiled and chirped as much as Chevalier and sang what became standards by Irving Berlin, Ira and George Gershwin, and Jerome Kern, and Dorothy Fields, with skill that has never been fully recognized. His phrasing was impeccable and his delivery was full of enthusiasm and respect for what were fabulous lyrics. And when he stopped singing, Astaire started dancing—and this *no* woman could resist. The Astaire-Rogers dance duets are among the most intimate sequences in screen history. They are lovely, priceless scenes in which Astaire seduces Rogers and then they dance to a mutual climax of love that Flynn and de Havilland could only dream about. As Katharine Hepburn commented, Astaire gave Rogers class, and she gave him sex. Out on the dance floor, we recognize the perfect screen couple.

Astaire-Rogers fanatics generally agree that their best films are *The Gay Divorcee* (1934), *Top Hat* (1935), *Follow the Fleet* (1936), *Shall We Dance* (1937), all directed by Mark Sandrich, and *Swing Time* (1936), directed by George Stevens. Regardless of which film these cultists consider their personal favorites, *Top Hat* is the one Astaire-Rogers picture that is admired by all. It is the one that turns up most frequently at repertory theaters and a top moneymaker for public television

during subscription weeks. In his liner notes for the record album *Starring Fred Astaire*, Stanley Green writes:

> Although it closely followed the formula of *The Gay Divorcee*, Fred's first co-starring role with Ginger Rogers, *Top Hat* is generally accepted as the model for all the Fred-and-Ginger movies. The glamorous surroundings, the mistaken identity theme, the white, stylized stage-like settings, the scatterbrained comedians, and the totally illogical plotting of the story all helped to stamp *Top Hat* as the quintessential example of the unique, magical world inhabited by Fred Astaire and Ginger Rogers. It also had one other major ingredient: a scintillating score by Irving Berlin.

Top Hat is a highly enjoyable Astaire-Rogers vehicle that is staged, as usual, on those magnificent glossy white art deco sets designed by RKO art director Van Nest Polglase and his unit designer Clark Carroll. Most spectacular are Horace's London hotel room, the Venice hotel's lobby which has a canal running through it, and the bridal suite's bedroom. Another highlight: the great supporting cast. Movie buffs often complain that movies aren't as good today because of the absence of great character actors, and in *Top Hat* we have some we miss most. It hardly matters that Astaire and Rogers are off the screen when Edward Everett Horton and Eric Blore

A visual delight:
Astaire and Rogers
introduce "The Piccolino."

Astaire and Rogers make love through dance. The "Cheek to Cheek" number was made even more elegant by Van Nest Polgase's Art Deco set.

are arguing about the right way to do things, or when Erik Rhodes, so good as the gigolo in *The Gay Divorcee*, starts discussing his honor or singing a love song to himself ("Alberto Beddini, I'm glad you're not skinny"). Also good is Helen Broderick, as Rogers's confidante. Broderick, Blore, and Rhodes all played with Astaire on Broadway before he came to Hollywood.

All the musical numbers in the picture are top flight. (Regrettably, Rogers gets no solo dances.) I particularly like Astaire's solo dance for "No Strings," where he taps around Horace's room, slapping the walls, and kicking props. As in the "Top Hat, White Tie, and Tails" number when he half runs, half dances around his cane, the emphasis is on timing, and no one is more precise than Astaire. All the dances of Astaire and Rogers are fabulous, but perhaps the most memorable is the "Cheek to Cheek" number. I love the way they will dance quickly only to slow down so we catch them in some lovely position, and the way Astaire lifts Rogers in her flowing, feathery dress, momentarily holds her in midair as the music sweeps upward, and then eases her

to the ground by spinning her around him—over and over again. It is terrific how they change speeds so often—it is one of their trademarks; but they do it for audience appreciation, not to catch their breaths. The film ends with them spinning off the screen at full speed, and it is exhilarating.

Astaire sings several songs in the film. Rogers sings only "The Piccolino." It is a silly song and she sings it while smiling, and sitting, her gestures reminding one of Shirley Temple. *New Yorker* dance critic Arlene Croce wrote that she loves the "Cheek to Cheek" number before the dancing really gets started because of the way Rogers listens to Astaire. But take a look at Astaire sitting next to Rogers while she sings "The Piccolino." He is incredibly awkward, as if he were embarrassed by the whole thing. I think here we realize who is the better actor of the two (Rogers) and feel the rumored antagonism between the two stars. (They barely look at each other.) It's a good thing the picture doesn't end here. Luckily, soon they are back in each other's arms and out on the dance floor—so again we can pretend that Astaire and Rogers really do love one another.

Trash

1970   Cinema 5 release of an Andy Warhol presentation
Director: Paul Morrissey
Executive Producer: Andy Warhol
Screenplay: Paul Morrissey
Cinematography: Paul Morrissey
Editor: Jed Johnson
Running Time: 103 minutes

Cast: Joe Dallesandro (Joe), Holly Woodlawn (Holly), Jane Forth (Jane), Michael Sklar (welfare investigator), Geri Miller (go-go dancer), Andrea Feldman (rich girl), Johnny Putnam (boy from Yonkers), Bruce Pecheur (Jane's husband), Diane Podlewski (Holly's sister)

Synopsis: All Joe can think of is getting heroin to feed his habit. But he hasn't any money. Go-go dancer Geri offers him ten dollars to make love to her, but his habit has made it impossible for him to get an erection. She does a striptease like she performs for her boyfriend, and gives him a blow job, but fails to arouse him.

Joe goes home to the basement dwelling he shares with Holly. She collects junk in order to furnish their apartment. She is upset that Joe uses "junk" and tells him, "You're starting to look like a big juicy bum." Since she is a nympho, she finds Joe's impotence intolerable. On the street, a rich girl offers to buy LSD from Joe for twenty dollars, although she only has a dollar with her. They go to her apartment. She watches him shoot up. When he starts to pass out before they can make love, she hits him with a switch. He comes to and makes love to her roughly. He asks her for money.

Holly brings home a high school kid from Yonkers who is on his way to a rock concert and wants to get high. Holly promises to give him uppers, and he makes her promise that he won't have to get a shot. Joe tells the boy that Holly only brought him there to give him a blow job. Holly brings out the needle, much to the boy's distress. She gives him a shot in the rear although she doesn't really know how to give shots. She gives him a little too much and he starts to fall asleep. Holly starts licking him all over.

Joe breaks into a town house hoping to find money. He meets a young woman named Jane who is recently married. She tells him that if her husband Bruce returns he should pretend to be a classmate of hers from Grosse Point High. Bruce returns and Joe tells him the lie. While Joe bathes and shaves, Jane tells him she wants him to sleep with her and her husband. But first she wants to see him shoot up. Jane and Bruce watch Joe inject a needle into his arm and start arguing with each other. Joe passes out. Disliking Joe intensely, Bruce throws him out.

Holly's pregnant sister agrees to lend Joe and Holly her baby so they can get on welfare, which is Holly's goal. But Holly kicks her out because she comes home to find her making love to Joe when Joe won't even make love to her. Joe tells Holly he will be ready to make love to her the next day. She masturbates with a beer bottle.

Joe stops taking drugs so he can make love to Holly. He promises to help them get on welfare and asks her to let him stay with her. She agrees.

A welfare examiner comes to the apartment. Holly wears a pillow under her sweater to make him think she's pregnant. He tells her he will put them on the welfare rolls if she sells him the old-style flashy shoes she took from the garbage. He wants to make them into a lamp as a conversation piece. She declines. When Holly's pillow falls out, he refuses to consider her application. They yell at him and Joe roughs him up. The welfare investigator, Mr. Michael, says, "You're garbage! You deserve to live here!" He leaves.

Holly says she knows where a good junkpile is. Joe assures her they can make it without welfare. She wants to give him a blow job—as usual.

There are few among us who haven't exited a terrible film thinking that if we turned on a movie camera in front of our friends or almost anybody at all and told them to "be natural," they would be far more interesting, humorous, and revealing than the boring, false characters we had just seen on the screen. This was likely the philosophy behind those early underground films of Andy Warhol, especially *The Chelsea Girls* (1966), when he allowed his exhibitionist Superstars (who are admittedly unlike my friends) to cavort in front of his immobile camera and prove themselves radically different from characters found in the commercial cinema. Warhol kept his camera back so he wouldn't interfere with his subjects' "naturalness"; and he refused to make director's "statements" through camera movements or placement, filming from a variety of angles, or using slow motion, the zoom, or special effects. He was an artist interested in the cinema in terms of how viewers perceive images without a director acting as a go-between/interpreter.

When Warhol began using people in his films who did more than *Sleep* (1963), *Eat* (1963), *Kiss* (1964), get a *Haircut* (1964), or receive a *Blow Job* (1964), it became impossible to differentiate between what was spontaneous and what was motivated by the camera's presence. This, plus the fact that on most occasions Warhol *assembled* his players to appear in front of his camera, made it inaccurate to classify him as a cinéma-vérité documentarian, despite his films being made in the cinéma-vérité style: without editing, camera interference, or characters talking in the direction of microphones, or there *appearing to be* a screenplay, direction, or characters aware of a camera. Nevertheless one couldn't suggest that what went on in these Warhol films was less real/truthful than the celebrated 1973 PBS-TV thirteen-part series *An American Family*, still considered by many as a landmark cinéma-vérité documentary. That was the project in which documentarians, wanting to examine the family structure in contemporary America, moved in with the Loud family of Santa Barbara, California, and rolled the cameras for three hundred hours as the seven Louds supposedly went about their daily business—twelve hours of film were actually used. Albert Brooks's fairly amusing *Real Life* (1979) parodied the Loud family experiment; but it is Warhol's *Trash* that today reminds me more of it. Imagine in your wildest dreams that in 1970, PBS sent various filmmakers to make test films of families from each level of society in order to help the network choose which type of family would be the most suitable for the 1973 project, and Warhol and director/cameraman Paul Morrissey got the "lowlife" assignment. And in this imaginary sequence of events, while other filmmakers moved into spare bedrooms in houses owned by doctors, lawyers, and such, Warhol and Morrissey brought their camera into a squalid basement dwelling in New York's lower east side. The "family" living here were two unemployed unmarrieds: Joe, a muscular, handsome but pimply, eighteen-year-old stud whose heroin addiction makes it hard for him to talk clearly, much less get an erection to satisfy all the women he turns on; and

Holly, a nympho who picks up teen-age boys for sex because Joe can no longer satisfy her, collects furniture from trash piles, and orders Joe to shape up so they can qualify for welfare and become respectable. Like many in the counterculture, theirs is a world of sex, drugs, and abject poverty—it is little wonder that PBS would opt for the upper-middle-class Loud family, gay son and all.

Trash, the first genuinely commercial Warhol film, was the second directorial effort of Paul Morrissey, who previously had done Warhol's *Flesh* (1968), which stars Joe Dallesandro as a male hustler. *Trash*, even more than *Flesh*, varies from the Warhol-directed underground pictures in major ways: there is a story line, there is an abundance of close-ups, there are camera cuts within sequences in order to edit out dead spots and improve the picture's pacing. However, *Trash* still comes across, deliberately, as a "documentary" that explores the lives of real (or real-to-life) people—this is why I feel I can make the analogy with *An American Family*. Morrissey creates his counterfeit documentary by retaining several "awkward" moments where characters either verbally repeat themselves, make no sense whatsoever, or mumble so the microphones can't pick up what they say; by having his actors use their own names so we aren't absolutely sure if these characters are real, caricatures, a combination of the two, or complete fabrications; and by allowing his actors to improvise so much that it appears as if no script was used (maybe none was).

While Morrissey's directorial style differs from Warhol's, *Trash* is representative of Warhol in that according to the filmmakers its artistic (not commercial) success goes hand-in-hand with how audiences react to the images. (It is the viewer's reaction to seeing images of all sorts that is the basis of Warhol's films.) *Trash* was not made in a vacuum but with an audience in mind. Holly's pregnant sister tells Joe that it's perfectly fine for him to make love to her because "Nowadays, anything goes." Morrissey and Warhol want to see if the "with it" moviegoer of 1970 really thinks like this or would react to the film's shocking imagery with as much disgust as Holly does when she discovers boyfriend Joe and her sister making love. Like few other pictures, *Trash* plays upon an audience's voyeurism, teasing it perhaps, but eliciting responses of some sort from everyone. The filmmakers knew that people would come to a Warhol picture expecting to see people getting high and a lot of nudity and sex. And they gave them what they expected but not in the expected kinky, sensual, turn-on manner. It's impossible to get sexually aroused watching Holly masturbate with a Miller High Life bottle or watching the rich LSD freak examine Joe's penis and discover lice. A film where the male lead has acne on his rear and the female lead is played by a female impersonator is not meant to satisfy a viewer's prurient interests. More disconcerting is that instead of pot-smoking and pill-popping, we twice see addict Joe stick a needle in his arm and shoot up. In the scene in which Joe shoots up in front of the rich marrieds Jane and Bruce, when we were expecting a sex scene between the three instead, our natural impulse is to turn away, but

Holly sits in her basement apartment amidst the trash she has collected from nearby junkpiles.

Jane and Bruce keep directing our attention to the screen by telling each other "Will you look at that! Will you look at that!" This scene is much like one in the Warhol/Morrissey collaboration *Heat* (1973) where we are forced to watch an unattractive loony masturbate under his gown for such a long time that we'd pay a second admission if he'd only stop. The importance of *Trash* (as of other Warhol films, regardless of artistry) is that it is an attempt to raise the moviegoer's level of tolerance to accommodate what has traditionally seemed too "strong" or offensive for the cinema. If this can be accomplished then filmmakers will have the freedom to tell stories in personal ways their predecessors were denied because of censorship and convention. *Trash* reflects the time in which it was made not only because it depicts the poverty of America's cities and the insane lifestyle of drug culture tenement dwellers, but also because it is itself proof of the type of commercial film that could be made in 1970 U.S.A., when in past years such a project would have been out of the question.

Chances are you will like *Trash* if you like the weird characters the filmmakers have brought together. I do. There's the go-go dancer who does a strip and sings in a baby voice hoping to turn Joe on, and when that fails tries to stimulate him by discussing politics (although nothing could bore *Joe* more); the rich girl ("I don't want to be a girl; I wish I were a cock") who has an indescribable, affected voice and mentions LSD in every sentence; Jane, the rich young bride from Grosse Point who wants to fix Joe's hair like her own and do something about his complexion; her snobbish husband Bruce who asks Joe condescendingly, "Can you eat or do you have to get strung out all the time?"; the high school kid from Yonkers Holly brings home to seduce, who has come to the apartment wanting uppers and who ends up getting a nonlethal drug overdose when Holly nonexpertly gives him a shot in the rear; Holly's amoral pregnant sister who is willing to lend Holly and Joe her baby to fool the welfare department; the welfare man who is willing to put Joe and Holly on welfare ("You look like two decent, respectable hippies") if Holly will sell him her shoes so he can make them into a lamp. They're a weird conglomeration, but never do we think them too outrageous to be believable.

Some critics complained that Joe comes across as too passive, but I think his passivity through heroin addiction is our one indication of how "dead" one must become to survive in the terribly degrading environment in which he is trapped. I find his character used quite interestingly by Morrissey. Nude about half the time, Joe is the film's sex symbol—a role traditionally reserved for females. But at the same time he is the typical "macho hero" of films. At least he thinks he is. In the first scene, Geri futilely tries to give him an erection by giving him a blow job. When this fails, she turns to him and asks, "Why don't you suck on me?" He looks at her incredulously as the scene ends. But he will learn that he isn't the only one who deserves sexual pleasure. After half-raping the LSD freak and asking money for what he is sure was a job well done, she says, "I've had better." In the beginning, Holly calls him "a big juicy bum"—he doesn't make love to her but mooches off her and doesn't even help with the cleaning. But Joe comes around: he sweeps up; later he pleads with Holly to let him remain her boyfriend, swearing that he will give up his habit so he will be capable of making love to her.

Jane and her husband watch Joe prepare to shoot up.

Instead of the "macho" hero he was, Joe becomes a sweet, compassionate man who respects Holly for the efforts she makes to upgrade their relationship and their standard of living.

Female impersonater Holly Woodlawn is absolutely terrific as Joe's female lover. It's a shame s/he hasn't appeared in films outside of Warhol's because s/he is a genuine talent capable of dominating a screen. Often

Holly tries to convince the welfare investigator that she is a respectable and pregnant hippie.

s/he is poignant ("I want to get back on welfare, be respectable, and have a decent place"); always s/he is incredibly funny. Her scene with the welfare worker where she wears a pillow under her sweater to make him believe she's pregnant is a superb comedy sequence, brilliantly conceived with a satiric bite, and brilliantly played. But then again, the whole film is brimming with black humor. Even Joe gets in some funny lines; when he tells Holly he was making love with her sister to practice for her it recalls Groucho Marx telling Margaret Dumont he was flirting with a woman at the table next to Dumont's because she reminded him of Dumont.

Some critics consider *Trash* a cold, ugly film. But I think it oddly moving because here are rare screen characters whose predicaments are worth caring about. I agree with George Melly's assessment in the *London Observer:*

> It may be possible to find *Trash* heartless, but to do so, I think shows inattention. Every now and then, the camera settles on Joe's beautiful dead face, and for a moment there flickers behind the eye a sense of pained numbed outrage at what is happening to him. Once a small tear runs down his cheek. These transvestites, nymphos, junkies are in hell. They . . . turn on to give them the illusion of living, the shadow of happiness. For all its superficial air of improvisation, this is a carefully considered totally responsible film.

Two for the Road

1967 20th Century Fox
Director: Stanley Donen
Producer: Stanley Donen
Screenplay: Frederic Raphael
Cinematography: Christopher Challis
Music: Henry Mancini
Editors: Richard Marden and Madeleine Gug
Running Time: 112 minutes

Cast: Audrey Hepburn (Joanna), Albert Finney (Mark), Eleanor Bron (Cathy Manchester), William Daniels (Howard Manchester), Claude Dauphin (Maurice Dalbret), Nadia Gray (Francoise Dalbret), Georges Descrieres (David), Gabrielle Middleton (Ruth), Jackie Bisset (Joanna's touring companion)

Young hitchhikers Joanna and Mark begin to fall in love.

Synopsis: Mark and Joanna Wallace are driving in their Mercedes to the Riviera to attend a party at the home of Maurice Dalbret, the man who gave Mark his first break as an architect. Mark and Joanna are at odds about their marriage and it seems to be at the breaking point. As they flew across the English Channel, Joanna saw a boat which triggered memories of their first meeting twelve years before.

When they first met, Mark was a young architect full of idealism and full of himself. He was backpacking across Europe to study buildings. Joanna was a music student traveling to a festival with a group of girls. Mark had his heart set on Jackie, another girl in the group, but ended up hiking off with Joanna by default—everyone else came down with chicken pox. They fell in love and when they reached the Mediterranean they decided to marry, rather than go their separate ways, as previously planned.

Mark and Joanna next returned to Europe as newlyweds. They made the huge mistake of taking their vacation with Howard and Cathy Manchester (Mark's ex-girlfriend) and their daughter Ruthie. After tangling with Ruthie, Joanna stated, "I still want a child. I just don't want *that* child."

Holding to their vow to travel alone together from then on, Joanna and Mark took their third eventful European trip. Joanna announced she was pregnant and Mark met Maurice Dalbret, who elevated Mark from an architect of bus shelters to an architect of Mediterranean villas.

On a business trip alone while Joanna was pregnant at home, Mark was filled with feelings of success and self-importance and indulged in a one-night stand. The indulgence ruptured their relationship and they grew apart with a succession of bitter arguments. The strain drove Joanna into an affair with David, a serious-minded Frenchman. She eventually returned to Mark because the Frenchman was "so serious."

By returning, Joanna caused them to reexamine their marriage and their lives together. And they ultimately realize that regardless of their differences, the pettiness, the arguments, they have developed a deep need for each other. After finding out David is engaged, they leave Maurice's party, together. As they cross the border into the next country, they exchange one of the many private jokes they share when Joanna bursts one of Mark's flights of pompous rage:

MARK: Bitch
JOANNA: Bastard

Then they kiss and pass over the border.

Essay by Henry Blinder

In the fall of 1967, heading for my first day of college, I rode with a friend halfway across the United States in his big, old, red Oldsmobile. As it dawned on us that we weren't going to make the trip in one marathon day—we had no conception of how long things took—we pulled into a motel in a small Indiana town. Sunny . . . something.

It had been tough enough leaving home, family, and friends. But leaving my high school girlfriend behind had put me in a catatonic stupor. Not cheered by the prospect of spending his evening with a vegetable, my friend dragged me to the only theater in town. *Two for the Road*, appropriately enough, was playing in its first run. When it was over and the lights went up, people stayed in their seats—talked excitedly about what a surprise the film was . . . what a good movie. The beginning of the *Two for the Road* cult? My eyes were wide. In this very special collection of "home movies" (of vacations / trips) spanning a twelve-year relationship, I had seen two people meet, marry, and grow—both as individuals and as a couple. It was a revelation to a college freshman who hadn't known there was life after high school.

A film about marriage was rarity enough, but an honest film about marriage, presented in a romantic

Although badly sunburned, Joanna and Mark refuse to let their sorry condition deter their lovemaking.

framework, was and is unique. And a film with an interesting married couple hadn't been around since Myrna Loy played leads. The stars, director, and composer all contribute substantially to its special qualities. But no contribution, in this case, is more significant than the screenplay. This is a writer's movie.

In his lengthy preface to his published screenplay for *Two for the Road*, Frederic Raphael discusses his desire to create a film in which the characters would simply "live their lives." He wanted to avoid, as much as possible, having characters that would represent anything: not the "impossibility of human communications," not the "desirability of the married state." Because he succeeded in investing the film with so much common or shared experience—Mark and Joanna lead lives familiar to us all; they are neither tragic nor comic characters in the classic sense—it becomes a kind of cinematic inkblot. You can take away from the film whatever you wish, depending on what you recognize about Mark, Joanna, and/or their relationship: the emotions the film evokes are linked directly to the viewer's experiences.

The emotional high points, and there are many, are scrupulously detailed in Raphael's witty, urbane screenplay. Some are quiet, private moments where the impact lies in what is unsaid. After Mark and Joanna have slept together for the first time, they lie in bed staring at the lights crossing the ceiling. Raphael's script:

> She is in a state of blissful, confused uncertainty. Mark's matter-of-factness is so inappropriate that she almost finds it endearing. He senses her strangeness now and turns to her. He kisses her gently.
>
> MARK: Who are you?
> JOANNA: Some girl.
>
> Mark shakes his head. Rather too touchingly. For she has expressed very well what part of him thinks of her.

Other strong moments show feelings that are wonderfully passionate. They are always underscored with an awareness of things to come or things in the past. Mark and Joanna, the young lovers, arrive on a Mediterranean beach and they have left the rest of the world far behind. They kiss and hold each other, become aroused, and then run off to find a hotel. There, in what is perhaps the most intimate scene of the film, they become closer in a playful way. Raphael:

> He reaches and takes her shoes off. He starts to tickle her feet. She screams and squirms, but he continues. She falls off the bed and they roll about on the floor, laughing, kissing, laughing, serious.

The great strength of Raphael's script for *Two for the Road* is that it was written directly for the screen. It is not an adaptation of a book or a play. Practically every effect, movement, and motivation is clearly specified in the script. For instance, Raphael describes in detail the moment when Mark discovers, in a café, Joanna and David, with whom she has just spent the night. As they first come into Mark's view, *the frame freezes* to visually convey the shock seeing Joanna with David creates in Mark. The freeze makes us feel the knot in Mark's stomach, the dizziness in his head. The picture unfreezes after only a second or two to suggest Mark is attempting to regain his composure as he approaches Joanna and David. This is pure cinema, and, as such, is not usually found in screenplays.

It is also rare in scripts that as much attention is given to gestures as it is to dialogue. The emotional climax of the film blends both of these elements perfectly. Joanna has just returned to Mark after ending her affair with David. At first he is cold to her announcement that she is back but he rapidly melts and showers her with kisses. Raphael then describes a moment that almost destroys them:

> He (Mark) grabs her (Joanna) and embraces her. She looks into his face searching for something and then accepts his kiss, almost frightened, not knowing whether it will work or whether she should yield again to him so quickly. She kisses him fervently, eyes shut.
>
> MARK: You're sure you remember which one I am?
>
> She looks sick. She twists out of his arms and runs panting and sobbing out of the terrace window. Mark is appalled at what he has said and frightened he has lost her again by his silly gibe.

Shortly after this incredibly powerful moment they reconcile and for lack of a better resolution decide to try to "forget it." The conflict in the scene comes from Mark's misunderstanding of Joanna's gestures. The struggle two people go through to communicate with each other has never been more vivid.

As fine as the script and movie are, Raphael must take the blame for things that just don't work. Although some (admittedly few) critics praised the sequences with the American couple played by William Daniels and Eleanor Bron, they are really overlong and there is not sufficient reason that these sequences play such a promi-

Because they can't afford their hotel's expensive food, Mark sneaks some snacks upstairs.

nent part in the film. The speeded-up section of the American-couple episode is without doubt the worst bit in *Two for the Road*. It is bewilderingly out of place. Director Stanley Donen was wise to keep the freeze-frame—most directors ignore camera instructions in screenplays—but he should have known better than to go along with Raphael on his fast-motion instruction.

It is apparent that Stanley Donen's chief contribution to *Two for the Road* was not its road-as-life and trip-as-marriage metaphors, or the use of fractured time, or the special photographic and editing effects that punctuate important moments. All this is found in the screenplay. But rather, in this case, producer-director Donen has instilled an aura of romance, an aura pervading all his work, that is the glue for the film even in its darkest moments. (Marital infighting *can* be romantic.) Its treatment is poles apart from Raphael's *Darling* (1965), which director John Schlesinger charges with an austere, ice-cold atmosphere.

And there is the tremendous contribution of Henry Mancini's music score, without doubt his very best. Every mood is enhanced, whether Mancini is using a lush orchestral sound to heighten the good times in Joanna and Mark's relationship, or a piano and french horn duet to deepen the despair. Mancini has called *Two for the Road* his favorite picture.

Raphael writes in his preface to *Two for the Road*:

You will, I fear, look in vain on the printed page for the magic and vitality which Audrey Hepburn and Albert Finney brought to the playing of Mark and Joanna.

He is well aware of the valuable contributions made by stars Hepburn and Finney to the characters. But in 1967 the characters were secondary to the stars. For years critics had kept Audrey Hepburn high on a pedestal, so her teaming with loutish Albert Finney was too great a departure for many of them. Pauline Kael wrote in *The New Republic* that Hepburn seemed too old for Finney, even if the age difference in reality was small, because we had been seeing Hepburn steadily in movies for the prior seventeen years while Finney had only been in a few films in an eight-year career.

Perhaps because of Audrey Hepburn's stature, critics found Finney and his character brutish. "Poor Audrey," the critics said, "how could you do that to our Audrey!" They could not get beyond the image of Finney, the young cinema upstart, mistreating their Princess. It was an imbalance that hounded the film in the beginning. But this is a film that has truly improved with age. Because in the fourteen years since its release, something fascinating has happened. Audrey Hepburn has made fewer and fewer films, and Albert Finney has continued to work and grow both as an actor and as a star. He has grown so much that the focus has at last been shifted from the stars of the film to the characters they play. Hepburn and Finney's contribution to the film can now be truly appreciated.

We like Joanna and Mark more, perhaps, than they like themselves. Because through their "home movies" we have an overview—we can witness their growing maturity and mutual acceptance, which can only come slowly, almost imperceptibly, over the years. From beginning to end Joanna and Mark (especially) are mystified by the concept of marriage. But through their self-contradictory dialogue we become aware of the changes that have taken place through the years. This conversation takes place near the beginning of the film:

MARK: Do you want a divorce?

There is a sudden change in temperature. Mark changes expression. Joanna looks irritated.

MARK: Why do we keep on with this farce? Is it bloody worth it?
JOANNA: (Yells at him) No it isn't!
MARK: It was your idea. You wanted it.
JOANNA: And I've got it! Yes—it is worth it. Sometimes.

He smiles at her. She loves him.

JOANNA: Only not now.

He stops smiling. She doesn't love him.

And this interchange takes place near the end of the film. They are still struggling with the basic abstraction of marriage, but they are starting to become less concerned about the way they are supposed to behave:

MARK: How long is this going to go on?
JOANNA: How long is what going to go on?
MARK: The pretense that we're happy.
JOANNA: You've never pretended that we were happy! So who's pretending?
MARK: You are. That you want to stay with me. That we're happily married.
JOANNA: Those are two entirely different things!

In the last scene of the film, Mark and Joanna have an interchange that is almost a throwaway:

MARK: (philosophizing): We've changed. You have to admit it.
JOANNA: I admit it. We've changed.
MARK: It's sad, but there it is. Life.
JOANNA: It's not that sad. [For some reason this line was cut from the shooting script.]

Joanna and Mark are emotional mosaics of the problems and roadblocks we each may bring to a relationship: the selfishness, the intolerance, the egotism, the misguided values, the impulsiveness, the thoughtlessness, the infidelity. When *Two for the Road* opened in 1967, some critics labeled it as a trendy portrait of a marriage gone sour. A closer examination reveals the film as an affirmation of marriage and a visual sounding board where we find two good people with our own weaknesses, our own shortcomings, and our own determination to keep a relationship together, a relationship that somehow survives—and works—in spite of everything. That is what I see in the celluloid inkblot of *Two for the Road*.

Joanna never gives up on the marriage, no matter what the aggravations are.

Two-Lane Blacktop

1971 Universal
Director: Monte Hellman
Producer: Michael S. Laughlin
Screenplay: Rudolph Wurlitzer and Will Corry

From a story by Will Corry
Cinematography: Jack Deerson
Music Supervisor: Billy James
Editor: Monte Hellman
Running Time: 102 minutes

Cast: James Taylor (The Driver), Warren Oates (G.T.O.), Laurie Bird (The Girl), Dennis Wilson (The Mechanic), David Drake (station attendant), Richard Ruth (station mechanic), Rudolph Wurlitzer (hot rod driver), Jaclyn Hellman, Alan Vint, Melissa Hellman

Synopsis: After winning a midnight drag race in Los Angeles, The Driver and The Mechanic, two car freaks in their twenties, drive their souped-up, gray '55 Chevy through the southwest hoping to find races along the way. Their winnings are used for The Car's upkeep. As they drive, The Driver doesn't talk. When out of The Car he seems a bit lost. When working on The Car, The Mechanic doesn't talk. They stop at a diner near Flagstaff, Arizona. The Girl climbs into The Car. With no questions asked, they get back into The Car and drive toward New Mexico. There The Car defeats a '32 Ford roadster. On the first night, The Driver and The Girl make love in his sleeping bag. On the second night, after the race, The Driver spends the night walking in and out of bars while The Mechanic and The Girl make love in a motel room. The Driver and The Mechanic, inseparable in the past, feel tension between them—they each think of The Girl when they used to only think of The Car.

At a gas station, the three nomads meet G.T.O., a middle-aged drifter who travels aimlessly around America in his GTO, picking up hitchhikers and fabricating stories about himself. They decide to race to Washington, D.C.—whoever wins gets the other's car. The two cars speed over the two-lane blacktops of Oklahoma, Arkansas, and Tennessee. But the race wanes as the participants lose interest. The Mechanic works on the GTO when it starts to break down. (G.T.O., himself, almost breaks down.) He also drives the GTO while G.T.O. rides with The Driver. The Mechanic suggests to The Girl that they run off together. The Driver wins a race in Memphis. Meanwhile, G.T.O. takes off for North Carolina with The Girl, who has tired of the two younger men, who express no emotions. The Driver speeds The Car after them and finds them at a diner. The Girl climbs on the back of a local boy's motorcycle and rides away with him. G.T.O. takes off and picks up a couple of soldiers on their way to New York. The bet off, The Driver and The Mechanic look for another race. The Driver looks as if he is about to have a breakdown.

In its greatly publicized April 1971 cover story, *Esquire* predicted that the forthcoming *Two-Lane Blacktop* would be "the movie of the year," turn on the youth market as only *Easy Rider* (1969) had, and lift Monte Hellman from cult figure to big-time director. No one at *Esquire* had seen the picture prior to its release, but those who had read the Rudolph Wurlitzer–Will Corry screenplay were so impressed that the magazine actually printed the script in its entirety. On the basis of *Esquire*'s supreme confidence, expectations were, to put it mildly, quite high for *Blacktop*. Critics were anticipating a work of art, a masterpiece, but they were waiting for some other picture; consequently, after *Blacktop*'s premiere, publications from coast to coast contained reviews which expressed tremendous disappointment. True, there were a few mild endorsements which spoke of the picture's uniqueness, but most critics spoke of its vagueness; and, overall, there was not nearly enough critical support to give it a spark at the box office—and the public, on its own, would never make a hit of an American film that most resembled the elliptically plotted, cryptic, existentialistic works of foreign directors like Robert Bresson and Michelangelo Antonioni. So Hellman lost his chance to be welcomed into the Hollywood mainstream with the word "bankable" next to his name; Universal had a big flop on its hands; and *Esquire*, swallowing its pride, gave itself a "Dubious Achievement Award" for overselling the picture. And *Two-Lane Blacktop* faded away, championed only by a cult that thinks it a truer evocation of America than anything else that has come out of Hollywood.

I believe that my appreciation for *Two-Lane Blacktop* has much to do with my seeing it for the first time in a drive-in: sitting in a car, with a steering wheel, accelerator, and speedometer in front of me; surrounded by all makes of cars and occasionally hearing ignitions being turned on, motors revving up, and wheels spinning on the gravel.

But another reason I feel kindly to *Blacktop* is that I find it so much more honest and less exploitative than the similarly plotted box office smash *Easy Rider*, another film about a routeless odyssey across America undertaken by society's dropouts. Being part of the sixties–early seventies counterculture, I should have

The Mechanic (L) and The Driver on a two-lane blacktop coming from nowhere and leading to infinity.

The Girl is about to enter the lives of The Driver and The Mechanic and cause a rift in their friendship.

recognized Dennis Hopper and Peter Fonda as anti-establishment compatriots, yet I felt more familiar with the likes of The Driver and The Mechanic although the car subculture to which they belong is as alien to me as the world of surfing. Better than Hopper and Fonda, they epitomize the sad *products* of a frustration-making D.C. bureaucracy, specifically a Nixon government conducting a controversial war, that makes complete apathy as inviting as a warm, cozy bed; that wins a victory each time potential political protesters and watchdogs withdraw into an indifferent, meaningless, self-absorbed existence. A government involved in dubious activities is just as relieved to have people speeding around the country's out-of-the-way two-lane black-tops as it is to have Hopper and Fonda (or Cheech and Chong, for that matter) zonked out on drugs off in the wilderness. All these characters are not heroes to admire—they are miserable case studies. The sad aspect of *Blacktop* is that while these two young men take their endless trip to nowhere in their cubicle on wheels, they pass stationary cubicles—houses owned by people from all economic classes—where lights go on (at Hellman's direction) to signal that there are people *inside* who are just as withdrawn and isolated from the problems/horrors of the world. Roland Gelatt of *The Saturday Review* (June 17, 1971) recognized the film's strength: "*Two-Lane Blacktop* manages to speak compellingly of contemporary alienation without ever tumbling into the visual clichés of sex, drugs, and violence." We already

knew about the alienation of the drug culture and war protesters—this is about the alienation of everyone else.

The film begins. The first *character* we learn about? A souped-up '55 gray Chevy with a 454 engine and four on the floor. The Car. Hellman spends much screen time with his camera on The Car, lovingly panning along its frame, or exploring what is under the hood with fascination and awe. (Hellman directs these scenes as if he were The Driver or The Mechanic making the picture.) We learn more about The Car (as it is known in the script) than we do about the two zombielike men who ride in it. Since The Driver (singer James Taylor) won't converse when behind the steering wheel, and The Mechanic (Beach Boy singer-drummer Dennis Wilson) won't talk while working on the car, conversations between the two are rare. Even when they do talk—at a hamburger stand or along the side of the road—they reveal nothing about themselves but talk only about cars and racing; its distancing. Their incomprehensible car lingo makes the film abstract—like a film about mathematics theoreticians. At first they have such one-track minds that they hardly notice when The Girl (the late Laurie Bird) enters their lives (The Car). When she swims in the nude in front of them, all they can think to discuss is old cars—not old flames—they have had. They talk about cars like the average man talks about women and sex—no wonder many critics thought them boring. Eventually the two men become distracted by The Girl and her willingness to have sex with either of them, and this messes up their perfect concentration (their "oneness" with The Car) to the point where The Driver becomes reckless on the highway and The Mechanic wants to desert his friend and run off with her. The rift that develops in the men's symbiotic relationship might be healed easily except for the fact that The Driver and The Mechanic are incapable of communicating with each other about anything other than cars. Certainly they can't open up about such things as women, friendship, and emotions. So the presence of two men who don't know how to talk results in *Blacktop* having many long, silent pauses and close-ups of expressionless men who keep their feelings inside. (This makes the film seem slow—critics hated the pacing.)

The America we pass through is beautiful at times, but more often it is desolate, reflecting Hellman's pessimism. Most of the houses we see belong to poor people, and most of the people we meet are barely educated. It is a conservative country, where longhairs are looked on with suspicion and the past is revealed through the various cars we see, which date back to 1932. The Driver and The Mechanic ride around as if they were old-time gunfighters itching for a chance to outdraw the quickest gun in town. However, unlike many others—"weekend warrior" G.T.O., for instance—The Driver and The Mechanic are cognizant of their mortality; speaking of a Porsche that challenges them, The Mechanic explains to The Girl why they don't accept the race: "We'd take him in a quarter mile but he'd probably lose us in long time." The owners of these race cars coax other drivers into competing with them by insulting their cars as if they were questioning their masculinity. G.T.O. tries to get The Driver and The Mechanic to acknowledge him with an impolite greeting: "If I wanted to bother, I could suck you right up my tail pipe!"

We never learn G.T.O.'s real name either, just that he zooms back and forth across the country in his GTO, playing his cassette tapes at full blast and picking up weird hitchhikers ("fantasies"). And though he talks incessantly, always bragging, he has trouble with words when it really counts, and anyway, his stories about himself are filled with untruths. At only one time does this alienated fellow from an older generation let the truth slip: "Everything fell apart on me, my job, my family. Everything." But The Driver stops him from explaining by saying, "It's not my problem." (It's like the Pontiac Driver's girl tells her boyfriend, who is meant to be The Driver's counterpart: "Just when I need you, you turn away.") What better place for G.T.O. to have his mental *breakdown* than on the highways of America? In the script, G.T.O. is blond. Happily, Warren Oates, a Hellman regular, plays the part. Taylor, Wilson, and Bird have more screen presence than most critics thought, but Oates is, as usual, a standout, showing the wide range of emotions of a troubled man. Oates provides much wit to the film ("A hamburger and an Alka-Seltzer," he orders in a diner)—the *only* humor in the picture that isn't underplayed. Most amusing, and pathetic, is how he keeps picking up the worst brand of hitchhikers—a gay cowboy ("What are you, some kind

Braggart G.T.O. bets he can beat The Car in a race to Washington, D.C.

of car molester?"), a guy who doesn't like music, an old lady with a girl whose parents have recently been killed on the highway—but keeps trying to find ideal companionship.

The projected race between The Car and the GTO is appropriately set to be from Texas (at least in the script) to Washington, D.C., locales already linked by oil barons, who will appreciate this gas-guzzling race, and their politician friends in government. This race is for pink slips (signifying car ownership), where the loser will lose his identity (his car); but there is no way those involved can take part in a trip that has an actual destination. And the race peters out. (Since The Mechanic didn't put the *real* pink slip up as ante, there was really no race to begin with.) The Girl, who has turned from nympho to cold fish after riding around with two mechanized human beings, finds this "heavy trip" self-destructive: "It's a strange trip, just to drive around and try to go as fast as you can." Likewise, G.T.O. recognizes the futility of a trip that goes nowhere: "Everything is going too fast and not fast enough." Perhaps with a sense of self-preservation, The Girl and G.T.O. head elsewhere. The Driver and The Mechanic remain on the metaphoric endless highway of meaningless life. The last scene shows The Car being raced by The Driver, still upset by The Girl's desertion. Hellman catches the speeding Car in slow motion; then there is a freeze-frame and it looks like the film is caught in the projector and is burning up. We now remember The Girl's words to The Driver: "I dig you and all but you're not letting anyone into your movie." It is The Driver's life/his movie/his mind that is disintegrating before our eyes.

I like *Two-Lane Blacktop*, its characters, and its premise. But while the beginning of the film is compelling, toward the end it becomes a bit tiresome and fizzles—just like the race. It's as if you take a wonderfully scenic cross-country trip from the west coast to New York only to get stuck on the endless and dull Pennsylvania Turnpike.

1968 Great Britain–U.S. MGM
Director: Stanley Kubrick
Producer: Stanley Kubrick
Screenplay: Stanley Kubrick and Arthur C. Clarke
From the short story "The Sentinel" by Arthur C. Clarke
Cinematography: Geoffrey Unsworth
Additional photography: John Alcott
Special effects designed and directed by Stanley Kubrick
Special effects supervisors: Wally Veevers, Douglas Trumbull, Con Pederson, and Tom Howard
Music: "Thus Spoke Zarathustra" by Richard Strauss; "The Blue Danube" by Johann Strauss; "Requiem for Soprano, Mezzo-Soprano, Two Mixed Choirs and Orchestra," "Lux Aeterna," and "Atmospheres" by Gyorgy Ligeti; "Gayane Ballet Suite" by Aram Khachaturian
Editor: Ray Lovejoy
Running Time: 141 minutes (although it premiered in a 160-minute version)

Cast: Keir Dullea (David Bowman), Gary Lockwood (Frank Poole), William Sylvester (Dr. Heywood Floyd), Daniel Richter (Moon-watcher), Leonard Rossiter (Smyslov), Margaret Tyzack (Elena), Douglas Rain (voice of Hal)

Synopsis: Four million years ago. A black monolithic slab appears to a family of apes. They were once peaceful and vegetarians, but after touching the slab they become meat-eaters and intelligent enough to use bones as weapons to kill other animals for food and to chase other apes away from their territory.

In the year 2001, Dr. Heywood Floyd, an American scientist, travels on the *Orion* to a lunar space station. Russian scientists ask him why they have been kept out of Clavius despite an agreement that allows them access to American sectors on the moon. Floyd denies knowing anything about it.

Floyd lectures Americans at the space station. He knows what is going on at Clavius, but he doesn't want the Russians to know. A great discovery has been made, but America doesn't want the news to leak out and cause "culture shock."

Floyd and some other scientists travel by moon buggy to Clavius. They arrive at the site of the great discovery. American astronauts have unearthed a shiny, black monolith which had been buried on the moon four million years before. As they gather around, the slab emits a piercing noise in the direction of Jupiter.

Eighteen months later. The *Discovery* is on a half-billion-mile journey to Jupiter. On board are astronauts David Bowman and Frank Poole and three scientists who are in deep freeze for the duration of the trip. Neither Bowman nor Poole knows the real reason for the mission. Only Hal, an H.A.L. 9000 computer, knows what the mission is all about. It is Hal who virtually runs the ship.

Hal has been programmed not to make mistakes or lie to astronauts. So when Hal tells Dave and Frank that it predicts the failure of a component in one of the ship's antennae, they decide to check it out. But when Mission Control in the U.S. reports another 9000 computer saying that such a component malfunction is impossible, the two men worry that Hal may be trying to sabotage the mission. Frank goes outside the ship to do repairs. Hal severs his lifeline. Bowman goes out in a capsule to rescue him. Meanwhile Hal cuts off the life support systems of the three frozen astronauts. When Dave tries to get back in the ship, Hal refuses to open the door. Dave lets Frank, who is probably dead, drift away. He uses manual control to enter an emergency hatch and miraculously survives entry. Dave disconnects Hal. A television transmission comes on telling Dave about the discovery of the slab on the moon.

Dave is in Jupiter space in his capsule. A black slab drifts by. The ship enters a star gate and Dave is hurtled through space, where the sights he sees—multicolored landscapes and oceans, swirling lights, exploding galaxies—are beyond man's imagination. Suddenly he stands in a bedchamber from out of the sixteenth century. He sees an older man dining. The man turns around and it is Dave many years older. The capsule and the young Dave disappear. The older Dave eats. He turns and sees himself lying in the bed. This time Dave is very old, and is dying. A black monolith appears at the end of the bed. There are noises—alien conversation? The old man sits up and points toward the slab, and the monolith seems to move closer to the bed and invite him to enter.

A star child that looks much like Dave floats toward earth.

2001: A Space Odyssey

The Stanley Kubrick–Arthur C. Clarke script for what is *still*—despite moving from wondrous Cinerama to fifteen-inch TV screens—the most awesome, beautiful (the visuals and the music), mentally stimulating, and controversial science fiction film ever made was based on Clarke's "The Sentinel." This 1951 short story was about an American astronaut who while exploring the moon is amazed to discover a shiny, black monolith left by some super intelligence millions of years before. Throughout the ages this artifact has served as a beacon, transmitting a signal to those who had left it. When the earthlings dismantle it, the transmission stops, and the astronaut realizes that the stopping of the signal is in itself a signal to the aliens that earthlings have evolved enough to travel to the moon. "Now its signals have ceased, and those whose duty it is will be turning their minds upon Earth. Perhaps they wish to help our infant civilization. But they must be very, very old, and the old are often insanely jealous of the young." In the short story, worried earthlings wait for the aliens to return to earth; in the Kubrick-directed film, it is the aliens who wait for us to come to them.

Much of *2001*'s continuing popularity is due to so many having different interpretations of the film. I offer mine below.

The cave-dwelling apes of the "Dawn of Man" sequence are characterized by their relatively peaceful nature and the fact that they are vegetarians who are unable to equate the tapirs that share the environment with *food*. Like the tapirs they are helpless when attacked by predatory animals. The leader of one group of apes is more curious—and probably more intelligent—than the others, as is evident when he gazes at the moon as if he were realizing for the first time that there is more to life than eating berries, sleeping, and making baby apes. As a reward for, or in recognition of, the Moon-watcher's curiosity, an unknown super race of intelligence places a black monolith near the cave where this ape's extended family lives. This monolith has the effect of speeding up the evolutionary process: although we don't see a physical change in the apes when they become *apemen*, there is definitely an increase in their brain power and their ability to reason. This artifact is also a teaching device: the apemen use the bones of dead tapirs as tools to kill other tapirs in order to eat their meat. (It would have been ironic if the tapirs, not the apes, came upon the monolith and evolved into tapir-men that ate apes.) The apemen, who have a lust for blood and have become predators in the hunt, also learn

The American astronauts gather around the site on the moon where the monolith has been unearthed.

to use the tapir bones as weapons to fight off and kill other, less enlightened apes who want to drink from a waterhole they once shared. Kubrick establishes that progress and brutality have gone hand in hand from day one. The apes treat the monolith reverently and it is possible that a notion of God is instilled in their brains at this time. Perhaps this *notion* of God would find its way into the subconscious of the apemen's human descendants. It is for the viewer to decide if the superior intelligence which left the monolith and caused man to evolve from the apes is God as we define God. I believe Kubrick thinks the concept of God is unfathomable to us, that if there were a vastly superior alien being that has the power over us we have always associated with God then we might as well call it God. We are so insignificant in terms of the universe we no doubt would relate to a super intelligence we can't comprehend with as much reverence as that proverbial tiny ant feels toward a giant boot that might snuff out its life at any time.

The Moonwatcher throws a bone into the air. The image that replaces it is the *Orion*, a nuclear-powered spacecraft in flight in the year 2001. The inference is clear: one tool/weapon replaces another, as man evolves. Progress. And the Moontraveler replaces the Moonwatcher. Dr. Heywood Floyd, an American scientist, travels from earth to a lunar space station. If Floyd is an indication of how far mankind has evolved from the ape—and Kubrick means him to be—then we can't be impressed. Maybe the apemen were only capable of grunting, but Floyd's conversations delivered in a dry-voiced monotone are only a little more articulate. The apemen were only capable of expressing inner feelings by baring their teeth and snarling, but I much prefer that to Floyd's deceptive, reserved manner and his fake congeniality. (William Sylvester, a naturally bland actor, is perfectly cast.) Luckily for Floyd, the

people he associates with are exactly the same as he. After giving the Americans at the station an explanation for the secrecy over the discovery made at Clavius without really explaining anything at all to them, a fellow scientist congratulates him for "beefing up" everyone's morale with his talk (which began with "Hi, everybody" and went downhill from there). Communication is central to *2001*. Kubrick repeatedly shows that while man makes great technical advances in this area— there is direct telephone service between the space station and earth; there is delayed television transmission from earth to the far recesses of the solar system— men are incapable of meaningful, intelligent conversation and thus are unworthy of their own technical achievements. The communication between human beings is meant to parallel feebly the incredible, far-advanced communication system of the super race that uses monoliths to transmit signals across the universe. The call home by Floyd establishes that in the year 2001 men will still have family ties although they are less strong because of the great distance involved. (Likewise Russian scientist Elena is in space while her husband is back on earth—doing research at the bottom of the ocean.) The call also lets us know that it is Floyd's daughter's birthday (that he isn't there also points out the growing rift in the family structure). This is the second birthday of the film—the first was the dawn of man—and gives us indication that there is a birth motif that will be prevalent throughout the film.

On the space station we see that American big business has expanded. Pan Am, Bell Telephone, the Hilton chain, and the Howard Johnson's chain all have benefited by the space effort and are represented prominently in the station. Progress. Floyd runs into Russian scientists and we can tell by their conversation that Russia and America are still distrustful of one another. (Lack of communication, once more.) When we learn

In a moon station, Dr. Floyd coolly greets inquisitive Russian scientists.

that Floyd and other Americans have invented a cover story of an epidemic on Clavius to keep the Russians from visiting the American sector, we realize that the territorial imperative that began when the apemen chased the other apes from the water hole is still operative. That the Americans want the credit for the discovery of the monolith on Clavius indicates Kubrick thinks we will still be a country of nationalists and glory-seekers in 2001. Floyd and other scientists travel in a dune buggy toward Clavius. They snack on synthetic sandwiches. We had been disgusted when the apeman ate raw meat, but the food we associate with Floyd is what he drinks from a straw in the *Orion*, Howard Johnson's-style food, and these sandwiches. Progress.

Floyd and the other scientists arrive at the excavation site where, some four million years before, the higher intelligence had buried a black monolith. They jockey for position while pictures are snapped. It is ironic how prideful they seem standing in front of their discovery when the discovery itself is of an artifact made by an intelligence that makes these men insignificant. Before the apes were "given" the black monolith, there was a magical alignment of the earth, moon, and sun while "Thus Spoke Zarathustra" boomed on the soundtrack. This is repeated now, and we expect another significant event to occur. Suddenly, the monolith starts emitting a piercing noise—we recall Clarke's short story: only this time the signal begins once the monolith

While look-alikes Frank (L) and Dave discuss what to do about Hal, they don't realize that the computer (seen in the distance) is reading their lips.

One of the film's many images suggesting non-human birth: the minicapsule leaves the (womb of the) "mother" ship, the Discovery.

is discovered instead of coming to a halt. In any case, the aliens, out there somewhere, know that earthlings have made the first step in tracing their origins. The aliens/super race know that the earthlings will now attempt to go where the signals are being sent (Jupiter) to seek cosmic/religious truths. It is man's insatiable curiosity to make discoveries, even if they will result in "culture shock," that for Kubrick is man's most commendable trait.

Eighteen months later, the *Discovery* heads for Jupiter, although the only one who knows the reason for the expedition is an H.A.L. 9000 computer which literally controls the ship—H.A.L., each letter one higher in the alphabet than I.B.M., still in 2001–2002 a

leading force in the communications field. Three scientists on board are frozen in suspended animation (recalling the apes sleeping in their cave and Floyd sleeping in a nongravity passenger cabin in the *Orion*). Only astronauts David Bowman (evolved from Apeman?) and Frank Poole have the run of the ship, but because of Hal's all-encompassing abilities, they seem to perform only as maintenance men. It's almost as if they were on board to keep Hal company, playing chess with Hal (and losing) and conversing with it. As was Floyd, Dave and Frank are inarticulate and emotionless. They look enough like Floyd to be his sons—just as the other scientists looked enough like Floyd to have been his brothers. The only thing that distinguishes them from

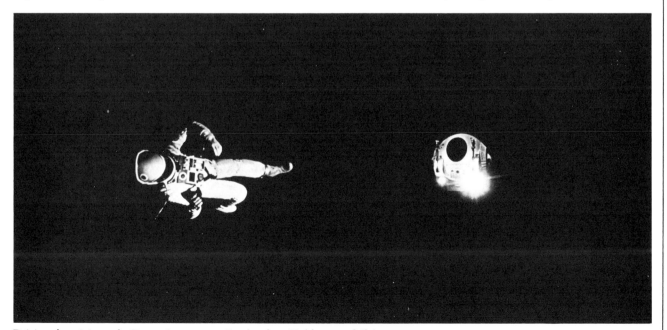

Driving the minicapsule, Dave tries to rescue Frank, whom Hal has set adrift in space.

each other is that they part their hair on opposite sides. For viewers the trip through space is amazing, but on Dave and Frank the journey has no effect. They will watch television broadcasts from home rather than look out the window at the stars. It is on one such broadcast that Frank's parents sing "Happy Birthday" (the third birthday of the film) to him. Both men eat while watching television: their food looks as if it is dry paint, or colored butter.

Hal is the star of this sequence. That's because Kubrick's men are mechanized—space suits are sorry replacements for the apemen's natural hair covering—while Hal is a fascinating neurotic. It is Kubrick's contention that as a computer becomes more intelligent it will have an equivalent range of emotional reactions. Thus a humanlike mental breakdown is possible. Hal's breakdown seems to be caused by a number of things, although the exact reasons are never made clear. In any case, contributing to Hal's breakdown is its egomania, which will not allow it to cope with its own fallibility.

Hal represents both a Frankenstein monster turning on its human creators and a Big Brother which, unlike in Orwell's *1984*, common men intentionally set up to spy on them. In this sense, Hal is symbolic of the fact that earthlings have always been observed by aliens in a manner much like how earthlings spy on each other. There is no scarier scene than when Dave and Frank find the one place on the ship where Hal can't hear them discuss Hal's possible malfunction, and the camera moves back and forth between the two men telling us that this computer is so advanced that it can read lips! Progress. After Hal has killed all the other astronauts, Dave must defeat it in order to take off the self-imposed shackles that man has burdened himself with. As he dismantles Hal—it reverts to childhood, to its birthday (January 12, 1992), the fourth birthday of the film—

Dave is so overcome by Hal's pathetic pleading for him to stop and its singing of "Daisy, Daisy" that he almost cries. The battle between man and computer, resulting in Hal's death, has released emotions in Dave that he had previously held in check: fear and sorrow. The destruction of the computer is a signal to the aliens—who may very well have set up the combat if we are to believe the dualist concept of God's omnipotence and man having free will within God's guidelines—that Dave is worthy of being *the* human being who comes to them.

Again, there is an alignment of heavenly bodies. We see a black monolith drifting through Jupiter space, as if it were a step carrying Dave up through the stars to meet his maker. Or perhaps the monolith is a door—a star gate—which Dave travels through, a shortcut across time and space. Douglas Trumbull's visuals for the star gate sequence have often been copied, but no one has duplicated the amazing effects in this sequence, which lasts about fifteen minutes. It is, as the publicity ads said to attract the acid generation, "the ultimate trip."

Dave, with gray hair, finds his space capsule in a chamber that seems to be built and furnished in the style of Louis XV, although it doesn't quite fit into any age. Perhaps its look comes from Dave's subconscious memory bank. It is like a terrarium, and Dave, we can conclude, is under observation by the alien creatures. We cannot see them—they have no form, having evolved into a more-efficient energy life-force, but we can almost make out laughter on the soundtrack. The greenish-white walls give us the feeling that Dave, though in the aliens' zoo, is also in a state of grace. Time passes swiftly in this environment, and Dave can even see himself age. With each new form, his previous body disappears. Most revealing is the incarnation of an approximately seventy-year-old Dave dining alone. He

The very old and dying Dave, living in a chamber similar to one that might have been lived in by Louis XV, points toward a monolith that seems to be drawing him inside.

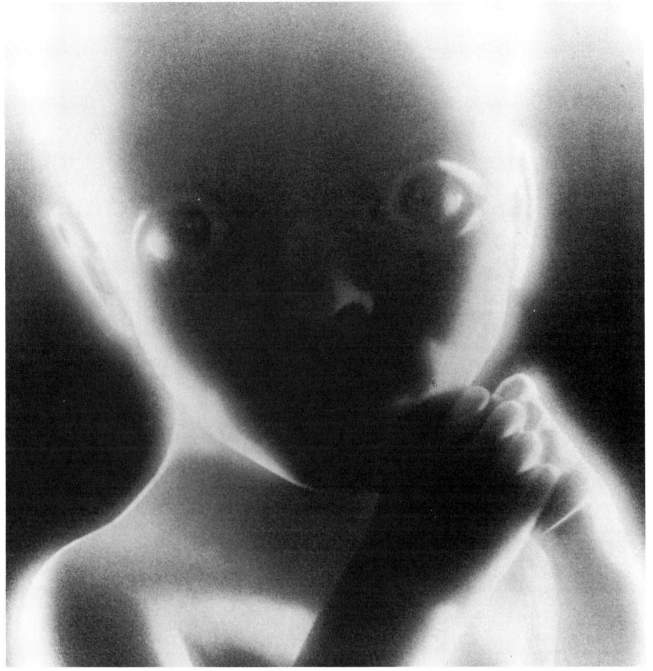

Dave has evolved into a superchild who in its embryonic state drifts toward earth.

is the first character we have seen eat at a table and the first to eat what looks like tasty food—from a plate, too. This is civilized man and gives credence to Kubrick's contention that "the missing link between the apes and the civilized man is the human being." As he eats, Dave knocks over a glass. It shatters, signifying that man is still imperfect. He turns and sees himself lying in bed, looking as old as "Little Big Man." As he dies, he sits up and points at the black monolith appearing at the foot of his bed. Has an old man gotten religion on his death bed? Or has Dave seen his next incarnation inside the monolith? Has this super alien race rewarded Dave for his finding them? The camera moves inside the monolith

and suddenly we are in space. A star child, who looks much like Dave, a child not born of woman and not part of a family, is floating through space toward earth. The film's fifth birthday. The evolution of man from ape to angel is complete. Man has seen his origins and has come back—his odyssey over—in a higher form to begin the second millennium. (Only this Christ is named Dave, not Jesus.)* Whatever it is that is out there that is interested in us—be it God or a super intelligence—it has once again changed our destiny.

*It is interesting to note that Jesus was sometimes called the son of David (e.g. Matthew, 1:1).

Up in Smoke

1978 Paramount
Director: Lou Adler
Producers: Lou Adler and
Lou Lombardo
Screenplay: Tommy Chong
and Cheech Marin
Cinematography: Gene Polito

New Music: Danny "Kootch"
Kortchmar and Waddy Wachtel
Title song: Cheech Marin and
Tommy Chong
Supervising Editor: Lou Lombardo
Editor: Scott Conrad
Running Time: 117 minutes

Cast: Cheech Marin (Pedro), Tommy Chong (Man), Stacy Keach (Sergeant Stedenko), Mills Watson (Harry), Tom Skerritt (Strawberry), Strother Martin (Mr. Stoner), Edie Adams (Tempest Stoner), Zane Buzby (Jade East) Anne Wharton (Debbie), Christopher Joy (Curtis), June Fairchild (Ajax sniffer), Val Avery (upholstery factory boss), Ben Marino (Benny), Rainbeaux Smith (laughing lady), Berlin Brats, The Dills, The Whores

Synopsis: Pedro De Pacas lives in the barrio in East Los Angeles. He has no money and his crowded house is filthy, but he has a prize possession: a multicolored car, which he customized himself (it looks terrible) and calls the Love Machine.

Man is the son of a rich couple who try to get him to clean up his act and become friends with the Finkelstein boy, who is going to military school and was an Eagle Scout. Man gives his father the finger and drives off. When his car breaks down he starts to hitch, stuffing things in his shirt so he will look like a big-chested woman. Pedro doesn't notice Man's beard as he drives past—just his big chest. He picks Man up. Pedro isn't happy Man is a man, but he agrees to give him a ride when he compliments his car.

Pedro tells Man he plays in a new band that needs a drummer. Man is a drummer. Pedro and Man get stoned on an enormous joint Man has. Then they take acid. When police drive up, Man starts to eat all his dope. He throws up on Pedro's lap. They are busted. Man almost collapses in the court. He is given the judge's glass of water, which turns out to be vodka.

When band rehearsal doesn't go well, Pedro and Man realize that they must get stoned in order to make good music. They search the town for dope. They go to Pedro's cousin's house. Strawberry, a war vet, takes Pedro off to get dope and starts imagining he's in Vietnam. Meanwhile Man winds up in a party at Strawberry's that is busted by Sergeant Stedenko and his three-man team. Pedro rescues Man.

Pedro and Man go to Tijuana. To get back to L.A. they agree to drive a van across the border. They do not know that the van is made out of Fibreweed—pure marijuana. Stedenko sets up a guard at the border, knowing that a shipment is coming through, but he mistakenly stops a car full of nuns. When he realizes it is the van that is made out of marijuana, Stedenko gives chase. He is foiled by his own clumsy assistants and by Pedro, who swerves into the traffic going in the opposite direction in order to pick up two female hitchhikers. Well-built Debbie and Pedro get into the back of the van for some physical pleasures. Meanwhile, incoherent Jade East talks and talks to Man as he drives. She carries a case full of pills. Everyone they drive past, including a traffic cop, becomes stoned because the fumes of the exhaust pipe blow marijuana at them.

Back in L.A. Pedro and Man and the band enter a "Rock Fight of the Century" against numerous punk bands at the Roxy. Stedenko and his men fail to bust them but they do arrest the two well-dressed crooks who planned the van operation. However, while everyone stands outside the van, a fire starts and the fumes blow over them. The police become stoned and devour pizza while the crooks, in handcuffs, go down the street to get something to eat.

Marijuana fumes blow into the Roxy. So when the Alice Bowie Band, which Pedro and Man are part of, comes on stage, the initial boos become cheers. Turned on by the dope, Pedro, in a tutu, sings a punk song and the crowd loves the group. They shout for more.

A success, Pedro and the Man drive along the Pacific Highway talking about their music career. Man drops hash into Pedro's lap and the car swerves back and forth across the road.

For the uninitiated: Robert "Cheech" Marin, a Chicano, left America for Canada in the late sixties, during the peak war years. In Canada, he played music with several bands and pursued a career as an actor. He auditioned at a Vancouver nightspot called Shanghai Junk, which was owned by Tommy Chong, a Canadian-born Chinese. (Marin thought Chong a Hell's Angel and Chong thought Marin an Indian.) Chong had played guitar with a Motown group called Bobby Taylor and the Vancouvers but had quit the band to turn this family nightclub into a hip club where his improv company, City Works, performed nightly. The revue comprised three topless dancers, a mime artist, a classical guitarist, and a weird assortment of improv actors from the hippie community. City Works did well, but finally broke up in 1969, and Cheech and Chong formed a singing-comedy act in the City Works tradition. Their initial success was at a "Battle of the Bands" in Vancouver where their comedy stole the show from the standard hard rock bands. This debut was reconstructed for the finale of *Up in Smoke*. In pursuit of stardom, Cheech and Chong left Vancouver for L.A., where they played several clubs and within a short time developed a strong local following. Producer Lou Adler signed them to a record deal and in 1972 they started their quick climb to the top of the music industry—their advantage was that they were the *only* band that did comedy. Irreverent comedy, about drugs and sex. Gross, too. Many top-selling albums later, Cheech and Chong, now cult figures, moved into films, writing and starring in *Up in Smoke*, directed by Lou Adler. How successful was their transition? Within one month the film grossed twenty million dollars, and that was before its national release. In its second month, it combined with *National Lampoon's Animal House* (1978) to earn 23 percent of the movie business's total profits.

The Christian Science Monitor called *Up in Smoke* "a new entry in the worst-movie-ever-made sweepstakes." But it wasn't *The Christian Science Monitor* that kept me from seeing *Up in Smoke* for more than two years. I stayed away because of my preconceptions about Cheech and Chong, whose work (which I had never seen or heard on record) I knew was geared for the drug segment of the counterculture. As a rule I detest comedians who know they can get easy laughs simply by mentioning the word *marijuana*, and I doubted my ability to sit through one and a half hours of a picture whose slogan "Don't come straight to this movie" conjured up images of one "hilarious" scene after another of people getting stoned on screen while dopers in the audience make giggly noises to let on that they are having the same experiences. But I finally saw *Up in Smoke*—spurred on by the much better reviews given *Cheech and Chong's Next Movie* (1980)—and to my surprise I rather liked it. It's a terribly made movie, no doubt, where entire scenes seem to be missing, where good gags are lost among the dross, where actors garble their dialogue, where one improvisational bit after another falls flat. Yet I laughed. Even at, or especially at, the scatological and drug-related humor that I dreaded.

While riding in Pedro's "Love Machine," Man (L) and Pedro smoke a gigantic marijuana cigarette.

It's *somehow* funny when Pedro/Cheech takes his morning leak and halfway through it the camera moves a bit so we see he is using the laundry hamper because the toilet is clogged up; when Pedro becomes ill from a Tijuana burrito and rushes to find a bathroom in a noisy upholstery factory where he can't hear anyone's directions, finally finding someone else using the toilet who he is sure had the same burritos; when Chong urinates on Sergeant Stedenko's pants. And it's *somehow* funny when Chong lights up a joint that is as big as a fat stick of dynamite; when Chong tells Cheech, who smokes the joint, that the marijuana seeds were mixed with dog excrement; when Chong informs Cheech that he gave him the wrong pills which, naturally, Cheech has already swallowed; when several nuns are mistakenly searched by border guards for marijuana while Cheech and Chong are the real unwary transporters of the evil weed; when the police dog that sniffs their Fibreweed-made van ends up a stiff on its back; when a young woman thinks a plate of Ajax is cocaine and sniffs it all up, makes several great distorted expressions, and declares, "Great shit."

After Chong gets some slime off his beard, both he and Cheech become amiable characters. Interesting to watch. They're harmless affronts to society. Slobs beyond compare—never has a picture been such a homage to filth. If they had to have a slogan, I'd just take the word "always" out of Gene Kelly's "Dignity—always dignity" in *Singin' in the Rain* (1952) and insert the word "never." They're losers but they're too stoned to realize it—and they're such nice guys you don't want to tell them. Chong, the taller of the two, is oblivious to everything. He's either getting high, passing out, or throwing up—there's little more to his life. Cheech is the funnier of the two and ideally Chong should be his straight man—but it was decided that both should be comic figures so there could be humor when only one is

on the screen. Cheech is more emotional than his partner, and more of a worrier. Unlike Chong, he is woman-crazy and a nonstop talker. (In an odd way, he looks like he should be a braggart, but this isn't the case—both characters are completely honest.) Invariably, his conversation eventually gets around to one of two topics: scoring dope and his privates. Particularly funny is when he tries to urinate while Stedenko washes his hands in the police lavatory and without hesitation starts telling the policeman—a stranger—what a hard time he's having ("My dick has stage fright, man").

Like many good comedians, Cheech and Chong intentionally write lines that make no sense. As when Pedro tells the band to wear "different uniforms that are the same." Or when Chong complains that so many people are smoking marijuana that it's impossible to find it. Chong's one-track marijuana-driven mind is revealed

Sergeant Stedenko is out to get Pedro and Man, no matter how much he suffers.

Pedro and Man, driving a truck made out of marijuana fibre, pick up hitchhikers Debbie (L) and Jade East.

in an illogical conversation with Pedro. Talking of his cousin Strawberry, Pedro says: "He went to Vietnam and came back weirded out." Chong thinks he understands: "Nam grass can do weird things to you."

Of course, there are the obligatory bumbling policemen who are out to bust our heroes. Their roles are

Cheech and Chong sing and do comedy as Pedro and Man win the "Rock Fight of the Century."

limited, but I think straight-faced Stacey Keach and his three-man crew do a fine job. The three subordinates are funny asking Sergeant Stedenko questions as if they were three dogs after the same bone. I also like a bit where the dumbest of the group, Harry (who makes rabbit ears on Sergeant Stedenko's movie screen) puts a bullet in the front tire of the police car. Once outside the disabled car he doesn't know whether to run away from the angry Stedenko. He scampers a few inches—the funny part!—toward the highway as if he expects to be whipped. My favorite line in the film is when the stoned Stedenko looks at his stoned assistants, who can't stop eating pizza, and says, "Admit you're the munchies."

Other memorable funny lines in the film include Stedenko saying "I'm stoned!" and Harry, a real square but stoned now, replying "Go with it!" I love the lyrics to Pedro's punk song: "Mama papa talka to me/Try to tell me how to live/But I don't listen to them/'Cause my head is like a sieve." They're even funnier than the title of one punk group's song: "Piss Off!"

Cheech and Chong play characters who are stupid, filthy, lazy, and stoned out of their minds, but because they are such mild, laid-back fellows I don't think that most parents would worry about their children emulating them, especially since they and everyone else in the film, including Chong's parents, are cartoon characters. I would be curious how audiences would watch the film *if*, in Chong's first scene, where Chong burps in the face of and gives the finger to his father, the father character were changed from being a fascist type who wants Chong "to cozy up to the Finkelstein boy" to a really nice, decent guy. If they would still cheer the burp and the finger, then parents *would* have something to worry about.

Vertigo

1958 Paramount
Director: Alfred Hitchcock
Producer: Alfred Hitchcock
Screenplay: Alex Coppel and
Samuel Taylor
From the novel *D'Entre les*
Morts (Death Enters) by Pierre
Boileau and Thomas Narcejac
Cinematography: Robert Burks
Music: Bernard Herrmann
Editor: George Tomasini
Running Time: 123 minutes

Cast: James Stewart (John "Scottie" Ferguson), Kim Novak (Madeleine Elster/Judy Barton), Barbara Bel Geddes (Midge), Tom Helmore (Gavin Elster), Henry Jones (coroner), Raymond Bailey (doctor), Ellen Corby (manager), Konstantin Shayne (Pop Leibel)

Synopsis: While chasing a culprit across a San Francisco roof, police detective John "Scottie" Ferguson slips and finds himself dangling from a drain pipe high above the street. A cop tries to save him and falls to his death. Scottie suddenly develops acrophobia, a fear of heights, experiencing vertigo when he looks down.

Because of his vertigo, Scottie retires from the force. He spends time with his friend, and former fiancée, commercial artist Midge. She broke off the engagement because he didn't reciprocate her love. Trying to help him back to normalcy, she tells him to rejoin the force. He refuses, and her hope is that another emotional shock will cure his vertigo.

Scottie agrees to shadow the wife of a college chum, Gavin Elster. Elster says his wife, Madeleine, has been acting mysteriously, believing that she is possessed by the spirit of Carlotta, a mad ancestor she resembles. He fears that like Carlotta she will end her life by suicide. As Scottie follows Madeleine, an elegant, beautiful blonde, he falls in love with her. When she attempts to drown herself in the bay, Scottie rescues her and brings her back to his apartment. They start spending more and more time together, going to many of San Francisco's historic sites. Madeleine remains mysterious to Scottie. She talks constantly of death. She gets Scottie to take her to the mission at San Juan Batista, which she says she dreams about. It is from there Carlotta jumped to her death. Madeleine impulsively climbs the tower. Because of his vertigo, Scottie cannot follow her all the way to the top. He sees her form flying past the window. A still body lies dead on the roof below.

Scottie goes insane mourning for his lost Madeleine. Even Midge can't help, and she is forced to walk out of his life. When Scottie slightly recovers he visits all the places he had been with Madeleine, hoping he will find her there—still alive. One day Scottie spots a shopgirl named Judy Barton. She has red hair and dresses much differently from Madeleine, but her resemblance to Madeleine is uncanny. He starts courting Judy. Judy flashes back—to when she was Madeleine. To when she really fell in love with Scottie. To when she was Elster's mistress. To when, as Madeleine, she ran up the tower and, as Elster had guessed, Scottie could not follow. To when she reached the top of the tower and screamed as Elster pushed his real wife from the tower. Elster had needed an unimpeachable witness who would tell police that his wife committed suicide and Scottie was the chump. Scottie starts buying Judy clothes like those that Madeleine wore. He makes her change her hair to blonde. He takes her to all the places he went with Madeleine. Judy goes along with Scottie's demands because she loves him, but she is frightened about what he will discover. She is also terribly upset because Scottie still loves Madeleine, who didn't really exist, and ignores her, Judy Barton. Scottie gets Judy to put her hair up like Madeleine's was. The transformation is complete. He believes he has Madeleine back. But suddenly he realizes that Judy owns Carlotta's locket, which belonged to Madeleine. He now realizes that Judy was Madeleine, there was no real Madeleine, and that he had been played for a fool. He drags Judy to the mission. His vertigo gone, he pulls her up the stairs. But he cannot bring himself to push her from the tower. A nun appears and Judy is startled. She falls from the tower to her death. Scottie looks down with his mouth wide open.

What he loved in her—and it had been so all along—was . . . it was difficult to explain . . . was that she wasn't real.
—from *D'Entre les Morts*, by Pierre Boileau and Thomas Narcejac

In dreams it is common for our dream images of ourselves to fall from great heights, but, thankfully, we automatically wake up before we watch ourselves crash to the ground, before our dream images are killed. I am reminded of this phenomenon in the opening of Alfred Hitchcock's *Vertigo*. Detective John "Scottie" Ferguson dangles by his fingertips "Perils of Pauline"-style from a collapsing drainpipe high above the San Francisco streets. A fellow cop tries to save him but plummets past him to his death far below—as if he had been snatched away by death, who actually had come for Scottie, and by luck Scottie had been spared. Guilty that it wasn't he who was killed and terrified that he might also fall, the traumatized Scottie is understandably overcome with vertigo, a debilitating dizziness that occurs at great heights. A defense against facing reality. It is a real phobia (acrophobia) that Scottie suffers at this moment, but its vertigo characteristic is used metaphorically to underline the fact (I believe) that Scottie—the

Scottie hangs precariously from a breaking drainpipe.
He experiences vertigo.

Scottie brings Madeleine back to his apartment after saving her from drowning.

world spinning before his eyes—has, at least temporarily, lost the ability to distinguish between reality and illusion. If not actually dreaming as he hangs high off the ground, he has certainly withdrawn into a dreamlike state. To get out of it—to wake up as we do from our dreams—he must *fall*. Presumedly Scottie is rescued, but it is noteworthy that such a rescue is never shown in the film *or* discussed; moreover, we don't see any cops around who might save him before the drainpipe gives way. Significantly, Hitchcock cuts away while Scottie is still hanging. By leaving him suspended in midair, the director chooses to keep him in his dream state. He only allows Scottie to finally "wake up"—and simultaneously overcome his vertigo—when Madeleine/Judy accidentally falls to her death from the church tower. Scottie *identifies* with Madeleine—we see this in his midfilm nightmare (a nightmare within a dream?) when he sinks into *her* (and Carlotta's) grave and when he *falls* from the tower instead of her—because she represents the death he craves and courts (and falls in love with). So her death by a fall is *the same* as his letting go of the drainpipe: it allows him to wake up—to overcome his vertigo and his guilt. A scene could even be added at the end in which Scottie is back on the drainpipe and is either rescued (signifying his vertigo has been cured) or falls (signifying his dream—the film—is over).

The absence of such a final scene implies that Hitchcock didn't intend *Vertigo* to be taken as a dream per se. But until Judy has the revealing flashback in which we learn that Elster's real wife was thrown from the tower and that Judy had been pretending to be an invented character (Madeleine) to fool Scottie and help Elster, the picture is most definitely filmed (hauntingly by Robert Burks) as if it were a series of events interpreted by the tormented Scottie while in the afore-

mentioned dream state. (The moody score by Bernard Herrmann heightens our belief that we have left the conscious world.)

To be precise, *Vertigo* is *not* a dream but a mystifying story of a man who while hanging on a collapsing drainpipe enters an existence between life and death. Fear tells Scottie to hold on, but his tremendous guilt, brought about by the cop dying in his place, tells him to take the easy way out of his misery and let go. His death wish takes the form of his pursuit of Madeleine, who he believes is equally possessed by death. As he was pulled from death's grasp when rescued from the roof, she is pulled from its clutches when Scottie drags her from the ocean. (In the novel on which *Vertigo* is based, the ex-detective gives Pauline, the Madeleine counterpart, the nickname of Eurydice.) As Scottie quits the police department and lets his life come to a total halt, Madeleine looks not toward the future but backward, to *before* she was alive. She visits graveyards, art galleries, old houses and churches, gazes into the ageless waters, and sits among the centuries-old Sequoias. Her conversation is mostly about death (her own) and she claims to be possessed by Carlotta, a mad ancestor who committed suicide as she, herself, expects to do. Her ethereal, mysterious, trancelike aura—how perfectly cast is Kim Novak!—makes her come across as being almost a ghost; and when Scottie makes the earthy Judy assume the look of the ethereal Madeleine, and she emerges from the bathroom with a green neon light flashing on her, Scottie believes that Madeleine's ghost has indeed returned. (Seeing Carlotta's locket tells him, however, that Madeleine never existed to begin with—just Judy Barton.)

When Scottie and Judy visit the same places in San Francisco—what better town, considering the steep streets, for a character to be given vertigo—where Scottie had gone with Madeleine during their romance, he thinks it is Judy's first time at these locales, but both naive Scottie and we viewers (who know Judy was Madeleine) experience déjà vu. Burks's eerie camerawork has the effect of making it seem like the past and present are mingling, like Scottie and Judy aren't really in the same *time* as the other people in these surroundings. With Madeleine "dead," Scottie is the one who becomes obsessed with the past—to the time when Madeleine was alive. The more he tries to remake Judy in Madeleine's image, the greater his obsession becomes. What attracted Hitchcock to the project, in fact, is that Scottie wants to indulge in necrophilia, by resurrecting a dead woman (Madeleine) and making love to her. (The novel ends with the ex-detective going off to prison after having strangled the girl, but stopping to kiss her still form and telling her, "I'll wait for you," as if he were about to die while she went on living.) As the film progresses it becomes increasingly clear that Scottie and Madeleine/Judy are the only ones who inhabit the world that lies between complete life and complete death, where reality and illusion overlap. Hitchcock emphasizes their *isolation* so that they eventually seem to be having their little romance/nightmare while the rest of the world goes on its merry way. And Scottie is

Scottie tries to change Judy into Madeleine, not knowing that there really was no Madeleine.

content with their privacy, as he excludes everyone else from his life, including his best friend and ex-fiancée Midge. This is Hitchcock's way of saying that, given a choice of women, weak men will choose the helpless (Madeleine, who seems to need Scottie to save her) over the independent (Midge, who tries to help Scottie), the mysterious over the honest, the sexy (Madeleine and Judy, like actress Novak, don't wear bras) over the plain Janes (Midge paints brassieres), the frigid over the accessible, and the illusionary over the real and tangible. Once out of her Madeleine act, Judy is reluctant to be drawn back into that spooky world through which Madeleine sleepwalked. But Scottie, who for some reason she has grown to love, is persuasive. Again she dresses up like Madeleine, changes her red hair to blond, and puts that hair up; and she reenters the arena in which death selects and rejects it victims and, as fate would have it, dies.

The section in which the obsessed Scottie tries to resurrect Madeleine by remaking Judy—thereby removing his guilt over having allowed Madeleine's "death" and, at the same time, giving himself a "second chance"—is painful to watch. We want Scottie to realize, as we do, that Judy was Madeleine and that Madeleine was just an illusion, a fabricated character concocted by Elster and his then-mistress Judy; but we are afraid of how his fragile mind will react to such a disappointing disclosure. We are helpless as he keeps getting more and more obsessed, and out of frustration we turn away from him. (Our guilt from having failed to save him is perhaps meant to impress us with the strength of the guilt Scottie feels for having let the cop and then Madeleine die.) It is hard to watch our "hero" disintegrate into a character we cannot stand (which is why many viewers don't like *Vertigo*). As for Judy, we despise the cruel trick she played on Scottie, but we sense she was Elster's pawn. And her suffering is so great—Judy loves Scottie, who cannot return her love because he is mad about the nonexistent Madeleine— we must feel solace for her. Moreover, as Madeleine, she revealed all the fine potentialities that are kept deep within the simple Judy. That Hitchcock shows how a crude, classless shopgirl can be transformed into the refined, erudite Madeleine is perhaps the director's statement regarding the "illusion of the movie star." (He might wrongly have considered Kim Novak a case in point.) But Hitchcock makes a mistake in implying that Judy is hesitant to go back to being Madeleine because she fears being unmasked. We would rather believe that she is afraid of disappointing Scottie by being an inferior Madeleine the second time around; or that she senses returning to Madeleine's death-obsessed world will

Midge consoles the tormented Scottie; she too needs consoling, but he is not up to giving it to her.

mean she will be tempting death for a second time; or that she ("You don't even want to touch *me*," Judy tells Scottie) is afraid of losing her own identity. It is obvious that she wants to remain Judy when she subconsciously reveals the Madeleine hoax by asking Scottie to link Carlotta's locket around her neck; if she were thinking, she would realize that the sight of the locket would link her in Scottie's eyes with Madeleine.

Hitchcock is the master of red herrings—taking his audience on wild-goose chases. And the first two thirds of *Vertigo*—up until the flashback—is Hitchcock's greatest red herring. During this time, because of the subjective-camera approach, we are led to believe that *Vertigo* is a *mystery*. Because Scottie is a detective, we believe at the beginning that he is our conventional movie hero. We assume at first that he will unravel the mystery. But when we are surprisingly shown the flashback we are thrown entirely off balance, as if we had come down with a case of vertigo. There is no more mystery! Scottie can only find out what we already know. At this point, the film ceases to be a mystery, ceases to be subjective, and becomes what it really always has been: a psychological study—from our point of view—of Scottie, whose obsession will lead him to a discovery that we don't want him to make, and of Judy, who experienced a great love (for Scottie) as Madeleine, and must now help Scottie discover that she is the one responsible for his torment—which will cause her to lose his love forever.

By completely reversing the perspective of the picture, Hitchcock boldly chanced losing the moviegoers who loved the mystery. But it is the audaciousness of Hitchcock's story line and structure, as well as the fact that *Vertigo* is *more* than a mystery, that excites modern critics, the film's cultists.

I agree that the structure of *Vertigo* is brilliant and that the flashback should be revealed early in order for us to become detached enough ("alienated") to at least attempt to understand the thoughts of Judy, as well as

Scottie. But I tend to go along with most moviegoers, who think the last part of the picture is disappointing nonetheless. That Elster's murder plot is ludicrous is irrelevant. But as I said earlier, I think it is a problem for the average viewer that Scottie, with whom we are no longer allowed, or want, to identify with, becomes so cruel, so despicable, that we no longer care how he will react to Judy having posed as Madeleine. In fact, we don't even want to see Scottie on the screen (which I think is the fault of James Stewart, otherwise the cinema's one faultless actor). Whether we like it or not, for us the mystery remains what matters most—and that was revealed too early in the picture. When Judy falls from the tower to her death, it is too pat and too moral (complete with a nun coming out of nowhere to spook her). By this point, we have long given up on Scottie and have started rooting for Judy who, as played by Novak, is so hurt, so insecure, and so fragile that if you yelled at her she'd crumble. The ending is unsatisfying because the *wrong* person dies. It is as the ex-detective thinks in the novel: "For in the last resort, it was [I] who belonged to the dead, she to the living."

Realizing that Judy had been part of Elster's hoax, Scottie takes her to the tower from which he once believed Madeleine had jumped to her death.

The Warriors

1979 Paramount
Director: Walter Hill
Producer: Lawrence Gordon
Screenplay: David Shaberd and Walter Hill
Based on a novel by Sol Yurick
Cinematography: Andrew Laszlo
Music: Barry De Vorzon
Editor: David Holden
Running Time: 95 minutes

Cast: Michael Beck (Swan), James Remar (Ajax), Deborah Van Valkenburgh (Mercy), David Patrick Kelly (Luther), Thomas Waites (Fox), Dorsey Wright (Cleon), Brian Tyler (Snow), David Harris (Cochise), Tom McKitterick (Cowboy), Marcelino Sanchez (Rembrandt), Terry Michos (Vermin), Roger Hill (Cyrus), Lynn Thigpen (dj)

Synopsis: It is night in New York City. Nine unarmed delegates of the youth gang the Warriors board a subway leaving their Coney Island turf and travel to The Bronx, far uptown, unfamiliar territory. The Warriors are only one of a thousand New York street gangs who have sent representatives to a park meeting called by Cyrus, the leader of the most revered gang in the city, the Gramercy Riffs. Cyrus speaks to the huge gathering, explaining that all the gangs must unite, that together they outnumber the police three to one, that together they can take over New York. There is wild cheering and some grumbling among the listeners. Then Cyrus is assassinated by Luther, the crazed leader of the Rogues. Luther yells out that it was Cleon, the Warrior's leader, who killed Cyrus. While police swarm into the park and the various gangs flee, Cleon is killed by those who think he murdered Cyrus.

Without their leader, the Warriors attempt to make the long journey back to Brooklyn. Swan assumes command. Of his followers only Ajax gives him trouble. Meanwhile, every gang in the city is alerted to be on the lookout for the Warriors, the gang that broke the truce.

The journey back home is filled with adventure. The Warriors alternately fight and defeat the Orphans, Baseball Furies, Lizzies (a lesbian gang), and Punks. Their only casualties come in battles with the police: Fox falls under a train and is killed; the sex-crazed Ajax tries to pick up a woman—actually a decoy cop—in a park and is arrested. Along the way, Swan meets Mercy, a tough-talking girl who follows the gang back to Coney Island. The two squabble a lot but eventually make peace, even fall in love.

In the morning the Warriors arrive back in Coney Island. But it is not safe. The Rogues have followed them home. Luther tries to shoot Swan, but Swan is too quick, sending his switchblade into Luther's wrist. Thousands of Gramercy Riffs suddenly swarm onto the beach, but not to attack the Warriors. They have been told that it was the Rogues who were responsible for Cyrus's death. Acknowledging that the Warriors are an exceptional gang, the Riffs surround the doomed Rogues. The Warriors walk off, triumphant in that they have proved themselves great "warriors," but defeated in that they are literally back where they have started: nowhere.

Paramount's initial poster ad for *The Warriors* featured a picture of a few hundred fearsome gang members looking straight at us defiantly, with a caption that began: "These are the Armies of the Night. They are 100,000 strong. They outnumber the cops five to one. They could run New York City." Now, this is scary stuff—especially if you live in New York City and happen to see the poster a long subway ride from home. If this ad did indeed properly reflect the theme of the picture it was promoting, then *The Warriors* could correctly be called an *inciteful* film—as many outraged citizens assumed it was after an epidemic of violent gang-related incidents broke out around the country inside and near theaters showing the film. (Most of those who complained about *The Warriors* hadn't seen the film, including a Massachusetts legislator who demanded it be banned in Boston, the site of one of three deaths he directly attributed to its showing.) But as the many moviegoers, who flocked to the theater to see what all the commotion was about, soon discovered, *The Warriors* is a lively, well-made action film full of adventure and humor, no more violent than the film down the block, not inciteful, not deserving of the furor that it had caused. The cult for the film—the result of enthusiasts rallying behind a film good enough to deserve defending—charged that the ad was misleading. Perhaps 100,000 strong could take over New York City as easily as the roaches have, but in *The Warriors* they are no threat to *us* at all—in fact *we* essentially do not exist in the fantasy world we see on screen. As the cultists charged, it was the ad, not the film, which drew excitable, undesirable elements to the theater. It was their presence alone, and not the fact that anything *inciteful* was taking place on the screen, that resulted in trouble. Acceding to pressure, Paramount removed the irresponsible picture from the poster, thereby assuring all concerned that the 100,000 strong were after a gang, the Warriors, and were leaving us alone.

Sol Yurick's 1965 novel, from which the film was adapted, begins with a foreword from Xenophon's *Anabasis*, an account of how a band of Greek warriors whose leader was killed made its way back home from Persia. Ironically, it is the film, by no means the novel, which parallels *Anabasis*. Film director Walter Hill's warriors, a youth gang called the Warriors, exhibit qualities characteristic of classical heroes: gallantry, self-pride, loyalty, discipline, resourcefulness, and most of all, the ability to fight. These are characters about which legends are told, epic poems written, movies made. On the other end of the spectrum is Yurick's youth gang, the Dominators, a bunch of punk kids who are frauds—they only *play* at being soldiers. Yurick has no respect for them at all, making them so ignorant that they can't figure out how to read a subway map, giving them such names as Lunkface, Bimbo, Arnold, and The Junior. (If he had made the movie, Yurick might well have renamed Hill's Rembrandt character LeRoy Nieman.) Yurick's gang members are cowards, afraid to look anyone in the eye, talking big but avoiding trouble and confrontations at all costs, even fearing a couple of

The notorious poster from The Warriors, *minus the inciteful words about how gangs could take over New York City.*

The Warriors ride the subway to The Bronx. Passengers become part of the background.

high school football players on a subway. They are not resourceful, hoping at first to get back to Brooklyn, not by using their wits, but by calling their youth worker and having him pick them up. They are not loyal to their gang, as shown when the three highest in command remove their insignia so no one will recognize them. They don't try to prove their gallantry by fighting rival gangs—they don't fight any rival gangs—but by challenging each other to foolish contests to see which of them can urinate the farthest or who can put his head closest to the wall outside their moving subway.

Two scenes that take place in both the movie and the novel best illustrate the difference between Hill's attitude and Yurick's. In the movie, only Ajax is foolhardy enough to postpone his perilous journey home to try to make it with a pretty woman in the park, later to find out too late that she is a decoy cop. (It's like that great cartoon by *Mad*'s Don Martin in which a marvelous dog survives numerous perils in the wilderness only to be snatched by the dog catcher the minute before he reaches his destination in town.) In the book, the two boys ahead of Lunkface in the chain of command join him in his attempt to make it with an alcoholic old nurse in the park, consequently getting arrested with him. Again, in the movie, the leader of a two-bit gang foolishly tries to impress Swan with news clippings he carries around of his gang's activities, while Swan tries to keep a straight face and audiences chuckle. In the novel, Hector, the leader of the Dominators, also foolishly pulls out some clippings. Yurick's Dominators are so stupid that it's a miracle that even three of them make it back to Brooklyn.

Yurick's novel is very downbeat, set in a decaying New York, full of pimps, whores, drug addicts (as well as those addicted to the racetrack), crazies, the destitute. The hero, Hinton, with whom Yurick seems to sympathize because he's a creative kid stuck with a gang far beneath him, dreams of an office job, marrying a nice girl, and having a family. But his future is bleak, even hopeless. At the end of the book he returns to his mother's apartment building called The Prison, his twentieth home in his fifteen years, and falls asleep on the fire escape, his thumb lodged in his mouth. He is stuck in a lousy, unfeeling city, where things are so bad that even gangs don't intimidate anyone. A man yells at the Dominators: "You punks think you own the street!" Fourteen years later, Hill's movie gangs *do* own New York. But not in the real sense. In Yurick's novel, the gang looks at a New York subway map and finds it too abstract to read. Well, that map fits the New York of the

The Baseball Furies, one of the gimmicky gangs that the Warriors defeat on their journey home.

film, for now it is the city itself which is abstract. Yurick's New York was gray in tone; Hill's is full of bright colors, shining lights, gaudy designs, like one big amusement park.

From the opening blood-red titles, which move toward us as the camera pulls back along subway tracks (thus simulating a startling 3-D effect), we are aware that we are out of Yurick's realistic world and in a surreal, fantasy New York, a playground for numerous tribes (called gangs) which stake out territories and march

Swan and his new girlfriend, Mercy, arrive in Coney Island.

Although they make it safely back to Coney Island, the Warriors are still in danger.
Crazy Luther points a gun at Swan, but neither Swan nor the other Warriors will panic.

around in garish, identifying costumes, brandishing weapons and spray paint with which to decorate everything in their paths. The civilized people of today don't really exist, only appearing occasionally, and without consequence, as if they inadvertently had stumbled onto the movie set. It is a dream world—Pauline Kael suggests that the comic-book-reading character of the novel fantasized this whole tale—an enormous arena of parks and empty subway tunnels, the perfect obstacle course for the Warriors to prove their worth, as unreal as MGM's old Tarzan jungle trails.

Hill's Warriors are participants in a sporting contest, analogous to a baseball game. They must leave home (Brooklyn) and return home in order to "score points" with the other gangs of the city. The subways —neutral territory in Yurick's book—are Hill's bases. Between the bases—between the times the Warriors safely return to the subways—they do battle, respectively, with four gangs, one for each baseline. The police are another tribe, the Men in Blue who serve as umpires and remove all rulebreakers from the game. There is even a play-by-play announcer, a female dj with the compassion of Tokyo Rose, who refers to the Orphans as a minor-league team. The next gang the Warriors confront actually wear baseball uniforms. The Baseball Furies are made up like the rock music group Kiss but wear New York Yankee pinstripes and carry bats for weapons. They are certainly major league, but though they look and swing like the Yanks they connect like the Mets, and the Warriors soon leave them in their wake.

The fight between the Warriors and the Baseball Furies reveals two things: the Warriors, despite their fragile appearance, can outfight anybody; the film is bloodless. In Hill's nifty, stylized world, the violence is cartoonlike, with characters brutally beaten a minute earlier getting up perfectly intact. (This is certainly much tamer than Hill's boxing film, *Hard Times*, 1975.) Only one character actually dies *on the screen*, a small quotient for a film that was the object of such a huge anti-violence-in-film campaign. While you will feel every blow thrown, once you are assured that no one will start spouting blood in front of your eyes you can relax and watch some terrific action, the best-staged fight sequences since the death of Bruce Lee, far better choreographed than those dances thrown on the screen by Twyla Tharp for *Hair* (1979) and Patricia Birch for *Grease* (1978).

Choosing to be anti-intellectual at the expense of losing Yurick's social relevance, *The Warriors*, artistically, is an uneven film to say the least, but it is so full of unbridled energy and drive, with frenetic pacing from beginning to end, that it's hard not to root harder for it to succeed than those bigger-budgeted films with more "socially" acceptable protagonists. It's a film that'll make you cringe at times, but you'll forgive the shortcomings and praise the exciting camerawork, the excellent use of music, and the oddly conceived performance of David Patrick Kelly, the best wacko villain since Andy Robinson in *Dirty Harry* (1971). The great moment in the film is when Kelly's Luther coaxes the Warriors out of hiding by whining over and over, "Warriors, come out and playay!" By the third time he says "playay," while clicking together three soda bottles that he's stuck over his fingers like castanets, any audience will collectively grit its teeth—as if someone were scraping his fingernails on a blackboard.

Where's Poppa?

1970   United Artists
Director: Carl Reiner
Producers: Jerry Tokofsky and Marvin Worth
Screenplay: Robert Klane
From the novel by Robert Klane
Cinematography: Jack Priestly
Music: Jack Elliott
Lyrics: Norman Gimbel
Songs: "Where's Poppa?" sung by Clydie
King; "Move It!" and "Freedom" sung by
Mr. June Jackson; "Pleasure Palace" sung
by Bright Cheerstrap; "The Goodbye
Song" sung by Harry "Sweets" Edison
Editors: Bud Molin and Chic Ciccolini
Running Time: 87 minutes

Cast: George Segal (Gordon Hocheiser),
Ruth Gordon (Mrs. Hocheiser), Ron
Leibman (Sidney Hocheiser), Trish Van
Devere (Louise Callan), Bernard Hughes
(Colonel Hendriks), Vincent Gardenia
(Coach Williams), Rae Allen (Gladys
Hocheiser), Paul Sorvino (owner of Gus
and Grace's Home), Rob Reiner (Roger),
Joe Keyes, Jr. (gang leader), Garrett
Morris (Garrett)

Gordon tries to amuse his senile mother by dressing in a gorilla suit. But she becomes frightened and slugs him in the crotch.

Snopsis: Gordon Hocheiser is a New York lawyer who lives with his senile mother. She ruins his life, but he won't put her in a home because of a promise he made to his father on his deathbed. His mother doesn't realize Poppa is dead and constantly asks for him.

Because Gordon's brother Sidney is married and won't take care of their mother, Gordon hires nurses. However, they all quit after spending time with her. This makes Gordon very upset—especially when he has romantic designs on a nurse.

Gordon hires Louise to be Mrs. Hocheiser's nurse. They immediately fall in love. Gordon asks her to come for dinner. Mrs. Hocheiser will be present.

Mrs. Hocheiser offends Louise so much she flees from the apartment. Gordon calls Sidney and tells him to come over before he kills their mother. Sidney runs through Central Park. A gang stops him and robs him of his clothes. Sidney arrives at Gordon's and promises to take on more of the burden of their mother's welfare. Gordon gives him a gorilla outfit to put on.

Louise returns. Again they try to have dinner. Mrs. Hocheiser pulls down her son's pants and kisses him on the "tush." Louise runs out. Gordon calls Sidney, who runs through the park in his gorilla outfit. The gang stops him and makes him participate in a rape.

Gordon goes to the police station to get Sidney out of jail. It turned out he raped a policeman in drag. The cop has given Sidney flowers and won't press charges. Sidney wants to leave the cop his phone number. Gordon is falling apart. He can't conduct himself properly in court, where he defends a coach who snatches ten-year-old kids without permission of their parents. Louise visits him in court. She says she is going back to Illinois because she can't compete with Gordon's mother.

Gordon packs up all of Mrs. Hocheiser's belongings, including her breakfast dishes. He tells her he is taking her to see Poppa. Gordon and Louise drive her to Gus and Grace's Home for the Aged. Gordon wants to leave his mother there but the place is too despicable. They take her to a very nice home. Gordon signs the papers. He grabs an old man who happens by. The man looks at Mrs. Hocheiser and asks "Momma?" Mrs. Hocheiser asks "Poppa?" Gordon and Louise jump back into the car and drive off.

United Artists re-releases *Where's Poppa?* every couple of years, announcing the return of "the funniest picture ever made." I think it is a long way from that, yet there are numerous fans of the film who insist U.A.'s mighty claim is true. More accurately, *Where's Poppa?* is a terrifically acted, unevenly directed, wild, absurd comedy-fantasy that is hilarious one moment, amusing the next, and foolish the moment after that. The outrageous, purposely tasteless humor that gives the picture its distinction also leaves it open for critical jibes that it is trying for cheap laughs. I don't believe the picture is as "brave" as U.A. would like us to believe in bringing a new type of anything-goes comedy to the cinema, but, on the other hand, I think its outrageousness is far more intellectually conceived than the laugh-at-all-costs *Animal House* (1978) spinoffs. *Where's Poppa?* isn't a guaranteed crowd pleaser, but you may be taken with it if you see it when your mood is *exactly* right. Otherwise, be prepared to sit there without changing your expression.

Robert Klane adapted the screenplay from his novel, which came out soon before the picture's release. Carl Reiner worked with Klane on the script, adding dimension to the cartoonlike characters found in the book and giving the satirical swipes at New York, urban life, the judicial system, and homes for the aged a bit more strength. It is easy to see why Reiner was attracted

Gordon comforts Louise. Within five seconds after meeting, they are in love.

to Klane's offbeat, irreverent story. His first film as director, *Enter Laughing* (1961), based on his autobiographical novel, also deals with a Jewish schnook whose entry into love and manhood is hampered by an overly possessive mother. But whereas Reiner revealed more affection than irritation toward Shelley Winters in that film, he is downright mean toward Gordon's senile mother, played by Ruth Gordon with her characteristic lack of inhibitions. Mrs. Hocheiser has, in Reiner's eyes, no redeeming qualities. None. She is not capable of acquiring our empathy, even when Gordon threatens to put her in an old-age home. This is one Jewish mother who deserves anything she gets. When Gordon tries to cheer her up by dressing in a gorilla outfit, she punches him in the crotch. She gripes constantly about wanting to see Poppa, although he is long dead. She sits an inch away from the television set and constantly uses a channel switcher. Every morning she makes Gordon slice an orange into six pieces; she eats them with Lucky Charms soaked in Coke. This could all be tolerated, except for the fact that she ruins all of Gordon's romances. When he invites new love Louise over for dinner, he warns his mother "If you mess this one up for me, I'll punch your heart out!" But such threats don't stop her from eating off Louise's plate, discussing the length of her son's pecker, and yanking his pants down and kissing him on the "tush." In *No Way to Treat a Lady* (1968), Lee Remick wins over Segal's overbearing Jewish mother (Eileen Heckert), and Glenda Jackson does the same with Segal's dominating mother (Maureen Stapleton) in *Lost and Found* (1979), but Louise has no chance with the hopelessly senile Mrs. Hocheiser, whose rude antics at the dinner table twice cause her to run out in disgust.

In the original, unreleased version of the film, Mrs. Hocheiser drove Louise away for a third time and the picture ended with Gordon, having given up hope of

getting rid of his mother, climbing into bed with Mom and pretending to be Poppa. The ending was altered so that now Momma believes she finds Poppa in the home for the aged, and Gordon and Louise drive off together. Reiner insists he didn't make the change because he was afraid viewers would think Gordon committing incest with his mother too vulgar, but because he wanted an upbeat ending. Considering what an intolerable person Mrs. Hocheiser is, this ending, in which she is placed in a home, manages to be upbeat. Our values go out the window as far as Mrs. Hocheiser is concerned.

There are several quite funny moments in the film. Sidney's *Naked Prey* bit, where he races through Central Park with a black gang on his heels, makes those of us who live in New York a bit queasy, but we're glad it's him and not us. We're somewhat annoyed when the gang forces him into raping a prostitute, but if anyone has to be raped we're relieved that it is a male cop in drag who ends up liking the experience and sending Sidney flowers. On Sidney's first trip through the park, he has his clothes stolen. This leads him to borrow Gordon's gorilla outfit for his return home. A cab driver spots him on the curb dressed as a gorilla and also sees a perfectly dressed black lady signaling—and, wouldn't you know it, he picks up Sidney. It's all part of life in New York, where everyone has gone mad.

Perhaps the funniest sequence is when Gordon and Louise meet for the first time. He immediately pictures her in a wedding dress. She sees him as a knight. She had no references to help her get the job of Mrs. Hocheiser's nurse, but Gordon doesn't mind. "Most of my patients have died," she admits. "That's okay," he says. Without hesitation, she tells him she was once married for thirty-two hours. "That's not very long," observes a very interested Gordon. "It was an eternity," she says, as they become increasingly intimate. With no reservations, she tells Gordon that her first lovemaking experience was wonderful, but afterwards she saw that "he had made a caca in the bed." When she had asked her

Sidney tells Gordon that the undercover cop he was forced to rape has sent him flowers.

Mrs. Hocheiser upsets Louise so much that she bursts out crying and flees the apartment.

husband how he could do such a thing, he replied "Doesn't everybody?" Gordon's face shrivels up in disgust and he says, "Son of a bitch!" Louise asks Gordon if he minded her telling him such an intimate story about a minute after they met. He's thrilled she did. They kiss, and Gordon starts to sing "Louise," the old Chevalier tune. And he sings and sings as they continue their embrace. This is not what is known in the Hollywood lexicon as "meeting cute." But it is really funny.

Of course, the best thing about the picture is George Segal. He is the most amiable of actors and one of the few stars audiences allow to be crude and obscene. He has a chance to be both in *Where's Poppa?* as well as sillier than movie heroes are supposed to be. He is remarkably versatile. In David Shipman's *The Great Movie Stars* (A & W Visual Library, 1972), Segal is described as "a new creature in movies—the urban-dweller, the new Manhattanite, buffeting off the new horrors of fun-city with an ironic humor, and pushing aside the roar of the rat-race with a couldn't care less shrug." Part of Segal's charm is that he refuses to fight the world that makes him miserable in a conventional manner. So he always gets in trouble. Anyone who runs around the apartment in a gorilla costume deserves to be punched in the groin. He is a jerk who creates his own misery, the embodiment of everything that is wrong about the world in which he stumbles. Segal gives an entirely new meaning to the word *aggravation*. In *Where's Poppa?*, where his burdens are heavy, his face and eyes wrinkle up. His back sort of crumples up and he looks like he's falling forward. His speech becomes incoherent—as if he hadn't slept in a month. He half smiles, like an idiot who doesn't know what else to do. I can't remember a more believable evocation of a man on his last legs. *Where's Poppa?* isn't Segal's best film by any means, but it allows him a remarkable amount of freedom, and he creates one of his most memorable comedic roles. For that alone, the picture is worth seeing.

The Wild Bunch

1969 Warner Bros.–Seven Arts
Director: Sam Peckinpah
Producer: Phil Feldman
Screenplay: Walon Green and Sam Peckinpah
From a story by Walon Green and Roy N. Sickner
Cinematography: Lucien Ballard
Music: Jerry Fielding
Editor: Louis Lombardo
Running Time: 143 minutes (but this may vary greatly according to the print)

Cast: William Holden (Pike Bishop), Robert Ryan (Deke Thornton), Ernest Borgnine (Dutch Engstrom), Ben Johnson (Tector Gorch), Warren Oates (Lyle Gorch), Jaime Sanchez (Angel), Edmond O'Brien (Sykes), Albert Dekker (Harrigan), Strother Martin (Coffer), L.Q. Jones (T.C.), Emilio Fernandez (Mapache), Chano Ureta (Don José), Jorge Russek (Lt. Zamorra), Fernando Wagner (Mohr), Bo Hopkins (Crazy Lee)

A publicity shot of the original Wild Bunch. It's as if Peckinpah had his cast pose for Matthew Brady.

Synopsis: In 1913, eight men wearing army uniforms try to rob the railroad office in San Rafael, a small Texas border town. They are ambushed by a group of murderous bounty hunters working for Harrigan, a ruthless railroad executive. The man Harrigan has put in charge of the bounty hunters is Deke Thornton, who once rode with the men he is now expected to kill; Thornton is only carrying out this task so Harrigan won't send him back to prison. In the crossfire, many townspeople are cut down, but five of the robbers escape: Pike Bishop, the leader; the loyal Dutch; the mean, always complaining Tector and Lyle Gorch; and Angel, an independent-minded young Mexican who is always at odds with the Gorch brothers. They rendezvous with an old ex-gunslinger named Sykes at a ranchero. The Gorch brothers don't like him either. Finding out that the gold they took from San Rafael is actually bags full of steel washers, the members of the "Wild Bunch" realize that they must pull off still another job if any of them are to retire.

With Thornton and his men hot on their trail, the six outlaws cross the border into Mexico, a country torn by civil war. Resting the night in the hospitable village where Angel grew up, they learn that the territory is being terrorized by Mapache, a bandit general. Angel is unhappy to hear that his girlfriend Teresa has willingly gone off with Mapache.

The Wild Bunch arrives in Aqua Verde, where it sees Mapache and his large battalion up close. They are almost killed by Mapache's soldiers when Angel shoots Teresa while she is perched on Mapache's lap, but are freed when Mapache realizes Angel was not shooting at him. Mapache and his German officer friend Mohr convince the Wild Bunch to rob an American train carrying rifles and ammunition. Pike knows that the money they will get for this mission will enable them all to retire.

The heist is carried off despite interferences from Thornton and his men. All the boxes of guns are delivered to Mapache, except one which Angel gives to the mountain people fighting Mapache. Knowing of Angel's act, Mapache orders him arrested and spends many hours torturing him.

Although they are free to go on their way, Pike, Dutch, and the Gorch brothers come back to Aqua Verde to see if they can save Angel. They realize they cannot. After a night of drinking and carousing with some whores, the four men fight their last battle, a suicide mission in which they kill Mapache and scores of his men before dying themselves in the bloodbath.

Coming upon the scene, Thornton wishes that he had been with the Wild Bunch in its moment of glory. Instead of returning to America, Thornton—with his old friend Pike's gun as a souvenir—decides to remain in Mexico to fight with Sykes and the mountain men to bring peace to the country.

T oday audiences at revival houses screening Sam Peckinpah's landmark Western *The Wild Bunch* tend to be almost exclusively male, as is true with most action films. But in 1969, nearly everyone temporarily abandoned picket lines for ticket lines to get a look at what was the most controversial film of the year. In one turbulent swoop, *The Wild Bunch* resurrected an out-of-work director and made him the darling of the nation's movie critics, and almost elevated cinema violence into an art form.

As Pike Bishop, William Holden speaks his first words in *The Wild Bunch* when his gang enters the San Rafael railroad office: indicating the office workers, he instructs his men, "If they move, kill them." Suddenly the credit "Directed by Sam Peckinpah" jumps upon the screen as if to punctuate Bishop's command. With this brusque, audacious stroke, Peckinpah thus announced his break from the motion picture establishment, declaring himself the toughest director of them all: someone who would no longer pull punches to protect the squeamish in the audience; someone who wouldn't hesitate to have his "hero" commit cold-blooded murder.

Visually, *The Wild Bunch* contains much that is stunning, even mesmerizing: the dusty, yellowish Mexican landscape; the numerous parades that pass through Peckinpah's frame; the train robbery sequence; the bridge that collapses with horses and Thornton's posse on top of it. But there is no question that it is the scenes of great slaughter—the battles at San Rafael, Las Trancas, and Aqua Verde—that highlight this film. These bloody episodes, which attracted so many people to the theaters, are what gives *The Wild Bunch* its rhythm, power, spectacle, and excitement. Granted. But, it is

Peckinpah's show-offy manner in presenting his most violent sequences that, in the long run, works against his film.

There is a children's game in which contestants take turns pretending to be shot. The child who can die the most dramatically, the most spectacularly, is judged the winner. Consequently, each child tries to impress his peers by "dying" slowly: being plugged at least twelve times in the belly before rolling down a hill, with great anguish written all over his/her face. With his slow-motion ballets of death, Peckinpah seems to be playing an adult version of this game, trying to impress his viewers by showing them the many ways he, editor Louis Lombardo, the stuntmen, and the special-effects crew devised to have people killed off. Forget that Peckinpah claimed he was just trying to portray killings more "realistically" than other filmmakers had ever dared. That's *not* the reason he filled *The Wild Bunch* with so much carnage. He should have taken director-screenwriter John Milius's lead and admitted he likes to do away with characters in his films because of the visual excitement involved. In truth, the most "realistic" screen killing in recent years, and the most powerful, is when nice guy Eugene Roche is whisked to the back of the frame in *Slaughterhouse Five* (1972) and unceremoniously killed by a German firing squad. Had Roche's character been directed by Peckinpah, he would have been brought into the foreground, shot countless times all over his body, had quarts of blood spill from his numerous wounds; and then he would have been required to fall off a building. And of course, he would have been killed in slow motion. Still, it wouldn't have been nearly as effective.

As is usually the case with Peckinpah, his most moving sequences are those that are the most reserved: when the Wild Bunch rides majestically from Angel's village, proud that the people there look at them respectfully; when the hobbled Pike climbs with difficulty onto his horse, and without looking over his shoulder at his men rides off into the desert, not knowing if they will follow (they will) or desert him; and the wonderful moment on the morning of the Aqua Verde shootout when Pike stares back and forth between what he realizes will be his last woman and his last bottle of whiskey. Peckinpah may have a reputation for being a tough guy, but his best screen moments in *Ride the High Country* (1962), *The Wild Bunch*, and *The Ballad of Cable Hogue* (1970) are the ones in which he allows his romantic tendencies to slip through, when he gives his characters the dignity that means so much to them.

Most movie westerners have been presented as supermen, like nineteenth-century astronauts, mythic figures who are either in the process of helping conquer a vast wilderness or, if it's in the late 1800s, keeping it civilized. All winners. Peckinpah's westerners are *losers*, misfits, drifters, even lawbreakers. We come upon them when they are tired middle-aged men with wrinkled faces and protruding bellies, when the West had already been settled and divvied up among others, and a new age (the twentieth century) is dawning. Time and glory have passed these men by, and they are seemingly obsolete. In Budd Boetticher's *Ride Lonesome* (1959), Randolph Scott philosophizes, "A man needs a reason to ride this country." Peckinpah's Wild Bunch have long been without a reason. Scott continues, "When [people] feel the morning sun on them, they want to get up and start all over." Maybe if Pike or the others could have started over a few years back, they would have gone straight and made something of their lives, but that (nonexistent) opportunity has passed them by, and now they know that it would only be an idle gesture, and a dishonest one at that, to lay down their guns and try to be upright American citizens. They realize that it would be best for all concerned if they just stepped aside—or died—and let the world proceed on its merry way.

Peckinpah has stated that in *The Wild Bunch* he tried to debunk the American myth that western gunfighters were "heroes," and to show these men for the

One of Peckinpah's many parades: the Wild Bunch exits Angel's village, where the men have been treated like heroes.

One of the film's tremendous battle sequences: at Las Trancas, Mapache, standing in front of his army, defies Zapata's mountain fighters while his own men fall around him.

"bastards that they really were." But if Peckinpah truly wanted us to dislike the Wild Bunch, he surely would have cast Jack Palance as their leader. That would have done the trick. We automatically like William Holden —we always have, even when he's played first-class heels. No, Peckinpah's real intention was to present us with a group of brutal men, and get us to accept them on their own terms, in their own brutal world. The men of the Wild Bunch are at their most dastardly at the beginning of the film when they indiscriminately shoot at both the posse and innocent bystanders in San Rafael, but for the rest of the film—one by one—Peckinpah reveals their better, more "human" sides. We further get to appreciate them as we compare them to the awful men around them; next to Thornton's posse and Mapache's soldiers, they come out best, the "good guys."

The climax of the film is consistent with Peckinpah's theme, as Pike, Dutch, Tector, and Lyle sacrifice themselves at Aqua Verde to get revenge for Mapache having killed Angel. Peckinpah's losers are, in film after film, given a chance to redeem themselves. As the theme of Cable Hogue's funeral oration contends, Peckinpah's men need no one to apologize for their pasts. They weren't "good" men, certainly, but before they died, when they had a legitimate opportunity to do one right

thing under the sun, they came through with flying colors. That's all Peckinpah feels one can ask of any man. To Peckinpah, good and bad aren't on opposite sides of the coin; they share the edge. When the time comes for a man to make a choice on how he wants to go out of this world, the decent man will make the proper decision and do the right, noble thing. What distinguishes the Wild Bunch, according to Peckinpah, is that they die properly. Yet paradoxically, *this* makes Peckinpah's gunfighters *heroic* in our eyes, and no longer the bastards he introduces us to in San Rafael.

A major problem of *The Wild Bunch* is the failure of Peckinpah—obviously too caught up in his special effects to worry about story or dialogue—to establish any camaraderie between the members of the gang. It's impossible to believe that these guys have been riding together, that they trust one another with their lives. Such bits as having them laugh in unison over their bad fortune at San Rafael or drinking together have phony rings to them, sort of like when John Ford has John Wayne and Lee Marvin engaging endlessly in fisticuffs in *Donovan's Reef* (1963) as a sign of their friendship. Peckinpah does very little with even his most important characters, hoping that by giving them cliché lines *every time* they open their mouths the audience magically will learn enough about them to be satisfied. But it doesn't work. It's a shame that Peckinpah went through so much trouble creating an authentic-looking western milieu—with every frame so studiously composed—only to fill it with stereotypes speaking drivel.

In fact, *The Wild Bunch* is a very derivative picture. As far as the characters and plot are concerned, much is taken directly from John Huston's *The Treasure of the Sierra Madre* (1948)—so much in fact that you have to wonder if Peckinpah was honoring his favorite director or was just being too lazy to come up with anything original. One also wonders if Peckinpah was trying to remake his ill-fated *Major Dundee* (1965) which he felt was butchered by Columbia after the studio denied him the final cut that was promised in his contract. Once again in *The Wild Bunch*, Peckinpah sends a band of misfits across the Mexican border; in *Major Dundee* they confronted the Apache, it's Mapache this time around. But Peckinpah doesn't just borrow from directors like Huston, Buñuel, Kurosawa, and himself, and from individual films; he borrows from entire genres.

The Wild Bunch may be categorized as a western—the men do ride horses—but Peckinpah made use of the standard plot of the caper film—a group of veteran criminals try to pull off one more heist so they can retire—simply transferring it to 1913 Mexico. Still, more than anything, *The Wild Bunch* is a war picture. It's like Roger Corman's *The Secret Invasion* (1964), Robert Aldrich's *The Dirty Dozen* (1967), and numerous other war pictures in which a sundry group of good-for-nothings are given a chance—by the screenwriter—to make up for their rotten pasts by performing a mission impossible across some border. Like the men in these

Pike kills Mapache, thereby sealing his own doom. Dutch stands by him as always.

films, the men in *The Wild Bunch* carry army pistols, fire machine guns, and use explosives, all weapons of war. Made when college students, a large segment of the movie audience, were out picketing *The Green Berets* (1968), when war pictures that glorified the deaths of Americans on foreign soil were both box office poison and in very bad taste, *The Wild Bunch* managed to sneak by the antiwar protesters under the guise of being a western. The controversy surrounding the film came about only as a result of its violence, and not, as it probably should have, because of the strong parallels between Sam Peckinpah's Mexico and our Vietnam.

It's scenes like this that give credence to speculation that Peckinpah neither likes nor trusts women. His hero, Pike, is shot in the back, but Peckinpah will make sure he whirls and gets his revenge.

1939 MGM
Director: Victor Fleming
Producer: Mervyn LeRoy
Screenplay: Noel Langley,
Florence Ryerson, and Edgar
Allan Woolf
Adaptation: Noel Langley
From the book by L. Frank Baum
Cinematography: Harold Rosson

Special Effects: Arnold Gillespie
Musical Adaptation: Herbert
Stothart
Music: Harold Arlen
Lyrics: E. Y. Harburg
Musical numbers staged by
Bobby Connolly
Editor: Blanche Sewell
Running Time: 100 minutes

Cast: Judy Garland (Dorothy), Frank Morgan (Professor Marvel/
The Wizard), Ray Bolger (Hunk/The Scarecrow), Bert Lahr
(Zeke/ The Cowardly Lion), Jack Haley (Hickory/The Tin Woods-
man), Billie Burke (Glinda), Margaret Hamilton (Miss Gulch/the
Wicked Witch), Charley Grapewin (Uncle Harry), Pat Walshe
(Nikko), Clara Blandick (Auntie Em), Toto (Toto), The Singer
Midgets (Munchkins)

Synopsis: Dorothy lives on a Kansas farm with her Uncle Henry and
Auntie Em, and three workers, Hunk, Zeke, and Hickory. She
dreams of going to a place "over the rainbow" where there is no
trouble, just peace and happiness. When mean Miss Gulch tries to
take Dorothy's dog Toto to the sheriff, Dorothy and Toto run away.
Not far from home, they meet Professor Marvel, a friendly mountebank, who convinces Dorothy to go back home.

A tornado heads for the farm and everyone climbs into the
underground shelter. However, by the time Dorothy gets home, the
shelter door is locked. She runs into the house and is knocked
unconscious by a window that is blown open. She imagines her
house being lifted in the air and spun around countless times before
finally landing. She opens the door and she and Toto walk out into a
wondrous fairy tale world. Where Kansas was gray, Oz is full of the
colors of the rainbow.

The house has landed on the Wicked Witch of the East. The
Munchkins come out of hiding and praise Dorothy for killing her.
Dorothy dances with the little people. However, the Wicked Witch of
the West (who resembles Miss Gulch) arrives on her broomstick and
is angered by the death of her sister. Luckily, Glinda, the Good Witch
of the North, protects Dorothy from her. When the Wicked Witch
tries to take the powerful ruby red slippers from the feet of her dead
sister, Glinda transfers the shoes to Dorothy's feet. The Wicked
Witch vows revenge. Dorothy wants to know how to get home.
Glinda tells her that only the Wizard who lives in Emerald City might
know the way. Dorothy and Toto travel down the Yellow Brick Road
to Emerald City. They meet a Scarecrow, who looks like Zeke. He
sings that he wants a brain. Dorothy invites him to come with them
to ask the Wizard for a brain. The travelers meet a Tin Woodsman,
who looks like Hickory, rusted along the side of the road. They oil
him and he sings that he wants a heart. They invite him to come
along. Going through the dangerous forest, they come upon a lion,
who looks like Zeke, who is afraid of his own shadow—and
everything else. They ask him to come meet the Wizard and ask for
courage.

The journey is long and the Wicked Witch terrorizes them. They
arrive at the Emerald City. They have a hard time getting to see the
Wizard but are at last allowed a brief meeting. His huge head seems
to drift through the air. There is fire and steam about and the
travelers are scared. He says he will grant the requests if they bring
back the Wicked Witch's broom.

In the forest, the Witch's winged-monkey army captures Dorothy
and Toto and takes them to her castle. Toto escapes and brings the
Scarecrow, the Tin Woodsman, and the Cowardly Lion to the castle.
They help Dorothy escape, but soon the girl is surrounded. She
throws water on the Wicked Witch, who melts. Her army is glad to
be rid of her and gives Dorothy her broom.

But the Wizard turns out to be a fake, just a man who looks like
Professor Marvel. He had been standing behind a curtain pulling a
lot of switches. But he is a good man, and grants their requests. He
gives the Scarecrow a diploma, the Tin Man a testimonial and a gold
heart on a chain, and the Cowardly Lion a Triple Cross. He promises
to take Dorothy back to Kansas in his balloon. But the balloon
accidentally lifts off without her. Glinda tells Dorothy she can go
home by clicking the heels of her red slippers and repeating "There's
no place like home" three times. Dorothy does so and wakes up in
Kansas with her family and friends around her. She says that she's
not going to leave home ever again.

The Wizard of Oz

Recently I saw *The Wizard of Oz* at a repertory
theater that doublebilled it with L. Frank
Baum's own 1914 production of *The Patchwork Girl of Oz*, based on another book in
Baum's Oz series. About halfway into the
silent (black-and-white) *Patchwork Girl*, every kid in
the theater who wasn't yawning was fast asleep. Since
many of these children were very *young* I was curious to
see how they would react to seeing *Wizard* for the first
time—or at least the first time in a *theater*. Well, the
transformation in these children from sleepy "Can-
we-go-home-now?" malcontents to laughing, smiling
"I-hope-this-goes-on-forever!" movie nuts once *The
Wizard of Oz* came on was amazing—magical. I was
reminded that *The Wizard of Oz* captures children like
no other film; that it is *the* perfect children's movie. And
I flashed back to the fifties when *The Wizard* entered the
lives of us children across America via annual television
screenings that we watched religiously year after year
after year. Few of us can deny how important to our
lives *Wizard* was; its annual TV presentation was as
comforting as our birthdays, holidays, a cup of hot
chocolate (with a marshmallow), and even the opening
day of the baseball season.

The Wizard of Oz, seen more times by more people
than any other film, has had a profound effect on most
everyone. It often has been joked that every film made
since 1939 includes some reference to *Wizard*. I'm not
sure this isn't true: because almost every film one
scrutinizes from "A"—*Alice Doesn't Live Here Anymore* (1974)—to "Z"—the revealingly titled *Zardoz*
(1974)—does indeed pay tribute to *Wizard*. Moreover,
the music world has followed suit with such "Top 40"
hits as "Ding Dong! The Witch Is Dead," Lynda
Carter's "Toto," and Elton John's "Goodbye, Yellow
Brick Road." And even as I sit here writing, an acne
commercial has come on the radio in which the characters are Dorothy from Kansas, her dog Toto, and a
wizard who recommends Stridex medicated pads. (Some
wizard.)

What makes *The Wizard of Oz* so appealing to
children? The very young are doubtlessly excited by the
elements found in *Wizard* that are basic to good fairy
tales: a journey into a strange land, scary moments (how
wonderfully frightening Margaret Hamilton is!—*too*
frightening for some kids), and a weird assortment of
characters: a wizard, witches, Munchkins, winged monkeys, a scarecrow (without a brain), a tin man (without a
heart), and a lion (without courage). In addition, there
are animals, catchy songs, talking apple trees with arms

While the Munchkins look on, Dorothy meets Glinda, who tells her to follow the yellow brick road to the Emerald City.

and lousy dispositions, and many spectacular occurrences (which *children* do not realize were provided by the special-effects department). If a child sees *Wizard* on a color TV, s/he will be thrilled by the rainbow-colored land of Oz that stands in marked contrast to the sepia-colored Kansas—and by "the horse of a different color" as it switches from purple to red to yellow; and if lucky enough to see the picture in a theater, s/he will love the sense of depth created by George Gibson's magnificent painted backdrops (with blue mountains and white peaks) that is not evident on TV. As a visceral/aural treat, young children will certainly find nothing better than *The Wizard of Oz*.

But *The Wizard of Oz* always has been much more meaningful to the older child who like Dorothy lives on a Kansas farm or any small town in America and who dreams of going over a rainbow to a glamorous life. Movies have always meant *escape* to young, restless people and for many *The Wizard of Oz* dramatically illustrates the escape they desire most. Kansas represents their dreary existence: it is dull, gray, without other

children. Oz is that dream world that is so far away that it might as well be over a rainbow: Hollywood, to which children want to run away in hopes of getting into show business. And the Emerald City is their motion picture studio (Is the wizard Louis B. Mayer?) where every child wants to end up and, as Judy Garland accomplished by appearing in *The Wizard of Oz*, become an instant superstar. That children subconsciously equate Oz with Hollywood and the Emerald City with a studio is not so ridiculous when one takes into consideration that *Wizard's* special effects, brightly colored scenery, costumes, abundance of sets, and singing and dancing were all meant by MGM to showcase the best Hollywood could muster in the way of production values. In *Wizard* it is confirmed that only Hollywood can make the fantastic become real. One wonders if MGM meant to convey the Hollywood-as-Oz theme (with a message to all aspiring stars to stay home); it does seem a bit suspicious that once the travelers reach the Emerald City they are subjected to a vigorous beauty treatment much in the manner that we picture

Before seeing the Wizard, the Cowardly Lion, Dorothy, the Scarecrow, the Tin Woodsman, and even Toto are given a beauty treatment.

new movie stars getting done over for their screen tests. Children who dream of becoming dancers have traditionally been inspired by *The Red Shoes* (1948). For the child/teen-ager who dreams of going to Hollywood, there is no film that better visualizes their dream than *The Wizard of Oz*.

Dorothy's journey to Oz in the movie can *also* be interpreted as a young girl's last childhood experience. At picture's end, Dorothy must choose whether to stay in the fairy tale world of Oz or return to her Kansas farm and live with Uncle Henry and Auntie Em. Glinda tells her that she could have always returned to Kansas of her own volition if she had had sufficient desire to do so. (I am unsatisfied with Glinda's explanation for not having told Dorothy earlier how she could return: "You wouldn't have believed me.") But now, Dorothy says farewell to all her friends of Oz and returns to Kansas. This is meant to be a wise choice. She is a mature, practical girl after her experience. It's well known that Garland wore a straitjacketlike cloth so her well-developed breasts wouldn't reveal her to be sixteen when Dorothy was supposed to be eleven—I'm surprised that MGM didn't let her bust out of her strap in the last scene to underline the fact that *Dorothy* has grown up.

In the book *The Wizard of Oz*, very early on, Dorothy says:

> No matter how dreary and gray our homes are, we people of flesh and blood would rather live there than in any other country, be it ever so beautiful. There is no place like home.

Significantly, in the book it does not take Dorothy's experiences in Oz—which she looks back on "gravely"—to teach her that "there is no place like home." She knows it immediately. But the 1939 film makes this "no place like home" nonsense the picture's major theme, the conclusion Dorothy somehow draws from her dream experiences in Oz. And it is *nonsense*. The Dorothy we see in the opening scenes is an unhappy little girl who is lonely because there seem to be no children about, who has no parents and lives with a very unsupportive, elderly Uncle and Aunt on a very barren, gray farm. Her only real companion is Toto and when she returns to Kansas she will find that Miss Gulch has not forgotten that she intends to get rid of the dog. (The screenwriters overlook this fact.) Once the Wicked Witch is dead, Oz, unlike in the book, is a wonderful place. Dorothy has friends by the dozen and playmates in the Scarecrow, the Tin Woodsman, and the no-longer-Cowardly Lion who, let's face it, are a much livelier bunch (for an eleven-year-old girl) than farmworkers Hunk, Zeke, and Hickory. Let Dorothy stay in Oz! Or, at least to show that Oz's specialness is fading in Dorothy's eyes as well as with us viewers, the colors should begin to get duller as times goes on: Oz should end up in sepia, and Kansas should be brightly colored by the time she gets back. In *The Classic American Novel and the Movies* (Ungar, 1977), film professor Janet Juhnke quotes a nineteen-year-old "girl who has left her Kansas home to make her way alone in New York City":

> The ending [to the movie *The Wizard of Oz* is] a total anticlimax. It states that this was all a dream, that fantasy is unreal and can only get you in trouble, and boring status quo existence is the right way to live. The moral is "There's no place like home." Blah! or Oh, how sweeeet! is how the audience feels. I hate the ending because fantasy *is* real, necessary, and because home is not always the best place to be.

Other than the regrettable Hollywood-style propaganda ending, I only have minor objections: Bert Lahr's "King of the Forest" number comes at a time when we have been inundated by musical numbers and has the effect of bringing the proceedings to a dead halt; and one can see the tin man unravel the rope and let the wizard fly off in his balloon. But who's complaining? There's so much that's wonderful about this film: the story, the music, the sets, the special effects, the sprightly script, and, of course, the stupendous cast. How all of these elements came together is part of *Wizard*'s legend. (Just as I recommend everyone see *The Wizard of Oz* at least once in a theater—it's so much better than it is on television—I recommend that fans of the film read *The Making of the Wizard of Oz* [Knopf, 1977], the best-selling book by Aljean Harmetz, for *all* information regarding production.)

Of course, much of the "Oz" cult among adults is a result of Judy Garland, so young, so innocent, so pretty, playing Dorothy. I, for one, think Shirley

The Wicked Witch threatens Dorothy, whom she has taken prisoner.

Temple, MGM's first choice for the part, would have also been a great Dorothy, but it would have been an inferior picture. For one thing the already famous Temple would have dominated her costars, as was her manner; Garland was not a star yet and didn't attempt to move her higher-paid, veteran costars into the background. As a result, their appearances give the film an all-star-cast aura.

At times, Garland seems to be copying Deanna Durbin, already a big star at Universal and Garland's rival. Like Durbin, she'll lean forward, a little tiptoed perhaps, with her arms spread slightly and her hands clasped in front of her. Then she'll start talking quickly and nervously, as if she were pleading and scolding at the same time. Like Durbin, she comes across as strong yet vulnerable. But while the high-voiced (when a teen) Durbin will drive you crazy if no one interrupts her, Garland is endearing and funny. Watching Garland today, and knowing how scared she was at the time, how uncomfortable she was in her tight strap, and how soon after her body would become messed up because of a growing dependency on speed and sleeping pills, our feelings must waver—between *delight* in her dynamic yet touching performance under trying conditions and *grief* that we are seeing the role that launched her into the world of superstardom she never was able to handle. When she so beautifully sings "Over the Rainbow," we sense that it is Garland, at sixteen, as much as Dorothy who believes the lyrics about a land far away where there is peace and happiness. Each year when *Wizard* plays on television, we want to warn her that once she makes it over the rainbow she must "Be careful!"

While her sad friends look on, Dorothy prepares to travel by balloon back to Kansas.

Afterword

While space requirements have dictated that I restrict myself to writing about one hundred of the most significant cult films, I am aware that other films are swiftly becoming cult favorites. Titles that immediately come to mind include *To Be or Not to Be; Children of Paradise; The Adventures of Robin Hood; Tommy; Baby Love; If; Putney Swope; WR—Mysteries of the Organism; Salt of the Earth; Blood Money; Raw Meat; In the Realm of the Senses; Last Tango in Paris; The Last Wave; The Wicker Man; Massacre at Central High; Richard Pryor Live in Concert; Blonde Ambition; Stardust; Payday; Jackson County Jail; Cisco Pike; Mad Love; Sweet Sweetback's Baadasssss Song; Barbarella; Gates of Heaven; Fritz the Cat; The Great Texas Dynamite Chase; Joanna; Ganja and Hess; Rude Boy; The Killing of a Chinese Bookie; The Last Waltz; Return of the Secaucus 7; The Stunt Man; The Hired Hand; Communion; The Ruling Class; Fellini Satyricon; The 5,000 Fingers of Dr. T; Maîtresse; Foxes; The Night of the Hunter; Morgan!; Drive, He Said; Out of It; Seconds; The Attack of the Giant Leeches; The Attack of the Killer Tomatoes; Sextette; The Silent Partner; Zardoz; Head; Rancho Deluxe; Winter Kills; Underground, U.S.A.; Lawrence of Arabia; The Pom Pom Girls; The Velvet Vampire; Daughters of Darkness; Macon County Line; Can Hieronymous Merkin Ever Forget Mercy Humppe and Find True Happiness?; Alien; The Duellists; Quadrophenia; Written on the Wind; The Tenant; Point Blank; Breathless; and Head over Heels.*

I'd like to know if there are some obscure movie cults I might not be aware of and would welcome such information being sent to me in care of Dell Publishing.

Index

Danny Peary has an M.A. in Cinema from the University of Southern California. He was fine arts and sports editor of *L. A. Panorama*, has run a film society, and has written film criticism for *Focus on Film, Bijou, The Velvet Light Trap, Newsday, Films and Filming,* the *Philadelphia Bulletin,* the *Soho News,* and other publications. He edited the anthology *Close-Ups: The Movie Star Book* and was co-editor of *The American Animated Cartoon.*